DATA COMMUNICATIONS:

BEYOND THE BASICS

Edited by John Turpin, Tandem
Computers and Ray Sarch,
Executive Technical Editor,
Data Communications

 **Data Communications** Book Series

McGraw-Hill Information Systems Company
1221 Avenue of the Americas
New York, New York 10020

Data Communications Book Series

- **Basic Guide to Data Communications.** Edited by Ray Sarch, Executive Technical Editor, Data Communications. 1985, 360 pages, softcover.
- **Cases in Network Design.** Edited by William E. Bracker, Jr. and Ray Sarch. 1985, 275 pages, softcover.
- **Computer Message Systems.** By Jacques Vallee. 1984, 176 pages, clothbound.
- **Data Communications: A Comprehensive Approach.** By Gilbert Held and Ray Sarch. 1983, 441 pages, clothbound.
- **Data Communications: Beyond the Basics.** Edited by Ray Sarch, Executive Technical Editor, Data Communications. 1986, 307 pages, softcover.
- **Data Network Design Strategies.** Edited by Ray Sarch, Executive Technical Editor, Data Communications. 1983, 273 pages, softcover.
- **Interface Proceedings.** Edited by Data Communications Magazine. Annual publication, softcover.
- **Linking Microcomputers.** Edited by Colin B. Ungaro, Editor-in-Chief, Data Communications. 1985, 310 pages, softcover.
- **The Local Network Handbook.** Edited by Colin B. Ungaro, Editor-in-Chief, Data Communications. 1986, 387 pages, softcover.
- **McGraw-Hill's Compilation of Data Communications Standards, Edition III.** Edited by Harold C. Folts. 1986, 3,000 pages, clothbound.
- **Teleconferencing and Beyond: Communications in the Office of the Future.** By Robert Johansen, with others contributing. 1984, 206 pages, clothbound.
- **Teletext and Videotex in the United States: Market Potential, Technology, and Public Policy Issues.** By J. Tydeman, H. Lipinski, R. Adler, M. Nyhan, L. Zwimpfer. 1982, 312 pages, clothbound.

Library of Congress Cataloging-in-Publication Data

data communications.

(Data communications book series)
"These articles, which originally appeared in Data communications, should be considered supplemental to those in an earlier volume, Basic guide to data communications"—Pref.
Includes index.
1. Data transmission systems. 2. Computer networks.
I. Sarch, Ray. II. Data communications. III. Basic guide to data communications. IV. Series: McGraw-Hill data communications book series.
TK5105.B364 1985 Suppl.   384.3   86-2892
ISBN 0-07-606950-8

DATA COMMUNICATIONS:

BEYOND THE BASICS

Edited by John Turpin and Ray Sarch

Table of Contents

Preface

These articles, which originally appeared in DATA COMMUNICATIONS, should be considered supplemental to those in an earlier volume, "Basic Guide to Data Communications." The topics in this volume range widely, from digital transmission, data compression, and transport protocols to artificial intelligence and anticipated network architectures.

The articles are grouped into five sections, but for some, not easily. If the reader feels that an article has been misassigned, so be it. The classifications represent the thinking of the editors and are readily open to argument.

But the reader should not dwell on what belongs where. Rather, one should regard this volume as a sampling of today's and tomorrow's data communications technology in many of its varied aspects. Most of the authors represented here are acknowledged experts in the subject areas they discuss. Serious data communicators will find much material that will prove beneficial and which they may well wish to pursue to even greater depth.

Therefore, if the reader, at the least, considers any of these articles as instigators for further study, then the editors feel that they have accomplished one of their major purposes in their efforts.

Section 1
Planning & Design

Robert B. Fish, Network Equipment Technologies Co.,
Menlo Park, Calif.

Considerations for picking a corporate backbone network

There is more than idle
speculation to setting the
stage for flexible video,
voice, and data integration.

The Bell System divestiture
has drastically changed the environment in which the
network communications manager operates. And it
appears that a continued state of volatility will exist for
some time. Therefore, in addition to the normal pressures of corporate needs such as the proliferation of
microcomputers, the replacement of outdated PBXs,
and the increasing usage of customer-operated data
terminals, the network manager must deal with additional divestiture-related issues. These include substantial rate increases, loss of a single point-of-contact for
service provisioning, increased services and product
offerings from multiple vendors, and decreased availability of competent telecommunications personnel.

Rather than trying to solve these and other issues
across the entire network, many managers have divided their current multiservice networks (voice, data,
video, and so on) into two generic transmission categories: backbone and non-backbone. Generally, a backbone transmission requirement exists if two or more
sites have significant concentrations of network-based
activity flowing between them. Corporate locations that
have either low levels of intracompany traffic or no
discernible communities of interest (areas with a consistent need for communications between specific locations) are generally not considered part of a backbone requirement.

Because of the high concentrations of traffic within
these backbone communities of interest, economies of
scale can be used to reduce both overall cost and cost
per traffic unit. Hence, many Fortune 500 corporations
have focused their attention on solving the backbone
networking issues before addressing the communications needs of locations where voice/data traffic is
relatively light. The recent availability of high-speed
digital facilities provided by common carriers, resellers,
and vendors of bypass technologies has allowed large
corporations to deploy utility backbone networks (see
"Likely candidates for private bypass networks"). Because of the aggregate price differential between one
T1 (1.544-Mbit/s) facility and the equivalent 24 voice-
grade or 56-kbit/s Dataphone digital service (DDS)
lines, corporate networks with defined backbone requirements are incorporating T1 links in their
strategies.

Figure 1 illustrates the relationship of the per-channel
costs between different types of transmission facilities,
based on current AT&T tariffs. The per-channel cost
shown for the T1 line is based on the use of pulse code
modulation (PCM) encoding, which results in twenty-
four 64-kbit/s channels. As shown, DDS cannot compete with T1 on a per-channel basis over short distances with a low number of circuits. The standard
voice-grade circuit fares better than DDS and even
shows a positive price relationship to T1 at around 500
miles.

Further, recent advances in voice processing are
projected to make T1 even more attractive. Both the
CCITT and AT&T are proposing a new encoding standard called adaptive differential pulse code modulation
(ADPCM), which will use a mere 32 kbit/s to represent
a voice signal. This bit rate is twice as efficient as the
current PCM standard, and allows up to 48 toll-quality
voice channels to be carried by a single T1 facility. The
result is that the per-channel costs of T1 will probably
be cut by half of what is shown in Figure 1. Hence, the
viability of replacing standard voice-grade lines with T1
links is increased for almost any distance whenever a
significant number of tie-lines are involved.

Since the T1 link passes information in a digital
format, subscribers can simultaneously transmit voice,
data, video, and other types of digital traffic through it.

1. Cost comparison. *On a per-channel basis, T1 comes out the cost-performance winner at distances under five hundred miles. DDS lines offer few cost savings.*

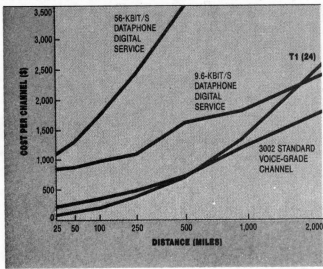

The signal regeneration technique used in T1 repeaters ensures low levels of noise and better transmission quality than those used to amplify analog signals. These factors make T1 the medium of choice when laying the groundwork for a fully integrated corporate backbone network.

Despite the demonstrable economic incentives, a T1-based backbone network is not necessarily the optimal solution for every company's needs. Nevertheless, because of the amount of information that can be carried, and its importance to the company, T1 links should not be viewed as simply a replacement for multiple individual telephone company circuits. Implementation of any network component must be combined with a well-thought-out strategy if it is to support the business needs of the corporation. An ill-planned or incorrectly implemented digital backbone network could easily become a liability rather than an asset to a company.

Uncharted waters
The many issues surrounding the incorporation of an integrated backbone network into a corporate network strategy often require an information executive or network manager to venture into previously unknown territories. Some of these issues relate directly to the network—such as financial considerations, network design and performance goals, and action item time frames. Other issues pertain more to non-network problems such as positioning for future growth or enhancement. Also, in many corporations planning and implementation for voice and data have taken place separately. Many organizations have even physically separated the two. The creation of an integrated network, therefore, can have an impact on the organizational structure of management information systems at the corporation. Considerations such as these need to be addressed if the backbone network is to mesh well with a corporation's information management structure.

In dealing with the technical considerations involved in planning and implementing a T1 backbone network, it is necessary to focus on:
■ The logical relationship to overall corporate network architecture
■ The physical T1 facility media
■ The physical relationship to premises equipment
■ T1 bandwidth resource control
■ Network management considerations
■ Topological considerations relating to traffic flow.

In this article, problems faced by major corporations will be demonstrated using an actual example of a corporate planning exercise. Since the corporation described requested anonymity, it will be referred to as XYZ Corp., with 4,000 employees and 150 branch offices scattered across a wide geographical area. XYZ has concentrated its major administrative and data processing activities at five locations. Figure 2 depicts these large concentrated sites of activity. However, the 150 outlying branches are not shown. The executive offices and major headquarters location is labeled "HQ," while its three large regional branch offices are R1, R2, and R3. The primary data center is labeled "PDC," and the backup disaster center is labeled "BDC."

At the beginning of the planning, the MIS director at XYZ Corp. entertained and concurred with a network communications department recommendation to explore the feasibility of building a corporate backbone T1 network. This proposed network would connect HQ, PDC, BDC, R1, R2, and R3 and replace all existing application-specific transmission facilities between those locations. The first step in the evaluation process was to establish two concurrent task forces to investigate the feasibility of this network, internally dubbed "zee-net."

The task force A was made up of administrative and financial personnel whose objective was to resolve the myriad non-network issues. The task force B was staffed by network personnel from the data and voice network planning units and was charged with putting out a request for information (RFI) for zee-net components. At the end of their research, the RFI was to be sent to various telecommunications products and services vendors in preparation for a final network funding recommendation to XYZ's senior management. This article will focus on task force B to illustrate the steps involved in the actual network planning.

The process
It is critical to the success of both the entire planning effort and the backbone network's operation that the first planning milestone be the review and analysis of the company's major business requirements. A planning group must understand the details of the business environment and the possible impact of an integrated network on that business. That understanding is essential to developing network design criteria truly responsive to corporate needs. For example, if customer-operated terminals, such as automated tellers, are accessing the backbone network, both response time and downtime will be critical to management. By

prioritizing business problems according to their importance, the analysts also gain insight about how weighting factors should be associated with each RFI selection criterion.

At XYZ Corp., for instance, task force B reviewed the entire three-year MIS business plan for voice, data, office automation, and video teleconferencing. They also reviewed and documented the current network configuration, traffic usage patterns, and locations of major voice/data processing resources.

As depicted in Figure 2, the data network is SNA-based with large terminal concentrations at R1, R2, and R3. The host computer at PDC has a job entry system 3 (JES3) to send files nightly to the BDC for backup. Inquiry traffic (not shown) from the 150 branches is directed to the PDC via multipoint circuits.

The voice network is an electronic tandem network (ETN) with nodes located at R1, R2, R3, and headquarters. The area branch voice traffic is homed (targeted) into the regional branches. The network also carries voice-band asynchronous data traffic to and from minicomputers located within each regional branch. All downstream (from the HQ node) switches are considered by the ETN nodes as main sites and are linked directly to the nodes for tandem switching.

The senior management of XYZ Corp. decided to use video teleconferencing to support the weekly meetings held by senior managers at all five primary administrative sites. They requested that this capability be ready for daily use sometime within the nine months following network startup.

Architectural considerations

After fully assessing XYZ's business requirements, task force B constructed a common framework of reference in order to avoid continually defining and redefining terms and meanings that vary between the voice and data disciplines. To accomplish this, the task force defined the logical relationship of the backbone network (controller devices and T1 transmission facilities) as it relates to the data and voice networking architectures currently in place. In the case of SNA, the data network, the architectural boundaries between layers of functionality are already well defined. An ETN, on the other hand, does not implement a formal network architecture like SNA. However, there are reasonably well-defined boundaries between some functional ETN layers that do parallel the SNA model. Transmit and receive lines on a two- or four-wire interface, for example, are toggled or "winked" to establish a connection between the PBX and the phone company's central office (CO). A certain combination of winks, for instance, on a two-wire arrangement (an "on" condition on the one wire and an "off" condition on the other) might indicate a call request from the PBX.

Further, depending on the amount of functionality defined within the backbone network environment, formal definitions permit the initial network implementation, and future enhancements, to be made without necessitating a massive re-system-generation of the mainframe or front-end processor software. Clear architectural definition can also avoid a corporate-wide

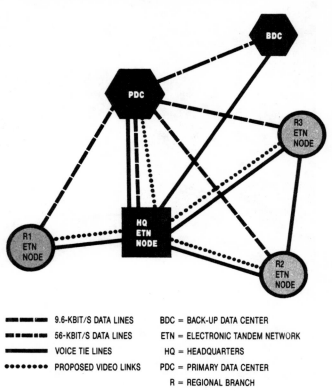

2. The way it was. All voice traffic on XYZ's private network was routed toward headquarters. Teleconferencing links connect regional branches R1, R2, and R3.

▬ ▬ ▬ 9.6-KBIT/S DATA LINES	BDC	= BACK-UP DATA CENTER
▬■▬■▬ 56-KBIT/S DATA LINES	ETN	= ELECTRONIC TANDEM NETWORK
▬▬▬ VOICE TIE LINES	HQ	= HEADQUARTERS
•••••• PROPOSED VIDEO LINKS	PDC	= PRIMARY DATA CENTER
	R	= REGIONAL BRANCH

conversion of any current voice-station numbering plan.

For the purpose of developing an evolutionary backbone network strategy, the voice network analysts may wish to build a functional ETN model. Once this is done, the entire task force team can then map both SNA and ETN models into a common corporate network architecture (CNA) like that shown in Figure 3. In the case of XYZ Corp., the task force analysts consider it essential for zee-net to be transparent to layers 2 and 3 of the CNA and be complementary to the current transport layer capabilities at XYZ Corp.

The details of CNA are important only in relation to the MIS strategy of XYZ Corp., and only transport layer functions are relevant to this article. Generally, the task force defined the transport layer as having the range of functions required to efficiently manage the T1 bandwidth. Each company that applies this architectural approach may find it appropriate to include more or less functionality in a backbone network. This range could be anywhere from the minimal capabilities offered by a pair of wires, up to the sophisticated capabilities of a highly intelligent value-added network.

From the perspective of the premises equipment interface, CNA layer 1 relates to zee-net as follows. Currently, the data communications equipment at XYZ Corp. uses RS-232-C and CCITT V.35 interfaces for low-speed and high-speed data, respectively, while the voice equipment uses four-wire E&M (rEceive & trans-

3. Not visible. *The physical layers on the voice network (ETN) and data network (SNA) connect, and are transparent to the CNA transport layer.*

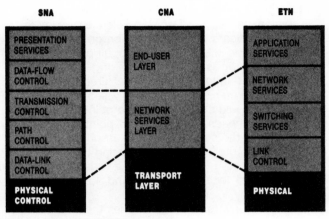

SNA = SYSTEMS NETWORK ARCHITECTURE
CNA = CORPORATE NETWORK ARCHITECTURE
ETN = ELECTRONIC TANDEM NETWORK

Mit) leads. Therefore, the RFI specified that the T1 link-control equipment should support at least those interfaces for data and voice equipment at network startup.

Working considerations

After defining the CNA and delineating the functional limits of the backbone network as a transport subnetwork, the network task force needs to consider the various functions performed within that subnetwork. These can be broken down into two major areas:

1. The physical transmission media upon which the backbone will be built
2. The link-management equipment that optimizes media use.

Cost and service factors are the major criteria in analyzing the transmission media area. The zee-net sites are scattered across a wide area, and, due to the geographic dispersion of locations, a private network (microwave and fiber optic) cannot be economically justified. Also, because some of XYZ's transaction-processing networks still use binary synchronous communications (BSC) protocols, satellite links can be eliminated for all but backup purposes because of the excessive propagation delay due to using BSC. Additionally, the voice users may find the time lag encountered on satellite circuits quite annoying.

These same cost and service factors are also important in weighing the various leased terrestrial service offerings. For XYZ Corp., the analysts found that the most economical situation is a combination of two different T1 offerings. The AT&T Accunet T1.5 service is cost-effective for the administrative center and regional branches. The data centers, however, are located within the same local access and transport area (LATA). As a result, the links connecting PDC and BDC were found to be less expensive if obtained from the intra-LATA carrier. To increase the effectiveness of the

planning process, the final network configuration was not designed until the link controller requirements were in place. Therefore, installation orders for these zee-net trunks were completed only after the approval for the funding recommendation had been obtained from management.

There are at least two direct results of this decision. Since at least some of these T1 trunks will be from AT&T and will require support of AT&T's forthcoming 193-bit clear-channel frame format by 1985, the RFI included this criterion. And, since two carriers will be involved, zee-net will not be able to use a digital cross-connect scheme based on a carrier CO implementation. Because the XYZ Corp. philosophy is to have managerial and operational control over their own networks, this was not an important consideration.

Defining activities

The second area in the CNA transport layer is the scope of its activities beyond just providing a physical transmission path. Some of these activities include bandwidth allocation, call routing, channel service unit functions, diagnostics, encoding and decoding of data, multiplexing and demultiplexing, and operational monitoring and synchronization. The intent of the network is to be a utility within itself and yet remain as transparent as possible to the end-user applications—in other words, to appear as a copper wire.

Rather than deciding where and how these functions should be performed, analysts should simply specify what activities must be performed and allow the different vendors to respond with either individual components or entire networks. This provides the network design team with a range of options that allows them to select the scenario best suited to their company's environment. There are some functional implementations, however, that may be clearly undesirable to any individual company. In the case of XYZ Corp., there were some major business considerations, such as cost constraints and time-frame requirements. In an effort to target the RFI to vendors who can comply within these business considerations, the zee-net task force had to continue refining the parameter specification list.

As stated, the range of capabilities that must be supported by the link-control equipment goes far beyond those found in a D4 channel bank. This device only handles the interfaces to premises equipment, the digital signal encoding, and the multiplexing function. A more appropriate generic descriptor applied to the required range of capabilities is the term transmission resource management (TRM).

An integrated backbone network, by definition, must support a wide range of traffic disciplines, time frames for future implementations of new features, and projected levels of data flow—both on a day-to-day basis and for longer timetables. At XYZ Corp., for example, the normal workday usage mixture was a large amount of voice (and voice-band data) calls in addition to the regular transaction-processing data traffic. And at scheduled intervals throughout the week, there were to be video conferences between the major operations centers. At night and on the weekends, however, the

Likely candidates for private bypass networks

The divestiture of AT&T and the deregulation of the telecommunications industry may have had the desired effects of stirring up competition and lowering long-distance toll rates. On the negative side, however, service performance has deteriorated and confusion has spread over which organization has responsibility for the various elements of the telecommunications network.

In today's deregulated environment, large corporate and institutional users believe that dependable telecommunications networks have become essential to the success of their businesses and have searched for and found ways to take control of the total telecommunications functions. A recent in-depth market analysis by Decision Sciences Corp. shows why and how large users are changing their approach toward telecommunications. In particular these users express very strong needs for:
■ Secure, reliable, and responsible installation, repair, and maintenance service for the total network, guaranteeing minimal downtime of voice and data equipment
■ Control of telecommunications cost
■ Acquisition of productivity- and efficiency-improving features to ensure technological compatibility with future voice/data office automation networks.

How are the largest organizations in the country trying to fill these requirements? In its market studies Decision Sciences found that, aside from installing an occasional station management detail reporting system or dealing with an alternative common carrier, the majority of larger users are taking a comprehensive approach by installing private or bypass telecommunications networks.

What are the private networks? Decision Sciences finds that the building blocks of private networks are typically large third-generation voice/data PBXs and long-haul transmission schemes such as microwave and private leased circuits. These PBXs are installed at the organization's major location. They are then directly connected, either through leased lines or preferably through more economical alternatives such as microwave, satellite, coaxial cable, optical fiber, or copper links. Frequently, a central control center is installed. This center continuously controls and monitors the entire network, performing line diagnostics, remote software analysis, billing, network routing, and other functions. Most installed networks transmit and switch both voice and data communications. They frequently incorporate advanced features such as electronic mail, voice mail, and teleconferencing.

The private network meets the large user's needs better than conventional telecommunications schemes in three major areas. First, by gaining full control over its network, the organization gains control of service and maintenance. It may opt for an in-house repair and maintenance staff or subcontract this function to a dependable facilities management organization. The latter frequently turns out to be the initial supplier of the hardware, though several third-party organizations have started to make inroads in this service market. The Decision Sciences survey respondents indicate that either option or a combination has resulted in better service repair performance and more responsiveness in making equipment moves and changes. Many users, tired of finger-pointing repairmen, had specifically searched for a vendor who could serve as a single point of contact for all service needs. Under a single-point-of-contact arrangement, the service provider assumes responsibility for the total network, eliminating the need for the user to locate problems or call a variety of different hardware, local-exchange, and long-distance vendors.

Second, a private network enables the user organization to contain costs. For example, replacement of leased local or long-distance facilities by more economical private microwave, satellite, or fiber links will reduce transmission cost. Point-to-multipoint microwave can connect intra- or interlocal access and transport area calls directly to the lowest-cost long-distance carrier or value-added network provider, bypassing the local telephone company plant and its charges. The PBX's least-cost routing features optimize use of the private network and cut toll charges. Statistical voice and data multiplexers can reduce long-distance capacity requirements by 50 to 60 percent, resulting in drastically reduced lease expenditures or limitation of transmission facility investments. On the basis of these capabilities, many users estimated that the payback period for private networks would fall in the three-to-five-year range.

The third major advantage is that a private network can be designed to incorporate features and network options that meet the specific needs and requirements of the individual user. Instead of being dependent on the limited offerings of the main lessor of the network, users can integrate a variety of elements from any vendor. In particular, the aggressive interconnect manufacturers frequently offer strong price/feature performance, allow integration of communications equipment with existing computer installations, and provide or interface with advanced features such as electronic- and voice-mail equipment, local networks, or teleconferencing gear.

Decision Sciences' market research provided an in-depth understanding of requirements and a detailed profile of existing and potential private-bypass-network users. Most private-network users are large corporations, educational institutions, or government organizations, including those distinctive needs of specific market segments that Decision Sciences identified and analyzed, such as Fortune 500 manufacturers, large financial institutions, transportation and distribution firms, wholesale/retail organizations, large service companies, utilities, educational institutions, and federal, state, and local governments. The research shows that approximately 1,200 U. S. organizations have requirements that could justify installation of private integrated bypass networks.

Likely candidates for bypass networks usually have high communications and information processing costs. Many financial and insurance companies, for example, have communications and information processing expenses as high as 20 to 30 percent of their operating costs; communications budgets in excess of $30 million annually were not unusual. Many potential user organizations are also geographically dispersed and have a strong need for specialized communications services, such as high-speed data transmission, electronic mail, or extensive intracompany communications.

Typically, potential users were dissatisfied with their existing (usually common-carrier provided) network and network services. Top management frequently recognized telecommunications as a vital business tool and had instituted a large planning staff devoted to telecommunications development, backed by substantial budgets. But some organizations without the planning expertise or advanced technology needs were simply seeking a replacement of predivestiture AT&T equipment, in order to take care of all service problems, reduce cost, and furnish external planning and maintenance expertise.

In general, the needs for improved service, cost containment, and advanced technology were prime motivators for all 1,200 potential users of private bypass networks, although certain specific needs differed between market segments.

To date, approximately 200 of the 1,200 organizations have had private networks installed. Decision Sciences estimates that this number will grow to more than 600 by 1988—a penetration rate of over 50 percent of the potential market. Analyzing the profiles of the existing installation, Decision Sciences found that the new private bypass networks cover a number of the major locations of an organization and range in cost from $5 million to $15 million. In addition to the initial outlays, many organizations have budgeted further expenditures for network upgrades and expansion with smaller nodes.

Only a few companies have the ability to supply large user organizations with total private bypass network solutions. The criteria for vendors are stringent, and few have successfully penetrated the market. Users expect their vendors to be fully capable of providing high-quality support. Installation forces must be able to design and install state-of-the-art networks around the country; maintenance forces must be able to service and repair these systems around the clock. Above all, vendors must also be able to design total network solutions, frequently incorporating thelatest digital telecommunications hardware and software components geared to provide the required cost savings or advanced features. Most users start to consider cost only after the service and technology hurdles are passed.

To date, only a handful of large interconnect and telephone operating companies have been able to meet the requirements and compete effectively in the private-network market. The major advanced PBX manufacturers dominate the market. Decision Sciences' research showed that Northern Telecom, with its large-capacity SL-1 and SL-100 switches, strong network features, and nationwide sales and service capabilities, had the greatest single share of the installed base: 20 percent. Northern was followed by Rolm, Intecom, and NEC. Of the divisions of independent telephone operating companies, GTE, through its Communications Systems Division, commanded the largest share, followed by Centel and Contel, which frequently install Northern Telecom equipment. This business, however, has not been very profitable for GTE and Contel. To date, the new AT&T Information Systems unit has only a very small part of the installed base, since Decision Sciences excluded the nonprivate predivestiture electronic-transmission networks. This top end of the PBX market, however, is a major target for ATTIS, which intends to supply its Dimension 85 and Number 5 ESS switches. Several of the new regional Bell operating companies, such as Bell South, Bell Atlantic, through its Bell Atlanticom Systems subsidiary, and U. S. West, through its Interline subsidiary, may also become major private-network vendors in the future.

The market analysis did not show usage of local network or CATV-type technologies as a basis for large private networks, so, consequently, no local network, data processing, or data-switching vendors were identified as major competitors, though their role is expected to increase. CATV technology, however, can form the basis for efficient local and wide-area network transmission, and thus CATV technology vendors could become major private bypass network suppliers in the future.

The competitive scenario is not expected to change drastically over the next three to five years. The large participants are expected to expand their market shares, which should result in increasing performance standards and product development for advanced network applications. The industry's distribution structure is expected to change when the regional Bell operating companies begin to develop as competitors in the large private-network market. Since the market should mature toward the end of Decision Sciences' five-year-analysis time frame, price competition is likely to increase. This trend, in combination with high investment and service requirements, will probably result in a shakeout of most minor manufacturing and interconnect participants.
— *Donald F. Blumberg*

Blumberg, president of Decision Sciences Corp., a Jenkintown, Pa., management consulting firm, specializes in data communications service planning and strategy.

major use for zee-net was to be the transmission of large batch files between the regional branch and the primary data center (PDC) as well as the database file transmissions from PDC to the backup disaster center (BDC).

Nodal soup

A good area to start with is the T1 trunk interface and bandwidth management. Since more than one T1 trunk will terminate in each of the six zee-net nodal locations (four in the case of HQ) and since future growth is expected, the RFI will specify that each TRM be field expandable to support at least six concurrently operating T1 trunks. To optimize the bandwidth use on these trunks, the TRM should view trunks with common destinations as a "pool" of bandwidth and manage that pool with maximum efficiency. Basically this means that a TRM must be able to build a "path," or link, between any two locations over more than one actual trunk facility, as needs dictate.

This capability is important for several reasons. For path redundancy purposes, it provides the TRM with the ability to dynamically route traffic over an alternate path should the primary trunk encounter high error rates or fail completely. Also, each TRM would then support the ability to drop and insert channels at interim locations (and should not demultiplex the information channels that are just passing through the nodes).

The business requirements associated with using T1 bandwidth highlight the need at XYZ Corp. for several different call-processing capabilities. The ongoing mixture of voice and data calls, occasionally intermingled with large video bit streams, did not lend itself to a full-period channelization scheme, since it would result in significant bandwidth waste. Due to the types of usage patterns that occurred on zee-net, the efficiencies brought about by a dynamic bandwidth allocation scheme were most applicable. With this scheme, bandwidth for voice, voice-band data, and video calls would be allocated only when the origination terminal created an off-hook condition. The bandwidth would be assigned to these classes of calls only for the duration of the call. Only the bandwidth required to support the data calls associated with the transaction-processing applications would be reserved for the entire workday in order to give them fast response time.

By opting for a dynamic bandwidth assignment scheme, the zee-net task force needed to specify customization parameters that would enable the TRM bandwidth assignment algorithm to adapt to the varying traffic mixtures. One of these parameters would be a call prioritization capability that allowed more important calls to be connected before lesser ones. A link-routing parameter was also needed to allow calls to be placed over the most appropriate T1 link for that type of call (such as a satellite facility for batch file transfers). This capability freed up the bandwidth on other facilities for the classes of calls that required them.

Another feature should provide the ability to reserve bandwidth before it is needed so that wideband video or file-transfer calls could be gracefully scheduled into the traffic flow rather than just grabbing huge chunks of bandwidth whenever the transmission occurred.

Speech processing

A second major call-processing criterion that needs to be studied by a network planning group is the use of an enhanced speech-encoding technique, which allows more than 24 voice calls to be placed on a single T1 line. A network planning group can spend hours debating the merits of the various techniques available today. While the subjective voice quality derived using any of the various voice digitization techniques over a point-to-point link is quite good, ADPCM has been proven by Bell Laboratories tests to be the least susceptible to reduced signal quality in a multihop (node-to-node) network. For the zee-net analysts the decision was made easier by the corporate requirement to position the company to take advantage of future capabilities. They therefore specified the ADPCM algorithm running at 32 kbit/s because this was recommended by both CCITT and AT&T. ADPCM also has an extremely high probability of becoming the domestic and international low-bit-rate voice (and voice-band data) encoding technique within the next year.

The next area to be considered is the network timing or synchronization requirement. A digital network must be synchronized to a single clock source. This is to keep "slips," or framing, errors from occurring at the various nodes. Since zee-net was to have more than one carrier's T1 facilities in it, the RFI specified that the TRM entities would:

A. Provide clock to the whole network
B. Accept a station clock, or
C. Accept clock from one of the carrier's links and use it to synchronize the rest of the network.

There should also be a provision for immediate use of a backup clock source when the primary one fails. Since XYZ Corp. would be using the Accunet T1.5 service in some areas, the heaviest weighting was given to that alternative so that the implemented network would derive primary clock source from one of those Accunet links.

Since a significant amount of corporate information would be passing through the backbone network, a major failure between any two points could be disastrous. Thus, uptime was critical, and the task force needed to spend considerable time and effort delineating the business issues and translating them into RFI criteria.

From a destination perspective, uptime translates into the availability of access to resources when required, such as the on-line computer programs. Therefore, a planning group should consider the merits of an alternate destination capability, both within a single site and to a second site. In this manner, a call would automatically be forwarded to a second destination address if the first was unavailable. Using the XYZ Corp. example, if one computer at PDC fails, a connection must be rapidly established to the backup mainframe running the application programs. Also, if the entire PDC complex is put out of service, data transactions would be automatically rerouted to the BDC once the TRM had been commanded to invoke this capability. The zee-net task force would specify, in its RFI, the ability for the TRM to handle automatic alternate destination delivery of calls.

Network operation
Another element critical to reliable network operation is the ability to diagnose specific failures and get them repaired quickly. This requires the TRM to have an effective, and easy to use, network operator interface. There should be central access to all TRMs in the network. This should provide the ability to run diagnostic tests on all of the logic boards, as well as run remote and local loopback checks on all circuit interfaces. Continuous monitoring of trunk bit error rate (BER) is very important—so is the ability to interrogate all TRMs via both in-network and out-of-network diagnostic channels.

An effective network control environment will need all network events and alarms to be communicated to a network control center where they can be acted upon immediately—and where network usage detail records can be extracted for analysis and planning purposes. It is important to include the operations personnel when determining this section of the RFI criteria. At XYZ Corp., for instance, the operations representative to the zee-net task force requested that standard network "health" information be displayable in graphics format on the control console. These statistics include, among other things, buffer usage over specified time periods, errors incurred, and number of executed processor cycles. This task-force representative also wanted the various alarm levels to be color coded for immediate identification of critical failures.

A practical scheme for the TRM equipment was to have three basic levels of service disruption: catastrophic, major, and minor. A catastrophic failure was one that removed the entire TRM from service. To reduce the chance of the latter, the RFI specified that common equipment, such as power supplies, be either fully redundant or that the logic components be spread across multiple power supplies to reduce the possibility of equipment failure. To reduce the possibility of a major failure (which, for instance, may affect the voice encoding routines), all common-logic components within a TRM should have on-line redundancy or hot standby replacements. For minor disruptions, such as a trunk or port-card failure, the TRM should provide for either on-line or standby redundancy or the ability for operation personnel to swiftly replace the faulty board without having to power-down any equipment.

Strategic issue
At XYZ Corp., largely because of the architectural decision to implement and operate zee-net as a utility transmission subnetwork, the XYZ's task force eliminated the current premises equipment (voice and data) as the primary transmission resource manager. Following are a few reasons supporting this line of action:
■ The wideband video transmission requirements were beyond the capabilities of their current premises equipment

4. Off premises. *An efficient TRM between premises equipment and the T1 links will optimize the backbone network for digitized voice, data, and video.*

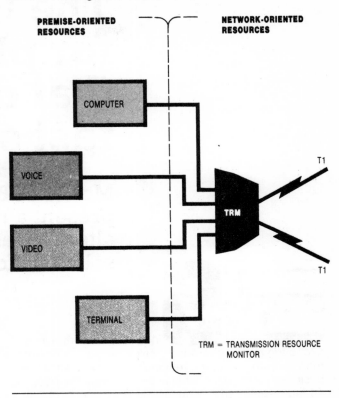

TRM = TRANSMISSION RESOURCE MONITOR

■ The differing response-time characteristics of the various applications
■ The desire for enhanced T1 link-management capabilities
■ The corporate benefits of network control gained from having vendor independence between the premises-oriented and transmission-oriented equipment
■ Positioning for future enhancements even though the standards (such as ISDN) are still being defined
■ The desire to upgrade the zee-net subnetwork as new capabilities are needed, while not having to wait for their possible incorporation into a large expense item such as a PBX or communications controller.

Figure 4 summarizes the design for the premises that the analysts recommended as a functional and flexible solution to their needs. By locating an efficient TRM capability between the customer-premises equipment and the T1 facilities, zee-net would be able to optimize the use of the backbone network for voice, high-speed data, video, and other types of traffic—gaining extremely useful call-processing and network management capabilities. Being separate from the premises equipment, the TRM and/or any piece of premises equipment could be upgraded without affecting the other. ■

Bob Fish, manager of customer network design at Network Equipment Technologies, attended the University of Virginia.

Michael W. Patrick, Ztel Inc., Wilmington, Mass.

The heat is on for phone switches that do a lot of fast shuffling

Modern PBXs and local networks present a range of alluring alternatives as voice/data solutions for automated office.

Since the first commercial exchange began operating, in New Haven, Conn., more than a century ago, the telephone has been a tool for business communications. In recent years the PBX has added a variety of functions—such as flexible calling, holding, and transferring—to office workers' desks. Lately, innovations in minicomputers, terminals, and microcomputers have brought technology to the point where it is economically feasible to provide desktop computer access to every office worker.

Now two new technologies are competing for a place in the foundation being set for improved communications services: voice/data PBXs and local networks. The new PBXs, by digitizing voice directly at the handset, readily support data rates at speeds up to 64 kbit/s (the standard data rate for digitized speech). The new local networks offer computer links able to carry data at speeds greater than 1 Mbit/s.

Not surprisingly, many information processing managers have trouble weighing the relative merits of PBXs and local networks. Requirements vary for voice and data communications in medium to large offices, and managers could use some criteria to compare the benefits and drawbacks of local networks and PBXs.

PBX voice features

Today the PBX is so ensconced in the office environment that almost no one disputes its ability to enhance voice communications. Modern PBXs provide upwards of 150 separately identified features, although many of them are not obvious to the typical user. One such PBX feature—responsible for major cost savings—is least-cost routing. This enhancement automatically selects the cheapest trunk for outgoing long-distance calls. Newer PBXs will permit bypassing the local telephone exchange entirely when connecting corporate facilities directly to the company's long-distance carrier of choice. The newer switches also permit tracking of each telephone call with the station message detailed recording function.

The more visible PBX features alleviate the major gripe with telephone calls—the frustration encountered when the called party is away from his or her phone, or is busy on another call. The ability to reroute calls automatically (call forwarding), have calls answered by another party (call pickup), and automatically redial an unanswered call (call-back, no answer) are all features that permit the caller some recourse other than hanging up when the called party does not answer.

Notification of incoming calls (call waiting), automatically redialing a called number when it becomes available (call-back when free), dialing a specified series of numbers in a group when no one answers on the original number (hunting), and a variety of "hold" options can put two parties in touch if the called party is busy on another call. Other popular features include call transfer and conferencing.

The most important—and most difficult—challenge in meeting an organization's data communications and processing needs is to determine the functional requirements of its users. Planning personnel often emphasize only the hardware required, concentrating on the most visible initial cost. They attempt to determine, say, how many minicomputers, disks, terminals, and microcomputers are required for a given organization. Unfortunately, most planners discover far too soon a variant of Parkinson's Law: The use of a resource expands to exceed its current capacity.

To circumvent such resource bottlenecks, planners should carefully analyze the application programs required by potential users. Thus, planners can anticipate the processing power, memory, disk storage, and communications capabilities that will be needed.

To determine the best way to meet users' needs, managers must first examine the job responsibilities of each user or user group. For example, organizations are typically divided into groups that perform special functions:
- Engineering, responsible for the creation of new products.
- Operations, in manufacturing firms, responsible for the assembly, testing, and shipment of products; and in service companies, responsible for the performance of the service offered.
- Marketing, responsible for sales and customer support.
- Control, responsible for financial accounting and analysis.

Also, to identify data communications requirements, it is useful to assemble all managers and secretaries into a separate functional group—managerial/secretarial, responsible for leadership and clerical support of other activities.

The application programs typically required for each function are shown in Table 1. Virtually all the applications listed deal with the manipulation of disk-based databases. Most other programs require random access for inquiry, entry, or update operations on a database. Such programs are considered transaction-based because the only information exchanged between a terminal and a program is a transaction request entered by hand plus the subsequent displayed data. Note that for all transaction-based programs the database involved requires access by several users. Therefore, some means of sharing that database is required.

Table 2 summarizes the results of a survey of business data communications network installations done by International Data Corp. of Framingham, Mass. The networks in this survey were usually dedicated to a particular purpose. They connected remote terminals or minicomputers to a host mainframe to run a particular set of applications.

Table 1: Computing requirements

FUNCTION	APPLICATIONS
ENGINEERING	CIRCUIT DRAWING, SIMULATION, TEXT EDITING, COMPILATION
OPERATIONS	MATERIALS RESOURCE PLANNING, PRODUCTION PLANNING, FACTORY MACHINE, CONTROL, SERVICE RESERVATIONS
MARKETING	ORDER ENTRY, SALES FORECASTING
CONTROL	EXPENSE CONTROL, ASSET MANAGEMENT, PORTFOLIO ANALYSIS, ACCOUNTS PAYABLE, ACCOUNTS RECEIVABLE, SPREADSHEET ANALYSIS, PERSONNEL RECORDS
MANAGERIAL/SECRETARIAL	WORD PROCESSING, PHONE MESSAGES, PROJECT PLANNING, EXPENSE CONTROL/FORECASTS; CAPITAL BUDGETING
ALL	INTEROFFICE MAIL, PHONE MESSAGES

Table 2: Data communications requirements

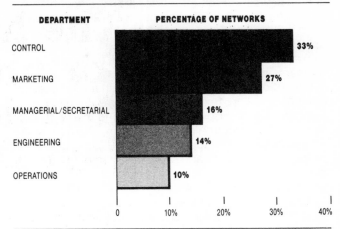

The survey results showed that data networks for the control functions of financial, accounting, and payroll applications constituted a third of the installed networks, though the personnel performing these functions formed less than 5 percent of the office workforce (according to the 1980 U. S. Census). Overall, the transaction-based networks for control, sales/marketing, and operations formed 70 percent of the data communications requirements. The key implications are that the bulk of traffic in an office's data communications network is for transaction-based database updates and not disk-based file transfers.

Common access
Local networks permit disk resources to be shared among several processor or memory devices with little consequent loss in throughput. For hard-disk drives (such as Winchester-based devices), the throughput between disk and memory is often limited by the standard defining the interface between the disk and controller. Most small computer hard-disk interfaces limit data transfer to 5 Mbit/s.

The transfer rate between a floppy disk and memory is limited by the disk itself and falls between 250 and 500 kbit/s. Hence, modern local networks, capable of providing burst throughput rates of 4 to 50 Mbit/s, introduce little delay in the transfer of disk storage to system memory. High-performance minicomputers (such as Digital Equipment Corp.'s recently announced Venus) that use a high-speed local network as the primary connection between CPU/memory and storage subsystems are now evolving. Data communications managers, then, should concentrate on the separate requirements for both terminal-to-program data flow and program-to-disk data flow.

The 64-kbit/s limit
For transaction-based programs, the throughput consists of terminal-to-program traffic of several information fields and, at most, one full terminal screen at a time. Because human entry and review is involved, a maximum of about two transactions per second should be supported (typical scrolling speed when perusing a

file). Conversely, the transaction-based program should have a turnaround of less than 0.5 seconds. Assuming a 24-line, 80-character-per-line display sent every half-second, the terminal requires up to 30.72 kbit/s. Hence, the 64-kbit/s limitation of PBX-based terminal connections easily surpasses the needs of transaction-based applications.

Exceptions to this requirement for shared access to one database are text-editing programs. In this case, users develop their own documents and then distribute them in either electronic or paper form. Microcomputers are ideal for this application because the text-processing CPU time and disk activity required for development of the document need not affect other users. If microcomputers are not used, a text-editing program on a shared minicomputer or mainframe suffices. The network must handle the communications between the terminal and the text-editing program. In that case, the load of text-editing programs is similar to the load required by transaction-based programs.

Most organizations, however, do not provide terminals at every potential reader's desk, so most electronically stored documents are eventually printed. Because of the high-density one-way traffic, document printing then places the greatest load on an internal communications network. Yet the fastest line printers available, which provide speeds of approximately 1,200 lines per minute, require only 19.2 kbit/s.

The new laser printers, which rely on stored fonts, can print 100 picture elements, or pixels, per inch but are nevertheless limited to transmitting the standard 80 characters per line. Still, a 66-line page requires 42.24 kbit/s (66 lines multiplied by 80 characters multiplied by 8 bits per character), so a PBX link at 64 kbit/s limits a laser printer to less than two pages per second. Standard blank compression techniques, however, can push that limit to approximately four pages per second.

Even so, high-speed printers are quite expensive and are usually justified only for the high-output requirements of a mainframe computer room. For economic reasons, the more common laser printers distributed throughout a work area will be limited to throughput of 1 to 10 seconds per page for several more years. Hence, the 64-kbit/s maximum throughput of a PBX data link will suffice for distributed printer applications.

Most memoranda are limited to less than two pages. Program source-code modules (following generally accepted programming principles) are limited to only a few pages as well. Based on an estimate of 66 lines of 80 characters per page with no blank suppression, a data rate of 64 kbit/s transfers over 1.5 pages per second. Therefore, most edits can be transferred in a few seconds. Even a 1-Mbyte file is transferred in only two minutes.

The most frequently cited requirement for high-speed local networks is the connection of intelligent engineering workstations. In a hardware engineering department (whether electrical, mechanical, or chemical), the primary documents produced are graphic drawings and their accompanying text. Engineering workstations with displays providing 1,024-by-1,024-pixel resolution are becoming economical for individual use in large design engineering departments. A unit with such high-resolution display on a black-and-white screen requires approximately 1 Mbit/s of display memory; a color display requires about four times that amount.

Graphics

The display memory size is important because the entire memory must be updated when the screen is redrawn. Studies have shown that user productivity significantly drops and dissatisfaction results when screen redraw times exceed one second. Therefore, graphics terminals require at least 1-Mbit/s channels between the programs that generate the display data and the display memory. But an intelligent workstation includes a program to generate graphics data; and the workstation display memory resides in the high-bandwidth system bus of a program in the terminal itself. It is not necessary, therefore, that an intelligent graphics-based terminal require a megabit-per-second connection to a host computer running a graphics application program.

On graphics terminal applications, usually there is a language of higher-level primitives to define certain graphics operations (such as a single command to draw a line). Furthermore, many graphics terminals define custom fonts, or character representations, within the terminal and then select an 8-bit character code to designate that font.

Based on a benchmark of 1,024-by-1,024 pixels per 8.5-by-11-inch page, a video screen showing a third of a page could display 24 lines of 80 characters each, where each character defined 12 pixels across and 16 pixels down. Thus only 19,200 characters would have to be transmitted to fill the screen. That is the number required by today's terminals.

In such applications, the most annoying factor is actually downloading the font from the host to the terminal. In the example, each character requires 192 (12 times 16) bits; a font of 256 characters therefore requires that 49.152 kbit/s be sent. At the de facto standard of 9.6 kbit/s using asynchronous protocols, the font download requires more than 6 seconds. With the newest PBXs, however, graphics terminals can transmit synchronously to their hosts at up to 64 kbit/s for a font download time of only three-quarters of a second. Even for graphics terminals, then, PBXs' 64-kbit/s transfer rates are acceptable.

Cost considerations

The costs of an office data communications network can be divided into three areas—equipment costs, wiring costs, and adapter costs. The equipment costs include the terminal or microcomputer cost as well as that of the equipment required at the host to connect the terminal. Wiring costs include the cost of any physical media and attendant installation costs. Adapter costs include the expense of any adapter required between desk equipment and the data communications network.

The communications equipment typically found on an office desk includes a telephone and one or more electronic keyboards. Keyboard costs vary widely, depending on the type of equipment they are attached to:

Coaxial-cable-connected
display head: $2,400—$3,000
Word processor: $2,000—$6,000
ASCII terminal: $500—$2,000
Microcomputer: $1,600—$9,000

The industry-standard IBM 3270 display uses coaxial connections between dumb display heads (models 3278, 3279, 3178, 3179) or printers (model 3287) and an intelligent terminal controller (models 3274 and 3276). The terminal controller connects either directly to the mainframe through a channel attachment or remotely with a synchronous communications link. Other mainframe manufacturers offer similar coaxially connected display systems. The price tag of $2,400 to $3,000 includes not only the cost of the terminal but also a prorated fraction of the controller's cost.

Word processors have traditionally been standalone items, but several products (Wang Laboratories', for example) offer a coaxial connection to a common control element for communications with other displays or printers. The cost per station can vary widely, depending on the number of per common control elements and the type of printer selected.

ASCII terminals are the primary interface to minicomputers and microcomputers. They transmit data asynchronously using either RS-232-C or current-loop protocols. The so-called dumb terminals with few display and scrolling options fall at the lower end of the cost range. Terminals offering multiple fonts and sophisticated features fall at the high end. Because minicomputer application programs often take advantage of all terminal characteristics, many terminal manufacturers offer modes that emulate the full-feature terminals of the minicomputer manufacturers (DEC's VT100, for example).

Microcomputer prices primarily reflect the amount of disk storage they provide. Units that accommodate just one floppy disk fall at one end of the price range. Those with 10-Mbyte Winchesters tend toward the high end. Because disk storage and printer peripherals represent the bulk of a microcomputer's cost, a cost-effective data communications network permits several microcomputers to share a disk or printer. The most popular configuration attaches the microcomputers to a common minicomputer or mainframe, which in turn controls the common disk and printer resources.

Wiring costs
Today, computer terminals are typically hardwired to a computer. When an office worker moves, the host connection (and the terminal itself) has to move with him or her. Whenever a new application is required, existing terminal equipment becomes obsolete. As more office workers require electronic keyboards, the need for flexible means of attaching terminals to other equipment grows. Otherwise the cost of physically rewiring a terminal connection over several years can

exceed the cost of the terminal itself. This situation contrasts with telephone wiring, which is routed to each workplace when a building is constructed or before office furniture is put in place.

Data communications wiring installed after initial building construction has been completed is usually set in raised ceilings and other environmental plenums. Because of this, smoke-resistant insulation such as Teflon is required for the media, adding significantly (as much as three times that of preconstruction wiring) to wiring costs.

Most terminal equipment is wired in a star fashion, with the terminal directly wired to a host computer or controller. Telephones are wired in the same manner; all wires are brought to a central wiring closet. Within an office, the average length of the wire between a workplace and a host computer is about 150 feet. Using industry-standard conventions for the placement of wiring closets, an IBM study demonstrated an average workplace-to-closet wiring distance of 85 feet. The latter figure is relevant because telephone wiring must be bundled into cables containing 25 to 300 pairs for connections between closets. The labor charges for laying such a bundled cable must be prorated across each connection.

Table 3 lists five of the most popular data wiring options and compares the cost of an average connection. PBX-based front-end wiring consists of quad wire from the wiring closet to each workplace. The connection from the wiring closet (the intermediate distribution frame) to the PBX (main distribution frame) would normally be by 50-pair cables. Because the labor cost of laying the 50-pair cable is shared by the 25 stations thus connected, the labor costs for PBX wiring are low.

As shown, telephone wiring is by far the least expensive of wiring options. And it becomes even more attractive in light of the fact that all other front-end connection schemes (except the IBM Cabling System) must also add the cost of connecting telephone wiring to their initial costs. If four-wire telephone connections are already set up, a company can take advantage of considerable savings by using existing wire rather than installing new media.

For connection to minicomputers, such as the popular DEC VAX, RS-232-C-based wiring is used. In general, only four connections are required for an asynchronous terminal connection: send data, receive data, signal ground, and protective ground. Data rates up to 19.2 kbit/s across these wires are possible, but 9.6 kbit/s is typical. Wiring for a minicomputer connection costs more than $100 in parts and labor.

Coaxial cable is used for most mainframe terminals, including IBM 3270 displays. For local connections, the 3274 or 3276 controller is attached to the CPU in the computer room, requiring coaxial cable to run from the computer room all the way to the workplace. This type of wiring scheme costs approximately $117 per connection (Table 3). For remote connections, the 3274 or 3276 controller may be placed in the intermediate distribution frame, saving about $14 in cable costs and $35 in labor.

Unlike other schemes, Ethernet connections are not

wired in a star fashion. Instead, the main Ethernet cable, a specially developed coaxial cable, is routed throughout a building. For each station to be attached to the network, a transceiver unit is tapped into the cable. The station is then attached to the transceiver unit by a separate transceiver cable (with four twisted pairs). This analysis assumes a main cable is routed once through each area of 10 feet by 10 feet (10 feet of main cable per user).

Based on recent average list prices, a fixed cost of $90 for the transceiver cable (including connectors and the labor required to make the cable) is used. If a building is prewired with main cable and transceiver cable (but no transceiver tap) for each desk, the cost of wiring to each desk will be about $186 per workstation. In this case, when a user moves, a new tap must be placed on the main cable. If, for convenience, a tap is provided for each user, another $270 must be spent, bringing wiring costs to $456 per workplace.

IBM recently announced the IBM Cabling System. With this approach, a combination voice/data wire is routed between each workplace and a wiring closet at the time of building construction. The cable used

includes four twisted-pair wires for each telephone connection and two twisted-pair wires within a metal shield for data. At the wiring closet, the telephone wires and data wires are separated and brought out to separate patch panels. The shielded twisted pairs, or data-grade media, can replace virtually any coaxial connection within a building.

A data-grade media cable is used to connect the patch panel of the wiring closet to a terminal controller or host in the computer room. With this scheme, both voice and data cabling networks can be established at a cost of $186 per workplace. Although the IBM Cabling System can be used to provide universal connection for coaxial-based terminals, IBM has also announced that they intend to provide a token-ring-based local network using the data-grade media within two to three years.

Adapter costs

The adapter costs depend on the type of communications network used. A point-to-point connection between terminals and computers incurs no additional adapter cost because the circuitry to transmit and receive the data is built into the terminal and host equipment. If a local network is used, a separate adapter to the network is required at both the terminal and host sides.

The average cost of a single connection to a local network is currently more than $900. To lower the per-connection price, many local network adapters (terminal servers) allow eight to 24 terminals to connect to the local network, providing transparent RS-232-C connection across it. Such terminal servers can provide a per-terminal cost in the range of $400 to $500 but require an unwieldy and inflexible scheme combining both RS-232-C and local network wiring.

A PBX data adapter, which adds data capability to a telephone connection, however, costs only $200 to $500 and can be attached to any workplace. The difference between local network adapter and PBX data adapter costs—a factor of two—is due primarily to the following:

■ The local network connection requires additional memory to buffer the high-speed data between the terminal's system memory and the local network.
■ The local network adapter requires additional processing power to implement mechanisms for distributed error detection, reporting, and recovery.
■ The local network adapter requires additional logic to implement the access control mechanisms to the local network.

Only the latter is amenable to cost reduction through the use of local network chips. Also, because of the plethora of local networks and the widespread acceptance of RS-232-C, lower-speed UARTs/USARTs will always enjoy a significantly higher volume of shipment. For these reasons, it is expected that low-speed (less than 64-kbit/s) terminal connections will remain significantly cheaper than local network connections, and that the economic justification for a separate front-end network involving point-to-point terminal wiring connections will remain sound.

Table 3: Average data-wiring costs

FRONT-END NETWORK	WIRING	WIRE COST[1]	CONNECTOR COST[2]	LABOR COST[3]	TOTAL COST
PBX	QUAD WIRE	$3.62	$3.00	$45.74	$52.36
RS-232-C	4-WIRE, 22-GAUGE UNSHIELDED	18.76	4.00	80.00	102.76
COAXIAL	RG58	31.36	6.00	80.00	117.36
ETHERNET	STANDARD ETHERNET AND TRANSCEIVER CABLE	100.00	6.00	80.00	186.00
IBM CABLING SYSTEM	TYPE 2 TO WIRING CLOSET; TYPE 1 TO CPU	81.25	26.00	80.00	187.25

NOTES: 1. BASED ON A DISTANCE OF 85 FEET FROM WORKPLACE TO INTERMEDIATE DISTRIBUTION FRAME AND 65 FEET FROM THE INTERMEDIATE DISTRIBUTION FRAME TO THE MAIN DISTRIBUTION FRAME, WITH NONPLENUM WIRING COSTS AS FOLLOWS:

	COST/1,000 FEET
PBX QUAD WIRE	$36
RS-232-C 4 CONDUCTOR	125
RG58 COAXIAL	209
IBM VOICE/DATA	650
DATA ONLY	400
ETHERNET MAIN CABLE	985
TRANSCEIVER CABLE	90 (50-FOOT DROP)

THESE COSTS ARE BASED ON THE MANUFACTURER'S RETAIL PRICE FOR JUNE 1984. THE ACTUAL PRICES PAID UNDER A VOLUME CONTRACT WILL PROBABLY BE LOWER.

2. WIRING CONNECTORS, FACEPLATES, WALL MOUNTS, AND THE LIKE; DOES NOT INCLUDE TRANSCEIVER FOR ETHERNET STATION ($270).

3. TWO HOURS FOR CABLE CONNECTOR ASSEMBLY, LAYING, AND DISTRIBUTION FRAME WIRING AT $40 AN HOUR CONTRACT LABOR.

Five in one. Host computers and PBXs may be connected in several ways, including: via common data banks, by direct T1 links, and through terminal servers.

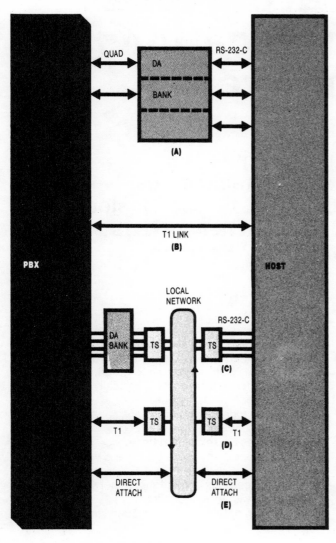

DA = DATA ADAPTER   TS = TERMINAL SERVER

While local networks are not cost-effective as front-end networks, they are necessary for the interconnecting computers with disk resources, major shared peripherals, and other computer peripherals. The backbone local network connects the mainframes, minicomputers, and any smaller department-specific local networks. It is required for the high-speed file transfer between hosts. The backbone local network is also necessary to accomplish the transparent connection of applications running in one host accessing files in disks attached to another.

A fiber-based local network, such as the IEEE 802.5 ring supported by IBM, is optimum for this purpose. Other possibilities include the 100-Mbit/s fiber distributed data interface local network under development by the ANSI X3T9.5 committee. Fiber-optic connection is desirable for its high speed and immunity to radiated noise. Further, because it is immune from electromagnetic interference, it is an excellent choice for connection between buildings.

One problem managers encounter is how to make the connection between the front-end network provided by digital PBXs and an organization's computers and local networks.

How to connect

The accompanying figure shows five separate mechanisms for interconnecting computers or local networks with PBXs. Today, the primary mechanism is a direct connection between a PBX and a host through a bank of data adapters that transform the PBX's internal 64-kbit/s stream to an asynchronous or synchronous stream at a standard data rate of 300 bit/s to 19.2 kbit/s (Fig. 1A). Each lower-speed terminal link is then separately attached to a serial port of the host.

To reduce the cost of this solution, two standards have been proposed to multiplex up to 24 terminal links on a T1-carrier link between a PBX and host (Fig. 1B). Northern Telecom and DEC have proposed the Computer-to-PBX interface, and AT&T and Hewlett-Packard Co. have spearheaded the development of the Digital Multiplexed Interface (DMI). One mode of DMI conforms to the provisions of common channel signaling specified in the emerging ISDN standards.

When a local network is involved, the PBX can provide connections for its terminals in one of three ways. A proprietary terminal server connection, such as those provided by Ungermann/Bass or Interlan, can be used to provide several transparent data streams through the local network. The PBX then attaches to those streams with each individual terminal link (Fig. 1C). Combining the approaches of Figures 1B and 1C, a T1 link could connect the PBX and host to the proprietary terminal servers (Fig. 1D). The most cost-effective approach, of course, is for the PBXs to directly attach to the local network (Fig. 1E). This scheme, however, requires a standard for providing virtual terminal service on a local network, a standard that does not yet exist.

Next to come

Because no standard exists for combining both voice and data on a high-speed local network, separate networks are required for voice and data connections. Future local network standardization work should address this problem by including both types of terminal traffic, thus allowing a single medium to be used for both networks. In addition, when designations of the geographical right-of-way do not exist, or the distances between buildings are greater than those handled by a local network, a fourth-generation PBX is able to provide full transparency of voice and data across a wide-area public network. ■

Michael W. Patrick, senior research associate at Ztel, received his B. S. and M. S. in computer science from Massachusetts Institute of Technology. Formerly, Patrick worked for Texas Instruments as a systems architect for the company's microprocessor division.

David P. Levin, Netcomm Inc., New York, N. Y.

Comparing local communications alternatives

What are the strengths and weaknesses of the techniques? When should a PBX be used instead of—or with—a local network? Is optical fiber viable? Read on.

Data communications facilities are rapidly expanding, and the recent boom in microcomputer and workstation usage is fueling this growth. These trends reinforce the importance of integrating all of one's local and remote data and voice networks. And as it turns out, most major organizations in the United States plan to integrate their different communications networks.

Many organizations are currently experiencing rapid business expansion. To meet this growth, new facilities are typically acquired within a company user group's geographic area—such as a campus environment's previously uninhabited section or a building's newly occupied floor. This expansion into new locations raises issues of how to provide access to data processing resources as well as providing voice communications. The most cost-effective approach in terms of flexibility and growth is some type of local communications—specifically, a PBX, a local network, or some combination of the two.

Another consideration: Many organizations not only have a growing mainframe-based data communications network but also a growing number of specialized data devices requiring communications. Most have a growing voice communications network as well. Alternatives to local transmission solutions obviously include those provided by the local telephone company.

Figure 1 details several alternatives to channels provided by the telephone company (bypass services) and the distances best spanned by each service. Note that local networks are defined here as parallel-bus-based installations typically used for linking mainframe computers. These local networks normally span distances of less than 1,000 feet. Campus and institutional networks typically use coaxial cable as a transmission medium and span distances up to five or six miles. CATV networks cover distances of between one and 20 miles and are otherwise similar to the campus network. Optical fiber and regional microwave services span distances both equal to and greater than CATV networks. Satellite transmission typically spans distances greater than 100 miles.

Alternative local communications solutions for most organizations include:
- PBX facilities for selected data services.
- Telephone company voice-grade and wideband services.
- One's own campus or institutional network, using coaxial and twisted-pair cabling.
- CATV, which provides wideband services (see "Bidirectional broadband").

The current leader

Baseband networks represent the most popular local network today and use both twisted-pair and coax as a transmission medium. Datapoint's Attached Resource Computer (ARC) product is the most widely installed baseband local network, with more than 6,000 installations. Xerox's Ethernet is the second-most popular, with approximately 800 installations.

Broadband local networks represent the greatest bandwidth of the local communications technologies. Broadband networks are typically more costly to implement and maintain. They require testing at least once a year to ensure proper operation. Today only broadband (and fiber) networks can support full-motion video as well as multiple channels of 1.544 Mbit/s, the telephone company's basic T1 carrier service.

Regarding PBXs, most manufacturers offer exclusively digital switches. The notable exception to this is AT&T Information Systems (ATTIS) with its actively marketed Dimension analog-product line. More re-

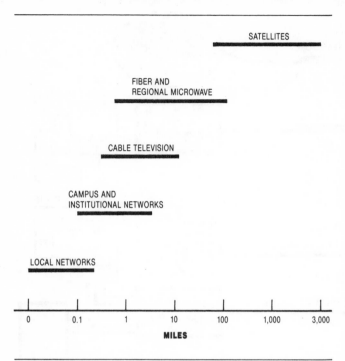

1. Bypass alternatives. *Shown here are technologies that may be used instead of channels provided by the telephone company, with their optimum distances.*

SATELLITES

FIBER AND
REGIONAL MICROWAVE

CABLE TELEVISION

CAMPUS AND
INSTITUTIONAL NETWORKS

LOCAL NETWORKS

| 0 | 0.1 | 1 | 10 | 100 | 1,000 | 3,000 |

MILES

cently, ATTIS has offered digital switches, called the System 85 and System 75.

An analog PBX transmits voice signals with a bandwidth of 300 to 3.3K Hz. The analog switch creates a distinct analog signal path from each extension to a trunk line, line card, or another extension. A digital PBX transmits a digital signal representing binary digits and—depending on the data rate—requires less bandwidth than an analog signal. (For example, a 1.2-kbit/s signal needs 1.2 kHz; analog voice, 3 to 4 kHz).

Analog technology uses amplifiers to boost signal strength. This technology has the disadvantage of amplifying noise and distortion as well as the actual information signal. Digital technology overcomes this limitation: Digital signals are boosted using repeaters rather than amplifiers. A repeater senses whether the signal is a zero or a one and then generates a completely new signal without distortion.

Continuing conversions

Digital technology and facilities are currently replacing analog throughout the country. Approximately 60 percent of all telephone facilities are digital. This conversion will continue, with the most populous cities converted first and rural areas last. Because of the cost of conversion, it is uncertain how long analog facilities will remain in operation. It is safe to assume, however, that some analog facilities will be in use for at least the next ten years.

A PBX can serve as a local communications hub for both voice and data transmissions (Fig. 2). Depending on where voice signals are digitized, data communica-

tions traffic may be combined at the telephone instrument or at the line-card location within the PBX. If the voice signals are digitized in the telephone instrument, data traffic may be multiplexed onto the same workstation cable using time-division multiplexing techniques. If voice is not digitized at the phone set, data traffic may be provided through separate cable pairs from the workstation location to the switch. Rolm, for example, makes use of the former architecture in its CBX-II product, while Northern Telecom uses the latter architecture in its SL-1 product.

The development of an integrated voice/data PBX is a fairly recent occurrence. The first digitized-voice PBX became available in the mid-1970s. The potential economics of using an existing facility, a currently installed voice network, to satisfy growing data communications needs are obvious. The early entry of the PBX in competition with local networks, the PBX's already large installed base (about 100,000 units in the United States), and recent technology advancements should enable digital PBXs to capture over half the installed base of local data communications by 1988.

The typical PBX uses twisted-pair wire for each device on its network, including telephone, data terminal, printer, or facsimile machine. A device signals the PBX when it wants to establish a session. The user enters switch-signaling characters or a destination identification. Through its digital switching matrix, the PBX completes the connection and establishes the session. This is similar in concept to how long-distance voice telephone networks perform.

The older analog PBX products accept digital data as input, convert the information to analog via a modem, and switch and transmit it. A modem at the remote end converts the signal back to digital form. The newer digital PBX switches accept digital data as input and eliminate the interim digital-to-analog conversion and reconversion.

The digital data transfer rate for the newer generation of digital PBXs is 56 kbit/s for each line. The number of lines simultaneously available on a PBX varies from less than 100 to several thousand, depending on the model. Since all data is fed into the PBX's

Bidirectional broadband

Even though the Federal Communications Commission requires that new cable TV networks install two-way capabilities, the use of this feature for data transmission varies considerably among the states, primarily because of politics. In New York, for example, Manhattan Cablevision provides 2.4-, 4.8-, 9.6-, and 56-kbit/s data channels. The company actively competes with New York Telephone in this area. In Connecticut, the situation is different. Southern New England Telephone, for example, has pressured the Connecticut Public Utilities Commission to strictly interpret the definition of a telephone public utility. Consequently, none of the CATV operators has been able to offer any data channels.

2. Datacomm center. *A PBX may serve as a local communications hub for both digitized voice and data transmission. If voice signals are digitized in the telephone instrument or workstation, data traffic may be multiplexed onto the same telephone-workstation cable using time-division multiplexing techniques.*

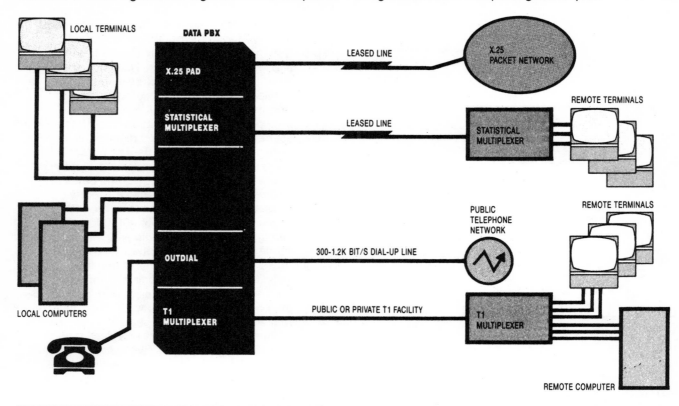

dedicated set of wires, PBX networking is usually based upon time-division multiplexing. Most PBXs use 64-kbit/s pulse code modulation (PCM) encoding, resulting in good data transmission properties and limited data storage requirements (as determined by the PCM encoding) within the switch.

PBX processors vary considerably in their architectures, speeds, and memory configurations. Several small PBXs, such as the GTE Omni series, use the 8-bit Intel 8080 and 8085 microprocessors. The Mitel SX-2000 uses the 16-bit Motorola MC68000, one per 128 ports. Intecom's PBXs use one of the most powerful 32-bit processors, with 3 to 4 MIPS (million instructions per second): the Perkin-Elmer PE3205. Northern Telecom uses a proprietary 16-bit processor in its SL-1 and SL-100 switches. Rolm uses a proprietary 16-bit processor in its VSCBX and a proprietary 32-bit processor in its CBX-II.

RAM variations
Memory configurations also vary considerably among PBXs. Northern Telecom's SL-1M uses only 32 kbytes of random access memory (RAM). The Rolm VSCBX is configured with 144 kbytes of RAM. Larger PBXs, such as Intecom's S/80, Mitel's SX-2000, Northern Telecom's SL-100, and ATTIS's System 85 are all configured with 4 Mbytes of RAM.

The number of voice and data conversations that can be simultaneously switched by a PBX depends on the processor speed, the amount of memory in the switch, and the controlling software. The number varies from several hundred to tens of thousands. The Rolm VSCBX supports 94 simultaneous calls; the Northern Telecom SL-1M, 2,100; the Intecom S/80, 6,000; the Northern Telecom SL-100, 15,000; the ATTIS System 85 (single-switch configuration), 7,636.

The new ATTIS System 75 PBX seems to be the little brother of the System 85 but represents a change in architecture when compared with the basic 85. The System 75 has many features that make it attractive as a node in a distributed-architecture network.

The System 85 is basically a large switch using a centralized architecture. Since its introduction in late 1983, the 85 has evolved considerably. Originally announced as a single-node PBX supporting a maximum of 2,250 trunk lines, it was recently enhanced to accommodate 15 nodes supporting more than 10,000 trunks in a distributed architecture. Among other new features is a voice store-and-forward capability.

One could divide the leading PBX products into two types, based upon their architectures:

1. Centralized
ATTIS System 85
ATTIS Dimension 2000
Northern Telecom SL-1
Mitel SX-2000
GTE Omni III

2. Distributed
ATTIS Systems 75 and 85
Rolm CBX-II
Northern Telecom SL-100
Nippon NEAX 2400
Intecomm

Northern Telecom recently enhanced its line of integrated-voice-and-data PBXs. The SL-1 and SL-100 enhancements are called Meridian Integrated Services Networks (ISNs). Also, a new unit, the Meridian DV-1 Data/Voice System (DVS), has been added.

The SL-1 and SL-100 upgrades add packet transport equipment (PTE), which includes two 40-Mbit/s signal buses that act as redundant time-division highways carrying digitized voice and data. The PTE uses multiple Motorola MC68000 microprocessors, self-contained RAM, and the new proprietary operating system XMS (Extended Management System). The PTE permits microcomputers and Northern's new 4020 workstation to communicate within a 2,000-foot radius of the centrally located PBX at 2.56 Mbit/s over two twisted pairs of wires.

The 4020 uses Unix-based software and the Motorola MC68000. The terminal emulates the IBM 3101, Digital Equipment VT100 and VT220, and Data General Dasher. Northern Telecom calls its digitized voice and data network LANlink. With the appropriate microcomputer interface cards, the LANlink emulates IBM's PCnet local network, operating at 1 Mbit/s.

The new Meridian DV-1 may be configured as either a data-only or an integrated voice/data PBX. It fits between a multiline telephone (key system) and another PBX. The DV-1 supports up to 100 simultaneous nonblocking voice and data users. Two 20-Mbit/s signal buses carry voice and data independently.

Ethernet et al.
Baseband technology is enjoying a newfound popularity in networking communities of minicomputers and microcomputers that exchange file and database information. Time-division schemes and ring or bus topologies are used to divide a single signaling channel to accommodate multiple users. Typically, baseband networks operate at 5 or 10 Mbit/s and support up to 100 data devices. Ethernet-compatible products are expected to dominate the baseband market in the future.

As for broadband, the leading local network offerings include Ungermann-Bass's Net/One, Sytek's Localnet 20, Interactive Systems/3M's Videodata, and Wang's Wangnet. When considering this technology, one must be aware of two common impairments, signal attenuation and tilt (a type of waveform distortion), both of which are directly affected by temperature variations. Signal attenuation on most coaxial cable changes at the rate of 1 percent for every 10 degrees of temperature change. This could amount to a 10 to 15 percent change over the temperature range typically found in the United States.

The relationship between temperature and frequency in the broadband network is considered in the design process through the operational window concept. The operational window is the amount of allowable radio frequency (RF) signal change that can take place without degrading network performance. Network amplifiers must compensate for the cable loss (signal attenuation), signal tilt, and temperature variations experienced in normal operation.

Other factors may affect broadband network performance. If the coax cable is compressed during installation or manufacturing, its attenuation and distortion characteristics may change. As amplifiers, taps, and splitters are installed, additional signal attenuation is introduced. A structural-return-loss test (transmitting in one frequency; receiving in another) should be run on coaxial cable before and after installation to detect structural problems. The maximum usable length of a broadband trunk is determined by the number of amplifiers that can be connected in series without signal degradation. Up to 30 amplifiers may be connected to span a distance of up to 30 miles. One important criterion when selecting trunk amplifiers is the distance that the connecting trunk lines must cover. Although broadband trunks can run up to about 30 miles, the usual length is less than five miles.

The strengths and weaknesses
PBX-based networks typically support data rates from 300 bit/s to 9.6 kbit/s, with 56 kbit/s technically possible but rarely used. Baseband local networks typically support devices starting at 2.4 kbit/s, with aggregate channel rates from 1 to 10 Mbit/s; they usually do not support voice transmission. Broadband networks typically support data rates from 9.6 kbit/s to 20 Mbit/s; they may also support several baseband transmission schemes on allocated frequency bands.

PBXs have about one-fourth of the market shared with local networks. Due to their design, PBX networks are best suited to devices with data rates of 300 bit/s to 2.4 kbit/s, with less than 10 percent utilization. Traffic is typically from communicating word processors, communicating copiers, microcomputers, interactive minicomputers, terminals, and printers. Other applications emerging on PBX-based networks include voice/data store and forward and gateways to other networks. Most PBX networks will continue to be limited to 56-kbit/s traffic, with the most currently installed office automation devices transmitting at less than 10 kbit/s. By 1988, PBX-based networks will be the most popular, having nearly two-thirds of the market that it shares with local networks.

The PBX-based network approach has many strengths. These include: proven technology, low-storage requirements (less than 64 kbytes per port), least-expensive alternative for users with an existing telephone switch, use of existing twisted-pair wiring, extreme flexibility when moving user devices, availability of data service wherever there is a telephone, and support both for remote terminal controllers and for individual asynchronous terminals.

The PBX-based network does have weaknesses. Throughput is typically limited to 100 to 500 simultaneous digitized voice-and-data sessions. The data-transfer rate is limited to 56 kbit/s. Most PBX-based networks depend on a centralized, nonredundant controller for network management. (However, the distributed-architecture PBX is similar to a local network in eliminating this potential single point of failure.) PBXs are not typically used to switch transmissions from terminals with utilizations greater than 30 percent, such as those of 3270-type data-entry applications. This traffic load would saturate the typical blocking-type PBX, preventing any additional user transmissions.

One remedy for the traffic-load situation is to upgrade the digital multiplexer paths within the PBX. As an example, the Rolm CBX-II may be upgraded from supporting an aggregate 74-Mbit/s throughput to the Rolmbus 295 configuration that supports 295-Mbit/s throughput. This type of upgrade is available from a limited number of PBX vendors—another being Northern Telecom. The upgrade price is typically 15 to 25 percent of the original PBX cost.

Where it fits
Broadband, CATV-based local networks are best suited to applications requiring large bandwidth (typically more than 3 kHz) and high volume (typically more than 10 percent station utilization). These most suitable types of traffic applications include:
■ Video.
■ 56-kbit/s (and higher) data workstations.
■ High-volume (greater than 10 percent utilization) print stations, including laser printers.
■ Integrated voice-and-data workstations.
■ CPU-to-CPU communications.
■ Response-time-critical applications (requiring two to three seconds).

These applications are most feasible, economical, and efficient on broadband local networks. The multiple channels, high data-transfer rates, and sophisticated access schemes make broadband networks attractive. Broadband currently accounts for less than 10 percent of the local network market. Growth over the next few years will be slow and steady.

The strengths of broadband local networks include:
■ Data-transfer rates (attached devices may operate at rates as high as 56 kbit/s or more).
■ Channel bandwidth greater than 3 kHz.
■ Multiple channel types, including video.
■ Up to 400-Mbit/s traffic capacity.

The weaknesses of the broadband approach include:
■ Most expensive type of local network.
■ Difficult to design (the placement and gain setting of the amplifiers are critical).
■ Adding stations is difficult among dense terminal populations (the addition would cause a reduced signal level that might require the installation of an additional amplifier).

Baseband networks have characteristics that make them best suited to traffic and applications that are different from those of either PBX or broadband networks. Because of its relatively low cost, its somewhat-higher-than-PBX data-transfer rates, and its implementation flexibility, baseband networking is best suited to linking interactive terminals, intelligent workstations, and executive workstations.

The strengths of baseband networking include:
■ Usually less expensive than broadband networks.
■ Multiple access methods.
■ Can utilize twisted-pair or coaxial cable.

The weaknesses of the baseband approach include:
■ Limited capacity (usually limited to office machines; no video).
■ Limited growth capabilities (less than those of the PBX or broadband networks).
■ Limited cable distances (typically 1,500 feet) supported.

Suitabilities
Another local network consideration is the access method. Access methods may be divided into two general categories: carrier-sense multiple access (CSMA)—with either collision detection or collision avoidance—and token passing. The CSMA methods are best for an aggregate network utilization of less than 30 percent with terminal devices utilized between 10 and 40 percent. CSMA local networks are comparatively inefficient when accessed by constantly used devices. They are best for asynchronous terminals; they are not advised for synchronous terminals with utilizations greater than 30 percent. CSMA is inefficient for supporting digitized voice mixed with data traffic.

The token-passing access method is more efficient than CSMA schemes when applied to terminals with utilizations greater than 30 percent. Token passing provides guaranteed device access, with each device taking its turn on the medium. It is typically implemented for scientific and engineering workstations, real-time process control, and factory automation applications. The choice between CSMA and token passing depends mostly on the user's device- and network-utilization loads.

Baseband networks fall between PBX and broadband networks with respect to function and capacity. For this reason, the economics of a PBX network have eroded the baseband market share on the low end (less than 30 stations), while the capacities of a broadband network have captured the high end (more than 100 stations) of the market. This leaves baseband networks with a limited and specialized market. However, it is a stable and fairly well-defined technology due to Ethernet-like products and other well-known early entries into local networking. Although baseband networks account for about two-thirds of the local network market today, their popularity is expected to significantly decline in the future.

The accompanying table details some of the key considerations when planning and implementing local communications technologies. Both baseband and lightwave networks use a single transmission path and time-division multiplexing techniques to serve multiple users. PBX-based and broadband networks typically use multiple transmission paths within the same—as well as different—transmission medium. These networks use time-division and frequency-division multiplexing techniques to serve network users. Broadband and lightwave networks are best suited for graphics and other specialized workstations that commonly re-

Comparing local communications technologies

KEY CONSIDERATIONS	TWISTED-COPPER	BASEBAND	BROADBAND	FIBER OPTICS
TERMINAL TYPES	DUMB OR INTELLIGENT	INTELLIGENT ONLY	DUMB OR INTELLIGENT	DUMB OR INTELLIGENT
CENTRAL INTELLIGENCE	YES, PBX	NOT REQUIRED, BUT MAY BE DONE	YES, TRANSLATOR	NO
BANDWIDTH	3 MHz	50 MHz	440 MHz	VIRTUALLY UNLIMITED
VIDEOCONFERENCING	YES, BUT NOT FULL MOTION	NO	YES	YES
GRAPHICS CAPABILITY	NO	LIMITED	YES	YES
CAPACITY FOR HIGHER SPEED	DIFFICULT	VERY DIFFICULT	EASY	EASY
DISTANCE	LIMITED EXCEPT WITH MODEMS	1 MILE	40 MILES	UNLIMITED
REPEATER REQUIREMENT	STANDARD PHONE NETWORK	EVERY 4,500 FEET	EVERY 2,000 FEET	EVERY 4,000 FEET
MAXIMUM CHANNEL SPEED	56 KBIT/S	50 MBIT/S	10 MBIT/S	200 MBIT/S
TYPICAL CONFIGURATION	POINT-TO-POINT/MULTIDROP/ RADIAL	RADIAL/RING/POINT-TO-POINT/ BUS	TREE AND BUS	POINT-TO-POINT OR LIMITED MULTIDROP
TRANSPARENCY	YES	ONLY VIA SPECIAL INTERFACE	YES, ON DEDICATED SUB-CHANNELS	YES, ON DEDICATED FIBER
BIT ERROR RATE	1 IN 10^5	1 IN 10^7	1 IN 10^9	1 IN 10^{10}
RFI/EMI VULNERABILITY	HIGH	MODERATE	LOW	VERY LOW
DATA SECURITY	LOW	MODERATE	VERY HIGH	VERY HIGH
MAINTENANCE	EASY	MORE DIFFICULT	MORE DIFFICULT	VERY DIFFICULT
MODIFYING NETWORK	EASIEST	MORE DIFFICULT	MORE DIFFICULT	IMPOSSIBLE TODAY
WIRING IN PLACE	LIKELY	UNLIKELY	UNLIKELY	VERY UNLIKELY
MAXIMUM DATA RATE PER CABLE	1.5 MBIT/S	10 MBIT/S	UP TO 400 MBIT/S	300 TO 450 MBIT/S

RFI = RADIO FREQUENCY INTERFERENCE   EMI = ELECTROMAGNETIC INTERFERENCE

quire transmission rates in excess of 56 kbit/s.

Each local communications technology has its own special appeal. Twisted-pair-based PBXs appeal to those who have wiring in place, where the users are scattered throughout an office building, and device operation is at 1.2-to-9.6 kbit/s asynchronous and synchronous. The baseband local network appeals to those who have concentrations of users sharing information or application programs within their department. Broadband networks appeal to users requiring distribution of video signals and T1 transmission paths.

'The tie that binds'
Bridges are devices that allow interconnection of local networks with common protocols—thus extending similar network services geographically. Bridges allow interconnection of local networks that have different media or different access methods. Bridges do not perform protocol or code conversion but do perform speed conversion and support flow control. Bridges link local networks that have the same high-level protocols up to the network layer of the seven-layer International Organization for Standardization's Open Systems Interconnection model.

Gateways allow the limited connection of devices in dissimilar networks. Typically, gateways support speed conversion, code conversion, flow control, and protocol conversion. Gateways connect local networks to wide-area and remote networks, supporting interconnection of networks with different high-level protocols from the network layer and above. Also, gateways usually connect local networks to value-added networks such as Telenet, Tymnet, and Uninet, as well as to common-carrier public dial facilities.

Typical local network applications of gateways and bridges occur when:
■ The distance between nodes exceeds the maximum backbone length of a single network.
■ The cable run between nodes is complicated by right-of-way problems.
■ Interconnecting networks use different media.
■ Interconnecting networks are located in different organizational units or departments.
■ Interconnecting networks from different vendors have different equipment (such as cable-interface units).
■ Interconnecting different network protocols is required due to the applications required.

Bridges and gateways differ in their performance and the services they support. When comparing them, users should take care to compare factors that are truly

3. Technology mix. *Devices connected to a PBX may communicate with each other, with the telephone company's dial network, or with a value-added network* *through an X.25 gateway. Through a separate gateway for each network, the PBX-connected devices may communicate with devices that access local networks.*

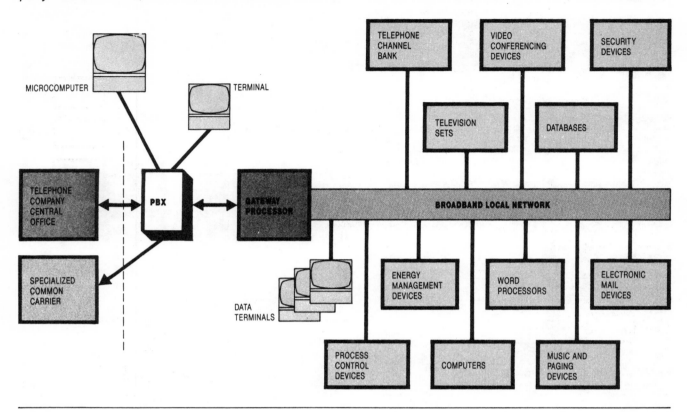

required by the applications being considered.

Figure 3 illustrates how a PBX is used to link terminals to a local network. Typically, low-usage (10 percent or less) 300-bit/s-to-2.4-kbit/s asynchronous terminals or microcomputers are connected to the PBX. These devices may communicate with each other, with a minicomputer connected to the PBX, with local network devices, and may connect to the telephone company's dial network. The devices may also communicate through multiplexers to remote computers as well as with a value-added network through an X.25 gateway connected to the PBX.

Through a different gateway, the devices connected to the PBX may communicate with devices connected to a baseband, broadband, or other PBX-based network. Separate gateways would be required for each particular local network to which the user wishes to connect. These gateways handle the forwarding of traffic from one network to another on a packet-by-packet basis, supporting both virtual circuit and datagram protocols.

A disadvantage of bridges, compared with gateways, is that more bandwidth is needed for packet headers because of the independent routing decisions made within each bridge. Gateways usually yield the best use of bandwidth for 300-bit/s-to-2.4-kbit/s interconnections because complete routing information is not contained in each packet. Destination and function information is implied by the dedicated virtual-circuit connection. Gateways support single-function uses of the connection between networks, except when additional multiplexing functions are used.

What's new

Lightwave transmission is the latest development in local network technologies. While most fiber-optic components are still manufactured manually, assembled-equipment sales reached $200 million in 1983. Most current applications have concentrated on developing integrated telephone transmission networks. The market for fiber-optic local network components is dominated by small, highly specialized, privately held companies such as Canoga Data Systems, American Photonics, and Fibronics.

Most of today's products consist of Ethernet-compatible transceivers that extend the location of terminals away from the backbone 3270-type coaxial-cable multiplexers, and of devices that extend EIA RS-232-C cable distances. Fiber optics uses photon counting instead of amplitude or phase detection of electromagnetic signals. As such, fiber-optic transmission is similar to baseband local network technology in that a single signaling source uses time-division multiplexing and cannot support frequency-division multiplexing. Fiber-optic transmission typically has one error in 10^9 bits (compared with one in 10^5 or 10^6 for copper-based transmission) and is not affected by frequency-dependent losses characteristic of twisted-pair or coaxial

4. Lightwave and local networks. *Tapping into optical fibers is not currently practical. But this newest networking medium may be readily applied to point-to-point applications. One application offered by Ungermann-Bass and Xyplex enables a fiber-optic star topology to interconnect local networks.*

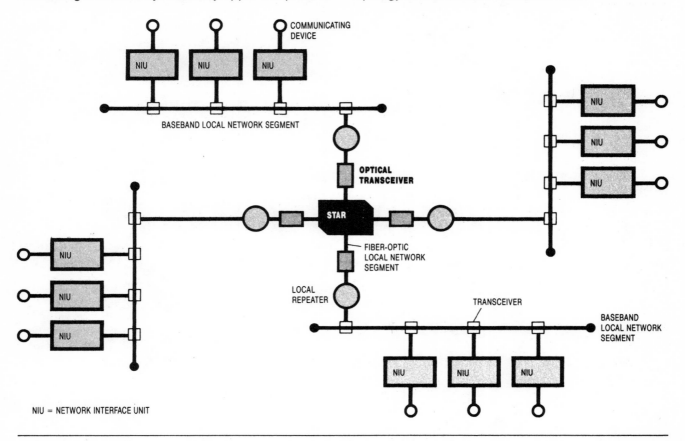

cable. Bandwidth is a function of light dispersion in the fiber, which depends on length. Optical fiber currently supports a minimum bandwidth of 25 MHz (300 to 450 Mbit/s) per 30-kilometer link without repeaters.

Fiber-optic technology currently accounts for less than 10 percent of all local network equipment components. As the expected economies of scale in manufacturing become commonplace over the next five years, fiber is expected to account for the basis of 30 to 40 percent of all local network equipment components, equaling $500 million in value during 1988.

The advantages of fiber-optic over coaxial and twisted-pair cable are many. The signal energy is confined totally within the fiber, with no radiated energy or crosstalk between fibers. The considerably greater bandwidth equates to a range of 25 to 1,500 MHz per kilometer, as derived from today's multimode fibers. A 3-inch diameter 900-twisted-pair copper cable can be readily replaced by a single 50-micrometer-diameter optical fiber. Fiber cable is easier to install although considerably more difficult to tap or splice without a major signal loss. Optical fiber is made from dielectric material, which is plentiful. The extensive shielding required by conventional copper cable is unnecessary. Also, fiber is considerably safer than copper cable, since it cannot short-circuit or cause sparks (poorly installed or eroded copper can and does). Fiber offers considerably lower attenuation, 1 to 10 decibels per kilometer, as compared with the 25 to 140 decibels per kilometer of loss typical of coax.

Fiber optics has considerable promise for local networking. The present difficulty in tapping into the cable without a degrading signal loss is a major hindrance to its widespread user application. The number of repeaters required is determined by both cable length and the existence of taps (if any). Currently, taps are not typical in fiber-optic installations.

The present economics of fiber make it unattractive for most users, except those requiring extensive bandwidth or immunity to radio frequency or electromagnetic interference. Ungermann-Bass and Xyplex are two of the few vendors offering local network technology using fiber optics. Both use point-to-point-type topologies (Fig. 4). The current cost of cable, installation, and attached components is about five times that of coax, making it difficult to cost-justify fiber-optic local networks on a widespread basis. ∎

David Levin, president of Netcomm, is a consultant specializing in network design, management, and control. He has worked on projects that combine communications, management, and operations research. He received graduate and undergraduate degrees from Rensselaer Polytechnic Institute.

Wen-Ning Hsieh and Israel Gitman, DVI Communications Inc., New York, N.Y.

How good is your network routing protocol?

All networks, public and private, employ a specific set of rules for transporting packets. Users should understand these protocols and their impact on network performance.

Introduced by the Department of Defense in the late 1960s, packet-switching technology is used in many public data networks and the proprietary network architectures. The effectiveness of this method of data delivery hinges on the fragmentation of a message into packets, the independent transport of the packets to the destination node, and the ordered reassembly of the packets into a meaningful message.

Clearly, the method of routing packets to their destination heavily impacts network cost and performance. Yet, routing receives very little attention from users obtaining a packet-switching technology of their own, or by users of public data networks. This lack of attention may be due to insufficient understanding, as well as the difficulty of evaluating alternative routing procedures.

Less-than-optimal routing procedures can have a variety of adverse effects on a network. For instance, an inefficient routing technique may transport packets over longer routes than necessary, hence consuming excessive transmission facilities. An ill-designed routing algorithm may end up forming loops that not only reduce efficiency, but also create situations in which these data units do not reach their destinations at all.

Another performance element is the capability to transport data units by priorities—thus matching delays to applications requirements.

Network reliability is also impacted by the routing protocol (that is, the protocol machinery on the network nodes that collectively perform the routing function). An important issue here is how quickly routing patterns adapt and change in the face of failures in the network. Several questions become relevant: Does the user perceive a link or node failure? Could there be loss of data because of the failure? What is the delay in re-establishing communications? Finally, does the routing change in a damaged network alter to adapt to the new network configuration?

A number of networks are discussed in this article in terms of the routing functions and the associated network performance. The public networks include Arpanet, Tymnet, Telenet, and Datapac; the proprietary ones include IBM's SNA (System Network Architecture) and Digital Equipment Corp.'s DNA (Digital Network Architecture).

In most of these, the routes used to forward data units are generated automatically by the network. To make efficient use of network resources, the routes selected are required to be of minimum "cost" with respect to some specific cost criteria. Typical costs are the number and type of communications channels on the route, the utilization levels of the channels, and the average delay incurred in transporting a data unit along the route. The cost of an entire route is the sum of the costs of the constituent links.

The routing function may be divided into three general categories:

■ **Routing network definition.** The "routing network" is commonly defined in terms of nodes and links. But exactly what are the "nodes" and "links" of the network? A "routing network" could be different from the underlying physical network; the routing network may not take into account certain physical elements, such as clusters of switches in a single node site, parallel transmission facilities between a pair of nodes, or the data concentration subnetwork. The link-cost function must also be defined, as well as a method of determining the link cost.

■ **Route generation.**
What information is needed for route generation? Where are the routes computed?

What events trigger the computation of (new) routes?

■ **Packet forwarding.** Some networks route packets on a session-oriented basis—all packets belonging to the same session are routed over the same path. In other networks, routing decisions are made independently for each packet. In both cases, a related factor is the type and amount of information that is kept at each node in order to route the packets to their destination.

Basic concepts

A "link" in the routing network may consist of single or multiple parallel communications facilities interconnecting the two switching nodes. Use of multiple parallel facilities reduces the chance that a link may become inoperative. On the other hand, it makes message transport over the link more complex, because a decision must be made about which facility to use to transport a packet. Furthermore, preserving the order of the message (if this is required) on a multiple parallel transmissions facility requires more than just the link level protocol.

Some network representations allow at most one link joining a pair of nodes; in these cases a link can be denoted simply by its two end nodes. If the actual network provides more flexible message routing by implementing multiple links, this requires more complex link representation. For example, two adjacent nodes may be joined by a terrestrial facility and a satellite facility. Representing these facilities as two distinct links would permit, for example, the routing of interactive traffic on the terrestrial link and file transfer traffic on the satellite link.

Link-cost functions for routing protocols usually take one of two basic forms. In the first, the link cost is a function of the capacity (bandwidth) of the channels that comprise the link. Alternatively, the link cost is considered a function of channel utilization. This function may depend on the packet type. In other words, the same link can have different costs, depending on the application—which itself determines the packet type—and on the instantaneous link utilization.

The first type of cost function is essentially static. The cost of a link will change only with a change in the link's operational status or in the link's composition. The second cost function provides a better assessment of routing data through the link. However, it also requires many more processing and transmission resources. Moreover, the measurement (averaging) interval for the link-cost function becomes critical. If the interval is too short, excessive fluctuation in the link cost can result, which leads to instability; if the interval is too long, the link-cost function is no longer effective.

Shortcut

There are two basic approaches to computing where the shortest path is located. The paths may be centrally computed at a supervisory-node/network-control center, or calculated in a distributed fashion at all network nodes.

The centralized approach requires far fewer processing and storage requirements at most network nodes.

On the other hand, the entire routing operation becomes vulnerable to supervisor node failure and to network partition (due to the failure of certain nodes or links, or both). If this happens, the network or some of its components may be left without any supervisor node. Contingency measures, such as the provision of hot standby supervisor nodes, must be provided.

With a distributed approach, more processing and storage are needed at each network node. The routing operation is, in general, more resilient against network component failure. However, due to the inherent complexity of distributed operation, the routing protocol needs to be designed carefully to avoid anomalies, such as inaccurate routing data at one node disrupting the entire network.

Shortest-path algorithms are used to compute the least-cost ("shortest") path between a pair of nodes, based on the link costs in the network. These algorithms are usually much more efficient when they are used to compute the shortest paths from one node to all other nodes, or the shortest paths between all pairs of nodes, rather than computing the shortest path between a pair of nodes.

Shortest-path computation is a discipline that derives many of its results from graph theory. Work in the field has demonstrated that the shortest paths can be computed in a distributed fashion. To accomplish this, each node computes its shortest-path cost estimate to a given destination and exchanges that information with its neighboring nodes.

Computational efficiency

The computational efficiency of the algorithms is important, as are the databases generated and maintained for routing purposes. In general, there are two databases needed. One of them maintains the path cost by outbound link, which defines the "cost" of routing a packet from the given node to a given destination using the specific outgoing link. The other database contains the shortest-path cost estimates and the successors for the shortest paths (called the shortest-path database). The protocol packet that exchanges path cost estimates between neighboring nodes is called the path-cost-update packet.

The information required at each node to perform the packet-forwarding operation depends critically on whether the packet routing is performed on a session-oriented basis or on a datagram-oriented basis.

With datagram-based routing, the information required at each node is simply the shortest-path database (in other words, the outgoing link to use for each destination). The minimum information needed in the packet header is the destination field. If desired, the source field may be included as well. This allows the packet to be routed back to the source node if the packet's destination cannot be reached from an intermediate node.

With session-oriented routing, the situation is more complex: At each node along the path, the route that is selected for the session has to be distinguished in some way from the routes that are selected for other sessions.

1. Session oriented. *Paths for Tymnet packets are to be established on the basis of an entire session. Each node maintains a logical channel association table,* *which it uses to correctly modify the packet's logical channel number field. For destination and source nodes, the logical channels are actual ports.*

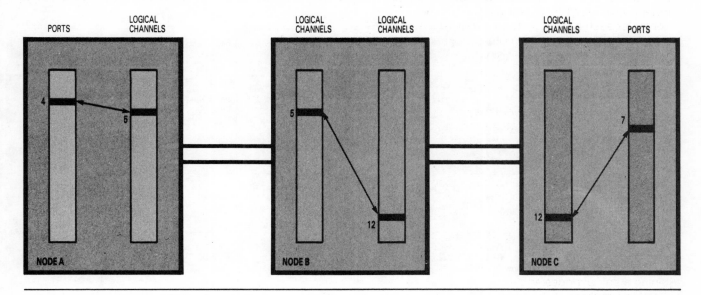

A straightforward implementation technique is to identify each active connection at a node (the connection could be specified by the source, destination, and a connection number). The outgoing link is assigned to each active connection and stored in the connection database at the node. This approach, however, potentially requires either excessive processing, excessive storage, or both, at the nodes.

A much more efficient approach is suggested by the Tymnet implementation, in which each link is allocated a number of "logical channels." Each active connection at a node is assigned a logical channel on the inbound link (or a port number, if this is the source node) and a logical channel on the outbound link (or a port number, if this is the destination node). The association between the inbound logical channel number and the outbound logical channel number is established at each node along the end-to-end path as part of the session set-up process.

Modification

The logical channel number is carried in the packet header. As an illustration, consider the example in Figure 1, in which the end-to-end path is already established. At A, the source node, the source port number (4) is known. Based on this number, the outbound link for a packet belonging to the session is known, and the packet will be assigned a value of 5 in the logical channel number field (5). Node B knows, from the value in the logical channel number field (5) and the logical channel-to-channel association table, the appropriate outbound link for the packet at node B. Consequently, it modifies the logical channel number field in the packet header to 12. At the next node, based on the logical-channel-to-logical-channel association table, the packet is forwarded to the appropriate destination port (number 7).

Tymnet implementation strategy substantially reduces packet overhead. The logical channel number field is used both for routing at the network level (at all nodes along the path) and for connection identification at the transport level (at the end nodes).

Table 1 provides a summary of the routing protocol characteristics of these networks.

Developed by the Advanced Research Project Agency (ARPA), the ARPA Network (Arpanet) was an experimental network exploring computer-system resource sharing. It became operational in 1969 and today supports more than 100 computer systems interconnected via close to 60 switching nodes throughout the United States and Europe. It was the first network developed in the United States that employed packet-switching technology.

Two features of Arpanet's routing protocol merit attention:

■ **Route generation operation.** Route generation in Arpanet is performed in a distributed fashion, with each node computing the shortest paths to all other nodes. Each node maintains a network database of complete network topology and link costs. Based on this database, each node independently computes the outbound link corresponding to the shortest path for each destination node. To update the network database consistently, each node broadcasts the link cost of its incident links to all other nodes in the network every 10 to 60 seconds, or whenever changes occur in the link operational status.

Prior to May 1979, Arpanet employed a distributed algorithm with the path-cost-update packet exchanged between neighboring nodes at 128 msec intervals. This protocol created a number of difficulties. For instance, whenever there was a link failure, it took a long time to update fully all the shortest-path databases. Consequently, the routing protocol was modified to the

Table 1: Summary of routing protocol implementation

ATTRIBUTE	ARPANET	TYMNET	NETWORK SNA
ROUTING NETWORK LINK DEFINITION	AT MOST ONE LINK BETWEEN EACH PAIR OF NODES	AT MOST ONE LINK BETWEEN EACH PAIR OF NODES	MULTIPLE LINKS (TRANSMISSION GROUPS) MAY EXIST BETWEEN A PAIR OF NODES*
A FUNCTION OF LINK COST	AVERAGE PACKET DELAY	■ OVERLOAD CONDITION ■ TYPE OF TRANSMISSION FACILITY ■ TYPE OF SESSION TO BE SUPPORTED (HIGH SPEED, LOW DELAY, ETC.)	USER SELECTABLE FOR EACH COS CLASS: ■ HOP COUNT ■ PACKET DELAY ■ LINK CAPACITY ■ SECURITY, ETC. ALL CRITERIA ARE LOAD INDEPENDENT
LOCATION OF ROUTE GENERATION	DISTRIBUTED AT ALL NETWORK NODES	CENTRALIZED AT NETWORK SUPERVISOR	CAN BE EITHER DISTRIBUTED OR CENTRALIZED
LINK COST UPDATE FREQUENCY	EVERY 10-60 SEC., OR WHENEVER TOPOLOGICAL CHANGE OCCURS	APPROXIMATELY 16 SEC. IF CHANGES IN LINK COST EXCEED THRESHOLD	WHENEVER NETWORK IS RECONFIGURED
OCCASION FOR ROUTE GENERATION	LINK COST CHANGE	AT SESSION SETUP AND SESSION RESET	AT SYSGEN ONLY
PACKET-FORWARDING OPERATION	DATAGRAM-ORIENTED	SESSION-ORIENTED	SESSION-ORIENTED
PACKET ORDERING	ORDERING PERFORMED END-TO-END VIA HIGHER LEVEL PROTOCOL	ORDERING ENFORCED ON EACH HOP	ORDERING ENFORCED ON EACH HOP
PACKET-TRANSPORT PRIORITIES	2 LEVELS (NETWORK MSG. ALWAYS AT THE HIGHER LEVEL)	2 LEVELS (NETWORK MSG. ALWAYS AT THE HIGHER LEVEL)	4 LEVELS: ■ NETWORK/MSG. HIGHEST PRIORITY ■ 3 USER-PRIORITY LEVELS

*A LINK MAY BE COMPOSED OF MULTIPLE TRANSMISSION FACILITIES, USUALLY OF THE SAME TYPE.

present version. It should be noted that, with appropriate modifications, the original algorithm would have performed satisfactorily. The Decnet implementation demonstrates this.

■ **Link-cost function and measurement.** The Arpanet link-cost function is the average packet delay experienced in routing over the given route, computed over a 10-second interval. The packet delay on an outbound link is measured by the difference between the time the packet arrives at the node and the time the acknowledgment is received from the next node. In general, if the average is taken over a period much less than 10 seconds, the average exhibits too much variation from measurement period to measurement period to be useful.

Tymnet is a commercial value-added network oper-

ated by Tymshare Inc., of Cupertino, Calif., that has been in operation since 1971. The original network, called Tymnet I, was designed to connect low-speed terminals to a few timesharing computers. Because of a substantial increase in the user population, network size, and network traffic, plus an increased diversity of traffic types, Tymnet I is being gradually replaced by Tymnet II. The new network uses more powerful network processors as well as somewhat different network control strategies. With approximately 1,000 nodes, Tymnet covers the United States and Europe.

In Tymnet, the routes are computed centrally by the supervisor node. Each route is generated separately for a specific user session, either at session setup or during session reset when the original path has to be dismantled due to a failure on the path. The link costs that are

DNA	DATAPAC	TELENET
AT MOST ONE LINK BETWEEN EACH PAIR OF NODES	AT MOST ONE LINK BETWEEN EACH PAIR OF NODES	MULTIPLE LINKS ARE ALLOWED BETWEEN A PAIR OF NODES
LINK CAPACITY	LINK CAPACITY	GLOBALLY AT NCC: ■ LINK CAPACITY LOCALLY AT EVERY NODE: ■ LINK CAPACITY ■ NO. OF ACTIVE CONNECTIONS
DISTRIBUTED AT ALL NETWORK NODES	DISTRIBUTED AT ALL NETWORK NODES	BOTH CENTRALIZED (INITIAL STAGE) AND DISTRIBUTED (FINAL STAGE)
WHENEVER TOPOLOGICAL CHANGE OCCURS	WHENEVER TOPOLOGICAL CHANGE OCCURS	AT NCC: WHEN NETWORK IS RECONFIGURED AT NETWORK NODES: WHEN A VC IS SET UP/TORN DOWN
NETWORK TOPOLOGY CHANGE	NETWORK TOPOLOGY CHANGE	AT NCC: WHEN NETWORK IS RECONFIGURED AT NETWORK NODES: DURING CONNECTION SETUP/RESET
DATAGRAM-ORIENTED	DATAGRAM-ORIENTED	SESSION-ORIENTED
ORDERING PERFORMED END-TO-END VIA HIGHER LEVEL PROTOCOL	ORDERING PERFORMED END-TO-END VIA HIGHER LEVEL PROTOCOL	ORDERING PERFORMED END-TO-END VIA HIGHER LEVEL PROTOCOL
2 LEVELS: ■ NETWORK MSG. ■ USER MSG.	3 LEVELS: ■ NETWORK MSG. ■ 2 USER PRIORITY LEVELS	2 LEVELS: ■ NETWORK MSG. ■ USER MSG.

used in each shortest-path run are assigned by the supervisor, and they reflect the desirability of the links to the particular session.

Inbound-outbound association
As mentioned, the path for a connection in Tymnet is represented by a logical channel number on each link along the path. At session setup, a buffer pair is assigned to the session at each node along the path, one for each direction. The buffer location is stored in a table, called the "permuter table," assigned to the logical channels. The association between the inbound logical channel and the outbound logical channel of the same path is provided by the buffer pair.

The path setup is handled by the "needle" packet generated by the supervisor, and path dismantling is accomplished by the "path-zapper" packet. The needle contains all the nodes along the path. It is first sent from the supervisor to the source node and is then passed from node to node, acquiring the logical channels and data buffers along the way. If resources are not available somewhere along the path, the needle is made into a path zapper and sent back to the source, releasing the logical channels and data buffers along the path.

A major objection to a centrally directed network is the consequences of a supervisor going down. (Existing paths are totally unaffected by a supervisor going down.) Tymnet's solution is to provide a hierarchy of four supervisors. Only one supervisor is active at a time, and it keeps the others dormant by sending them "sleeping pills" on a regular basis. If a supervisor goes down, one of the dormant supervisors will be awakened—either by direction from the operator or by the expiration of its sleep time—and it will take control of the network. Although sleep times are staggered, it is possible to have two supervisors trying to take control of the network at once. This situation is resolved gracefully when the less dominant supervisor discovers the activities of the more dominant supervisor and puts itself to sleep. A supervisor can take control of the network in 2 to 2.5 minutes.

Tymnet link costs are assigned by the supervisor each time it computes a path for a session. The link cost is a function of a number of factors, including link capacity, type of transmission facilities, link load condition, and the type of the session making the route generation request. Some of the factors that are needed in the link-cost assignment are supplied by the network nodes, such as message delay and link operational status.

Overhead conditions
A number of link overload conditions are defined in Tymnet, each of them identifying a condition that is detrimental to specific application type. For example, a link is said to have reached "high-speed overload" if it cannot support additional printer output at full speed. If such an application requests a route, then this link is assigned a high cost. On the other hand, if a low-speed interactive application requests a route, the same link is assigned a low cost because the performance of the application will not be adversely impacted by the link (the interactive traffic will have higher priority than the printer-output application in transport). The link is said to have reached "low-speed overload" if the messages transmitted over the link have experienced frequent excessive delay over the measurement interval. When this occurs, a link is assigned a high cost for interactive application.

The message forwarding operation in Tymnet is similar to that performed by a typical statistical multiplexer. When a link is ready to send data, it will examine its associated logical channels. For each of those logical channels that has data in the associated buffer, a logical record is formed whose maximum size is specified by the associated congestion-control parameter. Each logical record is identified by the cor-

2. Mapping. *Each SNA virtual route is mapped to an explicit route, which is an ordered sequence of actual transmission facilities.*

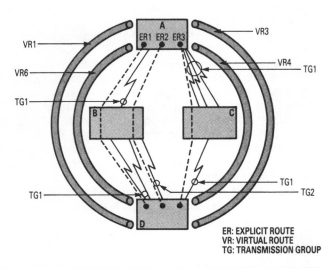

ER: EXPLICIT ROUTE
VR: VIRTUAL ROUTE
TG: TRANSMISSION GROUP

responding logical channel number. The logical records are then combined into a physical record, together with the physical record header and checksum. The physical record is the basic unit of transport over the link, with the data associated with each logical record read from the buffer location identified in the permuter table. When a physical record is received over the channel, the content of each logical record is stored into the appropriate buffer, whose location is identified in the permuter table.

The system network architecture formally defines the function of various IBM network system components, thereby allowing IBM to develop a unified set of products for distributed data processing configurations. The architecture has grown from supporting a single-host configuration in its earlier versions, to current multiple-host networks.

In SNA terminology, there are four node types. Type 1 nodes are terminals, type 2 nodes are terminal controllers, type 4 nodes are front-end processors, and type 5 nodes are the host. (There are no type 3 nodes.)

Hierarchical architecture
The current release of SNA supports a two-level hierarchical architecture with the type 4 and type 5 nodes forming a distributed backbone. The type 1 and type 2 nodes are peripheral nodes, each attached to a specific type 4 or type 5 node. Type 4 and type 5 nodes are called the subarea nodes. The nodes in each subarea form a tree, rooted at the controlling subarea node. The higher-level network of SNA subarea nodes are the most relevant here; for clarity, the subarea nodes will simply be called nodes.

A "link" in the SNA routing network is called a transmission group, which may consist of multiple parallel transmission facilities with the same characteristics. Multiple links (transmission groups) are al-

lowed between two adjacent nodes (Fig. 2).

The explicit routes (ERs) are used to provide the physical representation of the routes. An ER is composed of an ordered sequence of transmission groups traversing from the source node to the destination node (Fig. 2). Up to eight ERs may be defined between a pair of nodes.

For end-to-end control purposes, a logical entity called a virtual route (VR) is defined. Each VR is mapped onto a specific ER. Multiple virtual routes can be mapped onto the same ER.

Between each pair of subarea nodes, three classes of service (COS) of VRs are defined; each class may have up to eight VRs, in predefined order of preference. Several sessions of the same class may use the same VR simultaneously. The specification of the explicit routes, the mapping of the VRs onto the explicit routes, and the ordering of the VRs are all defined during the initial system definition.

Explicit routes
The specification of explicit routes in SNA is a complex undertaking. An IBM field development program, called routing table generator (RTG), was introduced in 1981 to facilitate this process.
■ The explicit route at a node for a given destination must map onto the explicit route with the same explicit route number (ERN) at the next node for the same destination.

For example, consider the network configuration shown in Figure 3. Suppose the two explicit routes from B to A are:

ERO: BA/TG1
ER1:   BC/TG1 - CA/TG1,

where BA/TG1 denotes the transmission group TG1

3. Numbering constraint. *Part of SNA's complexity is in labeling the explicit routes. All routes to the given destination must be considered simultaneously.*

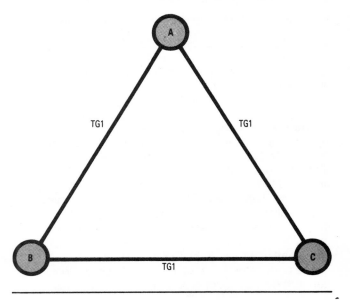

4. TRT. *Each SNA node contains a Transit Routing Table that maintains pairs of subareas and explicit routes. Each packet has a destination subarea and explicit route that maps to a specific cell in the TRT. This cell specifies the actual transmission facilities that will be used to transport the packet.*

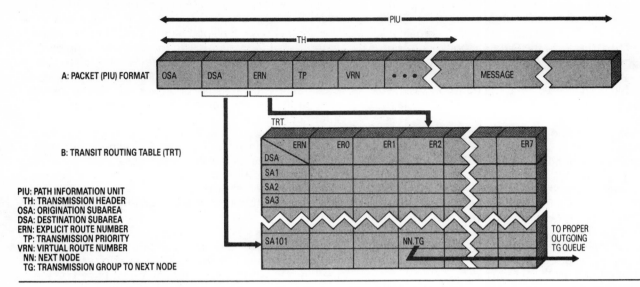

A: PACKET (PIU) FORMAT — OSA | DSA | ERN | TP | VRN | ... | MESSAGE

B: TRANSIT ROUTING TABLE (TRT)

PIU: PATH INFORMATION UNIT
TH: TRANSMISSION HEADER
OSA: ORIGINATION SUBAREA
DSA: DESTINATION SUBAREA
ERN: EXPLICIT ROUTE NUMBER
TP: TRANSMISSION PRIORITY
VRN: VIRTUAL ROUTE NUMBER
NN: NEXT NODE
TG: TRANSMISSION GROUP TO NEXT NODE

from B to A. Suppose there are two explicit routes from C to A: CA/TG1 and CB/TG1 - BA/TG1. These two routes cannot be conveniently numbered ER0 and ER1, respectively, because that would force ER1 for routes from B to A to be BA/TG1 (to be consistent with the numbering for CB/TG1 - BA/TG1). However, this conflicts with the assignments above.

To avoid conflict, the ERN assignment process must simultaneously consider all routes selected for the given destination node.

■ A route is said to be a migration route if it traverses one or more nodes from specific previous SNA releases. A migration route has to be numbered zero in the routing table.

■ Multiple (up to eight) explicit routes need to be selected for each source-destination pair, which is much more complex than selecting only one route. This is due to the fact that the number of possible sets of routes increases drastically as the number of routes increases.

■ For an explicit route to be acceptable, its reverse explicit route (i.e., the same physical path but operating in the reverse direction) must also be defined in the routing tables.

■ As the network configuration changes, with nodes and links being added, moved, or deleted, changes in the routing tables should be kept to a minimum. This makes the preceding constraints even more difficult to implement. (Overall, these considerations make SNA routing algorithms much more complex to develop than those of other networks.)

Deactivating

The set of explicit routes and virtual routes between a pair of (subarea) nodes is essentially fixed after initial system definition. However, not all the routes are necessarily activated. For example, a virtual route is deactivated if there is no session using it, thereby

freeing up the VR control block. A set of protocol packets is defined for the activation and deactivation of virtual routes and explicit routes.

The routes are specified on an end-to-end basis for each session. All packets belonging to the same session will traverse along the same end-to-end explicit route. If any of the transmission group on the explicit route used becomes inoperative, the session will be disconnected. The user needs to request, specifically, session reinitialization and to use an operating explicit route for the re-established session.

To enhance flexibility, the RTG provides the user with the capability of specifying the type of routes desired. This capability allows the user to specify the inclusion of specific explicit routes, the number and maximum number of hops for ERs between a node pair, the exclusion of certain nodes that are to be used as intermediate nodes, and the selection of route selection criteria (for example, hop count, packet delay, or route availability level).

Session packets from the source node will always be transported over the first ordered (operative) virtual route for the COS that is associated with that session. (The user, however, can use an exit routine to reorder the virtual routes, so that a route other than the first ordered can be used for a particular session.)

As shown in Figure 4, an explicit route is specified at each node along the path via the set (DSA, ERN, NN, TG). The packet header uses the DSA and ERN fields for routing purposes.

Changes

As with most networks, Digital Equipment's DNA/ Decnet has evolved over time, with capabilities added in each of the newer releases. For instance, the earlier version of Decnet allowed communications only between directly connected nodes. The more recent releases (Phases III and IV) significantly enhance networking capability by allowing routing and switching.

Datapac is the TransCanada Telephone System's public packet-switched network, based on the Northern Telecom SL-10 Packet-Switching System. Beginning commercial service in June of 1977 with five installed SL-10 nodes, the Datapac network has grown to include 14 installed nodes and 24 trunks connecting those nodes.

As Table 1 illustrates, the routing protocols in DNA and Datapac are essentially the same and are fairly straightforward.

Telenet is a commercial value-added network operated by GTE Telenet, founded in 1972 by the principal architect of Arpanet, Dr. Lawrence Roberts, and later acquired by GTE in 1979. Approved by the FCC in 1973, it was among the first value-added specialized carriers. From an initial network of seven central offices, Telenet has grown to an international network providing services in over 250 cities in the United States and interconnections in over 40 foreign countries. It currently supports over 1,000 host computers and an estimated 100,000 terminals.

There are three types of Telenet nodes. The TP4000s are full-fledged packet switches; the TP3000s are asynchronous/synchronous X.25 PADs; and the TP5000s are network control centers (NCCs). The routing protocol of Telenet is illustrated by the TP4000s and the NCCs.

At each system configuration/reconfiguration—that is, when adding, changing, or deleting either nodes or links—the NCC generates a new routing table for each node (TP4000) in the network. The routing tables generated are downloaded to the associated nodes in the network, and they remain static until the next reconfiguration.

Outbound links

For a given node, the associated routing table identifies, for each destination node, the primary outbound links and the secondary outbound links. Figure 5 is a sample routing table for a node with four outbound links. In the current Telenet implementation, the primary outbound links correspond to the least-cost paths to the given destination. The secondary outbound links correspond to the remaining links. The link cost is based on the link capacity.

When there is a network component failure, the NCC will be notified by the nodes adjacent to the failed component. However, the routing tables residing at the network nodes will not be updated.

At the point of session setup, an end-to-end path is selected by the connect request packet in the following manner. At each node along the path, the entries that are in the routing table for the given destination are examined. The next outbound link is the least-saturated primary outbound link that does not form a loop with the partially completed path (assuming that not all of the primary links are saturated). To allow the inspection of loops, the connect request packet contains the list of nodes traversed. The criterion for the link saturation level is based on both the link capacity and the number of active virtual circuits.

If all of the primary outbound links are ineligible, then the secondary outbound links are examined. Assuming that not all of the secondary links are saturated, one of them is chosen by the same criteria that were used with the primary links. If all of the outbound links are either saturated or form a loop with the partially completed path, then a connect reject packet is returned to the source. This process continues until either a path to the destination is established or a connect reject packet is returned to the source node from a node that is intermediate.

The path set-up operation is also performed automatically by the TP4000s when an existing path has to be dismantled due to link/node failure.

In summary, the route generation process in Telenet involves both centralized computation at the NCC and distributed outbound link selection at every node in the network.

In a scheme similar to Tymnet, a path for a Telenet connection is represented by a logical channel number on each link along the path. After session setup, a packet is forwarded from node to node, based on the association between the link/inbound and the link/outbound logical channel numbers.

Side by side

To compare the performance of the routing protocols, a number of attributes must be examined:
■ Protocol overheads introduced by the routing-related operations;
■ Impact on routing operations due to network component failure;
■ Capability for congestion adaptation and load balancing; and
■ Matching of route selection to traffic characteristics.

The three distinct areas of routing-related operations are link-cost computation, route generation/update, and packet forwarding. Each of these operations can consume three types of computer resources: transmission, processing, and storage.

The link-cost function used in both Arpanet and Tymnet takes into account traffic-sensitive factors, such as link loading, packet delay, and so on. Consequently, factors related to the cost of the link have to be measured and updated continuously at all network

---

5. Distinctions. *Telenet routing tables maintain each node's primary and secondary links. Some nodes may not have two of each type available.*

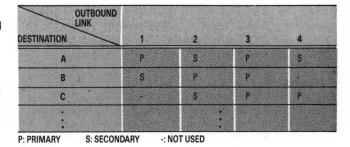

DESTINATION \ OUTBOUND LINK	1	2	3	4
A	P	S	P	S
B	S	P	P	-
C	-	S	P	P
⋮		⋮		

P: PRIMARY   S: SECONDARY   -: NOT USED

nodes. Thus, the processing overhead that is associated with link-cost computation for these two networks is quite high.

In Telenet, the link cost used in the local route selection process is based on the ratio of channel capacity and the number of active virtual circuits; this is a relatively easy quantity to track and does not change quickly. Consequently, processing overhead is relatively low.

In DNA and Datapac, the link cost is only a function of the link capacity, which should change rather infrequently. The processing overhead associated with link-cost computation is essentially minimal.

In SNA, the routes are only generated during the network definition. Consequently, in normal operation, there is no overhead for link-cost computation.

To provide Arpanet routes that are sensitive to changes in network traffic conditions, a link-cost update packet is broadcast from each node to all other nodes at fairly frequent intervals (every 10 to 60 seconds). The link-cost-update packets always trigger shortest-path computation at all nodes. Consequently, the overhead in transmission and processing for route generation is relatively high.

Route generation and update overhead

In Tymnet, the routes are also generated based on a traffic-sensitive link-cost function. However, the link-cost updates are forwarded only to the supervisor node, rather than to all nodes. Moreover, the route generation, circuit set-up, and circuit dismantle operations are usually invoked only once for each session. The transmission and processing overheads are typically lower in Tymnet than in Arpanet.

The processing overhead in Telenet for route selection is higher than it is in Tymnet, because each node needs to perform a fair amount of processing in checking for loops, selecting the most preferred outbound link, and fulfilling various other functions. On the other hand, the transmission overhead in Telenet is lower than it is in Tymnet, because the information on the link saturation level (based on the number of active virtual circuits) is only used locally and is not forwarded to the NCC.

In SNA, the routes are defined at the time of system definition and remain fixed during normal operation. The processing overhead is quite high at system definition time because of the complexity of the route generation and route numbering requirements. In normal operation, though, the only overhead associated with route maintenance is on the activation and deactivation of virtual routes and explicit routes. Consequently, the transmission and processing overheads are minimal.

In DNA and Datapac, failure-adaptive routing techniques are used, rather than traffic-sensitive ones. Consequently, the routing updates are performed rather infrequently. As a result, the transmission and processing overheads associated with route generation and update are minimal.

The amount of storage space requirements associated with the route-generation operation is also an important concern. Arpanet requires two databases at each node: the network database and the shortest-path database. Each node in DNA and Datapac needs a similar shortest-path database. In addition, the path-cost-by-outbound-link database is needed, which has storage requirements comparable to those of the network database.

In SNA, the routing database maintained at each node is more complex than those used in the other networks. For each destination, there can be up to 24 virtual routes at each node, and up to 8 explicit routes. Each entry of the virtual route table contains information on the associated explicit route and the transport priority. The explicit routes are specified by identifying the next node and the outbound transmission group. The storage requirement for SNA thus appears to be the largest.

The storage requirement at a typical node (except the supervisor) in Tymnet is relatively small. An active circuit through a node is specified simply by the two-way association between the logical channels on the inbound and outbound links associated with the circuit. In addition, storage is required at each node to allow the computation of link-cost estimates for all incident links. At the supervisor node, storage is required on the current network topology and link costs, as well as all of the active circuits.

Three databases are required in Telenet. One of them keeps the association between the inbound logical channel and outbound logical channel. Another database tracks the primary or secondary outbound links for each destination. A third contains the link saturation level, in other words, the number of active virtual circuits. The storage requirement for these three databases is comparable to that of Arpanet, DNA, and Datapac.

Packet-forwarding overheads

Excluding the routing databases, the overheads associated with the packet-forwarding operation are relatively small in all networks.

In Arpanet, Decnet, and Datapac, path-independent routing is used. The only field needed in the packet header for routing purposes is the destination field. At each node the destination field and the shortest-path database determine which outbound link is the appropriate one.

In both Tymnet and Telenet, session-dependent path routing is used. Only one field, the logical channel number, is needed in the packet header for routing purposes.

Based on this information, the appropriate outbound link and the logical channel number on the outbound link is readily found from the permuter table. Note that the logical channel number field needs to be updated at each node along the path. As noted in the packet-forwarding database requirements, the same field also serves at the end nodes to identify the session and connection. Consequently, the overall packet-header overhead is much reduced with this type of implementation.

SNA also uses session-dependent routing. Two

Table 2: Routing protocol performance characteristics

| NETWORK | PROTOCOL OVERHEADS | | | ATTRIBUTE |
	LINK COST COMPUTATION	ROUTE GENERATION/ UPDATE	PACKET FORWARDING	IMPACT ON NETWORK OPERATION DUE TO LINK COST COMPUTATION AND ROUTE GENERATION/ UPDATE
ARPANET	HIGH PROCESSING OVERHEAD AT ALL NODES	HIGH PROCESSING AND TRANSMISSION OVERHEADS AT ALL NODES	SMALL	NO DIFFERENT FROM NORMAL OPERATIONS TRIGGERED BY OTHER TYPES OF LINK COST CHANGES
TYMNET	HIGH PROCESSING OVERHEAD AT ALL NODES	■ HIGH OVERHEADS AT SUPERVISOR ■ LOWER PROCESSING AND TRANSMISSION OVERHEAD THAN ARPANET AT NETWORK NODES ■ MINIMAL STORAGE OVERHEAD AT NETWORK NODES	■ SMALL ■ MUCH MORE EFFICIENT THAN OTHER NETWORKS IN THE USE OF TRANSMISSION RESOURCE. A SINGLE "LOGICAL CHANNEL NUMBER" FIELD SERVES BOTH THE NETWORK AND TRANSPORT LEVELS	■ ROUTES USING THE FAILED COMPONENT WILL BE DISMANTLED, AND NEW ROUTES NEED TO BE ESTABLISHED FOR THE AFFECTED SESSIONS ■ MINOR USER-PERCEIVED IMPACT
SNA	NO OVERHEAD IN NORMAL OPERATION	■ VERY HIGH PROCESSING OVERHEAD IN NETWORK DEFINITION/ RECONFIGURATION ■ MINIMAL PROCESSING/ TRANSMISSION OVERHEADS IN NORMAL OPERATION ■ HIGHER STORAGE OVERHEAD THAN OTHER NETWORKS	SMALL	■ VR AND ER USING THE FAILED COMPONENT WILL BE DEACTIVATED ■ AFFECTED SESSIONS WILL BE ABORTED ■ USER INTERACTION IS NEEDED TO REESTABLISH THE SESSION
DNA/DATAPAC	MINIMAL OVERHEAD DUE TO LOW FREQUENCY OF LINK COST COMPUTATION	■ MINIMAL PROCESSING AND TRANSMISSION OVERHEADS ■ STORAGE OVERHEAD COMPARABLE TO ARPANET	SMALL	NO DIFFERENT FROM NORMAL OPERATIONS TRIGGERED BY OTHER TYPES OF LINK COST CHANGES
TELENET	LOW OVERHEAD (IN TRACKING NO. OF ACTIVE VCs ON A LINK)	■ VERY LOW TRANSMISSION OVERHEAD ■ HIGHER PROCESSING OVERHEAD THAN IN TYMNET ■ STORAGE OVERHEAD COMPARABLE TO DNA/DATAPAC/ARPANET	SIMILAR TO TYMNET, EXCEPT NO PACKET RE-ORDERING PERFORMED ON EACH HOP	■ SIMILAR TO TYMNET, EXCEPT THAT THE ROUTING TABLES ARE NOT UPDATED IN NEW ROUTE SELECTION ■ MORE LIKELIHOOD OF LINK FAILURE THAN OTHER NETWORKS

fields, destination subarea (DSA) and explicit route number (ERN), are needed in the packet header for routing purposes. At each node, based on these two fields, the appropriate outbound link (next node/-transmission group) is found from the routing table.

The impact of node or link failure on the routing operations must be examined in two separate dimensions. The first is the link-cost computation and route generation/update operation. The second is the packet-forwarding operation.

First, the impact on the link-cost computation and the route generation are examined. In Arpanet, DNA, and Datapac, network component failure triggers link-cost update and route generation/update operations,

NETWORK COMPONENT FAILURE		
PACKET FORWARDING	CONGESTION ADAPTABILITY AND LOAD BALANCING	MATCHING OF ROUTE SELECTION TO TRAFFIC CHARACTERISTICS
PACKETS QUEUED FOR THE FAILED LINK ARE DISCARDED	PROVIDES CONGESTION ADAPTABILITY ON A PER-PACKET BASIS	NO
TRANSIT PACKETS BELONGING TO THE AFFECTED SESSIONS ARE DISCARDED	PROVIDES CONGESTION ADAPTABILITY ON A PER-SESSION BASIS	YES, CHARACTERISTICS SUCH AS: ■ HIGH THROUGHPUT ■ LOW DELAY, ETC.
TRANSIT PACKETS BELONGING TO THE AFFECTED SESSIONS ARE DISCARDED	NO CONGESTION ADAPTABILITY, BUT PROVIDES SOME DEGREE OF LOAD BALANCING (NEEDS MANUAL INTERVENTION)	YES, ALLOWS SPECIFICATION OF A VARIETY OF COST CRITERIA, SUCH AS CAPACITY, DELAY, SECURITY, ETC.
PACKETS QUEUED FOR THE FAILED LINK ARE DISCARDED	■ NO CONGESTION ADAPTABILITY ■ NO LOAD BALANCING	NO
TRANSIT PACKETS BELONGING TO THE AFFECTED SESSIONS ARE DISCARDED	PERFORM LOCAL LOAD BALANCING AND CONGESTION ADAPTATION. NOT AS EFFECTIVE AS TYMNET AND ARPANET	NO

active logical channels on the link) are dismantled, using the path-zapper packets. This process starts from the nodes incident to the link.

■ The supervisor updates the topology and link-costs database, and generates new circuits to replace the dismantled circuits.

■ The supervisor's trigger packet causes the circuit information to be stored at each node along the paths.

In addition, if the failed link causes the network to be disconnected, one of the sleeping supervisors isolated from the active supervisor will awake in a few minutes and take over route-generation functions for that part of the network. If there is no supervisor in that section of the network, then no new sessions can be established for nodes in that section. When the previously separated section is reconnected due to the failed links becoming operational, all but one of the supervisors are made inoperative again.

When the active supervisor fails, one of the sleeping supervisors will be awakened in a few minutes. It establishes control of the network and keeps other supervisors in the sleep state. In short, extensive activities are triggered by a failed network component in Tymnet. This is primarily due to the session-based routing methodology employed.

When links fail
In Telenet, when a link becomes inoperative, the following activities take place:
■ The nodes that are incident to the failed link will notify the NCC.
■ All paths that use the failed link will be dismantled, starting from the nodes that are incident to the link.
■ The source node will trigger path-rebuilding operations with an X.25 reset packet.

Since Telenet does not permit a link to be composed of multiple transmission facilities, the likelihood of link failure in Telenet is higher than in other networks. In addition, NCC failure in Telenet has essentially no impact on the routing operation, because the NCC is not involved in path setup.

In SNA, when a link (transmission group) becomes inoperative, all explicit routes using that link will be deactivated, which in turn deactivates all virtual routes mapped into these explicit routes. Since the routes are static, no path-rebuild operation takes place (as in the case of Tymnet). However, all sessions using the deactivated virtual routes will be aborted. Thus a failed link necessitates higher-level user interaction to reestablish the aborted sessions, and the impact of a failed link becomes more noticeable to a human user of the network.

The impact of link or node failure on the routing operation can also be examined in terms of the packet-forwarding operation. Consequently, examining the impact due to link failure is sufficient (except when the failed node is a supervisor).

When an Arpanet link becomes inoperative, the affected packets are those that have been queued for the failed link. But other packets are not affected by an inoperative link.

In Decnet and Datapac, the impact of link failure on

which are essentially no different from operations triggered by other types of link-cost change.

In Tymnet, when a link becomes inoperative, the following activities take place:
■ The nodes incident to the failed link generate update packets to the supervisor.
■ All circuits using the failed link (identified by the

the packet-forwarding operation is similar to Arpanet. In this case, though, the path-cost-by-outbound-link database could be used to select an alternate outbound link for an affected packet. The routing mechanism can be modified to allow the packet-forwarding operation to proceed even in the event of a partial or complete link failure.

When a link becomes inoperative in Tymnet, Telenet, and SNA, all packets that are in transit on circuits using the failed link will be discarded because all of these circuits will be dismantled. In Tymnet and Telenet, the use of end-to-end retransmission (via the transport layer) reduces the disruption to the end-user processes. This is not done in SNA, because the affected sessions are aborted.

In both Arpanet and Tymnet, the link-cost function is partially based on the link's saturation level. Consequently, when there is sufficient change in link loading, an update packet is generated and forwarded to the appropriate node (to all other nodes in the case of Arpanet, and to the supervisor node in the case of Tymnet).

Congestion adaptation and load balancing
In Arpanet, the packet-forwarding decision is made at each node, independent of the specific sessions generating the packets. Consequently, the routing mechanism itself will tend to steer packets to less congested areas. Unless the measurement interval for link loading is appropriately chosen, this type of routing mechanism can lead to excessive oscillation and instability. This is why the routing measurement and update interval in Arpanet was changed from 64 msec to 10 to 60 seconds.

Tymnet has a contrasting approach. Here, the up-to-date link-loading information is used at the supervisor for the selection of new routes for session request. However, that information is not used for the routing of packets belonging to the established sessions. Consequently, the use of network resources may not be as effective as it is in Arpanet. On the other hand, the link-loading levels tend to be more stable.

In Telenet, an estimate of link loading is made — based on the number of active VCs — and is used locally for path setup. This allows for some degree of local congestion adaptation and load balancing. In general, however, the routes selected do not use network resources as efficiently as routes selected in Tymnet and Arpanet. In these networks, route selection is based on global loading information, rather than just local loading information.

In Decnet, Datapac, and SNA, the link loading is not used in either the route-generation operation or the packet-forwarding operation. The routing mechanism in these networks is not adaptive to congestion, so congestion control is provided by separate mechanisms. The routing protocols in these networks are more concerned with reliability and availability than with the most efficient use of network resources.

In SNA, due to the availability of multiple explicit routes between a pair of nodes, some load balancing can be achieved by assigning different sessions to different explicit routes. However, manual assignments must be performed to use routes other than the first-ordered virtual routes.

Matching route selection to network traffic
In Tymnet, several different traffic categories are distinguished, such as high throughput (for example, an application for high-speed printer output), and low delay (exemplified by interactive, transaction-oriented applications). Different link-cost functions are applied to different traffic categories. This allows the selection of routes to be optimized to the traffic category under consideration. Thus, for example, it is appropriate to add an interactive session, but not an RJE session, to a link already overloaded with high throughput traffic. On the other hand, a satellite link is appropriate for a high throughput session, but is not appropriate for an interactive session.

SNA routing protocol provides a similar capability by allowing the user to specify different cost criteria for different classes of virtual routes. Arpanet, Telenet, DNA, and Datapac provide no such feature. Major extensions to these routing protocols would be needed to provide such a capability. Table 2 contains a summary of the performance comparison of the various routing protocols.

References
1. H.C. Folts, "A Long-Awaited Standard for Heterogeneous Nets," DATA COMMUNICATIONS, Vol. 10, No. 1, January 1981, pp. 63-73.
2. J.M. McQuillan, G. Falk, and I. Richer, "A Review of the Development and Performance of the Arpanet Routing Algorithm," IEEE Transaction on Communications, Volume COM-26, December 1978, pp. 1908, pp. 711-719.
3. J. Rinde, "Tymnet I: An Alternative to Packet Technology," in Proceedings of the Third ICCC, Toronto, Ontario, Can., August 1976, pp. 268-283.
4. L.W. Tymes, "Routing and Flow Control in Tymnet," IEEE Transactions on Communications, Volume COM-29, No. 4, April 1981, pp. 392-398.
5. A.J. Hedeen, "IBM Approach Aids Control of Multisystem Nets," Data Communicaitons, Vol. 9, No. 7, July 1980, pp. 97-100.
6. IBM Corp., Routing Table Generator, Program Description/Operation Manual, SB21-2806-1; available through IBM branch offices.
7. K. Maruyama, "Defining Routing Tables for SNA Networks," IBM Systems Journal, Vol. 22, No. 4, 1983, pp. 435-450.
8. S.W. Johnson, "Architectural Evolution: Digital Unveils Its Decnet Phase II, DATA COMMUNICATIONS, Vol. 9, No. 3, March 1980, pp. 85-90.
9. M. Thurk and L. Twaits, "Inside DEC's Newest Networking Phase," DATA COMMUNICATIONS, Vol. 12, No. 9, September 1983, pp. 215-223.
10. D.E. Sproule and F. Mellor, "Routing, Flow, and Congestion Control in the Datapac Network," IEEE Transactions on Communications, Volume COM-29, No. 4, April 1981, pp. 386-391. ■

David Stern, ITT Advanced Technology Center, Stratford, Conn.

A quick model for getting network response time close to perfect

The efficiency index, a relative newcomer to network analysis, can reduce packet delay and speed user throughput. It computes fast, too.

One of the most difficult problems facing a data communications network designer is deciding how to allocate network capacity in an optimal fashion or, similarly, how to assign packet flow. As corporate networks grow, such decisions have to be made more frequently by both network managers and consultants in their employ. Tools are needed to help network designers and managers do each of the following:

■ Allocate lines with the correct bandwidth or relative capacity in the predesign stage.

■ Increase capacities by adding lines of proper bandwidth to existing networks.

■ Reroute traffic to improve terminal response time, either by reducing the flow on overburdened lines or by increasing it on those that are underutilized with respect to their neighbors.

The results of various optimization methods are customarily measured in terms of least cost and/or minimum packet delay, which, of course, yields optimal response time. These areas of research are referred to specifically as the assignment problems for flow and capacity.

Computer networks are often modeled in terms of queuing theory. Mathematical algorithms can achieve optimal results with theoretical networks. However, the problem with using such algorithms to construct models is that, in the real world, they often do not match the existing network with any degree of precision. Moreover, the available optimization techniques are complicated, time-consuming, and computationally expensive. While mathematical modeling may suffice for researchers, simpler methods, such as approximation algorithms or heuristics, are always being sought by designers of real data communications networks for a more practical approach to these problems.

Recently such a heuristic was introduced, derived from the information-theoretic measure of mutual information: I. The measure I was presented as a way to determine a network's efficiency. For a discussion of this approach, see Joseph T. Johnson, "Universal flow and capacity index gives picture of network efficiency," DATA COMMUNICATIONS, February, p. 171. Johnson's method is appealing because of its simplicity of implementation. When the new measure I is applied to the analysis of a hypothetical network, it can be shown to perform well in terms of a meaningful and widely accepted measure of network performance, namely delay.

Moreover, the new measure is useful in reducing the delay and in honing the response time of real networks. I can be used as the central algorithm in a computer program the goal of which is the optimization of either network flow or capacity. The additional fact that I, a Swiss army knife of an algorithm, can optimize either flow or capacity is of particular importance since most others handle only one or the other. In fact, I presents a simpler method to tune a network, regardless of whether flow or capacity can be varied in that particular network.

The efficiency index

Given a network with n channels, each channel "i" is associated with a number c_i that represents the channel's portion of total network capacity $C(N)$ taken as a unit. Thus, $0 <= c_i <= 1$ and $C(N) = c_1 + c_2 + \ldots + c_n = 1$. The flow on a channel i over some period of time, taken as a percentage of the total network flow over the same period of time, is represented as f_i. As with c_i, $0 <= f_i <= 1$. Similarly, total network flow is taken as a unit and $F(N) = f_1 + f_2 \ldots + f_n = 1$. (Note that Johnson used raw percentages, rather than frac-

An easier approximation

The efficiency index I can be incorporated into a computer program in a much more efficient form than was given by Joseph T. Johnson (DATA COMMUNICATIONS, February, p. 171). If a program uses Johnson's equation, each iterative sampling of a network and test for I requires calculation of a logarithm, which is computationally costly. Henri Thiel (*Principles of Econometrics*, New York: Wiley, 1971) proved that I can be approximated without using logarithms. His equations, listed below, can cut computation time and make the job easier.

If the differences between each pair of elements f_i and c_i are not too large and if the efficiency index is defined using the natural logarithm, then I can be approximated in the following manner:

$$I = 1/2 \sum_{i=1}^{n} f_i \left(\frac{c_i - f_i}{f_i} \right)^2$$

$$= 1/2 \sum_{i=1}^{n} \frac{(c_i - f_i)^2}{f_i}$$

For networks with dynamic routing, where routing decisions are made in real time, Thiel's approximation lends itself well to quick, ongoing determinations of network performance. Existing methods for analyzing such networks take repeated "snapshots" and analyze them as if the network were static. With a costly or computationally complex algorithm, fewer and more infrequent glimpses can be taken for study, yielding a coarser approximation of performance. The index I is faster than published analytical methods, even more so if logarithms do not have to be used.

Other properties of the efficiency index include:
(1) If $I = 0$ then the network is behaving as expected.
   a. $I = 0$ is the lower limit.
   b. Even though separate index values for any channel can be less than zero, the index value for the network as a whole must be equal to or greater than zero.
   c. Theoretically, I could be infinitely large, creating a situation where the average packet experiences infinite delay. In this case, the network becomes a kind of "black hole," in that packets are never seen again once they enter the network. (Fortunately, no black-hole networks could ever be constructed, although terminal users might occasionally beg to differ.)
(2) In the case of $n = 2$ channels, if either channel's index value is equal to zero then the other channel's index term also equals zero.
(3) More generally, if $n - 1$ channels have index terms equal to zero then the nth channel's index term is equal to zero.

tions of a unit. Other differences between Johnson's equations and those that follow are merely notational.)

Johnson gives an equation for the efficiency index of a given network:

$$I = \sum_{i=1}^{n} f_i \ln \frac{f_i}{c_i}$$

For networks where the traffic is exactly proportional to the allocated capacity on all channels, the index I will equal zero, since $f_i = c_i$ means that the log term is zero for each i. However, in situations where there is much disparity between actual network usage and the allocated capacity, the index will be a nonzero, positive number. The larger the I value, the more severe the disparity between network data flow and capacity allocations.

Johnson's view of I assumes that good network design is a matter of proportions. If flow and capacity are assigned in proportion to one another for each link, the entire network will be functioning at its peak. This perspective is akin to the notion that the good of the whole is nothing but the sum of the good of the parts. It can be demonstrated that, in the case of the design of communications networks at least, this assumption is valid.

The classical method

The problem of determining the proper amount of flow or capacity to assign within a computer communications network has been the subject of considerable research in the past 20 years. Kleinrock, in particular, has devoted much attention to this subject, while many others have added to his original work (see Kleinrock, L. *Queueing System, Volume II: Computer Applications*, chapter 5. Wiley, 1976, and note the references for related work in the field).

The flow and capacity assignment problems normally strive to optimize parameters that are considered crucial to network performance. Perhaps the most important measure of network efficiency, as far as users are concerned, is packet delay, which is the time it takes a packet to travel through the network. This cumulative delay has a direct effect on how long a user has to wait at a terminal to get a response from the host.

Delay is also considered by theoreticians to be one of the most important classical figures of merit in packet-switching networks. Classical analysis calculates the overall network performance T by using parameters such as:
■ The average interarrival rate in packets per second (λ), which is analogous to data flow.
■ The average time it takes a network node to process a packet (μ), which is known as the average service time.
■ Channel capacity (C).

Both the flow and the capacity parameters are related to Johnson's terms. In these terms, each line is represented as a portion of the entire network; therefore, $f_i = \lambda_i / \lambda$ and $c_i = C_i / C$.

With Kleinrock's model, both flow and capacity are

1. Rudiments. In (a), channel 1 has twice the capacity but half the load of channel 2. Proportion is reached in (b), and the overall network delay declines. The routing table reflects the asymmetrical connections between the nodes, while the analysis table shows the results of a classical study of the sample networks.

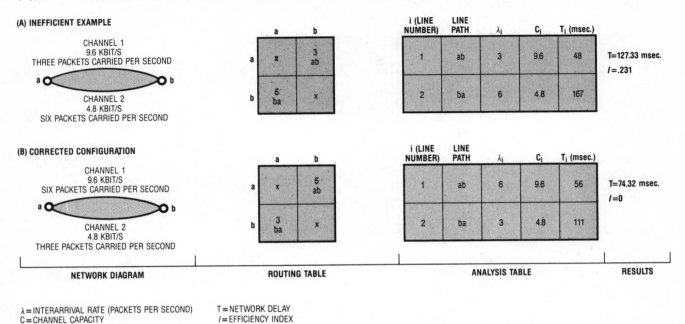

(A) INEFFICIENT EXAMPLE

CHANNEL 1
9.6 KBIT/S
THREE PACKETS CARRIED PER SECOND

CHANNEL 2
4.8 KBIT/S
SIX PACKETS CARRIED PER SECOND

	a	b
a	x	3 ab
b	6 ba	x

i (LINE NUMBER)	LINE PATH	λ_i	C_i	T_i (msec.)
1	ab	3	9.6	48
2	ba	6	4.8	167

T=127.33 msec.
I=.231

(B) CORRECTED CONFIGURATION

CHANNEL 1
9.6 KBIT/S
SIX PACKETS CARRIED PER SECOND

CHANNEL 2
4.8 KBIT/S
THREE PACKETS CARRIED PER SECOND

	a	b
a	x	6 ab
b	3 ba	x

i (LINE NUMBER)	LINE PATH	λ_i	C_i	T_i (msec.)
1	ab	6	9.6	56
2	ba	3	4.8	111

T=74.32 msec.
I=0

| NETWORK DIAGRAM | ROUTING TABLE | ANALYSIS TABLE | RESULTS |

λ = INTERARRIVAL RATE (PACKETS PER SECOND)
C = CHANNEL CAPACITY
T = NETWORK DELAY
I = EFFICIENCY INDEX

used in calculation. In addition, the average time must be known in order to calculate the average network delay.

Kleinrock computes the average delay for line i using equation 1 (see "A primer: Queuing in packet networks"), and the total delay of the network with equation 3. These expressions are important since they allow a designer to determine how long it will take for the average packet to flow through a network. They can also provide a widely accepted and understood yardstick for judging Johnson's efficiency index I.

Simple case

The validity of manipulating I to improve average network delay can be demonstrated by examining a very simple data network, such as one with two channels and two nodes (Fig. 1a). Channel 1 has a capacity of 9.6 kbit/s, while channel 2 is rated at 4.8 kbit/s. Measurements over a period of time indicate that channel 1 has transmitted 3 packets of data per second while channel 2 has transmitted 6 packets per second. Thus, $c_1 = 2/3$, $f_1 = 1/3$, $c_2 = 1/3$, and $f_2 = 2/3$. Therefore, using Johnson's equation, $I = 1/3 \ln (1/2) + 2/3 \ln (2) = 0.231$. It would be of interest to see if Johnson's measure can be used to reduce network delay; thus, delay must be computed for the network.

Classical network analysis involves the construction of a routing table and the derivation of queuing statistics, as in the primer. The routing table for the two-node network is shown in Figure 1a. Each element in the table consists of two items:
■ The path traveled by packets going from a source node to a destination node.

■ An integer indicating the total number of packets per second that the overall network contributes to each channel on the predetermined routing path.

This routing table and the capacity assignments given can be used to derive the analysis table in Figure 1a. It is assumed that the nodes can process 400 bit/s on average; that is, $\mu = 1/400$. Then, to find each line's delay T_i, the line's capacity and average packet flow can be combined with μ in equation 1 in the primer. Applying equation 3 to values in both tables gives the mean delay T of this network, 127.33 msec. Can it be shown that the value of T is related to the I value of 0.231?

Johnson implies that using his measure to reassign the network flow or capacity until $I = 0$ would make the overall network more "efficient." Since the capacity of line "ab" is twice that of line "ba," it makes sense to reassign the flow over line "ab" to give it twice the traffic.

The new network and routing and analysis tables appear in Figure 1b. How has reassigning the flow affected average network delay? Recalculation of T yields a delay of only 74.32 msec., now that $I = 0$. Thus, the theory would seem to hold quite well in this case.

Textbook case

A good many network analysts and consultants with contemporary training have learned from Andrew S. Tanenbaum's excellent text *Computer Networks*. The measure I can be tested against T more rigorously and in a more universally acknowledged context by borrowing a network description from this book (p. 63). Once it is derived, I can be increased and the routing and

A primer: Queuing in packet networks

Thinking of a data communications network in terms of a two-dimensional matrix can be useful. Along one axis of the matrix lie all nodes that can send a packet, and on the other are all those that can receive a packet. If all nodes can both send and receive packets (the usual situation), the result is an n-squared matrix where n is the total number of nodes in the network. Each element in the matrix represents a routing definition for a specific source-node/destination-node pair.

The definition contains two pieces of information: the mean number of packets per second (γ_{ij}) that are transmitted from a source node "i" to a destination node "j" and the "node path" along which packets travel in their journey between the source and destination nodes. (It is assumed that the network uses static routing tables.) For example, to get from a source node "s" to a destination node "d," imagine that nodes "x," "y," and "z" would also have to be traversed. In this case, "s, x, y, z, d" would be the node routing path.

To better understand the above description, consider a hypothetical network with five nodes: a, b, c, d, and e. They are connected as shown in the network diagram (A). The routing table (B), which defines the packet flow, indicates that the traffic from b to e is very heavy. Also note that, since none of the nodes sends packets to itself, the matrix is empty along its diagonal.

The routing table is useful in deriving a great deal of information about the behavior of the network. This information plus the line capacities and the service-time distribution, which is related to the average packet-processing rates, make it possible to determine with certainty how much delay the average packet will experience in its travels through the network.

How is this accomplished? First, all the elements' packet flow terms γ_{ij} in the table should be summed to form a variable γ. The next variable to be considered is the amount of packet flow that each source-node/destination-node pair contributes to the total flow over a given link. For example, the link between nodes a and d will handle 16 packets per second. This figure, known as λ_{ij}, is derived by summing the packet flow for node pairs ad, ae, cd, and ce. Adding all λ_i's together gives λ, which then represents the total network flow.

The capacity of each link, C_i, usually expressed in bits per second, must also be known. Summing C_i over all links yields C, the total network capacity. The last basic parameter used in this analysis is the average service time, referred to as μ. This is the average number of bits per second that any given node is able to process.

In the hypothetical network, all capacities are 64 kbit/s. Also, in any second, a given network node can process an average of 1,000 bits of information, meaning that $\mu = 1$ kbit/s. Looked at another way,

$1/\mu$ provides the average service time per bit over all nodes.

From these parameters, queuing theorists have developed specific expressions that present useful information about packet-switching networks. In particular, the equation for delay on an individual line i is as follows:

$$T_i = \frac{1}{\mu C_i - \lambda_i}$$

(Equation 1)

Another important result is the average number of hops (nodes) a typical packet will traverse in its journey through the network. This is expressed as another equation:

$$\text{hops} = \frac{\lambda}{\gamma}$$

(Equation 2)

These two equations can be used together to derive a widely used measure, namely the total network delay:

$$T = \sum_{i=1}^{M} \frac{\lambda_i}{\gamma} T_i$$

(Equation 3)

where,
M = the total number of channels in the network.
λ_i = the number of packets arriving each second on channel i.
(λ_{ij} = the traffic in packets per second between adjacent nodes i and j).
$1/\mu$ = the average service time per bit.
C_i = the capacity for channel i.

To understand the derivation of these equations, the reader is referred to Kobayshi and Konheim, Hayes, Tanenbaum, and particularly Kleinrock (see references).

In the hypothetical network, application of equation 1 permits the completion of the analysis table (C). Note the delay for line 6 in the analysis table, for example. By equation 1, $T_6 = 1/[(64,000/1,000) - 24] = 1/40$ sec., or 25 msec.

Since $\lambda = 113$ and $\gamma = 71$ from the analysis and routing tables, respectively, the average number of hops = 1.6. Also, T = 33 msec. It might seem that T can be found by taking an average of all T_i. However, each path of multiple hops contributes to delay. Comparing equations 2 and 3 shows that the total network delay takes into account the portion each line contributes to average network hops. This delay figure can be approximated by multiplying the average number of hops, 1.6, by the average of all the line delays, roughly 19. (This approximation is meant to serve as an illustration only.)

Queuing theorists have defined a variable ρ, which is also known as the traffic intensity factor. This is just the average arrival rate of packets multiplied by the average service time; that is, $\rho = \lambda / \mu$ (remember that the service time is $1/\mu$). One meaningful result that uses ρ is the expression that shows the average number of packets in a queue:

$$\bar{N} = \frac{\rho}{1 - \rho}$$

This formula indicates that, as the arrival rate λ gets closer in value to the service rate μ, the network delay approaches infinity. The equation is shown graphically in the diagram of traffic versus queuing (D).

Moving to the left along this graph suggests that, after a certain critical "traffic jam" point has been reached, upgrading a network's ability to service packets has a large payoff in reducing its overall delay.

It might seem that processing packets on average as fast as they arrive would cause no network congestion. However, this assumes a constant rate of arrival and service, whereas the equations presented above are valid for the class of queuing networks where the arrival and service processes are exponentially distributed.

Real networks do exhibit an exponential distribution, which can be likened to packets occasionally arriving at a node "in bus loads" and arriving very infrequently at other times. Also, not all packets can be processed in the same amount of time by each network node.

Most network analysts assume that the arrival process and the service process are exponentially distributed (see Kleinrock, Hayes, or Tanenbaum). The technical literature refers to such networks as being composed of M/M/1 queues. The first letter (M in this case) refers to the interarrival time distribution, the second letter to the service time distribution, and the integer (1) to the number of servers. M stands for exponential distribution. Calling a network M/M/1 assumes that each node is a single server of incoming packets. It further assumes that all packets are serviced first-come, first-served, and that the population of packets is infinite.

Kleinrock and others have shown that a packet-switching network of type M/M/1 will degrade very rapidly (that is, T will become very large) as the traffic intensity ratio ρ approaches one. Thus, the closer the traffic intensity ratio is to zero, the better the delay performance will be in a computer communications network.

Unfortunately, the methods currently in use to minimize the traffic intensity ratio, and hence the delay parameter "T," are time-consuming and complex. The measure "I" (which is relatively easy to compute) is similar to the traffic intensity ratio in that, as it approaches zero, the resulting delay parameter in a network is improved. The accompanying article attempts to demonstrate the index's value through a heuristic argument.

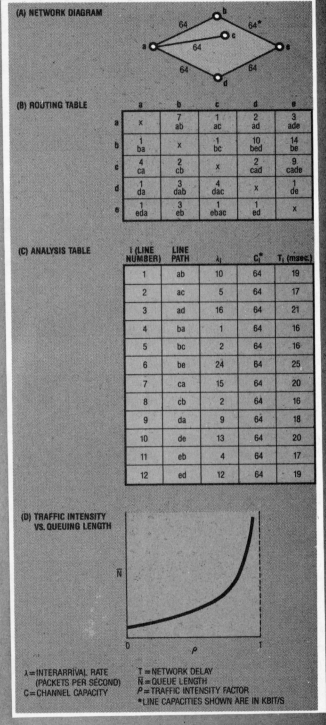

(A) NETWORK DIAGRAM

(B) ROUTING TABLE

	a	b	c	d	e
a	x	7 ab	1 ac	2 ad	3 ade
b	1 ba	x	1 bc	10 bed	14 be
c	4 ca	2 cb	x	2 cad	9 cade
d	1 da	3 dab	4 dac	x	1 de
e	1 eda	3 eb	1 ebac	1 ed	x

(C) ANALYSIS TABLE

I (LINE NUMBER)	LINE PATH	λ_I	C_I^*	T_I (msec.)
1	ab	10	64	19
2	ac	5	64	17
3	ad	16	64	21
4	ba	1	64	16
5	bc	2	64	16
6	be	24	64	25
7	ca	15	64	20
8	cb	2	64	16
9	da	9	64	18
10	de	13	64	20
11	eb	4	64	17
12	ed	12	64	19

(D) TRAFFIC INTENSITY VS. QUEUING LENGTH

λ = INTERARRIVAL RATE (PACKETS PER SECOND)
C = CHANNEL CAPACITY
T = NETWORK DELAY
$\bar{N}$ = QUEUE LENGTH
ρ = TRAFFIC INTENSITY FACTOR
*LINE CAPACITIES SHOWN ARE IN KBIT/S

2. Variations on a theme. *A reference network (a) is varied to see the effects of changes on the efficiency index and the network delay measure. First, traffic is routed around a high-capacity line (b); then, the network is improved slightly by using this link (c); finally, optimum is reached by juggling capacity (d).*

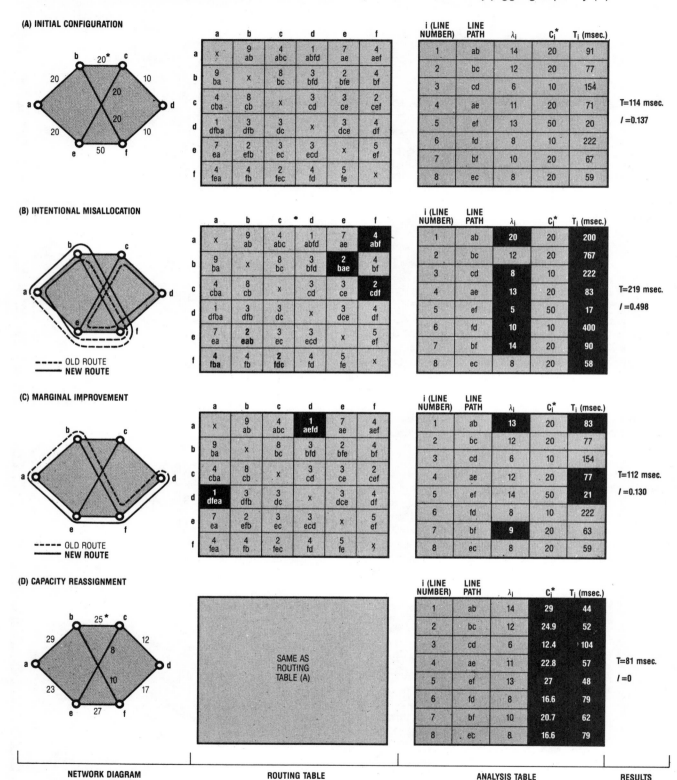

(A) INITIAL CONFIGURATION

Routing Table (A)

	a	b	c	d	e	f
a	x	9 ab	4 abc	1 abfd	7 ae	4 aef
b	9 ba	x	8 bc	3 bfd	2 bfe	4 bf
c	4 cba	8 cb	x	3 cd	3 ce	2 cef
d	1 dfba	3 dfb	3 dc	x	3 dce	4 df
e	7 ea	2 efb	3 ec	3 ecd	x	5 ef
f	4 fea	4 fb	2 fec	4 fd	5 fe	x

i (LINE NUMBER)	LINE PATH	λ_i	C_i^*	T_i (msec.)
1	ab	14	20	91
2	bc	12	20	77
3	cd	6	10	154
4	ae	11	20	71
5	ef	13	50	20
6	fd	8	10	222
7	bf	10	20	67
8	ec	8	20	59

T=114 msec.
I =0.137

(B) INTENTIONAL MISALLOCATION

- - - OLD ROUTE
——— NEW ROUTE

	a	b	c	d	e	f
a	x	9 ab	4 abc	1 abfd	7 ae	4 abf
b	9 ba	x	8 bc	3 bfd	2 bae	4 bf
c	4 cba	8 cb	x	3 cd	3 ce	2 cdf
d	1 dfba	3 dfb	3 dc	x	3 dce	4 df
e	7 ea	2 eab	3 ec	3 ecd	x	5 ef
f	4 fba	4 fb	2 fdc	4 fd	5 fe	x

i (LINE NUMBER)	LINE PATH	λ_i	C_i^*	T_i (msec.)
1	ab	20	20	200
2	bc	12	20	767
3	cd	8	10	222
4	ae	13	20	83
5	ef	5	50	17
6	fd	10	10	400
7	bf	14	20	90
8	ec	8	20	58

T=219 msec.
I =0.498

(C) MARGINAL IMPROVEMENT

- - - OLD ROUTE
——— NEW ROUTE

	a	b	c	d	e	f
a	x	9 ab	4 abc	1 aefd	7 ae	4 aef
b	9 ba	x	8 bc	3 bfd	2 bfe	4 bf
c	4 cba	8 cb	x	3 cd	3 ce	2 cef
d	1 dfea	3 dfb	3 dc	x	3 dce	4 df
e	7 ea	2 efb	3 ec	3 ecd	x	5 ef
f	4 fea	4 fb	2 fec	4 fd	5 fe	x

i (LINE NUMBER)	LINE PATH	λ_i	C_i^*	T_i (msec.)
1	ab	13	20	83
2	bc	12	20	77
3	cd	6	10	154
4	ae	12	20	77
5	ef	14	50	21
6	fd	8	10	222
7	bf	9	20	63
8	ec	8	20	59

T=112 msec.
I =0.130

(D) CAPACITY REASSIGNMENT

SAME AS ROUTING TABLE (A)

i (LINE NUMBER)	LINE PATH	λ_i	C_i^*	T_i (msec.)
1	ab	14	29	44
2	bc	12	24.9	52
3	cd	6	12.4	104
4	ae	11	22.8	57
5	ef	13	27	48
6	fd	8	16.6	79
7	bf	10	20.7	62
8	ec	8	16.6	79

T=81 msec.
I =0

NETWORK DIAGRAM — **ROUTING TABLE** — **ANALYSIS TABLE** — **RESULTS**

λ=INTERARRIVAL RATE (PACKETS PER SECOND)
C=CHANNEL CAPACITY

T=NETWORK DELAY
I=EFFICIENCY INDEX

*LINE CAPACITIES SHOWN ARE IN KBIT/S.

analysis parameters monitored for change. It can also be improved (that is, decreased) to see if the network delay T can be reduced and thereby made more efficient.

The network given in Tanenbaum's text is defined by a topology and a routing map. Six nodes are interconnected with eight full-duplex channels. The network configuration and line capacities are defined as shown in Figure 2a.

Since the eight channels are full duplex, the analytic relationships between nodes go both ways. Thus, the network actually contains sixteen half-duplex channels. The routing table in Figure 2a depicts the routing algorithm for the network, while the analysis table presents the performance numbers. (These results are from Tanenbaum.) Since the lines are full duplex, routing is the same in either direction, and the routing table is symmetric (as was not the case in the two-node network).

For this network, the total delay T equals 114 msec. As was mentioned earlier, the terms f_i and c_i can be derived from the analysis table. By calculation, $I = 0.137$.

Will the standard figure of merit T deteriorate if the network is manipulated to make I increase? Johnson has indicated that disparity will rise if traffic over the highest-capacity channel is restricted. The routing in Figure 2b has been modified to this end. As much traffic as possible has been restricted between the nodes e and f, except for direct packet exchanges between the two nodes, which would not make sense to redirect.

The rerouting of packets (flow reassignment) affects six elements in the table. The new analysis table reflects the changed state of the network. As indicated, delays change on all the lines, increasing significantly on most of them.

Using these new parameters, the total network delay almost doubles to T = 219 msec., while $I = 0.498$, increasing by a factor of 3.6. Thus, reassigning the flow so as to increase the index I affects delay T in a like manner.

To get the opposite, and preferred, effect, T must be decreased. Thus, it would seem appropriate to place more traffic on the channel that has a 50-kbit/s capacity, since f_i for this channel is only 0.16, although c_i is 0.294. Manipulating the original routing scenario produces the routing and analysis tables that are shown in Figure 2c.

Two extra packets per second have been placed on channel "ef" while the same number have been removed from lesser-capacity channels. For channel "ef," the flow f_i increases to 0.171 from 0.16. The net effect of this manipulation is to reduce I from 0.137 to 0.130, resulting in a 2-msec. savings to T (from 114 msec. to 112 msec.). Thus, even small changes to I affect T, indicating that the efficiency index could be used to fine-tune a network.

Finally, allowing I to equal zero can dramatically affect the delay time T. As before, changes will be made to the original network, but this time in terms of capacity rather than flow. In the previous two examples

data flow was varied by rerouting traffic. Changing the flow of real networks is easier in most cases than changing their capacity. Even if changing lines (or capacities, as with software-defined networks) is possible, optimization is limited by discrete increments of bandwidth (9.6-, 19.2-, and 56-kbit/s channels, for example).

However, by precisely matching capacity ratios to flow rather than vice versa, it is possible to force $I = 0$. In so doing, a new set of tables is generated (Fig. 2d).

Applying equation 3, the delay T is equal to 81 msec. It can be proven that this figure is within 1 percent of the theoretical optimum. Since, in the original definition tables, the delay parameter was 114 msec., minimizing I produced a savings of 29 percent. Such a savings might well be noticed and appreciated by users of a real network. ∎

For further reading

Hamming, R. *Coding and Information Theory.* Prentice-Hall, 1980.

Hayes, J. *Modeling and Analysis of Computer Communications Networks.* Plenum Press, 1984.

Huynh, D., H. Kobayshi, and F. Kuo. "Optimal design of mixed-media packet-switching networks: Routing and capacity assignment," *IEEE Transactions on Communications.* vol. 25, no.1, 1977, pp. 158-69.

Inose, H. and T. Saito. "Theoretical aspects in the analysis and synthesis of packet communication networks," *Proceedings of the IEEE,* 66:11, 11-78, pp. 1409-22.

Johnson, J. T. "Universal flow and capacity index gives picture of network efficiency," DATA COMMUNICATIONS, February, 1985, p. 171.

Kleinrock, L. *Queueing Systems Volume I: Theory.* Wiley, 1976.

— —. *Queueing Systems Volume II: Computer Applications.* Wiley, 1976.

Kobayshi, H. and A. Konheim. "Queueing models for computer communications system analysis," *IEEE Transactions on Communications.* vol. 25, no.1, pp. 2-29, 1977.

Kuo, F. *Protocols & Techniques for Data Communication Networks.* Prentice-Hall, 1981.

Papadimitriou, C. H. and K. Steiglitz. *Combinatorial Optimization: Algorithms and Complexity.* Prentice-Hall, 1982.

Tanenbaum, A. *Computer Networks.* Prentice-Hall, 1981.

Theil, H. *Principles of Econometrics.* Wiley, 1971.

David Stern is a principal member of the technical staff at ITT's Advanced Technology Center in Stratford, Conn. He holds a Bachelor of Arts degree from the University of Cincinnati, a master's in information science from The City University, London, and is currently completing a master's in computer science with a concentration in computer communications engineering from Rensselaer Polytechnic Institute at the Hartford Graduate Center. Stern has developed a microcomputer program based on the methods described in this article.

Gilbert Held, 4-Degree Consulting, Macon, Ga.

Expanding the uses of data compression

Besides cutting costs, errors, response time, and illegal entry, having a reduced data stream can alter the structure of networks.

In recent years, the data communications industry has been paying more attention to data compression—especially the techniques and algorithms used in reducing and reconstructing a data stream. Equally important, however, is a thorough understanding of how compression products can change various network structures. What are their benefits and potential effects?

In many cases, network configurations that are otherwise efficient are less than optimal when viewed in terms of compression-performing products. This can be corrected if managers know how to exploit data compression and can alter their networking strategies accordingly.

Data compression is commonly thought of as a technique used to reduce the duration of a transmission session. When researching the potential benefits of compression, network planners are therefore likely to concentrate on the potential cost savings from sending less data over the national dial telephone network. While this is a major benefit derived from data compression, there are several additional advantages. Compression can reduce the probability of transmission errors. Since it increases efficiency it may reduce or even eliminate extra workshifts. Moreover, by converting text that is in a conventional code (such as standard ASCII) into a different code, compression algorithms may offer some security against illicit monitoring. Compression also reduces the character transmission charges accrued with packet networks.

Highly effective data compression techniques may allow a reduced transmission data rate. Since the bit error rate (normally expressed as the expected number of bit errors per 100,000 transmitted bits) is proportional to the transmission rate, lowering the data rate will lower the bit error rate. Figure 1 illustrates this by showing the effect of a noise burst on two similar sets of data pulses, with each set of pulses transmitted at a different data rate.

Note that the duration of the noise burst is not great enough to affect 1 bit at a 300-bit/s data rate. Consider, however, the effect of the same noise burst on a higher data rate. Since the data pulses at 1.2 kbit/s are one-fourth the duration of pulses transmitted at 300 bit/s, they are more susceptible to error. As shown in figure 1, up to 2 bits could be erroneously transformed by the same noise burst that has no effect on data transmitted at 300 bit/s. Thus, if data compression techniques can allow a lower data rate, the data will be less susceptible to random errors. This increases transmission efficiency in a synchronous environment by reducing the number of negative acknowledgments and necessary retransmissions of data blocks.

Less overtime, more security

In many remote batch processing environments, data compression has been successfully employed to reduce or eliminate workshift operations. Typically, the primary function of second- and third-shift operations is the retrieval of output from deferred batch jobs run on a central computer in the evening. Since the limiting factors for this type of shift operation are the processing power of the central computer and the communications link data transfer rate, increasing the data transfer rate through compression may result in the elimination or reduction of a remote batch workshift.

The security of compressed data is enhanced because with compression algorithms data is transmitted in an encoded form. While some compression algorithms allow an easy reconstruction of the original data stream, others present a much tougher challenge.

1. Impact. *Since the pulses are four times shorter at 1.2 kbit/s than at 300 bit/s, a noise burst at the higher speed may make two '0' pulses appear '1's.*

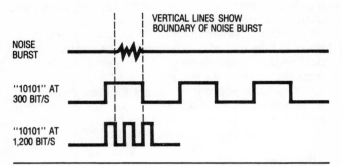

Thus, data compression implies some security against illicit monitoring. The degree of security varies with the compressibility of the data and the data compression algorithm or algorithms employed.

For installations using a service that depends on the quantity of data transmitted, compression can have another cost benefit. Typical among such services are packet-switching or value-added carriers. They usually charge a fixed fee per thousand packets, with packet size variable depending on the specific carrier and the format of the data. By decreasing the number of characters actually transmitted, compression reduces not only the transmission duration but also the character or packet charge associated with value-added carriers.

Structural change

Although data compression can result in a variety of benefits for the end user, its ability to alter the structure of a communications network may be its most promising feature. How such a change might occur can be seen in a brief examination of a few application areas. Consider two typical point-to-point network segments and a multidrop segment as illustrated in Figure 2. In most cases they represent one or more portions of many large networks.

Figure 2a shows a remote controller, or modem-sharing unit, used to connect (via one leased line) a number of remote terminals to a central computer facility. Although most controllers permit the physical attachment of up to 32 terminals, normal practice is to connect 20 or less. An application requiring the support of 30 remote terminals in one geographical area would probably necessitate two remote controllers, two leased lines, and four modems to connect the terminals to the host computer. Such a network has an inefficient structure, but it would be the most commonly chosen alternative to the unacceptable response time produced by connecting 32 terminals to one remote controller.

The major bottleneck in this configuration is the data transfer rate between the remote controller to the computer. Consequently, increasing the amount of data that flows across the line per unit time will decrease terminal response time. This is usually accomplished by replacing the existing modems with

higher-speed devices. Yet, because of fixed delays—including the modems' internal delay time, equalization delay, request to send and clear to send delay time, and the propagation delay time—doubling the modem data rate usually causes a far smaller increase in the actual rate of data transfer. By installing a hardware device or implementing appropriate software routines to compress data, a user will reduce the actual quantity of data transferred between the terminal and the controller.

This, in turn, increases the information transfer across the line and reduces the response time of the remote terminals. With data compression reducing terminal response time, additional terminals can be added to the controller; in the example, it might even be possible to eliminate the second controller and its required modems and leased line.

A second common network segment is illustrated in Figure 2b. A multiplexer is remotely located from a computer center that services a mixture of dial-in and directly connected terminals. With a conventional time-

---

2. Efficiency. *In networks* a *and* c, *compression algorithms decrease terminal response time. In* b, *compression increases the TDM's effective capacity.*

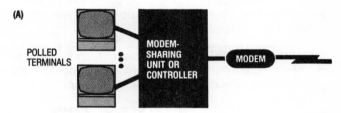

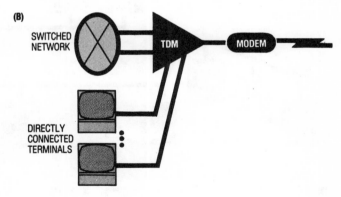

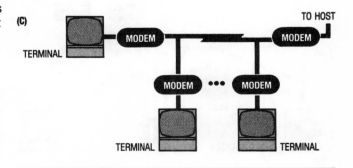

division multiplexer, the aggregate input data rate from the connected terminals cannot exceed the data rate of the high-speed line between the multiplexer and the computer. Because it dynamically allocates time slots depending on how great the demand for them is, a statistical multiplexer would permit many additional terminals to be serviced.

The proportion of the number of terminals serviced by a statistical multiplexer to those supported by a conventional multiplexer is known as the service ratio. This service ratio depends on many factors (among them, the activity of terminal users) and typically varies from 2:1 to 4:1. For instance, if a 9.6-kbit/s leased line were used to connect a multiplexer to the host computer, a conventional time-division multiplexer could service eight 1.2-kbit/s terminals. In comparison, a statistical multiplexer with a 2:1 service ratio would be capable of servicing 16 such terminals.

Suppose an installation were required to support 20 simultaneous terminal users at the remote location. Planners would be faced with two alternatives: simply install a second multiplexer for the extra traffic or cause response time through the statistical multiplexer to degrade by configuring one multiplexer to support 30 terminals. Once again, a compression-performing product might enable 30 terminals to be serviced by the multiplexer while maintaining an appropriate level of response time to each terminal.

Several vendors offer statistical multiplexers that perform data compression. Among these devices the compression and decompression function is most commonly performed within the multiplexer. The algorithms used in this method compress the aggregate data obtained by concentrating the input from several data sources that are active during one scan interval. Vendors whose compression products permit selective reduction of the data stream use a different method. With this latter approach channel adapters are equipped with a microprocessor programmed to compress and decompress data at the channel level before the input data sources are multiplexed.

Efficiency increase
Regardless of the specific technique, the end results are similar: a reduced quantity of data transmitted. Since the leased line operates at a fixed data rate, more information per unit time will pass over the line. This lowers the probability of the statistical multiplexer becoming a communications bottleneck and causing a decrease in response time. Thus, a statistical multiplexer performing data compression has an increased service ratio, allowing additional terminals to be connected to that device.

A multipoint or multidrop network segment is illustrated in Figure 2c. In this type of configuration, the benefit of data compresson is the reduction in re-

---

3. Quick 'n simple. *With compression techniques, one can often reduce the number of multidrop circuits. Since the response time is decreased, it may be possible to* *replace two circuits with one—without increasing the terminal response. Without compression, the response on one circuit might be unacceptable.*

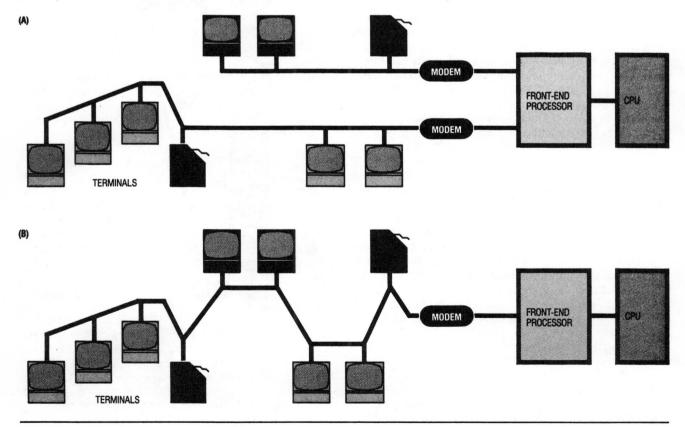

sponse time of terminals connected to the common line. Since terminal response time is the major factor governing the number of drops configured on a multidrop circuit, any mechanism that causes less data to be transferred permits additional drops to be added to the line.

In Figure 3, two multidrop circuits are used to connect a total of nine terminals to a host computer. Assume that the network planners estimated the activity of the terminals and determined that if only one circuit were used, the response time of the terminals would be unacceptable to the users. As a result, the planners decided that two separate lines were necessary.

As noted, if data compression is implemented on the multidrop lines, the actual data traffic carried by each line will be reduced. (The level of data reduction depends on how efficiently the compression algorithms work on the specific type of data traffic.) Since there is less total traffic, there is a reduction in the time it takes the computer to poll and service each terminal. The result of this is that users experience an improved response time. While simultaneously, planners may be able to combine two or more circuits (Fig. 3b).

Data compression can be implemented on multidrop circuits in a variety of ways. Although perhaps the most difficult method, providing compression through software offers the greatest flexibility. On the one hand, this method requires the user to have programmable terminals and to determine and code the the compression algorithms that are most appropriate to the type of data being transmitted. Yet, this same characteristic can be viewed as an advantage in that it provides an opportunity for custom tailoring the compression algorithms. This can result in optimal compression performance.

For users unwilling to invest the time and effort required to implement compression through their software, several vendors market hardware compression devices. Since the compression routines must be suited for general purpose, they may not be ideal for a particular user's actual data. Still, in some cases the general-purpose algorithms provide data reductions of 50 percent or more.

Two types of hardware compression devices warrant consideration for use on both point-to-point and multidrop lines: the standalone compression unit and the data compression modem. The use of each is illustrated in Figure 4.

The standalone compression unit fits between the terminal and the modem at the remote end of the line and between the computer port and modem at the central site. This device compresses data before it is modulated and decompresses data after it is demodulated. The intelligence of the standalone compression unit is in the form of a microprocessor programmed to examine and operate one or more compression algorithms on the data stream. Since most modern modems use microprocessors for a variety of signaling functions, adding routines to compress and decompress data permits the compression function to be integrated into a modem. Currently one modem vendor

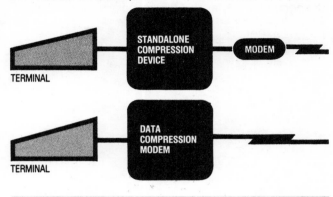

4. Supplementary? *Some hardware compression devices work with standard modems. Others incorporate the modem and compression functions into one unit.*

markets a data compression modem, but reliable industry sources indicate that several other modem manufacturers may introduce this type of modem in the near future.

Representative products

During the last five years approximately 20 compression-performing data communications products have been introduced. Table 1 lists 6 products representative of the spectrum offered.

The turbo-MUX multiplexer contains a Z80A microprocessor and a mixture of read only memory and random access memory. Employing a proprietary data compression algorithm, this device enables a doubling of the data rate through a Bell System 212A or equivalent modem.

In effect the turbo-MUX doubles the information transfer rate through a 1.2-kbit/s modem, permitting the user to multiplex two 1.2-kbit/s data sources or one 2.4-bit/s data source through a 1.2-kbit/s modem. In addition to doubling the throughput of the modem, the turbo-MUX performs automatic error detection and retransmission, greatly reducing the probability of undetected transmission errors.

The data flow compactor is a sophisticated compression device that supports a wide variety of protocols, including asynchronous TTY, bisynchronous 2780 and 3780, 3270, and HASP multileave. The product's adaptive six-level data compression algorithm often achieves data reductions of 50 percent or more. This device can be used either to reduce former wideband line requirements to much less expensive voiceband circuits or to replace multiple voiceband circuits with fewer such circuits (Fig. 5).

Paper images

Devices such as the FAX-COMP from Compression Labs can be used with a variety of facsimile machines to reduce the time required to transmit a document over the direct distance dial network. Most documents contain large runs of either black or white picture elements. Consequently, the compression of facsimile data is highly efficient and in most instances can reduce the transmitted data to one-fifteenth of the

Table 1: Representative data compression products

VENDOR	PRODUCT	DESCRIPTION
CHUNG TELECOMMUNICATIONS 4056 BEN LOMOND DR. PALO ALTO, CALIF. 94306 415-858-2456	TURBO-MUX	TWO-CHANNEL COMPRESSION MULTIPLEXER ENABLING TWO SEPARATE 1.2-KBIT/S OR ONE 2.4-KBIT/S DATA SOURCE TO COMMUNICATE VIA A 1.2-KBIT/S MODEM
DATA FLO 1301 CAMBRIDGE AVE. HOPKINS, MINN. 55343 612-933-2116 OR 612-437-2330	COMPLEXOR	USING AN ADAPTIVE SIX-LEVEL COMPRESSION ALGORITHM, CAN BE USED TO SUPPORT UP TO FOUR HIGH-SPEED DATA SOURCES ON UP TO FOUR CONVENTIONAL VOICE GRADE LINES
COMPRESSION LABS INC. 489 DIVISION ST. CAMPBELL, CALIF. 95008 408-866-1911	FAX-COMP	STANDALONE DEVICE ABLE TO COMPRESS FACSIMILE TRANSMISSION, REDUCING THE CONNECT TIME REQUIRED TO TRANSMIT DOCUMENTS ON THE DIRECT DIAL NETWORK
INFOTRON SYSTEMS CORP. CHERRY HILL INDUSTRIAL CENTER CHERRY HILL, N.J. 08003 609-424-9400	MICROCOMPUTER ASYNCHRONOUS COMPRESSION CHANNEL: ADAPTER MODULE	CAN BE USED IN SEVERAL OF THE VENDORS' MULTIPLEXERS TO COMPRESS DATA ON A CHANNEL BASIS, RESULTING IN IMPROVED HIGH-SPEED LINE UTILIZATION
KINEX CORP. 6950 BRYAN DAIRY RD. LARGO, FLA. 33543 813-541-6404	9600/DCM	CONTAINS A BUILT-IN COMPRESSION PROCESSOR THAT ACCEPTS DATA AT 14.4 KBIT/S AND AFTER PROCESSING PRODUCES A MODULATED DATA STREAM OPERATING AT 9.6 KBIT/S
T-BAR INC. 141 DANBURY RD. WILTON CONN. 06897 203-834-8227	DATA COMPRESSION RECORDER	COMPRESSES DATA PRIOR TO STORAGE AND CAN BE USED TO MONITOR AND RECORD EXTENDED TRANSMISSION

original. For example, the device can reduce a 3-minute transmission session to approximately 12 seconds.

The FAX-COMP unit is a standalone compression device containing internal memory that permits up to 3 pages of information to be stored for transmission. An optional floppy disk allows the storage of up to 10 pages of information. Transferring this amount takes under one minute with 9.6-kbit/s modems.

Assessing the suitability of a device of this type is not difficult. First a network planner would determine the approximate daily traffic volume of an organization's facsimile transmission. From this number, he or she could compute the potential cost reductions resulting from the use of the device. The calculation would enable the planner to determine whether or not the equipment cost was justified.

5. Less bandwidth required. A typical application for the Data Flo Complexor is replacing a wideband circuit with a less expensive voice grade circuit.

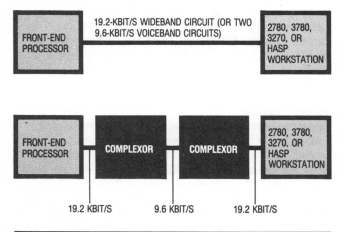

Multiplexer addition
One of the less well-known products of Infotron Systems Inc.'s line is the company's CA780/MAC3 Microcomputer Asynchronous Compression Channel Adapter Module. This module contains two input/output channel adapters, each of which are used to connect asynchronous channels to one or more of the vendor's statistical time-division multiplexers. A microprocessor and a mixture of read-only memory and random access memory are used to compress data at the channel level before it is multiplexed and to decompress data after it is demultiplexed. Performance tests have shown that by mixing five compression algorithms the product can achieve data reductions of up to 45 percent. Such reduction allows the statistical multiplexer to use less of the bandwidth in the high-speed line for each compressed channel. This, in turn, will make it possible for users to multiplex additional

Table 2: Compression efficiency of 9600/DCM

DATA TYPE	PERCENT REDUCTION BY COMPRESSION ALGORITHMS	EQUIVALENT EFFECTIVE BIT RATE
BASIC PROGRAM	35	14,688
COBOL LISTING	40	16,037
ENGLISH TEXT	36	14,926
ACCOUNTING FILE	39	15,744

channels or to operate the multiplexer in a lower high-speed line rate.

As noted above, compression techniques in a statistical multiplexer increase its service ratio. Thus, compressing the data at existing data sources (before it is statistically multiplexed) will, at the very least, reduce or eliminate some common sources of delay. Such delays sometimes occur when too many devices become active and the multiplexer has to inhibit terminal and computer port transmisson in order to prevent its buffer from overflowing.

Boosts the data

At first glance, the Kinex 9600/DCM is a standard 9.6-kbit/s modem that is compatible with the CCITT V.29 modulation scheme. In fact, however, the modem accepts data at 14.4 kbit/s, and its internal microprocessor compresses the data before modulating it at 9.6 kbit/s. Although noncompression 14.4-kbit/s modems are available, the price of the Kinex 9600/DCM is approximately one-third to one-half that of a conventional 14.4-kbit/s modem. In addition, unlike other high-speed modems, the 9600/DCM can operate over unconditioned lines.

The Kinex 9600/DCM has another key advantage in that it is much less sensitive to noise and other line impairments than are standard modems of the same capacity. Since bit errors cause the retransmission of data blocks, a high bit error rate can significantly reduce throughput. Remember that a lower level of line degradation causes more bit errors in higher-speed than in lower-speed transmissions. Thus, line conditions that could significantly impede information transfer using a 14.4-kbit/s modem may allow a modem like the 9600/DCM to operate at nearly 100 percent throughput.

Although the Kinex 9600/DCM has numerous advantages, it should be noted that the modem's effective bit rate is a function of the compressibility of the data. Table 2 lists the compressibility of four typical data streams by the algorithms contained in the modem; also included is the equivalent effective bit rate of each data stream. Since the modem's maximum clocking of data is 14.4 kbit/s, the actual compression rate is limited to that data rate. Currently the modem is designed to work with terminals and computers using a bisynchronous protocol. But a version of this modem

that would support the synchronous data link control (SDLC) protocol is expected to be released later in 1984.

Tight storage

The compression feature built into the T-bar DCR recorder represents a novel approach to the data recording problems experienced in many technical control centers. This compression device extends the storage equipment's capacity to record data, thus conserving storage media. In addition, technicians using this device may not need to monitor a transmission constantly to insure that the receiving device is not overwritten. They might thus use the time to perform other functions.

Although the T-bar data compression recorder uses a floppy diskette that can store up to 10 million bits, the actual quantity of data that can be recorded can vastly exceed the physical capacity of the diskette. When used to monitor and record a polled multipoint network, a device of this type can store 300 percent more data than can a device that does not compress data prior to storage. In more concrete terms, approximately 40 minutes of 9.6 kbit/s full duplex data can be recorded on one diskette before operator intervention is required to change diskettes.

Because prices are constantly changing, this discussion has avoided detailed cost-benefit analyses. Yet, the cost of compression products is typically 10 to 20 percent above that of standard devices. Most compression products provide a level of performance ranging from 30 percent to hundreds of percent above similar noncompression-performing products. From a price-performance perspective, these figures indicate that network managers should seriously consider compression equipment in most instances.

Further reading

Detailed information concerning practical ways to compress data for more efficient storage and transmission can be found in "Data Compression: Techniques and Applications." Many of the algorithms presented in this book are easily implemented via software and should interest those who wish to develop their own compression routines. Included in the appendix of the book is a Fortran program listing that can be used to determine which compression techniques best suit one's data traffic needs. Written by Gilbert Held, this $30.90 practical guide is published by John Wiley & Sons Inc., 605 Third Avenue, New York, N. Y. 10158 (212-850-6000). ■

Gilbert Held has the title of Chief, Data Communications, at the United States Office of Personnel Management and owns a consulting firm specializing in data communications and personal computers. A long-time contributor to DATA COMMUNICATIONS, Mr. Held has written a number of technical papers and books on the subject. His "Standards can increase efficiency and reduce cost of asynchronous personal computer transmissions" was a co-winner of the 1984 Harry R. Karp award for the best paper presented at Interface '84.

Captain Joseph T. Johnson, U. S. Air Force, Washington, D. C.

Universal flow and capacity index gives picture of network efficiency

This simple technique lets managers test for ways to make network configurations approach optimum performance.

The best-designed network can become inefficient over time. Growth, moves, changes, and other modifications can shift the internal traffic pattern toward disequilibrium. In an efficient communications network, high-capacity channels should carry a relatively large portion of the total traffic. Similarly, lines with lower capacity should be called on to carry a lesser load.

Gaining an overall picture of performance is difficult, however, when flow measurement alone is considered. A unified network-efficiency index could help managers determine the positive or negative effects of a planned reconfiguration. It could also be used to compare alternative topologies or even different networks. One such index can be derived from an application of information theory that was originally used to simplify complex budget problems.

Index *I* characterizes network inefficiency as a sum of variations among channels. In most data communications networks, the channels vary in terms of both throughput and capacity. Such variability makes it difficult to render a unified evaluation of the network's link configuration. One approach might be a technique that has been suggested by Henri Theil for use in cost accounting (see "How to worry about increased expenditures," by Henri Theil, *The Accounting Review,* January 1969). This technique culminates in a single index of the success of a company's budgeting process. One of its axioms is the idea that differences among the divisions of a company in terms of their ratios of actual expenditures to planned expenditures yields information about overall company budget variance. The key terms are "actual" and "planned." A divergence between actual and planned amounts can lead to useful information because it challenges expectations and raises questions.

In this analysis, network flow and capacity allocations are analogous to budget outlays, while channels are analogous to company divisions. "Capacity" here refers to the amount of bandwidth originally allocated to a channel. "Flow" is the throughput as measured on that channel. Flow/capacity ratios inform us about channel efficiency by comparing the traffic that actually occurs (flow) with that which is planned (capacity).

Efficient utilization in a network, as defined here, is based on two premises. First, if there is a significant difference between a channel's share of overall data flow and its share of overall capacity, that channel is inefficient. Second, variability among individual channels in their degree of flow/capacity inefficiency reflects how channels come together to create overall network inefficiency.

Simple channel ratios provide a basis for an index, but a good measure of efficiency requires associating individual channels with the whole network. Although they reveal information, individual ratios of actual-to-planned channel traffic do not, of themselves, provide a unified characterization of the network. Index *I*, therefore, associates each particular channel with the whole network by using each channel's portion of total network data flow or capacity as its basic unit. A channel's flow/capacity ratio becomes the ratio of the channel's share of total network flow to its share of total network capacity:

$$\frac{F_j}{C_j}$$

where F_j = (channel j flow) ÷ (total network flow) and C_j = (channel j capacity) ÷ (total network capacity).

These flow/capacity ratios of the channel's network

share are then bound into the unified channel Index I by means of computing a weighted sum of their logarithms in the following formula:

$$I = \sum_{j=1}^{n} F_j \log \frac{F_j}{C_j}$$

where n = number of channels in the network.

The use of logarithms to quantify information reflects the index's basis in information theory. The index rests on the premise that "information" about network inefficiency is obtained when early estimates prove inadequate. A given link, for instance, may have been expected to carry a small percentage of the total network traffic, leading planners to select a disproportionately low capacity channel. But their choice could then be contradicted by a high percentage of actual flow over that link. Index I is designed to highlight such an error.

As F_j in the numerator increases or C_j in the denominator decreases, the log term, and therefore the information index, gets larger. Multiplying the flow by the log term yields the highest values for links with ratios of high flow to low capacity. However, it also indirectly reflects the ratios of other links in the network. Since the flow and capacity percentages add up to 100 percent, a link with low capacity and high flow percentages will be somewhat offset by links elsewhere in the network with high capacity or low flow percentages.

Besides its ability to emphasize the inefficiency of inordinately low capacity, the log operation also allows the information content of the ratio to be interpreted as an arithmetic difference. Information in F/C is interpreted as log (F/C), which equals log (F) − log (C): the difference between information revealed in flow and information revealed in capacity. Thus, Index I characterizes the network by summarizing the variation, among individual channels, in the amount of information each one reveals in its ratio of actual (F) to planned (C) shares of data traffic.

Disparity and variation

The analytical power of the channel terms in Index I derives from disparity between flow and capacity. This is readily seen by supposing a channel's flow share equals its capacity share; then log (F/C) = log (1) = 0. When there is no disparity between actual flow share and planned capacity share, there is no information revealed by the flow/capacity ratio, so the channel's term is zero. The data communications networks in the following examples illustrate the influence of flow-capacity disparity on the size of the index. Since there is so little difference between flow and capacity shares of any channel in example 1, the informational value of each term is small. Consequently, the index is relatively small.

While individual channel disparity is one element of Index I, interchannel variation is another. Even though example 1 shows flow shares nearly equal to capacity shares, the network might still exhibit absolute disparity in the sense that the flow shares and capacity shares

might still be of widely different amounts. For instance, 20 percent of total flow might be 5 kbit/s, while 20 percent of total capacity might be 50 kbit/s. This absolute disparity between 25 kbit/s total flow and 250 kbit/s total capacity might be significant, but it reflects no interchannel variation and, therefore, contains no information for Index I. In other words, it reveals no information about how the individual channels come together to affect network efficiency. (Such information, of course, is not needed: The first step in improving the network would be reducing the overall absolute flow/capacity disparity rather than adjusting the individual shares of channels.)
Example 1.

	Link 1	Link 2	Link 3	Link 4	Link 5
% of total flow	10	15	30	25	20
% of total capacity	12	13	35	20	20

$I = 1.28$

Index I is designed to summarize the variation among channels in flow/capacity disparity, so the formula of the index weights each link's term to stress the informational importance of variation. The information measure of a channel, log (F/C), is weighted by F, the channel's share of total network flow, in each term of the equation. This weighting means that the links with the largest actual flows have the most influence on the size of the index. For example, a channel with a flow-share-to-capacity-share ratio of 60 percent to 30 percent would have more influence than a channel with an equal ratio of 10 percent to 5 percent.

Channels with flow shares greater than capacity shares, that is, where log (F/C) is greater than zero, lead to relatively high positive terms in the equation, since the positive value of the log is amplified by the flow weight. This is illustrated in example 2, link 1, where the formula for I has the relatively large log of 60 percent divided by 5 percent multiplied, in turn, by 60. In contrast, channels with flow shares less than capacity shares lead to negative terms, but not large negative terms. In link 5 of example 2, capacity share is much larger than flow share. Nevertheless, the large negative log term will only be multiplied by a small flow weight, and the index still has a relatively large positive value (Figs. 1 and 2).
Example 2.

	Link 1	Link 2	Link 3	Link 4	Link 5
% of total flow	60	20	10	5	5
% of total capacity	5	5	10	20	60

$I = 157.46$

If the flow value is large but still smaller than the capacity value, the negative log term will still be relatively small. This is illustrated in example 3, where the large flow share of 70 percent on link 1 is multiplied by a log term that is negative but approaches zero because 70 divided by 90 approaches 1 and log (1) equals zero. Large flow weights only have a large influence on Index I when log (F/C) = log (F) − log (C) has large absolute value; that is, when there is a large difference in information revealed by actual and planned data traffic.

1. Unforeseen. *Links can be designed for less traffic than they end up carrying. Link 1, below, was only meant to carry 5 percent of the network's data flow.*

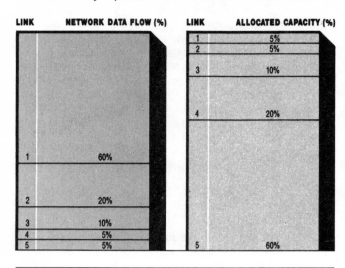

LINK	NETWORK DATA FLOW (%)	LINK	ALLOCATED CAPACITY (%)
1	60%	1	5%
		2	5%
		3	10%
2	20%	4	20%
3	10%		
4	5%		
5	5%	5	60%

Example 3.

	Link 1	Link 2	Link 3	Link 4	Link 5
% of total flow	70	12	10	5	3
% of total capacity	90	4	3	2	1

$I = 15.51$

The positive and negative effects of channel shares can be summarized by saying that Index I tends to amplify any gross disparity between flow shares and capacity shares—whether flow is much larger than

2. Disproportionate. *The width of each link corresponds to the share of network flow it carries, and to the share of bandwidth it was originally given.*

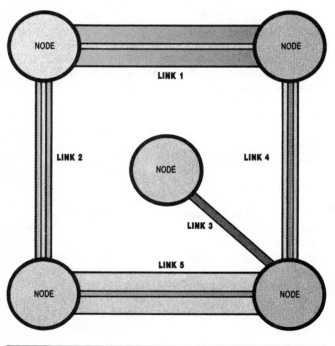

LINK 1

LINK 2   LINK 4

NODE

LINK 3

LINK 5

NODE

capacity or vice versa. This is because the percentage shares must add up to 100 percent. A large positive ratio (flow share much greater than capacity share) on one link must mean a large negative ratio (flow share much smaller than capacity share) on another link. As example 2 shows, such gross disparities lead to large interchannel variation. Large positive log terms combine with small negative log terms to yield a large overall index. This is as it should be: The larger the index, the more the channels vary in their difference between actual flow and planned capacity, and the greater the information revealed by Index I.

Calculating Index I requires measures of flow and capacity. The network might be measured for sheer physical efficiency. The manager could include overhead bits and delays in flow and compare this gross flow with raw line speed capacity. In this case, flow adjustments resulting from the calculation of I might include not just changes in user data flow, but also changes in the protocols that generate the overhead bits. Then again, the network might be measured by taking protocols as a given and including overhead bits and delays in capacity. The manager could compare this net capacity with the flow of data bits actually generated by users of data channels. The flow and capacity must be measured consistently so that the index is a sum of comparable terms.

There is no predetermined optimal value of Index I for a network. The purpose of calculating I is to provide a benchmark for adjusting the network so that a subsequent calculation of the index would reflect less interchannel variation. Thus the measurement is a relative one, being most useful when used to compare different networks or new configurations of the same network. For instance, if reconfiguring a network's flow and capacity allocation leads to a lower value of I, then the network is more efficient.

Index I treats total capacity as the sum of all the individual link capacities; so it treats two consecutive 10-kbit/s links as having a total capacity of 20 kbit/s. This does not mean that data can actually travel at 20 kbit/s from the beginning of the first link to the end of the second link. It does mean that Index I is not a measure of source-to-sink flow. Rather, the index is intended to be a measure of the composite effect of multiple network components, that is, data channels.

Data networks can present a complex analytical problem because of their multiplicity of interrelated data movements. Individual information parts (channels) are added up to form a whole that characterizes the sum of the parts (flow/capacity ratios). Thus Index I yields a simplified view of a network by tying the multiplicity of its components into a unitary measure that indicates how efficiently these components constitute the whole. This power to reduce analytical complexity provides ample reason for managers to consider applying the index to their networks' channel configuration. ∎

Captain Johnson is chief of the communications division in the Directorate of Functional Requirements at Bolling Air Force Base.

Mark P. Mendelsohn, Special to DATA COMMUNICATIONS

Bringing Unix machines within an IBM network

Without altering the standard operating system calls, Unix-based machines can be adapted to handle both BSC and SNA protocols. Just one uniform interface is needed.

As computer users increasingly recognize the importance of connectivity, communications managers face new challenges. For example, new Unix-based equipment (such as multi-user microcomputers or file servers) provide managers with great advantages in power and flexibility over batch-oriented equipment that may have been in place for several years. However, these Unix machines are designed for interactive applications, and implementing batch-oriented communications protocols is possible—though difficult.

A few vendors of Unix products provide this type of connection, and users should be cautioned about trying to implement a link themselves. Still, a very sophisticated user can build a reliable Unix-to-IBM batch link without altering the Unix kernel.

One approach is to utilize the half-duplex contention protocol, which is commonly used with devices that send large batches of data. The challenge is to implement the protocol using Unix's five basic system calls that (usually interactively) manage I/O devices. Since these calls can pass only a few arguments, there is a limited amount of information for controlling the communications. Despite this obstacle, it is possible to implement an interface between the user process (the program that manages the user's terminal) and the Unix operating system that provides full protocol support. An interface has actually been built for the 2780/3780 BSC (binary synchronous communications) terminals and 3790 SNA/SDLC peripherals used with the job entry system (JES).

Unix supports all I/O devices through the use of special files. As a result, device I/O is as similar as possible to file I/O, which means that a program can manipulate both a file and a device with equal ease. Standard output can be routed to either the terminal or the file without any changes in the user program. The terminal itself is a special file called TTYNN , where NN is a unique terminal number.

Five operating system calls facilitate the use of I/O devices in Unix: OPEN, CLOSE, READ, WRITE, and IOCTL (input/output control).
■ The OPEN system call attempts to obtain the named file or a special file as a resource, and, if the call is successful, it returns a file descriptor that is to be used with alter I/O calls.
■ The CLOSE system call attempts to release the resource obtained in the open system call and returns a value indicating the success or failure.
■ The READ system call attempts to write data from the resource indicated by the open system call into a specified area. A 0 return value indicates that an end-of-file has been reached. Any other return value indicates the number of bytes actually read.
■ The WRITE system call attempts to read (count) bytes of data from the specified area to the resource that is obtained by the open system call. The return value will then indicate the number of bytes that have actually been written.
■ The IOCTL system call, appears in the format of IOCTL ("file descriptor," "command," "argument") equals "return value." IOCTL is used for a variety of purposes dependent upon the special file indicated by the OPEN system call. In general the "command" is performed by using the information pointed to by the "argument," or it may return information to the location where "argument" is pointing. The "return value" may, in addition, be used to pass information from the special file resources to the user program.

The target of these system calls is the device driver, which is a set of subroutines of the Unix kernel. The different subroutines correspond to the five system calls, and each type of I/O device has a separate device driver. When a user program opens an I/O device, the operating system executes the open routine of the corresponding device driver.

Unsuccessful operating system calls result in a return value of "-1." The specific reason for the error may be found in the variable "errno," which is available to all user programs as an external variable. A successful OPEN of a device returns a value known as a file descriptor; this value is used for all subsequent system calls for that particular device.

Transmissions to and from asynchronous terminals usually occur one character at a time and without stringent requirements for the lapses between characters or the grouping of them. Since transmit and receive characters may pass each other on the communications link, protocols have little function to perform besides flow control. Moreover, there is no error detection beyond a parity bit.

In contrast, half-duplex contention protocols are usually batch-oriented. Large files of data are sent between computers that are typically unattended. Files are sent in logical groups, such as records and blocks, that may be sent in only one direction at a time. Because of the possibility that a great amount of data might be delivered, extensive error recovery mechanisms are built into the protocol to ensure accuracy. Since these protocols differ so greatly, significant enhancements must be made to I/O operating system calls designed for asynchronous terminals in order to use them with half-duplex contention.

A half-duplex contention protocol is one in which a device must request permission to transmit on the line from the receiving device. Once permission is granted, the transmitter may send data until the receiver is informed that the transmission is complete. Either device may then request permission in order to become the transmitter.

It is possible that both devices may request permission to transmit at the same time. This conflict can be resolved because one device is designated as the contention winner and one the contention loser. The loser must yield to the winner by granting permission to transmit and going into a receive mode. The loser waits until the winner has ended its transmission before trying to gain control of the line again.

This protocol is usually associated with devices that send large batches of data (as opposed to those that are based on interactive applications). The contention scheme is not unique to either character- or bit-oriented protocols.

Establishing the connection

Before a communications channel can be utilized, physical connectivity must be established. For devices employing the half-duplex contention protocol, the point-to-point access arrangements used can be either leased or switched. If the line is switched, it can be either dial-in or dial-out.

Information about the access arrangement must be propagated to the device driver. For dial-out, the device driver should be able to support a number of

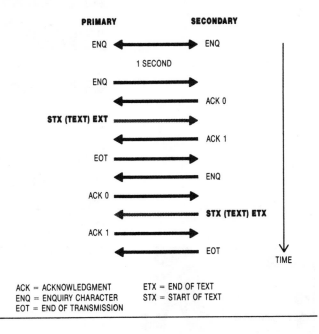

1. Who's in charge? *Although not shown in this sequence, the secondary device bids for master status once every three seconds.*

ACK = ACKNOWLEDGMENT
ENQ = ENQUIRY CHARACTER
EOT = END OF TRANSMISSION
ETX = END OF TEXT
STX = START OF TEXT

different automatic call devices. The number to dial may be part of the initial configuration parameters or provided later.

An IBM binary synchronous communications terminal may communicate with a similar unit or with an IBM mainframe. A device must request permission to transmit by sending a BID command to the receiving terminal. This terminal must grant permission by sending an acknowledgment back to the sending device before the transmission of data can commence. The transmitter indicates completion of the transmission by sending an end-of-transmission control message. Both devices on the communications link may again BID for control of the line.

Again, contention is resolved by designating one device on the link as primary and the other as secondary. A primary device bids every second until an acknowledgment is sent in reply; a secondary device bids only once every three seconds. If a secondary device sends a bid and then receives a bid from the primary device, the secondary one must acknowledge the received bid and prepare to receive data (Fig. 1).

The winner of a contention situation in the SNA protocol is specified as a bind parameter. A device must first BID or BEGIN BRACKET (which means either sending a request to transmit or actually beginning the transmission), depending on the parameters set at the beginning of the session, before the actual transmission of data can begin. The receiver will respond with either a positive response or an exception response and will begin its own bracket. The exception response may also contain a sense code, which indicates that a ready-to-receive (RTR) command will be sent at a later time when data can be accepted (Fig. 2). This scheme handles contention more intelligently than does BSC, which can encounter repeated unnecessary contention situations.

Information from the user process is needed to establish whether a device should assume the status of a contention winner or a loser. The user process must then request for permission to transmit, and this permission must be granted before transmission can begin. If permission is not granted, the user process must assume a receive mode. If permission is granted, the user process must inform the device driver when the transmit mode is being relinquished. If the user assumes the receive mode, the device driver must notify the user when it may attempt to transmit again. The device driver handles the contention based on the information provided.

As mentioned, the contention protocol lends itself to the transmission of large batches of data. Since these batches have no predefined length, they must be broken up into smaller pieces that are easier to manage. Each piece is checked for errors with cyclic redundancy check and retransmitted if necessary. It is crucial that the last "piece" of data of a large batch be handled correctly because this data signifies the completion of the entire data stream.

In the 2780/3780 BSC protocol, these smaller pieces of transmitted data are called blocks. Except for the last one, each block begins with a start-of-text and ends with an end-of-text block. The last block of the message ends in an end of text. The receiving station acknowledges the correct receipt of each block by using alternating affirmative acknowledgments (Ack 0 and Ack 1). A single transmission may contain multiple messages in order to cut down on the overhead of having to rebid before transmitting each message.

An EOT (end of transmission) following an ETX (end of text) block indicates a normal end of transmission. The acknowledgment to the ETX block is extremely important since it signifies to the transmitting device that the message has been received in its entirety. If the last block before the EOT ends in an ETB (end transmission block), the message is said to have ended prematurely, and all previously received data should be discarded. The entire message must be retransmitted from the beginning.

The 3790 SNA protocol breaks up its transmission a step further. An SNA bracket (analogous to a BSC transmission) is delineated by a begin bracket and an end bracket and can be made up of many chains. A chain, in turn, can be composed of a first-in-chain, any number of middle-in-chains, followed by a last-in-chain. The data is broken up into these pieces in order to ease error recovery. Unlike BSC, which requires retransmitting an entire message, the 3790 SNA protocol allows a bracket to be recovered at the beginning of any chain element (starting with the first element in the chain).

The user process must specify the end of a message or chain and the end of transmission or bracket. A Unix device driver can easily detect the beginning of the first element. The subsequent data before the last element becomes the middle element by default. Similarly, the same information will be provided by the device driver to the user process during reception. It is the respon-

2. Smarter. *Needless contentions can be avoided in SNA. For instance, the receiver may indicate that it will be ready to receive later.*

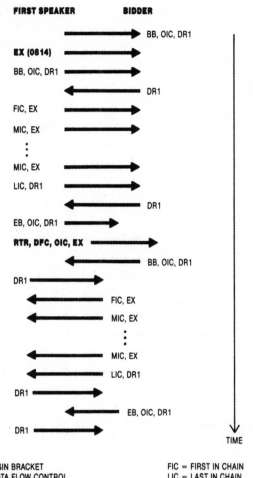

BB = BEGIN BRACKET	FIC = FIRST IN CHAIN
DFC = DATA FLOW CONTROL	LIC = LAST IN CHAIN
DR1 = DEFINITE RESPONSE 1	MIC = MIDDLE IN CHAIN
EX = EXCEPTION RESPONSE	OIC = ONLY IN CHAIN
EX (0814) = EXCEPTION RESPONSE WITH SENSE CODE	RTR = READY TO RECEIVE

sibility of the device driver to handle any retransmission or error recovery of data. Retry limits may be provided by the user process; otherwise, default values are used.

Device selection

A 2780/3780 communications terminal functions as three unit record devices. (A unit record device is an IBM term for a peripheral that can only handle records of one fixed length.) The card reader is the only device available for transmission, so no selection takes place. The line printer and the card punch are the two available output devices. If the user makes no particular selection, the default receiving device is the printer. Usually, any device can explicitly select the device with which it communicates. However, when transparent data (explained below) is used, the card punch must be selected, because only those devices can receive transparent data. It should be noted that IBM hosts, since they only act as readers, cannot accept component selection.

3. Just one more. *After sending a receive reverse interrupt, the secondary may still receive another block of text before the line is reversed.*

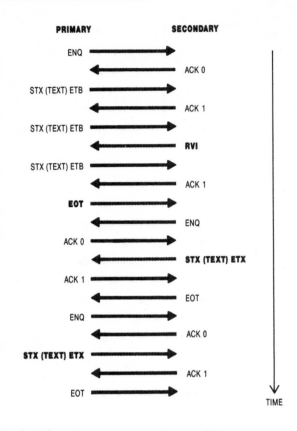

```
        PRIMARY              SECONDARY

      ENQ ══════════════►
               ◄══════════════ ACK 0
STX (TEXT) ETB ══════════════►
               ◄══════════════ ACK 1
STX (TEXT) ETB ══════════════►
               ◄══════════════ RVI
STX (TEXT) ETB ══════════════►
               ◄══════════════ ACK 1
      EOT ══════════════►
               ◄══════════════ ENQ
    ACK 0 ══════════════►
               ◄══════════════ STX (TEXT) ETX
    ACK 1 ══════════════►
               ◄══════════════ EOT
      ENQ ══════════════►
               ◄══════════════ ACK 0
STX (TEXT) ETX ══════════════►
               ◄══════════════ ACK 1
      EOT ══════════════►
                                        TIME
```

ACK = ACKNOWLEDGMENT   ENQ = ENQUIRY CHARACTER
EOT = END OF TRANSMISSION   RVI = RECEIVE REVERSE INTERRUPT
ETB = END TEXT BLOCK   STX = START OF TEXT
ETX = END OF TEXT

In addition, the 3790 SNA communications facilities include a console device that can be used for either input or output. As a result, it is necessary to select devices in both directions, even to the host.

When a message or a chain is begun, a user process may specify the device to which it intends to send data. Also, upon receiving data, the user process will receive an indication of which device is being selected.

A BSC message may consist of a mix of two block types, normal and transparent. A normal block contains displayable data and is restricted to only those characters that do not have significance as control characters or delimiters. A transparent block, however, may contain any of the 256 bit combinations of an 8-bit byte and is, therefore, only used in special situations.

The data within an SNA frame can be any one of the 256 bit combinations of a byte; however, communications of transparent data to JES on a mainframe requires a change in the format of the data. The transmission mode of data changes as well, and the user must specify this mode. Similarly, the device driver will inform the user process of the mode of the received data.

The 3780 bisynchronous terminal provides space compression in order to improve the throughput of the transmission of many consecutive spaces. The user process need not compress the data on output and expand on input; it can merely indicate compression procedures to the device driver through a configuration parameter.

The 3790 SNA protocol provides both compression and compaction capabilities if agreed upon at bind time. Through the use of SCBs (string control bytes), not only can consecutive spaces be compressed, but any consecutively repeating characters can be compressed. Also, an optional compaction table can be provided if the user expects that certain characters will occur frequently.

The user process need not be aware that this compression/compaction is occurring, since it is agreed upon at bind time. If desired, the user process may optionally provide a compaction table.

With half-duplex contention, an established transmission can be quite lengthy. Consequently, a facility for momentarily turning the line around for high-priority messages is important.

All BSC devices must be able to receive reverse interrupt (RVI) control messages. Upon receiving an RVI, transmission must be suspended as soon as possible so the transmitter can receive the high-priority message. Once the message is received, the original transmission may continue from exactly where it left off (Fig. 3). (Note that this is an exception to the recovery mechanisms mentioned earlier.)

To indicate a request for a line turnaround, 3790 SNA devices use a Signal DFC (data flow control) command on an expedited flow. This term refers to a high-priority message stream (indicated by an expedited flow bit in the header) that signifies a request for line turnaround. To comply with the turnaround request, the transmitter will end the chain that it is currently transmitting. In doing so, it will add indicators to the chain that signify that the direction has been changed and that all previous output is suspended. Thus, the device is free to send the high-priorty data. After the high-priority message is sent, the change direction indicator will once again be sent and the transmission will resume (Fig. 4). Both the device driver and the user device use these mechanisms to request a line turnaround during a transmission.

Solutions
The essential problem in implementing half-duplex contention protocols in the Unix environment is passing enough information to manage the communications link between the user process and the device driver. The solution lies in four areas. First, a configuration structure must be constructed to hold initial information that must be present before communications can begin. Second, IOCTL operating system calls can be used to both pass and obtain information that is not available on any other system calls. Third, an information header will precede all data passed between the user and the device driver. This will serve as the medium for communicating information about the data that may

4. Go ahead. *After it knows an important message must be send, the transmitter finishes the current chain and sends an indicator that the line will be reversed.*

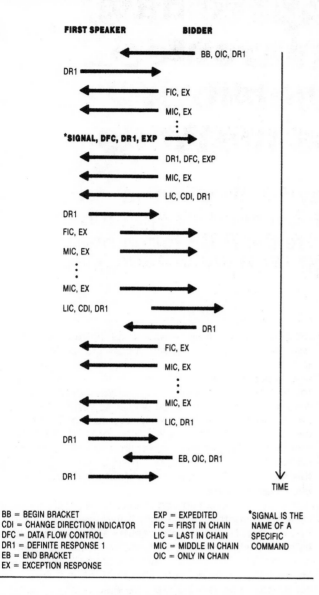

FIRST SPEAKER   BIDDER

BB, OIC, DR1
DR1
FIC, EX
MIC, EX
⁛
*SIGNAL, DFC, DR1, EXP
DR1, DFC, EXP
MIC, EX
LIC, CDI, DR1
DR1
FIC, EX
MIC, EX
⁛
MIC, EX
LIC, CDI, DR1
DR1
FIC, EX
MIC, EX
⁛
MIC, EX
LIC, DR1
DR1
EB, OIC, DR1
DR1

TIME

BB = BEGIN BRACKET
CDI = CHANGE DIRECTION INDICATOR
DFC = DATA FLOW CONTROL
DR1 = DEFINITE RESPONSE 1
EB = END BRACKET
EX = EXCEPTION RESPONSE

EXP = EXPEDITED
FIC = FIRST IN CHAIN
LIC = LAST IN CHAIN
MIC = MIDDLE IN CHAIN
OIC = ONLY IN CHAIN

*SIGNAL IS THE NAME OF A SPECIFIC COMMAND

change on each segment. Finally, by expanding the set of possible return values for all operating system calls, much of the needed status information can be made available to the user process. This information will indicate to the user not only success or failure, but also whatever subsequent action the user must provide.

Much of the information about a device is either needed or known by the user before communications have begun. Some of these items have been mentioned previously, such as error recovery retry limits, data formatting (compression/compaction), and access arrangement types. Other indicators, like the character set or identification information, should also be specified at configuration time.

To communicate this information, an open system call is first issued to obtain the device driver. Then an IOCTL call is issued to communicate the configuration

parameters. A set of default configuration values will initially be assumed by the device driver until the user process overrides it with new values. The user process will have the ability to read the configuration values currently used by the device driver. This facilitates the user process of reading the default values, changing a few of them, and then passing the whole set of values back to the device driver. Once physical connectivity is established (as will be discussed in the next section), the configuration structure cannot be altered. An error will be returned to the user process if any alterations are attempted.

The user process will use an IOCTL system call to inform the device driver when and how it wishes to establish connectivity with the remote device. Once the call is issued, control will not be returned to the user program until either the connection is established or a time limit for doing so has been reached. An "activate link" command will establish a leased or dial-in connection. A dial-out command (which includes the appropriate telephone number) will be used to establish dial-out connections. Once the connection is completely established, a successful return will be passed to the user process.

An IOCTL system call will be issued by the user process to request permission to transmit. If permission is granted by the remote device, the user process will receive a successful return from the system call; it may then begin writing data to the device. Otherwise, an error return indicates to the user process that it must immediately prepare to receive. (To do this, it issues a read system call.)

The write system call, along with the data to be transmitted, will contain a write header that will contain information about the data to be transmitted. The header contains the following information: the mode of transmission, whether this is the last element of data, whether master status is to be relinquished after transmission, and the destination device. The return value from a write system call goes beyond merely indicating success or failure; it reveals the reason for a failure or the subsequent action that must be taken after a success. Failure reasons include: communications link is down, retry limit is reached, and data is invalid for the mode or device selected. Of course, an otherwise successful write call may return an indication that a line turnaround has been requested and that a high-priority message will soon follow.

Along with the data that has just been received, a read system call will contain header information identical to that used by the write call. In addition, the error return will indicate "data lost" if the data stream ends prematurely. An inactivity time-out may be returned as an error indication to a read system call. The user process must then decide (by a predefined convention) whether to attempt another read or to bring down the data link. ∎

Mark P. Mendelsohn is an independent telecommunications consultant currently contracted to AT&T Information Systems, Enhanced Network Services Division, Lincroft, N. J.

Robert Carpenter, National Bureau of Standards, Washington, D.C.

A comparison of two 'guaranteed' local network access methods

Access delay can be a critical concern in local network operation. Compared are the IEEE token bus and the ANSI LDDI access schemes.

The best-known fully distributed, network-access arbitration schemes for broadcast-type local networks generally fall into three broad classes: the "send anytime you wish" scheme, the "listen before sending to see that the medium is free" scheme (known as carrier-sense multiple access, or CSMA), and the "listen before sending, listen while sending, stop if there is a collision" scheme (or CSMA with collision detection).

All these techniques result in occasional data loss caused by collisions—when two stations send at the same time. Also these schemes do not include any fixed method for scheduling/rescheduling access rights. As a result, local networks that employ these schemes cannot guarantee a maximum time delay before access to the network is achieved.

Two new schemes—one already standardized and the other nearing standardization—do guarantee a limit to the waiting time for any given station attempting access to the network. They are the IEEE 802.4 Token Bus (TB) standard and the ANSI X3T9.5 Local Distributed Data Interface (LDDI) specification.

The LDDI access method is a form of carrier-sense multiple access with collision prevention, or CSMA/CP. In this scheme, medium-access opportunities are based on the elapsed time in which the medium is free after the end of the previous occupancy (transmission). The first time period immediately after a transmission, called the Priority Access Opportunity (PAO), is 64 bit times in duration (see "Modeled network characteristics"). The PAO allows the recipient of the previous transmission to immediately send a high-priority response. Following the single PAO, each network station has assigned to it an access "slot" called the Arbitrated Access Opportunity, or AAO. These times are set up so that a station (called, say, N+1) can hear if the station immediately preceding it (station N) has captured the medium, in which case station N+1 defers.

This process, which is, in effect, an implied polling of the stations on the medium, is repeated each time the medium is free. If no station wishes to send, all station timers are then reset to zero and restarted. This is called the Resynchronization Time, or RT. The first station reaching its AAO is required to send either a normal information frame or a resynchronizing frame. In this manner, timers at all stations on the network are kept synchronized.

In order to have a limited medium-access delay for all stations, a control mechanism called the Wait Flag, or WF, is used. The Wait Flag is set by a station when it uses the medium during its AAO, and then it is reset when an RT occurs. Thus, all other stations reuse the same Wait Flag again. Actually, all of this is quite simple to implement in hardware without a programmed processor.

The IEEE's Token Bus access scheme relies on a token or frame, which all of the network's active stations pass along on the medium in the course of message exchange. A station is allowed to access the medium only when it holds the token. Naturally, the access delay in this case occurs while each station waits for the token. Not all stations on the medium need to be in the logical token-passing ring, but those outside the ring must wait until entry is specifically offered.

It should be noted that a considerable portion of the token-bus (TB) protocol is devoted to necessary functions such as recovering from a token loss (due to network noise or station failure), or resolving collisions that result when more than one station responds to the offer to join the token-passing ring. The token-passing

Table 1 Bit durations

LENGTH OF MEDIUM	DATA RATE (END-TO-END PROPAGATION DELAY IN BIT DURATIONS)				
	1 MBIT/S	10 MBIT/S	50 MBIT/S	100 MBIT/S	200 MBIT/S
10 m	.04	0.4	2	4	8
30 m	0.12	1.2	6	12	24
100 m	0.4	4	20	40	80
300 m	1.2	12	60	120	240
1 km	4	40	200	400	800
3 km	12	120	600	1,200	2,400
10 km	40	400	2,000	4,000	8,000
30 km	120	1,200	6,000	12,000	24,000

medium-access method involves conscious polling and response and requires that information concerning the state of the network be retained by each active station. Compared to the alternative LDDI, token passing is a software protocol layer.

Control variables

In order to compare the two access methods, all times used in this study are expressed in data bit durations. A bit duration is the time from one bit to the next as a function of data rate and cable length (see Table 1). Further, the comparisons made herein presume that all the modeled networks are limited to no more than 60 attached stations. The number of active stations in the token-passing logical ring varies from 4 to a maximum of 60. Traffic is assumed to be offered by two stations to all active stations. All stations are attached to a single linear bus medium, except in the one case where a head-end-based, two-channel bus configuration is specifically noted. In addition, the bus length is varied from 5 to 160 bit durations, with regard to end-to-end propagation delay. The corresponding mechanical lengths are presented in Table 1.

In most examples, the stations are attached to the network bus at fixed distances. However, an additional LDDI configuration is introduced wherein the access method is modified so that stations may be put anywhere on the medium.

Two different combinations of header/trailer frame design are presumed in the networks modeled in this study. The ANSI LDDI and the IEEE 802.3 CSMA/CD committees selected a frame preamble of 64 bits in order to ensure reliable network synchronization with a wide variety of physical interfaces. The token bus specification calls for a minimum of two microseconds of preamble, which corresponds to only 2 to 24 bit durations at the normal TB signaling rates (1 to 10 Mbit/s). However, since the preamble may constitute a major part of a token frame, the preamble length has a substantial impact on token-bus performance. This is also true for LDDI performance. Therefore, for standardization purposes, most of the comparisons in this study presumed a header of 64 bits and a trailer of 16 bits for LDDI.

Some of the token-bus calculations were made with a preamble of 20 bits, which corresponds to a transmission rate of 10 Mbit/s and a zero-length trailer. The LDDI physical interface characteristics are used for both LDDI and TB, since the TB specification does not define many of the critical timings, such as transmitter turn-on and turn-off.

Contention space

In addition to protocol performance considerations, individual-station failure rates limit the number of stations that should be connected to a single network segment. Network segments should be coupled by packet repeaters so that failed stations are not allowed to affect the network beyond their own segment. These store-and-forward devices isolate their two connected segments so that medium access on one segment is independent of the traffic on the other.

The IEEE token-bus standard demands that the chance for a network-disrupting failure be one in 10^6 per hour per station, or no more than one such failure every 114 years. Alternatively, the token bus specification requires that the aggregate mean time between failures (MTBF) for all attached stations be greater than 10,000 hours, which is an even stricter imposition when large network segments are employed.

Since equipment is built to commercial design and fabrication standards in a price-competitive environment, this study assumes that each station will suffer a network-disrupting failure every 10 years, which is considerably less than the IEEE-prescribed MTBF, though more realistic. Since failures are infrequent and presumably uncorrelated, a 44-station network segment would be expected to have an MTBF of about 2,000 hours, or about 12 weeks. This would be unacceptable in many applications, but this is one of the inherent drawbacks of most broadcast schemes. As mentioned, a partial solution would be to break the medium into segments by repeaters, which have enough intelligence to limit most failures to a single segment.

In addition, failure tolerance and the need to confine failures to only part of the network will drive realistic network implementers to limit the number of stations attached to one network segment (and therefore contention space) to fewer than 50. In view of these considerations, it is entirely appropriate in this survey to limit most of the modeled networks to a total of 60 stations.

Throughout the text and figures of this article, a number of parameters and variables are employed. Following are the key ones, along with a definition of what they describe:
- C1, the end-to-end length of the medium, in bit durations;
- Na, the number of stations attached to the medium;
- Ns, the number of stations that always have messages ready to be transmitted; and
- Nt, the number of stations in the token-passing logical ring.

1. Maximum access delay.

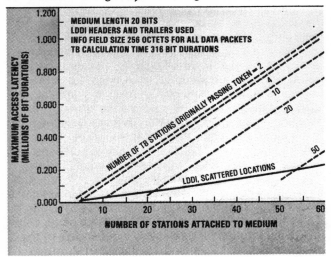

1. Maximum access delay. *Broken lines indicate to-ken-bus network performance as a function of the number of stations originally in the ring.*

Medium-access delay is the waiting time that a station suffers before the medium-access scheme allows it to access the network. A design goal of both LDDI and TB has been to provide a guaranteed limit to the access delay, assuming that bit errors are absent. Bit errors increase this delay in the token bus through damage to the token. Since the LDDI medium-access arbitration scheme depends on the presence of a signal—and not its content—its functioning is relatively unaffected by bit errors, as long as all stations on the medium sense the noise bursts. The physical layer interface specified by LDDI is already in commercial use, and it has been shown to be relatively error-free. Thus, this error effect is ignored in this performance comparison.

Maximum delay

In LDDI, the maximum medium-access delay calculation is straightforward. It is the sum of the AAO settings of all the stations on the medium, plus the sum of the packet's maximum duration that all these stations are allowed to transmit, plus the resynchronizing timer delay and resynchronizing frame durations. A resynchronizing frame is sent after all sending stations (Ns) have transmitted to guarantee that even the station with the last AAO has had a chance to transmit. If the station with the first AAO always has data to transmit, it will send data instead of a resynchronizing frame, which results in even better network performance than that shown.

The token bus situation is more complex. At regular intervals, each station in the token passing logical ring must offer the token to other stations not in the ring sequence. Upon the offer, more than one station may respond, which requires an iterative collision-resolution process. The frequency at which the token is offered sets the access delay for stations outside the passing ring, but it also increases the delay for the stations within the ring.

If an access offer results in a collision, up to eight

resolution iterations (the number of address bits divided by two) may be required. Each iteration requires some calculation by the polling station, and each repeated offer ties up the medium for a token duration, plus up to four round-trip medium-propagation delays, plus station reaction times. This sequence will be repeated to some extent for each station joining the logical ring, and a number of stations may respond to the same token offer.

A comparison of maximum medium-access delay for LDDI (where stations with successive AAOs are separated by one-third the cable length) and TB is shown in Figure 1. For TB, if few stations are originally in the ring, all stations not in the token-passing logical ring may join it before a station already in the ring can gain the token. Thus, curves are given for varying numbers of stations already in the ring (Fig. 1). The access delay includes time for all TB stations not in the token-passing loop to join it. Since, in LDDI, no station is "out of the loop," a single line represents all cases. Under most conditions, LDDI has less medium- access delay than TB.

Overhead

Most broadcast medium-access arbitration schemes use time on the medium that could otherwise be used for data transmission. In the case of LDDI, this overhead can be calculated exactly, since there are never any collisions and all stations connected to the medium are always in the "virtual polling" scheme.

In the case of TB, medium-access arbitration delay and overhead can be calculated exactly if no stations are entering the token-passing logical ring. Collisions can occur when stations attempt to join the ring, which result in considerable longer token transfer delays. This overhead, and the TB overhead caused by offering stations the opportunity to join the ring, are ignored in the following throughput calculations.

These calculations are made for a network in which the stations sending (of number Ns) use their access

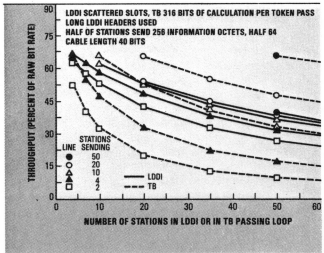

2. Throughput versus stations sending. *Throughput for token-bus networks is high when all or nearly all attached stations are sending.*

3. Improving token bus. *With a reduced token-passing calculation time of 100 bit durations, performance improves with the token-bus medium-access protocol.*

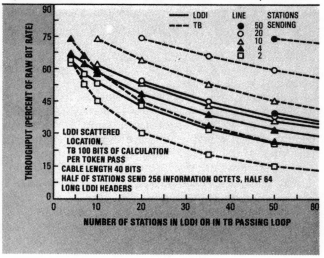

LDDI SCATTERED LOCATION, TB 100 BITS OF CALCULATION PER TOKEN PASS
CABLE LENGTH 40 BITS
HALF OF STATIONS SEND 256 INFORMATION OCTETS, HALF 64
LONG LDDI HEADERS

opportunity every time it is offered. That is, information to send is always queued in Ns stations. Note that Na is all of the stations attached to the network in LDDI and TB, while Nt of these are actually in the token-passing ring in TB (often only a portion of those connected).

Plotted results

In LDDI, all sending stations, Ns, are served before the wait flags must be reset by a resynchronizing frame (RF). On the average, the transmission grant will pass (Na-1)/2 stations after each transmission: that is, the average of 0 (the first station) and Na-1 (the last station). After all Ns stations are served, the next arbitration will allow the resynchronization timer (RT) to expire, thus resetting the wait flag. This allows all Ns stations to send their next frame. An RF (64 bits in duration) is then sent.

For TB, Nt stations are in the logical token-passing

ring, though only Ns of them are actually sending. The token is used by a sending station every time it is offered.

Figures 2 through 6 present data calculated for a medium with 40 bit durations of propagation delay. This corresponds to a medium length of about 200 meters with a 50-Mbit/s data rate, or 10 kilometers with a 1 Mbit/s data rate. Logically, succeeding "scattered" stations are assumed to be one-third of the medium length apart. Figure 2 presents a general picture of the throughput performance strengths for the two access schemes. Note that throughput is the total network throughput—the contents of all of the data link information fields of all of the sending stations. TB has high throughput if nearly all the stations in the token-passing ring are actually sending, but throughput is seriously degraded if the number of sending stations, Ns, is significantly smaller than the number of stations, Nt, in the token-passing ring. On the other hand, in LDDI, the throughput is relatively independent of the number of stations sending, Ns, though it slowly degrades as more stations, Na, are added to the medium. In many cases, the token bus Nt must be considerably less than Na to achieve the same saturated throughput.

Figure 3 illustrates the improvement in TB performance that can be gained by reducing the token passing calculated time to 100 bit durations.

Figure 4 differs from Figure 2 in that a star (or head-end bus) topology is used, rather than a linear bus. The stations are assumed to be evenly distributed from very near the head-end to a limit of 40 bit durations of propagation time away. Ordering of LDDI stations is of no benefit in this topology, so no "ordered" results are presented.

Figure 5 illustrates the case in which 20 stations are attached to a linear bus, and it shows the plotted data-link-layer throughput as a function of the number of these stations that are active, Nt, and the number sending, Ns. It differs from Figure 4 only in that both LDDI and TB have 20 stations connected at all times. It

4. Star performance. *A broadcast star and a head-end bus topology are compared for performance differences in both LDDI and TB access schemes.*

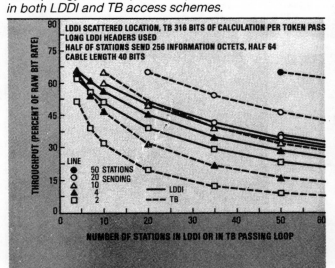

LDDI SCATTERED LOCATION, TB 316 BITS OF CALCULATION PER TOKEN PASS
LONG LDDI HEADERS USED
HALF OF STATIONS SEND 256 INFORMATION OCTETS, HALF 64
CABLE LENGTH 40 BITS

5. Limited numbers. *Throughput for 20 stations attached to a linear bus is plotted as a function of the number of those that are currently active.*

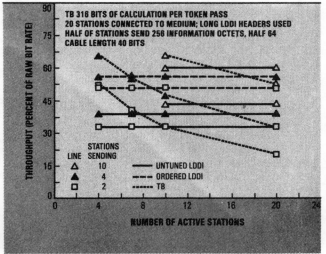

TB 316 BITS OF CALCULATION PER TOKEN PASS
20 STATIONS CONNECTED TO MEDIUM; LONG LDDI HEADERS USED
HALF OF STATIONS SEND 256 INFORMATION OCTETS, HALF 64
CABLE LENGTH 40 BITS

Modeled network characteristics

This study compares two medium-access protocols, the Local Distributed Data Interface (LDDI) and the Token Bus (TB), in terms of a number of parameters. Unless stated otherwise, it is assumed that half of the Ns stations are sending packets with information fields of 256 octets and that the other half are sending shorter frames, with 64 octets in the link-layer information field.

In the LDDI model, factors in the arbitration algorithm are the times required for the transmitter to become active (10 bits) and the receiver hardware to detect this (5 bits), and for the transmitter hardware to become inactive (15 bits) and the receiver to detect this (5 bits). The figure shows the LDDI frame design that has been used to compute bit overhead.

Three different station-location configurations are considered: Ordered, whereby stations are ordered by their Arbitrated Access Opportunity (AAO), the optimum situation; scattered, wherein stations are located approximately one-third of the cable length from the logically preceding station; and untuned, wherein the AAOs are large enough so that the stations can be placed in any physical location on the cable without readjustment.

For the P802.4 token bus, Na (active) stations have been assumed. When calculating throughput, it is further assumed that other stations attached to the network, but outside the logical ring (not active), do not cause overhead. In this case, no other stations are given a chance to join the token-passing ring.

CALCULATION TIME	NETWORK BIT RATE (IN EQUIVALENT BIT DURATIONS)			
	1 MBIT/S	10 MBIT/S	50 MBIT/S	100 MBIT/S
2 µs	2	20	100	200
5 µs	5	50	250	500
10 µs	10	100	500	1,000
20 µs	20	200	1,000	2,000
50 µs	50	500	2,500	5,000

µs = MICROSECONDS

Sixteen-bit medium-access-control (MAC) layer addresses have been assumed. Refer to the main text for a discussion about preamble size. The figure shows the TB frame designs that have been used in calculating bit overhead through the data-link layer. Note that the 8-bit DSAP and SSAP fields are not counted as overhead, since this function is not present in the data-link protocol layer in LDDI.

The TB medium arbitration method requires each node to perform certain functions before the token can be used or passed to the logically succeeding station. Comparisons are made for three values of TB calculation in each station: 100-, 316-, and 1,000-bit durations. Table 2 illustrates various calculation times in terms of bit durations.

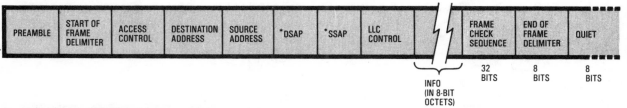

LDDI FRAME

PREAMBLE	FLAG	DESTINATION ADDRESS	SOURCE ADDRESS	LENGTH FIELD	INFO FIELD (IN 8-BIT OCTETS)	FRAME CHECK SEQUENCE	TRAILER	PRIORITY ACCESS OPPORTUNITY
64 OR 20 BITS	8 BITS	16 BITS	16 BITS	16 BITS		32 BITS	0 OR 16 BITS	0 OR 64 BITS

PACKET OVERHEAD PER LDDI INFO PACKET, EXCLUDING THE PRIORITY ACCESS OPPORTUNITY (PAO) = 168 BITS.

TOKEN FRAME

PREAMBLE	START OF FRAME DELIMITER	ACCESS CONTROL	DESTINATION ADDRESS	SOURCE ADDRESS	FRAME CHECK SEQUENCE	END OF FRAME DELIMITER	QUIET
64 OR 20 BITS	8 BITS	8 BITS	16 BITS	16 BITS	32 BITS	8 BITS	8 BITS

INFORMATION FRAME

PREAMBLE	START OF FRAME DELIMITER	ACCESS CONTROL	DESTINATION ADDRESS	SOURCE ADDRESS	*DSAP	*SSAP	LLC CONTROL	INFO (IN 8-BIT OCTETS)	FRAME CHECK SEQUENCE	END OF FRAME DELIMITER	QUIET
									32 BITS	8 BITS	8 BITS

TOTAL OVERHEAD PER TB INFO PACKET = 124 BITS.

*THE 8-BIT DSAP AND SSAP FIELDS NOT COUNTED IN OVERHEAD SINCE THEIR FUNCTION IS NOT PRESENT IN DATA LINK PROTOCOL LAYER IN LDDI.

6. Relative throughput. *LDDI and TB saturated throughput as a function of Ns, Na and Nt. The performance advantage of LDDI is shown. Refer to key.*

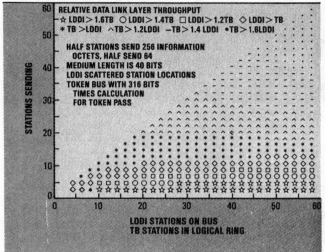

RELATIVE DATA LINK LAYER THROUGHPUT
☆ LDDI > 1.6TB ○ LDDI > 1.4TB □ LDDI > 1.2TB ◇ LDDI > TB
* TB > LDDI ∧ TB > 1.2LDDI — TB > 1.4 LDDI • TB > 1.6LDDI

HALF STATIONS SEND 256 INFORMATION
OCTETS, HALF SEND 64
MEDIUM LENGTH IS 40 BITS
LDDI SCATTERED STATION LOCATIONS
TOKEN BUS WITH 316 BITS
TIMES CALCULATION
FOR TOKEN PASS

STATIONS SENDING (y-axis)
LDDI STATIONS ON BUS
TB STATIONS IN LOGICAL RING (x-axis)

7. Throughput versus medium length. *Compared are LDDI stations' distributions and TB token-passing calculation times. Medium length's effect is shown.*

HALF OF STATIONS SEND 256 INFORMATION OCTETS, HALF SEND 64
NUMBER OF STATIONS SENDING, NS, IS 4
NUMBER OF STATIONS ON LDDI, NT, BUS IS 20
NUMBER OF STATIONS IN TB LOGICAL RING, NT, IS 20

LINK LAYER THROUGHPUT (PERCENT OF RATE BIT RATE) (y-axis)

100 BIT TIMES CALCULATION
ORDERED
SCATTERED
316 BIT TIMES CALCULATION
UNTUNED
1000 BIT TIMES CALCULATION

—— LDDI
- - - TB

MEDIUM LENGTH IN BIT DURATIONS (x-axis)

can be seen that the throughput of LDDI is independent of the number of active stations, since an AAO is provided for all attached stations, Na. Clearly, the performance of TB improves rapidly when only a small percentage of the attached stations are active (in the token-passing logical ring).

Figure 6 illustrates the relative saturated throughput of LDDI and TB as a function of Ns, Na, and Nt for the same parameter combination used in Figure 4. This illustrates the performance advantage of LDDI with small numbers of stations sending, even in large (60 or more) networks. There is less than a 20 percent difference when up to about 18 stations are sending. LDDI performance would improve even more with a shorter medium. The various shaded bands on this figure illustrate regions of relative performance, with the following symbol key:

■ Star denotes where LDDI throughput is at least 160 percent of TB;
■ Circle shows where LDDI throughput is at least 140 percent of TB;
■ Square shows where LDDI throughput is at least 120 percent of TB;
■ Diamond shows where LDDI throughput is at least equal to TB;
■ Asterisk (*), where TB throughput is greater than LDDI;
■ Caret (<), where TB throughput is at least 120 percent of LDDI;
■ Dash (-), where TB throughput is at least 140 percent of LDDI; and
■ Dot (.), where TB throughput is at least 160 percent of LDDI.

Figure 7 shows the relationship between throughput, medium length, LDDI station distribution, and TB to-ken-passing calculated time. Fixed values are used for Ns (the number of stations sending), and Na (the number of stations in the TB token-passing ring). The strong effect of medium length on LDDI is easy to see in this figure. It also illustrates the great performance

benefits if LDDI stations are ordered on the medium.

Arbitration in TB is essentially unaffected by medium length until cable propagation delay is greater than token duration. However, TB throughput is greatly affected by the time taken at each station to execute the required token-passing protocol routines. It is note-worthy that there would be no advantage to speeding up the token calculated time to the point where it took less time than the turn-off time delay of the transmitter.

A medium-access protocol that is well suited to arbitrating requests from many stations may not allow bursts of great throughput between a small number of the attached stations. This requirement is typical in applications such as file transfers, and such activity may occur in the presence of a continuing low level of other traffic — to communications multiplexers, printers, and other low-speed users that cannot be removed from the token ring. The situation of small Ns and considerably larger Nt represents this situation. An examination of figures 2 through 6 shows that the LDDI is well suited to this application. In fact, it was designed specifically for this application.

References:
1. Amer, P.D., R.M. Rosenthal, and R. Toense, "Measuring a local network's performance," submitted for publication in Data Communications, April 1983, p. 173.
2. Institute of Electrical and Electronics Engineers, Project 802, Local Network Standards, Draft C. Contact George Jelatis, Honeywell Inc., 10701 Lyndale Ave. South Bloomington, Minn. 55420.
3. Shock, J.F. and J.A. Hupp, "Performance of an Ethernet Local Network: A Preliminary Report," Local Area Communications Network Symposium, Boston, May 1979, pp. 113-125.
4. Burr, Wm. E., "An Overview if the Proposed American National Standard for Local Distributed Data Interfaces," Communications of the ACM, Vol. 26, August 1983, pp. 554-561.

Mike Hurwicz, Telco Research Inc., Nashville, Tenn.

MS-DOS 3.1 makes it easy to use IBM PCs on a network

No longer do software developers have to fashion their multi-user programs to the vagaries of each network. As a result, users will have a great deal more choice.

About a year ago, Microsoft announced its latest upgrade to the standard operating system of the IBM Personal Computer. The importance of this operating system—MS-DOS version 3.1—is often underestimated, although many astute observers of the communications industry realize that it may have tremendous long-run significance.

For the first time, a programmer can write a multi-user application that will run on all local area networks (LANs) compatible with the latest version of MS-DOS. Some even say that developers of MS-DOS-compatible multi-user applications may find it nearly impossible to market a program that does not run on all the major LANs compatible with MS-DOS 3.1. This is a dramatic change from the recent past, when a multi-user program needed a tailor-made version for almost every LAN.

At the root of this revolution is the fact that the new version of MS-DOS now provides solutions to some of the most basic problems of multi-user programming. In fact, it not only provides them, once they are invoked, it enforces their use until the computer is rebooted. Thus, MS-DOS 3.1 multi-user programming tools are forcing the standardization of applications running on LANs that accommodate MS-DOS-compatible computers. To remain truly MS-DOS-compatible (and therefore able to survive) these LANs must implement the MS-DOS 3.1 solutions.

The MS-DOS 3.1 standard has several implications:
■ Users will no longer have to select an MS-DOS-compatible LAN on the basis of available multi-user applications. Because such networks will run substantially the same software, users' hardware choices will be governed by their physical environment, performance needs, vendor preferences, and budget.
■ Many more multi-user applications will be created.

Since a single program can now reach a much wider market, software developers can expect a better return on their investment and will be encouraged to create more programs.
■ Data integrity will, on average, be improved. The standard operating system permits a significant improvement in data integrity for many LANs, primarily because MS-DOS 3.1 incorporates a "file server" rather than a "disk server."
■ Because the standardized world is richer and more flexible for users, more LANs will be sold. This will further encourage software development.

As of July 1985, there were three network operating systems (NOSs) conforming to the MS-DOS 3.1 standard on the U. S. retail market:
■ IBM's PC Network Program (being used by IBM and by Nestar Systems Inc., Palo Alto, Calif.).
■ Netware, from Novell Inc., Orem, Utah.
■ Tapestry, from Torus Inc., Redwood City, Calif.
(It should be mentioned that Microsoft Networks, also referred to as MS-NET, is available, but not at the retail level; it is licensed to vendors and provides them with a network operating system conforming to the standard. The author was not aware of any MS-NET-based NOS selling at retail as of July 1985, although apparently many were on the way.)

Some of the network operating systems have developed a following of their own. For example, at least 25 LANs are compatible with Novell's Netware, which means that 25 network manufacturers are conforming to the MS-DOS 3.1 standard. Numerous manufacturers are preparing to conform as well.

LANs that are believed to have leased MS-NET and are expected to conform to the standard include 3Com's EtherLink (perhaps the number one LAN in terms of installed bases), Ungermann-Bass's Net/

MS-DOS 3.1 compatibility

MS-DOS 3.1 is not always incompatible with previous MS-DOS versions, but it is usually incompatible with the other versions in a multi-user environment. Problems arise only for multi-user programs, and then only when the SHARE program is loaded.

In the standard network environment, the SHARE program will be loaded. Previous muti-user software is compatible with MS-DOS 3.1 only if SHARE is not loaded. Thus, previous multi-user software is not MS-DOS 3.1 compatible in the standard network environment. Each network has essentially two alternatives: It can run new standard applications and not load SHARE. This allows it to use any version of MS-DOS, including MS-DOS 3.1, without SHARE and to run previous multi-user applications. Or, the network can run new standard applications and load SHARE, which wreaks havoc with multi-user programs written for previous versions of MS-DOS. In the long run, almost without exception, networks will standardize, load the SHARE program as part of regular operations, and revise or abandon previous multi-user software.

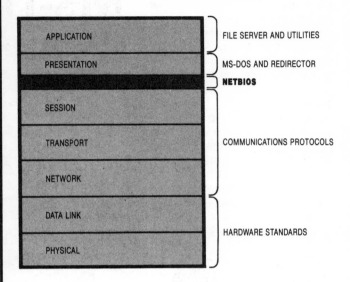

1. Spanning layers. *Netbios functions between the session and presentation layers, while MS-DOS 3.1 and the Redirector operate at the presentation layer.*

MS-DOS = MICROSOFT DISK OPERATING SYSTEM
NETBIOS = NETWORK BASIC INPUT/OUTPUT SYSTEM

One, Corvus's Omninet, and Orchid Technology's PCnet. Indeed, no vendor of an MS-DOS-compatible LAN can afford to ignore MS-DOS 3.1 because of the fact that old operating systems will be incapable of running the new multi-user applications being written for the new operating system.

Unless they are massively revised, multi-user applications running under old operating systems will not run under the new operating system. Thus, LAN vendors may wait until new or revised software is at least equal to software presently available before they make the changeover. For many LANs, this may occur sometime in 1986. (For a discussion of whether MS-DOS 3.1 is compatible with previous versions of MS-DOS, see "MS-DOS 3.1 compatibility.")

To understand the importance of the MS-DOS 3.1 standard, it is important to understand how it relates to the other emerging major LAN standard, IBM's Netbios (Network Basic Input/Output System), which is positioned to become the most widespread standard in local area networking (DATA COMMUNICATIONS, "IBM provides industry with a versatile local network standard," June, p. 195). While Netbios allows different operating systems to interface with any Netbios-compatible LAN regardless of the hardware used, it is MS-DOS 3.1 that plays the largest role in allowing a programmer to write one multi-user program that will run on all MS-DOS 3.1-compatible LANs.

The relationship between MS-DOS 3.1 and Netbios can be most easily summarized by referring to the International Organization for Standardization (ISO) seven-layer Open Systems Interconnection (OSI) model for network architecture (Fig. 1). Information starts at the application layer at one computer on the LAN. It is passed down the seven layers until it reaches the

physical layer, which includes the physical cable. At the receiving computer, it is passed upward through the seven layers until it reaches the application layer, which is the only layer that users handle.

Netbios is positioned just above the session layer, between the session and presentation layers. Netbios is an interface that offers the capabilities of the five lower layers to the two upper layers in the form of 17 commands, such as SEND DATA and RECEIVE DATA. These commands are designed to be generic so that nearly all LANs will be able to support them.

MS-DOS 3.1, in turn, operates at the presentation level and provides an interface between Netbios and application programs. Although applications can access Netbios directly, the MS-DOS interface is much more convenient for most purposes. Some estimates indicate that only about 5 percent of the MS-DOS-compatible multi-user programs presently being developed—mostly those for communications gateways—will go directly to Netbios rather than going through MS-DOS. (Single-user programs do not go to Netbios, either directly or through MS-DOS.) Thus, for most multi-user applications, the characteristics of MS-DOS 3.1 are all-important, for Netbios remains hidden behind MS-DOS.

Working hand-in-hand with MS-DOS is its "Redirector" program. When an application requests service from a local device (such as a disk), the Redirector can reroute the request over the network to a device at another computer. The Redirector (discussed more fully below) may, in general, be considered a part of the MS-DOS standard. It is also a service of the presentation layer.

In the past, a single-user program that ran under MS-DOS on a standalone computer would probably exe-

65

cute correctly when the computer was networked, regardless of the particular type of network being used. (This has remained generally true even though incompatibilities between a particular application and a particular network are possible.) A multi-user program, on the other hand, had a very slim chance of running on more than one network. Today, the status of the single-user program has not changed, but the status of the multi-user program has changed dramatically.

New tools
Today, MS-DOS 3.1 provides tools for multi-user programmers, and in order to run under the standard, the program must use the standard multi-user programming tools incorporated into MS-DOS 3.1.

The most important of these tools is the SHARE program, which implements the file-sharing facility. In the past, when opening a file, a user specified only an "access mode," which told MS-DOS of the desired operations on the file: "read only," "write only," or "read and write," for example.

With the SHARE program operating, however, the user can now also specify a "sharing mode." The sharing mode determines permissible access modes for subsequent users opening the same file. For example, an operator can open a file for read and write access, while specifying that subsequent users will only be able to read the file; this is called "read/write" access and "deny write" sharing mode. Such a file-sharing mechanism is obviously indispensable for a multi-user application. Each NOS designer need no longer invent a new file-sharing scheme.

Moreover, the SHARE facility cannot for practical purposes be ignored because there is no un-SHARE command. The standard way to deactivate SHARE after it has been loaded is to reboot (reinitialize the computer). Rebooting is generally avoided as much as possible on a network, since it cuts off communications with all other computers. Therefore, if one program runs with SHARE loaded, all programs on that computer must be able to run with SHARE loaded. This means that every time the user opens a file, MS-DOS is going to: (1) check its "sharing table" and, if the file is already open, determine the user's access according to the "sharing mode" specified by the person who opened the file, or (2) check the sharing mode specified by the user who is the first to open the file.

Of course, most programs today do not specify a sharing mode, since they were written before SHARE was available. When SHARE is loaded, files opened by pre-SHARE programs are automatically assigned "compatibility" sharing mode, which means that only one user can access them at a time. Thus, programmers who fail to take SHARE into account automatically write single-user applications. Once SHARE is loaded, these applications are unable to share files.

There is one exception to this rule: If the program only needs to read a file (and does not need to write to it), the ATTRIB command can be used to assign a "read-only" attribute to the file. Then, when a pre-SHARE program opens the file, MS-DOS will automatically assign a sharing mode of "deny write" (rather than

"compatibility") so that other users can also read the file. This allows pre-SHARE programs a limited file-sharing capability. The ATTRIB command is used extensively in adapting older programs to the MS-DOS 3.1 networking environment, but its applicability is limited to programs that need to read shared files but do not need to write to them.

Loaded simultaneously with SHARE is the "byte-locking" function, which is required when two or more users have simultaneous read and write access to a single file. This function allows a user to exclude all other users from accessing a particular range of bytes while the range is being updated by the original user. The standard procedure is to lock a range of bytes, read them, change them, and then unlock them. Without such a mechanism, two users attempting to update a file would be like two painters trying to paint on a single canvas, without being able to see all of each other's brush strokes. In the past, NOSs running under MS-DOS had to invent their own byte-locking methods, and naturally they tended to be incompatible with one another. Now, any program ignoring the standard MS-DOS 3.1 method is a renegade and unwelcome in the society of well-behaved applications.

In fact, the renegade might suffer more than the law-abiding citizens because not only would the renegade not be able to break their locks, but it might also be unprotected while it was updating. Suppose, for example, that the application "Renegade" opens a file with read/write "sharing mode." (Other users can read from and write to the file while Renegade is using it.) Locking bytes by using its own private method — a method other than the MS-DOS standard — Renegade updates the file.

When another user requests to write to the file, MS-DOS will check to see if a lock is active for the requested bytes. But MS-DOS will only check *its own* lock table, not Renegade's lock table. Therefore, MS-DOS — finding no locks in its table — will assume there is no reason not to change those bytes.

Suppose now that another user places a standard MS-DOS lock on a range of bytes, and Renegade tries to write to that area of the file. Normally, Renegade will go through MS-DOS to accomplish the write; MS-DOS, however, will check its lock table and will prevent Renegade from writing. Unless it goes around MS-DOS, Renegade cannot break the lock.

It is important to note that additional methods of coordinating access to files or records are not precluded by conformance to the MS-DOS 3.1 standards. Any program or operating system is free to impose additional access restrictions. Netware, for example, provides a whole set of locking mechanisms and semaphores that can be used in addition to those provided by MS-DOS. Tapestry provides several extra security features as well.

It is clear that MS-DOS now provides solutions to some of the most basic problems of constructing a multi-user application. (See "Network-related MS-DOS commands, interrupts, and functions.")

These "high-level network primitives," as they are called, will encourage the adaptation of popular single-user programs for network use, the adaptation of multi-user minicomputer programs for use on microcomputer networks, and the design of new network applications.

MS-DOS also allows the programmer to use the "Redirector" program, which reroutes requests away from local devices and sends them instead to remote devices.

Forces use of file server

MS-NET essentially consists of the Redirector, MS-DOS 3.1, and a file server. The MS-NET file server is fully compatible with the new standard, but it is not an integral part of it. IBM, for example, created a proprietary file server for the PC Network, as did Torus for Tapestry. Novell adapted Netware's existing file server. All are fully compatible with MS-DOS 3.1.

The inclusion of the Redirector forces LAN manufacturers to use a file server rather than a disk server, although the Redirector does not mandate the use of any particular file server. This distinction is very important and bears some explanation.

Disk-server software fools a computer into seeing a remote disk as a local disk. Each computer continues to believe it is the only one using that disk, and the disk-server software must coordinate requests from multi-users essentially without cooperation from them. Unexpected problems can result, the most serious being inconsistencies in the various computers' File Allocation Tables (FATs).

Each computer maintains a FAT to keep track of which areas of the disk have been used and which ones are still available. When numerous FATs are maintained—as is the case with a disk-server network—there must be a mechanism for constantly updating all the FATs, so that every computer can know which areas of the disk have been used by the other computers. If an error occurs in the updating procedure—an all too common occurrence—it is possible for computer A to be unaware that computer B has written to a particular area of the disk. Computer A may then overwrite areas of the disk that have already been used by B, thus corrupting B's files.

With a file server under MS-DOS 3.1, the Redirector determines when a request should be redirected to the file server and handles the exchange of information. When using a file server, the computer cannot perform remote disk storage and retrieval operations directly. For example, each computer does not maintain its own FAT. All the individual computer can do is send messages, via the Redirector, to the file server, which then performs the disk access operations, taking into account all other active or pending requests. Only one FAT is maintained by the file server. Compared with a disk server, the operation is more orderly and controlled, and it is less prone to failure.

File servers also make it easier to internetwork or use multiple operating systems on a single network. This is because file servers are more likely than disk servers to support "high level" requests, which tend to be generic (common across most operating systems). For example, the Redirector communicates with the file server using blocks of information called Server Message Blocks (SMBs). To update a file, the following SMBs might be sent: "start connection," "open file," "read byte block," "write byte block," "close file," and "end connection." Such commands are not operating-system dependent. This makes it much easier to create an interface between a non-MS-DOS computer and an MS-DOS file server. In theory, there is nothing to keep any machine, be it mainframe, mini-, or microcomputer, from sending and receiving these message blocks. And the message can be sent or received through a gateway to another network. (The server on the Appletalk network for Macintoshes, although it does not run MS-DOS, accepts requests from the PC Network, probably by translating SMBs into Appletalk commands.)

By way of contrast, note that disk servers frequently use direct or "absolute" disk input/output operations that address physical sectors of the disk and are operating-system dependent. Thus, disk servers wishing to service multiple operating systems have to partition the shared disk and allow each operating system to access only one partition. This is required because different operating systems format disks differently and cannot read one another's formats directly.

File servers have been standard equipment for many years in the mainframe and minicomputer environment. However, perhaps because a file server is harder to create than a disk server, they have been slow to catch on in the microcomputer LAN environment.

Netbios

The Redirector, a presentation layer service, talks to the session layer through Netbios. Although it is not necessary to have a general discussion of Netbios, there are some aspects of it that have particular importance to MS-DOS-compatible LANs.

IBM has made it clear that Netbios will be used in all its forthcoming networks, and that it intends for Netbios to become a standard; thus, vendors must take Netbios into account for future compatibility requirements. For most multi-user programs running on an MS-DOS-compatible LAN today, Netbios' significance lies in the role it plays in "extending" network protocols, adding basic multi-user functions that do not presently exist in MS-DOS. Suppose a programmer wants to allow a station to set its time-of-day clock to correspond with the time at a file server. If the programmer wants to maintain compatibility with MS-DOS and Netbios, a new SMB can be added to those that already exist (a "get time" SMB), the SMB can be defined at the server, and the SMB can be sent to the server when the function is desired. This procedure, which IBM has fully documented, allows the programmer to make a network function out of literally any operation available on the IBM PC. To use this powerful method, however, one must be able to send and receive SMBs; the standard way to do this is through Netbios. MS-DOS permits a programmer to access peripherals, such as disks and printers at a remote computer, but it makes no provision for sending a specified string of bytes over the cable. Netbios, on the

Network-related MS-DOS commands, interrupts, and functions

MS-DOS commands

ATTRIB allows the user to designate certain files as "read-only" files. In a multi-user environment, any number of users can open such a file in order to read it. In a standalone or multi-user environment, ATTRIB can be used to protect files, because a read-only file cannot be deleted or copied over.

SHARE is useful only in a multi-user, or at least multitasking, environment. It allows a single file to be opened by more than one user (or process). SHARE also loads the byte-locking function that allows one user to exclude all other users from a particular range of bytes within a file.

MS-DOS function calls

The following functions are called when an INT 21H interrupt occurs. (The "H" means hexadecimal.)

1. Open a file (function call number 3DH). Called the "extended" file open, this function allows the programmer to declare both an "access" and a "sharing mode." The "access" determines the tasks available to the user (or process) that opens the file. The "sharing mode" determines what subsequent users can do with the file.

2. Input/output control for devices (function call number 44H). This function, chiefly used for controlling disk drives, allows the programmer to send and receive control information. For example, this function call allows the programmer to change (a) the number of times MS-DOS will retry when it detects a sharing conflict before it sends a critical error message to the application, and (b) the length of time MS-DOS will wait between retries.

This function can also be used to get information about the channel over which the data passes. For example, the programmer can determine if a particular disk drive is local or remote.

3. Load or execute a program (function call number 4BH). This function call is equally useful in standalone or networking environments. It allows the programmer to execute a program, MS-DOS command, or network operating system command from within an application.

4. Get extended error (function call number 59H). Extended error reporting returns an error code, an error class, a suggested action, or an error locus. There is network-specific information in all categories, except "suggested action." For example, one locus (site of error occurrence) is "Net: Related to the network."

5. Create temporary file (function call number 5AH). Many applications use temporary "work files." Normally, these are not multi-user shared files. The "create temporary file" function helps ensure that each temporary file will be used by only one user. A closer look at the "create file" function will illustrate the usefulness of "create temporary file."

To use the old MS-DOS function for creating a file (function call 3CH), the programmer supplies a file name. MS-DOS will create a new file if no file presently exists with the specified name. If a file already exists by that name, MS-DOS truncates that file to zero, completely wiping out its contents.

In a multi-user environment, this type of file creation is extremely dangerous. In particular, if two users are using the same program in the same directory at the same time, they run a serious risk of truncating one another's temporary files if they use the old "create" function. For example, suppose the multi-user program creates a temporary file named "TEMP.FIL." First, user A creates a file by this name and stores some information in it. Next, user B creates a file by this name, wiping out all the information A just put in it, and stores different information. When A comes back to the file looking for his information, he gets a big surprise. Clearly, this is unsatisfactory.

A multi-user program that creates a temporary file needs to ensure that each user will use a different file name. The "create temporary file" does just that: It produces an arbitrary file name and attempts to create a file with that name. If a file already exists with that name, that file is left alone; it is not truncated or affected in any way. Then, a second arbitrary name is checked to see if there is an existing file by that name. This continues until a name is found that is not in use. A file is then created with that unique name.

6. Create new file (function call number 5BH). Many applications check for the existence of a particular file and, if it does not exist, create it. A problem can arise in a multi-user environment when user A checks for the existence of a file, but before he can create it, user B creates a file by that name. When user A finally does create his file, he destroys the one user B created. This function call checks for the existence of a file and performs file creation all in one step, eliminating such problems.

This function is very similar to the preceding one, except that here the programmer supplies the file name, and the file will not be created if a file with the same name is found. Again, the existing file is left undisturbed.

Thus, "create temporary file" creates a unique file no matter what—but the programmer has no control over the file name. "Create new file" creates a unique file or no file at all—and the programmer determines what file name, if any, will be used.

7. Lock/unlock file access (function call number 5CH). This is the standard MS-DOS "byte-locking" function that all MS-DOS 3.1-compatible multi-user applications will now be using.

8. Get machine name (function call number 5E00H). Netbios requires that a user communicate over the network using names that consist of 16 characters. The PC Network program considers one of these names to be the "computer name" that uniquely identifies each computer. Function call 5E00H sticks the machine name into a memory location defined by a user program.

9. *Printer setup* (function call number 5E02H). Allows a program to specify up to 64 bytes that will be sent to a network printer immediately before any file is sent to that printer. This is normally used to reset various printer controls to standard default values that a previous print job may have changed.

10. *Get redirection list entry* (function call number 5F02H). Returns the name of one redirected device. Each time the function is used, it returns the name of another device.

11. *Redirect device* (function call number 5F03H). This command intercepts operations intended for a local device and reroutes them so that they are actually performed on a remote device. The local device does not really have to exist. For example, users could redirect drive N, even if they do not have a physical drive N. The only requirement is that "N" be a legal drive specifier. All calls to drive N will then be redirected to the remote device.

12. *Cancel redirection* (function call number 5F04H). Undoes the work of the previous function. Calls to the local device will access the local device once again.

MS-NET network call (interrupt 5BH)
This interrupt is used by MS-NET for executing network commands.

IBM PC Network Netbios call (interrupt 5CH)
Used to execute Netbios commands, this interrupt goes directly to the IBM PC Network adapter.

Hardware-independent network call (interrupt 2AH)
1. *Check installation* (function call number 00H). Checks whether the interrupt 2AH interface is installed.

2. *Check direct input/output* (function call number 0300H). Ensures that "absolute disk access" is allowed to the device. If this is allowed, the physical sectors of the disk are addressed instead of particular files. "Absolute disk access" is forbidden with all shared network devices.

3. *Execute Netbios with error retry* (function call number 0400H). Currently, this function simply translates the request into an interrupt 5BH or 5CH, depending on the network operating system being used. This version also retries network commands upon receipt of certain error messages. For example, if the network is busy, the program can retry the request a number of times to ensure that it is not just a temporary condition. This function can also be used by programmers to add commands to Netbios.

4. *Execute Netbios without error retry* (function call number 0401H). Similar to the previous function, but with no error retry.

5. *Get network resource information* (function call number 0500H). Checks how many network names, network commands, and network sessions are available to an application. This operation is used by the application after the network operating system (NOS) is loaded in order to determine the remaining network resources.

Multiplex interrupt (interrupt 2FH)
1. *Get installed state* (function call number 00H). Checks whether the multiplex interrupt interface is installed.

2. *Print queue interface* (function calls 01H through 05H). These functions support the print queue by submitting or canceling print jobs, or reporting status.

3. *"Append" installation check* (function call number B700H). Checks to see whether the MS-DOS APPEND command is active.

4. *PC Network program installation check* (function call number B800H). Checks whether the PC Network program is installed. This function can also be used by other network operating systems to check for installation. It also provides information about which features are configured.

5. *Get current post address* (function call number B803H). After a "network event," instructions will be executed beginning at a particular address in memory referred to as the "post address" because the instructions at that address are executed "post-event" (after the network event). The instructions at this post address are called a "network event handler." Two network events are defined: a) message received and b) critical network error. This function allows the programmer to determine the current post address.

6. *Set new post address* (function call number B804H). Used with the previous function, this allows the programmer to "hook into" network events. For example, an application doing distributed processing may need to send messages back and forth between workstations, without user intervention. The application gets the current post address. Then the application sets the new post address to the address of the application's network event handler. Every time a message is received, the instructions in the application's event handler are executed. The application's event handler checks the message to see whether it belongs to the application and routes it accordingly. If the message belongs to another program, it is routed back to the event handler at the original post address. If it belongs to the application, then it is routed accordingly.

Multitasking interrupt (interrupt 15H)
Whenever Netbios encounters a busy condition or is about to enter a wait loop, it issues interrupt number 15H. Other programs can watch for this interrupt and use this "idle" time to accomplish their tasks.

2. Connections. *A similar sequence of events occurs when John and Mary establish a connection over one network (a) and through an intervening network (b).*

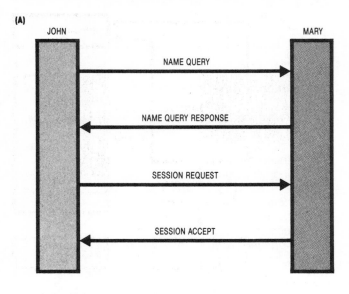

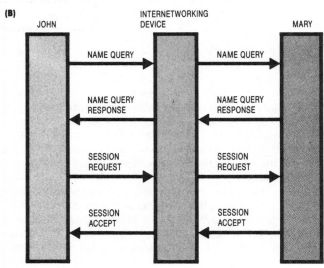

other hand, has just such a "send data" command. (Note: SMBs are used with the Redirector, so NOSs that provide their own redirecting function provide some mechanism parallel to SMBs as well.)

The inclusion of Netbios in the MS-DOS 3.1 standard has far-reaching—and perhaps troublesome—implications, particularly in the area of internetworking. Netbios assumes that each station will maintain a "local name table" of up to 16 names. When a connection or "session" is established between two computers on the network, Netbios sees it as a connection between the two names. Because IBM designed the PC Network to operate in a "peer-to-peer" fashion, there is no central controller that knows all the names on the network. If an entity called "John" on computer A wishes to establish a connection with "Mary" on computer B, computer A will send out a

Netbios "call" for Mary. This causes computer A's adapter card to broadcast a series of "name query packets" to all stations asking, in effect: "Is Mary out there anywhere?" If Mary resides on the network, Mary and John exchange packets in a prescribed order, and the connection is established (Fig. 2a).

If John and Mary are on two different networks connected by some type of internetworking device, a number of different approaches may be taken to establish the connection. In one approach, termed "Discovery" by Sytek Inc., the makers of the PC Network, the internetworking device receives the "name query packet" from John and rebroadcasts it onto Mary's network. The device continues to forward packets from Mary to John and from John to Mary (Fig. 2b). The process is transparent to John and Mary, who proceed as if they were on the same network.

Today, there are no MS-DOS-compatible devices that use "Discovery." The Discovery protocols are proprietary to Sytek (Mountain View, Calif.), although the company has announced its intention of making these protocols available on a leased basis. Thus, network manufacturers will find it relatively easy to become compatible at the MS-DOS, Redirector, file server, and Netbios levels, because all these items can be currently purchased "off the shelf" (the first two from Microsoft, the third from Microsoft or Novell, and Netbios emulation from Novell). Still, it remains practically impossible to become compatible with the PC Network at the packet level, which is what would be required to integrate with Discovery.

Even if the Discovery protocols become available at a reasonable price, they will probably be used only for linking IBM PC Networks or networks based on the same protocols (such as Sytek's LocalNet). The Discovery method assumes that: (1) the internetworking device can broadcast a packet on Mary's network, and (2) Mary can respond to John's "call" before John times out. These are not safe assumptions except when two IBM PC Networks are communicating (or an IBM PC Network and a network with very similar protocols). One reason for this limitation is that some networks do not support the broadcast mode of transmission; Corvus' Omninet is a prominent example. (A broadcast facility is, however, a part of the Netbios standard and will probably be incorporated in most LANs in the future.) Also, on the PC Network, timeouts and retries for the "call" are fixed and cannot be changed by the user; it is therefore likely that the PC Network timeout period and/or retry count will be inappropriate for some networks.

Nevertheless, internetworking is still possible with the PC Network. Novell, for example, uses a "clearinghouse" approach. In this scheme, an internet "name server," known to all stations, maintains a name-to-internet address map for every name on the internet. The name server handles the packet exchanges for setting up a connection. Since every station knows the address of the name server, broadcasts are not required. Furthermore, all names can be verified with equal speed, without reference to the performance of the network where the name is in use; the performance

3. PC Network. *When an application needs an operating system service, an INT 21h interrupt is issued to the operating system. If a network resource is needed, the* *Redirector routes the request to the proper place. The* SHARE *and PSPrint utilities are also available to route network requests correctly from the file server.*

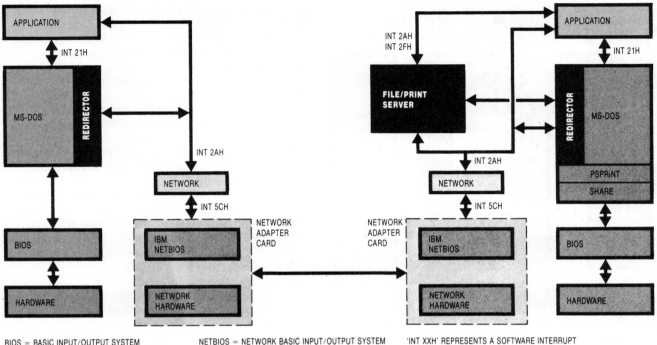

BIOS = BASIC INPUT/OUTPUT SYSTEM
MS-DOS = MICROSOFT DISK OPERATING SYSTEM

NETBIOS = NETWORK BASIC INPUT/OUTPUT SYSTEM
PSPRINT = PRINT SPOOL PRINT

'INT XXH' REPRESENTS A SOFTWARE INTERRUPT

of Mary's network does not affect how quickly John receives the "name query response packet," because John actually receives it from the name server on his own network. Furthermore, the name server, in setting up the connection with Mary, is free to use any appropriate protocol; it does not have to use PC Network-type packets.

The clearinghouse approach becomes less efficient as the number of names in use rises, while Discovery is equally efficient with any number of names. In selecting the Discovery approach, IBM may have been looking forward to the day when the PC Network would be used in very large networks that might do major internetworking. In such a situation, all the networks involved might have to be standardized at the MS-DOS, Redirector, Netbios, and packet levels.

How the pieces fit

Figure 3 shows how the various elements of the MS-DOS 3.1 standard work together on the PC Network. On the left is a workstation. On the right is a file/print server, which can also be used as a workstation. At the workstation, an application will normally talk to MS-DOS, which will, in turn, talk either to the local computer hardware through the BIOS (Basic Input/Output System) or to the network through the Redirector. At the server, an application has three additional options: talking directly to the file server, talking to the file server through MS-DOS and the Redirector, and going through the SHARE or PSPrint programs to reach BIOS and the local computer hardware. (PSP, the "Print

Spool Print" program, is the basis for printer sharing on the PC Network, just as SHARE is the basis for disk sharing.) Architectures incorporating the MS-NET file server are similar, except that no application can run at the MS-NET file server, which must be dedicated to printing and managing files.

There are other ways to put the pieces together. Figure 4, for example, shows how Novell uses a proprietary "Interface Shell" as a Redirector. At a workstation, the Interface Shell routes requests either to MS-DOS or to the network. At a server, requests are routed either to MS-DOS (for local workstation functions) or to the file/print server, which can then communicate with the network. The Interface Shell has direct access to network resources, without the intervention of MS-DOS. The elimination of MS-DOS as a middleman significantly increases efficiency.

LAN vendors have essentially three choices in constructing a standard network operating system:

1. They can use both MS-DOS 3.1 and the Redirector and create the rest of the network operating system themselves, either from scratch or by adapting present software. This approach requires a large investment of expensive programming resources, but some vendors may be pursuing it nonetheless. Torus is already pursuing this course, and 3Com may do so.

2. They can use MS-DOS 3.1, the MS-NET file server, and the MS-NET Redirector. MS-NET supports a somewhat limited number of commands and functions, so to this basic package vendors will be likely to add features that will distinguish them from other LANs follow-

71

4. No middleman. *In Novell's implementation, an interface shell at each workstation serves as the Redirector, routing requests to MS-DOS or to remote servers.*

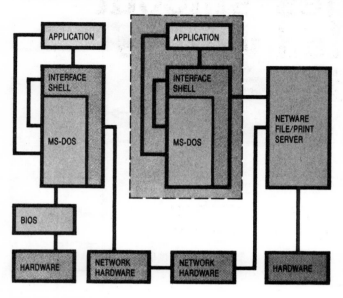

BIOS = BASIC INPUT/OUTPUT SYSTEM
MS-DOS = MICROSOFT DISK OPERATING SYSTEM

ing the same strategy. Perhaps the biggest weakness of such configurations is the dedicated MS-NET file server. Most LANs are small (a dozen stations or less), and dedicating a station to act as a file server raises the cost per connection significantly. Another weakness of MS-NET is in recovering from "orphan locks" that occur when a station locks a record and then, because of some type of malfunction (perhaps as simple as the station's cord getting unplugged), fails to unlock the record. On MS-NET, the malfunctioning station itself must unlock the record. Obviously, it would be preferable for the server to be able to clear the orphan lock, too, as is the case on IBM's and Novell's networks. However, it must be remembered that NOSs based on MS-NET have not yet appeared on the retail market, so no definitive statements can be made about their performance.

3. They can use MS-DOS 3.1 and the Novell Interface Shell and file server. Such a configuration will support concurrent workstation/server operation and recovery from orphan locks by the server. It will allow a greater number of commands and functions than either the PC Network or MS-NET. ∎

Mike Hurwicz has been a technical documentation liaison and consultant at Telco Research Inc. for one and a half years.

John H. Hart, Vitalink Communications Corp., Mountain View, Calif.

'Bridges' smooth troubled waters for wide-area networking

Data-link bridges are just hitting the market, but their impact on many transmission schemes could be long-standing.

Data-link-layer bridges need not know how an entire network configuration works in order to operate effectively. Instead, a well-designed bridge only needs to be able to interface with the network to which it directly connects. Ethernet or 802.3 local networks, for example, are currently being installed in droves, with a variety of office automation and data communications products attached. Once installed, many of these local networks become the data highway for interconnecting multiple products that use various network architectures. After installing one local network, many organizations go on to install others in different locations. In many cases, the need to link these intrabuilding local networks is, at first, ignored. Later, however, as communications managers begin to look at their options, they discover that the simple, multiple-purpose data highway environment that they assumed had existed within the building has disappeared.

Many traditional local network interconnection techniques support a single architecture and consequently a subset of the current or potential local network population. Also, since processes in the local network stations must assist in the interconnection, costly software upgrades may be required, and complex multivendor compatibility problems can occur. Which architecture to interconnect becomes an issue: Redundant configurations for the different internet protocols may be required, and some local network stations may not support an internet implementation at all.

In contrast, what are known as extended local networks, such as Vitalink's Translan, provide a simple and elegant local network interconnect solution that transparently extends the public data highway paradigm to local network interconnection. From the perspective of all interconnected local network stations,

such a wide-area interconnection scheme turns an arbitrary number of Ethernet or 802.3 local networks into a single network.

Ways and means
Figure 1 illustrates four Ethernet or 802.3 local networks that are bridged together across a satellite backbone network. The backbone operates in a fully connected broadcast mode: Any frame transmitted by one bridge is received by all others. Also, each bridge can be configured to transmit at the same or different speeds.

Thus configured, a fully connected satellite network is similar to an Ethernet or 802.3 local network. Both use broadcast transmission media, support a promiscuous (receive all frames) reception mode, and have low bit error rates.

Both Ethernet and 802.3 use an unacknowledged datagram protocol. Across the satellite backbone, the forwarded Ethernet/802.3 frames are simply enveloped inside the high-level data link control frame structure. That is, a single wide-area network bridge can concurrently relay messages between a number of different networks. For brevity, however, the following discussion configures each bridge with only two networks.

Tracking packets
When bridge 1 (designated B1 in Fig. 1) is powered on, it enters into listen-only mode. It remains in that mode for 10 to 60 seconds and operates in what is called a "promiscuous" reception mode relative to local network I and the satellite backbone. As a result, it receives all frames transmitted by local network stations A-C or bridges 2-4. No frames are relayed by B1 during listen-only mode.

73

1. Broadcast backbone. *Four Ethernet or 802.3 networks are bridged across a satellite backbone network. Frames transmitted by one bridge are received by all* *others. The backbone is, in fact, similar to Ethernet in that it is a broadcast medium, supports a "receive all" transmission mode, and has low bit error rates.*

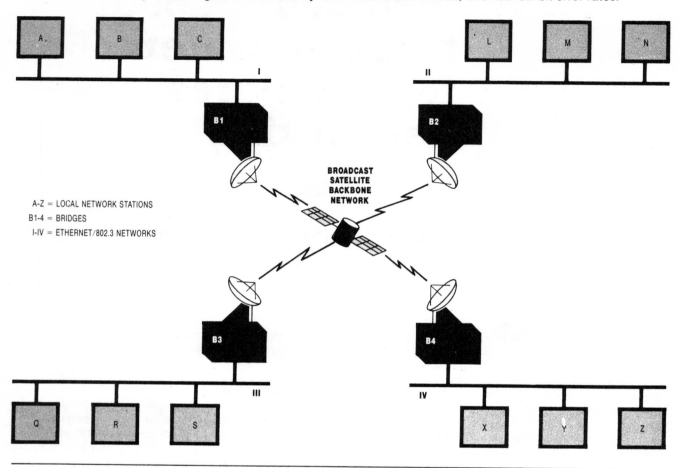

A-Z = LOCAL NETWORK STATIONS
B1-4 = BRIDGES
I-IV = ETHERNET/802.3 NETWORKS

During listen-only mode, B1 automatically creates a local database, termed the forward data store. A forward data-store entry is created from each frame received with a unique source address value. The entry contains the address and a local variable that identifies the source of the frame (local network I or satellite backbone). A bridge such as this can support a forward data store of up to 8,000 entries.

The following assumptions are made about the current activity within the Figure 1 configuration. Stations A and B, M and N, Q and R, and X and Y communicate only on local networks I, II, III, and IV, respectively. Stations N, S, R, and Z communicate with each other across the satellite backbone. Station C is turned off. As a result, the initial B1 forward data store contains the following entries:

Entry 1—address=A, source=LN-I
Entry 2—address=B, source=LN-I
Entry 3—address=N, source=satellite backbone
Entry 4—address=S, source=satellite backbone
Entry 5—address=R, source=satellite backbone
Entry 6—address=Z, source=satellite backbone

The entry source values of local network I or the

satellite backbone are locally assigned within B1. They are not globally administered or used as a global identifier between bridges.

After the listen-only time period, the bridge enters the forwarding mode. In this mode, the main foreground activity involves determining whether to discard or relay frames, while in the background the bridge continues maintaining the forward data store, based on source address.

Relaying rules
When a bridge receives a single Ethernet/802.3 destination frame, it creates a hash or lookup algorithm based on the address bits most likely to change. The hash is used to quickly locate a matching forward data-store entry. If the matching entry's source value identifies the frame's source network, the frame is discarded. Otherwise, the frame is relayed to the identified network. If no matching entry is located, the frame is relayed to all networks other than the source.

Since multicast or broadcast address values never appear as source addresses, forward data-store entries are not automatically created. As a result, multicast and broadcast frames are relayed like single-destination frames with no matching entries. However, this can be changed by configuring broadcast and multicast entries into the bridges. When this is done, multicast and broadcast destination frames are selectively filtered in the same way as single-destination frames.

Like routers, bridges store and forward frames. This means that routers, unlike repeaters, are able to selectively filter and discard frames addressed to local stations. Bridges keep local traffic on one local network from interfering with local traffic on the other local networks. As a result, bridge-to-bridge links can operate at less than local network speeds. In fact, in almost all configurations the same link speeds used to interconnect routers can be used to interconnect bridges.

Also, as with routers, the maximum number of stations that can be effectively serviced by a single local network is not a limiting factor. The stations can be spread among multiple bridged local networks. Since bridges operate at a lower layer than routers, they have less processing overhead and are capable of processing and relaying frames at higher rates.

The frames
Once in forward mode, B1 (Fig. 1) begins relaying and filtering frames as follows:

■ Frames received from local network I destined for A or B are not relayed to the satellite network.
■ Frames received from the satellite network destined for N, S, R, or Z are not relayed to local network I.
■ Frames destined for M, N, Q, X, and Y are not received on the satellite network because they are filtered locally by the associated bridge. These stations are not communicating with remote local network stations.
■ Frames received from local network I destined for L-Z are relayed to the satellite network.
■ Frames received from the satellite network destined for A or B are relayed to local network I.

In the forwarding mode, the bridges quickly learn the location of new local network stations. When station C is initialized, for example, it generates an initial multicast frame containing a "Hello" or "Help" message. This is normal behavior for many newly initialized local network stations. Bridge 1 relays the frame from local network I to the satellite backbone and creates the following forward data-store entry:

Entry—address=C, source=LN-I

Bridges 2-4 receive the "Hello" or "Help" message by all addressed local network stations and forward it to the respective local networks. Also, bridges 2-4 learn the relative location of station C as source=satellite backbone and appropriately filter and relay frames destined to it. If a bridge does not receive a frame containing a particular destination or source address value for about 15 minutes, the associated forward data-store entry is considered stale. Stale entries are automatically deleted. If station A in Figure 1 moves to local network II, the bridges forget that station's association with local network I—independently of any action by station A.

If station A—in less than 15 minutes—moves and generates, say, a "Hello" or "Help" multicast frame on local network II, the B1 and B2 entries change as follows:

B1 entry—address=A,
    source=satellite backbone (was LN-I)
B2 entry—address=A,
    source=LN-II (was satellite backbone)

The source value in the B3 and B4 entries remains satellite backbone. Hence, relative to B3 and B4, station A did not change position.

Experience has shown that the "no matching entry" case for single-destination frames is rare. When it

2. Room to grow. *Configurations can easily be expanded. The addition of bridge B6 results in B1-4 learning about more stations. For example, station D sends a* frame to Z, B5 *learns that station D's source address is the terrestrial link. However, B4 thinks D is located on local network IV; B5 appears as a network station.*

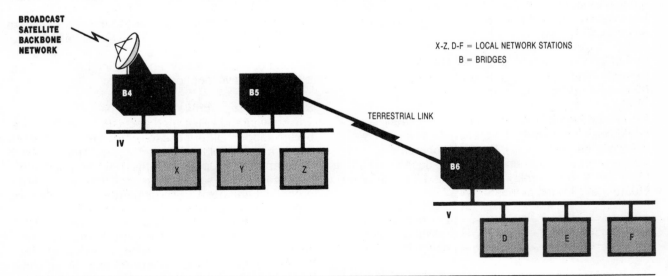

3. Two bridges. *Either broadcast or point-to-point links can be used to connect local networks. In both configurations, B1 and B2 are connected to a local network.*

When using a broadcast medium, B1 and B2 relay frames that are destined to remote local network stations onto a simplex broadcast channel.

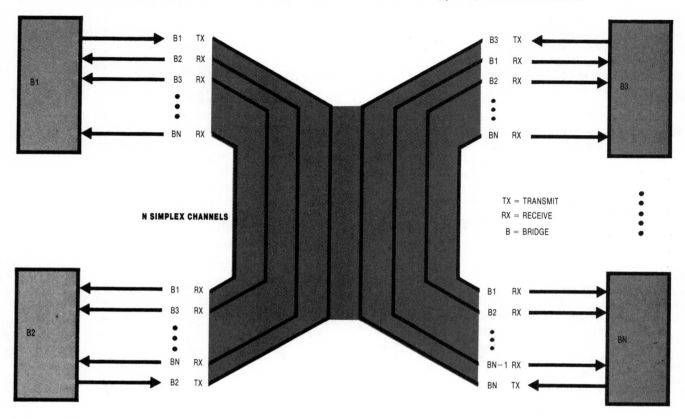

occurs, it is usually for one frame and never results in a bridge forwarding error. The frames always reach the addressed destination.

Network growth
The original configuration can be expanded, as illustrated in Figure 2. Through the addition of B6, it is possible for B1-4 to gain information about a greater number of stations. If, for example, station D generates a single-destination frame to station Z, the following entries are created:

B6 entry—address=D, source=LN-V
B5 entry—address=D, source=terrestrial link
B4 entry—address=D, source=LN-IV

Since B4 does not relay the frame to the satellite backbone (the B4 entry for station Z has a source value of local network IV), B1-3 do not create entries. Subsequently, if D generates a single-destination frame to station A, B4 will relay the frame and B1-3 will then create the following entries:

B3 entry—address=D, source=satellite backbone
B2 entry—address=D, source=satellite backbone
B1 entry—address=D, source=satellite backbone

If station E initializes and generates a "Hello" multicast

frame, B1-6 create the following entries:

B6 entry—address=E, source=LN-V
B5 entry—address=E, source=terrestrial link
B4 entry—address=E, source=LN-IV
B3 entry—address=E, source=satellite backbone
B2 entry—address=E, source=satellite backbone
B1 entry—address=E, source=satellite backbone

The bridges automatically adapt to the new configuration. The addition of B5 and B6, a terrestrial link, and local network V requires no configuration changes to existing bridges. The new and existing bridges simply learn the relative location of new stations.

Supported topologies
The configuration illustrated above indicates that the bridge supports interfaces to both a broadcast satellite network and a point-to-point data link. The network is also capable of supporting other point-to-point and broadcast media such as terrestrial microwave. Both broadcast and point-to-point interconnect media are supported by the network in a number of ways.

Two bridges can be interconnected using either a broadcast or a point-to-point interconnection. A broadcast and point-to-point configuration is illustrated in Figure 3. In both configurations, B1 and B2 are connected to a local network.

Layered devices

The figure illustrates a taxonomy for describing a local network interconnection. This taxonomy associates a local network interconnection device with an ISO reference model layer. A device is associated with the layer in which it relays information from one network to another. The term network in this context ranges from local network segments, satellite links, and terrestrial lines in the lower layers to network architectures (Decnet or SNA, for example) in the higher layers.

In this taxonomy it is important to note that the layer performing the relay does not use information from the higher layers. In fact, differing higher-layer protocols can concurrently use the same lower-layer relay. Generally, the higher the relay layer, the more specialized are the products and protocols serviced by the relay. Overhead and complexity also increase as the layer level increases.

The hardware devices of direct interest to network interconnectivity are repeaters, bridges, and routers, and they correspond to network layers 1 through 3, respectively.

Repeaters

These devices relay physical-layer protocol data and control signals (such as collision detection). They operate at the local network speed and add only a small amount of transmission delay (typically less than 1 microsecond).

Repeaters extend local network configurations by connecting channel segments directly or across an internal point-to-point link. In general, repeaters are transparent to local network station protocols. As general devices for interconnecting multiple local networks, repeaters are severely limited. The length of a single local network is limited by physical-layer constraints such as maximum round-trip propagation delay. This limits local network repeatered expansion to a few kilometers. The maximum number of stations that can be effectively serviced by a single local network is another limiting factor.

Since repeaters relay bits, they are unable to selectively filter data link frames. Consequently, local network expansion is restricted by maximum local network capacity. Another consequence of the absence of filtering is that links used by repeaters to tie two segments together must operate at local network speeds.

Routers

When using these traditional local network interconnect devices, local network stations must be able to distinguish between communications with a station on the same local network and a remote local network. Remote data communications links require local network stations to transmit and receive data link frames to and from a router on the same local network station.

The frames contain internetwork protocol data units (packets) created by the local network stations. Routers use the internetwork protocol control information in the packets and a local configuration topology table to determine how to relay a packet between the local network and other networks. When compared with repeaters, routers are not transparent to local network station protocols. They only work with local network stations having a compatible internetwork layer. Operating as a store-and-forward packet relay, routers add significant transmission delays compared with repeaters.

Since local network stations perform the packet filtering function for a router (by only sending it packets destined for a remote local network), the router-to-router links do not need to operate at local network speeds. Typical link speeds range from 9.6 kbit/s to 56 kbit/s. Also, the maximum number of network stations that can be effectively serviced by a single local network is no longer a limiting factor. These stations can be spread among multiple interconnected local networks.

Bridges

These devices interconnect local networks using the same media as routers but operate totally within the data link layer. Thus, local networks connected by bridges logically appear to the local network stations as a single local network.

Local network stations simply address data link frames to other stations as if they were on the same local network. Broadcast and multicast destination frames are handled properly. They are received by the addressed group of stations regardless of location. Local network stations do not address frames to bridges as they must with routers.

The frame check sequence (FCS) value created by the source system is delivered to the destination station. Bridged local networks have the same level of protection against corrupted data as is present on a single local network. With routers, the original FCS is removed by the first router and recreated by the last. Bridges are capable of effectively using high bandwidth links (1 to 10 Mbit/s) between local networks.

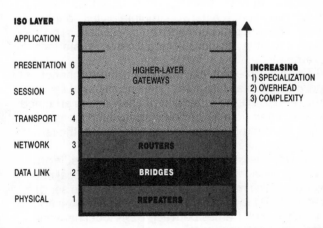

When using a broadcast medium, B1 or B2 relays frames destined to remote local network stations onto a simplex broadcast channel. Each receives the other bridges' transmit channel. When using the point-to-point medium, B1 and B2 each transmit on one side of the duplex data link and receive from the other.

Relative to both the broadcast and point-to-point configurations, frames transmitted by one bridge are almost always relayed and not filtered by the other. This occurs because each bridge normally filters frames received from its local network that are destined for local stations. As a result, only frames destined for stations on the other local network are transmitted.

Typically, a point-to-point medium (terrestrial line) provides the same transmit rate in both directions. In contrast, the concept of simplex broadcast channels encourages the use of different transmit rates to accommodate asymmetric data transmission requirements economically. For example, if most of the traffic consists of local network I stations transferring files to local network II stations, simplex broadcast channel support allows the transmit rate of the bridge attached to local network I to be much higher than that of a terrestrial link.

Star topology

The network can interconnect more than two bridges using a star topology. The medium used to interconnect the star can be broadcast or point to point. In both cases, the network automatically relays and filters frames as appropriate. Support of broadcast and point-to-point media is summarized below using the configurations shown in Figure 2. In both of the configurations, B1 through BN are each connected to a local network.

In broadcast star topology each Vitalink bridge has a simplex transmit channel. B1's usual format simplex channel is received by all remote bridges. Each remote bridge's transmit channel is only received by B1. This allows numerous remote local network stations to statistically share a high-speed B1 transmit channel. The B2-N transmit channels can be low speed in comparison.

In configurations where a large percentage of the data is transferred from a central site to remote locations, the broadcast star topology is particularly effective. In addition, the network maintains full connectivity (local network stations mediated by B2 can send frames to both B1 and B3-N local network stations, for example).

The point-to-point star topology is interconnected by individual duplex data links. One end of each link is attached to B1; the other end of each link is attached to a remote bridge. Each link can have a different transmit rate; but transmit rates for B1 and the remote bridge are always equal for a given line.

As with the broadcast star topology, the point-to-point network maintains full connectivity. Local network stations mediated by bridges B2-N can send frames to B1 local network stations and B1 will appropriately switch frames between B2-N local network stations. A fully connected topology is characterized by

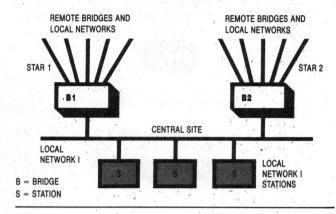

4. Star topologies. *Star 1 and Star 2 can be either broadcast or point-to-point configurations. Both B1 and B2 think they are relaying and filtering for network I.*

each bridge being directly connected to all other bridges.

Vitalink's Translan uses simplex channels to support a fully connected topology (Fig. 3). Each bridge has a transmit channel that is received by all other bridges. Thus, to fully connect the set of N local networks using a broadcast topology requires N simplex broadcast links. To fully connect a set of N local networks using a point-to-point medium requires N (N-1)/2 links. If N equals 3, 4, 8, or 16, the number of links equals 3, 6, 28, or 120, respectively. The number of broadcast simplex links required for the same N values is 3, 4, 8, or 16, respectively.

A fully connected broadcast topology is chosen over a star topology (see "Layered devices") when the information flow between the remote sites is balanced, not predominantly to and from a single central site. This does not imply that the transmit rate of each bridge must be the same. In fact, in a fully connected topology the network allows each bridge to have the same or a different rate.

The only restriction when mixing broadcast and point-to-point topologies is that the topologies cannot be configured together in such a way as to form a loop.

Figure 4 illustrates a configuration containing two star topologies connected to a local network in the central site. The star topologies and the local network are labeled in Figure 4 for the convenience of this discussion. There are no corresponding global identifiers.

The topology of Star 1 and Star 2 can be either broadcast or point to point, or one broadcast and one point to point. Each of the remote sites has a local network and a bridge and is one hop away from the central site and two hops away from any of the other remote sites.

As discussed earlier, a frame transmitted between remote sites on the same star is relayed by the associated central site bridge. The frame is not transferred to local network I. A frame transferred between a Star 1 remote site and a Star 2 remote site is relayed between B1 and B2 across local network I. Normally, relaying a frame across local network I will cause the

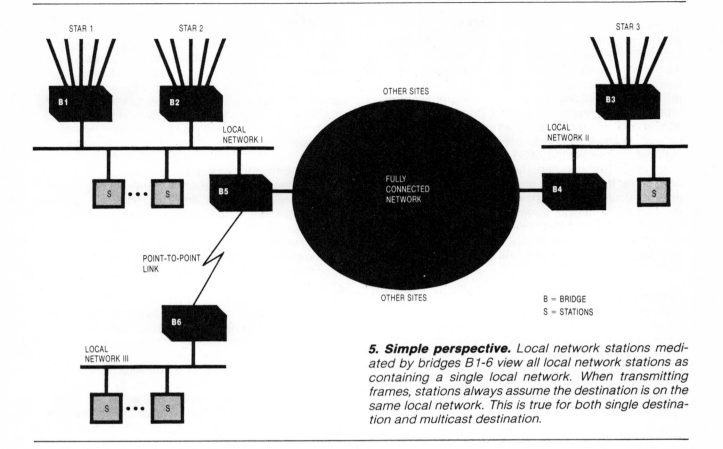

STAR 1

STAR 2

STAR 3

OTHER SITES

B1

B2

B3

LOCAL
NETWORK I

LOCAL
NETWORK II

FULLY
CONNECTED
NETWORK

S • • • S

B5

B4

S

POINT-TO-POINT
LINK

OTHER SITES

B = BRIDGE
S = STATIONS

B6

LOCAL
NETWORK III

S • • • S

5. Simple perspective. *Local network stations mediated by bridges B1-6 view all local network stations as containing a single local network. When transmitting frames, stations always assume the destination is on the same local network. This is true for both single destination and multicast destination.*

addition of only a few more milliseconds.

It is interesting to note the extent to which each bridge "understands" the network (Fig. 4). Both B1 and B2 think they are relaying and filtering for local network I and functioning as the center of Star 1 and Star 2, respectively. Remote bridges for Star 1 and Star 2 in turn think that they are relaying and filtering for their local network and are functioning as a remote

bridge in a single star. It is this characteristic that allows configurations to be so easily expanded. For example, the Figure 4 configuration can be expanded as illustrated in Figure 5. In the expanded configuration, the following occurs:
■ The perspective of all Star 1 and Star 2 bridges does not change.
■ The B3 and the Star 3 remote bridges have the same

6. Transparent exchanges. *Network management communications to and from bridges are able to exploit the simplicity of the bridge perspectives. When a frame*

having the local bridge destination address is received, it is passed along to the local bridge management process and is not relayed.

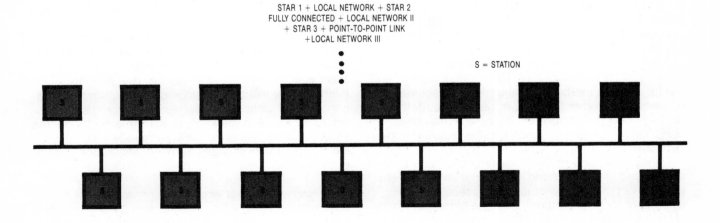

STAR 1 + LOCAL NETWORK + STAR 2
FULLY CONNECTED + LOCAL NETWORK II
+ STAR 3 + POINT-TO-POINT LINK
+LOCAL NETWORK III

S = STATION

relative perspective as either of the respective Star 1 and Star 2 bridges.

■ B4 is only aware of relaying and filtering for local network II and the fully connected broadcast network.

■ B5 is only aware of relaying and filtering for local network I, the fully connected broadcast network, and the point-to-point link. B5 is another example of a Vitalink bridge interfacing to more than two networks.

■ B6 is only aware of relaying and filtering for local network III and the point-to-point data link.

While the perspective of B1-6 in the Figure 5 configuration is greatly simplified, the local network stations have by far the simplest perspective (Fig. 6). The network configuration is viewed by all local network stations as containing a single local network. When transmitting frames, stations always assume the destination is on the same local network. This is true for both single-destination and multicast-destination frames.

Network management

Figure 6 illustrates the transparency of the network. However, providing this transparency elevates the need for distributed network management visibility and control. Fortunately, network management communications to and from bridges can exploit the simplicity of the single local network perspective. Each bridge automatically creates the following permanent forward data-store entry.

Entry—address=local bridge, source=self

When a frame with the local bridge destination address is received, it is passed to the local bridge management process and is not relayed. Entries are also created for certain bridge-multicast address values.

Entry—address=bridge-multicast-1, source=self
Entry—address=bridge-multicast-2, source=self

When a frame with a bridge-multicast destination address is received, it is copied for the local bridge management process and then relayed. To communicate with a bridge anywhere in the configuration, a local network station only needs to generate a frame with single bridge destination or multicast destination address. The frame will be received and processed by the Vitalink bridge(s) with a matching entry.

A bridge management process generates single destination and multicast frames. Except during listen-only mode, a bridge treats the local bridge management process like another network. A frame generated by the local bridge management process is relayed or filtered in the same manner as a frame received from a network.

During listen-only mode, bridge management frames are relayed to and from the local bridge management process or program. All other frames received during listen-only mode are filtered. One use of this capability is for loop detection. During listen-only mode a bridge transmits loop-detection multicast frames. If a loop-detection frame is received with a source address equal to the local-bridge address, the bridge does not enter forwarding mode. If it did, a loop would be created.

Each bridge maintains an extensive set of statistical and local configuration information. The local bridge management process provides an information access service. The service supports information retrieval and on-line reconfiguration. This service can be accessed by both network operators and peer management processes.

Network communications

Network operators can access a Vitalink bridge from one or more remote locations using terminals attached to network management stations. The management station communications with a bridge uses a virtual terminal protocol. An operator can establish up to 8 concurrent connections to different bridges from the same terminal. This allows an operator to view the perspective of several bridges concurrently. Optionally, an operator can access a bridge through its local console. The operator interfaces from the console and terminal are the same. Multiple bridge consoles and terminals (or printers) can be configured to receive alarms and statistical messages.

A Vitalink bridge supports a simple request/response protocol that is layered directly on top of either Ethernet or 802.3. When a request is received within an Ethernet or 802.3 frame, a bridge transmits the associated response using the same type of frame. The destination address in the response frame equals the source address value received in the request frame.

This request/response protocol provides the mechanism through which both Ethernet and 802.3 stations can communicate with a bridge. The protocol provides access to essentially the same information that is available to a network operator. In order to work properly, Ethernet and 802.3 bridges expect certain operating parameters and formats from a local network. Vitalink's Translan, for example, expects the following:

■ A promiscuous reception mode is supported.
■ All frames sent and received from a local network contain a 48-bit destination and 48-bit source address.
■ Frames contain a 32-bit frame check sequence (FCS) and can be between 64 and 1,518 octets (8-bit bytes) in length.

Local networks that are in compliance with these assumptions are required to support non-Ethernet local networks. The implementation difficulty ranges from no effort at all to developing an entirely new network interface. For example, changing the medium to broadband or fiber optics only requires a different transceiver. However, depending on the implementation, the effort required to change network speeds from 10 Mbit/s to 1 Mbit/s ranges from a configuration change to developing a new local network interface. ■

John Hart is assistant vice president for network architecture at Vitalink Communications Corp. He has a B. S. in mathematics from the University of Georgia in Athens.

Charles Solomon, Hewlett-Packard Co., Fort Collins, Colo.

Exploring the problems of internetworking

Network users not only ask that their incompatible computers talk over the same network, they want their varied networks to communicate as well.

Today's data communications manager faces a hodgepodge of networking technologies. Largely based on topology requirements, degree of interconnection desired, and application needs, it is small wonder that there is little standardization for these varied networking schemes. Predictably, however, demand for interconnectivity is growing in direct proportion to the number of user installations.

What is more, managers who try to simplify the problem by implementing only individual homogeneous networks are still finding the task of interconnecting networks somewhat more than trivial. Basically, the problems are similar to those faced by implementers of isolated networks; but when viewed at the internetworking level they become much more complex. The issues are:

■ The different levels of network interconnection and the mechanisms used to accomplish them.
■ Flow control across a collection of interconnected networks.
■ Routing strategies appropriate for an internetwork environment.
■ Security.
■ Addressing and naming.
■ Fault detection and isolation.

The techniques for network interconnection can be classified according to how the functions supported by the interconnection map into the layers of the OSI (Open Systems Interconnection) model. For this article, the internet (a series of connected subnetworks that make up a larger network) layer is assumed to contain the upper two sublayers of OSI's network level three: the subnet dependent convergence functions (SNDFC) and the subnet independent convergence functions (SNICF).

Interconnection of networks at the data-link level is predicated on a uniform address space across all networks involved. This usually requires that the data-link protocols are the same. Accordingly, data-link interconnections operate at a level higher than that of the relay, which is merely used to extend the reach of a particular medium.

The term "bridge" is used to indicate this level of interconnection. It is a routing function that is merged with the data-link protocol in the node interconnecting two or more networks. A bridge does not require a peer layer at the source and destination nodes because it does not function at a protocol layer. The bridge software in the gateway simply knows enough about the data-link protocol to be able to perform some minor routing functions based on its knowledge of which network provides access to which address groups (Fig. 1).

A typical bridge application is the interconnection of bus media found in local networks. These buses are connected into treelike structures via the bridges (DATA COMMUNICATIONS, " 'Bridges' smooth troubled waters for wide-area networking," March, p. 209). The address space is partitioned between the participating media—with each bridge having its individually tailored routing tables. It is also possible to limit the routing function to a set of filters that prevent packets with certain addresses from being propagated on certain links. The main advantages of the bridge in comparison with the relay are:

■ The signal is regenerated at each node, whereas relays tend to propagate and increase signal attenuation. This results in increased reliability and a larger possible perimeter of the internet.
■ The bridge removes messages that are destined to go to other subnetworks—thus allowing more immediate access by local nodes.

1. Bridges. *The bridge knows enough about the data-link protocol to do some minor routing based on which network gives access to which address groups.*

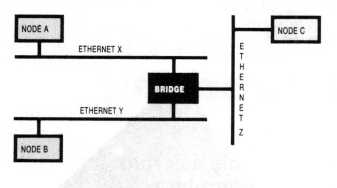

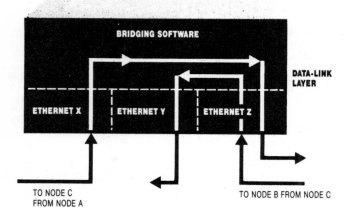

TO NODE C
FROM NODE A

TO NODE B FROM NODE C

In CSMA (carrier-sense multiple access) networking schemes, relays only increase the vulnerability period of all packets by increasing the propagation delay along the network.

Internetwork gateways

Nodes connected to more than one network that support internetwork traffic are called "gateways." Nodes that are directly connected to only one network and linked to nodes in other networks are called "gateway halves."

The problems associated with network interconnection at the gateway level are similar to those encountered in point-to-point networks. In fact, the internet model can be viewed as a hierarchical extension from the point-to-point network of nodes to a point-to-point interconnection of networks. For this reason, the internet protocol is relegated to an upper sublayer of the OSI model called the internet, or "3i," layer. (The "3" represents the third level of the OSI model; the "i" represents the internet layer.) Protocols supporting the interconnection of nodes in point-to-point subnetworks are relegated to the "3s" layer (the "s" equals subnet). The CCITT (International Telegraph and Telephone Consultative Committee) X.25 standard poses its own set of problems when attempts are made to map X.25 into this sublayered OSI scheme, since X.25

can either be used as a 3s protocol or viewed as a fully interconnected network.

The goal of providing 3i interconnection is to allow individual networks to use diverse lower-level protocols and, at the same time, provide access to resources in other networks with different protocols. Typically, this level of interconnection uses a specific protocol that has its own address domain and is recognized across the entire internetwork. Thus, each internetwork node must implement this protocol and have a unique address from a common internetwork address domain. This protocol should provide a subset of services that are supported by all intervening networks. Where special network-dependent services are presented by the internet protocol, mechanisms need to be provided that allow upper network levels to determine whether the target network can support such services (internet broadcast messages, for example).

Other questions

Issues also arise when determining whether intermediate networks are capable of supporting those services. However, the one service required of internet protocols is internetwork routing. That is, the protocol must handle the routing from a source node to the nearest gateway, from that gateway through other gateways and on to the gateway that is connected to the destination network — and then from the final gateway to the internetwork destination.

The way this works is that the gateway receives packets transmitted across one network using a particular set of protocols. The gateway resubmits the internet packet to the "next-hop" network for encapsulation in its particular set of protocol headers. In this fashion an internet packet is passed from gateway to gateway across different networks, until a gateway finally recognizes the destination network number of the internet packet as being a network to which it is directly attached. At this point, the appropriate gateway makes use of specific information (which it then retains for all of its directly connected networks) in order to provide a path to the final destination in the attached network.

The main advantage of the gateway over the bridge is that it can support the interconnection of networks that differ in their data-link layers. For example, point-to-point networks can be interconnected with bus-based local networks and with broadcast networks. It must be noted, however, that only the intersection of the services provided in the interconnected networks can be supported transparently. A broadcast-based bulletin-board service, for example, might have trouble making its service available on some point-to-point networks (Fig. 2).

Due to the lack of foresight and experience in network interconnection, many attempts at network interconnection occur at this level. Internetworking at the application layer must be resorted to whenever the incorporation of a global internet standard is not feasible. The main users of this technique are computer-based or electronic mail networks. Here the application uses globally administered client names to perform the required routing. It may also require the use of a presentation layer to convert character sets and formats whenever messages must be delivered into incompatible domains.

There are also approaches to network interconnection that do not subscribe to the conventional OSI approaches. That is, they can operate within the scope of the OSI model, but such interconnections may violate some of the straightforward notions about the layered network architecture.

Hybrids
Mutual encapsulation is a technique for using other networks as a "tunnel" for communicating with a peer node that lies on the other side of the incompatible network. The reason for this is that members of a particular internetwork community may be separated from each other by members of an incompatible internetwork domain. By encapsulating an internet packet of one type in the header of the intermediate domain, the intermediate network can be used to connect these otherwise partitioned networks.

For example, if a node on network A (Fig. 3) desires to communicate with a node on network C, that node encapsulates with a type X header and sends it to gateway G1. The gateway G1 must have implemented internet protocols X and Y and must also have routing tables that specify the type Y destination of gateway G2, YG2. When G1 receives the type X packet, it discovers that the next hop involves a "tunnel" through a type Y network. It then routes the packet through the type Y protocol; in the same gateway the original type X packet is additionally encapsulated with a type Y header that designates YG2 as the destination. When YG2 receives this packet, that gateway finds that the type Y header indicates that after disassembly, it should be sent to the type X protocol handler in the gateway for further processing. Once G2's type X internet protocol receives the packet, routing to its final destination is handled per the type X specifications. The term "mutual encapsulation" refers to a gateway's capability of encapsulating in either direction across incompatible network types.

Translating gateways are used in two circumstances. They are used either when one is operating with a very large installed customer base of incompatible internet architectures, or when the use of such an interconnection is great enough to warrant the development of gateways that are this specific.

The problem is that it is not always possible to guarantee that the protocols to be translated can be reasonably mapped into each other. For instance, file transfer protocol A may first prescribe the size of the file to be transferred, whereas protocol B may not commit the size of the file until the last packet has been transferred. This leaves the translating gateway with the burden of buffering the entire file when transfers occur from a B-type node to an A-type node. Further, while the transfer takes place to the A-type node, the sending B-type node may time out—assuming that the transfer failed. Nonetheless, application translation gateways do exist. These implementations pick and

choose the applications and domains within which the interconnection will work.

Moving from the lower to higher levels of interconnection, and then into the hybrid techniques, trade-offs are made in favor of simplicity over increased versatility. The appropriateness of a particular technique for the desired level of internetwork functionality must be considered.

A bridge, for example, is best suited to interconnecting a set of like networks that reside within the confines of a single administrative body and are limited to a small physical domain. In this kind of environment, no protocol translation needs to be performed, security concerns are minimal, and address management as it relates to implementing a rudimentary routing function between networks is feasible. The use of bridges at this level provides an effective way of expanding the capacity and physical reach of a facility's computer interconnection resources, while minimizing the performance costs associated with network interconnection at higher levels.

Gateways are useful where there is support across these networks to implement a common internet vehicle (like a protocol standard). This solution allows individual networks to tailor the lower-level protocols— from the 3s level on down—to their local requirements, while simultaneously providing access to resources available on other networks. Interconnection at this level can also provide a greater latitude in what the individual gateway routing policies might be; gateways may implement everything from static routing policies (which greatly simplify implementation) to dynamic policies, which can provide resiliency in the face of gateway or network failures. Additionally, gateways allow the administrative body of each network a certain amount of control over the access allowed from outside networks.

Interconnection at the application level can be done on an ad hoc basis between the networks and applications for which interconnection is desired. Even less standardization is required at the application level than

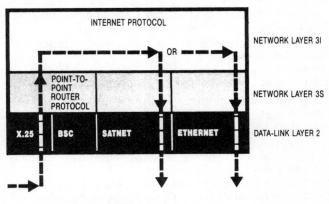

2. Bridge mix. *Bridges can be used to connect networks with differing data-link layers. Point-to-point networks can be linked with bus-based local networks.*

BSC = BINARY SYNCHRONOUS COMMUNICATIONS

3. Mutual encapsulation. *If network A desires to communicate with network C, A encapsulates its data with a type X header and sends it to gateway G1. G1 must* *have implemented both X and Y internet protocols and have the appropriate routing tables. G1 encapsulates the packet and tunnels it through to G2 on network C.*

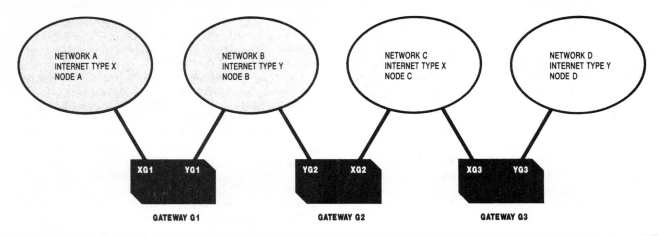

at lower levels of interconnection. Application implementations in the different networks may be uniform, allowing gateways to perform simple routing functions; or they may be disparate, thus forcing the gateway to perform application translation with its attendant liabilities.

Using a mutual encapsulation technique to interconnect networks is of value where two 3i protocol standards are in effect, and where their interconnection provides mutual benefit. In these situations the encapsulation strategy can become quite involved, since either each node on the interconnected networks must support both 3i protocols, or else the gateways must be sufficiently sophisticated to provide the address translation and mutual encapsulation to route packets across the disparate networks. Mutual encapsulation becomes impractical when there are more than two internet protocols.

Flow control
The object of internetwork flow control is to prevent the possibility of deadlock in the gateways and to provide graceful performance degradation when gateways are overloaded with internetwork traffic. The interpretation of what constitutes "graceful degradation" and what is a reasonable cost varies with the application using the internetwork. For instance, digitized voice does not work well when graceful degradation means graceful loss of throughput.

Another aspect of internetwork flow control is to minimize the effect of the longer propagation delay associated with internetwork traffic—as compared with that of local traffic. Much of the ability to adapt to the internetwork propagation delay depends on the OSI level 4 transport used. Nevertheless, the internet protocol should be able to convey a lot of useful information to assist the transport in this task.

Whether an internetwork service should be datagram or virtual-circuit oriented is controversial. The proponents of these two methods appear to be split along the Atlantic Ocean, with the ARPA (Advanced Re-

search Projects Agency) and Xerox community staunchly in favor of the datagram approaches designed into their networks, and the European-based CCITT (International Telegraph and Telephone Consultative Committee) propounding their X.75 internetwork virtual circuit. The latter operates on a large installed base of telephone equipment. If analyzed solely from the control aspect of flow problems, the virtual circuit does provide a much simpler implementation of internetwork flow control. The mechanism works as follows.

A call-request is first placed on the line. As the packet is routed, each gateway that receives this packet allocates the maximum resources required to support the connection. (Other aspects of the call-setup process exist but are not relevant to this discussion.) If the call-request is successfully routed, then the caller can be assured of uniform service during the life of the connection. If the call-request encounters congestion, the original attempt is aborted, and the caller is given no service at all.

In the above mode, users need not fear that their connection will experience any performance degradation once the connection is established. Further, throughput on the connection is enhanced because no routing is required at the gateway—since the original call-request routing serves to prescribe the route for subsequent messages. The concern with the virtual circuit is that its resource allocation is static and always at a maximum. This can easily result in wasted bandwidth in the gateway. A more specific complaint about the X.75 internet standard is that it only concerns itself with the interconnection of X.25 networks. In addition, the X.75 virtual circuit is difficult to reroute in the face of node failure.

On the other hand, datagram-based internetworks provide a dynamic allocation of resources and, therefore, increase the use of the gateway bandwidth. Resiliency in the face of gateway failure is also easily managed. The trade-off for providing this increase in resource use and failure rerouting is that datagram implementations offer an unreliable grade of service. Datagram internet networks should make a best effort at delivery where lost packets result from problems inherent in the datagram approach—such as link failure and intermittent lack of resources at a gateway. Reliability is relegated to the transport layer's retransmit policy.

The disadvantage of the datagram approach is that requests for resources beyond a gateway's bandwidth are rerouted or rejected on a real-time basis. This causes general performance degradation, which users of the service must be prepared to work around. Also, in contrast to the virtual circuit approach, each datagram must be routed at each gateway. In this way, the datagram approach reduces internetwork throughput on an end-to-end basis.

Ross Callon of Bolt Beranek and Newman Inc. has developed a connection-oriented internet protocol that defines a middle ground in the datagram/virtual-circuit debate. Callon concludes that it makes little sense to provide all of the functionality traditionally associated with connection services at the internet level. In particular, 100 percent reliability does not seem achievable where the definition of the internet protocol is to connect diverse networks. Further, the functions of managing data loss, packet duplication, and resequencing do not belong in the internet layer on a hop-by-hop basis. On the contrary, these functions, Callon maintains, are a concern of the end-to-end transport protocol.

As the internetwork grows, so will the amount of header space required to contain the route, which at some point becomes counterproductive. The persistent need for internetwork routing and high throughput make a connection-oriented approach very attractive. Nevertheless, datagram services are still appropriate for some applications, such as broadcast and request-reply functions.

Callon's proposal, then, involves substituting existing internet layers with a protocol that supports both this less-than 100 percent connection service and the datagram service. The proposed internetwork header format is identical for both "grades" of service.

Packet breakdown

The issue of fragmentation and reassembly affects flow control in that it is an internetwork function that can result in deadlock. The need for fragmentation at the internet level is because many networks have maximum allowable packet-size constraints. Gateways must honor these contraints in order to pass traffic across such networks to remote gateways. In bus-based topologies, the internetwork layer is the only layer available to provide fragmentation into the data-link layer's maximum packet size.

Problems occur when a gateway implementation has multiple reassembly attempts in progress—none of which are complete—and lacks the memory to add any new fragments that might complete and release a particular packet. To minimize the probability of this occurring along the internetwork route, the ARPA Internet Protocol (IP) allows a gateway to fragment on

an as-needed basis. No reassembly occurs except in the destination node. To prevent deadlock on the destination node (which incidentally may also act as a gateway), a timer is set in each reassembly attempt. If the timer expires, the attempt is terminated and all of that attempted circuit's resources are made available for another circuit. The duration of the timer is usually set to some estimated maximum transmit time for traffic coming from the internetwork perimeter. The value of providing a more definitive or dynamic time-out interval based on statistical analyses of traffic patterns is questionable in a datagram-based gateway. The reason is that OSI level 4 protocols usually provide their own end-to-end flow control and retransmission adjustments.

Transmission speed

Early implementations of Arpanet flow control included a message type called the quench message, which is part of the Internet Control Message Protocol (ICMP). The original purpose of quench was that it be sent to the internetwork source to slow the source transmission frequency and decrease the message interval until either it received a quench message, or the destination returned to its normal speed.

There are several problems with the quench technique. When the internetwork experiences global congestion, the quench message becomes added flow to an already congested internetwork. Many cases of internetwork congestion tend to be transitory, and by the time the quench message is processed by the source the problem has cleared up. The quench message is only useful in limited situations. For instance, the message can be read by the previous gateway of an internetwork route to try alternate routes for traffic originated by a particular network.

Another use for quench is in the first-hop gateway, when a source in a higher-speed network (10-Mbit/s Ethernet, for example) requires a transition to a slower-speed wide-area network (WAN) in the gateway. The quench technique can then be used to slow the sending data rate of the transmission source to more closely match the WAN speed.

Many level 4 transport protocols involve an acknowledgment scheme indicating to a local node that a remote peer has reliably received a particular packet. The local node relies on a timer to prompt retransmission if an acknowledgment has not been received in time. For communications within a single network, this time may be as short as 1.5 milliseconds. However, in communications that span an internetwork, the timer setting must be long enough to account for a packet's round-trip time in all but the worst-possible route. This interval can be entire seconds. If the interval is underestimated, the result floods the network with unnecessary retransmission and possible unnecessary loss of the level 4 connection; if over estimated, the end-to-end connection can experience significant loss of throughput. Moreover, the consequences of inappropriate timer settings for round-trip delay can be amplified if higher protocol levels base their timers on those of a lower level.

In addition to providing a realistic retransmission interval, it is important that the level 4 transport, which uses the internet protocol, be adapted to the long propagation delays of the internetwork. For instance, a file transfer application that runs effectively in a local network may perform poorly when used over an internetwork if the transport is of a request-reply type (which allows only one outstanding request at a time). As the propagation delays become greater than the single-event processing time on the remote node, the greater the advantages are of using a transport protocol that supports a sliding time-window scheme.

Source and sink

In this type of transport, a data source can place a series of packets on the internetwork before having to wait for an acknowledgment from the data sink. The sink can then process a packet, acknowledge it, and be able to process another packet, without waiting for the last acknowledgment to travel to the source. The internet protocol's knowledge of the data source and sink can also be used by the upper-level transport to adjust its window to a size that helps maximize throughput.

The term "routing" in the internetwork environment is a multifaceted concept. One must choose a protocol stack (at least through to the internet level) that is compatible with the protocols available on the destination node in the remote network. The source node must have a way of obtaining the local network address of the first gateway. Thereafter, the gateway needs to be able to pass the packets along a reasonably direct route to the destination. This routing may also involve some resiliency when a previously viable route fails. Additional restrictions on the route may evolve, including security criteria to avoid "hostile" or nonsecure networks. And finally, a packet needs to "get off the internet" and be routed to its final destination when a gateway determines that a packet has arrived at its destination network.

Selecting the stack

A main objective of the OSI model is to present the (N1) level with a packet that has been encapsulated with protocol headers. Further the packet should be easily broken down and properly routed upward to the peer level. On machines and networks that may support limited or varied sets of protocol options at any layer, it is important for a sending host to know whether it shares any viable subset with the remote host.

For now, let us assume that an application in the sending host has access to a remote name-server that resides in the network of the target host. This name-server can provide a list of the protocol options available in the remote host, as well as the addresses associated with each protocol option. This kind of attributed information can be of value to intranetwork communications on the same network if it consists of heterogeneous protocol implementations. In the internetwork, however, the only information that is of any value is that giving options and addresses that are in a layer above or pertain to the internet layer. The

internet protocol must determine how to get to the target network by itself.

The first step of getting an internet packet from the source into the gateway network is somewhat different from the gateway routing mechanism. The first problem the source has to solve is how to locate the first-hop gateway. This information may be preprogrammed into the node; or the gateway may broadcast a message where the first respondent is used as the first hop.

Each gateway could also notify potential internet-work sources of appropriate gateways by sending its routing vector to the nodes. A gateway could do this at power-up and at periodic intervals thereafter. A new source node would have the ability to request such information from all of its adjacent gateways.

The advantages of sharing routing vectors are two-fold. Not only can the source determine which gateway to use, but the other information such as hop-count could provide as well a number on which to base timer calculations for more effective flow control. The disadvantage is that such information may be overkill for large networks. That is, not every node needs to know routes to every, or any, network. Also, this approach may require too much processing power for small microcomputer nodes.

The best approach appears to be to allow the source to select any attached gateway and then to have the selected gateway inform the source of alternate gateways if the selection is inappropriate. Better still, a node may broadcast the desired internetwork destination as well as the gateway that is able to handle such traffic responds.

Internal routing

If a network contains more than one first-hop gateway, some interesting situations can develop in the source node. The main consideration is that the internet layer contain a "down-multiplexed" path. That is, a single upper end-point in the 3i layer may have several alternative lower end-points, each of which represents an alternate gateway. Usually, the first lower end-points are created when the source first attempts to reach the remote network. The other end-points may occur when a dynamic routing strategy on a remote gateway routes return traffic through the other gateways represented in the target node as additional lower end-points of the 3i protocol. In most cases, it would be appropriate for the

---

4. Node requirements. *A user wishing to share D via path B to D must now add memory requirements to D so that the path can be supported.*

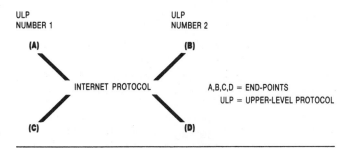

source node to send outbound traffic through the lower end-points on which it has most recently received inbound traffic. This is so because the activity in the end-point can be construed as an indication of the path's viability. The original path should always be retained as a backup should the other paths become nonviable.

Regarding Figure 4, assume that the memory overhead required to support paths through end-point C is greater than that required when using D. And suppose that path A-C was the original path used until path D-A came alive due to return traffic. The node in Figure 4 then decides to use A-D for all outbound traffic. Because the requirements of C are greater than those of D, the switch should pose no problems associated with inbound buffer shortages (assuming inbound buffers are a shared resource). Next, a new user wants to share end-point D using path B-D. This user must now add his memory requirements to D so that the new path can also be supported.

Talking down

The problem arises when something happens to end-point D. End-point C still provides viable support for A and B; however, the switch cannot occur transparently if the user is responsible for allocating memory resources to support his path. Further, the mechanisms for notifying the upper levels of the change and for prescribing how the upper levels should respond is potentially complex. The alternative solution is to provide the 3i level with the facilities for allocating and charging memory requirements to upper-level end-points. Associated with each end-point should be an accounting of what the upper level requirements are for that end-point. This would allow each layer to manage the memory to support its end-point paths in a transparent manner.

Path management is very similar to connection management. In a sense the two are identical—except that path management is defined independently of the connection (level 4) protocol. Maximizing the reliability of the datagram service leads to such internal implementation support of connectionlike behavior. Rarely is the path life expectancy limited to one or two packets. And in those cases where it is so limited, the chances of incurring this complex path management overhead are minimal.

The algorithms for routing between internetwork gateways (3i) are essentially the same as those available at the level (3s) in store-and-forward networks. The routing is accompanied by the same behavioral problem. The extreme static gateway implementation involves a table with a list of networks that might need to be contacted. Mapped with each network is the local network address of the "next-hop" gateway. No alternatives exist, and no verification of the next hop's viability is made. If the gateway is down, the packet will be sent regardless.

Source routing is the term applied when the route is prescribed by the source node. This usually entails a string of internetwork addresses and a pointer in the internet protocol's header. This pointer is moved from one address in the string to another, as each gateway routes the packets.

Source routing helps solve perceived problems in a dynamic routing environment and provides a way of routing through portions of an internetwork that may not be fully integrated. The mechanism can also be used when trying to diagnose internetwork problems.

Certain kinds of source routing can be dynamic. In this mode, a gateway can alter the route and modify the routing list. This list can then be used by the target node to route return traffic.

In static source routing, the gateway tries to route according to the gateway specified by the pointer routing-entry in the list accompanying the packet. No alternatives are permitted if the route is not viable.

In semistatic routing, the gateway is allowed to change the route recommended in the packet. The gateway records the alteration over the top of the proposed next hop. Route-recording allows the gateway free reign in how it routes a packet. Each hop is recorded on the packet's route list.

There are many things on which a gateway can base its routing decisions, such as congestion, precedence, performance criteria (throughput, delay, reliability), security, and cost. As shown, these aspects of routing are not unique to the internet layer. Congestion at the internet level becomes coupled with congestion in the subnet across which the gateway is trying to route its internetwork traffic. Also with precedence, some consideration has to be given at the subnet level as to what kind of traffic—local or internetwork—should be given priority.

The congestion may be caused by inadequate routing at the "subnet link" level, or it may actually be in the gateway. The determination of what is causing the low throughput and high delay can make a difference in determining whether there is any point in trying to reroute through other gateways on the remote side of the same attached network. If the entire network is congested, then all of the alternate gateways that are located on the other side of the subnetwork should be abandoned in favor of a hop through another attached network.

Precedence is also potentially important in managing the internetwork. The ability to force diagnostic packets around, and through, congested areas can provide internetwork management with a powerful diagnostic tool. Security is one of the most sensitive issues where internetwork connection is concerned. Data vulnerability is increased when it is directly exposed to "enemy" territory. Hence, it is important that large internetworks, which may have such "enemy" components, provide users with the capability of routing around such possibly hostile entities. ∎

(This is the first part of a two-part article. The security issue, as well as administrative network issues such as addressing and fault detection and isolation, will be dealt with in part two.)

Charles Solomon received his M. S. in computer science at Colorado State University, Fort Collins, Colo.

Charles Solomon, Hewlett-Packard Co., Fort Collins, Colo.

Getting the data there: Issues in network connectivity

Once large internetworks are in place, managers face getting data, intact and error-free, to the right location.

Security, addressing, and diagnostics all conspire to give data communications managers new headaches once their organizations' networks are successfully interconnected. What's worse, some single-network issues, which may not have been problematic before interconnection, seem to loom large after link-up. Security, for instance, has not traditionally been a major concern at the single-network level. Because single networks usually reside within single administrative bodies they can benefit from whatever local physical protection and organizational sanctions these domains may provide.

Once administrative bodies begin to interact, however, edges of the internetwork (a series of connected subnetworks) become exposed to uncontrolled areas, as shown in Figure 1. These areas make internetworks extremely vulnerable to intruders. As has been widely publicized, the ability of a computer "hack" to enter an internetwork through its weakest link and then roam about at will is a serious problem.

Link encryption is considered a solution to the problem of preventing intrusion, but this approach requires that every packet—whether or not it needs the protection—be encrypted at the link level. The overhead is passed on to all the users. In addition, needless encryption, which unnecessarily reduces bandwidth, must be performed on all links if security along the route is to be guaranteed. Further, encryption must vary from link to link in order to prevent a successful attack on one link from exposing all others.

Unless the link-level protocol is modified to carry more specific security information, there is only one security mechanism available to network bridge implementations. This security mechanism prevents specified link packets from traveling to another network on a case-by-case basis.

Security at the internetwork level should:
- Confine packets to a given perimeter.
- Permit an internetwork user to specify the boundaries beyond which specific information may not be routed by the gateways.
- Prevent data of some prescribed sensitivity from being delivered to or from certain nodes.
- Limit traffic to a local network by preventing unauthorized users from having access to the internetwork protocol.
- Prevent the routing across untrusted networks.
- Force gateways to route traffic through themselves in dynamic routing schemes. This would be accomplished simply by causing the gateway to advertise the shortest path to a given network or set of networks.
- Encrypt information that must pass through hostile territory.
- Provide public key encryption, for it holds some promise for data security. With this scheme, a public key is used to encrypt raw data. The key's algorithm, however, does not repeat itself. A second secure key decodes the public key's algorithm. This scheme's reliability hinges on the public key server's ability to accurately authenticate the client requesting the keys.

Another problem with implementing security at the internetwork level is that the protocols running on top of the internetwork layer are connection oriented (DATA COMMUNICATIONS, "Exploring the problems of internetworking," June, p. 177). The connection's grade of service is usually implemented with return packets that contain acknowledgment and flow-control information. The problem occurs when information is flowing from a low security level to a high security level.

Unless the internetwork layer is equipped with knowledge of the upper-level protocol—a violation of the Open Systems Interconnection (OSI) model—a low-to-

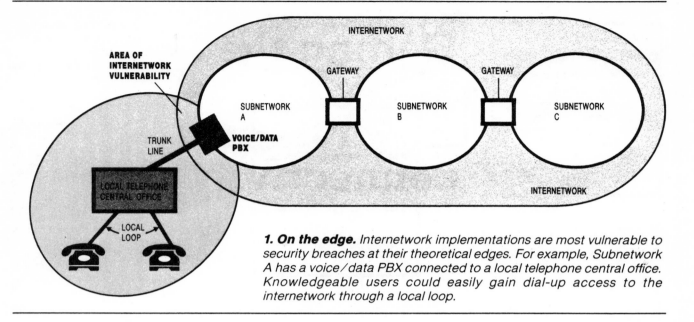

1. On the edge. *Internetwork implementations are most vulnerable to security breaches at their theoretical edges. For example, Subnetwork A has a voice/data PBX connected to a local telephone central office. Knowledgeable users could easily gain dial-up access to the internetwork through a local loop.*

high connection service cannot be supported. This limitation exists because one or both gateways will disallow the resultant high- to low-level transfers of the upper-level protocol's acknowledgments and flow-control packets. The result is that low- to high-level information transfers are limited to unreliable datagram service that requires no acknowledgment.

Ultimately, responsibility for the security of a particular piece of information should lie at the application level. Currently, security is a function that the OSI model places in the presentation layer. Yet the use and definition of security functions are determined and controlled by the application itself. Whether these functions occur in a separate layer is not important, since control must be provided to the application — telling it which services to invoke, and when.

The determination of what is and is not to be secured can be most effectively defined at the application level. Thus, only those who require the service need pay the price. Security in lower layers only paints things with an increasingly broad brush.

One security mechanism provided at the application level is the name server function. Most applications reference objects (destinations or resources) symbolically. The name server function translates these symbols into addresses and routes, which can be used by the other layers to provide connection with the remote object. Such a server can be implemented to control who gets what translation services and can then provide authentication.

The other security technique is encryption (possibly public key encryption), which the application can employ in an as-needed basis.

Addressing and naming
One of the purposes of interconnecting networks is to increase the number of shareable resources. As these resources increase, the less practical it becomes to require that the nodes maintain tables that indicate

where all of these resources are located.

At the internetwork level, the process of locating an object is as follows: A user requests the location of an object and the response carries an internetwork address that identifies the network and the host within that network. The internetwork level then translates the internetwork address into a route over which the internetwork gives access to the object.

Application programs may make use of remote internetwork objects, but in order to do so, the programs must first locate such objects. An object's location is defined by its address. An object such as a printer or a person's mailbox, however, may change its address from time to time. The object's name does not change. It therefore makes sense to code applications, particularly those that deal with internetwork objects, with a name or symbol that can be translated at run time. This internetwork translation service, called a name server, is very important.

Some name servers provide object-to-attribute mapping for any object entered into the database. These attributes may be lists of member objects, making the mapping hierarchical. The attributes are known by name (actual implementation assigns a unique number to individual attributes). It is possible then for an application to ask for the internetwork address-attribute of the hardware that belongs in the attribute member list of a particular higher-level object. For example, the application could ask for the internetwork address of a printer at the computer science department — which is on the member list of Colorado State University, which is a member of the object directory (Fig. 2).

First, the name server finds an entry in its object directory for "Colorado State University." It then checks its attribute member list to see if "computer science" exists. From there the name server tries to find another member list within the computer science object descriptor that matches the term "printer." If

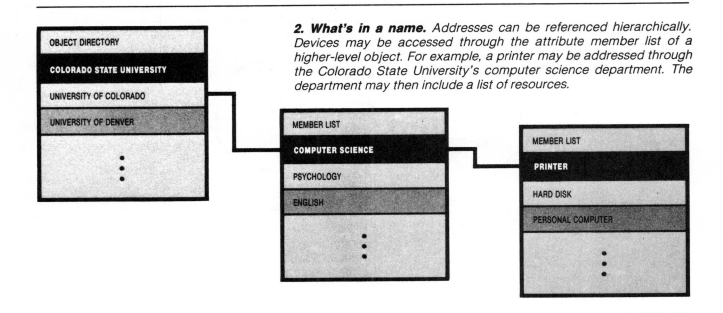

2. What's in a name. *Addresses can be referenced hierarchically. Devices may be accessed through the attribute member list of a higher-level object. For example, a printer may be addressed through the Colorado State University's computer science department. The department may then include a list of resources.*

found, the attribute list of printer is scanned for an internetwork attribute. An internetwork address value (or list of values) is then returned to the application process of the original caller.

The above description is a simplification of what must occur to locate an object in an internetwork. The sheer volume of objects forces the database of this name server to be decentralized. Hence, the local name servers contain assigned-object domains as master copies, in addition to caches of most recently referenced objects. Failure to find a particular object sends the local server off to locate the object in behalf of the caller.

This distributed approach also provides the means for hiding object locations from other networks by placing a name server or "sentry" on the gateways. The sentry location is well-known by the other networks. All name-server requests are handled by the sentry if they come to the gateway from a remote network. The sentry obtains the data from the local server and passes it back to the source of the request.

Authentication and access control are used to provide objects with security. With certain requests, users must provide identification and a password. The name server compares the user's identification against the object's authorized identification attribute and the corresponding access attribute values, as logged in the object's database entry.

One of the rudest awakenings occurs when independently administered internetworks try to interconnect. For instance, each internetwork has so far been managing its own internetwork address domains—which invariably start with zero and proceed upward.

Therefore, when the two internetworks attempt to interconnect, one or more of the network numbers is almost certain to be ambiguous. Currently, no internetwork is capable of detecting and reporting such a condition in the course of their normal operations. The results can be very frustrating to the user who is

unaware of the problem. A major administrative battle can ensue over who pays the cost associated with changing the network numbers in all of the hosts attached to the ambiguous network.

When dealing with a large internetwork, an organization charged with impartial troubleshooting and arbitration is a necessity. Because the internetwork is potentially very dispersed, it is worthwhile to have at least provided for remote diagnostic and recovery tools.

Regardless of how the internetwork is administered, the ability to service the internetwork effectively is related to the degree of standardization of the methods, formats, and protocols used in the tools. Managers can develop special translating gateways, compatible end-to-end applications, special service features, and so forth. But if the internetwork diagnostic and recovery tools are not standardized and supported across the internetwork, the notion of providing internetwork control facilities rapidly disintegrates.

The functions of internetwork control fall into four major categories:

■ Status polling—a control site can poll internetwork nodes for current status information.
■ Event reporting—any node can issue unsolicited messages that notify a control node of a particular event.
■ Diagnostic probing—messages can be sent that are designed to invoke particular responses from remote nodes.
■ Remote manipulation—a control site can directly manipulate the state of a remote node.

Status polling is used in the Arpanet (Advanced Research Project Agency's network) host monitoring protocol (HMP) to select nodes, from which status reports are obtained. The nodes use a double buffering technique with time stamps associated with each node. To keep overhead low, the responsibility of reliably obtaining a report is left with the control site. The site will retransmit polls to a node if the node fails to receive a report in a reasonable length of time. The node must provide an interval before switching buffers that is long enough so that the control site can guarantee that it will receive the older status buffer. Each buffer is time-stamped to let the control site reconstruct the situation involving all the nodes in a given time period.

When a node encounters an error, or is operating out of the ordinary, it may send this report to a control site for logging. The report must identify who it is from, the time the failure occurred (within reasonable resolution), and any associated particulars.

Probing and manipulating

A probe can address many areas, and there are many mechanisms for assessing the operational health of those areas. Remote loopback facilities can provide round-trip timing to determine the node's accessibility. Also, loopbacks can provide fairly exhaustive testing of the remote node's operation—depending on which protocol level the loopback operates. Source routing and route-recording can be used alone or in conjunction with remote loopback facilities to evaluate the status of the internetwork's routing tables and specific routes. Sometimes software versions can be dumped from all nodes to determine version incompatibilities.

Frequently, particular pieces of network equipment or software need to be reset. If mechanisms have been sufficiently standardized, this can be done by a control site. If the site wants to change its address, nodes from which it wants to receive event reports can be notified of the new location, and new software downloaded.

Artificial loading of a link or node is one additional tool that can be provided, since some diagnostic tools may require that the internetwork give preference to diagnostic functions through congested areas. One issue surrounding the placement of these diagnostic facilities is whether or not they should be centralized or distributed. The problem with centralization (like centralized routing) is that networks closest to the control site experience heavier traffic loads. Centralization also means complete loss of internetwork management when the node goes down. The advantage is that it is more cost-effective to place increased sophistication in a single site. The distributed approach decentralizes the diagnostic and remedial capabilities of the internetwork, but it also involves increased cost in terms of resources required to support the function.

It is important that these facilities be available to specific onetime requests that might come from an internetwork operator. These diagnostic facilities should also be available so that certain monitoring functions can be performed automatically.

Practical experience with the internetwork environment is still limited. New approaches and applications are frequently being discovered. In light of this, and the attendant liabilities of failures, those wishing to implement an internetwork solution should check recent literature for tips from others' experiences. ∎

Charles Solomon received his M. S. in computer science from Colorado State University, Fort Collins, Colorado. This is the second part of a two-part article.

Larry Orr, Hewlett-Packard Co., Cupertino, Calif.

Gateways to SNA offer multivendor network solutions

Having opted for non-IBM software and computers, managers are often stymied when trying to integrate into IBM networks.

Different types of IBM Systems Network Architecture (SNA) gateway implementations can provide high levels of multivendor computer integration, substantial cost savings, and flexibility for growth or network reconfiguration.

The basic capabilities included in many gateway products are IBM 3270 terminal and remote job entry (RJE) emulation. These gateways can be differentiated by the hardware that runs the emulation software, the number and type of terminals supported, other capabilities offered, or the associated cost savings. A more all-encompassing way of evaluating these products, however, is to consider the degree of multivendor integration they permit.

At the lowest integration level are the single-device protocol converters. These products may be software solutions for microcomputers or "black box" protocol converters that permit a single asynchronous terminal to appear to an IBM host as a 3270 terminal.

The highest integration levels include various gateway software implementations running on mainframes or minicomputers. The minicomputer implementations permit the application programs, terminal equipment, and networking solutions of another vendor to be totally integrated into an IBM network. Both quantitatively and qualitatively, the internetwork multivendor gateway is superior to the single-device protocol converter. Quantitatively, it can support a potentially large user population; and qualitatively, it encompasses the distributed-processing solutions of non-IBM vendors while providing access to IBM networks.

Between the extremes of multivendor gateways and the single-device converters are the 3270 cluster controller emulators designed to be used as substitutes for IBM or IBM-compatible 3270 control units. These cluster controllers can also provide a gateway from local

networks (including PBX data networks) or packet-switching networks. Like the single-device protocol converters, these products are designed primarily to provide better price/performance by permitting low-cost asynchronous terminals to substitute for the costlier 3270 terminals.

Any interface between non-IBM equipment and an IBM network that permits access to IBM host applications through an IBM binary synchronous communications (BSC) or synchronous data link control (SDLC) network can be called a gateway, regardless of the level of integration it provides. For clarity, however, this article will use the term gateway to refer to software interfaces on non-IBM mainframes, minicomputers, or dedicated communications processors. These gateways permit the terminal equipment, application programs, and networking facilities of a non-IBM network node to access IBM networks and user services.

Implementations

There are basically three types of gateways. Two types integrate alternate networking solutions into SNA, one (Fig. 1A) requiring a dedicated gateway processor between the networks and the other (Fig. 1B) using gateway software integrated with other applications on a processor. The third implementation (Fig. 1C) provides IBM access only for a single processor, either because the gateway cannot be accessed through the vendor's networking facilities or because no networking facilities exist.

An internetwork gateway with a dedicated gateway processor provides a single point of entry to an SNA network. Any terminal or application program on the independent, non-SNA network will access the SNA network via that single gateway. For example, Digital Equipment Corp. uses a dedicated PDP-11 gateway to

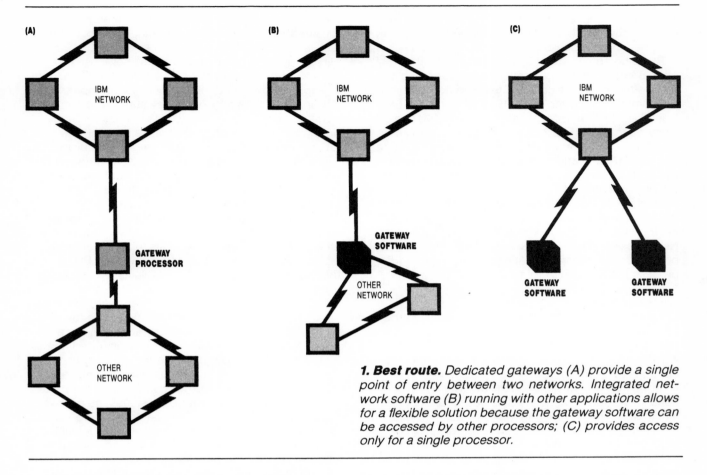

(A)

IBM
NETWORK

GATEWAY
PROCESSOR

OTHER
NETWORK

(B)

IBM
NETWORK

GATEWAY
SOFTWARE

OTHER
NETWORK

(C)

IBM
NETWORK

GATEWAY
SOFTWARE

GATEWAY
SOFTWARE

1. Best route. *Dedicated gateways (A) provide a single point of entry between two networks. Integrated network software (B) running with other applications allows for a flexible solution because the gateway software can be accessed by other processors; (C) provides access only for a single processor.*

permit a Decnet network to coexist with an SNA network. In this type of implementation, the vendor's proprietary network (in this case Decnet) is used for transmitting messages to the gateway. The dedicated processor then supports a potentially large concentration of messages directed to an IBM host through a single node.

An integrated internetwork gateway consists of application programs running parallel with other applications on the same processor. For example, Hewlett-Packard Co.'s SNA link for the HP 3000 minicomputer differs from a single-processor gateway in that the gateway software may be accessed by any other remote processor or terminal in the HP 3000 network. Users have the benefits associated with an internetwork gateway, even if the cost of a dedicated processor gateway cannot be justified by the expected volume of use. This implementation also may be used to provide several points of entry into SNA — distributing the volume of messages to be processed among several computers.

A single-processor gateway provides an interface to an IBM or SNA network only for the terminal equipment and application programs under the direct control of the one processor running the gateway software. Like the integrated internetwork gateway, gateway software runs parallel with other application programs. But if access to an IBM host is required by a terminal in the domain of a peer processor, gateway facilities and a

dedicated physical link to the IBM host must be supported by each processor.

Bottom line
All gateways offer cost savings and convenience, since any one terminal may be used to access both IBM and non-IBM processors. Each implementation, however, differs to the degree that it allows managers to optimize their physical network. The telecommunications expense of operating a multivendor network over time largely determines a gateway's cost-effectiveness.

A dedicated-processor gateway is most useful where the two networks are geographically separated because a single point of entry results in reduced leased-line costs. This might be the case where, through merger or acquisition, a non-IBM corporate network in one state must interact with an IBM host in an SNA network in another state.

A dedicated-processor gateway, however, may not be an ideal solution where two networks overlap geographically. A network topology similar to the one shown in Figure 2 illustrates why. If the traffic between Node A and Node 2 is heavy, a dedicated leased line between those nodes may be desirable based on performance requirements or capacity limitations. Future increases in traffic might force a manager to choose between another leased line or another dedicated gateway processor at Node A. In this respect, the integrated gateway is more flexible for changing communications requirements, since the capital investment for the communications software is significantly less than that for dedicated gateway processors.

By being able to share a leased line with other IBM node processors, the computer node supporting gateway software offers significant telecommunications economies. For example, an HP 3000 might share a leased line with an IBM System/38, an 8100, or a 3274 cluster controller (Fig. 3). Thus, users may substitute an HP for an IBM processor or introduce an HP node into an SNA network in place of 3270 cluster controllers and RJE devices, without significantly modifying the physical network.

Single-processor gateways are least flexible because a dedicated physical link to an IBM host is required for each processor to be integrated into the IBM network. Nevertheless, single-processor implementations are expedient solutions for integrating an existing non-IBM processor into the SNA fold.

Ways and means

Vendor mainframe and minicomputer gateway products are software interfaces that typically perform the following functions:
■ Control the devices and application programs that communicate with an IBM host
■ Permit non-IBM devices to emulate IBM RJE workstations, 3270 devices, and in some cases, SNA protocols
■ Establish sessions with an IBM host as directed by a terminal operator or application program
■ Control the physical link to an IBM front-end.

The gateway facility is composed of several applica-

---

2. Intersections. It may be cheaper for A to send data to 2 via a second dedicated gateway rather than having A relay data from node B to node 1 and then to 2.

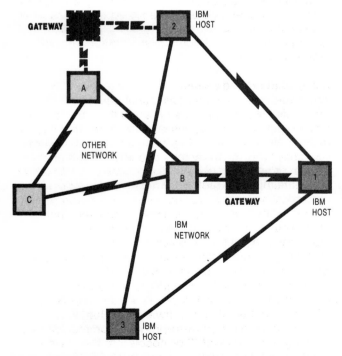

---

tion programs running concurrently with other applications under the computer's operating system, or by itself in a dedicated gateway processor.

In some cases, gateways provide interactive program-to-program communications. This facility permits an application on a non-IBM processor to appear to an IBM application as a 3270 display station. Less common and of more specialized use are pass-through facilities that permit IBM terminals to be operated in native mode while subordinate to a non-IBM processor.

The simplest implementation of a 3270 gateway uses independent application programs as software substitutes for 3270 cluster-controller emulators. Each program is recognized by an IBM host as a physical unit (PU) in the SNA architecture and supports a logical unit (LU) address for each terminal that requires IBM host access. If the number of terminals requiring access exceeds the number of LUs supported by a PU, another software program may be installed. Each program supports its own physical link to the host.

A more common and efficient implementation uses two or more application programs to provide the 3270 emulation facility. A separate program serves as a collecting point for messages to be transported across the physical link. This program is the gateway and is shared by one or more terminal-emulation software products. Each terminal-emulation program supports a finite number of concurrent LU sessions. The gateway program—not the terminal-emulation software—is recognized by the IBM host as a physical and logical component of the network. At a minimum, the gateway program handles the data link and path control protocols and establishes sessions with an IBM host "by proxy" for non-IBM terminals. The terminal-emulation software permits a non-IBM device to be used as if it were a 3270 terminal and supports basic 3270 editing and keyboard functions.

The initial gateway product offerings of the major mainframe and minicomputer vendors have generally been pre-SNA 3271 BSC or SDLC emulations. With the pre-SNA protocols, only terminal-emulation and lower-level protocols had to be emulated. The high-level SNA protocols required in an SNA environment may be supplied by the terminal-emulation program. Another approach is to implement high-level SNA protocols in a separate program that can be used by a variety of applications for program-to-program communications with an SNA host (Fig. 4).

A 3270 gateway differs from a conventional 3270 cluster controller in that there is no hard-wired connection between a terminal and an LU network address. As a result, terminals may be dynamically assigned to available LU addresses. This LU assignment is transparent to network routing software in the IBM host front-end. Terminals may be used alternately in 3270 emulation or in their native mode.

IBM host sessions may be established via the gateway or by terminals attached to another processor using the vendor's network. No special gateway communications software is required for routing a message to the gateway across a non-IBM network if the point of origin is an adjacent node. Terminal-emulation software

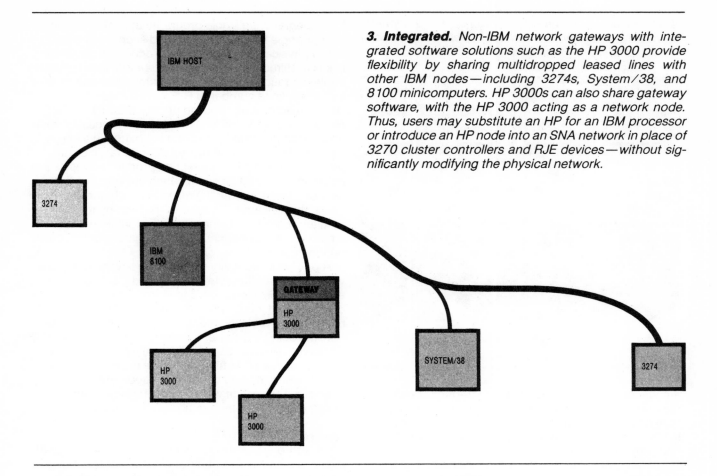

is accessed remotely over a point-to-point link between two processors. Certain communications vendors, for example, provide peer-to-peer networking through a star topology to provide work-sharing and load-balancing between processors. This type of network is designed specifically for communications at the node level of a distributed-processing network. These peer-to-peer networks augment the capabilities of hierarchical networks, such as SNA, similar to the way IBM 8100 peer-to-peer networking facilities augment SNA.

Where a vendor uses a hierarchical network architecture similar to SNA, the software required to manage a gateway facility is much more complex. To control communications costs, minimize response time, and manage the gateway's processing load, 3270 terminal-emulation software must reside on each node in the non-IBM network requiring such emulation. Only the gateway product is centralized at the gateway node.

In addition to terminal-emulation software, each node supports gateway management software that establishes sessions with the gateway node and provides the protocol conversion necessary to transport 3270-formatted messages. As illustrated in Figure 5, the software overhead required to support a gateway between two incompatible layered network architectures is high. Thus, response time may be increased if messages exchanged with an IBM host must be processed by gateway management software in intervening nodes in the non-IBM Network.

An application interface permits an application program resident on a non-IBM host to establish an LU-to-LU session with an application program on an IBM host. Data may be transferred interactively without the involvement of an operator or additional IBM host user-written software. In this way, the non-IBM application program appears to the IBM host as a 3270 display station or printer.

Many valuable solutions

The primary value of an application interface is its ability to store and process data locally rather than having to send transactions directly to the host through multiple SNA sessions. This ability reduces the average response time, the communications overhead on the central processing unit, and the volume of traffic on the link to the host. The IBM host database may be updated while the remaining data is either stored locally or kept on-line for access by local terminals. This capability combines the many valuable multivendor applications solutions with the ability to update host applications—all without additional programming or host application modification.

It is more difficult for a vendor to implement an effective 3270 application interface than to develop 3270 terminal-emulation software. For this reason, users who need program-to-program communications typically must write 3270 protocols into their own applications. In addition, if the high-level SNA protocols

4. Cross talk. *High-level SNA protocols in a separate software package allow a variety of applications to communicate with programs on an SNA host.*

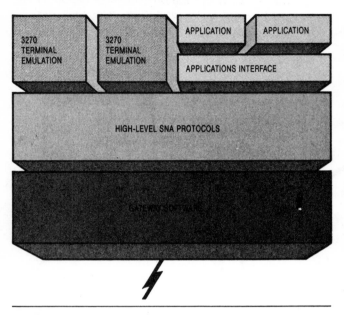

are inaccessible to the application interface (because they are integral to the terminal-emulation software), they also must be written into the application program. In effect, each application must contain its own 3270 SNA-emulation program.

The programming requirements for application access to an IBM host can be simplified by integrating an application interface into the 3270 terminal-emulation facility. Hewlett-Packard's interactive mainframe facility (IMF) is a good example of this. The IMF product, Hewlett-Packard's 3270 emulator for its 3000 minicomputer, provides simple macro commands that streamline software development in two ways. First, an IMF buffer maintains 3270 display-screen images that may be viewed or printed. Second, IMF implements 3270 protocols so that existing programs may be easily modified for interactive IBM host access, and new ones may be developed with no knowledge of 3270 data streams or SNA protocols.

Batch facilities

The gateways offered by major mainframe and minicomputer vendors generally provide BSC 2780/3780 or SNA 3770 RJE emulation, or both. These devices also provide all of the protocols—except job control language—for assessing job entry subsystem software in the IBM host. When a pure 2780/3780 or 3770 emulation is provided, a dedicated physical link to the IBM host is required—in addition to the physical link for interactive facilities. A dedicated processor gateway or an integrated internetwork gateway (such as the HP 3000 gateway based on IBM 8100 emulation) can typically provide batch and interactive communications over one physical link.

The efficiency with which RJE emulation is implemented varies from vendor to vendor. In the simplest

implementation, a single programmatic interface emulates a single RJE workstation and supports a dedicated physical link. A separate product and physical link is required for each RJE workstation. More effective implementations permit a single interface product to emulate a finite number of RJE workstations or a Houston automatic spooling priority (HASP) multileaving workstation. With a HASP processor, multiple batch job streams may be submitted in a single session. Where proprietary networking facilities are provided, a single RJE emulation product serves as a collecting point for files originating anywhere in the network. Users submit their files to batch queues. From there, the files are submitted to the host by the RJE emulation product. Generally, RJE emulation supports a number of I/O devices, including card readers, card punches, line printers, or disk units.

A powerful capability provided by several computer vendors is a feature commonly called job output management. This allows users to change the ultimate disposition of job output from the host. Thus they can route output to destinations that best fit their operation, including a disk file, a printer, or another user. RJE emulation also can be used to send information from a database on an IBM host to a node processor. In this way, the data editing can be off-loaded from the mainframe to a node with better interactive capabilities, modified, and then returned to the host.

Reverse access

A pass-through facility allows the data stream originating from a native IBM-compatible 3270 or RJE device to be routed through a non-IBM processor without modification. The IBM device is recognized by the IBM host as if it were attached through conventional connection methods. Both Tandem Non-Stop computers and Sperry Univac Distributed Communications Processor nodes support pass-through facilities.

The major advantage of pass-through by itself is the ability to reconfigure real 3270 and RJE workstations without having to modify path control macros in IBM's front-end Advanced Communications Function/ Network Control Program (ACF/NCP) software. This modification requires that the entire subarea be shut down until ACF/NCP is modified and regenerated. A processor with pass-through facilities, however, may be used to act as a front-end to an SNA network. The vendor's network transmits messages to the pass-through port, and the vendor's network management software keeps track of and monitors native 3270 systems that are transparent to ACF/NCP.

The advantage of a pass-through facility is increased when additional emulation software is provided that allows native IBM devices to access applications on the non-IBM host. However, the implication that this inverted terminal emulation provides full interconnectivity between two data communications networks is misleading. In reality, relatively few non-IBM applications can be accessed by IBM devices, because they are written for terminal equipment that has capabilities not provided by IBM equipment.

In short, pass-through facilities serve specialized

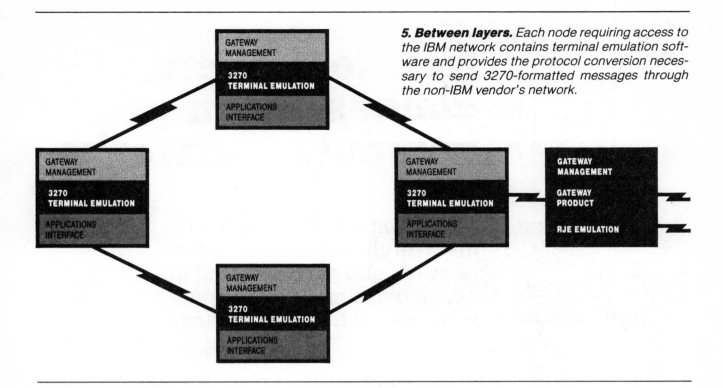

5. Between layers. *Each node requiring access to the IBM network contains terminal emulation software and provides the protocol conversion necessary to send 3270-formatted messages through the non-IBM vendor's network.*

applications where flexibility is required for frequent IBM terminal reconfiguration or for using IBM devices with specific applications on the non-IBM processor.

Selecting a gateway

A number of issues must be considered when determining whether a gateway offers a good solution to a particular requirement and in assessing the costs associated with various gateway implementations. These considerations include performance requirements, telecommunications costs over time, the capacity needed to satisfy users, and the flexibility for responding to changing communications requirements.

In terms of performance, no gateway facility is an adequate substitute for IBM or IBM-compatible 3270 devices for dedicated applications that involve continuous use by terminal operators. This is simply because the data rate between a gateway facility and a terminal is typically 9.6 kbit/s or less, whereas a 3270 terminal hardwired to a control unit receives data over coaxial cable at a transmission speed of approximately 2 Mbit/s. When a gateway message must be processed by management software in intervening nodes in order to use a non-SNA network to reach the gateway processor, costly delays are incurred.

The highest costs and least flexibility in gateway implementations result when numerous dedicated physical links are required for multiple 3270 and RJE-emulation products, for each gateway processor, or for both. The lowest costs and greatest flexibility are afforded by an integrated internetwork gateway, since it may serve as a single point or as multiple points of entry into SNA networks—depending on the most economical deployment of leased lines. The dedicated processor internetwork gateway is an efficient imple-

mentation where two networks are geographically dispersed. However, where overlap occurs, a more effective physical network may be at the expense of a second or third dedicated processor. In any case, the greatest economies in hardware and software and in leased-line costs are gained when a non-IBM processor can be introduced with little change to an existing physical network.

The capacity of various gateway implementations relative to hardware and software overhead is difficult to assess. The greatest amount of hardware and software overhead is required by a dedicated-processor internetwork gateway. In this case, gateway management software is required to route messages from a local terminal-emulation program to a dedicated gateway processor using proprietary protocols. The additional overhead, however, can be offset by a potentially large user population (up to 256 concurrent sessions per link) using the gateway. Most integrated internetwork and single-processor 3270 gateway products support a maximum of 32 concurrent sessions per terminal-emulation product.

One terminal-emulation product is usually sufficient for a single minicomputer node, since a greater number of terminals may contend for 32 LUs without inconvenience—depending on the average time each terminal is on line.

Single-processor gateways are an attractive entry point but can become costly if additional software and leased lines are required to integrate additional nodes into the IBM network. ■

Larry Orr, who is with Hewlett-Packard's Information Networks Division, has a B. A. in mathematics from Harvard and an M. B. A. from Stanford.

Wen-Ning Hsieh and Israel Gitman, DVI Communications, Inc., New York, N.Y.

How to prevent congestion in computer networks

Incremental traffic can clog the overall response in some heavily used networks, but the use of two simple techniques can prevent that occurrence.

One major advantage of packet-switching technology is its ability to share a network's resources among a community of users. This takes advantage of the fact that a typical network user transmits or receives messages rather infrequently. Great economy is achieved by not dedicating a portion of the network resources to any particular user. In an active environment, however, significant throughput degradation may occur unless the network traffic is carefully controlled. This has been observed in earlier communications networks, which sometimes have improper control disciplines. In these networks, system throughput can decrease as user demand increases, especially during heavy demand (the "Mother's Day syndrome").

Figure 1a illustrates graphically the congestion phenomenon. Curve A represents the idealized situation, in which network throughput is equal to the offered traffic up to a maximum level, and the throughput is equal to the "network capacity" from then on. In practical situations, one expects throughput to be worse, due to the necessary protocol overhead associated with message transport (curves B through E). Curves D and E illustrate cases in which the network is not controlled properly. The network throughput decreases as the offered traffic increases, which may be caused by several factors:

■ With more traffic in the network, alternate routes longer than the primary route may be used, tying up more network route resources.

■ More network traffic implies longer queueing delay for nodal processing and channel transmission. Consequently, buffers at each node are tied up longer.

■ If the packets are dropped because buffers are unavailable, the packets will be retransmitted mostly through the link-level control or the end-to-end trans-

port-level control. As a result, each successful packet transport to the destination consumes more resources and incurs longer transport delay.

■ In an improperly designed network, deadlock can occur (Curve E). Suppose message holding resource A seeks resource B, and intends to release A when B becomes available. In ill-designed networks, the availability of resource B might depend on the resources held by the requesting message. Under such circumstances, the message might wait indefinitely even though there are resources available for its use.

Although the problem of efficient control of traffic flow is complex, two simple mechanisms presented here can be implemented easily to achieve "near-optimum" performance. The mechanisms described were either partially or fully implemented in several operational networks. This is often not the case with some state-of-the-art technologies, and the result can be the oversizing of networks, as well as the inefficient utilization of system resources.

The two mechanisms are:
(i) Control of the number of outstanding unacknowledged packets on an end-to-end virtual circuit;
(ii) Control of packet buffers at a switching node, so that only a fraction of these buffers can be used for newly entered packets and the rest by transit packets.

Purposes

Flow-control strategies are the collection of control procedures applied to a communications network to achieve the following objectives:
1) Prevention of throughput degradation and loss of efficiency due to overload;
2) Deadlock avoidance;
3) Fair allocation of resources among competing users;
4) Speed matching between the network and its users.

Communications network functions may be partitioned into hierarchical layers of cooperative functions, in which the functions at a given layer use the services provided by functions at lower level layers. The reference model of the Open System Interconnection defines seven protocol layers, which perform the following functions:

■ *Application layer* serves as the window through which all exchange of information "meaningful" to the users occurs.

■ *Presentation layer* presents information to communicating application entities in a form that preserves meaning while resolving syntax differences.

■ *Session layer* provides the means for cooperating presentation entities to organize and synchronize their dialogue and manage their data exchange.

■ *Transport layer* provides transparent transfer of data between session entities. This layer relieves the user of any concern with the implementation details of data transfer.

■ *Network layer* provides network connections from any transport entity to any other, and relieves the

transport layer of any concern with switching, routing, and relaying.

■ *Data link layer* provides the functional and procedural means to activate, maintain, and deactivate one or more data link connections among network entities at adjacent nodes.

■ *Physical layer* provides mechanical, electrical, functional, and procedural characteristics to activate, maintain, and deactivate physical connections for bit transmission between data link entities (possibly through intermediate equipment).

Flow control may be applied at different levels in a packet-switched network. For example, at the data link layer, control can be applied to maintain a smooth flow of traffic between two neighboring nodes; at the network layer, control can be applied to throttle user input traffic, based on internal network congestion conditions, and to regulate traffic flow between neighboring nodes; at the transport layer, control can be applied to maintain a smooth flow of traffic on the end-to-end connection between the source process and the destination process.

The first control mechanism considered, called the Group ACK/CREDIT strategy, is applied at the transport layer to regulate message flow on an end-to-end basis between a source process and a destination process. The second control mechanism, called the input-buffer limit strategy, is applied at the network layer to regulate message flow into a node. This message flow comes from the higher layer processes or from other nodes.

As will be demonstrated, both control strategies are relatively straightforward. Without great difficulty, procedures for dynamic adjustment of the control parameters can be incorporated into the appropriate protocol layer to provide effective flow control.

Relevant yardstick

Before probing the strategies, a quantitative measure of flow control performance is required. This will facilitate assessing a flow control mechanism's performance, the impact of a specific parameter on a flow control mechanism, and differences between dissimilar flow control mechanisms.

One of the most widely used performance measures employed in the flow control studies is called the throughput. For a given offered load, the throughput represents the rate (in packets per second, for example) at which the network can deliver packets. This measure is useful in determining the "capacity" of a controlled configuration under heavy load or the critical offered load of an uncontrolled network. (Beyond this critical load, the network throughput actually decreases.)

A more complete measure than the throughput is the combined delay and throughput performance profile. This measure represents the average packet delay as a function of the network throughput (Fig. 1). In general, for a properly controlled network, the higher the throughput the higher the average packet delay. This ratio corresponds to the fact that the queueing time increases as more traffic is pumped through the net-

---

1. No degradation. *The throughput of a properly controlled network keeps increasing, even during heavy congestion.*

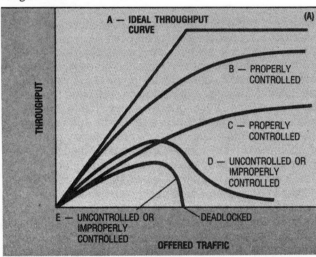

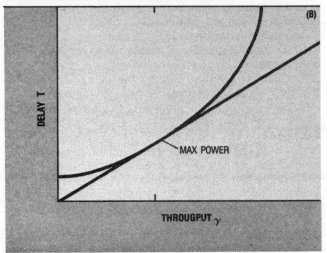

2. Empirical data.
Measurements from the Arpanet network and computer simulations both show that packet delays usually occur with an Erlang distribution.

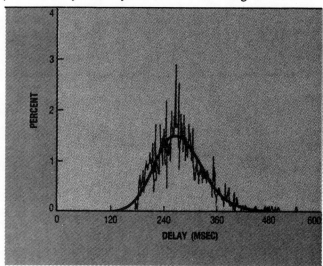

work. Often, the throughput (and hence the offered load) may be intentionally constrained in order to achieve an acceptable packet delay, even though the constrained level could be well below the maximum achievable throughput. Information required for this type of design would not be available with the throughput measure alone. The combined delay and throughput performance profile also allows the comparison of control strategies that exhibit comparable throughput performance but quite different delay characteristics.

In order to allow the selection of a single operating point that compromises between maximizing throughput and minimizing delay, some analysts use a single combined measure called power. The most simple definition of power is:

$$Power = \frac{Throughput}{Delay}$$

(Power is thus a function of the offered load.) This definition can be generalized to allow different weights to be assigned to throughput and delay.

As Figure 1b indicates, the point of maximum power corresponds to the "knee" of the delay-throughput profile, where a ray out of the origin is tangent to the performance profile. In many important cases, the maximum power occurs where throughput is approximately half the maximum throughput and the delay is about twice the minimum delay. This point represents a compromise between the two conflicting objectives.

ACK/CREDIT
The transport layer flow control mechanism regulates the traffic flow on an ETE connection between a source and a destination process. The regulated flow rate on the connection, or the throughput rate of the connection, must not saturate the transport network or the destination process. Stated symbolically:

$$\gamma \leq \mu_N$$
$$and$$
$$\gamma \leq \mu_R$$

where μ_N is the "network transport rate" for the connection and μ_R is the "destination process absorption rate" for the connection. These equations represent the speed matching conditions between the source and the network and between the source and the destination, respectively.

One noteworthy control mechanism is the so-called group ACK/CREDIT scheme. The ACK/CREDIT control mechanism and its variants are used in a number of transport layer protocols, such as the DECnet END communications protocol and the Department of Defense Standard TCP protocol (see DATA COMMUNICATIONS, September 1983, p. 215, and March 1983, p. 153). It operates as follows:
■ An ACK/CREDIT packet of the form (a,W) is sent periodically from the destination of the connection to the source, indicating that:
(i) All packets with sequence number smaller than "a" have been correctly received;
(ii) The source is allowed to send W packets with sequence numbers "a" through "a+W-1". Thus, up to W packets are allowed to be in transit on the connection simultaneously.
■ To reduce protocol overhead, the ACK/CREDIT packet is generated at the rate of one for every V data packets received. This is referred to as the

---

3. Tandem Queue Model.
The ETE Delay Distribution matches the Erlangian distribution. Also, the forward transport service can be modeled by K tandem M/M/l queues. The service rate in the queue is equal to the sum of the rate of Erlangian distribution and the connection throughput.

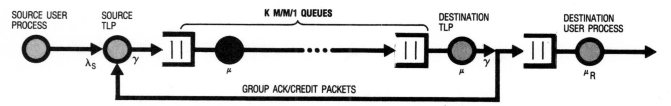

λ_S: SOURCE USER PROCESS EMISSION RATE (THE RATE PRIOR TO BEING REGULATED BY ETE FLOW CONTROL).

μ_R: DESTINATION USER PROCESS ABSORPTION RATE.
TLP: TRANSPORT LAYER PROTOCOL MODULE.
γ: CONNECTION THROUGHPUT

ACK/CREDIT group size V. An ACK/CREDIT packet will also be generated if the elapsed time from the time the last ACK/CREDIT packet was sent is longer than a predefined maximum time limit. This avoids prolonged delay when the source has no data to send.

By adjusting V and W according to prevalent traffic conditions in the network, the Group ACK/CREDIT scheme provides error control and flow control for the transport layer connection.

Note that V is primarily an error-control parameter. The larger V is, the longer it will take the source node to receive the acknowledgment. V should be sized based on considerations such as the source-emission rate, acknowledgment delay requirement, and source buffer availability.

On the other hand, W is primarily a flow control parameter. The larger W is, the more packets the source process can forward to the destination at any one time. Thus, W should be sized based on considerations such as the destination absorption rate, network transport rate, and destination buffer availability.

Credit allocation

A central issue with the ACK/CREDIT scheme (or any other window-based flow control strategy) is the specification of a procedure for determining value for W that provides "good" or "near-optimal" connection performance. The procedure for determining W should use information measurable at the transport layer module. One such procedure is presented below.

From past measurement and simulation studies, it was found that the density function of the ETE delay (for both one-way and roundtrip) in a distributed packet-switched network may be modeled by an Erlangian density function E(θ,K) with rate θ and degree K:

$$f(\theta, K, x) = \frac{\theta^K}{(K-1)!} x^{K-1} e^{-\theta x}, \quad x \geq 0$$

The degree K is dependent upon the average number of hops on an ETE path and on the traffic load on channels used in the ETE paths.

Figure 2 presents typical delay distributions obtained from measurements in Arpanet (a) and from simulations (b). As can be seen, the Erlangian distribution provides a reasonably good fit.

The queue of packets at the network nodes can be represented by an "M/M/1 queue," that is, a single-server queue with randomly arriving clients and exponentially distributed service time. According to observations from queueing theory, the total time in an M/M/1 queue with input rate γ and service rate μ is exponentially distributed with mean $\gamma - \mu$.

The network transport service for the connection can be represented by "hypothetical" end-to-end tandem queue with K M/M/1 queues, each with service rate μ given by:

$$\mu = \theta + \gamma$$

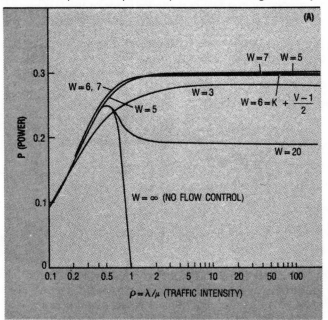

4. Sticky. All of the curves for $V <= 6$ have about the same optimum power. When V begins to get greater than 6, the point of optimum power moves significantly.

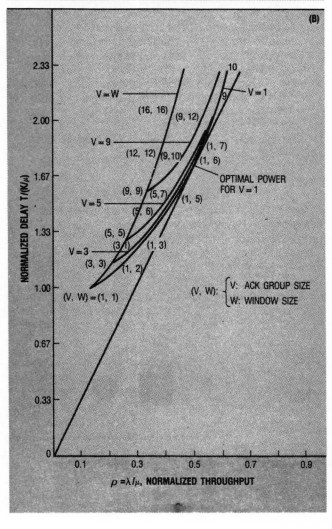

where γ is the connection throughput (Fig. 3).

The rate Θ and degree K of the Erlangian distribution, as well as connection throughput γ, can be obtained through transport layer measurements at the two end nodes and adjusted dynamically from time to time.

The above tandem queue model for the network transport service holds if packets belonging to a connection are being served by the network in a first-in-first-out manner. This is, in fact, a fairly accurate assumption for most computer networks in operation.

The window size W^* that would provide near-optimal performance (in terms of the power P) is found to be:

$$W^* = \begin{cases} K + [\frac{V-1}{2}] & \text{if } \mu \leq 2\mu_R \\ B + [\frac{V-1}{2}] & \text{if } \mu \geq 2\mu_R \end{cases}$$

where V is the group size. (The notation [X] denotes the smallest integer greater than or equal to X.) B is given by:

$$B = [K \times \frac{\mu_R}{\mu - \mu_R}]$$

The definition of W^* states that the "effective window size" should be set to either K or B, depending on whether the limiting constraint is the the network service rate or the destination service rate. Intuitively, this means that the best strategy is to "keep the connection pipe full" by having one packet at each of the K hypothetical queues, unless the source rate is faster than the destination rate. If the source rate is faster, then only B packets are allowed in the K forward tandem queues.

Numbers
Figure 4a shows the connection performance (in terms of the power P) as a function of the traffic intensity $\rho = \lambda_S/\mu$ for various window sizes W, for the case K=6, V=1. The recommended window size is given by:

$$W^* = K + \frac{V-1}{2} = 6$$

Note that the recommended window size provides near-optimal performance over the entire range of ρ. Moreover, the performance of the connection under W=6 improves monotonically with the offered traffic load. This is highly desirable. There is no improvement in monotonic performance when the credit allocation is too large (W=20) or when there is no control (W=∞).

The performance is acceptable as long as W is not too far from the recommended value (6). This indicates that we need not be overly concerned with the accuracy of the measurement of the ETE delay distribution.

Effect of group size
Figure 4a depicts the throughput and delay for various choices of V and W, for the case K=6, ρ=1. As can be seen, the performance is significantly worse under the case V=W than under the case V=1. The case V=W is the situation in which the ACK is sent only at the end of the window; the case V=1 corresponds to sending the ACK after each packet reception.

The performance degradation under the case V=W should be easily seen. After each group of packets is sent, the next group of V packets at the source has to wait at least one round-trip time delay before it can get permission to continue to send. However, as W increases, the throughput and delay performance curve for a fixed V rapidly approaches that for V=1, especially for small to moderate Vs.

It should be intuitive that the best performance for the forward direction is obtained under the case V=1, because the ACK/CREDIT packet is returned as soon as a packet is received at the destination. This minimizes the "wait time" at the source due to unavailability of credits. However, in practical operation, the case V=1 is highly undesirable, because it generates a significant amount of protocol overhead traffic. Note that for Figure 4b, the performance for small to moderate values of V (V=<6, for example) are comparable to the case V=1. Consequently, the Group ACK/CREDIT scheme is advantageous because the processing and traffic overhead from ACK/CREDIT packets (not captured in the model of Fig. 3) can be significant.

Input-buffer limit control
The function of the network layer flow control mechanism is to regulate the traffic flow into a subnetwork (one or many nodes). The amount of traffic accepted by the subnetwork must be compatible with the resources available in the subsystem. This is distinguished from ETE flow control, which regulates the traffic flow over an ETE connection.

One of the important flow control mechanisms is sometimes called the input-buffer limit scheme. The Canadian Datapac network employs this scheme, and variations on it are used by several currently operating networks. With the task of controlling traffic into a node, either from the user or from other nodes, it operates as follows:

■ Out of the total of N Network Layer packet buffers at a node, a subset of N_I buffers are designated as input buffers. The ratio IBL = N_I/N is called the input-buffer limit.
■ Newly arrived packets from the Transport Layer (i.e., from the user process) are buffered into the input-buffer pool. If the pool is exhausted, the source processes (the Transport Layer) are temporarily stopped.
■ Transit packets (those that have traversed at least one link on the transport network) may be buffered in any of the free buffers at the node. If all N buffers are exhausted, the incoming links to the node are put into a receiver-not-ready state.

The rationale behind the input-buffer limit scheme is quite appealing. The transit packets have already consumed some network resources, and will probably consume less network resources through the rest of their journey than the input packets. Thus, it is preferable to make more resources (buffers, in this case) available to the transit packets than the input packets.

In cases where end-to-end retransmission is done within the subnetwork, there is more incentive to give higher priority to transit packets. If such packets are discarded, they will be retransmitted into the network and result in wasteful reuse for network resources. Both network analysis and simulation have demonstrated that proper sizing of the IBLs can, in fact, provide effective congestion control.

Sizing

Again, we must define a procedure for determining the input-buffer limit (IBL), which would provide "good" or "near-optimal" performance for the nodal management. This procedure should use information measurable at the network layer module.

If the control mechanism is effective, the transit packet blocking will be minimal. This is because discarded transit packets imply that the network resources consumed for that packet thus far are completely wasted—they make no contribution to the total

---

5. Not too many. *When the number of input buffers is much less than the total number of buffers, actual performance curves parallel ideal ones.*

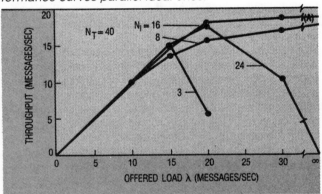

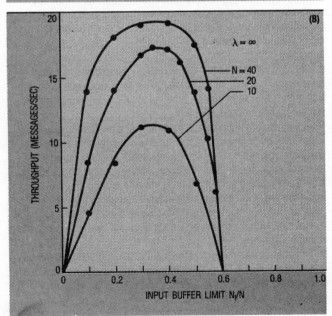

system throughput. Thus, one way to find a procedure for sizing IBL is to control the congestion problem at the source:
(1) Each accepted input packet should have a high probability of reaching the destination;
(2) Conversely, the source should not accept input packets that have a good chance of being discarded later in the network because of the unavailabiliity of network resources.

Under the above conditions, each accepted input packet will give rise to an average of n_{hop} transit packets in the network where n_{hop} = average number of hops for all ETE paths.

Consequently, the input traffic and the transit traffic over the entire network obey the following relationships:

$$\Gamma_T \simeq n_{hop} \times \Gamma_I, \text{ and}$$

$$\Lambda_T \simeq \Gamma_T$$

where

Γ_I = Total input traffic throughput (summing over all nodes);

Γ_T = Total transit traffic throughput (summing over all nodes); and

Λ_T = Total offered transit traffic (summing over all nodes).

In a homogeneous network—in which all nodes have the same amount of traffic loading—these equations imply the following constraint on the IBL at each node:

$$IBL \leq \frac{\gamma_I}{\gamma_I + \gamma_T} = \frac{1}{1 + n_{hop}}$$
where

γ_I = Input packet throughput at the node, and

λ_T = Offered transit packet traffic at the node.

Simulation studies show that IBL sizing based on this procedure does indeed provide good network throughput performance. Note that both λ_T and γ_I can be measured by the network layer module at each node.

In the general case, it was found that an effective uniform bound for IBL is (Equation 1):

$$IBL = \frac{\alpha}{1 + n_{hop}}$$

where
$\theta < \alpha \leq 1$.

The need for an adjustment factor α in non-homogeneous networks can be explained as follows. Since each node has a different input traffic and transit traffic composition, a bound on IBL based on Equation 1 at a particular node may cause too much transit traffic at other nodes and cause a high probability of blocking for these transit packets. This is in conflict with one of the primary design guidelines discussed earlier. Thus, IBL should be sized more conservatively, as suggested in Equation 2.

It was found from simulation studies that α critically depends on the expected frequency of traffic surge, severity of surge, and duration of surge. If only moderate surge is expected most of the time, a value of 0.7 for α is adequate. On the other hand, if the surge is expected to be quite severe and sustained, a value of 0.4 for α would be more suitable. In general, the more severe the traffic surge, the smaller the α should be.

Sample values

Figures 5a and 5b illustrate typical throughput performance under the input-buffer limit scheme. The curves are obtained with a homogeneous network with $n_{hop} = 1.25$. So, equation 1 states that the IBL will be sized no larger than 0.44.

In Figure 5a, the network throughput is shown as a function of the offered input load λ, for the case $N = 40$. If the IBL is properly sized (Curves $N_I = 8$ and $N_I = 16$), the throughput increases monotonically with the offered load λ, which is the desired feature of a properly designed control mechanism. On the other hand, if the IBL is sized too large (Curves $N_I = 24$ and $N_I = 32$), the network throughput decreases as the offered load increases beyond a certain point.

Figure 5a also illustrates that Equation 1 is quite effective. Note that the figure shows that throughput under $N_I = 16$ (IBL = 0.4) is typically comparable to or better than $N_I = 8$ (IBL = 0.2). However, a large IBL, in general, would induce a higher transport delay. Consequently, a smaller IBL (for example, 0.2) might be more desirable.

Figure 5b depicts the network throughput performance as a function of IBL for several different values of N, the total number of buffers at each node. Note that as N gets larger, the throughput curve has a relatively wide and flat region near the optimum. This suggests that as long as the packet buffer pool is reasonably sized, IBL can be designed to be substantially smaller than the constraint given in Equation 1, without causing too much loss in throughput.

In actual operation, the expected traffic rate cannot be estimated with certainty. As long as the IBL is sized conservatively, the network would provide a level of performance that is both satisfactory to users and relatively safe from shocks. ■

Section 2
Technology

Hugh M. Goldberg, General DataComm Industries Inc.,
Middlebury, Conn.

The why, how, and what of digital data transmission

Why is it better than analog? How is pulse-code modulation used for both? What new services are pending? Here are the answers.

Increasing attention is being focused on a new breed of data transmission: digital service. For the communications manager who has worked with modems, multiplexers, and diagnostic equipment over the years, this newer technology may hold some mystery. Yet digital service actually makes use of many elements required for current analog service.

Data processing equipment continues to place increased demands upon communications for faster data rates. While analog modem technology has kept pace so far, the theoretical voiceband limitation of 20,000 bits per second is rapidly being approached. The current class of 14.4- and 16.8-kbit/s modems represents a major milestone in data communications technology. But even these devices do not fully utilize the potential bandwidth available with the current subscriber-access lines.

Pulse-code modulation (PCM) transmission is a 1.544-Mbit/s carrier scheme—a digital scheme also used for analog transmission—that has been deployed in the United States for almost 25 years. Each of 24 channels uses 64 kbit/s of data bandwidth to carry 3,100-Hz voiceband information transmitted over a subscriber-access line. The 300-bit/s voiceband modems that support scores of microcomputers make use of less than 0.5 percent of the capability currently available in today's PCM installations. Digital transmission technology is the key that unlocks the potential inherent in each subscriber channel.

Digital techniques permit increased transmission rates by simplifying the local distribution scheme. PCM methods digitize the analog signal at the telephone company's channel-bank equipment. It is this analog-to-digital (A/D) conversion that requires 64 kbit/s to sample the 3,100-Hz signal. The removal of this A/D conversion—required for full digital implementation—makes the entire 64 kbit/s available for data transmission.

AT&T's Accunet Dataphone digital service (DDS), as well as DDS provided by the former Bell operating companies (BOCs), represents the most widely deployed private line digital services in the United States. Four data rates are currently available: 2.4, 4.8, 9.6, and 56 kbit/s. Each of the three lower (subrate) speeds may be grouped and subsequently multiplexed at the phone company's serving (central) office to form one 64-kbit/s PCM channel. In this manner, twenty 2.4-kbit/s, ten 4.8-kbit/s, or five 9.6-kbit/s channels share one 64-kbit/s DS0 (the lowest PCM digital signaling rate) data stream. Note that only 48 kbit/s of data bandwidth is used for subrate DDS; 8 kbit/s is used for framing, with the final 8 kbit/s for the transmission of control codes. While the 56-kbit/s DDS rate does not require the subrate's framing bandwidth, it does require 8 kbit/s for the network codes.

Unconfined digital
The primary difference between analog and digital data transmission can be directly attributed to the requirements imposed by the local distribution networks, since both techniques make use of identical interoffice PCM equipment. PCM is based on a multiplexed structure that starts with the 300-to-3,400-Hz voiceband provided to the subscriber. Both telephones and modems must confine their energy to this bandwidth. At the central office, the voiceband signals are digitized by an A/D converter that is integrated into the PCM channel-bank equipment.

Amplifiers, equalizers, and loading coils (Fig. 1) establish normalized (within specified limits) signal levels throughout. All of these elements are required to

1. The analog way. Each subscriber line must have certain amplitude and phase characteristics to assure reasonable voice reproduction. Amplifiers, equalizers, and loading coils establish normalized signal levels throughout. These elements are required to condition the analog signal prior to A/D conversion.

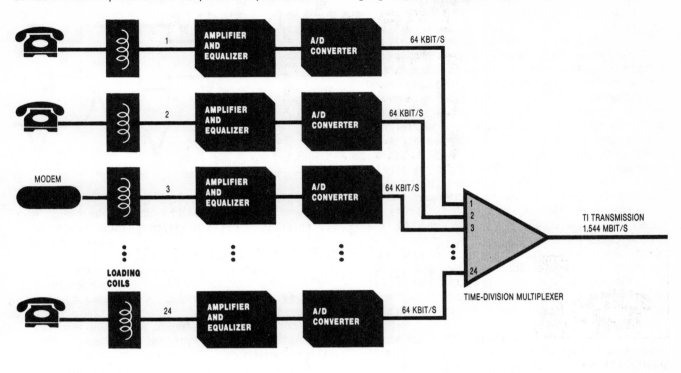

2. The digital way. Digital transmission uses the identical PCM carrier scheme and twisted-pair wires as analog. But all loading coils, amplifiers, and equalizers must be removed, leaving just the wires as the only element between the subscriber and the phone company central office's channel bank equipment.

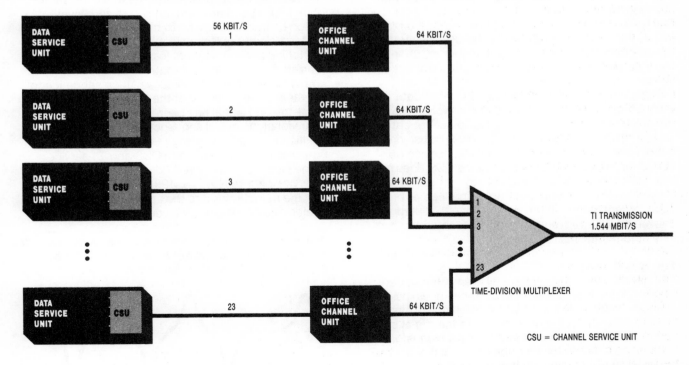

condition the analog signal prior to conversion to a digital form. The PCM gear requires the digital format to enable the signal to be multiplexed with other subscriber signals to form a T1 (1.544 Mbit/s) aggregate.

The A/D conversion is performed by sampling the analog signal at a rate of 8,000 samples per second. The sampling rate has been chosen so that a minimum of two samples is assured for the highest transmitted frequency, in accordance with the accepted Nyquist criteria. Each analog sample must assume the closest of 256 discrete levels. Since each digital representation is 8 bits long, a total of 64,000 bit samples per second (8,000 samples per second—each sample 8 bits long) is required to represent a 3,100-Hz signal. Twenty-four 64-kbit/s channels are then multiplexed to form a 1.536-Mbit/s data stream. With one network framing bit required every 192 data bits, the total T1 rate becomes 1.544 Mbit/s [(1.536÷192)+1.536].

While digital transmission makes use of the identical twisted-pair and PCM carrier technique used for analog, the local distribution scheme is very different (Fig. 2). All loading coils, amplifiers, and equalizers must be removed, leaving the physical twisted pairs as the only element between the subscriber and the central office's channel-bank equipment.

Services like DDS are terminated with either separate or integrated channel service units (CSUs) and data service units (DSUs) at the subscriber's premises—discussed in detail later—and office channel units (OCUs) at the phone company's central office. The OCU performs much like an integrated CSU/DSU to compensate for the line's effect on the received signal, to generate the transmitted signal, to provide both transmitter and receiver filtering, and to convert the received bipolar pulses back to serial digital data. The OCU also reformats this signal back to a 64-kbit/s frame. In a diagnostic operation, the OCU generates the commands that place the subscriber's CSU into a line loopback and the DSU into a digital loopback test mode.

Transmitting digital representations of the data and eliminating the analog-to-digital conversion at the central office permits current PCM gear to accept data at 64 kbit/s. Services such as DDS, however, use one bit out of every eight for network signaling, leaving 56 kbit/s for the subscriber's data. Since DDS does not use multilevel signaling—common to modern modems—the immunity from noise-induced errors is many orders of magnitude greater than that of modem-derived 14.4 kbit/s, although the data throughput is almost four times faster.

The way it's done
Virtually all current digital transmission in the United States utilizes a data encoding scheme known as alternate mark inversion (AMI) or bipolar transmission. While bipolar encoding does eliminate the signal's d.c. component permitting the use of isolation transformers, no classical modulation need be performed. Both line signal and data timing transitions occur at the same isochronous (equally timed) intervals, greatly simplify-

3. Bipolar encoding. *The unshaped signal is reduced to a 50 percent bipolar waveform and filtered. The spectral output exhibits zero energy at the data rate.*

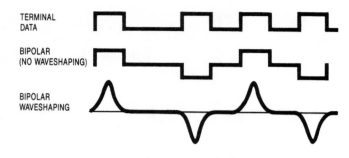

ing the design for the required equipment.

Figure 3 illustrates how a bipolar waveform is generated from a terminal's serial digital output. When an unshaped bipolar signal is filtered, its area is reduced to a 50 percent bipolar waveform. This elimination of the d.c. component and reshaping of the waveform permits use of transformer coupling. This coupling also enables line isolation from high voltages, such as from lightning strikes. Current digital services utilize filtered 50 percent bipolar waveshapes, which help eliminate high-frequency components that may interfere with other transmissions.

For 9.6-kbit/s transmission, the resulting transmitted output spectrum has no energy at either d.c. or 9,600 Hz and peaks at 4,800 Hz.

Normal bipolar transmission requires that each data pulse, representing a logical-one state, be transmitted with alternating polarity. A violation (of this rule) is defined as two successive pulses that have the same polarity (Fig. 4) and are separated by a zero level. Violation characters may be framed either to replace a long string of zero pulses (which could result in a loss of signal timing and subsequent loss of receiver synchronization) or to transmit control information. An example of the latter is a bipolar violation sequence to notify the remote station that the local terminal's request-to-send signal has been turned off. Another bipolar violation control sequence may be transmitted as notification that the network is out of service.

Equipment for connection to DDS and T1 service must be either grandfathered (identical devices placed into service prior to Nov. 18, 1983) or certified compliant by the manufacturer to the appropriate Bell Technical Reference and the requirements set forth by the

4. Violations. *A violation is two successive pulses with the same polarity, separated by a zero. Normal bipolar signaling requires alternating polarity.*

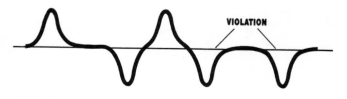

former BOCs. Final rules will be developed at industry meetings composed of carriers and equipment manufacturers. Once adopted, newly developed equipment will be registered under FCC Part 68, in a manner very much like today's switched-network modems.

Connection to digital service has progressed in a manner similar to that of the analog public-switched network. In June 1983—nine years after the first AT&T-provided DDS was deployed—the FCC declared that virtually all equipment interfacing digital service, and located at the customer's site, is defined as customer premises equipment (CPE). As such, it could no longer be provided by the regulated phone company.

Available CSU

Between 1974 and 1981, the equipment interfacing a terminal had almost exclusively been the Western Electric 500A-type integrated CSU/DSU. The portion of this device that performed the actual line-interface functions, the CSU element, was also available. To lease the CSU, the customer would have to buy a bipolar signal converter to interface the CSU to the data terminal. Since the difference between tariffs for the CSU and the full CSU/DSU was under $20 a month, almost all customers chose the latter as the more economical approach.

In response to industry and FCC pressure, AT&T established the CSU as the sole standard interface for all digital services in October 1981. The bipolar signal-converter portion was broken out of the 500A to form the 500B-type DSU. All equipment providers, including AT&T, were required to interface DDS via CSUs provided by the phone company.

As a result of the FCC's Computer Inquiry II ruling, neither AT&T nor the BOCs were permitted to install any equipment the customer could provide. This included the 500B-type DSU, which customers then sought from independent suppliers. Also, an FCC order eliminated the CSU from the regulated domain. While subscribers may still use separate CSUs, they must either purchase or lease them. Integrated CSU/DSU equipment may also be used instead of the separate devices.

So, two types of digital CPE may be found at the end of the subscriber's access line:

■ *Channel service unit.* Prior to Nov. 18, 1983, all digital services were terminated in a phone-company-provided CSU, known generically as network channel terminating equipment (NCTE). See Figure 5. The CSU performs certain line-conditioning functions such as equalization and signal reshaping. Also, the CSU incorporates the aforementioned line loopback test capability, used in troubleshooting procedures to isolate network problems. This loopback is activated by a command transmitted from the phone company serving office, causing the CSU to return the received line signal back to the phone company office.

■ *Integrated equipment (combined CSU/DSU).* Due to the recent changes classifying the CSU as customer providable, the functions of both the CSU and DSU may be integrated into one device. Unifying the equip-

5. The CSU and DSU. *The DSU functions as an interface to the data terminal; the CSU, to the digital line. The two are now available as one integrated device.*

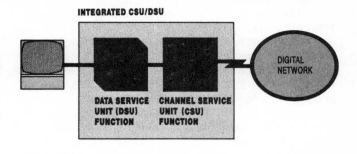

INTEGRATED CSU/DSU

DATA SERVICE UNIT (DSU) FUNCTION   CHANNEL SERVICE UNIT (CSU) FUNCTION   DIGITAL NETWORK

ment to contain both CSU and DSU functions saves cost by eliminating an enclosure, power supply, and interface cable. In response to the FCC order, AT&T proposed rules to register equipment for connection to digital networks, such as DDS, and to call for a standard 8-pin plug-and-jack arrangement. The older CSU/DDS connection was a far more cumbersome 15-pin connector, requiring the use of a screwdriver to secure the interface cable.

From its inception, digital transmission services, such as DDS, have been oriented toward very high availability at very low error rates. DDS is the first service ever tariffed with guarantees of 99.95 percent uptime and 99.5 percent error-free seconds.

Uptime describes the amount of time that a channel remains available for the user's data. Since there are 8,766 (365¼ × 24) hours in a year, the uptime guarantee translates into service interruptions not to exceed 4.4 hours per year.

Block transmissions

Error-free seconds is a common measure of a channel's signal quality under normal operating conditions. With a 99.5 percent guarantee, only one second in 200 may have an error, on average. Since most transmissions occur in blocks of characters, a total message retransmission may be required if an error is detected within a block. A typical 128-character block (8 bits per character) has 1,024 bits. An error rate of one in 10^5 bits, a commonly used criterion for analog transmission, implies a retransmission rate of about one out of every 97 data blocks.

With DDS, no more than one second in 200 is likely to contain an error. For single-bit disruptions at 9.6 kbit/s, each 128-character transmission would take 0.107 seconds—equivalent to about nine data blocks per second. This equates to one retransmitted block out of every 1,800 blocks—almost 20 times better than that commonly seen with analog transmission.

To maintain the quoted digital-service guarantees, AT&T has established elaborate testing procedures to pinpoint network problems. One Chicago-based test facility, owned by AT&T Communications Services, is known as automated bit access test systems (ABATS). ABATS controls remote bit access test systems (BATS) at the various serving offices. Thus, ABATS can test the entire digital network, including the subscriber's DSU. By accessing the bit stream, ABATS can actuate loopbacks at the remote DSUs. While the service provider cannot require the subscriber's CSU/DSU equipment to interoperate with the network test capabilities, customers will most likely opt for equipment that reduces the time required to troubleshoot a faulty installation.

Serving test center equipment controls two kinds of loopback tests at the customer's location, if the on-site equipment is designed to respond. The first, a line loopback (LL), returns the received bipolar signal from a remote CSU—after equalization and signal reshaping—to the network. This test is engaged by reversing the d.c. sealing current's polarity—under the test operator's control—which is sensed by the CSU. Sealing current is supplied between the transmitter and receiver pairs to reduce the possibility of corrosion between wire splices, which could result in an intermittent or open circuit.

The second or remote terminal (RT) loopback actually permits the phone company maintenance technician to perform a complete digital loopback at the remote DSU-data terminal interface. By sending certain repeated bipolar-violation codes, the test operator can direct the digital data—which was received and decoded by the DSU—to be transmitted back to the test center. Whereas the LL test returns the reshaped bipolar signal, the RT test verifies the data after it has been decoded, reclocked, and retransmitted.

When a problem is suspected, the subscriber calls a repair number to have the phone company begin diagnostic procedures. Note that control and maintenance of the digital network focuses around the serving test center, not the customer's host location. Also, when problems are reported, there must be agreement between the service provider and customer as to how and when the testing is to proceed.

Some communications managers are reluctant to choose digital service without customer-controlled diagnostics. Fortunately, independent equipment manufacturers have been able to offer these capabilities.

The nature of today's digital diagnostics provides network control via command codes within the data band. Since services like DDS offer no extra bandwidth for a diagnostic channel, it is not possible to send both primary and diagnostic data without somehow reducing throughput.

The DDS diagnostic schemes currently available do help the communications manager to pinpoint network problems. Diagnostics such as LL and RT, remote transmit inhibit (anti-streaming), and passing of control commands from master to remote business-equipment interface are all capabilities currently offered on an interruptive basis. But many communications managers would like to have the continuous network surveillance available with analog networks.

A new digital service is being proposed to the BOCs by Bell Communications Research, the network consultant owned equally by all seven regional BOCs. The service, called DDS with Secondary Channel, simultaneously provides both a full-rate data channel and an auxiliary channel. By using this latter capability, diagnostic data can be transmitted for remote surveillance and control, independent of the primary channel.

The proposed offering is based on a time-division multiplexed approach and the fact that central-office-to-subscriber signaling is performed at overspeed rates. For the subrates 2.4, 4.8, and 9.6 kbit/s, the transmission speed of the composite primary- and secondary-channel data is actually 8/6 the primary channel rate: 3.2, 6.4, and 12.8 kbit/s, respectively. At 56 kbit/s the composite rate is 9/7, or 72 kbit/s. The precise overspeed rate is dictated by a clever adaptation of the current PCM technique and the byte structure that it uses.

The subrate data is formatted into 6-bit bytes from the subscriber. At the phone company, one bit is added for subrate framing and a second bit to pass control information. By adding a ninth bit onto the composite data between the central office and subscriber equipment, the information is framed so that the network's control (C) bit may be passed to the digital terminating equipment. Timesharing this C bit as one secondary channel bit for every three frames provides a low-speed channel at $133\frac{1}{3}$, $266\frac{2}{3}$, and $533\frac{1}{3}$ bit/s for 2.4, 4.8, and 9.6 kbit/s, respectively. A customer-provided device will be responsible for formatting the data to the central office.

Higher-speed 56-kbit/s service derives its $2{,}666\frac{2}{3}$-bit/s secondary channel in much the same manner as for the subrates. But because 56 kbit/s makes use of 7 out of 8 bits for customer data (as contrasted with 6 out of 8 for the subrates), full primary and secondary data independence cannot be assured. Also, one of the C bit's network functions is to relay the status of the remote terminal's request-to-send interface lead. Because of the limitations involved, the proposed 56-kbit/s DDS with secondary channel is currently limited to point-to-point service.

Extension to the service

The conversion of phone company analog facilities to run digital services can be expensive. Besides having to clear the subscriber access line of loading coils, amplifiers, and equalizers (as described earlier), extraneous unterminated lengths of wire (such as bridged taps) must also be located and removed (discussed later). Finally, equipment at the central office must be replaced to enable acceptance of the digital, bipolar-encoded data by the PCM gear.

Some U. S. locations may not currently have the data subscriber base to justify the phone company investment necessary for digital service. These locations are usually from remote urban areas and cannot economically be brought directly into the digital network.

The method to extend DDS-type services (with data rates up to 9.6 kbit/s) to these remote areas makes use of existing analog facilities and modems (Fig. 6). By collocating a CSU/DSU and a modem at the nearest location accommodating digital service, data is retransmitted by the modem over a voice-grade leased line to the remote site. This leg of the network is referred to as an analog extension of digital service.

6. Analog extension. *To supply digital service to a remote location that is not economically justifiable for DDS service, a modem and a CSU/DSU are collocated at the nearest DDS location. The modem retransmits data over a voice-grade leased line to the remote site. Subtle clocking considerations must be observed.*

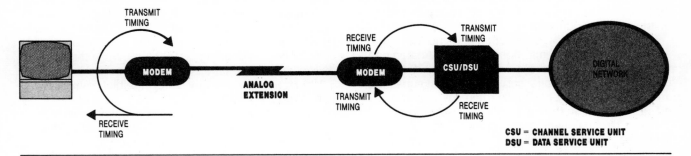

CSU = CHANNEL SERVICE UNIT
DSU = DATA SERVICE UNIT

Since all digital transmission services are centrally timed, subtle clocking considerations must be observed. Successful analog extensions require that the modem use the recovered network timing from its collocated DSU to supply timing to the modem's transmitter. At the remote site, the recovered receiver timing must also be looped back to supply timing to the remote modem's transmitter. Finally, the DSU collocated with the modem must have the transmitted data resynchronized with the digital network timing, using either a buffer or phase corrector. The requirement that network timing be retained by all elements of the analog extension must always be observed.

Acquisition scenario

Let us now outline the manner in which a data user orders digital service:

■ The customer must first contact the service provider to evaluate the configuration that is required. The provider may be a BOC for intra-LATA (local access and transport area) service. For inter-LATA service, contact should be made with a long-haul carrier such as AT&T Communications, General Telephone, Continental Telephone, or MCI. AT&T's Accunet DDS is offered exclusively as an end-to-end service: all coordination of facilities between AT&T Communications and local access providers is handled by AT&T.

■ Among the service considerations are data rates, number and distribution of the remote terminals, type of transmission (whether synchronous or asynchronous), as well as the host-facility requirements. At this time the service provider explains the various tariff charges related to service. Whether or not the user's volume of data warrants the expense of digital service should be thoroughly explored at these initial stages — not when the lines and equipment have been installed. New tariffs may well provide for minimum service provisions and contingent termination liabilities. This means that one may no longer be able to postpone service installation while awaiting other equipment. Once an installation date has been agreed upon, the customer will be committed to a minimum operational time — possibly as long as one year. It is important for the communications manager to get firm delivery dates for ordered equipment before establishing the service installation date.

■ The user must either purchase or lease the appropriate termination equipment. This will be either a separate CSU and DSU or a combined CSU/DSU device. These devices are available from communications equipment manufacturers, various phone company equipment subsidiaries, and distributors. While acquiring the termination equipment, the customer must also consider whether or not network diagnostics are required. Simple point-to-point installations may not justify the added expense. On the other hand, complex multipoint networks in critical applications — such as banking transactions — may dictate a well-integrated (analog and digital) network control design.

■ With the current interim direct-connection standards, DDS-type services are terminated in either "42A" blocks for single lines, or mass termination "punch-down" blocks for multiline installations. When final standards for direct connection to DDS have been adopted, the customer will most likely see the service terminate in an 8-pin phone company jack, similar to that used for terminating programmable 3002 analog private lines used by modems.

■ Once the service is installed, the customer attaches the CSU or combined CSU/DSU to the four wires that terminate the service. As in analog private line terminations, the red and green wires generally accept the subscriber's transmitted data signals, while the yellow and black wires provide the received signal from the network.

■ If separate CSUs and DSUs are used, an interface cable between them is required. All 550A-type CSUs use a standard 15-pin connector for this purpose.

■ The business equipment (terminal) connects to the DSU or combined CSU/DSU via one of the various standard connectorized interfaces. Most 2.4-, 4.8-, or 9.6-kbit/s equipment makes use of EIA RS-232-C, while the majority of 56-kbit/s equipment uses the CCITT V.35 standard.

It should be noted that analog transmission does have three near-term advantages over digital. First and foremost is availability. Dial-up analog voiceband service is provided on a worldwide basis. But the majority of data is transmitted via leased lines, between fixed points of concentration. This fact favors digital service in the long run, since the private line represents a substantially controlled environment.

Analog's second near-term advantage over digital lies in its ability to work with existing network elements, such as loading coils and bridged-tap remnant lines. But the vast majority of subscriber access lines are not loaded, and they have a manageable number and distribution of bridged taps.

Finally, analog local distribution does not have the access-line distance limitations of digital. Analog can work much further than the 15,000-to-18,000-foot limitation of 56-kbit/s digital service. Yet most subscribers are served within a 2-to-3-mile radius of a central office—well within the range of digital service.

Better digital network performance and higher efficiencies will be accomplished by improving the utilization of the local subscriber distribution. The installed twisted pairs that serve most telephones will support a far greater bandwidth than the 3,100 Hz currently used. Typifying new data transmission concepts that make more effective use of the subscriber access lines are local area data transport (LADT) and circuit switched digital capability (CSDC). LADT is geared toward more-localized data requirements and is therefore being scrutinized closely by the BOCs. CSDC, on the other hand, has been designed to provide nationwide service. Although access to the service will come via the BOCs, AT&T Communications—as an inter-LATA carrier—is spearheading the effort to make CSDC available throughout the United States.

LADT centers around a packet network such as the one deployed in Dade County, Fla., by Bell South and Knight/Ridder Publications. While LADT has the essentials of any packet network, great interest has been focused on the subscriber distribution scheme.

LADT is currently under trial in two forms. The first is dial-up access using standard full-duplex 1.2-kbit/s modems. Customers with an asynchronous terminal and modem dial into an access node when they wish to use the service. The second form makes use of dedicated communications facilities for immediate access, without the inconvenience of dialing first. It is this dedicated access that holds the most promise for widespread distribution of the various services to be carried. Dedicated access uses existing customer wires, employing modems that actually add a full-duplex 4.8-kbit/s data channel to the subscriber access line's voice capability.

Using a frequency-division multiplexing technique, the modem for LADT modulates the customer's data into two frequency channels well above the voiceband. These channels provide for communications to and from the phone company's central office. The analog channel, used for telephone service, remains within the 300-to-3,400-Hz band. The two-wire subscriber line then provides both voice and data service. Equipment at the central office splits off the data stream, passing it to the packet network, while the voice signals proceed normally to the PCM channel bank. While this method of adding a communications channel is similar to that used for many years to add an extra voice channel, LADT represents the first dedicated data application.

With LADT, the customer gets an apparent net gain of one data channel, piggybacked onto the standard switched phone network service already in place. This means that the majority of installed switched-network access lines become candidates for adding a full-time, independent data capability, without adding any lines.

Some subscribers may not be able to take advantage of the LADT scheme. Standard access-line installation procedures have required the addition of loading coils for lines exceeding 18,000 feet. While these devices may flatten the amplitude response in the 3,100-Hz voiceband, they distort the higher-frequency bands required by the data channel. Dispatching phone company personnel to remove these loading coils becomes an expensive proposition that neither the phone company nor the subscriber may want to bear. (Note that coil removal may affect analog speech quality.)

The other potential problem with installed access lines is the existence of bridged taps. A bridged tap is a remnant left from service disconnection and subsequent reconnection, or from replacing defective lines. Bridged taps add undesirable capacitance and disruptive discontinuities representing points for signal reflections that can distort the line signals. Fortunately, the majority of phone company lines are not loaded and do not have problems with bridged taps: most subscribers can be served by LADT.

While the current equipment used by Bell South provides a 4.8-kbit/s capability, new gear may well make higher rates possible, such as 9.6 and possibly 19.2 kbit/s. Even a 64-kbit/s capability may become an LADT offering in the not-too-distant future.

The next frontier

Private-line digital services are now entering their second decade. CSDC is the next digital service frontier.

By making use of the subscriber's two-wire access line and current PCM distribution facilities, CSDC will permit users to dial up various locations for 56-kbit/s data transmission. While CSDC makes use of existing digital facilities, the scheme for distributing the local data to subscribers is new. The technology chosen, time-compression multiplexing (TCM), is actually a time-division multiplexing technique that establishes adjacent frames of transmitted and received data. Like most digital transmission schemes, TCM requires that the subscriber access lines have no loading coils, but one or two bridged taps can be handled.

By alternating transmission bursts to and from the serving central office at double speed (2×64 kbit/s), a full-duplex link is established (Fig. 7). Separation or buffer spaces appear between the alternating frames to eliminate the possibility of collision between energy bursts. While CSDC will be first offered at 56 kbit/s, the structure of the transmission makes possible future 64-kbit/s clear-channel transmission. (Clear means entirely available to the user.) With the TCM composite (double speed) data rate at 144 kbit/s, and 128 kbit/s dedicated to customer's data, 16 kbit/s is left for a combination of dead-zone buffering, overhead, and control.

CSDC, as proposed, is made up of two functional blocks found on the customer's premises: the NCTE

7. Time-compression multiplexing. *TCM alternates transmission bursts at double speed to and from the central office, establishing a full-duplex link.*

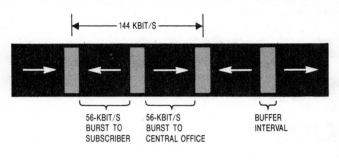

144 KBIT/S

56-KBIT/S
BURST TO
SUBSCRIBER

56-KBIT/S
BURST TO
CENTRAL OFFICE

BUFFER
INTERVAL

function and the terminal interface equipment (TIE) function (Fig. 8). The NCTE portion interfaces the subscriber's two-wire access line, converts the TCM transmission into a bipolar format, reclocks both transmitted and received data signals, and provides the TIE's voice/data interface. The TIE performs a bipolar-to-serial digital data conversion, interfaces both the data terminal equipment (CCITT V.35 for 56 kbit/s) and a telephone handset, passes interface-control information (such as request-to-send/clear-to-send and data-carrier-detect status), and commands the NCTE to enter the voice or data mode. Call setup is accomplished via the telephone's touch-tone keypad.

A second two-wire full-duplex transmission scheme is gaining support in Europe for switched digital local distribution. Called echo cancellation, it makes use of its equipment's adaptive capability to duplicate the attached line's parameters. This information, coupled with knowledge of the transmitted signal, permits the subtraction of the transmitted energy from the composite signal (transmitted plus received) at the two-wire interface.

With this subtraction, the desired received signal is extracted from the composite signal, amplified, and filtered prior to being decoded and sent to a terminal's received-data input. It should be noted that with either TCM or echo cancellation processing, the terminal

8. A step toward ISDN. *The proposed circuit-switched digital capability uses the NCTE and TIE functions. The NCTE provides the TIE's voice/data interface.*

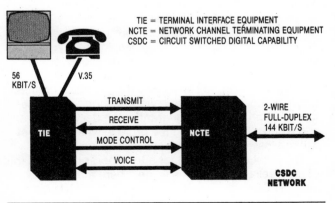

TIE = TERMINAL INTERFACE EQUIPMENT
NCTE = NETWORK CHANNEL TERMINATING EQUIPMENT
CSDC = CIRCUIT SWITCHED DIGITAL CAPABILITY

56
KBIT/S

V.35

TRANSMIT

RECEIVE

MODE CONTROL

VOICE

TIE

NCTE

2-WIRE
FULL-DUPLEX
144 KBIT/S

CSDC
NETWORK

equipment sees a steady data stream.

An echo cancellation standard is currently being formulated by the CCITT. The standard proposes to establish full-duplex 144 kbit/s over the two-wire access line. This standard would provide for two 64-kbit/s channels, with extra supervisory bandwidth per remote station.

Not yet cost-effective

While TCM, designed for CSDC in the United States, uses the same transmitted bandwidth as echo cancellation, it has one-half the latter's channel capability. But the technology to do cancellation, especially at the proposed speed, is not yet considered cost-effective as far as both equipment and integrated-circuit manufacturers are concerned.

While CSDC initially offers 56 kbit/s to the user, 64 kbit/s is in the offing. Current protocol makes use of a network control bit for every seven bits of customer data. By giving this control bit to the subscriber for data, a full 64 kbit/s can be accommodated.

Nationwide deployment of a switched digital capability has its problems. Subscriber access historically deals with analog voiceband signals. Electromechanical relay and crossbar switching equipment (space switches) once represented the most economical means of handling these signals. Space switches route the voiceband signals prior to the A/D conversion required by interoffice PCM transmission. In many cases, local calls routed through such switches do not require digitizing, since both calling and called subscribers share the same routing equipment.

Large-scale integration has tipped the scales away from space switches so that increasing numbers of installations are moving toward time-division digital switching devices. Unfortunately for CSDC, however, a great number of devices already installed are space switches. To be cost-effective, CSDC requires digital switching. This means that investment in new equipment may be required at the local BOC level.

Though CSDC will be deployed initially as a data communications service, its switched network aspects have far-reaching implications. This service could be a major step toward an integrated services digital network (ISDN).

LSI (large-scale integrated) technology has made possible analog-to-digital conversion within each telephone via a coder-decoder (codec). This component can now be made at a cost such that the price of a digital handset is comparable to that of an analog one.

CSDC coupled with the digital handset clears the way for the integration of voice and data over the same network. In this manner the outputs from the telephone and from the data communications equipment become indistinguishable. New equipment such as 56-kbit/s facsimile and full-frame video (though not full-motion) now becomes more economically feasible. ■

Hugh Goldberg's General DataComm assignments have included directing the baseband marketing activity and engineering development of modems and data service units.

William Stallings, Honeywell Information Systems, McLean, Va.

A primer: Understanding transport protocols

Mechanisms for managing data encapsulated at the transport protocol layer form the basis of communications architecture.

The transport protocol is the keystone of the whole concept of a computer communications architecture. Within the structure of a communications architecture, it is the transport protocol that provides a reliable mechanism for the exchange of data between processes in different computers. The protocol typically ensures that data is delivered error-free, in sequence, with no loss or duplication. The transport service relieves higher-level software of the burden of managing the intervening communications facility. Because the transport protocol provides for high-quality service, and because it may need to deal with a range of communications services, it can be the most complex of all communications protocols.

The transport layer shields applications from the details of the underlying communications service. This is depicted in Figure 1. Stations 1 and 2 each have one or more applications that wish to communicate. For each such application (for example, electronic mail) an application-oriented protocol is needed that coordinates the activities of the corresponding application modules and assures common syntax and semantics. The transport protocol in turn makes use of a network's services module, which provides access to the intervening communications network (for example, using X.25).

The basic service provided by a transport protocol is the transfer of data between two transport users, such as a session protocol or an application. Data is passed from a transport user to a transport protocol entity. This entity encapsulates that data into a transport protocol data unit (TPDU), which contains the user data plus control information, such as the destination address. Beyond this basic service, there are a number of other services offered to the transport user:

■ *Connection type.* This provides for the logical connection between transport users. Connectionless service transmits each unit of data independently and generally does not guarantee delivery.

■ *Grade of service.* Transport users can specify the grade of transmission service, such as acceptable error and loss levels, desired average and maximum delays and throughput, and priority.

■ *Connection management.* With this connection-oriented service, transport entities are responsible for establishing, maintaining, and terminating logical connections between endpoints.

■ *Expedited delivery.* This is an interrupt mechanism used to transfer occasional urgent data, such as a break character or alarm condition. The sending transport entity endeavors to have the transmission facility transfer the data as rapidly as possible; the receiving transport entity interrupts the user to signify receipt of urgent data.

■ *Status reporting.* This service allows the transport user to receive information on the condition or attributes of a transport entity or connection.

■ *Security.* The transport entity may be able to request security services from the transmission facility.

The complexity of a transport protocol depends upon the type of service it provides and the type of service it receives from the communications facility below it. Typically, a transport protocol provides a connection-oriented service. That is, a logical connection is established between two transport users. The transport protocol may guarantee the delivery of data over such a connection in the order in which it is sent with no losses or duplication.

The most difficult case for a transport protocol is that of an unreliable network service. There are two problems: TPDUs are occasionally lost; and TPDUs may arrive out of sequence due to variable transit delays. As we shall see, elaborate mechanisms are required to cope with these two interrelated network deficiencies. We shall also see that a discouraging pattern emerges. The combination of unreliability and nonsequencing creates problems with every mechanism. Generally, the solution to each problem raises new problems. While there are problems to be overcome for protocols at all levels, it seems that there are more difficulties with a reliable connection-oriented transport protocol than with any other sort of protocol.

The four key transport protocol mechanisms are:
- Ordered delivery
- Connection establishment
- Error control
- Flow control

Ordered delivery
If two entities are not directly connected, there is the possibility that TPDUs will not arrive in the order in which they were sent, because they may traverse different paths. In connection-oriented data transfer, it is generally required that the TPDU order be maintained. For example, if a file is transferred between two points, we would like to be assured that the data in the received file is in the same order as in the transmitted file, and not shuffled. If each TPDU is given a number, and numbers are assigned sequentially, then it is a logically simple task for the receiving entity to re-order

received TPDUs on the basis of sequence number.

Thus, the header in the TPDU contains a sequence number field. The only hitch in this scheme is that sequence numbers repeat; when the maximum number is reached, the numbering sequence starts over again at zero. It is evident that the maximum sequence number must be greater than the maximum number of TPDUs that could be outstanding at any time.

Connection establishment
To provide connection-oriented service, any transfer of data between transport entities must begin with a connection-establishment procedure.

Connection establishment serves three main purposes:
- It allows each end to assure that the other exists.
- It allows negotiation of optional parameters (for example, TPDU size and grade of service).
- It triggers allocation of transport entity resources (for example, buffer space and entry in connection table).

Connection establishment is by mutual agreement and can be accomplished by a control TPDU (a TPDU that contains no user data, just control information). The side wishing to initiate a connection sends RFC X, which is a request for connection, and indicates that the requesting entity will begin issuing data TPDUs with sequence number X. The other transport entity accepts the connection by issuing an RFC Y, indicating that it

1. Shielded from details. The transport protocol layer shields applications from the details of the underlying communications service. The two stations depicted here have applications that wish to communicate. Therefore, an applications protocol is needed that coordinates activities and assures common syntax and semantics.

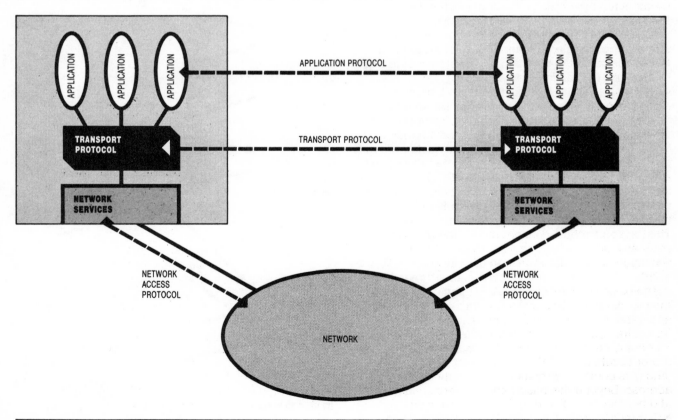

will send data TPDUs beginning with sequence number Y. Note that either side can initiate a connection, and if both sides initiate a connection at about the same time, it is established without confusion.

As with other protocol mechanisms, connection establishment must take into account the unreliability of the network service. Suppose that A issues an RFC to B. It expects to get an RFC back, confirming the connection. Two things can go wrong: A's RFC can be lost or B's answering RFC can be lost. Both cases can be handled by using a retransmit-RFC timer. After A issues an RFC, it will reissue the RFC when the timer expires.

This gives rise, potentially, to duplicate RFCs. However, if A's initial RFC is lost, there are no duplicates. If B's response is lost, then B may receive two RFCs from A. Further, if B's response is not lost, but simply delayed, A may get two responding RFCs. All of this means that A and B must simply ignore duplicate RFCs once a connection is established.

Now, consider that a duplicate RFC may survive past the termination of the connection. RFC X arrives at B after the connection is terminated. B assumes that this is a fresh request and responds with an RFC Y. Meanwhile, A has decided to open a new connection with B and sends RFC Z. B discards this as a duplicate. Subsequently, A initiates data transfer with a TPDU numbered Z. B rejects the TPDU as being out of sequence.

The way out of this problem is for each side to explicitly acknowledge the other's RFC and sequence number. The procedure is known as a three-way handshake. With this strategy, the transport entity hesitates during the connection opening to assure that any RFC that was sent has also been acknowledged before the connection is declared open. Plus, there is an additional control TPDU to reset (RST) the other side when a duplicate RFC is detected.

Figure 2 illustrates typical three-way handshake operations. An RFC is sent that includes the send sequence number. The responding RFC acknowledges that number and includes the sequence number for the other side. The initiating transport entity acknowledges the RFC acknowledgment in its first data TPDU. Next shown is a situation in which an old RFC X arrives at B after the close of the relevant connection. B assumes that this is a fresh request and responds with RFC Y, ACK X. When A receives this message, it realizes that it has not requested a connection and therefore sends a RST, ACK Y. Note that the ACK Y portion of the RST message is essential so that an old, duplicate RST does not abort a legitimate connection establishment. The final example shows a case in which an old RFC ACK arrives in the middle of a new connection establishment. Because of the use of sequence numbers in the acknowledgments, this event causes no mischief.

Error control
If the underlying communications facility is unreliable, the transport facility must cope with lost or damaged data TPDUs. For this purpose, a positive acknowledgment (ACK) scheme is used: the receiver must ac-

knowledge each successfully received TPDU. For efficiency, we do not require one ACK per TPDU. Rather, a cumulative acknowledgment can be used. Thus, the receiver may receive TPDUs numbered 1, 2, and 3, but only send ACK 3 back. The sender interprets ACK 3 to mean that number 3 and all previous TPDUs have been successfully received.

Now, if a TPDU is lost in transit, no ACK will be sent. To cope with this situation, there must be a timer associated with each TPDU as it is sent. If the timer expires before the TPDU is acknowledged, the sender must retransmit.

So, the addition of a timer solves that problem. Next problem: At what value should the timer be set? If the value is too small, there will be many unnecessary retransmissions, wasting network capacity. If the value is too large, the protocol will be sluggish in responding to a lost TPDU. The timer should be set at a value slightly longer than the round-trip delay (send TPDU, receive ACK). Of course, this delay is variable even under constant network load. Worse, the statistics of the delay will vary with changing network conditions.

---

2. Three-way handshake. *Here are three examples showing connections initiated, accepted, acknowledged, or rejected before transmission begins.*

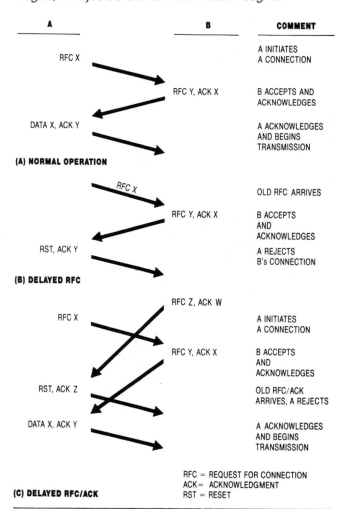

A	B	COMMENT
RFC X		A INITIATES A CONNECTION
	RFC Y, ACK X	B ACCEPTS AND ACKNOWLEDGES
DATA X, ACK Y		A ACKNOWLEDGES AND BEGINS TRANSMISSION

(A) NORMAL OPERATION

RFC X		OLD RFC ARRIVES
	RFC Y, ACK X	B ACCEPTS AND ACKNOWLEDGES
RST, ACK Y		A REJECTS B's CONNECTION

(B) DELAYED RFC

	RFC Z, ACK W	
RFC X		A INITIATES A CONNECTION
	RFC Y, ACK X	B ACCEPTS AND ACKNOWLEDGES
RST, ACK Z		OLD RFC/ACK ARRIVES, A REJECTS
DATA X, ACK Y		A ACKNOWLEDGES AND BEGINS TRANSMISSION

(C) DELAYED RFC/ACK

RFC = REQUEST FOR CONNECTION
ACK = ACKNOWLEDGMENT
RST = RESET

116

Two strategies suggest themselves. A fixed timer value could be used, based on an understanding of the network's typical behavior. This solution suffers from an inability to respond to changing network conditions. If the value is set too high, the service will always be sluggish. If it is set too low, a positive feedback condition can develop, in which network congestion leads to more retransmissions, which increase congestion.

An adaptive scheme has its own problems. Suppose the transport entity keeps track of the time taken to acknowledge data TPDUs and sets its retransmission timer based on an average of the observed delays. This value cannot be trusted, for three reasons:
■ The peer entity may not acknowledge a TPDU immediately. Recall that it has the privilege of cumulation acknowledgments.
■ If a TPDU has been retransmitted, the sender cannot know whether the received ACK is a response to the initial transmission or a retransmission.
■ Network conditions may change suddenly.

Each of these problems is cause for some further tweaking of the transport algorithm; but the problem admits no complete solution. There will always be some uncertainty concerning the best value for the retransmission timer.

If a TPDU is lost and then retransmitted, no confu-

---

3. Exhausted. *When the sequence space is exhausted, A cycles back to the original TPDU 0, which is accepted by B before the duplicate TPDU 0 arrives.*

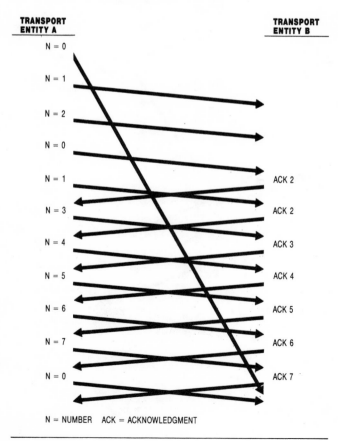

N = NUMBER   ACK = ACKNOWLEDGMENT

---

sion will result. If, however, an ACK is lost, one or more TPDUs will be retransmitted and, if they arrive successfully, they may be duplicates of previously received TPDUs. Thus, the sender must be able to recognize duplicates. The fact that each TPDU carries a sequence number helps, but, nevertheless, duplicate detection and handling are not easy. There are two cases:
■ A duplicate is received prior to the close of the connection.
■ A duplicate is received after the close of the connection.

Notice that we say "a" duplicate rather than "the" duplicate. From the sender's point of view, the retransmitted TPDU is the duplicate. However, the retransmitted TPDU may arrive before the original TPDU, in which case the receiver views the original TPDU as the duplicate. In any case, two tactics are needed to cope with a duplicate received prior to the close of a connection:
■ The receiver must assume that its acknowledgment was lost and therefore must acknowledge the duplicate. Consequently, the sender must not get confused if it receives multiple ACKs to the same TPDU.
■ The sequence number space must be long enough so as not to "cycle" in less than the maximum possible TPDU lifetime.

Figure 3 illustrates the reason for this latter requirement. In this example, the sequence space is of length 8. A transmits TPDUs 0, 1, and 2 and awaits acknowledgment. For some reason, TPDU 0 is excessively delayed. B has received 1 and 2, but 0 is delayed in transit. Thus, B does not send any ACKs. A times out and retransmits TPDU 0. When the duplicate TPDU 0 arrives, B acknowledges 0, 1, and 2. Meanwhile, A has timed out again and retransmits 1, which B acknowledges with another ACK 2. Things now seem to have sorted themselves out, and data transfer continues. When the sequence space is exhausted, A cycles back to sequence number 0 and continues. Alas, the old TPDU 0 makes a belated appearance and is accepted by B before the new TPDU 0 arrives.

It should be clear that the untimely emergence of the old TPDU would have caused no difficulty if the sequence numbers had not yet returned to 0. The problem is, how big must the sequence space be? This depends on, among other things, whether the network enforces a maximum packet lifetime and on the rate at which TPDUs are being transmitted. As we shall see, the standard transport protocols allow stupendous sequence spaces.

A more subtle problem is posed by TPDUs that continue to rattle around after a transport connection is closed. If a subsequent connection is opened between the same two transport entities, a TPDU from the old connection could arrive and be accepted on the new connection. Similarly, a delayed ACK can enter a new connection and cause problems.

There are a number of approaches to this particular problem. We mention two of the more promising. First, the sequence numbering scheme can be extended across connection lifetimes. This requires that a transport entity remember the last sequence number that it used on transmission for each terminated connection. Then, when a new connection to a transport entity is attempted, the RFC contains the sequence number to be used to begin data transfer. Of course, this procedure is symmetric, with each side responsible for declaring the sequence number with which it will commence transmission.

The above procedures work fine unless a crash occurs. In that case, the transport entity will not remember what sequence number was used last. An alternative is simply to wait a sufficient amount of time between connections to assure that all old TPDUs are gone. Then, even if one side has experienced a crash, the other side can refuse a connection until the re-connection timer expires. This, of course, may cause undesirable delays.

Flow control

Flow control is the process of controlling the flow of data between two points. This seemingly simple concept leads to a rather complex mechanism at the transport layer, primarily for two reasons:
■ Flow control at the transport layer involves the interaction of transport users, transport entities, and the network service.
■ The transmission delay between transport entities is generally long compared with actual transmission time and, what is worse, is variable.

When a transport user wishes to transmit data, it sends that data to its transport entity. This triggers two events: the transport entity generates one or more TPDUs and passes these on to the network service. It also acknowledges to the user that it has accepted the data for transmission. At this point, the transport entity can exercise flow control across the user-transport interface by simply withholding its acknowledgment. The protocol entity is most likely to do this if the entity itself is being held up by a flow control exercised by either the network service or the target transport entity.

In any case, once the transport entity has accepted the data, it sends out a TPDU. Some time later, it receives an acknowledgment that the data has been received at the remote end. It then sends a confirmation to the sender.

At the receiving end a TPDU arrives at the transport entity. It unwraps the data and sends it on to the destination user. When the user accepts the data, it issues an acknowledgment. The user can exercise flow control over the transport entity by withholding its response.

Now, the target transport entity has two choices regarding acknowledgment back to the source transport entity. Either it can issue an acknowledgment as soon as it has correctly received the TPDU, or it can wait until it knows that its user has correctly received the data before acknowledging. The latter course is the safer. In this latter case, the acknowledgment is in fact a confirmation that the destination user received the data. In the former case, it merely confirms that the data made it through to the remote transport entity.

With the above discussion in mind, we can cite two

reasons why one transport entity would want to restrain the rate of TPDU transmission over a connection from another transport entity:
■ The user of the receiving transport entity cannot keep up with the flow of data.
■ The receiving transport entity itself cannot keep up with the flow of TPDUs.

How do such problems manifest themselves? Presumably, a transport entity has a certain amount of buffer space. Incoming TPDUs are added to the buffer. Each buffered TPDU is processed by examining the transport header and the data sent to the user. Either of the two problems mentioned above will cause the buffer to fill up. Thus, the transport entity needs to take steps to stop or slow the flow of TPDUs to prevent buffer overflow. Due to the annoying time gap between sender and receiver, it is not always easy for the

---

4. Credit allocation. *In this example of a credit allocation protocol, data flows in one direction. Sending machine A is granted a credit allocation of 7.*

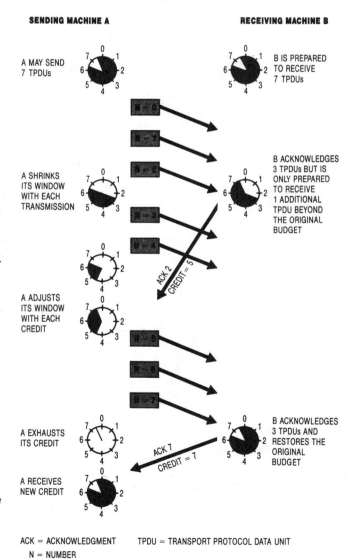

SENDING MACHINE A   RECEIVING MACHINE B

A MAY SEND 7 TPDUs

B IS PREPARED TO RECEIVE 7 TPDUs

A SHRINKS ITS WINDOW WITH EACH TRANSMISSION

B ACKNOWLEDGES 3 TPDUs BUT IS ONLY PREPARED TO RECEIVE 1 ADDITIONAL TPDU BEYOND THE ORIGINAL BUDGET

A ADJUSTS ITS WINDOW WITH EACH CREDIT

ACK 2 CREDIT = 5

A EXHAUSTS ITS CREDIT

B ACKNOWLEDGES 3 TPDUs AND RESTORES THE ORIGINAL BUDGET

ACK 7 CREDIT = 7

A RECEIVES NEW CREDIT

ACK = ACKNOWLEDGMENT   TPDU = TRANSPORT PROTOCOL DATA UNIT
N = NUMBER

ISO and DOD TPDU fields

ACKNOWLEDGMENT NUMBER (32 BITS)
A piggybacked acknowledgment.

ACKNOWLEDGE TIME
An estimate of the time taken by the entity to acknowledge a DT TPDU. This helps the other entity select a value for its retransmission timer.

ALTERNATIVE PROTOCOL CLASS
Specifies whether only the requested protocol class (2 or 4) is acceptable, or if both classes are acceptable.

CAUSE (8 BITS)
Reason for rejection of a TPDU.

CHECKSUM
For the ISO standard, the result of checksum algorithm for the entire TPDU. The checksum is used only for Class 4 and, within that class, it is mandatory for all CR TPDUs and for all other TPDUs when the checksum option is chosen.

CHECKSUM OPTION
For the ISO standard, it indicates whether checksum should be used.

CLASS (4 BITS)
Protocol Class 2 or 4.

CREDIT (CDT) (4 BITS)
Flow control credit allocation. Initial credit is granted in CR and CC, subsequent credit is granted in ACK. As an option, a 16-bit credit field is used with ACK and is appended after the TPDU-NR field.

DATA OFFSET (4 BITS)
Number of 32-bit words in the header.

DESTINATION PORT (16 BITS)
Identifies destination service access point.

EOT (1 BIT)
Used when a user letter has been fragmented into multiple TPDUs. It is set to 1 on the last TPDU.

FLAGS (6 BITS)
URG: Urgent pointer field significant
ACK: Acknowledgment field significant
PSH: Push function
RST: Reset the connection
SYN: Synchronize the sequence numbers
FIN: No more data from sender

FLOW CONTROL CONFIRMATION
Echoes parameter values in the last ACK TPDU received. It contains the values of the TPDU-NR, CDT, and sub-sequence number fields.

LENGTH INDICATOR (LI) (8 BITS)
Length of the header (fixed plus variable), excluding the LI field, in octets.

OPTION (4 BITS)
For the ISO standard, specifies normal (7-bit sequence number, 4-bit credit) or extended (31-bit sequence number, 16-bit credit) flow control fields.

OPTIONS (VARIABLE)
At present for the DOD standard, only one option is defined, one that specifies the maximum TPDU size that will be accepted.

PRIORITY
Priority of this connection.

REASON (8 BITS)
Reason for requesting a disconnect or rejecting a connection request.

RECEIVER TRANSPORT SUFFIX
Service access point that identifies the calling transport user.

REJECTED TPDU
The bit pattern of the rejected TPDU up to and including the octet that caused the rejections.

RESIDUAL ERROR RATE
Expresses the target and minimum rate of unreported user data loss.

SEQUENCE NUMBER (31 BITS)
Sequence number of the first data octet in this TPDU, except when SYN is present. If SYN is present, it is the initial sequence number (ISN), and the first data octet is ISN + 1.

SOURCE PORT (16 BITS)
Identifies source service access point.

SOURCE REFERENCE (16 BITS)
Reference used by the transport entity to give a unique identifier to the transport connection in its own networks.

SUB-SEQUENCE NUMBER
Number of the ACK that assures the sequentially correct processing of ACKs with the same TPDU-NR.

THROUGHPUT
Specifies the user's throughput requirements in octets per second. Four values are specified: the target and minimum acceptable throughput in both the calling-called direction and the called-calling direction.

TPDU CODE (4 BITS)
Type of TPDU:
- Connection request (CR)
- Connection confirm (CC)
- Disconnect request (DR)
- Disconnect confirm (DC)
- TPDU error (ER)
- Data (DT)
- Expedited data (ED)
- Acknowledgment (ACK)
- Expedited acknowledgment (EA)
- Reject (RJ)

TPDU SIZE
Maximum TPDU size in octets. The range of options is from 128 to 8,192 in powers of 2.

TRANSIT DELAY
Specifies the user's delay requirements in milliseconds. Four values are specified: the target and maximum-acceptable transit delay in both directions.

URGENT POINTER (16 BITS)
Points to the octet following the urgent data. This allows the receiver to know how much urgent data is coming.

VERSION NUMBER
Version of protocol to be followed. The current version is number 1.

WINDOW (16 BITS)
Flow control credit allocation, in octets.

transport entity to meet this requirement.

The most commonly used transport flow control technique is credit allocation, and it makes use of the fact that the TPDUs are numbered. At any time, the sender is allowed to transmit only a "window" of sequence numbers. Each time a TPDU is sent, the window is narrowed by 1. From time to time, the receiver will issue a credit, allowing the sender to widen the window by the granted amount. Credit allocation and acknowledgment are independent of each other. Thus a TPDU may be acknowledged without granting new credit and vice versa.

Credit allocation

Typically, the credit allocation scheme is tied to acknowledgments in the following way: to both acknowledge TPDUs and grant credit, a transport entity sends a control TPDU of the form (ACK N, CDT M), where ACK N acknowledges all data TPDUs through number N, and CDT M allows TPDUs numbers N + 1 through N + M to be transmitted. Figure 4 illustrates the protocol. For simplicity, we show a data flow in one direction only. In this example, TPDUs are numbered sequentially modulo 8. Initially, through the connection establishment process, the sending and receiving sequence numbers are synchronized, and A is granted a credit allocation of 7. A advances the trailing edge of its window each time that it transmits, and advances the leading edge only when it is granted credit.

This mechanism is quite powerful. Consider that the last control TPDU issued by B was (ACK N, CDT M). Then:
- To increase or decrease credit to X when no additional TPDUs have arrived, B can issue one credit (ACK N, CDT X).
- To acknowledge a new TPDU without increasing credit, B can issue (ACK N + 1, CDT M - 1).

In the credit allocation scheme, the receiver needs to adopt some policy concerning the amount of data it permits the sender to transmit. The conservation approach is to only allow new TPDUs up to the limit of available buffer space. If this policy were in effect in Figure 4, then the first credit message implies that B has five free buffer slots, and the second message implies that B has seven free slots.

A conservative flow control scheme may limit the throughput of the transport connection in long-delay situations. The receiver could potentially increase throughput by optimistically granting credit for space it does not have. For example, if a receiver's buffer is full but it anticipates that it can release space for two TPDUs within a round-trip propagation time, it could immediately send a credit of 2. If the receiver can keep up with the sender, then this scheme may increase throughput and do no harm. If the sender is faster than the receiver, however, some TPDUs may be discarded, necessitating a retransmission.

The credit allocation flow control mechanism is quite robust in the face of an unreliable network service. If an ACK/CDT TPDU is lost, little harm is done. Future acknowledgments will resynchronize the protocol. Further, if no new acknowledgments are forthcoming, the sender times out and retransmits a data TPDU, which triggers a new acknowledgment. However, it is still possible for deadlock to occur. Consider a situation in which B sends (ACK N, CDT M), temporarily closing the window. Subsequently, B sends (ACK N, CDT M), but this TPDU is lost. A is awaiting the opportunity to send data and B thinks that it has granted that opportunity. To overcome this problem, a window timer can be used. This timer is reset with each outgoing ACK/CDT TPDU. If the timer ever expires, the protocol entity is required to send an ACK/CDT TPDU, even if it duplicates a previous one. This breaks the deadlock and also assures the other end that the protocol entity is still alive.

An alternative is to provide acknowledgments to the ACK/CDT TPDU. With this mechanism in place, the window timer can have a quite large value without causing much difficulty.

ISO transport protocol standard

The International Organization for Standardization (ISO) has developed a family of transport protocol standards tailored to various levels of service and communications facilities. (For further reference on the ISO transport protocols, as well as on the similar Department of Defense transmission control protocol discussed below, see "ISO and DOD TPDU fields.") The ISO has defined three network types:
- Type A: Network connection with acceptable residual error rate and acceptable rate of signaled failures.
- Type B: Network connection with acceptable residual error rate but unacceptable rate of signaled failures.
- Type C: Network connection with residual error rate not acceptable to the transport service user.

In this context, an error is defined as a lost or duplicated network protocol data unit. If the error is caught and corrected by the network service in a fashion that is transparent to the transport entity, then no damage is done. If the network service detects an error, cannot recover, and signals the transport entities, this is known as a signaled failure. An example would be the notification by X.25 that a reset has occurred. Finally, there are residual errors, that is, those which are not corrected and of which the transport entity is not notified.

In order to handle a variety of user service requirements and available network services, ISO has defined five classes of transport protocol:
- Class 0: Simple
- Class 1: Basic error recovery
- Class 2: Multiplexing
- Class 3: Error recovery and multiplexing
- Class 4: Error detection and recovery

These classes are related to the three types of network service defined earlier, as follows: Classes 0 and 2 are used with Type A networks; Classes 1 and 3 are used with Type B networks; and Class 4 is used with Type C networks.

Class 0 was developed by CCITT (International Telephone and Telegraph Consultative Committee) and is oriented to Teletex, a text-transmission upgrade to Telex. It provides the simplest kind of transport con-

5. Fixed. *Shown below are the fixed-header formats for the International Organization for Standardization transport protocol. Fixed headers are required in a TPDU.* *The fixed header contains the frequently occurring parameters. CC and CR use parameters from a variable header field in the connection establishment process.*

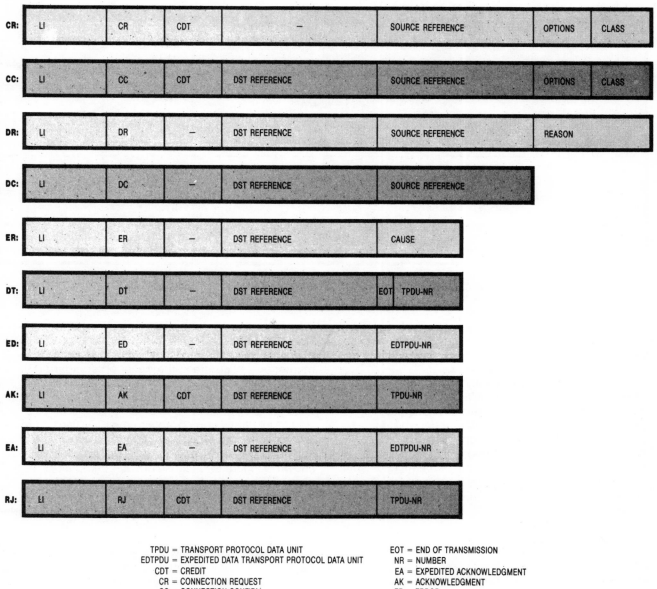

CR:	LI	CR	CDT	—	SOURCE REFERENCE	OPTIONS	CLASS
CC:	LI	CC	CDT	DST REFERENCE	SOURCE REFERENCE	OPTIONS	CLASS
DR:	LI	DR	—	DST REFERENCE	SOURCE REFERENCE	REASON
DC:	LI	DC	—	DST REFERENCE	SOURCE REFERENCE	
ER:	LI	ER	—	DST REFERENCE	CAUSE	
DT:	LI	DT	—	DST REFERENCE	EOT TPDU-NR	
ED:	LI	ED		DST REFERENCE	EDTPDU-NR	
AK:	LI	AK	CDT	DST REFERENCE	TPDU-NR	
EA:	LI	EA	—	DST REFERENCE	EDTPDU-NR	
RJ:	LI	RJ	CDT	DST REFERENCE	TPDU-NR	

TPDU = TRANSPORT PROTOCOL DATA UNIT
EDTPDU = EXPEDITED DATA TRANSPORT PROTOCOL DATA UNIT
CDT = CREDIT
CR = CONNECTION REQUEST
CC = CONNECTION CONFIRM
DR = DISCONNECT REQUEST
DC = DISCONNECT CONFIRM
DST = DESTINATION

EOT = END OF TRANSMISSION
NR = NUMBER
EA = EXPEDITED ACKNOWLEDGMENT
AK = ACKNOWLEDGMENT
ER = ERROR
RJ = REJECT
LI = LENGTH INDICATOR
DT = DATA

nection. It is assumed that a Type A, connection-oriented network service is available. Transport connections are mapped one-to-one onto network connections (for example, an X.25 virtual circuit). No explicit ordering, or error control, is provided.

Class 1 was also developed by CCITT and is designed to run on an X.25 network and provide minimal error recovery. Its key difference from Class 0 is that TPDUs are numbered. This allows the protocol to resynchronize after an X.25 reset. When the network resets its virtual circuit, some TPDUs may be lost. Each

transport entity informs the other of the number of the TPDU that it received last. In this way, the lost TPDUs may be retransmitted. Expedited data transfer is also provided.

Class 2 is an enhancement of Class 0 that still assumes a highly reliable network service. The key enhancement is the ability to multiplex multiple transport connections onto a single network connection. A corollary enhancement is the provision of explicit flow control, since a single network connection flow control mechanism does not allow individual flow control of

6. TCP header. *The transmission control protocol, whose header format is shown here, functions similarly to the International Organization for Standardization* (ISO) Class 4 protocol. TCP uses only a single type of TPDU. One header performs all protocol mechanisms, and the TCP header is longer than ISO's.

BIT POSITION

| 0 | 1 | 2 | 3 | 4 | 5 | 6 | 7 | 8 | 9 | 1 0 | 1 1 | 1 2 | 1 3 | 1 4 | 1 5 | 1 6 | 1 7 | 1 8 | 1 9 | 2 0 | 2 1 | 2 2 | 2 3 | 2 4 | 2 5 | 2 6 | 2 7 | 2 8 | 2 9 | 3 0 | 3 1 |

SOURCE PORT	DESTINATION PORT

SEQUENCE NUMBER

ACKNOWLEDGMENT NUMBER

DATA OFFSET	RESERVED	U R G	A C K	P S H	R S T	S Y N	F I N	WINDOW

CHECKSUM	URGENT POINTER

OPTIONS	PADDING

URG = URGENT POINTER   RST = RESET THE CONNECTION
ACK = ACKNOWLEDGMENT   SYN = SYNCHRONIZE THE SEQUENCE NUMBERS
PSH = PUSH FUNCTION   FIN = NO MORE DATA FROM SENDER

transport connections. A credit allocation scheme can be used.

Class 3 is basically the union of the Class 1 and 2 capabilities. It provides the multiplexing and flow control capabilities of Class 2. It also contains the resynchronization and reassignment capabilities needed to cope with failure-prone networks.

Class 4 assumes that the underlying network service is unreliable. Thus, most, if not all, of the mechanisms described in this article must be included.

The protocol makes use of 10 types of TPDUs:
- Connection request (CR)
- Connection confirm (CC)
- Disconnect request (DR)
- Disconnect confirm (DC)
- TPDU error (ER)
- Data (DT)
- Expedited data (ED)
- Acknowledgment (ACK)
- Expedited acknowledgment (EA)
- Reject (RJ)

Each TPDU consists of three parts: a fixed header, a variable header, and a data field. The latter two need not be present in a TPDU. The fixed header contains the frequently occurring parameters, as shown in Figure 5, and the variable header contains optional or infrequently occurring parameters. Each parameter field in the variable header consists of three subfields: a parameter code (8 bits), a parameter length (8 bits), and the parameter value (one or more octets). Most of the parameters are used by CC and CR in the connection establishment process.

The ISO transport protocols have only recently been approved as international standards. There are, conse-quently, comparatively few vendor-supported implementations. In contrast, the transport standard (MIL-STD-1778) from the Department of Defense (DOD), known as TCP, is well-established and implemented on a variety of machines.

TCP functions comparably to the ISO Class 4 protocol. It has, however, considerably more overhead bits. TCP uses only a single type of TPDU. The header is shown in Figure 6. Because one header must serve to perform all protocol mechanisms, it is rather large. Whereas the ISO fixed header is from five to seven octets long, the TCP header is a minimum of 20 octets.

Summary

ISO has been working away at its own protocol standard, which is now an international standard. It appears that the ISO standard will get early and widespread acceptance by computer vendors. As evidence of this, a number of vendors participated in a multivendor demonstration of the Class 4 protocol at this year's National Computer Conference. In addition, DOD has committed to eventually abandoning TCP in favor of the ISO Class 4.

The long-awaited arrival of standard transport protocols is welcome news for the customer and user. Customers can now begin the migration from proprietary protocols to the ISO standard. The widespread use of that standard is the key to open systems interconnection. ■

William Stallings is a senior communications consultant at Honeywell Information Systems. This article is based on material in his book "Data and Computer Communications," published by Macmillan Inc.

John Payton and Shahid Qureshi, Codex Corp., Mansfield, Mass.

Trellis encoding: What it is and how it affects data transmission

Hardware-implementable, the scheme doubles modem immunity to noise, enabling data rates of 14.4 kbit/s over leased lines.

Users are transmitting increasingly higher data rates over the widespread telephone network that was originally developed for voice communications. Trellis-coded modulation (TCM), as implemented in a new generation of modems, permits 9.6-kbit/s transmission over ordinary dial-up telephone lines and reliable operation at 14.4 to 16.8 kbit/s over good quality (D1-conditioned or better) leased lines.

Operation at such high data rates is possible because a TCM modem tolerates more than twice as much noise power as a conventional modem at the same block error rates. At the same signal-to-noise ratio (SNR), a TCM modem provides significantly higher throughput by reducing the error rate by about three orders of magnitude. For example, a TCM modem may require retransmission only once every 10,000 blocks, whereas a conventional modem—at the same SNR—typically requires retransmission once very 10 blocks.

A modem's fundamental signaling (baud) or symbol rate is limited by its channel bandwidth. Therefore, a high-speed (above 4.8 kbit/s) modem transmitter collects and sends multiple bits per symbol interval.

In amplitude modulation, a carrier signal is modulated by another signal of n amplitude selected by the incoming data bits. For example, to send two bits per symbol, in each symbol interval one of four (2^2) levels from the set [-3, -1, 1, 3] can be selected to modulate the carrier wave. (Note that the representation of levels is such that the difference between adjacent levels equals two. A suitable mapping would result in the bits 0,0 selecting -3; 0,1 selecting -1; 1,1 selecting +1; and 1,0 selecting +3.)

All modern high-speed modems use a form of quadrature amplitude modulation (QAM). In QAM, two carriers in quadrature (cosine and sine waves) are amplitude modulated and combined to produce the transmitter output. The receiver separates and demodulates the two in-quadrature signals, thus recovering the transmitted information. The modulation for each symbol interval is characterized by a pair of amplitudes, called a signal point.

A 9.6-kbit/s QAM modem sends 4 bits per symbol interval at a rate of 2,400 symbols per second. In each symbol, the modem maps the possible 4-bit combinations into one of 16 (2^4) possible signal points, or pairs of rectangular coordinates, which are then used to modulate the in-quadrature cosine and sine carrier signals. The x-axis ordinate is low-pass filtered, then modulated by the cosine carrier. The y-axis ordinate is similarly filtered, then modulated by the sine carrier.

The plot plan

The set of possible signal points is graphically described by a two-dimensional signal-space diagram, known as the signal constellation. Each point is placed at the x-y coordinates representing the modulation levels of the cosine carrier and the sine carrier. The signal constellation used by a 9.6-kbit/s leased-line CCITT-V.29 modem is shown in Figure 1.

At the receiver, after equalization and demodulation, a pair of received coordinates is generated. These coordinates are then fed to the decision circuit to make the best "guess" as to what signal point was transmitted from the signal constellation used by the modem. If the channel were ideal, the received signal-point coordinates would be identical to the signal point that was transmitted.

In practice, line impairments—such as noise, phase jitter, and nonlinear distortion—cause the received point to be displaced from the ideally received signal point. The best decision strategy at the receiver is to select the signal point that is closest to the received

1. Dot plot. *A 9.6-kbit/s QAM modem sends four bits per symbol interval at 2,400 baud. A plot of the 16 possible signal points is the signal constellation.*

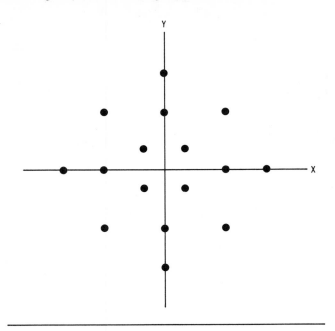

point as the one that was transmitted. When line impairments are large enough to cause the received point to be closer to a signal point other than the transmitted one, a symbol error is made.

The telephone company limits the signal power (proportional to the average squared amplitude of the signal points) that can be transmitted onto the line. The higher the modem data rate, the more significant is the effect of channel noise. This can be seen by noting that an increase in the number of bits per symbol from six (using a signal constellation of 2^6, or 64, points) to seven (using 2^7, or 128, points), while maintaining the same signal power, brings the signal points closer together. This reduces the modem's immunity to noise: Only about half as much noise power is needed to produce the same error rate.

The performance of a modem is characterized by the error rate as a function of the signal-to-noise ratio, which is measured in decibels (dB). High-speed synchronous modems are typically used in conjunction with synchronous link protocols employing error detection and retransmission—that is, automatic repeat request (ARQ). The throughput efficiency of such protocols is directly related to the modem's block error rate (BLER): the number of received blocks (each block consisting of 1,000 bits, for example) that contain one or more bits in error divided by the total number of blocks transmitted. Once a block of received data has an error, the actual number of bits that are erroneous is not important, because the entire block will be retransmitted. Therefore, in synchronous data links with ARQ, BLER is usually a better measure of the modem error rate than bit error rate (BER).

To achieve bit rates higher than 9.6 kbit/s over the telephone network, more than four bits must be sent per transmitted symbol. Each additional bit per symbol doubles the number of signal points in the signal constellation. The inherent noise immunity decreases and rapidly becomes unacceptable as the signal points move closer together.

Shannon's original work on information theory in the 1940s produced a fundamental theorem: It is possible to transmit information with an arbitrarily small probability of error over a channel, provided that the transmission rate is less than a value known as the channel capacity. Under the assumption that the random channel noise has Gaussian (normal) amplitude distribution, the theoretical capacity of a channel can be computed from the channel's bandwidth and the received signal-to-noise ratio.

The capacity of telephone channels cannot be precisely computed due to the presence of non-Gaussian impairments such as nonlinear distortion and phase jitter. However, capacity estimates neglecting these effects and extrapolation from known technology suggest that there is considerable room for improvement, perhaps by as much as a factor of 2, over the 9.6 kbit/s that was accepted as the maximum generally attainable in the 1970s.

Besides the ARQ method, a binary forward error correction (FEC) coding technique—designed to avoid retransmissions—may be used to reduce received errors. An encoder at the transmission site processes the user's bit stream and generates extra or redundant code bits. The encoder output bit stream, containing both the redundant bits and the original user data (or a transformed version of the user data), is then transmitted. At the receiving device, the redundant bits are regenerated from the bit stream and compared with the received redundant bits. When there is a discrepancy, a decoding procedure selects the most likely message to have generated the received bit stream.

There are two general types of binary coding methods: convolutional and block encoding (DATA COMMUNICATIONS, "Special Report/The ABCs of FEC," May 1984, p. 64). For a given coding method, the minimum number of bit positions in which any two valid encoded bit sequences (or code words) may differ is known as the Hamming distance of the code. (For example, the Hamming distance between the patterns 1101 and 1000 is two, because they differ in two positions.)

Add complexity

The greater the Hamming distance of a code, the greater is its ability to correct a corrupted message. In general, a larger Hamming distance can be achieved by making a code more complex. For convolutional codes, the complexity (particularly of the decoding equipment) is dependent on its constraint length—the number of previously transmitted bits that the encoder uses to generate the redundant code bits.

The Hamming distance can also be increased by decreasing the code rate (the ratio per unit time of the message bits to the total number of bits transmitted). The lower this rate is, the higher the relative number of redundant bits and the greater the ability to correct errors. The user, however, must suffer a lower information-transfer rate, unless the channel bandwidth can be expanded. Over wideband satellite transmission facilities, where the SNR is limited by the available transmitter power, the bandwidth expansion is well worth the increased data integrity.

The modem signaling rate is restricted over sharply bandwidth-limited channels such as telephone circuits. Here, any decrease in user information-transfer rate is undesirable. Thus, if a traditional binary FEC encoder is appended to a conventional QAM modem with a fixed symbol rate, a greater number of bits per symbol must be transmitted to accommodate a higher-speed encoded bit stream.

The modem signal constellation becomes denser as a lower rate code with greater redundancy is used to obtain a greater degree of error correction. Unfortunately, the corresponding decrease in noise immunity—because of the denser signal constellation—overcomes most of the potential advantage gained by using FEC. At best, the net gain is minimal.

With traditional FEC, because encoding is done before the data stream reaches the transmitter, the transmitter does not differentiate between the redundant bit and the message bit. Therefore, the redundant code bits cannot be used in a systematic way (one code bit associated with each symbol) to select the sequence of transmitted signal points.

What's new

There now exists a more sophisticated method of combining coding and modulation that realizes more reliable data transmission at high rates over bandwidth-limited channels. This method is called trellis-coded modulation (TCM).

The TCM scheme adds one redundant code bit to the user data in each symbol interval as this data enters the encoder. At 14.4 kbit/s, the transmitter (Fig. 2) collects the user data bits into 6-bit symbols 2,400 times per second and encodes two of the six bits using

a binary convolutional encoding scheme. The encoder adds a code bit to the two input bits to form three encoded bits in each symbol interval. The resulting seven bits (the three encoded bits and the four remaining data bits) are mapped into a signal point selected from a 128-point (2^7) signal constellation.

In the example shown in Figure 2, the three encoded bits select one of eight (2^3) subsets—each consisting of 16 (2^4) points—from the signal constellation, while the four remaining data bits choose one of the 16 points from the selected subset. The redundancy introduced by the encoder ensures that only certain sequences of signal points are valid. Moreover, a good code (one with a relatively large Hamming distance, better able to correct signal-point errors) combined with a suitable mapping rule ensures that any two valid sequences of signal points are far apart. (The code distance measure used is the sum of the squared absolute distances between individual signal points that make up the two signal point sequences. Thus if X_1, X_2, X_3 and Y_1, Y_2, Y_3 are distinct sequences of signal points, the distance between them is $[X_1-Y_1]^2 + [X_2-Y_2]^2 + [X_3-Y_3]^2$.)

A different operation

The scheme described above is known as TCM because it is based on a convolutional or trellis code combined with a suitable subset mapping rule in the modulator. Remember that traditional forward error correction operates directly on the data stream.

At the receiver, the observed signal points will generally differ from the transmitted sequence of signal points because of probable, unavoidable impairments. The TCM decoder compares the observed sequence of signal points of all valid sequences and selects that valid sequence that is closest to the observed sequence. The binary convolutional encoder at the transmitter is designed to transmit certain sequences, and the subset mapping rule ensures that these sequences

---

2. A better way. *With the trellis-coded modulation scheme, at 14.4 kbit/s, the transmitter (shown here) collects the user data bits into 6-bit symbols 2,400 times* *per second, encoding two of the six bits. The encoder adds a redundant bit to the two input bits to form three encoded bits in each symbol interval.*

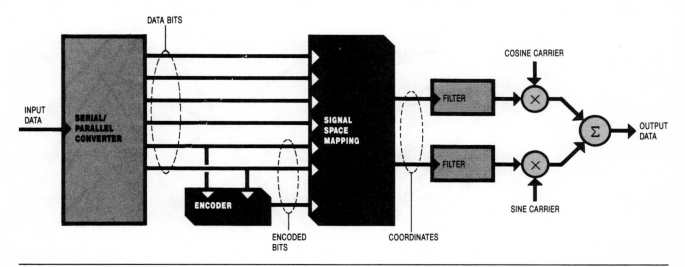

3. Implementing the scheme. *The three binary memory elements enable the encoder to be in one of 2^3, or eight, possible states, based on previous data.*

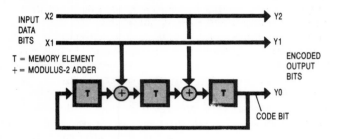

are going to end up being distinct from each other.

Let us now examine the TCM encoder and decoder more closely. Figure 3 shows a convolutional encoder with three binary memory elements. The encoder can therefore be in one of eight (2^3) possible states based on previous data. For each symbol interval, two new data bits cause the encoder to change its state and to generate three encoded bits (two data bits plus an extra code bit). Note that transitions from a given state to only one of the four next-interval states are permitted by design.

Figure 4 shows a state-transition, or trellis, diagram where states are represented by nodes and connecting lines are state transitions. Each transition has associ-

ated with it a combination of the three encoded output bits that determines the subset of the signal constellation from which the transmitted signal point is selected. The decoder does not know the state of the transmitter at any given time because errors may have occurred in the past. Therefore, an optimum decoder algorithm must search through all possible valid transmitted sequences, compare each to the observed sequence, and select the one that is closest (in code distance) to the observed sequence. The search over all possible encoded sequences is simplified by an efficient recursive procedure known as the Viterbi algorithm (DATA COMMUNICATIONS, May 1984, p. 64).

A decoder incorporating the Viterbi algorithm stores a path history of the most likely state transitions leading up to each possible state. Associated with each path history is a sequence of transmitted symbols and the corresponding accumulated code distance. As each new received symbol is observed, all possible extensions of the stored paths are considered (see trellis diagram, Fig. 4). The algorithm "prunes" the trellis by choosing the best (closest to the one received) of the four possible paths leading into each of the next states. This weeds out unlikely paths.

Figure 5 shows the pruned trellis with the previous state and only one transition into each next state. Notice that some previous states—having been discarded—are not connected. The paths terminating in these states will no longer be considered. In time, by

4. The trellis. *In this state-transition, or trellis, diagram, the states are represented by nodes, and the connecting lines are the state transitions.*

5. 'Pruning' the trellis. *The Viterbi algorithm selects the best of the four possible paths leading into each next state, discarding invalid paths.*

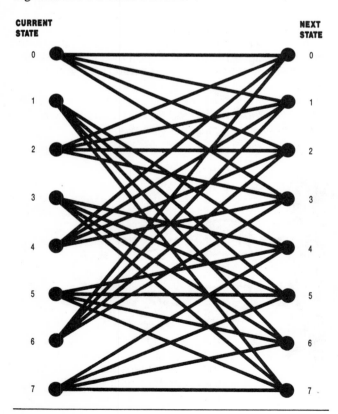

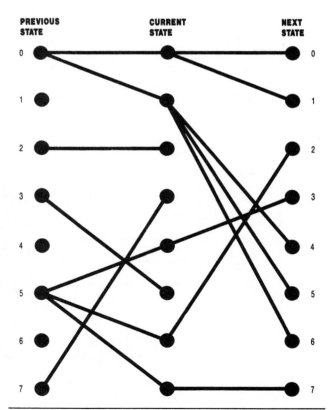

6. TCM vs. QAM. *Signal points are transmitted (A) and received (B) for 14.4 kbit/s. Conventional decisions: incorrect points (C); Viterbi chooses correctly (D).*

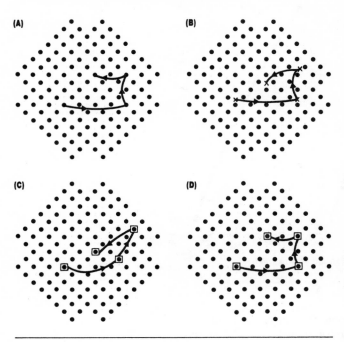

following the previous states back, all the paths in contention are seen as descendants of a single path. Thus, by applying the Viterbi algorithm (trellis search), the decoder can search back through the path histories to make the final decision. In practice, one truncates the path histories to a finite length, typically 12 to 16 symbols, at a negligible cost in performance. (For an excellent tutorial on the algorithm, see "The Viterbi algorithm," by G. D. Forney, Jr., referenced below.)

Doubling for dependencies
The key differences between a conventional QAM modulator and a TCM modulator are the encoder and a signal-point constellation. The TCM constellation contains twice as many signal points as does the QAM's. These extra signal points enable the encoder to introduce dependencies between successively transmitted signals by applying the prescribed algorithm.

In TCM, only certain patterns or sequences of signal points are valid. Other sequences are invalid and will never be transmitted. Thus, when channel noise or another distortion displaces the received signal-point sequence, the decoder detects if the received sequence is invalid and selects the valid sequence closest to the one that was actually received. This corresponds to the best guess of what was transmitted.

To illustrate with an example that might well happen using the trellis code, Figure 6A shows a series of signal points transmitted at 14.4 kbit/s. Figure 6B shows a corresponding series of displaced received points as seen by the receiving device after being distorted by line perturbations.

After receiving the distorted points, a conventional QAM receiver would make some incorrect decisions

about the signal points (Fig. 6C). These decisions would be based on an examination of each point independently and then a choice of the point in the signal constellation closest to the received point.

Figure 6D shows the TCM receiver making a correct decision about the series of signal points. This decision is based on the TCM receiver "knowing" that only certain signal-point sequencs are valid and choosing the valid sequence closest to the one received (best guess of what was transmitted). The signal point sequence that would have been chosen by a conventional receiver is not selected, because it constitutes an invalid sequence.

Closer is worse
The coding gain (or effectiveness of the coded modulation scheme compared with a QAM scheme) is determined by the distance properties of the subsets combined with those of the binary code. For example, a coding gain can be estimated by finding two distinct paths in the trellis that are closest (code distance). In the presence of noise, the decoder will tend to make errors between these paths more frequently than between paths that are farther apart.

Assume two closest paths in the eight-state (2^3) code. The error would involve mistaking the sequence 000, 000, 000 for the sequence 100, 011, 110. (The notation represents the output of the binary convolutional encoder.) The minimum distance with TCM (sum of the squares of the distances between points) equals 10 units. With QAM, when the transmitted power is the same as TCM, this distance equals 4 units. The coding gain is the ratio of the two, or 4 dB.

The performance of TCM and conventional QAM 14.4-kbit/s schemes may be compared theoretically in a plot diagram (Fig. 7). Performance is measured by block error rate in the presence of Gaussian noise, with a block size of 1,000 bits. The QAM modem uses a 64-point signal constellation, while the TCM modem uses the scheme of Figures 2 and 3 with a 128-point signal constellation.

Referring to Figure 7, QAM requires an SNR value of about 25.6 dB to achieve a block error rate of 10^{-2} (one errored block in 100), while TCM requires an SNR of only 22.2 dB to achieve the same BLER. The performance improvement of TCM is, therefore, more than 3 dB, which is more than double the immunity to noise as compared with QAM. Alternatively, for the same SNR (such as 24 dB in Figure 7), TCM has about three orders of magnitude lower BLER than QAM.

Field experience with TCM modems has shown that the theoretical improvement of TCM over QAM does indeed translate into increased end-to-end throughput on actual telephone circuits. In general, a TCM modem transmits at a higher rate for a given BLER than does a conventional QAM modem. Similarly, a TCM modem has a lower BLER than a QAM modem for the same transmission rate (thus reducing retransmissions).

The actual amount of throughput increase due to TCM use depends on the characteristics of each circuit. But field results indicate that TCM will replace QAM as the principal modulation technique for high-

7. Comparing BLERs. *Theoretically, at 14.4 kbit/s, to achieve an error rate of one in 100 blocks, TCM requires an SNR of about 22.2 dB; QAM, over 3 dB more.*

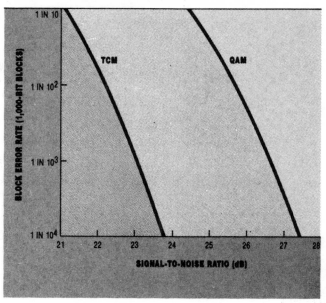

speed modems. International standards for TCM are already in place. CCITT Recommendation V.32 specifies a full-duplex 9.6-kbit/s two-wire dial-line modem that makes use of an 8-state TCM code. Draft Recommendation V.CC (temporary designation) covers a 14.4-kbit/s four-wire leased-line modem that uses the same TCM code. ∎

Further reading
Forney, G. D., Jr. "The Viterbi algorithm." *Proceedings of the IEEE,* March 1973, vol. 61, pp. 268-278.
Forney, G. D., Jr., R. G. Gallager, G. R. Lang, F. M. Longstaff, and S. U. Qureshi. "Efficient modulation for band-limited channels." *IEEE Journal of Selected Areas in Communications,* September 1984.
Hamming, R. W. "Error detecting and error correcting codes." *Bell System Technical Journal,* vol. 29, pp. 147-160, 1950.
Shannon, C. E. and W. Weaver. *A Mathematical Theory of Communication.* Illinois: University of Illinois Press, 1949.
Ungerboeck, G. "Channel coding with multilevel/-phase signals." *IEEE Transactions on Information Theory,* January 1982, vol. IT-28, pp. 55-67.

John Payton, principal engineer at Codex, designs high-speed voice-band modems. Payton has a B. S. in electrical engineering from Tulane University and an M. S. E. E. from Carnegie-Mellon University. Shahid Qureshi, senior director of research in transmission products at Codex, is working on signal processing applications to communications. Qureshi has a bachelor of science degree from the University of Engineering and Technology in Lahore, Pakistan, a master's degree in science from the University of Alberta, and a Ph.D. from the University of Toronto.

Brij Bhushan, GTE Business Communication Systems Inc., Reston, Va.

An architectural solution for voice and data integration

Using the newest-generation branch exchange technology, the author puts voice and data communications together.

Many users accept the axiom that anyone creating information in new formats will work better with desktop access to a database—whether a clerk answering yes or no on a credit check or a vice president calculating return on investment. Office workers, equipment designers, graphic artists, machine operators, salesmen, and many others can apparently multiply their productivity with ready access to computer-housed data. But while desktop devices to help these people are available, most often they are waiting in the wings for a director to stage appropriate entrances and exits to the corporate communications network.

The proliferation of devices and advances in network technology has complicated the job for those who must come up with a totally integrated voice and data solution. How to choose the right elements for such a network has developed into a controversial issue. An article on the subject in DATA COMMUNICATIONS, March 1983, was titled "Barriers to integrating voice and data." In the following issue, five executives contributed five different views on integrating voice and data. Another story in that same issue told of two PBX makers with different approaches who each hoped to establish a new industry standard and thereby guarantee themselves at least a slice of the market.

Still another recent article detailed an alternative to an integrated voice/data network. It listed 39 companies that are betting they can rewire much of the world with local networks. No wonder there is so much debate over and examination of proposed network anatomies. Decisions made now will prevail through the 1990s, and choosing the wrong path could prove very costly.

Despite the confusion, obstacles to an integrated voice/data network (IVDN) are starting to break down

rapidly. With its many advantages over alternative solutions it is sure to play a large role in corporate networks. The time is ripe for coupling this technology with the newest-generation PBXs.

Such a concept requires no radical or new technology, simply a fresh application and approach to the distributed PBX architecture. Beyond the benefits it can offer in the here and now, such integration also allows ease of expansion and future improvements.

Until recently, a PBX lifetime was 20 years. Now, telecommunications managers can often justify the cost of replacing these networks after just six years. The technology has expanded that rapidly. With the IVDN PBXs available from different manufacturers, managers can meet today's communications needs while keeping options open to embrace the productivity improvements that tomorrow will bring.

IVDN savings

The obvious benefit of an IVDN built around a PBX using existing telephone lines is the saving in installation costs over local networks or other types of equipment that require new wiring. Reduced administration and maintenance costs also weigh heavily on the side of IVDNs.

Less obvious—because they are not so easily measured—are benefits derived from reduced restrictions in network planning and implementation. Today, telecommunications managers and data processing managers have not so much an attitude of guarding their own turf as they have inherently different responsibilities and priorities. An IVDN forces these two positions into a synergistic relationship. Work is supported by a unified approach, consistent and accurate reporting of operations, and better centralized control. Such benefits, hard to measure at the outset, may be an IVDN's

129

greatest contribution to corporate communications.

These factors and the economy of the approach encourage rapid adoption of IVDN innovations. Moreover, the addition of elements of office automation such as electronic mail, voice mail, and word processing are greatly simplified in an IVDN.

Another advantage of an IVDN is that it allows many recently developed voice features in the PBX to be applied to data transmission. These features, which translate directly into productivity gains, can be applied to both voice and data calls originating in the same PBX. They include:

- Application of economical route selections
- Queuing features—to achieve optimum utilization of external analog transmission facilities
- Shared modem use (modem pool)
- Automatic camp-on with ring-back if a busy port is encountered
- Switched direct line (hot line) service
- Call message detail reporting for data calls
- Line lock out, i.e., line inactivity within a predefined time causes automatic release of the connection and the facilities
- Station hunting and uniform call distribution to send calls appropriately to high-occupancy ports
- Call-forwarding to divert calls automatically and selectively to another destination
- Three-way transfers to bridge or redirect an active connection to another port (e.g., printer)
- The permanent connection capability to provide full-period, point-to-point, high-capacity digital transmission channels.

Voice/data stepsisters
Traditionally, analog voice communications and digital data communications have developed like stepsisters widely separated by age, but with a lot to share if they can be brought together.

By converting one signal type to the other, voice and data signals can be joined and sent over a single set of wires to be decoded at a PBX for distribution. This avoids running separate wires for each device. Since the phone lines are already in place, there is a natural efficiency in using voice lines for data communications at speeds up to 19.2 kbit/s asynchronous and 64 kbit/s synchronous.

Let us examine the current alternatives offered by other PBXs. Generally, PBXs are built around the time division multiplexing (TDM) technique, which essentially allocates 64-kbit/s time slots for digitized voice as well as data switching.

In straight TDM, the PBX allocates a time slot for each I/O line coming into the PBX. Once signals get into the line card, the voice switch requires 64 kbit/s—or one time slot. However, data devices operate at various speeds. Data arriving at 56 kbit/s makes fairly efficient use of that slot. But the serious drawback of this approach is that if the device runs at 1.2 kbit/s or less (and many do), it is running at a very inefficient 2-percent use of that time slot. And a time slot is not only a costly commodity, but also expensive to expand. To get around this, the PBX requires a submultiplexing

scheme, which adds to cost. Even then, all data coming to one place in a multiplexed frame may not be destined for the same end point. So demultiplexing is required. This adds still more to complexity and cost.

Either many time slots must be made available—to handle the differing data and voice transmission speeds—or rearrangement must be executed. This is because the goal is a dynamic reconfiguration of the time slots. Remember too that once allocated to data, a time slot is not available for voice. This implies that the subsequent voice calls will encounter a greater amount of blocking in the switch, making the integration more and more difficult.

As recently as 1981, 90 percent of the 230,000 PBXs installed in the United States used only analog technology. To meet the need for high-speed digital communications, most new PBXs can handle data communications, though not in an economical and integrated fashion. For example, some PBX networks have separate wiring for voice and data. Others allow only one function at a time: either the user can use the phone wires to talk to another person, or he can use them to let terminals and computers talk, but not both at the same time. A PBX that is specially designed for both voice and data integrates the two modes and permits simultaneous voice and data communications.

Creating a modular IVDN
To create a modular, digital integrated voice/data network, several constraints must be satisfactorily addressed. First, the existing installation must be preserved as much as possible. Second, all interface connections must be standardized. Third, a modular construction should be sought to ensure future flexibility and economies. The approach detailed in Figure 1 takes these elements into account.

While the PBX designs were making great strides toward digitalization, data communications equipment makers were marching toward X.25 packet-switching standards. With the advent of microelectronics the distinction between technologies to implement voice and data switching was narrowing. As a result, it has become relatively easy to integrate the two forms of communications—analog voice and digital data—in a combined IVDN.

As shown in the diagram, the traditional analog phone continues to be supported by analog line cards that digitize and code voice samples. These samples are switched through the time slots under the control of microprocessors. This can be represented functionally as a pulse code modulated bus architecture. The control portion of the PBX can be either a distributed control or a central control—depending entirely upon the PBX design.

The innovative part of the integration is the addition of the second bus, labeled local packet bus. The data-only devices attach to a terminal block that converts the serial digital bit stream into packets and provides an X.25 packet assembly/disassembly (PAD) function. Since the internal switching mechanism of the data portion of the PBX is based on fixed-length packets (called minipackets), the terminal block converts these

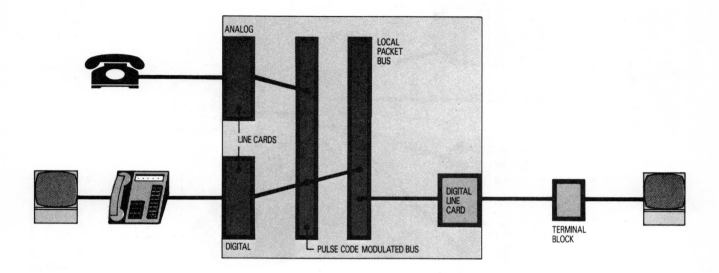

1. Getting together. *The corporate information network is based on two fundamental communications forms: conversations between people using telephones and computer-to-computer (or perhiperal) conversations. The architecture detailed here is designed to integrate both of these forms.*

data packets into minipackets. Each minipacket, like the traditional data packets, has a destination address associated with it.

Unlike the second-generation packet-switching equipment, in which the switching function was performed via software, this architecture takes advantage of the fixed-length minipackets and switches it via hardware. So 3 Mbit/s can be switched via this hardware instantaneously without throughput and delay degradation.

This assures that there are no bottlenecks in the packet domain for data switching, and that all data devices attached to the PBX can be supported at their rated speeds without degradation.

Dual bus
The digital phone shown in Figure 1 is capable of supporting a data terminal hooked into it via RS-232-C interface. It has the terminal block function built into it. The phone is truly integrating the digital voice samples and data stream via the use of minipackets. These multiplexed minipackets are carried over the installed single-pair wiring. The data and voice minipackets each have destination addresses associated with them. The digital line card in this case separates the voice minipackets and puts them on the pulse code modulation path—and puts data minipackets on the bus—to be switched simultaneously without affecting each other. As a customer's needs expand, more buses and switching hardware may be added to the PBX. This is the key to an efficient, expandable IVDN PBX design.

Additional packet buses do not steal capacity from the switch. In fact, they are almost like adding another data switch to the voice PBX. As mentioned earlier, with this type of approach, at the end-user (phone) side of the PBX, there is a card that will combine the

voice and data transmissions into a single signal to be carried to the PBX line card. The PBX line card also separates this information back out so it can be properly routed.

Segregating functions
One reason the dual bus concept has not previously been exploited stems from the PBX designer's consideration of his installed base. How would he retrofit? Unlike other PBXs, this proposed approach implies field upgrading of dual buses because it employs distributed processing concepts in the PBX. The same approach may not be viable for a majority of installed PBXs since they do not have distributed processing architectures.

In designing a distributed architecture for a PBX, the total PBX functions can be segregated into two distinct classes. The first class of functions can be the real-time scanning of the lines, digit collection, and maintenance-related functions of the line. The second category would include the voice-call processing functions, which constitute a majority of the PBX feature-processing and database-related activities. If the design were modular, these functions would be put on separate microprocessors linked together via a message interface and in constant communication via processor buses.

The microprocessor that performs the first class of functions can be sized to handle n lines simultaneously. Let us call this a peripheral complex. The central processor can be sized to handle m such modules, giving a total port capacity of mn lines. Further, these modules can be packaged physically so that the implementation is modular for customers having a diverse range of line-size requirements. The central processor is the boss of the two, implying that the architecture is hierarchical. The switching and process-

2. Networked PBXs. *Continued introduction of improved PBXs and increased use of data communications transmission standards (such as the X.25 packet-* *switching specification) will foster multiple PBX networks, allocating applications functions while improving overall efficiency via integration.*

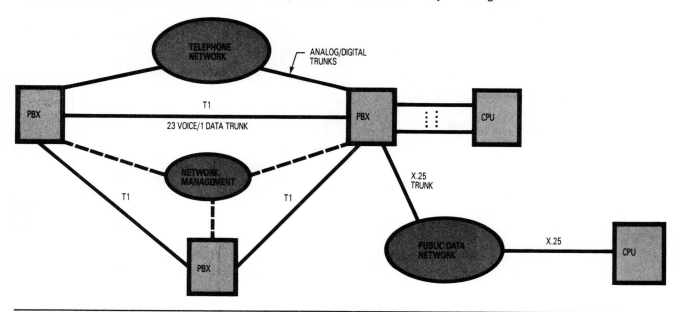

ing is accomplished under the control of the central processor.

In the voice and data integrated architecture described here, the peripheral complex has a virtually unlimited lifetime. For example, in an extreme case, one could design a peripheral complex to handle ordinary simple telephones only. As long as the customer wants to support these telephones, the peripheral complex need never change. Electronic phones and data communications terminals could be supported via another peripheral complex or they could be designed as part of the original peripheral complex.

The new line cards supporting devices such as the electronic phones could go into a different peripheral complex, allowing the older peripheral complex to coexist. This would protect the customer's investments and minimize both the cost and the downtime required to introduce new features and new technologies. By so doing, a major concern of communications managers is alleviated: the accommodation of future developments.

Performance of this new architecture, with the add-on bus concept, generates economies because it provides virtually unlimited bandwidth. This is accomplished by allowing the addition of buses and switching hardware when needed. Data throughput is in the megabit-per-second range through the switch. For example, with 256 lines running at 19.2 kbit/s, up to 6 Mbit/s can be pushed through the data highway in the PBX. Error rate, depending on whether retransmission capability or error detection is provided, is as good as 10^{-9} or better. In a synchronous environment, the individual line speeds are as high as 64 kbit/s.

Networking IVDNs
PBXs can be interconnected with each other and provide cost-effective networks. The interconnection

between PBXs can also be achieved with T1 digital trunks if the PBX offers T1 interface card support. Figure 2 shows three PBXs interconnected with T1 links. In traditional PBXs—even those with circuit-switched data capability—the data networking will require additional trunking above and beyond that necessary for the voice traffic. To configure the network for data communication applications, the communications manager must use an analog trunk or a 64-kbit/s channel of the T1 interface for every connection that has to terminate at the next PBX, thus increasing the cost of the network.

For example, assume an installation has a PBX with 500 voice ports and 100 data ports. Suppose 20 percent of its trunks is sufficient for voice applications, and 10 percent for data applications. The total number of trunks required is 50 + 10 = 60. The 10 data trunks will require 10 modems. To provide a similar level of service, one can use the modem pool feature and have 10 modems as before; but instead of 10 trunks dedicated to data application, one can now provide a total of 56 trunks (adding 6 trunks instead of 10) and let the data calls contend for all 56 trunks. This will save the cost of 8 trunks. To allow an improvement in service to data calls, one could have the on-hook/off-hook queuing feature invoked for data calls and give data calls a priority over voice calls.

In either of these scenarios, this situation is analogous to the time-slot usage discussed earlier. There is no inherent multiplexing capability in the traditional PBX, and the trunk bandwidth utilization is inefficient.

In IVDN architecture, however, X.25 packet-switching protocol implementation offers the multiplexing of virtual circuits. The transmission bandwidth, either analog or digital, can be utilized efficiently.

To illustrate, consider the earlier example. The 64-

kbit/s link between PBXs shown in Figure 2 (one channel of the T1 stream) can carry data from at least 60 asynchronous terminals and is capable of carrying data for as many as 200 terminals. This allows a communications manager to save as much as 9 trunks as compared with the previous example, thus utilizing this one data channel very efficiently and providing a data network superior to that in the previous example. Even in the absence of higher-speed digital transmission, a 9.6 kbit/s leased line link can carry between 20 and 80 virtual circuits without appreciable throughput or response time degradations. This provides up to 80 terminals to access host machines simultaneously, compared with 10 as in the previous example of circuit switching.

Flexible control

Network management in such a network can be centralized at any location—either a PBX location or a location removed from any PBX. The function of such a control center is to manage the network for both voice and data, thus offering the ultimate in voice and data integration.

The X.25 packet-switching integration also offers access to public data networks as shown in Figure 2. This access capability allows the terminals dispersed worldwide to reach—in a cost-effective and efficient way—the hosts implementing applications such as electronic mail attached to the private network. In addition, this capability can be used at peak periods for diverting data communications traffic to public data networks designed to carry the load. Finally, this capability permits the data portion of the network to handle average loads, thus reducing the communication costs even further.

Not radical

Beyond the benefits detailed here, planners should note that the IDVN and PBX approach will allow easy expansion and future improvements. It is certain that with the obstacles to truly integrated voice data environments falling rapidly, their role in corporate networks is set to grow significantly. The approach of coupling an IVDN and a PBX as described here means that no radical change is required on the user's part. Using available technology, and a fresh view of application needs, the integration problem can be neatly solved.

The data communications economics equations have recently changed in favor of users. This trend—toward faster equipment turnover—will continue as traffic grows. Only by adopting truly integrated solutions will data communications managers be able to keep up with such rapid changes. ■

Walter C. Roehr, Jr., Telecommunication Network Consulting, Reston, Va.

Inside SS No. 7: A detailed look at ISDN's signaling system plan

Here is the integrated network's
central nervous system.
But few users know about it
or understand what it provides.

Signaling System No. 7, in the final stages of specification by the International Telegraph and Telephone Consultative Committee (CCITT) and formulated in basic accord with the Open Systems Interconnection (OSI) reference model recommended by the International Organization for Standardization (ISO), differs greatly from most other data communications signaling techniques. The differences are neither accidental nor capricious. Rather, they are due to the real-time functions it provides. And these differences account for the power of SS No. 7 to flexibly interconnect clear 64-kbit/s channels—the essence of the Integrated Services Digital Network. Without the new signaling system, ISDN could probably offer none of its features and services. Yet, for all its power and importance at the heart of ISDN, SS No. 7 remains unknown to most users.

SS No. 7 came into being because the telephone industry planned a future array of enhanced features and services that users could reach rapidly and without disruption. To provide the access, the telephone industry needed something—in this case, SS No. 7—analogous to the central nervous system of a living organism, something to coordinate the functions while remaining completely separate from the organism's other parts and not actually performing their function. Without the nervous system's coordination, the organism—in this case, ISDN—could not perform.

SS No. 7 has much to coordinate for ISDN. Among its many features and services, ISDN will offer:
- User access to a full 64-kbit/s channel with no bits "stolen" for signaling or synchronization.
- Rapid establishment or modification of the destination and characteristics of the connection.
- Transmission of user data without disturbance to the existing connection.

Such features and services require the "central nervous system" function provided by a "common channel signaling system." On ISDN access facilities, this duty is performed by the D channel, part of the ISDN 2B + D interface.

On the backbone network, between telephone company switches, SS No. 7 will take on the common channel signaling task. A common channel signaling link is basically just a specialized point-to-point data link. There are two reasons for making it special:
1. It has a set of special tasks to perform.
2. It must operate as a network, rather than as a collection of independent links, so that it can perform as part of the total signaling complex.

In a modern telephone network, where switches are computer-controlled devices, use of a data link to interconnect switches appears trivially reasonable—why do it any other way? However, it is important to realize that telephone switches predate computers by many years. And it is only recently that computers and communications protocols have become sufficiently reliable to put entire trunk groups under their real-time control. Beyond that, sufficiently large trunks, and the signaling protocols to handle these trunks, must come into existence before common channel signaling becomes economical. Dedicating voice-channel-size capacity to a signaling link requires that the common channel handle one or hundreds of channels before it is justified.

As a backdrop to SS No. 7, it would be helpful to review ISDN. ISDN's fundamental concept is subscriber access, via standardized interfaces, to the digital transmission capability of the public telephone network. After more than 10 years of debate and discussion, the CCITT has decided that the standard bearer channel for this access will be an unrestricted 64-kbit/s path.

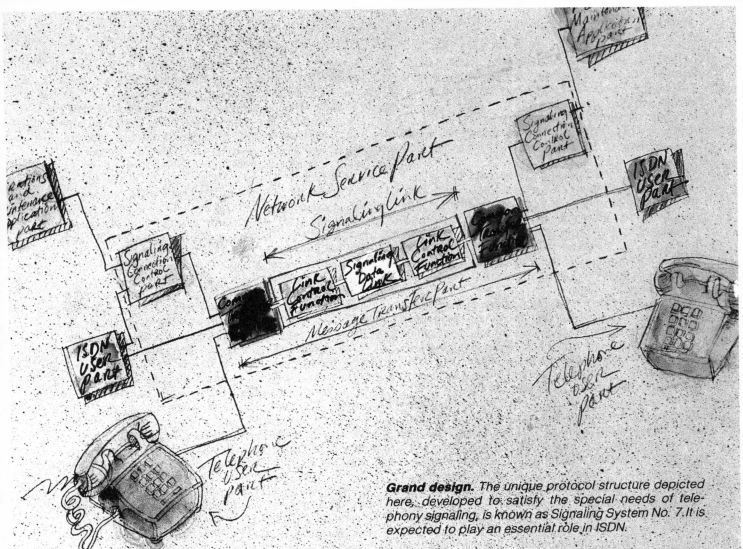

referred to as "B channel." All bit patterns are acceptable user data and none of the bits are to be "stolen" for signaling. Any digital source—such as a digitally encoded voice signal, a facsimile signal, a graphics file, or a data file—can be transported without prior arrangement if it fits in 64 kbit/s.

The flexibility of the B channel leads to problems in providing signaling capability. Since the 64-kbit/s channel can be used for a variety of purposes, there is the desire to allow rapid reconnection of the channel (for example, "Put this connection to the word processing facility on hold and connect me to the database so I can retrieve some facts for this report"). Furthermore, because any bit pattern can be included in the subscriber's data, there cannot be special "escape" or "break" sequences that indicate to the network that the associated information is for the network (for example, "I want to hang up. Please disconnect and stop charging me"). Provision must be made for a signaling channel outside the subscriber's channel. Both of these requirements are satisfied by the common channel signaling capabilities built into ISDN.

Essentially, common channel signaling provides a separate transmission capability for signaling. On ISDN access links, this signaling capability is known as the D channel and is multiplexed with a number of B chan-

nels—two B channels for a "Basic Interface" yielding the 2B + D capability and 23 or 30 B channels for a "Primary Rate Interface." (Signaling via a stolen eighth bit every sixth frame is the current North American standard. These stolen bits, and the sensitivity of 1.544-Mbit/s T-carrier repeaters to long strings of zeros, account for the limitation of digital data links in North America generally to a maximum rate of 56 kbit/s—8 kbit/s of the nominal 64 kbit/s provide the signaling and timing capability.) On the backbone trunks between telephone company switches, much larger groupings of B channels must be handled and there are more functions to be supported (for example, billing, routing, credit card checks, 800 service, and maintenance). A different, more efficient signaling technique was needed, and so SS No. 7 came into being.

With the emergence of its fundamental requirements, it became apparent that the signaling system must support, in real time, call establishment and disconnection, billing and financial administration, and supervision of the connection.

To do that, the signaling system must possess the following characteristics:

Speed. Routes must be found and established during the post-dialing interval while the caller waits on the line. During this interval significant resources are dedicated to an attempting call, but billing cannot begin until the connection is established. Similarly, once a caller disconnects (hangs up), facilities must be released and charging stopped.

Accuracy. Errors will cause, at best, lost or misconnected calls. More serious consequences can include billing errors or unnecessarily removing facilities from service.

Reliability. If the signaling system fails, the entire communications facility is useless. Each component of the signaling system must be highly reliable, be thoroughly tested before it is put in service, and incorporate self-checking capabilities. The signaling architecture (software, hardware, and operating philosophy) must accommodate redundancy so that a single failed component does not halt operation of the entire telephone system.

Transaction orientation. Each phase of every call is treated as a separate transaction. Establishing and holding a separate signaling connection (physical or virtual) for every call would not be practical; the time delay would be intolerable and literally thousands of simultaneous connections would be needed. Therefore, a connectionless mode must be used.

The next major development in telephony signaling was the use of registers that receive the customer's dialed digits, store them, and output a switch operating signal. The register's output need not be identical to the input signal; the register is an electromechanical implementation of a lookup table. Direct control of switches by the customer's dial pulses does not allow for alternate routing, uniform numbers for Direct Distance Dialing, or flexible assignment of switch ports, but registers provide for all these capabilities. Simultaneously, the register disassociates the representation used to transfer the information (the signaling) and the operating signal used by the switching machine. Signaling by tones, which can be much faster and more reliable, is possible.

By the 1960s, computer controlled switches changed the role of the register. Instead of many registers working in parallel to directly control a relatively slowly responding electromechanical device, the registers now operated as data buffers — accepting the slow signaling messages from the lines and rapidly inputting these messages into the central processor. For coordination between backbone switches a much simpler solution becomes obvious — interconnect switch processors with high-speed data links and completely avoid the need for registers. This high-speed data link arrangement is known as a common channel signaling system.

Since end subscribers were still using simple analog telephones without the capability of participating in a data link dialog with the access switch, there were no plans for common channel signaling on access lines. (ISDN, with its digital terminals will change this situation. Terminal devices also will have the capability of participating in a high-speed data link exchange with the access switch, and thus be capable of using a form of common channel signaling.)

The CCITT has developed two common channel

signaling system recommendations: SS No. 6 and SS No. 7. No. 6 was designed in the late 1960s and early 1970s to operate over analog trunks, using 2.4-kbit/s modems. The low data rate made efficiency a prime consideration. The data link protocols were very carefully optimized to carry trunk identifiers and address digits: Signaling messages are carried in "signaling units" composed of 20 information bits and eight check bits.

One SS No. 6 frame is composed of 11 of these information signal units, along with a twelfth signal unit (of identical 20 + 8 format) used for control. Clearly this is not a protocol designed by computer scientists (no binary value numbers); it is designed by signaling gurus. The protocol is not layered — it is one monolithic specification from the link control to the application code. There are two reasons for this monolithic structure: (1) in the 1960s layered protocols were virtually unknown, and (2) there was an overriding demand for the efficiencies that monolithic protocols can deliver.

"A signaling system for digital [pulse-code modulation] trunks" was the mid-1970s CCITT charter given to the SS No. 7 working group. Some of the group's initial considerations centered on minimum modifications to the No. 6 system, but it soon became apparent that the higher data rates (56 or 64 kbit/s rather than 2.4 or 4.8 kbit/s) and the lower error rates (typically one error in 10^9 rather than one error in 10^5) demanded a dramatically different protocol architecture. By the time that the 1980 CCITT recommendations were published (CCITT operates on a four-year study/publish cycle) the value of layering was well appreciated, bit-oriented protocols (HDLC, SDLC, ADCCP) were widely accepted, and at least the lower layers of SS No. 7 resembled standard computer protocols.

While SS No. 7 is layered, and it uses many of the devices of other bit oriented protocols (for example, the eight-bit flag sequence of 01111110 to open and close frames) it still is a unique protocol suite tailored to the special needs of telephony signaling.

Historical development

Revisions and realignments of SS No. 7 are still being made. Much of the current work is bringing No. 7 into greater conformance with the ISO's seven layer OSI reference model (CCITT Recommendation X.200). This continuing evolution is more understandable when the context in which No. 7 developed is appreciated. In the late 1970s, when work started on No. 7, open systems and a universal hierarchy of protocols were still academic concepts. Furthermore, the designers of No. 7 considered themselves to be primarily telephone signaling people rather than computer data link people.

While ISDN was under study (Special Study Group D had been given this mission during CCITT's 1972-1976 study period), it became apparent that No. 7 was likely to be the signaling system for the integrated network. But there certainly was no consensus as to what an ISDN should look like or what services it should provide. And it must be remembered that SS No. 7 had a destiny of its own, independent of ISDN. No. 7 is the signaling system for all circuit-switched digital net-

1. The layers compared. *SS No. 7 does not match the OSI reference model layer for layer. For one thing, No. 7 was developed before the wide acceptance of OSI and was kept "closed." For another, No. 7 was not intended to be a general-purpose network model. Still, recent changes to No. 7 have been made in line with OSI.*

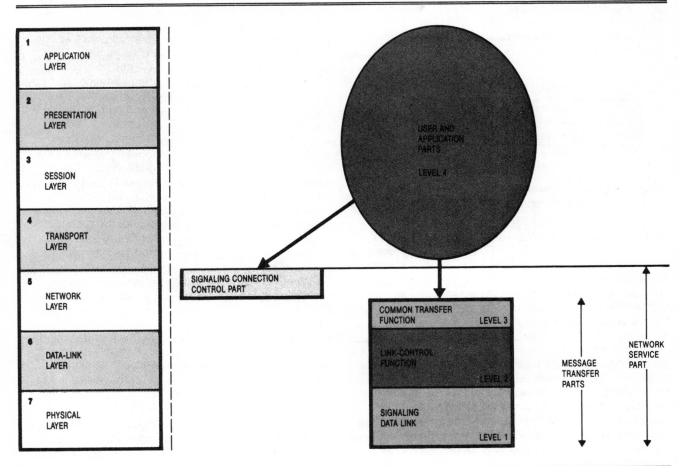

works. It so happens that ISDN is the most discussed network at this time, but No. 7 has provisions for plain pulse-code modulation telephone networks and other provisions for circuit-switched data networks.

The signaling system was defined as all of these environmental factors evolved. It is probable that No. 7 would look somewhat different if it were first conceived today—there undoubtedly would be a greater use of OSI layering principles, standard lower-layer protocols that are now available in large-scale integrated hardware, and more consideration of ISDN. However, the signaling system has been evolving (mainly through the addition of new modules rather than the elimination of existing layers) and further conformance with the OSI model is to be expected.

This ability to evolve gracefully is one of the reasons that there is virtually no talk of starting work on a replacement for SS No. 7—everyone is confident that No. 7 will be able to be extended to accommodate their needs. In addition, there is widespread appreciation of the tremendous investment of time that would be necessary to develop a replacement. The current

emphasis within the switching community is focused on getting on with the work of practical implementation and application of No. 7.

The layers

The original SS No. 7 design focused on efficient transport of circuit-switching control messages between switch processors—a closed system application. The objective for the cross-office delay at a relay point (last bit received to last bit transmitted) is 25 to 90 milliseconds—there is little room for unnecessary protocol features. Thus, though No. 7 is layered, the layers are not identical to the OSI reference model layering scheme. Figure 1 compares the layering of the OSI model to the layers used in SS No. 7. In some large part the differences are due to the quest for efficiency in the signaling system.

The value of a reference model is the structure it provides for defining information exchange procedures (protocols and interfaces). A new user function, that has been independently developed, can readily interface to an existing network if both the network and the

2. Link control. *While the frame format looks unique, SS No. 7's link control function shows the influence of typical bit-oriented link protocols.*

BASIC FORMAT OF A MESSAGE SIGNAL UNIT (MSU)

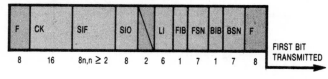

F	CK	SIF	SIO	LI	FIB	FSN	BIB	BSN	F
8	16	8n,n ≥ 2	8	2	6	1	7	1	7	8

FIRST BIT TRANSMITTED ➡

FORMAT OF A LINK STATUS SIGNAL UNIT (LSSU)

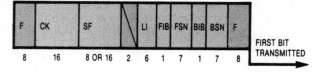

F	CK	SF	LI	FIB	FSN	BIB	BSN	F
8	16	8 OR 16	2	6	1	7	1	7	8

FIRST BIT TRANSMITTED ➡

FORMAT OF A FILL-IN SIGNAL UNIT (FISU)

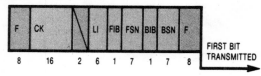

F	CK	LI	FIB	FSN	BIB	BSN	F
8	16	2	6	1	7	1	7	8

FIRST BIT TRANSMITTED ➡

BIB = BACKWARD INDICATOR BIT
BSN = BACKWARD SEQUENCE NUMBER
CK = CHECK BITS
F = FLAG
FIB = FORWARD INDICATOR BIT

FSN = FORWARD SEQUENCE NUMBER
LI = LENGTH INDICATOR
SF = STATUS FIELD
SIF = SIGNALING INFORMATION FIELD
SIO = SERVICE INFORMATION OCTET

---

application have built their protocol and interface interchanges in accord with the same reference model.

Since SS No. 7 was being built as a closed system, there was little concern with how additional applications would interface. This was a signaling system, not a general-purpose network. Furthermore, there was not a good (that is, widely accepted) reference model during the early definition stages. The growth in the use of data networking within the telephone industry (for administration and control of the network) and the current widespread acceptance of the OSI reference model has changed the situation. Many of the recent additions to No. 7 have either been in accord with the reference model or have increased the compliance of the signaling system.

In the following descriptions of each of the layers the degree of OSI compliance and recent shifts will be specifically noted. In addition, those aspects of the CCITT recommendations that have been changed by ANSI's T1X1 committee, for use in North America, will also be noted:

The message transfer part (the lower three levels of SS No. 7). Within the recommendation documents, the three lower levels of SS No. 7—collectively called the "message transfer part"—are universally referred to as the MTP. Each of the levels are never referred to by their full names but rather as "level 1, 2, or 3 of the MTP." (It should be noted that the No. 7 recommendations use the terminology "level" rather than OSI's "layer." This may seem trivial, but semantics are a vital issue when working in an international organization that publishes its recommendations in French, Spanish, and English.)

The MTP provides a service similar (but not quite equivalent) to an X.25 network. It accepts packets of data and reliably delivers them to their destination.

Signaling data link (OSI's physical layer). No. 7's signaling data link is in full compliance with the OSI definition of a physical layer. The signaling system is conceived for use on digital (for example, pulse-code modulation) links and has such things as timers and block lengths chosen for use on 64-kbit/s connections. CCITT allows for the use of switched connections to the data link, lower speeds, and the use of analog links with modems. The link is bidirectional and can be routed via a satellite.

The North American implementations are more restrictive, demanding the use of either 56- or 64-kbit/s links. In those cases where it is necessary to use analog facilities to support a No. 7 link, a wideband (56 kbit/s) modem must be employed.

Link control function (OSI's data link layer). The link control function shows the influence of the typical bit-oriented link protocols (HDLC, SDLC, LAP-B) but it definitely has a unique frame format, as is shown in Figure 2. The standard flag (01111110) is used to open and close the frame, bit stuffing is used to suppress strings of more than five 1's, and there is the standard CCITT CRC-16 checksum at the end of every frame. That much looks familiar.

The single-octet address field that is found in most bit-oriented link protocols is gone. It usually does not serve much purpose on the point-to-point links used with packet switching and the use of multipoint links with No. 7 is a topic for further study.

The forward and backward block-numbering schema is pretty much standard "extended mode" HDLC. One octet is allocated for each direction, a bit in each octet is used for control (ACK/NAK or new/retransmit), and the remaining seven bits allow modulo 128 block numbering. (Blocks are numbered from zero through 127. The block following block 127 is numbered zero.) Only signal units used for message transfer are uniquely numbered; overhead signal units use the number of the last message signal unit.

Two retransmission strategies are available. The "basic error correction method" is a typical go-back-N technique; upon receipt of a NAK the transmitter rolls back to the block received in error and retransmits everything from that point. When there is no data to be transmitted fill-in signal units are transmitted. The second strategy, "error correction by preventive cyclic retransmission," is designed for satellite and other high propagation delay links.

The basic design insights are recognition that (1) the link is frequently idle, (2) most of the messages are short, and (3) the signaling system operates in a connectionless mode wherein each signal unit is independent and delivery order is not critical. In that environment it is advisable to not wait for a NAK before making a retransmission. Whenever the link is idle cyclic retransmission of all unacknowledged signal units is started. Only positive acknowledgements are

3. Signaling work. *SS No. 7's signaling network functions cover routing, discrimination, and distribution, as well as traffic, link, and route management.*

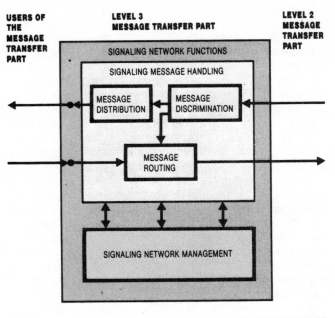

USERS OF THE MESSAGE TRANSFER PART

LEVEL 3 MESSAGE TRANSFER PART

LEVEL 2 MESSAGE TRANSFER PART

SIGNALING NETWORK FUNCTIONS

SIGNALING MESSAGE HANDLING

MESSAGE DISTRIBUTION

MESSAGE DISCRIMINATION

MESSAGE ROUTING

SIGNALING NETWORK MANAGEMENT

sent by the receiver and provision is made to retransmit unacknowledged signal units on a priority basis whenever the transmitter runs out of sequence numbers.

The next field in the signaling link control frame is a length indicator. In addition to allowing a cross-check on the closing flag and pre-allocation of buffer space (normal functions of a length indicator), the length indicator provides the signal unit type. Message signal units must have data portions larger than two octets. Status signal units have a data field of one or two octets, and fill-in signal units have a zero length indicator. All messages are an integral number of octets long. Flow control is provided through use of a status signal unit sent back by the receiver whenever congestion occurs. Timeouts on the flow condition alerts the level 3 entity if the "stop transmitting" condition lasts longer than 200 milliseconds without contact (including repeated "stop transmitting" status signal units) or 10 seconds with contact.

Up-down counts are used to confirm initial alignment and detect high error-rate environments. Prescaling of "good" counts by a factor of 256 allows detection of noisy physical links. A sustained block error rate of 1 error in 255 blocks will result in an alarm and taking the link out of service.

The signaling network functions (bottom half of OSI's network layer). The signaling network functions are divided into three categories:

1. Routing—determines where a message is to be sent.

2. Discrimination—determines if the message is at its destination or needs relaying.

3. Distribution—determines the user part to which a message should be delivered.

The relationship between these functions is shown in

Figure 3. In addition, there are signaling system management functions (management of the traffic, link, and routes) that must be handled by this level.

A 32-bit label is used for level 3 addressing. It is composed of 14-bit origination and destination addresses (called signal point codes) and a four-bit signaling link selection field that is used to distribute the traffic among alternative routes. The North American version of No. 7 uses 21-bit signal point codes to allow utilization of the signaling system in a larger network.

From an OSI point of view, this limited addressing capability is the primary deficiency of the signaling network functions. Signal point codes are basically node addresses; level 3 of the message service part does not provide for addressing (per se) anything beyond a node. (Roughly the equivalent of being able to address a packet switch and not being able to address the processors or processes attached to that packet switch.) The fixed-format user-part messages that SS No. 7 carries provide the information necessary for distribution. Message signal units contain a service information octet that designates the user part, or equivalent, and the network national or international.

This "peeking inside the envelope" is in direct violation of the spirit of the OSI philosophy, wherein each layer is responsible for providing all of the information necessary for its proper functioning. If each layer accepts this responsibility, the upper layers can be changed without changing the lower layers. The corner cutting that No. 7 uses makes it efficient for its signaling purpose. However, applications, such as signaling system management, have arisen that find the rigid format requirements of SS No. 7's third level onerous. Therefore, an additional level that provides full OSI addressing, called the signaling connection control part, has been established.

The signaling link selection field is made part of the address (presented by the user part) so that conflicting demands can be satisfied. From a user part point of view, it is useful if messages that must be associated upon receipt (such as all the messages associated with a single call) are directed along the same route and therefore generally arrive in order. Although the signaling system's connectionless mode allows for proper functioning despite out-of-sequence delivery, sequenced delivery reduces the user part's work load.

From the message transfer part's viewpoint traffic should be distributed uniformly over all available alternate routes. Both levels can be satisfied if the user part puts a value in the selection field that appears to be selected at random and the message transfer part uses a function of this field to determine the route to be taken. CCITT recommends that the least significant bits of the circuit number or a similar entity be used for the signaling link selection field. Such a number will be the same for the entire call, but it will vary uniformly from call to call.

The bulk of the signaling network functions specification is concerned with overcoming link degradations (failures or congestion). Procedures are detailed for rapidly determining that a link has degraded, removing it from service, rerouting traffic, and later bringing the link back into service. The overriding concern for signaling network reliability is evident in these procedures. The goal is no more than 10 minutes of unavailability per year for any route (available 99.998 percent of the time). This goal is achieved through redundancy and rerouting rather than emphasis on super reliability of any given link. Quasi-associated signaling, wherein the signals take a path different than the call to reach a given end point, is a fundamental part of this scheme.

The North American versions of the signaling system accept the CCITT recommendations and then go several steps further in specifying the redundancy that is to be available and the alternate routing techniques that are to be used. There is heavy reliance on a configuration called a quad, shown in Figure 4, which consists of signal transfer points deployed in pairs. The two members of the pair are interconnected by a link (shown as a vertical link in the diagram) that is used solely for restoration purposes. A source or sink node (typically a circuit switch) would be connected to both members of the pair. Backbone interconnections are made to other paired signaling transfer points by means of four signaling links.

Signaling connection control part (upper half of OSI's network layer). To provide full OSI addressing capability the message transfer part is supplemented with the signaling connection control part (SCCP). The combined capability is called the "network service part." In addition, it is planned to have the signaling connect control part eventually provide connections, while the message transfer part will only provide connectionless service.

The message transfer part addresses in the international version of SS No. 7 are limited to 14-bit signaling point codes. This would be equivalent to only allowing addressing packet switches in an X.25 network. For signaling applications this is an adequate solution. All signaling messages have a format that allows extraction of the additional information required for message distribution.

However, this can lead to additional complexity when nonsignaling applications are supported by the signaling network. Each of these nonsignaling applications could be designed as user parts, and provide their own routing and distribution functions. This would result in a number of applications implementing the same function, and clearly would not be in the spirit of the OSI model.

To solve this problem, the designers of SS No. 7 have chosen to add another layer, the SCCP, that looks to the message transfer part to be another user part. This added layer is responsible for services the OSI model assigns to the network layer. This not only allows the message transfer part to retain its efficient character, but also permits SS No. 7 to offer full OSI network layer service. In North America, there is greater emphasis on the SCCP and more tendency to use OSI layering.

The SCCP can accept signaling point codes (as does the message transfer part) or global titles (such as dialed numbers) or subsystem numbers as addresses. The SCCP has access to routing information that allows associating any of these addresses with a signaling

point code, which the message transfer part understands. At the destination signaling point, the message is passed to the local SCCP, which takes responsibility for delivery to the user.

There are five classes of service that are defined in the SCCP:

Connectionless

0. Basic (unsequenced) connectionless class.

1. Sequenced (fixed signaling link selection number) connectionless class.

Connection-oriented

2. Basic connection-oriented class.

3. Flow control connection-oriented class.

4. Error recovery and flow control connection-oriented class.

SS No. 7 user parts (upper layers of OSI reference model). The original SS No. 7 architecture had monolithic user protocols. These protocols directly interfaced with the message transfer part. The well-defined services and closed system environment of a classical signaling system made transport, session, and presentation levels unnecessary. The two oldest user parts— the telephone user part and the data user part—were designed this way.

Each user part is complete and independent. The user parts can generally connect directly to the message transfer part, thus providing end-to-end signaling service with only four levels of protocol. Several different user parts could operate in parallel (multiplexed) over a single message transfer part facility.

As other uses for the pervasive signaling network were found, the need for OSI type services increased. Thus, the SCCP and the newer user parts are taking on more of an OSI appearance.

The telephone user part and data user part recommendations jump immediately into long lists of signaling message groups—forward address messages, forward set-up messages, and backward set-up messages. Within each group there are a number of messages—initial address messages, and subsequent address messages. The hierarchical structure that is typical of modern layered protocols is not in evidence. A hierarchical structure allows the addition of newer user features with little fear of conflict with the existing messages.

Detailed instructions are given as to the content of each field of every message, which fields are mandatory, optional, fixed length, and variable length. These rigidly defined formats allow rapid parsing of message content and efficiency in setting up circuit-switched connections.

The telephone user part is still being actively refined for use outside North America. The data user part has largely been supplanted by the ISDN user part. And several more interesting user or application protocols are starting to emerge. The ISDN user part is one of them. The rigid formats of the older user parts are difficult to use with the more fluid parts of the ISDN. Therefore, while the routine signaling functions of the ISDN user part are similar to the old telephone user part, the more innovative features, such as end-to-end signaling (used to modify the nature of a call that has already been set up) and user-to-user data are likely to require the services of the SCCP. (This particular topic is still a matter for discussion within the standards community.) Since the ISDN user part can be used for non-ISDN telephony or data networks, it can completely supplant those user parts. In North America, only the ISDN user part will be supported.

Even more OSI-like in nature is the operations and maintenance application part. It is structured to support the SS No. 7 network, providing functions such as routing data management, route verification, long-term measurement collection, on-occurrence measurement reporting, delay measurements, clock initialization, real-time control, operations, and testing. Many of these services are less well-defined in nature. (Addressing a trouble reporting process running in a number of different switch control units is an example of this type of service.) To support these unstructured tasks there is heavy reliance on the OSI-like services and a complete dependence upon the SCCP.

In North America, an interesting set of application protocols have been developed to allow transport of SS No. 6 messages over the SS No. 7 network. These protocols do not allow a No. 6 end point to interact with a No. 7 end point, but do allow continued economical transport for the well-established No. 6 facilities.

As SS No. 7 matures, users can expect the new application protocols to look like the operations and maintenance application part. A key to identifying these newer protocols is likely to be the term "application," rather than "user," in their title. Within North America, this trend is already well underway. ANSI's T1X1 committee has recently introduced a complete OSI layered structure entirely within the SCCP for the purpose of maintaining the SCCP's routing tables.

Carrying No. 6 traffic over the No. 7 network
Within North America, there is extensive deployment of CCIS6 (an analog common channel system based on CCITT Signaling System No. 6). Several internetworking protocols that provide SS No. 7 support for these CCIS6 installations have been defined. These include:
■ AT&T's Embedded CCIS6 (ECIS6) for transmission of CCIS6 messages over a single No. 7 link. At each No. 7 signaling point traversed, there must be a CCIS6 process to accept the message and reroute it, if necessary.
■ AT&T's Destination CCIS6 (DCIS6) that uses the routing capabilities of the SCCP to allow routing to distant CCIS6 nodes.
■ Telecom Canada's CCIS6 (TCIS6) that adds enough processing in the "interworking unit" (protocol convertor) to provide valid No. 7 envelopes (including destination point codes) for CCIS6 messages.

The problem is how to route CCIS6 messages consistently through a No. 7 network. ECIS6 avoids the problem by falling back to a simple "hop at a time" routing to CCIS6 entities. DCIS6 uses the full OSI routing capability of the SCCP in No. 7. TCIS6 puts the routing burden on the CCIS6 side of the interface.

Note that none of these internetworking techniques

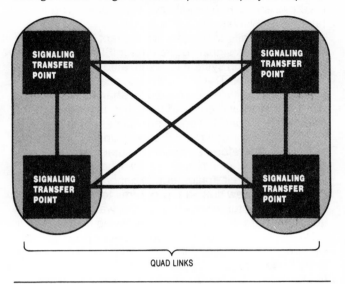

4. North American variations. One twist to SS No. 7 concerns redundancy, with heavy reliance on the quad configuration—signal transfer points deployed in pairs.

allows transfers between CCIS6 and No. 7 end points—they are just a means of allowing CCIS6 end points to communicate via a No. 7 network.

When and where
SS No. 7 is just now reaching the point where it will be operationally deployed in North America. Overseas, there have been a number of installations, mostly employing versions of the telephone users part. In the United States, the main driving forces are the installation of ISDN and the desire of the regional Bell operating companies to take on more sophisticated control functions, particularly In-WATS (800 number) and credit card validation services.

In the switch market, those driving forces have resulted in several organizations (ITT, Digital Switch Corp., Integrated Technology Inc., and AT&T) announcing signal transfer points (STPs). An STP is a processor hub joined to a number (typically over a hundred) of switches via No. 7 paths. The STP can be just a relay point, acting as a packet switch, but, generally, additional database capabilities are installed at the same location. These databases contain 800 routing and billing information and credit-card validity lists. ITT has sold the central processor units of its System 12 switches (without the switching matrix) to Southern Bell and Pacific Bell for use as STPs. ITT has announced that it will enter into an agreement with a computer vendor to provide the database function. Digital Switch Corp. has announced an STP wherein the database is kept on a Stratus fault-tolerant computer. Integrated Technology Inc. has an STP that it has jointly developed with Tandem Computers Inc., the fault tolerant computer pioneer. AT&T has developed what it calls a 2STP that will support both SS No. 7 and SS No. 6. The database in an AT&T installation will reside on an AT&T 3B computer.

An STP is a major purchase, typically selling for close

to $1 million. However, it is expected that the total market is relatively modest, totaling only $500 million through 1990. Vendors see the market's main value to be the opening an STP sale provides for winning future telephone switch sales.

It is worthwhile to underscore the fact that SS No. 7 will be the trunk signaling system for ISDN. A common channel signaling system is essential for providing the services of ISDN. The only common channel signaling system being developed for digital channels is SS No. 7. SS No. 7 will come to fruition independent of the fate of ISDN, but ISDN could not succeed if there were not a responsive common channel signaling system to support it. Therefore, all major manufacturers of central-office switches have, or soon will have, No. 7 appliques for their equipment. In general, these appliques are just new software programs for the switch, but some manufacturers are adding hardware modules to accommodate the additional processing load.

While the prime emphasis in the development of SS No. 7 has been interexchange (trunk) signaling, there is likely to be increased opportunity for users to avail themselves of SS No. 7 once ISDN access lines are available. Interfaces to the ISDN will consist of several 64-kbit/s B channels (used for voice, circuit-switched data, or wideband packet-switched services) and a D channel (used for signaling, telemetry, or low-speed packet-switched services). The D channel (and it's deviant brother, the E channel) are our primary focus.

The link layer protocol to be used on the D channel is LAP-D. It is a protocol that is similar to LAP-B (the balanced HDLC version used on X.25 connections) except for its two-octet address field that is used for statistically multiplexing the various services provided on the D channel. The signaling formats to be used above LAP-D, and when LAP-D should be replaced with the message transfer part of SS No. 7 (thus becoming the deviant E channel), require discussion.

The E channel is a leading candidate for PBX access. Using the SS No. 7 message transfer part on PBX links would allow the PBX to fully exploit the ISDN opportunities. The PBX would become more nearly an exchange switch. Signaling would be rapid and more features could be provided. In particular, information concerning users behind PBXs (called or calling party's availability, capability, and identity) could be made available and be passed through the signaling network.

End-to-end signaling to modify calls in progress and user-to-user data yields further application possibilities. End-to-end uses would open the possibility of user fraud—the high-tech "blue box." Current thinking about that protection focuses on limiting the signaling messages from the PBX to the first exchange, but the topic is still under discussion.

CCITT has a recommendation for the PBX interface. It is entirely concerned with what an E-channel message transfer part should look like (much like a normal message transfer part but with fewer arrangements for detecting failures and restoring service) and how it could be protocol converted from a standard D-channel interface, if necessary. The questions of when and why the E-channel format should be used, and what

the user part should be are topics for study and are not included in the latest version of the CCITT recommendations.

The other interface where the user community may come in contact with SS No. 7 protocols is at OSI Level 3, above a LAP-D link layer. The protocols to be used on a basic or primary access D channel are still under consideration by the ISDN specifiers. There is a drive to keep these protocols as simple as possible for low-cost user terminals, but there is also a drive to provide specialized services when required. A simple (but fully compatible) subset of the ISDN user part for simple terminals and a more sophisticated version for full function terminals is a possibility. A fascinating possibility, if the fraud protection approach allows it, is the access to a connectionless data service provided over the signaling network. The datagram service within X.25 has died and there is still an unfulfilled need for a simple transaction-oriented data service, for items such as credit checks. The network service part (that is, message transfer part plus signaling connection control part) of SS No. 7 provides a high performance connectionless service.

Implementation plans

At the current time the lowest three levels of No. 7 (the message transfer part) are fully specified and are probably stable. Implementation work can get underway. The SCCP is also fairly well-defined (although it is notable that there are some differences between the North American version and the CCITT version). Users can plan on having full OSI addressing available.

Above the network service part the situation is somewhat more fluid. It is not clear whether the telephone user part will become widely used outside North America and inside North America there are no plans to use it. The ISDN user part is still in a state of flux, but work is progressing rapidly. Application parts, which use the full OSI layering of the higher protocols, probably will become more prevalent.

The plans of AT&T and Telecom Canada for support of CCIS6 provide one sensible model for moving ahead—using the lower levels and developing a unique upper level, if necessary. The degree of layering that is incorporated in No. 7 allows that flexibility.

One thing is sure, No. 7 cannot be ignored by those who are building or buying telephone equipment that will be used over the next five to ten years. No. 7 will be a central component in the ISDN and, independent of ISDN, No. 7 will be the key to a number of enhanced services for telecommunications users. ∎

Walt Roehr heads Telecommunication Network Consulting, a firm he founded in 1984. Roehr has 20 years of experience as a telecommunications engineer, working for a variety of commercial and government clients. He holds a bachelor's degree in electrical engineering from City College of New York and an M. S. E. E. from George Washington University. An expert on Signaling System No. 7, he has presented tutorials on the ISDN signaling technique for Omnicom Inc., an OSI advisory firm in Vienna, Va.

Jeffry Parker and Hadi Ibrahim, Advanced Micro Devices Inc.,
Sunnyvale, Calif.

Bipolar and MOS make the best of all possible network worlds

Analog line interfacing and high voltage boost bipolar technology. Low-power signal processing applications make MOS ideal.

Tech focus

The standard requirements for the present telephone networks were designed prior to the advent of semiconductor devices. Because the implementations are so deeply entrenched, however, all new telephone equipment and components must work with these requirements in order to remain compatible with the existing telephone network. Nevertheless, with today's technology, implementing a given telephone function may favor one semiconductor over another.

For example, network component designs must meet certain requirements for high-voltage capability, power, size, reliability, and international standards. Telephone lines use relatively high voltages for a number of reasons. In the first place, about 50 volts are needed to send signals over the line, typically several miles long. In addition, around 120 volts at 20 Hz are needed to ring a telephone. Because the telephone line operates in a harsh environment (lightning strikes of 1,500 volts or power surges of 120 to 240 volts, for example, are typical), any components connecting to the telephone line must have extended protection circuitry in order to withstand surge voltages. Such an environment favors bipolar technology.

Conversely, power used by telephone components must be kept to a minimum. A set of batteries power central office equipment to ensure that a subscriber's telephone will work, even if the local utility's power fails. Components within the exchange should use minimal power in order to reduce the need for large expensive batteries. Further, any power dissipated by the components on a line card builds up as heat, which must be removed to ensure equipment reliability. Low-power circuits not only reduce cooling needs, but also allow components to be packed more tightly on a line card—hence, allowing for smaller network compo-

nents. Finally, at the telephone handset, only about 40 milliamperes (ma) of current remain, so that all handset circuitry must be able to operate with this limited power. In these applications, designs based on either n-channel metal-oxide semiconductors (NMOSs) or complementary metal-oxide semiconductors (CMOSs) are preferred.

Smaller telephone-switching equipment, derived from the integration of discrete components into silicon chips, benefits the user in many ways. Because line cards make up a major portion of switching equipment, overall system efficiency increases with smaller line cards or with more lines being placed on a card of a given size.

Bipolar vs. MOS technologies

After reviewing the requirements for a telephone system, it becomes clear that no single integrated circuit (IC) technology is ideal for implementing all the telephone interface functions. The requirements for high voltage, low power, and less cost are mutually exclusive. This is a result of the physical characteristics needed for chips to support high voltages that generally result in large high-cost dies with high power dissipation.

From a systems point of view, however, a two-chip set can be developed that draws on the strengths of each technology. For example, power feed circuits operate on 50 volts (v) and operational amplifiers that must both source (transmit) and sink (terminate) anywhere from 100 to 150 ma of current. Bipolar circuits can also implement low-noise, precision analog functions that are essential to meet stringent transmission specifications. Due to their high drive, high speed, and high breakdown voltages (see the preceding article, "Bipolar technology: Choice for network tasks"), bipo-

1. Chip duets. *The pairing of an SLAC with an SLIC combines the best of two IC technologies. NMOS-based chips on the SLAC must perform filtering and channel selection using little power and high speed. The bipolar-based SLIC ICs must withstand high voltages and perform loop supervision and signal transmission.*

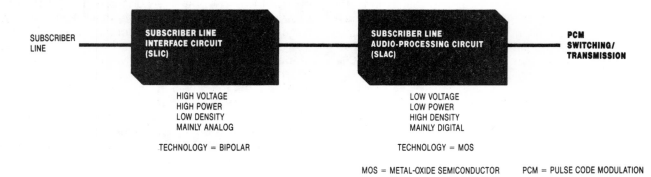

2. SLIC functions. *The two-wire interface provides both two- to four-wire and four- to two-wire conversion. The power feed controller supplies the d. c. feed current to the subscriber line using a programmable resistance that is set with an external resistor. The feed voltage and the feed resistance are independent of the battery.*

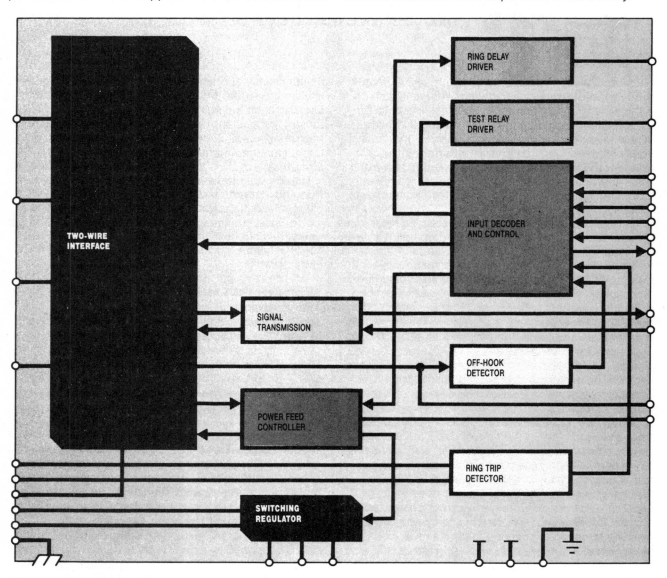

lar ICs can perform the inherently analog signal functions of battery feed, line interfacing, and overvoltage line protection.

Low-voltage, low-power metal-oxide semiconductor (MOS) ICs, on the other hand, can perform the remaining communications functions, which are mostly digital. Very large scale integrated circuit (VLSI) technology allows for a dense, small, low-cost NMOS or CMOS die that incorporates many capabilities. By using a digital signal processor, programmable features can be implemented in firmware; this eliminates the need for external components traditionally used to set operating parameters.

Analog subscriber lines

An example of a dual bipolar/MOS implementation (Fig. 1) is the pairing of a subscriber line audio-processing circuit (SLAC) and the subscriber line interface circuit (SLIC). The SLAC, built in NMOS, performs the codes and the filtering functions that are necessary in digital voice-switching machines. The SLIC, implemented using a 70-volt bipolar technology, performs the telephone local loop interface functions, including signal transmission, battery feed, as well as local loop supervision.

The SLIC and SLAC were both designed to take advantage of their respective technologies. The SLIC handles all of the high-voltage signals associated with the subscriber line. Thus, it is responsible for supplying the direct current feed voltage; detecting off-hook

(when the handset is picked up) and ring trip (when the handset is lifted during ringing); and driving the ring and test relays.

The SLIC could potentially dissipate many watts of power in order to supply 75 ma from a 60-volt battery, but an internal switching regulator minimizes wasted power. The SLAC handles all of the other functions that require only a low voltage and involve a large amount of processing. Using microprocessor techniques, the SLAC does, for example, all the filtering, channel selection, and noise suppression.

The SLAC makes the most of NMOS capabilities. It uses two independent digital signal processors for all of its filtering, converting an analog input signal into pulse code modulation (PCM) output and, conversely, converting a PCM input into an analog output. User-programmable digital filters allow gain adjustment, trans-hybrid balancing, and two-wire impedance adjustment.

The SLIC functions are shown in the block diagram of Figure 2. The two-wire interface block provides both the two- to four-wire, and four- to two-wire conversion. Through this block, the two-wire termination impedance is set via an external impedance. Additionally, the two-wire impedance could be effectively modified with the use of an impedance adjustment filter inside the SLAC.

The user-network interface in an Integrated Services Digital Network (ISDN) is at the "S" interface specified by the International Telegraph and Telephone Consul-

3. ISDN-four. *Four devices can adequately implement an ISDN at the "S" interface. The partitioning of the devices is based on optimum use of bipolar and MOS technologies. For example, high-voltage functions are done in the bipolar SPC, while low-power functions (in the DSC and DEC) are accomplished with CMOS.*

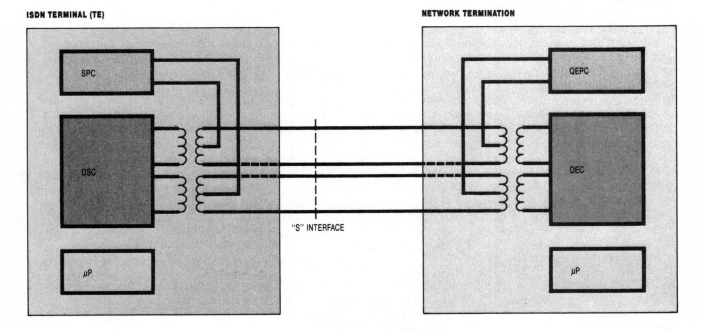

DEC = DIGITAL EXCHANGE CONTROLLER
DSC = DIGITAL SUBSCRIBER CONTROLLER
QEPC = QUAD EXCHANGE POWER CONTROLLER
SPC = SUBSCRIBER POWER CONTROLLER
µP = MICROPROCESSOR

4. Power to the interface. *The quad-exchange power controller (QEPC) provides regulated 40v power to four "S" interfaces. Input voltages may be up to 60v.*

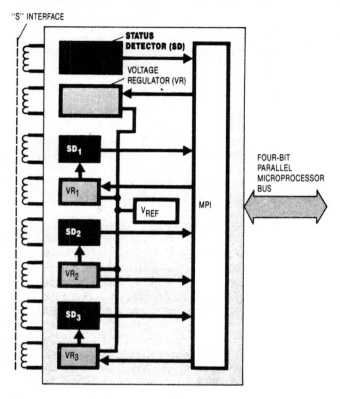

"S" INTERFACE

STATUS DETECTOR (SD)

VOLTAGE REGULATOR (VR)

SD$_1$

VR$_1$

V$_{REF}$

MPI

SD$_2$

VR$_2$

SD$_3$

VR$_3$

FOUR-BIT PARALLEL MICROPROCESSOR BUS

MPI = MICROPROCESSOR INTERFACE
SD = STATUS DETECTOR
VR = VOLTAGE REGULATOR
V$_{REF}$ = REFERENCE VOLTAGE

tative Committee (CCITT). At this interface or reference point, the CCITT specifies the physical link and network-level functions. The subscriber's installation contains terminal equipment (TE), which may operate in point-to-point or point-to-multipoint (bus type) arrangements; the physical medium is four wires, over which two 64-kbit/s channels (designated B1 and B2) and one 16-kbit/s channel (designated D) are transferred between the TEs and the network termination (NT).

In many cases, the NT function would be included within a private branch exchange (PBX). The B1 and B2 channels carry digitized voice and/or data, whereas the D channel contains only signaling and control information. Power may also be delivered to the TEs over the "S" line interface from the PBX by means of a phantom feed arrangement.

As with the SLIC and SLAC, the functional partitioning of ISDN devices is based in optimum usage of bipolar and MOS technologies. Thus, for example, the high-voltage and high-power functions would be included within the bipolar subscriber power controller (SPC) and the quad-exchange power controller (QEPC) chips (Fig. 3). These two devices control the transfer of power and the associated test and maintenance features.

All other functions that are essentially low-voltage and require high-density logic are designed in CMOS technology and are incorporated into the digital subscriber controller (DSC) and the digital exchange controller (DEC). The DSC forms the heart of ISDN terminal equipment and contains the "S" interface transceivers, audio processor, D-channel handler, serial interfaces to peripherals, and parallel interfaces to a microprocessor. The DEC may reside on a PBX line card, and it contains the "S" interface master transceiver, D-channel handler, system interface to PCM highways, and a parallel microprocessor interface.

Voltage in

Although input voltage (VIN) on the "S" interface is limited to 40v, the SPC has been designed to operate over a much wider input range (15 to 60v). A switch-mode regulator is essential in order to meet the power conversion efficiency requirements of the basic TE. Since the 5v supply is used to power sensitive circuits within the DSC, the SPC exhibits the high performance criteria that are characteristic of bipolar circuits, such as low ripple (small amounts of alternating current in a direct current circuit), low impedance, and high stability.

When power goes down in an emergency situation, the minimum power available at the TE is 400 milliwatts (mw). The NT notifies the TEs of such a condition by reversing the polarity of the "S" wires. Due to the limited power available under such conditions, basic telephony capability is provided to the "priority" TE on the bus; all other TEs are denied power. A diode bridge is connected across the input pins of the SPC in the "priority" TE. This SPC can detect voltage polarity reversal and inform the microprocessor that the "S" interface bus is currently operating under unusual emergency conditions.

The basic function of the QEPC (Fig. 4) is to provide a regulated 40v power source to four "S" interfaces (S0-S3). The device may be operated either in a saturated or in a regulated mode. In the saturated mode, the input supply is from a centrally regulated source: two to three volts above the required output voltage. In the regulated mode, the input supply may be up to 60v. In this case, if on-chip power dissipation specifications are exceeded, an external transistor may be connected to dissipate excess power. With current technology, the SPC and QEPC ICs are most efficiently implemented in bipolar; the high voltage handling capability of these devices illustrates perfectly one of bipolar's inherent strengths. But as pointed out, CMOS also has a role to play in telecommunications networks. ∎

Jeffry Parker received his B. S. E. E. from Lehigh University, Bethlehem, Pa., and his M. S. E. E. from Stanford University, in Palo Alto, Calif. Hadi Ibrahim earned his B. Sc. from D. J. Science College, Pakistan, in 1971 and his M. S. E. E. from Leeds College, Leeds, England, in 1975. Prior to joining Advanced Micro Devices, Ibrahim worked for GEC Telecom Ltd., Coventry, England.

Ben Barlow, Xerox Corp., Rochester, N. Y.

Microcomputer use on SNA networks is a balancing act

Protocol converters and microcomputers can be a cheap, flexible substitute for 3270 terminals and controllers, but their use demands careful planning.

Micro

Increases in data communications costs and availability of inexpensive hardware often make microcomputers and protocol converters in IBM networks an attractive alternative to the standard solution—the 3270 terminal, controller, and dedicated leased circuit. When dial lines can connect remote microcomputers to the protocol converter, service can be extended to users where dedicated service had been unaffordable. In addition, the computing power in today's microcomputers provides an added benefit for users, who can now use microcomputer functions such as word processing and spreadsheets, browse remote databases, and execute transactions on an IBM host computer from a single workstation.

But these benefits are not free. Applying protocol converters can be a complex and risky business for the data processing department that is unprepared to accept the higher degree of planning and support that accompany a mixed-mode network. The success of an implementation actually calls for the planners, implementors, and users to juggle many factors. This article examines those factors and points out some potential pitfalls.

Having microcomputers dial into protocol converters is not the answer to every networking problem. Indeed, careful, comprehensive planning is necessary to make sure the technology is not misapplied. Examples of instances where a dial-up protocol converter network may pay off include cases where many locations have single users needing occasional access to host computers, or when small sites move from building to building (or city to city) on short notice making dial-up access an ideal way to maintain network connections. Generally, the technique can be applied when dedicated circuits and controllers are impractical because of cost or inflexibility, and when security is not an issue.

The result will be a network similar in appearance to the illustration in Figure 1.

In the typical scenario, a user with a task to do sits at a microcomputer, runs a program that emulates a terminal, and dials a telephone rotary or resource switch that connects to a protocol converter that converts the terminal's ASCII protocol to the IBM SNA or bisynchronous protocol used by the host network. The user then enters transactions just as would be done on a dedicated terminal and theoretically notices no difference except the increased response time caused by the low-speed dial-up connection. When the task is complete, the user hangs up, freeing the protocol converter port, the telephone line, and the user session at the host.

Components

In this scenario, at least nine factors must be balanced if the computer and network architecture are to meet their goals of effectiveness and user satisfaction. The microcomputer and its software, the dial-up lines and their modems, the protocol converters, SNA circuit, host software, network planning, user training, and support tasks all need to work together smoothly. The better these pieces fit together, the more favorably will the network's users perceive them and the less expensive will the network's operation and maintenance be.

The ninth factor, security, though receiving a lot of notice in the press, is not within the scope of this article. The definition of overall security requirements, determination of likely threats, and analysis of products are complicated processes worthy of their own treatment. We consider security determination to have been made for the purposes of this article.

An unbalanced implementation generally leads to frustration among the users of the network, which in

1. Network structure. *A typical dial-up configuration, which usually ends up being the most expensive route that can be taken when designing a network.*

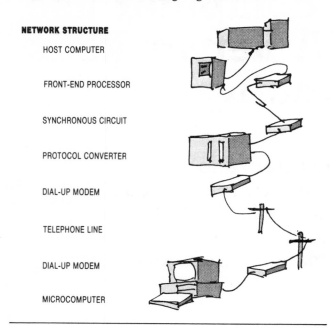

NETWORK STRUCTURE

HOST COMPUTER

FRONT-END PROCESSOR

SYNCHRONOUS CIRCUIT

PROTOCOL CONVERTER

DIAL-UP MODEM

TELEPHONE LINE

DIAL-UP MODEM

MICROCOMPUTER

turn can lead to higher support costs, loss of productivity, or even to total replacement. User satisfaction is the most critical single determinant of success and should be kept constantly in mind during the project by inviting users to participate in the planning and testing stages, and requiring that developers and trainers use the emerging network. Building a sense of participation will pay benefits—people are always more willing to accept, and less likely to criticize, a decision that they have helped to form than one that has been imposed on them.

One pitfall that can cause frustration is the belief that standard transaction design philosophies can be applied to dial-up protocol converter networks. The increase in response time caused by the dial-up link requires that design techniques be applied that will minimize the data transmitted across the link. Long response times definitely frustrate users.

The belief that a network with dial-up protocol converters will be as easy to operate as a vanilla network because of built-in software is another potential pitfall waiting to snare network planners. The vagaries of the dial-up connection, the mysteries of SNA (if that is the network's protocol), untrained users, lack of vendor support, and the increase in the amount of software in the communications path all point toward greater complication and higher support costs.

The balancing act
Attention needs to be paid to both human and network components to ensure the successful installation of microcomputers on 3270 networks (Fig. 2).

Microcomputer
The component of the network closest to the user is

the microcomputer that serves as the terminal. Although more expensive than the inexpensive ASCII terminals available, its use can often be justified by the increased function it offers, by the higher level of diagnostics and assistance its software can provide, and by its insurance against obsolescence.

When selecting a microcomputer, examine the present and future functions required (is it used simply as a terminal, or will it be called upon to run a spreadsheet or word processing program? Will it receive data files from the host computer for off-line processing?), ergonomic factors such as screen size, color (monochrome green, white, or amber, or full-color display?), keyboard comfort, programmability, and function keys. Good documentation of the machine's components and operating system are critical if you anticipate special communications programming. An internal modem card can sometimes save costs or simplify operations, but because installation and removal require opening the microcomputer's case, it may be more difficult to diagnose and service when problems arise. User participation in the selection of this hardware is very useful, and the results should be published for the user community.

Microcomputer software
Software for the microcomputer is extremely important. It is here that the user interface is defined and the goal of ease of use will be achieved. The decision of whether to buy or build this software is an important one, and the success or failure of the project depends to a great extent on the quality of the decision, regardless of which path is chosen.

Desirable features in the software should make it easy for the user to determine the status of the communications port, the modem, the connection path, and provide machine-based HELP functions, and statistics gathering (how many connections, when made, problems detected, and how long?). These features can be invaluable when tracking down persistent problems, and can also affect the degree of user training needed and the level and amount of support that must be provided after the implementation; a microcomputer program that is difficult to use or troubleshoot can easily take twice the support of one that provides assistance.

The terminal emulation chosen must, of course, be one of those offered by the selected protocol converter, but attention should also be given to the efficiency of the protocol being emulated if the protocol converter offers a choice of terminal types. Some terminals require lengthy control sequences to position the cursor or set field attributes—sequences that must be transmitted at low speed.

Murphy's Law, which states that everything that can go wrong will go wrong, applies here, so some method of software distribution must be considered to change the operating software after implementation. Automatic transmission of new software seems ideal, but making sure that transmitted changes are made to backup disks, avoiding the flooding of the network with time-consuming file transmissions, and maintaining synchronization with the host programs (if required) is difficult to accomplish. Mailing disks may be a better approach, although some of the same problems remain. Of course, thorough testing and good quality control for both made and purchased software help ensure that bug correction releases will not be necessary.

Dial-up lines and modems
Selection of a modem in a dial-up network is obviously an important decision. Testing can be very useful in determining which modems work well, and which ones are sensitive to noise. Although few organizations have sophisticated telephone line simulators for testing, some simple tests involving transfer of known data between machines several miles apart can be used to develop error rates for comparison. Visiting a few of the user sites with a microcomputer and modem and running tests on the actual telephone lines that will be encountered on the network will produce results indicative of live operation.

A modem that allows the microcomputer program to exercise software control of communications (which avoids the problem of users making incorrect settings), and detects call-progress signals (especially dial-tone detect, busy, and carrier detect) is extremely valuable. The microcomputer program can then include automatic trouble detection and resolution code or can record an event log to which the user can refer when calling the support center to resolve a communications problem.

The speed of this modem is the biggest contributor to the network component of response time. Since a 1,600-character screen will take a full 14 seconds to transmit at 1.2 kbit/s, the fastest modem should be chosen, taking into account affordability and the amount of tolerable error. Remember that the terminal's control sequences, though not visible, also get transmitted, and in carelessly designed applications they can account for more characters than are visible.

The lines on which the user places the calls to the protocol converters need to be identified and tested. If terminals will be calling through a PBX, testing should be used to determine the effect the PBX may have on the call. Data calls through PBXs, which are much longer than the average voice call, can catch the attention of the switchboard operator who may think that something is wrong with the line and may break in to find the problem. Noise from that interruption, or other noise generated within the PBX, may require that extra cost-measured business lines outside the PBX be used. In addition, few PBXs are configured for data calls that can degrade the voice service by tying up external lines for a long period, limiting the number of outside voice calls that the PBX can make or accept. Although too complex a subject to be discussed here, the selection of a proper PBX is another critical factor in network design.

Protocol converters
Protocol converter vendors abound, and the machines display many esoteric features as manufacturers strive

2. Balancing act. *Hardware, software, and human factors make up a checklist for juggling microcomputers on SNA networks.*

NETWORK COMPONENTS

- MICROCOMPUTER
- SOFTWARE
- DIAL LINES AND MODEMS
- PROTOCOL CONVERTERS
- SNA (OR BISYNCHRONOUS) CIRCUIT
- HOST SOFTWARE

PEOPLE COMPONENTS

- NETWORK PLANNING
- USER TRAINING
- SUPPORT FUNCTIONS

for product differentiation. Although some features such as file transfer capability, virtual printer, or operation as a remote batch terminal may seem of little use to the application, they may be important enough to another user on the network to justify a vendor selection decision.

The microprocessor revolution has spawned dozens of companies producing excellent and innovative protocol converters. Few of them have been around long enough to establish much of a track record, however, so the selection of the protocol converter supplier should consider the vendor's financial viability as well as some measure of the support provided for hardware or (more likely) software problems likely to ensue.

Ensure selection of a company that will be around and available to help resolve problems and provide equipment for future expansion. If the IBM network protocol is SNA/SDLC, bear in mind that SNA is not a simple architecture and is tightly woven into many levels of IBM software. The protocol converter vendor that can get all that software right (hundreds of thousands of lines of code) and offer desired and esoteric features, too, is rare. In such a state of flux there is no substitute for hands-on testing, at length and in depth. There is no such thing as too much quality assurance.

Operational and diagnostic capabilities are important. Can someone tell by looking at the machine or console if it is operating properly? Will they need to? If it is to be placed outside the data processing department, can it be accessed remotely for troubleshooting? Will the machines be maintained by the data processing department? Are maintenance procedures complete and readable? Is the equipment designed for ease of maintenance? Is the software on disk or based in ROM? Disks are easy to change when software updates are required, but their mechanical parts and additional hardware logic introduce some measure of unreliability. Read-only memory (ROM) chips are very reliable, but their change is difficult, requiring disassembly of the machine and replacement of the out-of-date or broken chips.

IBM 3270 terminals do not disconnect at random times as do dialed-in protocol converter connections, and one can anticipate problems in the interface. At worst, a user calling the converter may be connected into the session vacated by a user who has just hung up (or was disconnected by a network problem). Clearly, this is an unacceptable security breach, for the newly connected user has not had to pass any security checks. In fact, this type of failure is so common that it is one of the first-used tools in the bag of the hacker attempting to break into a computer. Other problems may result in the ASCII port being disabled forever while waiting for an SNA response that will never come, the result of an attempt by the protocol converter software to tear down the session connection in the host computer through several protocol levels. The result is that the protocol converter slowly dies as its ports succumb to failure one by one. Thorough testing with several terminals should uncover these problems if they exist.

Protocol converters generally emulate several terminals, giving software specifiers or programmers choices and introducing yet another set of decisions. Selection of which terminal to be emulated should take into consideration microcomputer software and the performance characteristics of the protocols of the various terminals offered. Although the ubiquitous ADM3-A terminal protocol tends to be efficient, it may not offer the variety of attributes required. In addition to the obvious differences resulting from the terminal protocols, the protocol converter itself may respond inefficiently to 3270 commands sent from the host: Empty fields may not be transmitted, but useless and redundant attribute setting sequences may be. The host application software may cause inefficiencies as well; some applications send a single-character CLEAR SCREEN command to clear the screen while others send a REPEAT-ADDRESS command, which may cause the protocol converter to transmit a full screen of spaces. Figure 3 shows a sample chart that can be used to measure transaction sizes (from existing applications, if programs aren't yet running) to get an idea of transaction characteristics. There is no substitute for some hands-on time with a datascope.

IBM SNA and bisynchronous circuits
Determining the circuit configuration for protocol con-

verters can be done in a manner similar to that used for 3274 multidropped controllers, since most converters can be multidropped on circuits along with existing 3274s of the same type (bisynchronous or SNA/SDLC).

It may be desirable to avoid intermixing of traffic and place the converters on their own circuits until the architecture can be proven under fire. To minimize response time, circuit speed should be the maximum affordable.

A problem of identification can arise if the protocol converter does not uniquely identify itself at connect time. If a user calls the support center with a communications problem, the answering diagnostician must know to which protocol converter and to which port the user is connected; however, only the protocol converter can determine this. Converters that send out a status line with controller and port addresses, or transmit a screen with that information in response to a special key-in, attempt to solve this problem, but even these steps may not avoid the necessity of giving every converter a different controller I.D. to ensure unique identification. When several converters on several circuits are involved, each circuit may have a converter named "C1," so a controller address alone may not suffice for uniqueness.

The view the protocol converter presents to the host computer operator needs to be determined, and new procedures may need to be defined for dealing with this new type of equipment. Be sure to match the network generation characteristics between the converter and host front-end processor.

Host software
In many situations, it is tempting to use dial-up terminals to execute existing transactions on the host computer or design new transactions as if they were to be run on 3278s. If designers are unaware of the unique nature of the network's architecture, however, the application design may be out of step with the network. Transactions that have been designed for 3278s running at higher speeds (4.8 kbit/s to 9.6 kit/s) will be greatly delayed by the low speed (1.2 kbit/s) of the dial-up link. Because of the link's low speed, the transactions should be designed (or redesigned, if resources permit) to minimize the data flow across the path. The more data that must be passed, the longer it takes, and the longer the user waits. The microcomputer can be a tremendous plus in this situation if one is willing to invest in the programming, for there are several techniques that can be employed to reduce data flow. One technique involves storing the fixed data from the screens (the format) in the microcomputer and calling formats up to the display with just a few characters of identification. Another beneficial technique stores the application menu screens in the microcomputer and executes them locally, interacting with the host computer only for meaningful transactions. Programmers should design ease of use into their applications in a way that also minimizes the bandwidth required.

While converter-to-terminal data flow should be cut

to the bone, transmission in the other direction makes little difference when the converter is emulating a nonblock-mode terminal. As each character is typed, the terminal emulator software sends it to the converter so data does not accumulate in the microcomputer, and the protocol converter is ready to respond positively to a poll the instant a return is typed.

Network planning

Planning the network for dial-up protocol converter applications involves analyzing two separate sets of network characteristics since there are actually two networks involved. The first is the dial-up network used to reach the protocol converters, and the second is the IBM SNA or bisynchronous network used to reach the host computer. The requirements for each of these networks must be carefully determined, generally in conjunction with planning for the future users of the network.

There is always some amount of contention designed into a dial-up network—some probability that an incoming call will not reach a free port, but instead get a busy signal. Nonblocking networks, where there is one incoming telephone line and port for every potential user, are seldom cost-justified unless users are expected to be connected full time (in which case dedicated circuitry or 3270s may be indicated). No one wants to think of being delayed when trying to connect to the network, though, so network planners must educate users to understand the trade-off between cost and a nonblocking network. Users can generally agree on an acceptable level of service (for example, incoming calls receive a busy signal no more than 5 percent of the time). If the user is willing or able to manage call activity by restricting callers to certain times of the day, a fairly high degree of contention can be accommodated. This results in fewer ports and lower costs. The same Erlang tables and models that are used to develop facilities requirements (the telephony needs of a site) in the voice world can be applied to this portion of the data network with a fair degree of success.

If the SNA or bisynchronous network is of appreciable size, network models should be used to estimate response time and determine the optimum topography. Network modeling begins by asking users what their typical applications look like—how many transactions of which type are run when, and what sizes the transactions will take on the communications lines. Terminology is important here, for the word "transaction" can often have different meanings, depending on the speaker and the function of his or her department (one person's business transaction may be equal to five of another's network transactions).

The user population and locations must be determined. When all data is collected and agreed upon, constraints must be specified on desired response-time targets, maximum acceptable circuit costs, operating characteristics of specific equipment, and software characteristics.

The sites for protocol converters must be picked. This decision depends on several factors. The closer

3. Transaction analysis. *A form such as this can be used to measure network transaction sizes. This is helpful in creating an accurate network model.*

TRANSACTION _____

	SYNCHRONOUS SIDE (HOST TO PROTOCOL CONVERTER)	ASYNCHRONOUS SIDE (PROTOCOL CONVERTER TO TERMINAL)
INPUT		
SYNCHRONOUS CHARACTERS		
BLOCK CONTROLS		
CHECKSUM CHARACTERS		
CURSOR ADDRESSING		
ORDERS/ATTRIBUTES		
DATA CHARACTERS		
SUBTOTAL		
OUTPUT		
SYNCHRONOUS CHARACTERS		
BLOCK CONTROLS		
CHECKSUM CHARACTERS		
CURSOR ADDRESSING		
ORDERS/ATTRIBUTES		
DATA CHARACTERS		
SUBTOTAL		
TOTAL		

the protocol converters can be located to the terminal users, the lower the cost of the telephone calls to reach the converters will be. With a widely dispersed user population, this may take some fairly extensive modeling to determine. Other factors to consider include the degree of human intervention required at the protocol converters for operation, diagnostics, and changes. The least-expensive location for the converters in terms of telephone charges may have only unskilled operators, implying that the converters must be unattended or remotely operable. In this case, another site more expensive to reach and with trained operators might be a better choice.

After collecting all the data and specifying the targets (response time, cost, and so on) it is time to run a model of the network to predict response time and cost. The more complete the model, the more accurate are the results that can be expected. Bear in mind that all data at this point is no more than an estimate. Be sure to run some what-if cases with higher and lower volumes to get a feel for how much of a problem will be faced when a user comes back and says, "I just found out that the 'typical terminal operator' will execute 32 transactions an hour, not the four that I told you before."

The definition of response time may need to be rewritten to include the converter to terminal screen paint time. This is a substantial amount of time (10-15 seconds for a busy screen at 1.2 kbit/s), and it implies lower transaction rates than those for similar 3270 applications. Internal processing delays in the converter, which can be on the order of a second or two (compared with milliseconds for 3274s), should be determined by testing. The converter can delay transmission of data to the terminal until a complete screen is assembled, affecting response time to the user. It can also delay block responses to the SNA host, affecting line use, decreasing the number of terminals that can be supported on the circuit, and increasing costs. A good network model (such as Contel's MIND modeling programs) should be able to accommodate various delays.

User training
User training in this type of network is critical, since the network generally involves new equipment and new operating methods. These invoke the normal human fear of the unknown. The better the training, the more comfortable the user will feel, and the fewer trouble calls that cause misunderstanding or confusion. Training must cover not only the business transactions, but the operation of the microcomputer serving as a terminal and its software, the connection to the network, some basic troubleshooting techniques, and directions about how to obtain help or service when the basic troubleshooting doesn't get results.

If the host computer has a computer-aided instruction package of some sort, constructing a short familiarization course and providing it to new users can help by giving them practice and an opportunity to familiarize themselves with the technology without the pressure of an actual problem.

The need for clear, accurate, and usable documentation goes without saying. The microcomputer can help here, if it is possible to put an abridged manual on the disk and use it as an built-in help facility.

User perception
The perception that the user has of the application and the network will determine its success. All the numbers in the world that show response times better than targets, down time better than planned, and of line use of less than 35 percent won't matter if the users perceive the network to be slow, unresponsive, or trouble-ridden. Many times, user dissatisfaction can be caused by mismatched expectations, resulting in the perception that the operation is not doing what it should.

Perception can be managed, however, by making sure that the users know what they can expect. User involvement in the process of requirements definition and development, constant updates on progress and decisions in user terms, and meetings featuring demonstrations will get the user community primed on what to expect, and remove the likelihood of their expectations being too far removed from the designer's goals.

Support functions
Once the application is installed, the users are trained, and daily operations begin, support functions become vitally important. User support should provide a user with an answer to a question about an application problem or telecommunications problem with a single telephone call. This requires that the receivers of the calls be well trained, and understand both the application and the telecommunications involved, and are in touch with the data center where the application is run. Plans for training these support people must be laid out well in advance of implementation; the necessary knowledge and procedures should be developed during the equipment selection and testing process. After the network is running, sending these support people to the actual user sites for a day is money well spent. They will better understand the users' needs for timely and accurate help, and will feel more like active participants. Telecommunications support is a necessity in a network with many pieces of equipment most likely from multiple vendors. The presence of software in every box can help identify problems, but it can also cause or mask problems, leading to frustrated users and management. The presence of knowledgeable experts, with the ability to understand and quickly track down problems in any of the pieces of equipment is invaluable. Vendor responsibilities need to be defined early; the user training package must include information about how to get equipment repaired, and the support organizations must know who to contact to obtain repairs of the network equipment. If the network is large, it may make sense to centralize this function and funnel all requests for service, maintenance, and enhancements through one point. In any case, some mechanism for tracking equipment performance should be built into the process.

With so much software in networks, a specialized software support function is also necessary, particularly if you have chosen to develop your own terminal software for the microcomputer. Although a few bug-free programs have been written, you can rest assured that they are not running in your protocol converters or terminals. Some infrequent combination of conditions will cause a critical component to fail, almost certainly at the busiest time (since the conditions are most often related to load). Although proper testing can identify and eliminate some of these failures, others will remain, lurking to emerge when least affordable. Good vendor support coupled with your own software staff will be required to diagnose protocol converter or terminal problems, which can be especially difficult to track down since the fleeting conditions that caused them will have long since disappeared. ∎

Ben Barlow is manager of telecommunications planning for the Business Systems Group of Xerox Corp. He holds a bachelor's degree in mathematics from Ohio State University.

Bob Bradley, Digital Equipment Corp., Tewksbury, Mass.

Interconnection draws DEC, IBM networks closer

A structured approach to gateway design, influenced by international standards, has given the two environments an unprecedented freedom in the exchange of data.

The familiar, seven-layer model known as the Open Systems Interconnection (OSI) has been primarily concerned with the development of individual network architectures. Communications between heterogeneous networks has evolved on a more ad hoc basis. But recently, by applying similarly layered techniques to high-level activity between networks, Digital Equipment Corp. (DEC) has been able to connect its machines to those of IBM with levels of integration up to and including IBM's newest office protocols.

DEC has taken an OSI-style approach to linking two traditionally distant computing environments. For years, IBM mainframes have served corporate data centers, with DEC computers at divisional and departmental levels. Data communications managers satisfied the earliest requests for intervendor communications with point-to-point links between the mainframes and the distributed minicomputers. The market for such connections spawned products that emulated IBM's binary synchronous communications (BSC) protocol to provide remote job entry (RJE) batch access and 3270 terminal interactive access.

But users soon felt a growing need for a more sophisticated, bidirectional flow of information. While point-to-point BSC will always be important, IBM's announcement of Systems Network Architecture (SNA) Release 4 in 1980—confirming its full commitment to the SNA concept in its own future products—rather quickly shifted much of users' attention from BSC-oriented products to the SNA network environment.

For this reason, a gateway between DEC's local and wide-area networking software, Decnet, and IBM's SNA was designed to address multivendor installations (DATA COMMUNICATIONS, January 1984, p. 159). The Decnet/SNA gateway allowed users and applications

in a Decnet network to access computing resources distributed throughout an SNA network. While this gateway product was a major step in interconnection, DEC felt that long-term efforts rested on an adherence to the OSI reference model.

SNA product architecture

In late 1984, DEC introduced two gateway-based software packages to heighten its level of IBM integration. Whereas the initial gateway opened a door from Decnet into SNA, the distributed host command facility (DHCF) provided similar access in the other direction. With DHCF, 3270 terminal users in an SNA network could utilize computing resources throughout a Decnet network. Another product, the DISOSS (Distributed Office Support System) document exchange facility (DDXF), permitted a DEC user at a terminal connected to a VAX node to participate in an IBM office network based on the DIA/DCA (document interchange architecture/document content architecture) protocols.

Continuing enhancements to SNA make it clear that the architecture is not yet in its final form. Therefore, as SNA evolves, maintaining and improving the software and hardware that establish the Decnet/SNA connection will require a consistent development framework. DEC's SNA product architecture (Fig. 1) provides such a framework, one upon which higher-level software such as DHCF and DDXF is based.

The SNA product architecture is layered in much the same way as SNA and the Open Systems Interconnection model, with similar relationships between tasks in different layers. These tasks furnish specific modular functions in the connecting equipment, and all the layers are linked through standardized interfaces. As with the networking software itself, the modularity of

153

Evolution of an intervendor environment

In the early 1970s, the first interconnections between IBM mainframes and non-IBM devices were point-to-point links. Many vendors provided terminal emulation of the 2780 remote job entry (RJE) workstation. Binary synchronous communications (BSC) was used at the link level for batch file transfer and for processing between computers of different manufacturers. Interactive connections were provided after the introduction of IBM's 3270 line, when a number of firms developed 3270 BSC protocol emulation for their computers.

IBM and DEC announced their network architectures in the mid-1970s, and each has since introduced additional functions periodically in the form of releases for SNA and phases for Decnet (see table). As both networks progressed in functionality and number of installations, DEC/IBM interconnections had to evolve beyond the original computer-to-computer BSC emulation concepts. The DEC computers had been required to emulate unintelligent devices talking to IBM mainframes, and using this emulation was a multistep, often laborious process—far from transparent to the user.

Network topology

The development of internetwork links that required no additional software on the IBM side was compromised at first by major differences between the SNA and Decnet product capabilities. Typically, SNA networks have a hierarchical topology of one or more domains, each consisting of a host node, at least one communications controller and one cluster controller, plus the terminal nodes.

The numerous communications functions that are involved in supporting SNA network environments are distributed in a hierarchical fashion among software elements resident in the host, communications controllers, and cluster controllers. In the host, a telecommunications access method supports overall network management, and an application subsystem handles the data messages and control communications among computing resources in the network. In a communications controller such as the 3275, IBM's network control program provides such lower-level functions as error checking, polling and addressing of multipoint lines, and character translation.

Decnet networks have peer-to-peer network topologies. Each node processes its own applications and has its own databases. Each is equipped with the Decnet software and communications hardware needed to perform all the functions distributed throughout SNA networks.

SNA has defined IBM network communications in the form of logical units (LUs), each of which uses different protocols and furnishes different functions to its users. Whereas LU1, LU2, and LU3 describe characteristics of specific devices under the control of a host, new architectural enhancements such as LU6.2 support peer-to-peer communications.

After SNA Release 4, DEC's first standalone SNA-oriented software product was a protocol emulator that permitted PDP-11 minicomputers in a Decnet network to communicate with nodes in an SNA network. This emulator offered multiple software interfaces that allowed user-written programs on a PDP-11 minicomputer to exchange information with IBM application subsystems.

While providing computer-to-network access, the emulator was not intended to support the turnkey capabilities of RJE batch workstations or interactive 3270 terminals. Users were allowed to develop their own customized software to complete the connection. Since then, the Decnet/SNA product set was developed in response to market demand for a true network-to-network interconnection.

The growth of two architectures

	SYSTEMS NETWORK ARCHITECTURE (SNA)	DIGITAL NETWORK ARCHITECTURE (DNA)
1974	■ INTRODUCTION OF SNA ■ SINGLE HOST NETWORKS	■ INTRODUCTION OF DNA
1976	**SNA-1** ■ ABILITY TO ATTACH REMOTE 370X ■ ADDITIONAL PRODUCTS **SNA-2** DIAL-UP CAPABILITY ADDITIONAL PRODUCTS	**DECNET PHASE I** ■ PROGRAM-TO-PROGRAM ■ FILE TRANSFER ■ PDP-11s ■ DOWN-LINE LOADING
1978	**SNA-3** ■ MULTIPLE HOST NETWORKS	**DECNET PHASE II** ■ ALL MAJOR OPERATING SYSTEMS, PROCESSORS ■ REMOTE FILE/RESOURCE ACCESS ■ NETWORK MANAGEMENT ENHANCED
1979	**SNA-4.1** ■ SUPPORT NON-SNA DEVICES ■ DYNAMIC CONFIGURATION ■ 8100 INTRODUCTION	
1980	**SNA-4.2** ■ MULTIPLE ROUTING ■ GREATER 370X CONNECTIVITY	**DECNET PHASE III** ■ STANDALONE SNA SUPPORT ■ ADAPTIVE ROUTING ■ NETWORK TERMINALS ■ MULTIPOINT LINES ■ CCITT X.25 SUPPORT
1982		**DECNET PHASE IV** ■ ETHERNET ■ LARGE NETWORKS ■ COMMUNICATIONS SERVERS ■ DECNET/SNA GATEWAYS
1983-4	**SNA-5.0** ■ EXTENDED SDLC FRAME ADDRESSING ■ SNA NETWORK INTERCONNECT ■ APPC (LU6.2) ■ DIA/DCA FOR OFFICE	■ LARGER NETWORKS (1,000 DEVICES OR MORE) ■ EXPANDED DECNET/SNA SUPPORT

ACF = ADVANCED COMMUNICATIONS FUNCTION
SDLC = SYNCHRONOUS DATA-LINK CONTROL
APPC = ADVANCED PROGRAM-TO-PROGRAM COMMUNICATIONS
DIA = DOCUMENT INTERCHANGE ARCHITECTURE
DCA = DOCUMENT CONTENT ARCHITECTURE

1. Structure. *DEC's SNA product architecture furnishes a layered framework for developing software modules to functionally connect Decnet and SNA networks.*

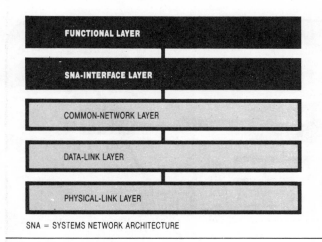

FUNCTIONAL LAYER

SNA-INTERFACE LAYER

COMMON-NETWORK LAYER

DATA-LINK LAYER

PHYSICAL-LINK LAYER

SNA = SYSTEMS NETWORK ARCHITECTURE

the SNA product architecture allows changes to be made in some layers without affecting the others. The interfaces make modifications to software at one level easy to integrate with other interconnection software.

The upper two layers of the SNA product architecture are implemented in software residing within individual DEC computers. The bulk of the development effort for DEC/IBM interconnection products is concentrated in these layers. For example, DHCF uses IBM's host command facility protocols to establish sessions for 3270 users on Decnet nodes. The IBM protocols are handled mainly in the functional layer. DDXF, however, implements IBM logical unit (LU) 6.2, a general-purpose protocol for communications among SNA nodes, in the SNA interface layer.

Support from the gateway

A structured architecture at the interface between networks provides freedom from proprietary changes on either side. In one implementation of the SNA product architecture, for instance, the lower three layers reside in the gateway. The common network layer handles routing from nodes in one network to nodes in the other. The data link layer, designed for error-free transmission at the boundary between Decnet and SNA, can accept modules to support various message protocols including SNA's synchronous data link control. And the physical link layer encompasses the physical and electrical characteristics of the transmission media, with modules for the V.24 (RS-232-C) and V.35 electrical interfaces. Any of these modules can be replaced or enhanced to adapt to network changes.

The Decnet/SNA gateway, which consists of special-purpose hardware and software, supports the operating systems of DEC VAXs and PDP-11s. Both types of machine can therefore be linked to SNA networks through gateways on wide-area or local networks (Fig. 2). Any such gateway on a local Decnet network can handle Ethernet protocols.

The gateways appear to IBM hosts as multifunction

cluster controllers (SNA physical units type 2). As a result, they can be linked to the 37X5 communications controllers in IBM's hierarchical topology. The number of Decnet/SNA gateways needed, all in remote, unattended operation, depends on the relative amount of traffic between the Decnet and SNA sides (DATA COMMUNICATIONS, February 1985, p. 153).

Computers in a Decnet wide-area network are typically linked by public communications facilities—telephone lines, microwave links, satellites, or a combination of these media—and can be installed side by side or scattered globally. The computers in a Decnet local network are linked over an Ethernet coaxial cable and are located within a limited geographical area, such as a group of office buildings or a university campus. IBM cluster controllers and terminal nodes, typically linked from the local to the remote sites with leased lines, perform device-specific control functions for various input/output devices.

Three types of emulation

The interconnection represented in Figure 2 requires a variety of networking software modules in the gateway and at each of the participating Decnet nodes (Fig. 3). This software consists of a gateway management access module and one or more of the gateway modules for various types of access to SNA. Computers in a Decnet network must contain gateway modules for only those types of SNA access they are expected to use. The modules include:

■ RJE gateway software, which effectively turns a DEC minicomputer running on Decnet into a remote SNA job entry workstation. This module allows the minicomputer to communicate with a job entry subsystem running under an IBM operating system such as multiple virtual storage (MVS). A user at a DEC VT video display or a similar terminal can submit data to an IBM host for batch processing, receive job output from the host, inquire about the status of jobs, and manipulate jobs, output, and devices.

■ The 3270 terminal emulation software, which permits a VT-type terminal to act like an IBM 3278 display attached to a cluster controller under SNA. Users invoke the Decnet/SNA interconnection by keying in a single command line. From a 3270-mode DEC terminal, three levels of computing resources can be accessed: machines on the local node only, those connected to any Decnet node, and any authorized IBM host.

■ The Decnet/SNA application program interface module, which allows programs running on a VAX or PDP-11 node to communicate interactively with programs running on an IBM host. This module, running in the common network layer of the SNA product architecture, is used mainly by programmers to develop custom application software that involves the Decnet/SNA interconnection. The application interface furnishes user-written programs with the SNA functions performed by the gateway.

When the Decnet/SNA gateway was designed, network-to-network access was meant to be transparent to Decnet users, who followed their customary routines and used a familiar command language and syntax.

2. Interconnection. *A Decnet network combining wide-area and local network segments is interconnected to multiple SNA networks through Decnet/SNA gateways.* *While SNA is based on a hierarchical topology, Decnet topology is peer-to-peer. SNA sees the gateways as cluster controllers.*

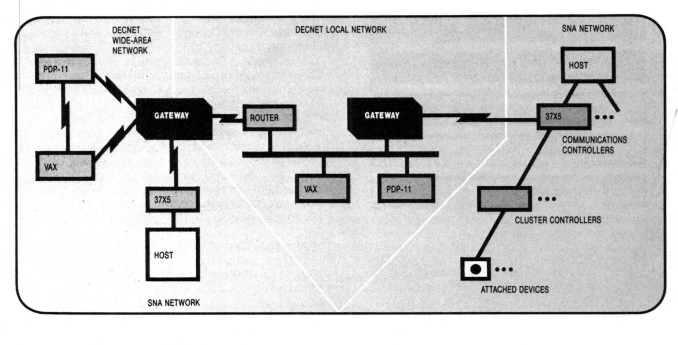

LOCAL CONNECTION   LONG-DISTANCE CONNECTION   SNA = SYSTEMS NETWORK ARCHITECTURE

Programmers developing internetwork applications were given closer contact with the IBM environment. They were able to incorporate standard IBM procedures and terminology into their Decnet/SNA software. For example, IBM job control language could be used to specify file transfers, and reference could be made to standard utility software in IBM host libraries. With IBM resources underlying the application, user interfaces could then be converted into the familiar DEC language.

A more perfect union

Such internetwork functions met the needs of users in 1982, when DEC announced the first version of its gateway. But users soon demanded more thorough access between the two environments. Although data and commands moved in both directions, transactions had to be initiated by users on the Decnet side. Firms operating both DEC and IBM computers wanted to offer users on either side the ability to start a session.

In addition, computers in the Decnet network could only access resources in the SNA network at the level of functionality of the IBM devices they were emulating. User demands for increased functionality prompted DEC to step up its interconnection activity and to develop the software necessary for two-way access and more complete SNA compatibility.

The DISOSS document exchange facility permits a user with a terminal connected to a VAX node to participate in an IBM Office Information Architecture network (Fig. 4). Such a user wishing to initiate a

document exchange signs on under DDXF with a simple, three-line command sequence.

DDXF conforms to IBM's protocols for DIA (document interchange architecture) and DCA (document content architecture) and to its definition of a compound electronic document (which may, in principle, include text, data, voice, image, and graphics elements). DDXF also implements IBM's LU6.2, otherwise known as advanced program-to-program communications (APPC). The DIA/DCA definition and LU6.2, which were announced by IBM in early 1983, together form the basis of an IBM office.

With DDXF running LU6.2 at local Decnet nodes, VAX users can now effect both revisable-form and final-form text document exchange. DDXF works in conjunction with IBM's DISOSS on an IBM host or, indirectly, with various IBM office configurations via the DISOSS host. The document-handling functions with DDXF include: filing locally or remotely retrieved documents on a DISOSS host; searching, retrieving, and deleting documents in a DISOSS host library; and requesting that the host distribute documents resident on the host or on the local Decnet node.

IBM access to DEC machines

Distributed host command facility (DHCF) software, also represented in Figure 4, allows interactive users on the SNA side to initiate sessions with a VAX computer on the Decnet side. A 327X display station under control of an IBM host becomes a virtual terminal on a VAX computer, giving its user the ability to reach and

3. Modules. *Exchange of data between DEC and IBM environments requires no special software in the SNA network. The Decnet side, however, must contain interconnection modules in the gateway node, plus gateway management and emulation software in other participating nodes. With emulation, a minicomputer mimics a remote job entry station, a terminal turns into a 3270 display, and an application program converses with its counterpart.*

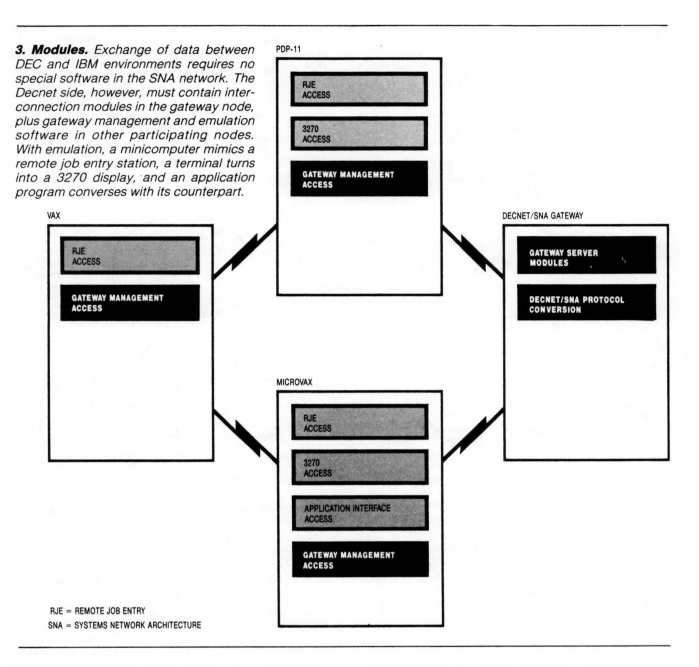

RJE = REMOTE JOB ENTRY
SNA = SYSTEMS NETWORK ARCHITECTURE

use computing resources at the VAX node. DHCF Decnet-side software communicates with the host command facility (HCF) program product, which IBM introduced to support a 327X user's access to remote 8100 processors in an SNA network.

A 327X user signs on under DHCF with the same command sequence, LOGON HCF and ACQUIRE LU, that is routinely entered to communicate with an 8100. In the DHCF mode, the referenced LU is the number or mnemonic character string assigned to software residing in the Decnet/SNA gateway. The user completes the access procedure by entering the DEC node name and then the user name, just as in a Decnet network.

The first version of DHCF provides IBM users with access to VAX computers in the line-edit mode. The 327X terminals can be used to run any VAX/VMS application programs that can be controlled from a

hard-copy terminal. These include reading VMS electronic mail, retrieving files, generating reports, developing programs, and, most importantly, configuring and controlling a Decnet network.

Managing Decnet from out of the Blue
IBM users are accustomed to the ability to monitor, control, and maintain a network from a single terminal. Management of an IBM network across vendor lines has been available for some time. The 3270 emulation permitted a Decnet user at a VT-type terminal to control interconnected Decnet and SNA networks. But now, using DHCF, a network manager at a 3270 station on the SNA side can similarly manage both networks. In this way, the network control center can use IBM's network management programs to account for and access all Decnet nodes.

4. Two-way access. *The 327X station users under SNA can interact with individual DEC nodes, provided that they can use IBM's host command facility (HCF). DEC* *devices become part of an IBM Office Information Architecture network through software that talks to the Distributed Office Support System (DISOSS).*

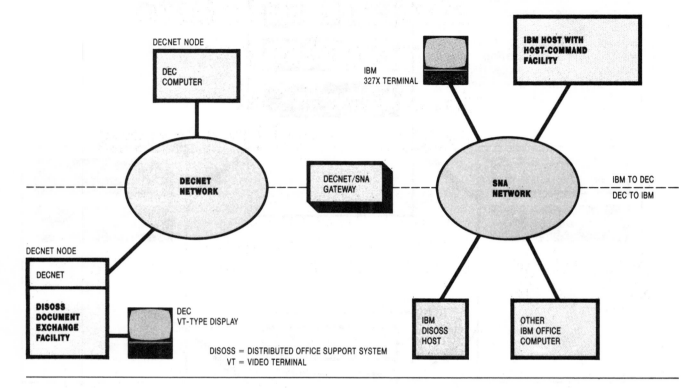

DECNET NODE

DEC COMPUTER

DECNET NETWORK

DECNET/SNA GATEWAY

IBM 327X TERMINAL

IBM HOST WITH HOST-COMMAND FACILITY

SNA NETWORK

IBM TO DEC
DEC TO IBM

DECNET NODE

DECNET

DISOSS DOCUMENT EXCHANGE FACILITY

DEC VT-TYPE DISPLAY

IBM DISOSS HOST

OTHER IBM OFFICE COMPUTER

DISOSS = DISTRIBUTED OFFICE SUPPORT SYSTEM
VT = VIDEO TERMINAL

Regardless of where network control originates, the authority the network manager normally enjoys is not compromised in any way by interconnection activity. The network manager can control such factors as CPU access priorities, disk space, and log-on authorization for both Decnet and SNA users. Traffic from an IBM host to a Decnet node will take an SNA-determined path to the Decnet/SNA gateway, but, from then on, the route is established by Decnet software.

A likely situation that might call for controlling utilization from both sides would be an interconnection between an SNA network in a data processing center and a Decnet network in a distant engineering department facility. On one side, engineers would typically ask for records in corporate databases. On the other, data processing people could, for example, run engineering's statistical analysis programs remotely on a VAX machine. A less convenient alternative would be to transfer corporate data over the communications link and then have the engineering department run the programs.

Other interconnection software
Broader use of the Decnet/SNA gateway in network interconnection requires gateway access modules that support DEC operating systems other than VMS and RSX and emulate other IBM devices. A 3287 printer-emulator module was introduced for VAX computers at the same time as the DHCF and DDXF facilities in order to provide downstream data transfer from IBM's application subsystems. Output data generated by existing

SNA applications specifically for the 3287 dot-matrix printer can now be stored on a VAX mass-storage device or printed on dot-matrix, high-speed, or laser printers.

Another approach to extending DEC's interconnection with IBM is the provision of multifunction standalone access to SNA networks, which can be particularly useful for microcomputers. Communications software has been developed to support point-to-point and point-to-multipoint connections by a microcomputer to computers in an SNA network. The connections can be used in the RJE batch mode, the 3270 interactive mode, or for the emulation of a downstream printer.

In its overall interconnection strategy, DEC is committed to developing the hardware and software resources necessary to support the transparent exchange of information between DEC and non-DEC machines and their users. A basic objective of DEC's strategy is to better accommodate the multicomputer, multifunction environment that will ultimately evolve from broad adherence to the Open Systems Interconnection model. It is now clear that the benefits of such adherence can be gained by incorporating OSI into devices residing between, as well as within, network architectures. ∎

Bob Bradley is product manager for networks and communications at DEC. His responsibilities in nearly a decade with the company have included network software development and consulting.

Philip L. Arst and Willie Ivey, Equatorial
Communications Co., Mountain View, Calif.

Hybrid satellite networks for distributed data applications

With post-divestiture telephone line tariffs heating up, users might do well to look skyward for bypass solutions.

Until recently, the data communications industry tended to view two-way transmission as essential for almost all applications. But dramatic changes in the communications industry—highlighted by the divestiture of AT&T's operating companies—have prompted users to seek less expensive and more efficient methods of moving data within a communications network. Significantly higher tariffs, requested by the majority of the common carriers for private-line services, tend to reinforce this mandate for efficiency. Hence, users need to examine usage patterns and new technologies to offset both the higher private-line costs and the loss of their predivestiture one-stop shopping with Ma Bell.

In current corporate communications usage patterns, for example, a significant portion of traffic flows from a central location (often a company headquarters) to many widely distributed network sites. Such applications generally use costly four-wire (two-way) facilities, even though the return path is used only for communications protocol handshaking and supervisory commands. The return lines—while paid for—are often used only 0.1 percent of the time.

But satellite-based point-to-multipoint data networks with low-cost micro earth stations and new protocols of the broadcast type can complement or, in many cases, replace existing communications methods and offer cost reductions of 50 percent or more. Other transmission methods available to the data communications user include copper wires, microwave, and fiber optics. The unique advantage of satellite transmission, however, is its ability to efficiently broadcast a single message to any number of remote stations.

Using either individual or group broadcast addresses, messages can be routed to individual stations, groups of stations, or an entire network community without the need for terrestrial message-switching processors and communications handshaking. This so-called data multiplier effect is superior to terrestrial line approaches that require a single message to be sent to a number of locations—once for each location. A satellite message is transmitted only once for a given broadcast.

New thinking

For the potential user, the most fundamental challenge of satellite transmission comes from eliminating the concept and the communications methods of terrestrial data communications lines. For if satellites are applied in data communications networks only to emulate existing terrestrial lines, the satellites are being used inefficiently.

But because any number of locations can be reached with one satellite broadcast, implementing all of a company's data communications lines on a single-broadcast packetized channel optimizes efficiency (Fig. 1). When one location temporarily experiences a great deal of traffic, for example, that location can borrow bandwidth from the other locations on the same channel and then return that capacity to the network when finished.

Also, whereas terrestrial network lines must be individually sized for worst-case traffic, satellite-broadcast channel costs can be minimized by averaging use during peak hours across time zones. For example, combining on the same broadcast channel the communications to New York, Chicago, and Los Angeles—all with peak traffic at 10 A.M. in their respective time zones—enables each city to communicate efficiently and economically during its peak hour. Since satellite channels are simplex, one-way, and have variable capacity, they can be tailored to data flow.

159

1. Land locked. *Terrestrial networks use separate lines. A single satellite broadcast channel can serve all these locations by dynamically assigning bandwidth.*

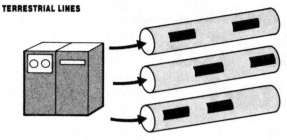

TERRESTRIAL LINES

SATELLITE CHANNEL

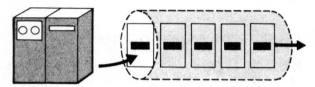

TERRESTRIAL
- MULTIPLE LINES
- SOME LINES UNDER-USED BUT THERE FOR CONNECTIVITY
- COSTS CAN BE REDUCED BY ELIMINATING RETURN PATH IF NOT NEEDED

SATELLITE
- ONE BROADCAST CHANNEL (LARGE LINE FOR ALL DATA)
- SIZED AND OPERATED AS A FULL NETWORK WITH NATIONWIDE AVERAGING
- SINGLE TRANSMISSION CAN SERVE ALL STATIONS
- GREATER BANDWIDTH EFFICIENCY

Consider a large distribution company with branches throughout the United States. Each receives a constant flow of information but issues only an occasional return message. In this case, adequate bandwidth can be provided to dispersed locations by simplex satellite channel operations. Individual dealers can then respond, if necessary, over dial-up terrestrial lines at a much lower overall cost.

With satellite-based communications, cost does not increase with distance from the message source as it does with terrestrial lines. The reason is that satellites — which are positioned in the geosynchronous equatorial orbit, approximately 22,300 miles from earth — remain stationary relative to the earth. Thus they are able to broadcast efficiently to all points within their "footprint" (Fig. 2).

Network flexibility is a second advantage. Since stations can be located anywhere in the satellite's footprint, they can be relocated without requiring network reconfiguration. Also, micro earth stations located directly on customer premises allow network users to bypass a terrestrial network completely. In this way, users avoid the costs of local loop connections as well as the substantial communications mileage costs from the information source.

A typical satellite bit error rate (BER) is less than one error in 10^7 bits, which greatly reduces the number of retransmissions required for an error-free information exchange. This contrasts sharply with the typical BER for terrestrial links — less than one error in 10^5 bits.

Other savings accrue to satellite networks due to their eliminating the need not only for line charges but also for modems, data concentrators, and the expensive switching processors required for most older data communications networks.

Newton defied

The laws of physics would seem to prohibit the use of small antennas and micro earth stations two feet in diameter. The smaller the diameter of the receiving antenna, the wider the angle of view. Thus, an earth station two feet in diameter at satellite radio frequencies of 4 GHz has a half-power beam width of 9 degrees when pointed at the equatorial orbital arc where the geostationary satellites are positioned. Therefore, with satellites spaced 2 degrees apart as the Federal Communications Commission has recently ordered, each small earth station is susceptible to interference from five satellites (Fig. 3).

The use of small-diameter antennas, however, is made possible due to implementation of a variant of spread-spectrum technology. This transmission modulation technique has become available to low-cost, high-volume commercial applications as a result of microprocessor implementations. As the name implies,

2. Pennies from heaven. *Satellite technology has specific advantages over terrestrial lines. Satellite transmission offers low BER and distance insensitivity.*

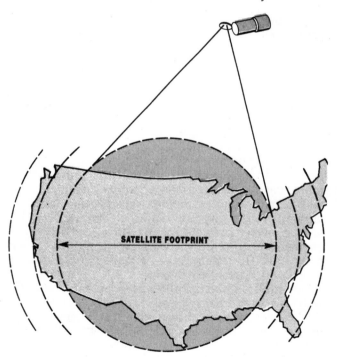

SATELLITE FOOTPRINT

- DISTANCE INSENSITIVE
- BROADCAST OPERATION
- VERY LOW BIT ERROR RATE (LESS THAN 1 ERROR IN 10^7 BITS)
- FLEXIBLE, QUICK LOCATION PLACEMENT
- DYNAMIC RESOURCE ALLOCATION

more frequency bandwidth is required for spread-spectrum signals than for conventional narrowband signals at comparable data rates. For this reason the technique has not been extensively used in commercial terrestrial applications where bandwidth is at a premium. Briefly, spread-spectrum technology divides each bit by 128. Each 1/128th of a bit is called a chip. The chips, however, are sent using a special pseudo-random algorithm, which is implemented at either end of the link. Special pseudorandom patterns indicate ones and zeros. Even though many of the chips can be garbled, their status can be inferred by chips received correctly at the other end of the link.

Bandwidth, conversely, is relatively inexpensive in point-to-point satellite networks with many small earth stations. Hence, satellite links spread the signal over bandwidth that would otherwise go unused. Also, use of microprocessors to recognize signals provides network advantages at a low cost. The interference-rejection property of spread-spectrum transmission permits small earth stations to coexist with terrestrial microwave in urban environments. It also permits them to operate within current satellite-spacing specifications as well as within the narrower (2-degree) spacing proposed by the Federal Communications Commission.

Data network solutions

The technology underlying micro earth stations and point-to-multipoint networking offers several new solutions to communications problems. The basic network configuration is a star topology with four major components (Fig. 4):
■ The host computer data link is either a terrestrial or satellite line used to transfer customer host computer data to the master earth station for relay.
■ A master earth station is used to send data up to the satellite for distribution to all micro earth stations and to provide network management and control for the entire network (operating in packet delivery mode).
■ Satellite capacity may be obtained in either large or

3. Crowding the arc. *Spread-spectrum technology allows two-foot diameter micro earth stations to ignore signals from sources other than the target satellite.*

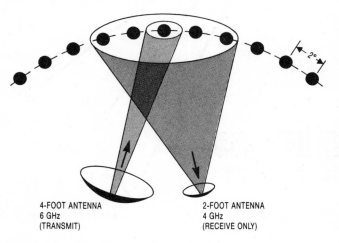

4-FOOT ANTENNA
6 GHz
(TRANSMIT)

2-FOOT ANTENNA
4 GHz
(RECEIVE ONLY)

small increments for use in relaying uplinked data to the micro earth station.
■ Micro earth stations receive satellite broadcast data and transfer it to a variety of customer terminals or computers through RS-232-C interfaces.

Figure 5 illustrates the distribution of data packets that may represent electronic mail, facsimile images, or even voice communications. Also, two major levels of service integrity are available:
■ *Best-effort delivery.* Basic point-to-multipoint communications provides best-effort delivery at a BER of less than one error in 10^7 bits. This is sufficient for applications, such as general and financial news distribution, that require continually updated information. In the unlikely event of an error, human recognition and correction is acceptable for these applications.
■ *Guaranteed delivery.* Where a higher level of data integrity is needed, guaranteed point-to-multipoint delivery can be implemented with either a standalone or a hybrid communications configuration and intelligence at each end. Standalone guaranteed delivery requires only the addition of a minimal-usage, data-acknowledgment return-path facility, such as a modem connection for dial-up retransmission requests in case of error.

A hybrid configuration is achieved by adding satellite communications to an existing terrestrial network. This approach offers advantages when a network becomes congested and users are faced with the alternative of increasing the capacity of the terrestrial network at great expense. The satellite network would manage all broadcast traffic, leaving terrestrial lines free.

Upgrading a point-to-multipoint network to provide sophisticated message delivery by using a return path for message acknowledgments involves adjustments in guaranteed-delivery protocols of the conventional automatic request for repetition (ARQ) type.

The return path may be any class of service that operates as a hybrid with basic outgoing delivery service. Dial-up message toll service, a public data network, or piggybacking on an existing private network are alternatives for this function. The secret of economical operation of this hybrid network is in minimizing traffic on the measured message-service return path used for handshaking. This is accomplished through two mechanisms.

Transmission accuracy can be enhanced by supplying a forward error correction (FEC) code on all outgoing messages. These codes, which in their simplest implementation send every message twice, create a level of data integrity that can result in an average of one unrecoverable error for every several weeks of full-time service per station.

A large satellite window is obtained by adding a large message-sequence number to the basic link-control protocol and using a type of negative acknowledgment called selective reject. The large message-sequence number allows many frames to be outstanding before an acknowledgment is required. And the selective-reject response simultaneously requests retransmission of faulty frames. Thus, traffic can be sent continuously for long periods without the need for numerous reverse-channel acknowledgments.

4. Star link. *Micro earth stations may be run in a star configuration by a master station. Data can be sent from the host to the network for delivery by terrestrial links or* *by satellite. If by satellite, the data would uplink to the transceiver and then be sent to the master station and rebroadcast to the smaller antennas.*

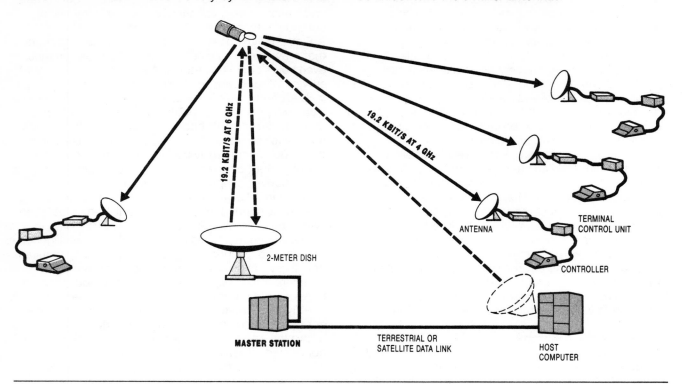

19.2 KBIT/S AT 6 GHz

19.2 KBIT/S AT 4 GHz

2-METER DISH

ANTENNA

TERMINAL CONTROL UNIT

CONTROLLER

MASTER STATION

TERRESTRIAL OR SATELLITE DATA LINK

HOST COMPUTER

5. Mail call. *Data packets transmitted on a broadcast satellite channel may be dynamically addressed to a single receiver, a group of receivers, or all the receivers in* *the network. The data may represent databases, electronic mail, facsimile transmission, or other applications. Two major levels of service integrity are available.*

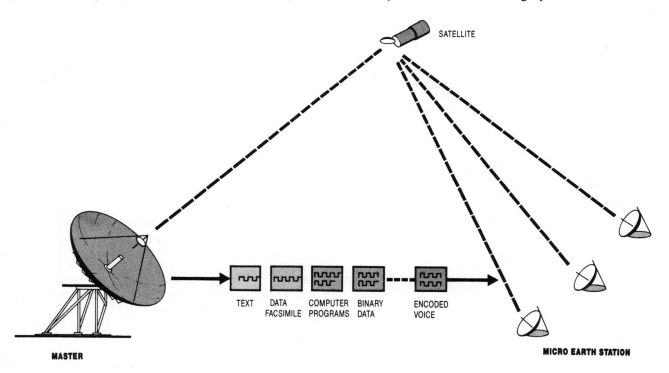

SATELLITE

TEXT

DATA FACSIMILE

COMPUTER PROGRAMS

BINARY DATA

ENCODED VOICE

MASTER

MICRO EARTH STATION

The basic protocol is "bullet-proofed" by periodically sending certain supervisory messages. These audit messages tell each station what message-sequence numbers it should have received—thereby catching stations that malfunction or miss messages. If a discrepancy is found between the send and the receive sequence, the missing messages are retransmitted to the stations that did not receive them.

This guaranteed-delivery service adds overhead to the basic communications traffic. The overhead—anywhere from 20 to 50 percent—can be eliminated entirely on traffic that is not critical and for which an occasional error is acceptable. The guaranteed-delivery service may be provided within the point-to-multipoint equipment or implemented by the network user. With the basic guaranteed-delivery service in place, many new applications become cost-effective.

Future uses

Simple point-to-multipoint transmission is most viable for applications such as national news distribution, which requires timely data distribution in real time to thousands of nationwide locations. Examples of this usage are found in radio and television broadcasting and in newspaper publishing. Data need only be distributed on a best-effort basis in this environment; an occasional character dropout causes little problem because human correction of missing or incorrect characters is an acceptable method of FEC.

Another ideal application is financial information distribution. Commodities prices, currency prices, quotas, and business news must all be delivered in real time and continually updated. A transmission error in a price quotation, after being detected by a validity check, would be overwritten by the next information cycle. Thus, point-to-multipoint best-effort distribution is the most cost-effective method of communicating this information.

In related applications, point-to-multipoint technology can be combined with microcomputers to give the data recipient a real-time stock-trend analysis and alarms capability. Here, a broadcast channel distributes information to stockbrokers throughout the nation, each with a microcomputer used both for account management and for real-time stock-trend analysis.

A more recent development in point-to-multipoint communications is its use for real-time digital voice transmission. This capability allows many remote locations to receive voice messages from a single source. Because the front-end of such a system can be connected via a dial-up telephone circuit to any field location, a reasonably flexible audio conference resource can be implemented as a form of corporate communications. Field offices could call in to corporate headquarters, for example, much the way a listener calls in to a radio talk show.

The microcomputer market explosion and subsequent demand for distributed processing applications has created complications in database delivery and control. Without timely and synchronized database updates, control over some distributed activities could easily be lost.

6. Distributed data. *Large databases are accessed from terminals via land lines. With satellites, updates may be downloaded to all sites at once.*

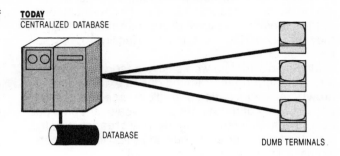

TODAY
CENTRALIZED DATABASE

DATABASE

DUMB TERMINALS

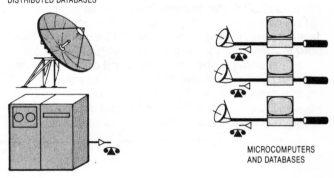

FUTURE
CENTRALLY UPDATED
DISTRIBUTED DATABASES

MICROCOMPUTERS
AND DATABASES

The guaranteed-delivery point-to-multipoint network offers a cost-effective solution by providing accurate simultaneous updates to all stations (Fig. 6). This approach eliminates the need for a dedicated terrestrial data communications network while providing the necessary delivery integrity and database control to make the application successful.

Software delivery can improve with the use of point-to-multipoint networks. Distributed microcomputers need occasional software updates as new capabilities are added or glitches are found in the basic package. This function may be provided on a standalone basis by manufacturers who distribute updates to hundreds of field offices and major customers.

Point-to-multipoint networks may also be used for on-demand delivery of software to microcomputer stores or retail outlets. This approach eliminates the need for and expense of stocking thousands of software programs for a comprehensive customer selection. And in distributed microcomputer applications, a point-to-multipoint network could serve the dual purpose of maintaining the databases during the day and delivering software updates at night.

With a message delivery mechanism in place, electronic mail also becomes a natural point-to-multipoint application. The headquarters of large corporations typically generate many documents that must be distributed to hundreds of field locations in real time. Such documents might include pricing changes for sales offices, product safety or repair bulletins, corporate announcements, and individual electronic mail messages.

Time-critical information distributed by electronic mail is not limited to text. Since a point-to-multipoint system broadcasts bits of digital information, these bits may represent data, text, images (facsimile), or voice messages.

Many terrestrial networks have become congested and their performance limited due to extensive traffic growth. An examination of traffic sources and destinations of some of these networks reveals (not unexpectedly) a heavy increment of one-way broadcast traffic from the headquarters to outlying sites. In some networks, 30 percent of all traffic is of this type.

The guaranteed-delivery point-to-multipoint network can provide relief during congested periods by acting as a low-cost second network to offload outbound administrative traffic from the main transaction processing network. When operated in this way, the existing terrestrial network is used to satisfy the return-path requirement for the point-to-multipoint network.

Finally, both point-to-multipoint and guaranteed-delivery networks can serve as interconnect media for local networks. Within the next few years, local networks will be standard facilities in most offices. Using satellite technology, they can serve as intrafacility distribution mechanisms for broadcast traffic received via the point-to-multipoint network. A bridge between two networks (and a common addressing structure) would be the only additional device necessary.

As post-divestiture tariffs firm up, the cost of using terrestrial lines as the primary data link in private data communications networks will continue to increase. Dramatically higher prices for local loops, plus sustained high prices for long-distance trunk lines and multidrop systems will result in basic cost increases of 15 to 100 percent for large network users. Network designers and users must carefully reexamine their data communications traffic patterns and consider the cost-effectiveness of augmenting existing data distribution mechanisms with the new approaches that are made possible by guaranteed-delivery point-to-multipoint networks using low-cost micro earth stations with two-foot diameter antennas. ∎

Philip Arst, director of marketing for Equatorial Communications, graduated from the U. S. Naval Academy, where he earned a B.S.E.E., and the University of Chicago, where he received an M.B.A. Most recently, Arst worked on specifications for an Ethernet chip at Intel Corp. Willie Ivey, product manager at Equatorial, earned a B.S. in computer science from the University of Virginia.

Dennis P. Waters, Waters Information Services Inc., Binghamton, N. Y.

Surfacing: FM radio provides a new alternative for carrying data

Even though it is limited to one-way transmission, FM is being refined with numerous hybrid, economical techniques.

One of the most malleable communications media, FM radio broadcasting is poised for yet another twist. In the 1960s, for example, FM radio was brought from relative obscurity to high visibility by broadcasting so-called underground music, such as psychedelic rock-and-roll, and providing alternative programming to Top-40 AM stations. Then, in the 1970s, FM radio displaced AM for most music broadcasting, with AM relegated to talk-show, call-in, and all-news formats. In the 1980s, FM finds itself being touted for something completely different: data transmission.

This latest development stems from an FM station's needing only a portion of its licensed transmission capacity to deliver audio programming to its listeners. Thanks to deregulation, the leftover capacity of FM radio — called the subcarrier baseband — can be used to transmit data. The transmission is one way, point-to-multipoint, within a metropolitan area. Users should find FM subcarrier to be reliable and cost-effective (see "FM tutorial").

More than 4,500 FM radio stations are operating in the United States, and the majority can transmit a usable signal for a distance of 40 miles. In flat terrain, some can regularly be heard 100 miles away. A large metropolitan area (1 million or more population) typically has 10 or more of these powerful (50 kw or more, depending on antenna height) FM transmitting facilities, and each is able to piggyback data onto the regular programming.

A recent series of Federal Communications Commission (FCC) deregulation orders has expanded the range of applications available for FM subcarrier technology, while eliminating virtually all of the paperwork that broadcasters had previously faced to exploit their excess capacity. The FCC also increased the bandwidth of the subcarrier baseband and removed certain modulation constraints, both developments that make the technology more attractive for data users. (Bandwidth and modulation details are discussed below.)

Before deregulation, the principal application for hundreds of FM subcarriers was local distribution of commercial background music services, such as Muzak. While this is strictly an analog application, it is a useful illustration of the subcarrier's capabilities.

A typical Muzak operator wants to distribute music in real time, 24 hours a day, to customer locations scattered throughout a metropolitan region. One way to do this is by leasing dedicated circuits from the local exchange carrier — one for each user — and then watch distribution costs pile up quickly. The preferred option is to lease a subcarrier channel from an FM radio station and then install a subcarrier receiver at each customer location. With this approach, distribution costs incurred by adding users rise more slowly than with leased lines.

Muzak operators have been using subcarrier in lieu of telephone lines for more than two decades, making the subcarrier one of the oldest of the so-called bypass technologies. With deregulation, the subcarrier economies that have been available to Muzak operators are now available to data users as well.

What has the FCC done to open the subcarrier to digital transmission? Deregulation has taken place in three areas: applications, technology, and operations.

Until deregulation, only broadcast applications such as Muzak were permitted. Now the subcarrier baseband can be used for, in the words of the FCC's order, "any legitimate communications purpose." This is a broad charter, consistent with the goal of the present FCC to maximize efficient use of the radio spectrum. It means, simply, that anything that legally can be trans-

FM tutorial

What is an FM subcarrier? Any reasonable answer first requires a brief introduction to FM radio broadcasting.

The FM broadcast band lies in the VHF (very high frequency) spectrum, from 88 to 108 MHz, and is divided into 100 channels, each 200 kHz wide. These channels are identified by their center frequencies, such as 97.1, 97.3, and 97.5 MHz.

Since an FM station's programming consists only of the audio frequencies between 20 Hz and 15 kHz, it is reasonable to ask why 200 kHz of bandwidth is required. At first blush it would appear that 30 kHz would do just fine. However, the transmission of stereophonic programming requires that two channels of information be provided. And this is where the subcarrier comes in.

The figure shows the baseband frequency spectrum of a broadcast FM station. Prior to deregulation, the baseband extended to 75 kHz. In its deregulation order, however, the Federal Communications Commission stretched the baseband out to 99 kHz, thereby providing additional bandwidth for subcarriers.

The region up to 15 kHz is the monophonic, or "left plus right," channel. Located at 19 kHz is the stereo pilot, an inaudible tone that activates the stereo circuitry in a receiver when a stereo program is being transmitted. Centered at 38 kHz—double the pilot frequency—is the stereo, or "left minus right," (called that because of the technique used) subcarrier.

Beyond 53 kHz is the subcarrier baseband. Figure 2 shows a conventional configuration with two 10-

kHz subcarriers, one centered at 67 kHz and the other at 92 kHz. Each of these can carry data at 9.6 kbit/s, or 5 kHz audio.

Two innovative configurations for the subcarrier baseband are being proposed. One is an FDM (frequency-division multiplexing) approach advocated by McMartin Industries of Omaha, Neb. The baseband is divided into five discrete subcarrier channels, each of which—the company claims—is capable of transmitting data at 4.8 kbit/s.

The other new approach uses a wideband subcarrier, developed by Electronic Publishing Systems of Mountain View, Calif., that occupies almost the entire baseband above 53 kHz. The firm claims a data transmitting capability of 38.4 kbit/s for this scheme.

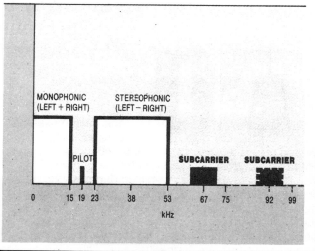

mitted, can be transmitted by subcarrier.

This applies even to uses traditionally associated with common carriers, such as paging. FM stations may now operate simultaneously within two different frameworks: as broadcasters on the main channel and as common carriers on the subcarrier baseband. The FCC has gone so far as to preempt state regulations that might block or impede the entry of common carrier subcarrier operations.

Deregulation has increased the data capacity of the subcarrier baseband. Previously, all subcarriers had to be frequency modulated. Now, digital techniques such as frequency-shift keying (FSK) and phase-shift keying (PSK) can be employed. In addition, the FCC has increased the available subcarrier bandwidth from 22 to 46 kHz and doubled from 10 to 20 percent the amount of power a stereo FM broadcaster can allocate to subcarrier channels. (Incidentally, the 10 percent reduction in the station's main-channel power translates to about a 1-dB FM broadcast reception loss at the user site.)

Deregulation has eliminated many of the headaches broadcasters faced in operating a subcarrier, such as maintaining logs and filing applications. Also, broadcasters are now permitted to transmit subcarrier sig-

nals even when their main channel is not being programmed. Previously, subcarrier transmissions had to sign off whenever the main programming left the air.

What are the characteristics of subcarrier transmission? In many ways, they resemble those of satellite transmission—in somewhat reduced terms. The first similarity is distance-cost insensitivity. Just as it costs the same to transmit 1,000 miles or 100 miles by satellite, it costs no more to transmit 40 miles by subcarrier than it does four miles.

The second similarity is point-to-multipoint capability. Adding new users to a satellite network is merely a matter of furnishing them with earth stations. Adding new users to a subcarrier network is just a matter of furnishing them with receivers. A third similarity is wide-area coverage. Just as a satellite can blanket a continent, a subcarrier can cover a 5,000-square-mile metropolitan area.

The principal difference between satellite and subcarrier transmission is that subcarrier is one way. If a return path is needed, it must be implemented via another medium. This limits subcarrier applications to those such as paging or to those that are overwhelmingly one way. The latter—sometimes known as "flood out/trickle back" applications—are exemplified by database queries. Here, 98 percent of the data flows in one direction, 2 percent in the other.

This unidirectional limitation can be offset by the cost-effective economies of the subcarrier. Since it piggybacks onto an existing transmission scheme, there are no large up-front capital costs. The antenna, tower, and transmitter of the FM station are already being paid for by its main-channel programming. Adding a 9.6-kbit/s data subcarrier capability requires a one-time capital expense of less than $5,000.

The cost of each user installation for 9.6-kbit/s service, using off-the-shelf hardware, is typically in the $500 to $1,000 range, depending on what is needed for local reception conditions. FM broadcasting is a line-of-sight medium, subject to shadowing (having a signal-reducing obstruction), multipath reflections (which are discussed below), and related propagation problems. In most cases an outside antenna is needed, although a company based in New York City, American Data Transmission, claims to have developed a microprocessor-controlled indoor antenna that overcomes many of these propagation difficulties.

The only recurring cost involved in subcarrier use is the monthly lease payment to the broadcaster. In the largest metropolitan areas, the going rate is $5,000 to $10,000 per month, while in smaller communities (having populations of 500,000 or less) $1,500 per month is more typical. Many broadcasters are also willing to lease on a revenue- or profit-sharing basis, with a smaller monthly minimum charge.

Another happy consequence of the piggyback nature is reliability. Most data communications carriers lose only their user revenue from a service interruption. But when a broadcaster goes off the air, lost as well is the advertising revenue from all the commercials that do not run. Hence the reliability of subcarrier transmission is kept high. An outage typically occurs once or twice a month and is measured in minutes.

Help from above
One additional factor that makes FM subcarrier transmission a useful technology is the growth of satellite communications in the radio broadcasting industry. All of the major national radio networks have converted their signal distribution facilities to satellite. As a result, thousands of broadcasters have satellite earth stations already installed, making it convenient to drop off data by satellite for local distribution via subcarrier. The transmission path is from satellite to earth station, to FM station, to subscribers/users. The cost of adding a data card to an existing earth station is typically under $1,000.

Since transmission costs remain essentially constant, the more FM subcarrier users there are, the more cost-effective the medium becomes. Which applications are most suitable for this technology? They include real-time delivery of financial information, downloading of video games and other microcomputer software, and electronic mail for large retailers.

Real-time financial market information is the oldest and largest digital application for FM subcarriers. In a simple scenario, the market information is transmitted in a short, endlessly repeating loop that is updated regularly. The user keys in the identification of the particular piece of information desired, and the receiver grabs the requested data the next time that portion of the loop passes by. This can give a strictly one-way service the appearance of being interactive.

The better way
The first users served by FM subcarrier were farmers and grain-elevator operators in the Midwest who needed access to information from the commodities exchanges. Because of the distances involved, dedicated leased lines were not economical. But because the terrain was flat, a powerful (50 to 100 kw) FM station could serve hundreds of users. Hence, in the mid-1970s, a business was born. Companies providing this service include a unit of United Telecommunications called Market Information, Omaha, Neb., and a unit of Knight-Ridder Newspapers called Commodity News Services of Leawood, Kan.

More recently, several companies have begun to provide stock market information via subcarrier. Two in particular—Telemet America of Alexandria, Va., and Dataspeed of San Mateo, Calif.—transmit this information to hand-held receivers. This enables brokers and traders to follow the market when they are away from their offices. Telemet and Dataspeed both recently announced subcarrier receivers that allow their respective quote streams to be loaded into a user's microcomputer. Telerate of New York City, a leading supplier of bond and currency-market information, recently launched its PDQ service, which also transmits via subcarrier to a hand-held device.

During the past two years, a great deal of attention has been given to downloading ("teledelivery") of video games and other microcomputer programs. Many executives in the software industry agree that some scheme for transmitting programs directly to users will eventually replace the present method of prerecorded cartridges and floppy disks.

What they disagree on is the most desirable delivery medium. Cable television and dial-up telephone lines have already been tried without great success—mainly because of unacceptable pricing and mismanagement. Satellite broadcasting and the vertical blanking intervals of broadcast television stations are contenders. Recent interest has focused on the FM subcarrier. At least two companies—Electronic Publishing Systems (EPS) of Mountain View, Calif., and National Information Utilities of Vienna, Va.—have announced plans to use it for software downloading.

EPS's home computer software service is aimed at owners of Commodore 64s, Apple IIs, and IBM PCs and compatibles. The subcarrier receiver has an RS-232-C port to deliver the software to the computer. For $9.95 per month, a subscriber gets unlimited monthly use of 40 different programs that are typically used on home computers, such as educational, checkbook, and games software (see "Digital techniques").

One difficulty with software downloading is the elimination of bit errors. With ordinary text transmission, an occasional mistake in an ASCII character can be

Digital techniques

What exactly are the digital capabilities of the FM subcarrier? The ultimate answer to this question is not yet clear. With deregulation less than two years old, the newly developed schemes for transmitting data via the FM subcarrier baseband are only now beginning to move into field tests. It is already clear, however, that deregulation has resulted in a significant increase in subcarrier data capacity and a substantial decrease in the cost of receivers.

Before deregulation, subcarrier data transmission was authorized by the FCC only on a case-by-case basis. Less than 5 percent of the FM broadcasters used their subcarrier capacity for this purpose.

The digital transmission technique used then—and still most common today—has come to be known as indirect modulation. FCC rules permitted only frequency modulated subcarriers, so subcarrier channels had to be modulated with audio frequency signals. This was furnished by ordinary 1.2- or 2.4-kbit/s modems. The subcarrier channel was treated like a leased line (using a modem), with audio output of the modem feeding an analog subcarrier generator. The resulting subcarrier was then multiplexed into the main FM channel. At the receiving end, the process was reversed.

Compared with the digital techniques available since deregulation, indirect modulation was expensive and inefficient. Every user required a subcarrier receiver and a modem, bringing the typical hardware cost for a 2.4-kbit/s installation to $1,000 to $1,500. Today, with "direct" modulation of the subcarrier, a 9.6-kbit/s user installation can cost anywhere from $500 to $1,000.

Direct modulation eliminates the need for the modem. Instead of frequency modulating the subcarrier with audio, the subcarrier is modulated directly by the data (see A in the figure). The demodulation process is shown in B in the figure.

While in principle any technique for encoding data into a radio frequency can be used, in practice binary frequency shift keying (2-FSK) is most common. The author is aware of more-sophisticated circuits using 4-PSK and 8-QAM (quadrature amplitude modulation) techniques that are under development by several vendors.

Electronic Publishing Systems of Mountain View, Calif. (owned by Activision—same location—and the Pittsburgh-based venture capitalist Hillman Co.) has announced a 38.4-kbit/s subcarrier data scheme with a receiver that costs $150. EPS's subcarrier generator plugs into an expansion slot in the back of an IBM PC XT located at the transmitting station.

While this technology has yet to receive extensive field tests, if it meets specifications, it will provide an order-of-magnitude increase in transmission speed and—simultaneously—an order-of-magnitude decrease in receiver cost compared with indirect modulation. Johnson Electronics of Winter Park, Fla., recently announced a similar design that provides a throughput of 38.4 kbit/s.

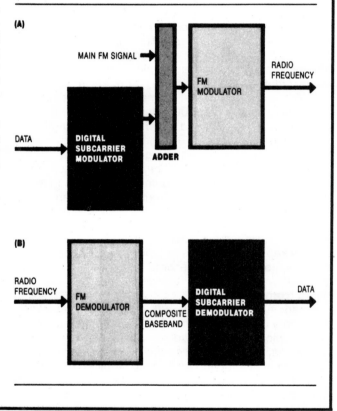

tolerated. With software, however, a single erroneous bit can make the entire program inoperable.

To date no rigorous public testing of the bit error rate (BER) of subcarrier channels has taken place. Various suppliers claim uncorrected rates of one error in 10^6-to-10^7 bits. EPS says it will function with a BER as high as one in 10^4, although with some noticeable degradation in response time. It is generally agreed that the most critical factor affecting error performance is multipath, a common propagation problem arising when radio signals reflect off hillsides or buildings. Multipath distortion is often heard when listening to FM stereo in a moving automobile.

A third application that is emerging for subcarrier technology is electronic mail. Large retail chains and other businesses with many geographically dispersed locations often need the means for transmitting messages from headquarters to all sites immediately and simultaneously. A two-tiered scheme using satellite for national and regional coverage and subcarrier for local coverage is a cost-effective method.

For example, the satellite portion, using full capacity, costs $5,000 to $10,000 per month; in the Bonneville network (discussed below), the FM subcarrier "second tier" costs $7.50 per 1,000 characters, irrespective of the number of users. A typical packet network cost is

Two-tier, plus. *The information is received at the radio station from a satellite (one tier) and distributed to users—stores here—via FM subcarrier (the second tier).* *In addition, the data originates at a packet-network node, so that the users may communicate with headquarters: in effect, a two-way scheme.*

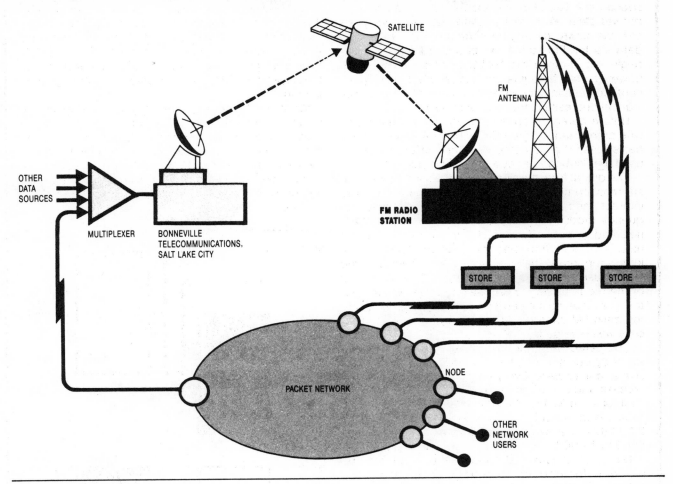

$0.05 per 1,000 characters per user. Therefore, once the number of users goes beyond 150, the FM subcarrier becomes cost-effective. (Note that costs are as of December 1984.)

The Data Systems Division of Bonneville Telecommunications, Salt Lake City, Utah, installed such a network (see figure) in the Southern Food Division (of Lucky Stores), a 300-store supermarket chain based in Buena Park, Calif. The Bonneville electronic-mail design, called Radio Writer, serves these stores via the subcarriers of FM stations in nine cities in California, Nevada, Arizona, and Texas. The equipment is fully addressable—that is, a receiver may be individually or group-addressed—and is used to transmit information on price changes, inventory, and the competition.

To implement two-way service, Bonneville recently signed a joint marketing agreement with GE Information Services of Rockville, Md. Under this agreement, Bonneville's customers will have access to GE's Marknet packet-switching network to receive asynchronous data, such as electronic mail and stock market information. GE customers will have access to Bonneville's 40-city subcarrier network for point-to-multipoint outbound traffic. More recently, Bonneville

concluded a similar agreement with a second packet-network carrier, San Jose, Calif.-based Tymnet.

The Mutual Broadcasting System, an Arlington, Va.-based radio network owned by Amway Corp., plans a similar electronic mail scheme for its parent company. Amway is a direct-sales business with 40,000 distributors. The planned implementation, called Multicomm, will allow updated product and price information to be sent to all simultaneously.

At present, about 150 FM radio stations use some or all of their subcarrier capacity for digital transmission. Half of these are in the 30 most highly populated cities. The author expects that by 1987 more than 500 stations (again, half in the top 30 cities) will be transmitting data via subcarrier, and that data communications will be the number one application for subcarrier technology in those cities. ∎

Dennis P. Waters is president of Waters Information Services and editor of the newsletter SCA: Radio Subcarrier Report. *He holds an M. S. in advanced technology from SUNY-Binghamton, where he is currently a Ph.D. candidate. Earlier, he was program director for NBC's WYNY-FM in New York City.*

Section 3
Application

Edwin R. Coover and Michael J. Kane, Mitre Corp., McLean, Va.

Notes from mid-revolution: Searching for the perfect PBX

The Washington, D. C., operations arm of an engineering firm embarks on a reconnaissance mission for its new in-house PBX.

ate in 1983, Mitre Corp. began planning. Mitre, an independent, not-for-profit organization that works in a variety of areas—including computers, communications, public health, and environmental protection—counts among its major clients the Department of Defense and the Federal Aviation Administration. Although over 18 months distant at the time, the convergence of two events—the expiration of the lease on its AT&T Dimension PBX (Private Branch Exchange) and the scheduled completion of a new, 300,000-square-foot building—demanded action.

Mitre's 2,300-person staff in Washington, D. C., would be consolidated from nine present buildings into four closely grouped buildings requiring voice, data, and video services. On the data side, the organization's Sytek LocalNet, a broadband local network, would have to be extended and reconfigured. Many of the 900 terminals, hundreds of microcomputers, two IBM mainframes, 10 VAXs, and other specialized processors would be affected by the relocation. IBM PCs are the most common microcomputer used by Mitre, followed closely by Apple Macintoshes. The corporation has something of everything: symbolic Lisp machines, Digitial Equipment Corp. (DEC) Rainbows, Apple IIs, Sun workstations, and so on. On the voice side, Mitre's aging Dimension switch and a satellite voice/data Rolm CBX II needed to be replaced, along with all station equipment. Mitre's new switch needed data capabilities, but a broadband coaxial cable would have to form the primary communications network for ASCII terminal-to-host transmissions. Mitre wanted the flexibility to use broadband, local networks, or PBXs.

Mitre's approach was systematic. A Mitre-wide advisory group was formed with members from every division who were then surveyed and interviewed. The data about their requirements was consolidated, re-viewed, and revised. Vendor product and capabilities information was culled from sources such as Datapro Research on PBX original equipment manufacturers (OEMs) who sold switches in the 2,000-4,000 line range. The data was digested, manufacturer representatives interviewed, and a Lotus 1-2-3 database created. Management was briefed, an RFP (request for proposal) written, and a vendor meeting held in which 14 different organizations were present, with four different bidders representing NEC-America equipment. At a subsequent meeting, building blueprints were distributed and a physical inspection of extant wiring took place. Mitre is currently awaiting proposals.

Although the replacement and procurement process is proceeding routinely enough, the quest itself turned out to be an awakening. Mitre's investigation revealed that in the last half-dozen years substantive changes have occurred on the digital PBX scene. New PBXs have radical designs that, if commercially successful, will, by their superior cost/performance margins, redefine PBX economics.

Microcomputers and data terminals can now plug into the back of streamlined telephone sets. (Perhaps, more ambitiously, hybrid microcomputer/telephone devices will become common.) Furthermore, in the future it will be less likely that PBXs will appear to the uninitiated as a DEC PDP-11 minicomputer look-alike stood on its head, with cables flowing out the top, and ensconced in a large, wire-crammed, heavily air-conditioned room in the basement. Instead, it is probable that a discreet peek into a telephone closet will reveal a compact device—often no larger than an under-the-counter refrigerator—that, in concert with similar switching nodes, will handle thousands of voice or voice/data devices.

What has happened, and why now? How may one

broadly characterize these new devices?

■ *Microprocessor-based.* Where conventional PBXs were once built around 16-bit and, later, 32-bit minicomputers serving as principal processors, high-performance microprocessors have usurped these functions. As with other similarly replaced equipment, the substitution has generated a benign ripple effect: greater performance, less power, less heat, drastically less space, and, most compelling, less cost. The 32-bit Motorola 68010s used in the Ericsson MD110, CXC Rose/Western Union Vega, and Mitel SX-2000 cost approximately $128 each.

■ *Parallelism and hierarchy.* The cost/performance advantages of high-performance microcomputers have allowed PBX designers to further increase parallelism in their switch architectures. Up until recently, conventional PBXs usually featured 8-bit microcomputers servicing the station equipment (analogous to cluster controllers in orthodox data processing shops). A fairly large minicomputer ran the more complex applications, such as least-cost routing and the central directory. Usually, a second standby minicomputer was offered as part of the package in arrangements of 400 lines or greater. The extra minicomputer served as a hot standby or alternated in regular use with the primary minicomputer.

The new generation of microcomputers allow creative extensions to this parallel, hierarchical architecture. The low cost of the microprocessor allows cold or hot standby processors at both the line cards and the application processors, thus augmenting fault tolerance. The proliferation of bus-connected 16- and 32-bit microprocessors results in significant capacity for parallel processing. Even more than that, however, they form high-speed proprietary local networks.

In the future, PBXs are likely to develop that have multiple processor complexes executing in lockstep and vote in a manner similar to that of Stratus Computer's fault-tolerant computers. This means that the processors are synchronized to a particular clock and execute instructions in parallel, comparing the results. Further, the bus designs allow the attachment of application processors for specialized (and usually extra cost) optional functions, such as voice and text mail, local network control, traffic analysis, protocol conversion, and the like.

■ *Local network architecture.* Fundamental to the newest designs (Ericsson MD110, CXC Rose/Western Union Vega) is that they are, or are capable of becoming, processing nodes on a geographically extensive local network. Among the older switches, Rolm's has implemented this capability in software, although the space and air-conditioning requirements of PBXs call into question its practicality.

In distributed cases, the PBX architecture resembles a packet network. Standing alone, the node is usually capable of handling about 200 ports. If the growth is in a contiguous area, the node grows by adding colocated processors. If the growth is not contiguous, a local network is implemented, connecting a network of physically distributed, homogeneous processing nodes. This can occur in either a physical ring or a physical

star. In either configuration, the node forms the hub of the wheel in a hub-and-spoke connection with the station equipment.

By contrast, in the traditional data processing context, local networks have been most frequently used to replace terminal wiring, as in the typical installation of physically distributed Ethernet or IBM PC Network. Less frequent are local networks with multiple processors. Where network control and homogeneous multinode operating systems are involved, the processing nodes are more likely to be contiguous—as in Tandem's 6700 Fiber Optic Extension and DEC's Massbus—due both to the requirements for computer-room operating environments and to the signal/media limits. Much less frequent is the combination of network control and heterogeneous operating systems, as in Network Systems Corp.'s Hyperchannel and Hyperbus or host-to-host Ethernets.

Finally, among the distributed PBXs, the preferred local network medium to link the nodes is fiber-optic cable. In addition to fiber's environmentally resistant qualities, it is able to support the very high speeds (up to 50 Mbit/s) employed in internode communications.

■ *Local/global software.* Where the local network physically implements the distributed architecture, local/global software conceals the local network from the user. By "local/global," it is meant that typically all routine call-handling software is present in every node; specialized functions, such as calculating the least-cost supplier for long-distance calls, may not be present in every node. Take the case of a multinode network on a campus or a multibuilding corporation. If the user dials within the building, the call will be processed by the local node; if the user dials outside the building but within the campus, the call is processed both by the local node and, through the local network, by the node in the distant building; if the user dials long-distance, the independently trunked local node normally runs the routing program and processes the call; if the user dials long-distance and the local node's central office trunks are busy, the call can be routed to the next node through outside trunks for processing according to a pre-established succession and depending on the class of service assigned.

A secondary, but important, aspect of local/global software and nodal trunking is resistance to failure. When the errant backhoe severs one set of trunks, calls can be alternately routed to surviving trunks. An equipment-room fire cannot damage the critical main distribution board because there is none. Should the node maintaining the network's directory fail, its predesignated successor assumes the task. Although ultimately dependent on building power and batteries, the distributed switching nodes can deliver a more robust PBX by eliminating single points of failure.

■ *Digital throughout.* The appearance of the digital Northern Telecom SL-1 and Rolm CBX in 1975 pointed the PBX market in a direction from which it has not retreated. Nonetheless, these and subsequent switches have had to accommodate, primarily for reasons of cost, analog station devices. The inevitability of the analog/digital conversion, performed by codecs at the

1. Power requirements. *The actual figures in kilowatts for the 3,200-line switches in this diagram are SL-1, 7.5; CBX, 16.45; IBX, 45; MD 110, 8.5; NEAX 12.12; Vega, 22.7; 20-20, 10. Battery needs and types of power, not shown in this diagram, should also figure into switch cost-benefit analysis.*

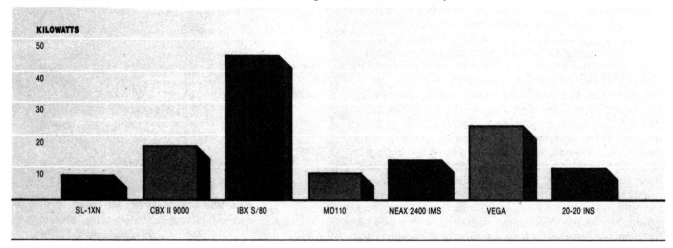

line cards, forced their designs to accommodate this mixed mode. With the falling cost of codecs, and of electronic station equipment in general, the newer switches are designed to routinely service digitized voice and data—usually, but not always, multiplexed—from the stations. While all manufacturers continue to support analog devices (commonly the ubiquitous 2500-type instrument), increasingly these devices are perceived as a technological burden that not only require special and sometimes costly accommodation at the node but also impose subtle penalties in operational flexibility. For instance, a Mitre study concluded that retaining 2500-type instruments can be costly if the overall mix of station instruments necessitates switch-side rewiring upon moves and changes. Further, each PBX OEM has handled the analog versus digital line-card design and cost, and the line-card impact on switch size and cost, in individualistic and unpredictable ways.

■ *Packet switching.* Similarly evolving is the technique of packet switching, which in the context of a digital switch performing time-division multiplexing (TDM) can be seen as further multiplexing the time-division multiplexing. The earliest accommodation of circuit switches to packet-switch technology appeared with gateways. Northern Telecom, Rolm, InteCom, and others ran circuit-switched, TDM data into a protocol converter to let terminals at user stations access X.25 public data networks. More recently, the Western Union Vega, Rolm CBX, and AT&T System 85 have used packetization to combine what is usually a digitized voice and ASCII data stream from station to switch. Next, apparently already in test with GTE and Western Union, is a hybrid packet/circuit switch where the digital voice is packetized and switched in a datagram fashion (DATA COMMUNICATIONS, "Packetized voice could move out of the laboratory soon," February, p. 45).

The data is handled similarly, internally employing—within the PBX network—a stripped-down high-level data link control packet that retains a virtual-circuit operations model. Although increasingly complex con-

ceptually, it may not be appreciably more costly given the falling price of microprocessor-based PADs (packet assembler/disassemblers). The returns are real: higher and higher data rates, fewer data errors, and most importantly, dynamic and highly efficient bandwidth employment.

■ *High-level languages, intensive software.* For performance reasons, the earlier minicomputer-based PBX software was usually written, all or in part, in assembly language. The use of assembly language kept software development, maintenance, and enhancement costs high. The coincidence of the high-performance microprocessors, the availability of powerful high-level languages such as Pascal and C, and the availability of integrated software development packages have effected dramatic changes.

Although technological conservatism is still present—AT&T largely rehosted its Dimension feature package from its analog pulse amplitude modulation (PAM) switch to the digital TDM hardware on the System 85—many of the new switches makers (CXC/Western Union, Mitel) choose to develop their software in these new languages because they come equipped with a variety of programming tools. These tool-intensive programming languages employ a full array of routine libraries, run-time debuggers, test data generators, cross-assemblers, and software configuration support aids. In the typical case this involves a programmer working on a DEC VAX running Unix or VMS coding in C and then downloading the object code to the Motorola 68010s. At least in theory, these new application software suites should be more sturdy, require less maintenance, and be easier to enhance than the older models. The real lesson, however, is probably different—that there is no substitute for thorough testing.

■ *Remote service.* At present, most PBX makers employ service technicians, either their own or trained by their company, at the customer site. These technicians are augmented by time-shared remote diagnostic services. Almost needless to note, these technicians are costly not only to train but also to retain.

As the switch architectures increasingly employ massive parallelism on multiple microprocessors, and in some cases with hot or cold standby processors, it is likely they will move in the self-maintenance directions employed by fault-tolerant computer manufacturers. For instance, most operating systems accumulate a record of all nonroutine events. With most fault-tolerant computers, when a nontransient failure occurs, the failing component is automatically switched off and a redundant unit takes over. Among the fault-tolerant makers, Stratus even employs an autodial modem so that each Stratus computer, like the Hollywood kids' hero E. T., calls home. A maintenance scheme diagnoses the information, and where replacement is necessary, arranges that a new component board is mailed to the site. Actual replacement is then performed by the customer's staff while the machine is still operating. As the PBX switch architecture more closely resembles commercial fault-tolerant architecture, and technician costs continue to rise, it is likely that on-site service will become similarly automated.

■ *Components.* At one time, particularly with AT&T and Western Electric, all major components of a switch were produced by the vendor. Gradually switch makers began to acquire their main processors from minicomputer makers—Northern Telecom/Danray from Data General, United Technologies from DEC, and InteCom from Perkin-Elmer. This reduced costs.

Not only did the PBX manufacturers not have to design and build a major component, but smaller ventures could take advantage of the production efficiencies achieved by the major minicomputer OEMs. This tendency has accelerated, especially in microprocessors, memories, and storage devices, to where a small startup like CXC can field equipment with lower production costs than their larger, more highly capitalized competitors.

■ *Specialized applications processors.* At a higher level of integration, but similar to the situation with components, the earlier tendency was that the vendor provided—often designed and manufactured—all major applications. These combinations of hardware, software, and firmware gave the PBX its distinctive features and functions. Although this was appropriate to a highly capitalized, monopolistic environment, it made little sense to smaller firms wishing to compete in a cost- and features-driven marketplace. As a consequence, many modern PBXs implement new features on specialized applications processors provided by other suppliers.

Present functions such as voice mail and electronic mail, protocol conversion and gateways, building monitoring, traffic analysis, and local network controllers are typically supplied in this fashion. Future features such as compressed video and cellular telephone interfaces are likely to be added in a similar manner.

Office environments
Earlier it was noted that PBXs are undergoing a physical transformation, changing drastically in appearance. The microprocessor, large-scale integration, and local

2. Cold air. BTUs are SL-1, 25,613; CBX, 67,250; UTX, 36914; IBX, 136,791; MD 110, 29,100; System 85, 75,632; NEAX, 27,000; Vega, 6,710; 20-20, 20,000.

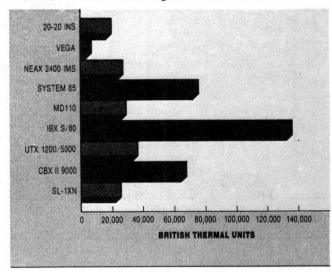

network architecture have combined to miniaturize and bring the PBX physically into the office.

Figures 1 through 4 present statistics for power, air-conditioning, and space for a model 3,200-line network. The data was provided by manufacturer representatives for a 3,200-line configuration for Mitre Corp.'s Washington-area campus.

One must note, however, several paradoxes regarding the physical space examples. First, compact, distributed switches like the Ericsson MD110 and CXC Rose/Western Union Vega can be physically configured in multiple nodes—a single site serving multiple buildings, multiple nodes in multiple buildings, or one or more switching nodes per floor. In places where floor space is expensive, the optimal location—space permitting—is in one or more telephone closets. In this instance, no additional building space need be allocated for PBX equipment.

Battery use itself has changed over the last 10 years. The old AT&T Dimension used small batteries to protect memory during the 18-second switch to backup power during emergencies. This generally preserved working connections but caused a service interruption when new calls were attempted during the 18 transitional seconds. Older digital switches such as the SL-1 ran off of large batteries at 48 volts d.c. with commercial power used to charge the batteries. The PBX was not directly connected to external power sources. This was an improvement, but these batteries required venting in separate battery rooms. Further, many PBXs required their own fallback generators. The most recent tendency, exemplified by CXC, is for switch makers to use very small, nonventing batteries, physically contained within the switch, that provide temporary backup to the PBX that operates on standard 110/115 volt a.c. power.

Building codes play an interesting role in this drama, part obstructionist, part progressive. While many municipalities now stipulate that new buildings must

3. Centralized space requirements. *Where office space is more expensive than $17 per square foot, differences in bulk may be an important factor.*

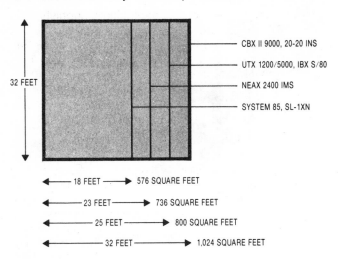

32 FEET

- CBX II 9000, 20-20 INS
- UTX 1200/5000, IBX S/80
- NEAX 2400 IMS
- SYSTEM 85, SL-1XN

- ◄— 18 FEET —► 576 SQUARE FEET
- ◄— 23 FEET —► 736 SQUARE FEET
- ◄— 25 FEET —► 800 SQUARE FEET
- ◄— 32 FEET —► 1,024 SQUARE FEET

COST OF OFFICE FLOOR SPACE:
WORST: 1,024 SQUARE FEET AT $17 = $17,408 PER YEAR
BEST: 576 SQUARE FEET AT $17 = $9,792 PER YEAR
DIFFERENCE: $7,616 PER YEAR

USUALLY HEAVY AIR-CONDITIONING; SQUARE FOOTAGE INCLUDES SPACE FOR BATTERIES

have automatically activated emergency generators, getting rid of the need for extra generators dedicated to serving a PBX, some also demand venting for batteries, ignoring the existence of the new, nonventing batteries.

In Figures 3 and 4, the actual square footage consumed by the multiple nodes can, in some cases, exceed that consumed by a single central switch. The reason is that several of the distributed designs (CXC/Western Union) require front and rear access. Interestingly, in virtually all the distributed switches the door swings require more space than the switch itself, raising the possibility that future, perhaps military, versions may come with sliding doors. Third, the lower

power, low air-conditioning, and small space requirements of the newest distributed switches are aimed at coexisting with office workers. Sites where building management routinely powers down their air-conditioning on weekends may find calculating the difference in savings complex: keeping the air-conditioning on to sustain a cost-saving PBX or switching it off and running the risk of damaging the switch is not a simple trade-off.

User interface

The least revolutionary aspect of the new switches is often the user interface. Part of the reason is cost. The large number of units associated with station equipment leads to a large line item and, often, a go-slow attitude. Some will undoubtedly continue using 2500-type station equipment for these reasons, though it is hoped that few will wonder why switchhook-initiated features are seldom used. Perhaps no failure has been so complete as the effort to piggyback advanced features on the 2500 telephone. Well-meaning lectures, slide shows, and faceplates aside, people who, from their earliest days, learned that pressing the switchhook resulted in a dial tone are hard to convince that it is part of the proper procedure to press the button to transfer the Boss's "very important call."

At the high-end, the voice station cum microcomputer has several entries with GTE's icon-directed Omni-Action, a friendlier approach than Rolm's Cedar (a midget IBM PC) and Northern Telecom's Display-phone, a shrunken smart terminal.

The major failure, however, has been in imagination. Station features continue to be added in an add-a-feature, add-a-button manner, with more and more buttons—often of small size or doing dual duty and with tiny print—appearing in a reduced, desk-amenable "footprint." Unfortunately, the employment of all these features is not intuitive nor is it likely that potential users will willingly digest a user manual to access them. To employ another parallel from data processing, the add-a-function, add-a-button approach most resembles the IBM microcomputer and its large and complex keyboard. Contrast it with the software-driven, icon-and-mouse user interface em-

4. Distributed space requirements. *Some switches are so compact that their greatest need is to have adequate walk-around space to reach cabling in the back.*

The Ericsson MD 110 solves this problem by pulling its cabling through the top. Compact PBXs might eliminate this need through the use of sliding doors.

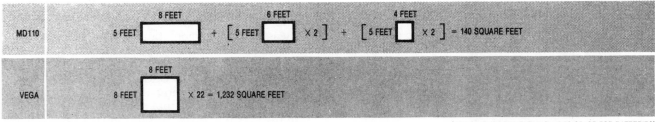

MD110   8 FEET   6 FEET   4 FEET
5 FEET [ ] + [5 FEET [ ] X 2] + [5 FEET [ ] X 2] = 140 SQUARE FEET

VEGA   8 FEET
8 FEET [ ] X 22 = 1,232 SQUARE FEET

(OFFICE ENVIRONMENT, INCLUDES SPACE FOR BATTERIES)

APPROACH:
- DISTRIBUTED PRIVATE BRANCH EXCHANGES PLACED IN TELEPHONE CLOSETS
- SAVINGS AT $17 PER SQUARE FOOT RANGE FROM $9,792 TO $17,408 YEARLY

ployed in the Apple Macintosh; other alleged merits and defects aside, the Apple product clearly has the superior user interface.

In their rush toward baby buttons and midget screens, the station equipment designers have overlooked the operant natural language: the spoken word. Although it required a great deal of intelligence at the switch (a human being), the earliest telephone networks were of the signal-and-voice-recognition variety. Later, five digits had to be remembered with two additional digits artfully camouflaged by easy-to-remember—and sometimes famous—exchange names (BUtterfield, MUrray Hill). At the moment, a 14-digit international direct-dial call seems unfriendly enough. Although incorporating an immediately unlikely economic development scenario, can one imagine the numbers unleashed should the First World personal communications trend in the United States, Western Europe, and Japan—a phone at home, at work, and in the car—extend to India and China?

Despite the fact that they have not as yet been embraced by a major vendor, the best prospects for an easier to use, more successful user interface seem to lie in the area of incorporating some kind of voice response/voice recognition capability. Already some major PBXs use voice response "helps" when using station equipment features. Current voice recognition gear is more limited. Although they permit one to say "Call...," they can only be programmed to recognize one voice, that of the instrument's habitual user. This excessively personalizes the device; in experimental military applications using voice recognition, some machines will recognize voices that imitate the original users, or at least make a statisticallly accurate guess about who within the switch's voice-recognition directory the speaker's voice most closely resembles. This is a far cry, though, from a commerically available general recognition capability based on an entire company's staff directory.

A chaotic environment
Some aspects of the new, postdivestiture PBX world have already been alluded to—Western Union, a large common carrier, adding data features to CXC's Rose and marketing it as the Vega. The present PBX vendor marketplace can be characterized as anarchistic at best. Large OEMs such as AT&T, Northern Telecom, and Rolm directly market and service the customer through regional organizations. Ex-Bell operating companies like Bell Atlantic distribute other PBXs through OEM arrangements (InteCom and NEAX 2400 in Bell Atlantic's case) while their regulated side pushes the PBX-like capabilities of the latest upgrade (Centrex III) of their central-office location switches. And everywhere loom relatively small local distributors, typically with low overheads, that market switches obtained directly from the OEMs at large discounts. Not infrequently, the local distributor's combination of low overhead and aggressive pricing provides the buyer with the same switch at lower cost than from the OEM. Nor is it clear who is likely to provide the best service support: a small, aggressive local company, an ex-Bell

regional company with multiple products and services, or a large, nationally or internationally based original equipment manufacturer

Unfortunately, the most technologically sophisticated PBX, particularly one launched by a startup company, may not be the one that wins bids. Since the financial status of the company, the ability to write a good proposal, and an established service record may often determine who wins a PBX sale, the Darwinian law of the jungle may be mitigated with PBX sales. Those who survive may not be the technologically fittest. More and more prevalent throughout the computer industry, this twist on the old truism is especially likely to apply to the PBX market. Just about every feature is available from every vendor, or can be bought off the shelf and added to any switch that appears lacking to a prospective customer. Comparison of features and functions becomes moot. PBX purchases become business decisions and not technology decisions, unless use of new technology drastically lowers prices: for example, the NEC switch is based on U. S.-designed Intel 8086 microprocessors manufactured in Asia and assembled by nonunion labor in Texas.

From the perspective of the first half of 1985, it is not clear where the revolution in PBXs is leading. Arguably, the U. S. PBX market is of insufficient size for so many switch vendors to make money. Nonetheless, a number of these switches (NEC, Ericsson, Mitel, Harris) are aimed at other national or world markets; success in the large U. S. market would be a boon but is not absolutely essential. Although the newest designs (Ericsson, NEC, CXC, Mitel) offer advanced features and should be cheaper to manufacture than conventional architectures, it is debatable to what extent they will carve out market share based on superior price/performance. Despite the fact that its present dominance remains largely based on the aging Dimension switch, the U. S. PBX marketplace remains an AT&T preserve, and new vendors must survive the IBM-like pull of AT&T. Nor is it self-evident who will best sell and service the switches. All three approaches—OEM, ex-BOCs, and distributors—offer both advantages and disadvantages to the buyer.

As for the revolution, the path of PBX technology seems most promising; what remains to be seen is whether the disorderly PBX market of today will postpone or accelerate it. As of this writing, Mitre expects proposals representing three different approaches: a Centrex III spin-off, minicomputer-based switches from vendors such as Rolm and AT&T, and microcomputer-based products such as CXC and NEC. ∎

Edwin R. Coover, who holds B. A. and M. A. degrees from the University of Virginia and a Ph.D. from the University of Minnesota, has been with Mitre Corp. since 1982 and is currently on staff in the Systems and Information Department. Michael J. Kane, who has been with Mitre since 1983, is a member of the technical staff of the Systems and Information Department. Kane earned a B. A. from La Salle College and an M. S. from American University.

G. Alan Baley, Strategic Inc., Cupertino, Calif.

One big headache: Incompatible operating systems and file transfer

A firsthand account of the trials and tribulations of transferring data between computers using CP/M, MS-DOS, and Unix.

ifferent types of computers exist today to accommodate the wide diversity of operating environments. While some serve only a single user, others handle several, or dozens, or even hundreds. Some are oriented toward certain software applications; others handle special peripherals. A host of different hardware architectures have evolved—and just as many different, and incompatible, operating systems to drive them. The result: Moving data between dissimilar operating systems remains a major headache, one that is likely to plague networkers through the foreseeable future.

It inevitably becomes necessary to transfer information, in the form of data files, from one computer to another. However, only under certain ideal conditions can this be done routinely. Specifically, both computers must:
■ Be hardware compatible.
■ Run the same operating system, or compatible subsets (or versions) of the same operating system.
■ Have compatible types of off-line storage media.
■ Run the same application program that uses the data.

If any of these elements is missing, which is likely to be the rule rather than the exception, then there are problems.

Strategic Inc., a market research firm located in California's Silicon Valley, has felt the pains of rapid growth and expansion, just like many other firms in this region. For Strategic, whose business is compiling and publishing market research reports and analyses, these pains have been most acutely felt in the effort to manage information flow.

Growth carries with it an ever-increasing need for automation, which invariably results in an increasing investment in computer equipment per employee. In Strategic's case, some new equipment replaced older

gear, but most was added over time as required to automate new functions in different departments. As do many firms today, Strategic has a variety of in-house computer equipment from different vendors. The inventory currently includes:
■ Two multi-user processors from Molecular Computing running essentially a CP/M-derivative operating system—one for accounting and electronic mail applications and another for administration, marketing, and text editing.
■ Four different processors running MS-DOS version 2.1: an IBM PC/XT for spreadsheet and plotting, a Texas Instruments micro for sales, a Compaq for use by authors, and a Logical LX for use by management.
■ Two different processors running Unix: a Sun Microsystems 2/120 (Unix 4.2) both for graphics and for publishing and a Plexus P35 (Unix 3.2) for database development.
■ A Tandy Model 100, running Microsoft Basic, for troubleshooting.

A broadband local network from Sytek provides communications links between the different computers and affords a flexible and consistent method of connecting terminals and modems to whatever computer is desired (Fig. 1). In addition, we found that the local network can be a valuable tool for managing a growing communications network. For file transfer, however, the role of the local network is minimal. It essentially enables users to electronically switch from one computer port to another, although it additionally provides for automatic speed detection and protocol translation between devices.

The need for file transfer between this diversified lot became unavoidable. Strategic's production procedures require that many departments be able to access and work on the same file at any stage of the cycle.

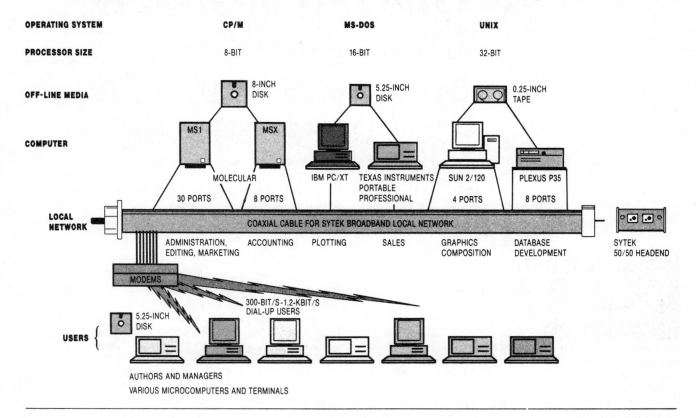

1. Mixed bag. *The in-house computer configuration at Strategic Inc. is shown. A broadband local network allows for the electrical connection of any user to any* computer, and between any two computers, but moving files between the different operating systems posed many problems that were finally solved.

OPERATING SYSTEM	CP/M	MS-DOS	UNIX
PROCESSOR SIZE	8-BIT	16-BIT	32-BIT

OFF-LINE MEDIA: 8-INCH DISK — 5.25-INCH DISK — 0.25-INCH TAPE

COMPUTER: MS1 / MSX (MOLECULAR) — IBM PC/XT / TEXAS INSTRUMENTS PORTABLE PROFESSIONAL — SUN 2/120 / PLEXUS P35

30 PORTS / 8 PORTS — 4 PORTS / 8 PORTS

LOCAL NETWORK: COAXIAL CABLE FOR SYTEK BROADBAND LOCAL NETWORK — SYTEK 50/50 HEADEND

ADMINISTRATION, EDITING, MARKETING — ACCOUNTING — PLOTTING — SALES — GRAPHICS COMPOSITION — DATABASE DEVELOPMENT

MODEMS — 5.25-INCH DISK — 300-BIT/S-1.2-KBIT/S DIAL-UP USERS

USERS — AUTHORS AND MANAGERS — VARIOUS MICROCOMPUTERS AND TERMINALS

This is due, in part, to the fact that the reports include numerous charts and graphs. A report is turned around several times in the production cycle to accommodate copy editing, review, and graphics integration.

Until 1982, all of these functions were performed on the same CP/M-based Molecular computer. Two things occurred about that time, however, that prompted a change in the status quo. First, many of our researchers and analysts acquired their own microcomputers and preferred using them to the existing 8-bit CP/M-based Wordstar application. Secondly, we found the graphics capability of the Molecular to be too limited, and the many graphics programs available for the IBM Personal Computer appeared to be far superior.

We began using IBM and compatible PCs for the initial draft text preparation and for advanced graphics work. This migration, undoubtedly experienced in many other organizations for many of the same reasons, is illustrated in Figure 2. And, as did many other companies, we discovered that we had to perform file transfer between the different operating environments.

MS-DOS to CP/M

We believed that transferring files from the MS-DOS PC to the CP/M-based Molecular computer would be a trivial matter. The Molecular had a communications software program called Modem-7, which reportedly was a compatible version of XModem, a popular CP/M

program in the public domain that employs a frequently used file transfer protocol. In addition, scores of communications programs are available for the PC, many of which claim to support the XModem protocol.

Our plan was to allow researchers and authors to transfer small files directly into the Molecular via dial-up phone lines at 300 bit/s or 1.2 kbit/s. Larger files, we anticipated, would first be brought in-house on floppy disks, and then read by a PC that was hardwired to communicate at 9.6 kbit/s directly to the Molecular.

Things were not, however, as simple as they appeared. Modem-7, we discovered, had been modified for the multi-user environment of the Molecular to the extent that it no longer supported the XModem protocol. (CP/M is traditionally a single-user operating sys-

---

2. Migration. *A common situation developed rapidly at Strategic, starting in 1982, users preferred their own MS-DOS to the in-house CP/M computer.*

	1ST DRAFT	→ EDIT →	NEXT DRAFT	→ GRAPHICS →	PRINTING
1982	CP/M	CP/M	CP/M	CP/M	CP/M
1983	MS-DOS	CP/M	CP/M	MS-DOS	CP/M
1984	MS-DOS	CP/M	CP/M	UNIX	UNIX

tem.) The problem, we found, was that our Modem-7 provided no form of flow control, which is necessary to prevent one computer from sending data to another faster than it can be received. To use Modem-7 to receive files, the sending PC would have had to transmit at a very slow rate—and delay about one second after sending each line of text. This was unacceptable as it would have tied up our in-house PC for long periods of time simply to transmit files, making it unavailable for other purposes.

We then tried another popular communications software package, PC-Talk. This did not work either, but for a different reason: We discovered that, with PC-Talk, control S characters that were part of the Wordstar file would cause PC-Talk to abort. (Wordstar, a flexible and ubiquitous word processing software product, makes extensive use of control characters for special functions, such as underlining and printer commands, but these can wreak havoc when files must pass through other software packages, which may interpret the unusual character strings differently.)

The answer, we thought, was to find a software vendor whose communications program had versions written both for the MS-DOS PC, as well as for the CP/M-based Molecular. Several vendors initially claimed to provide this, but only one of the many we contacted was actually able to deliver what we sought: Communications Research Group Inc., with its software product, BLAST.

BLAST, however, accommodates only one user at a time. When running on the multi-user Molecular, it locked out all other users from the system. It was not practical, we determined, to interrupt 30 users whenever one needed to transfer a file. So back we went to the drawing board.

By experimenting, we finally happened upon a reasonably acceptable solution. This, unexpectedly, involved using no communications software on the Molecular at all, but using a communications software program called Crosstalk, by Microstuf Inc., on the PC.

Procedure
The ultimate destination of the files being sent to the Molecular computer is the Wordstar application. So for editing, we experimented to see how fast Wordstar could accept text files sent directly from a PC. We found that 90 percent of the time, a sustained transfer at 1.2 kbit/s could be accommodated. The procedure we adopted, then, was as follows:
1. Start up Crosstalk on the PC and configure the transmission speed for 1.2 kbit/s.
2. Place Crosstalk into the terminal mode, which makes the PC look like an ordinary ASCII terminal to the destination device attached to the PC's communications port, in this case the Molecular.
3. Log on to the Molecular, specifying the user and account where the transferred file is to reside; the Molecular then views the PC as just another user typing at a terminal.
4. Load Wordstar on the Molecular and open a new file; then wait for Wordstar's prompt to begin entering lines of data.

5. Via a predefined function key on the PC, revert back to Crosstalk.
6. Enter the Crosstalk file transfer mode, and then enter the name of the file on the PC to be transferred.
7. File transfer begins, and the operator can observe lines of text on the screen as they are sent to the Wordstar program on the Molecular.
8. After the entire file is transferred, Crosstalk asks if another file is to be sent. If not, switch Crosstalk again into the terminal mode. Enter the Wordstar commands to save the file and exit (control K and X characters).
9. Log off the Molecular and, via another function key, revert back to Crosstalk. File transfer is complete.

This procedure works well unless the destination Molecular becomes loaded down, which in our experience, occurs less than 10 percent of the time. When this happens, however, switching to 300 bit/s will generally permit a sustained file transfer to be accomplished.

CP/M to Unix
At Strategic, after reports are edited and in final form on the CP/M-based Molecular, they must then be transferred to a Unix-based computer (in our case a Sun Microsystems supermini) where page layouts are done and graphics are added. And, as with the MS-DOS and CP/M computers, all the communications software tools seemed to already be there.

A communications software program for the Sun, called UModem, was provided to us by the retail vendor (not Sun, which is the OEM). Also, we had hoped that we could use Modem-7 on the Molecular to send files to the Sun. However, UModem came, and still does come, without the backup and background documentation normally accompanying a software product. What's more, the retailer's support representative in our area knew nothing about UModem (and also, as it turned out, knew little about Unix).

Being novice Unix users, we were again left to fend for ourselves. We decided to try the same approach that we used for the PC-to-Molecular file transfer. We discovered that a basic Unix command, DD, allowed information to be copied from a terminal (attached to the Sun) onto a disk file. We hoped that if we could get the Molecular, emulating a terminal, to connect to the Sun, then we could use this feature to snatch a file from the Molecular and write it to the Unix system's disk. We were wrong.

The Molecular computer is really an aggregation of several independent 8-bit processors, which share a common disk and housing. Each processor resides on its own card and bears two communications ports, labeled "A" and "B." The A port connects to a terminal and provides the user interface, while the B port normally interfaces to a printer.

When running Modem-7, however, the B port is used to connect to another computer. When in the "terminal" mode, everything typed at the terminal is read into the A port and routed immediately out to the B port, and vice versa (Fig. 3). We ran a four-wire cable from a Molecular B port directly to a terminal port on the Sun, making sure the speed, parity, and so on matched, and

3. CP/M to Unix. *Using Modem-7 software, data sent in to port "A" of the CP/M processor card is routed to port "B," which is hardwired to the Unix processor.*

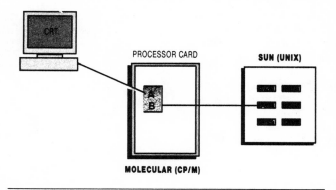

then we decided to conduct a test.

From a terminal connected to the A port on the Molecular (on the same card where the B port was connected to the Sun), we ran Modem-7 and selected terminal mode. We were then able to see the Unix log-in message prompt by typing a return. We were beyond ourselves with excitement. We logged on to Unix and listed a few files to verify the integrity of our connection.

We then entered the DD Unix facility by typing "DD, OF=TEST." (The "OF=" is the way of specifying the name of the output file, which in our case was the new file being created under Unix). To simulate a file being transferred, we entered a few lines, following each with a "RETURN," and then typed a control-D to denote the end of the file to Unix. The DD process finished and reported back the number of lines received. We examined the file "test" using another command ("CAT") and saw that it had the correct data in it.

We thought it was appropriate then to try the real thing, using basically the same procedure:
1. Log on to Molecular and run Modem-7.
2. Enter "terminal" mode and log on to the Sun.
3. Enter the DD command.
4. Interrupt Modem-7 (done by typing two special characters that are not sent out the B port).
5. Switch from "terminal" mode to "file transfer" mode and specify a CP/M file to be transferred.
6. Observe the lines of the file being transferred on the screen.

At this point, however, we saw a lot of garbage, and it was obvious the transfer was not working. We reduced the speed to 300 bit/s but met with the same results. We then connected our diagnostic Tandy Model 100 to the Sun and had the same problem: Data sent in a continuous stream from disk was being garbled while data typed at the terminal was being transferred correctly.

The problem appeared to be with the Sun. Through trial and error, we were able to correct the problem, via the Model 100, by specifying two stop bits per character. Unfortunately, the Molecular could not be configured to send two stop bits, and there was no provision in Unix for specifying one stop bit. Apparently stuck, we called the retailer who sold us the Sun. No help. We

called Sun directly and a special fix to Unix was sent the next day.

With the fix in place, we tried the transfer again. This time the DD command aborted near the end of the transfer and no data was saved. After much testing with the Model 100 at the Unix end, we discovered that Modem-7 sends a control Z character at the end of every file transfer which, we learned, aborts Unix commands.

We tried placing a control D character (Unix end of file) at the end of the file, hoping that Unix would see it before the control Z character and that the DD command would end normally. It didn't work; the command still aborted. We finally found that the control D character followed by about 60 spaces would do the trick.

This was hardly an elegant solution because it was complex and difficult for users to understand. Also, it limited file transfer to 1.2 kbit/s because of the lack of flow control at the Molecular end. We continued to search for a better way.

Thanks to a tip from an associate at Britton-Lee, a manufacturer of database machines in nearby Los Gatos, Calif., we finally came up with a much faster solution, and one that allowed us to control the file transfer process from the Unix-based Sun. As with the CP/M-to-MS-DOS file transfer, the answer was to have no communications program running on the Molecular. The configuration that we used, illustrated in Figure 4, worked. Using Unix configuration tables, we configured one of the Sun's terminal ports for connection to another host (computer) and named it "Molecular." We ran a four-wire direct cable between this port and an "A" port on the Molecular; the "B" port is not used. Then, any user on the Sun was able to initiate a file transfer using the following procedure:
1. Using the Unix TIP command, type "TIP MOLECULAR." A message then appears indicating that a link is established and the user is in terminal mode. Log on to the Molecular under the user and account where the file to be transferred resides.
2. Signal the TIP process to initiate a "receive file" sequence. This is done by typing two special characters. The user is then prompted to supply a name for the file to be created on the Sun.
3. The user is then asked to supply a command for the remote (Molecular) computer, which will initiate file

4. Unix-controlled. *To solve the CP/M-to-Unix file transfer dilemma, the TIP facility of Unix allowed an operator to retrieve files from the CP/M computer.*

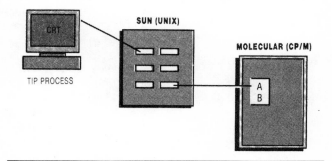

transfer. Type the CP/M command TYPE, and then the name of the file, followed by a "return." The remote Molecular views the command as if it were entered from a local terminal.

The CP/M TYPE command will cause a file to be displayed on the terminal. Of course the "terminal" in this case is the link to one of the Sun's terminal ports, which in turn is linked to the Sun terminal running the TIP facility. It is still necessary to append a control D character at the end of the file to be transferred from the CP/M computer, but this is a small price to pay for the resulting capability.

File transfer using this procedure will work at up to 2.4 kbit/s, and presumably it will work at even higher data rates. The TIP facility, by the way, also gives a running count of the number of lines transferred and, at the end, an elapsed time for the transfer.

The PC-to-Molecular and Molecular-to-Sun represent the extent of our direct experience with file transfers between different operating systems to date. Our next project, of course, will be to transfer files between MS-DOS-based PCs and Unix in both directions.

Nothing for granted

A number of tenets can be extracted from our experience, which should be of use to others who find themselves in the same situation:

1. Take nothing for granted.
2. Consider buying and using a troubleshooting portable computer equipped with every conceivable communications option (such as a Tandy Model 100). This, along with a breakout box (which lets you check the signals on communications lines), can save a lot of time.
3. Conduct initial tests at low speed, first by sending a few characters, then by transferring small files, and finally by transferring full-size files.
4. Use the same set of test files, which helps when problems occur.
5. Vary only one parameter at a time when looking for problems. This may require more tests, but it is easier than varying, say, data rate, parity and stop bits on two computers at the same time.
6. When looking for communications software, talk directly with vendor's technical representatives (salespeople generally are ill-informed), and ask questions about any functional restrictions or loss of capability evident on your specific computer when running their package. Also, make sure the control characters (if any) that are used to control a program will not appear inadvertently in the middle of the files to be transferred.
7. Above all, be patient, persistent, and methodical, and don't hesitate to check all possible resources for help. ∎

G. Alan Baley, a sales and marketing consultant currently employed by Strategic Inc., has over 16 years experience in the computer/communications industry. He has previously worked for the U. S. Department of Commerce, Stanford Research Institute, and Hewlett-Packard Co.

Tom Highly, Forte Data Systems, San Jose, Calif.

Strategies to link mainframes and microcomputers

Last year, 'micro-to-mainframe link' became one of the most overused phrases in the computer industry. Four categories can help clarify the confusion.

Over the past several months, hardware and software vendors have given data processing and communications managers better tools to satisfy microcomputer users' demands for improved mainframe access. Although many firms have rushed to please microcomputer users by implementing simple but uncontrollable types of micro-to-mainframe links, managers have remained justifiably cautious. That caution is about to pay off, because some of the latest micro-to-mainframe links offer microcomputer users the easy access they want, while still allowing managers of management information systems (MIS) control of that access.

Despite the emergence of these more complete micro-to-mainframe links, some managers are still confused about how to choose products. Part of the problem comes from the fact that the term "micro-to-mainframe link" is used to describe several different categories of products. When attempting to understand the micro-to-mainframe marketplace, some of the most important considerations to examine are the level of accessibility, the speed of the link, user transparency, and methods of controlling access.

Currently available micro-to-mainframe links tend to fall into one or more of four categories:
- Terminal emulators that simulate keystrokes entered by a human operator.
- File transfer programs that send data one screen at a time.
- Device emulators requiring microcomputer- and host-executed programs.
- Information-extraction packages for the selection of specified data.

A terminal emulator makes microcomputer transactions with the host look like operations on a dumb terminal (Fig. 1). The microcomputer merely stands in for the dumb terminal, except that the small computer can run software designed to ease access to the mainframe. The terminal emulator makes the microcomputer software appear as though a user were typing in commands at a terminal keyboard.

Limited uses, low speed
No matter how much a microcomputer-based software program seems to improve communications, the fact remains that this type of link is essentially a method of interfacing with a host-based editor rather than with a communications package. As such, the link can perform a very limited range of functions.

Beyond restricted functionality, one of the biggest problems with this type of link is its speed. Regardless of how fast the microcomputer software can generate command sequences, the standard 3270 terminal's coaxial cable can only accept data at about 120 characters per second. Transactions in either direction have essentially no error recovery because the terminal interface does not incorporate a communications protocol; this is not surprising, because the connection is intended only for dumb-terminal use.

Finally, an emulation link can deal only with text. Unless microcomputer users employ the formatting features of the editor on the host, this limitation prevents them from performing basic functions such as reformatting data and inserting control characters for a mainframe printer. At slow transfer rates, a host-based editor is clumsy at best and requires users to learn the details of the editor's operation in addition to learning to use microcomputer-based applications. In short, a link that only does emulation is rather primitive and permits neither ease of use for the operator nor data security for the MIS manager.

The second type of micro-to-mainframe link, the

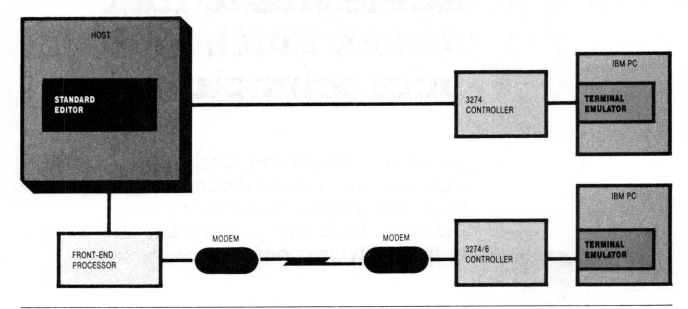

one-screen-at-a-time file transfer program, fares somewhat better in speed but suffers from the same fundamental problems that limit the emulation link. The microcomputer still interfaces with a host-based editor rather than with a communications package. However, the screen-oriented links do provide a significant speed improvement — to about 400 to 500 characters per second — by taking advantage of special software features on the host's editor that exploit the functions of 3270-type devices (Fig. 2). Still, this type of link uses the coax cable employed in the emulation link to accommodate the line speed and the interface specifications needed by IBM mainframes.

The specific characteristics of the screen-oriented link depend on the software running on the host, but in general, such products do not offer much error recovery. Again, this is because the interface is designed for use by a human operator using a terminal rather than for a microcomputer transferring entire files upon request.

Another limitation of these links is that, like emulation links, they can only transfer text. This restriction again requires the use of the host's editor to perform formatting functions such as controlling whether records are fixed or variable, expanding tabs, and allocating space.

Synchronized software

The third type of micro-to-mainframe link employs a device emulator, but it also uses special software that runs on both the microcomputer and the host (Fig. 3). The performance of such links depends almost entirely on the software, but there are some features common across a number of products. Because the link does not depend on standard interface software in either the microcomputer or host, the link can boost the transfer rate to 6,000 to 8,000 characters per second. (Data is

still transferred one screen at a time, however.) The user can also control the precise allocation parameters of a new file, and data can be directed to an internal reader or to a print spooler. Further, users can be given control of such functions as tab expansion and line numbering. The special interface can also implement a protocol for good error recovery and can handle any type of data.

The user's access to the mainframe can be made even more clear if the link software does data reformatting. Mainframe databases are too complex to be accessed freely without bringing a great deal of intelligence to the task of data extraction, but it is possible to reformat some host files into standard formats such as Data Interchange Format (DIF, a de facto standard format for spreadsheets) or Comma-Separated Variables (a format popularized by the microcomputer database management package dBase II).

It is not particularly important whether this reformatting takes place on the host or the microcomputer. What is important is that the reformatting operation be an integral part of the data transfer process so that the link will be easy to use. The transfer task is clumsy if files must be reformatted with one program and then transferred to the microcomputer with another program.

Software to implement this type of link usually comes bundled with 3270 emulation hardware. Thus, although this software is generally the least expensive way to link microcomputers and mainframes, it often represents little more than an enticement for buying the emulation boards. Data extraction features are not usually included in this free software, because extraction is difficult to implement in a way that incorporates both ease of use and data security.

The fourth type of link, which could be called the

2. More space. *In this type of micro-to-mainframe link, the file transfer program typically runs as an application in the Time Sharing Option of Conversational Monitoring* *System environments. Many of these products allow the user to access previously defined mass storage space or printing facilities.*

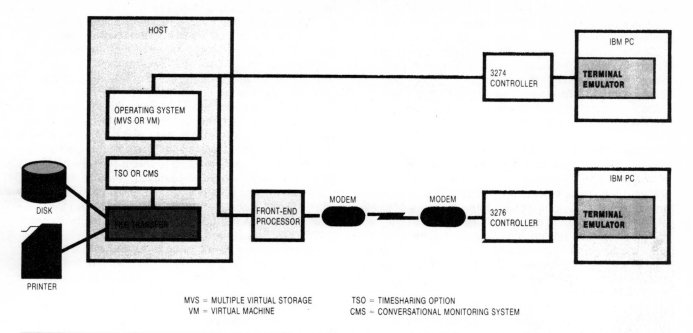

HOST

OPERATING SYSTEM
(MVS OR VM)

TSO OR CMS

FILE TRANSFER

DISK

PRINTER

FRONT-END
PROCESSOR

MODEM

MODEM

3276
CONTROLLER

3274
CONTROLLER

IBM PC

TERMINAL
EMULATOR

IBM PC

TERMINAL
EMULATOR

MVS = MULTIPLE VIRTUAL STORAGE
VM = VIRTUAL MACHINE

TSO = TIMESHARING OPTION
CMS = CONVERSATIONAL MONITORING SYSTEM

active information extraction package, actually represents an extension of the capabilities offered by the other types of links. In a sense, it is not a separate type of micro-to-mainframe link, since it employs one of the first three communications methods to allow users to interact with mainframe data. For illustrative purposes, though, it is useful to consider data extraction software as part of a complete link between the microcomputer user and the mainframe data.

The extraction link is also distinctive because of the difficulty of implementing the necessary extraction functions. These functions are in fact the most important capabilities that microcomputer users really want—the ability to freely access data kept on company mainframes without using esoteric search commands. Further complicating the issue is the fact that many microcomputer users also want to reverse the extraction process in order to use the database on the mainframe to store microcomputer data.

Products that offer these capabilities are almost always quite expensive (costing upwards of $75,000) and restrict users to closed environments (they work only with one vendor's mainframe product—typically a database management system). One reason for these restrictions comes from the nature of microcomputer and mainframe software: Since there is no standard file format, the link vendor must know what type of files the microcomputer software expects (Multiplan, Lotus 1-2-3, and Wordstar files are very different) and the particular format of the mainframe software files. This latter factor is particularly bothersome because the same database management system may have different file formats on different applications.

Another reason for the extraction package's limita-

tions is the difficulty of interpreting users' requests and converting those requests into appropriate actions. Because users need and want to be shielded from complex mainframe database manager commands that specify the data precisely, their commands will tend to be more simple and thus contain some ambiguity. The extraction package must have the intelligence to determine what data the user really wants when he or she requests, for instance, the sales figures for the

3. Advanced. *The link software in the mainframe and the microcomputer work in conjunction. They can achieve transfers of binary data files.*

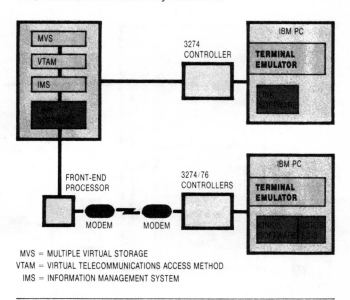

MVS

VTAM

IMS

LINK SOFTWARE

FRONT-END
PROCESSOR

MODEM

MODEM

3274
CONTROLLER

3274/76
CONTROLLERS

IBM PC

TERMINAL
EMULATOR

LINK
SOFTWARE

IBM PC

TERMINAL
EMULATOR

LINK
SOFTWARE

LOTUS
1-2-3

MVS = MULTIPLE VIRTUAL STORAGE
VTAM = VIRTUAL TELECOMMUNICATIONS ACCESS METHOD
IMS = INFORMATION MANAGEMENT SYSTEM

company's best-selling products. (Of course, this would not be done in English, but in a more restricted language that is less precise than a query language.) The intelligence required to translate ambiguous requests to specific ones is one reason why even closed-environment extraction programs are very expensive.

One way to ease this ambiguity problem is for users to employ data specification instructions that are understood by the extraction package. This approach forces users to learn the extraction package's language; thus it simply substitutes this language for the language of the mainframe's database manager.

The benefits are simple

The generation of micro-to-mainframe links now being introduced combines characteristics of the third type of link with the active extraction concept. The result is an environment that incorporates some measure of intelligence for interpreting users' data requests.

The benefits of this environment are neither complex nor obscure. One feature that is finding acceptance is the microcomputer's use of mainframe facilities for mass storage. In fact, it is possible to justify the cost of a micro-to-mainframe link solely on the basis of savings in mass storage costs. Instead of paying about $1,000 for 10 Mbytes of Winchester disk capacity at the microcomputer, users could take advantage of mainframe disk capacity that costs about $3,000 for 600 Mbytes. The large computer's storage is cheaper by a factor of 20 or more.

An additional advantage is that the mainframe capacity can be shared by many users. Each user can have an allocated capacity of, for instance, 32 Mbytes; but any unused capacity remains available for other users. On a microcomputer, in contrast, unused Winchester capacity is simply wasted.

Users cannot be relied upon to back up microcom-

puter data on a hard disk. Most users are very unfaithful to the time-consuming task of backing up data regularly, and almost no microcomputer users employ off-site archiving. Data stored on the mainframe, on the other hand, is subject to the regular backup procedures and off-site storage used for all mainframe data. With the extraction-based micro-to-mainframe links, the microcomputer user gets backup facilities that are free of hassles and encompass protection against disasters such as fire.

The extensive micro-to-mainframe links furnish on-line storage for each microcomputer user by maintaining a large file of virtual disk data and control data for each user. The control file specifies parameters such as the storage capacity entitled to the user and whether other users are authorized to have access to that data. Optimum access is usually obtained by using BDAM (Basic Direct Access Method) and an indexing file based on VSAM (Virtual Storage Access Method) or KSDS (Key Sequenced Data Set).

Access to host data can be furnished with a roughly similar strategy. To get information from a mainframe database, for instance, a microcomputer program requests a specific file. This block of data might be termed a pseudo-file, because it does not exist in the form of a previously defined file on the host. Defining the extent and parameters of the pseudo-file is the responsibility of MIS managers, who therefore control how much data a user can access.

To see how this method works, consider a microcomputer user running Lotus 1-2-3. To get some data, he or she might enter the following commands:

```
/FILE
RETRIEVE
X:SOMESTUF.DAT
```

---

4. Complete environment for downloading. *Active information extraction packages typically run under the Virtual Telecommunications Access Method and allow* *users private and common access to on-line storage facilities. In addition, users can usually employ the packages for accessing mainframe databases.*

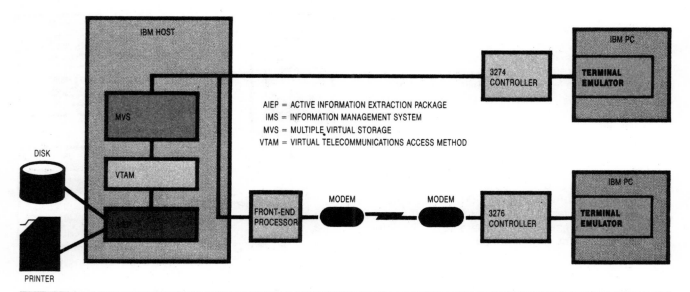

AIEP = ACTIVE INFORMATION EXTRACTION PACKAGE
IMS = INFORMATION MANAGEMENT SYSTEM
MVS = MULTIPLE VIRTUAL STORAGE
VTAM = VIRTUAL TELECOMMUNICATIONS ACCESS METHOD

The first two lines instruct Lotus 1-2-3 to retrieve a file, and the last line specifies the file. The "X" before the file name would normally designate the disk drive on which the file resides. But in this case, the "X" drive designation refers to a mainframe, and the user may know nothing else about accessing the host. Special link software running on the microcomputer traps the "X" and prevents the microcomputer's standard BIOS (basic input/output system) from interpreting the command as a reference to a drive that does not exist. The link software then follows the protocol needed to communicate the command to the host. From the host's point of view, the file SOMESTUF.DAT is a pseudo-file that must be interpreted by mainframe link software. This software makes the following conversion:

```
X:SOMESTUF.DAT =
IMS INFORMATION EXTRACT — LOTUS FORMAT
```

The link software extracts data to fill SOMESTUF.DAT from IMS (Information Management System) using a predefined information extraction procedure. It then converts the data to Lotus 1-2-3 format.

The pseudo-file approach creates an environment for host access in which the user manipulates only microcomputer files. Thus, MIS managers control access and prevent users from inadvertently damaging mainframe data. At the same time, users get the desired data and the ability to manipulate it with familiar programs. If the information extraction link is properly implemented, the mainframe transactions are almost completely transparent to the microcomputer user.

Control

Figure 4 shows the structure of a micro-to-mainframe link that provides both on-line storage and pseudo-file host access. It is identical to Figure 3 except that an MIS control file has been added to the mainframe software.

The MIS control file specifies what data each user can access on the host. For example, the control file might restrict a given user to mainframe data that has a high-level index equal to a certain value. The alternative to this arrangement is to simply give any raw data to a microcomputer program, which then puts the data into a standard file format (such as DIF). This method is easier to implement but allows no control mechanisms by the MIS department. However, since the link provides host access based on physical data content rather than the logical content, any security scheme implemented under the microcomputer's operating system will still be effective under the link.

In addition to ensuring data security, this type of micro-to-mainframe link should permit transparency of use. Specifically, no emulation session should be needed to log on to the mainframe because the link should automatically emulate the log-on procedure of the link facilities on the host. The part of the link that replaces the microcomputer's BIOS performs log-on functions, such as determining user identification, setting the microcomputer's clock, and checking for any available electronic mail. These actions are performed when the microcomputer is initialized.

In an active extraction link, there will likely be host software that establishes and maintains communications with the microcomputer. This software could be a VTAM (Virtual Telecommunications Access Method) application that runs as a started task on the MVS (Multiple Virtual Storage) operating system or a disconnected server machine on the Virtual Machine operating system. The software performs initialization housekeeping, then waits for its log-on module to be entered. The log-on module verifies the user's ID and password and establishes table entries to control the session and mark the user as being logged on.

Control information

At this point, the link's control structure will likely be used, if one exists. For example, a link's control structure might allow users different levels of access and be allocated so that users at one level cannot obtain data stored at a higher access level. After logging the user on, the log-on module would instruct the microcomputer to provide control information about the user, such as the user number and security number. With virtual floppy disks, for example, users whose access codes are lower than that of the disk's owner cannot use the disk, even if it is unlocked.

After the automatic log-on, the user might see a DOS (disk operating system) prompt, after which he or she can enter either normal DOS commands or link commands. The latter are in the form of DOS commands in order to simplify their use and may be exactly the same as the DOS versions. This would be most likely the case if the link implemented a virtual peripheral. Files are written to a virtual hard disk using the designation for a disk drive (C: or D:, for instance). To use the host's printer from an MS-DOS microcomputer, the user can employ either the DOS device name PRN or the control and PRTSC keys — exactly as though a physical printer were attached to the microcomputer.

Another important feature from the user's point of view is that high-overhead operations — such as extracting useful information from a host database — are done on the host. The data extraction task can run as a batch job on the mainframe.

Acts like the real thing

Primary features of a comprehensive micro-to-mainframe link are the virtual peripheral capability and a cross-system link that handles the microcomputer's interaction with host data. With virtual peripheral software, microcomputer users conceivably could have any mainframe device at their disposal, such as a virtual hard disk, virtual floppy disk, and virtual printer.

Although the mainframe obviously is not expected to incorporate any kind of real floppy disk, the link must — while still retaining terms that are familiar to users — distinguish between the virtual hard and floppy disks to provide two storage characteristics. From the user's point of view, the virtual hard disk should work just like a physical hard disk attached to the microcomputer. The virtual floppy disk should behave just like a physical floppy disk, except that the user cannot remove the virtual disk from the drive. The user should have facilities, however, to mount and dismount virtual disks, pass them to other link users, lock and unlock disks, and inventory and destroy disks. If constructed like this, the virtual floppy furnishes a method to share and temporarily store information; otherwise, the performance is essentially the same as that of the virtual hard disk.

The other virtual peripheral, the printer, could function just as a local physical printer, except that the host can spool several files before printing them. In this environment, all the files are collected and sent to the printer and stored in a file until the user enters a CLOSE command, which prompts the host to print all the data.

A cross-system link operates via the standard DOS COPY command. If this facility is implemented, the link software replaces the standard command with a version that permits users to specify a host file name as the source or destination of a copy. The link would ask the user to provide a minimal amount of information, if any, about the nature of the copy operation. The task would usually run as though both the source and the destination were files on the microcomputer's local disk drives.

Looking to buy?
Aspects of a micro-to-mainframe link that bear close examination include the extent of the virtual peripheral capability and the location of the software that implements the data extraction function. Some products limit the size of virtual disks to the same capacity available on a physical floppy disk (only 360 kbytes), although there is little reason to do so. Some products do not include a virtual printer capability, even though the savings compared with buying a physical printer for each microcomputer user are generally enough to pay for the micro-to-mainframe link. Finally, some products bring raw host data down to the microcomputer and perform data extraction routines on the microcomputer itself. This practice is inefficient as well as lacking in control for MIS managers.

As micro-to-mainframe links continue to evolve, they will incorporate many of the techniques being developed in artificial intelligence research. Such methods will enable much greater user interaction with host data regardless of its logical location or content.

More immediately, some links are beginning to offer electronic mail and the ability to run microcomputer-initiated batch jobs. With the addition of electronic mail, a micro-to-mainframe link can offer all the benefits associated with local networks, with some added advantages. While local networks are often limited by the computer used as a file server, for example, micro-to-mainframe links use the effectively unlimited resources of a mainframe computer as the file server. And at the same time, micro-to-mainframe links can go far beyond local networks by providing the ability to run mainframe batch jobs for large-scale data extraction or even performing remote job entry functions. ∎

For slightly over one year, Mr. Highly has been the director of mainframe software for Forte.

Talking true SNA over async links—why not?

Travelers' message to other IBM users: Shop around. Spurning dial SDLC and 800 numbers for packet nets and a micro-based SNA emulator saved over $1 million a year.

Microcomputers and packet-switching have changed the way The Travelers Insurance Companies does business. The Travelers is a financial services organization with assets of over $36 billion. It manages $38 billion in investment funds and has over $143 billion of life insurance in force. The company insures more than 5 million people for automobiles and homes and provides group life, health, and accident insurance for more than 8 million employees in 90,000 firms. A company this size might seem inertial, capable only of continued motion in its current direction and velocity. And yet, in data communications at least, The Travelers appears to be moving quickly in innovative ways.

Managing records and transactions in this paper-intensive enterprise has called for an aggressive approach to technology. The Travelers prides itself on the automation it employs in delivering its products and services. The company's extensive SNA network spans the country, joining over 11,000 devices. Upgrades to more sophisticated front-end processors, IBM 3725s, are proceeding apace, as are plans for the deployment of higher-speed links that will join these machines to a phalanx of IBM mainframes.

However, amidst this seemingly undiluted endorsement of SNA, The Travelers' telecommunications group is internally promoting an arrangement it designed to carry SNA data over public packet-switching networks to asynchronously connected dial-up microcomputers.

Plans for this configuration are, by any standard, ambitious. Micro-to-mainframe SNA emulation was conceived of two years ago and has been in production at The Travelers since November of 1984. Hundreds of non-Travelers employees are currently using it to communicate with The Travelers host applications via public packet networks. The goal of The Travelers' communications department is to provide 2,000 agents with SNA emulation by the end of 1985 (see table).

Many of the current users are companies, insured by The Travelers, that handle their own insurance portfolios and perform sophisticated risk management. With the SNA emulator, they can access claim information from the host databases through a specialized time-sharing service. Loading this data onto their microcomputers, they can summarize and manipulate it with their own spreadsheet software.

The SNA emulator seems destined to remake The Travelers' network. The first phase of the conversion to SNA emulation will be to seek a 40-to-50 percent cost savings over 800 service by implementing public packet network access in three-quarters of The Travelers' field offices. Phase two would be to provide larger cities, such as Atlanta, San Francisco, Chicago, New York, Boston, and Los Angeles, with their own packet assembler/disassemblers (PADs) connected via leased lines to a public packet network.

Commercial and technical motives

With its enormous investment in IBM-style networking, why is The Travelers at all interested in asynchronous communications and, in particular, public packet networks? The answer lies in the business and technological environment in which the SNA emulator was built.

The delivery of financial services has evolved in synchrony with its underlying technology. Before networking, there were large mainframes, accessible, though barely, from unsophisticated terminals. The first machine capable of telecommunications at The Travelers, a Univac 490 installed in the early 1960s, performed centralized number-crunching and record-keeping for the small field offices, which kept records manually, returning only summaries to the home office.

Development and growth of SNA emulation

	NUMBER OF USERS (INCLUDING FUTURE ESTIMATES)	
1983		
OCTOBER		REALIZED NEED, CONSIDERED POSSIBLE SOLUTION
DECEMBER		RESEARCHED AVAILABLE ALTERNATIVES
1984		
FEBRUARY		DEVELOPED ECONOMIC MODEL, BEGAN PROJECT
MARCH		CONSTRUCTED PROTOTYPE
EARLY APRIL		VISITED PACKET-SWITCHING NETWORK VENDORS
LATE APRIL		BEGAN FULL-SCALE IMPLEMENTATION; WROTE DETAILED DESCRIPTION OF A FULL-BLOWN SNA EMULATOR
SEPTEMBER		WORKING EMULATOR WITH LIMITED FUNCTION
NOVEMBER	5	PILOT PRODUCTION VERSION
1985		
APRIL	350	FULL PRODUCTION VERSION
JUNE	500	
AUGUST	750	
SEPTEMBER	1,000	
OCTOBER	1,250	COMPLETION OF APPLICATION PROGRAM INTERFACE (API)
NOVEMBER	1,500	
DECEMBER	1,750	
1986		
JANUARY	2,000	
DECEMBER	3,000	

Economies of scale, in terms of people, equipment, facilities, and management, led to the establishment of regional field offices. Such back-office functions as issuing policies, processing claims, and billing customers no longer had to be performed in Hartford, Conn. They could be consolidated into the large suburban field offices and handled closer to the agents' locations. The smaller offices were eventually left doing primarily marketing support.

Minicomputers hurried the consolidation of back-office functions. If a field office were large enough to justify its own machine, it could obtain a minicomputer and support multiple users. Many of these offices did a sufficient level of business to warrant a permanent, leased synchronous line to the home office.

The advent of microcomputers added another wrinkle to the scenario. Since many agents now had intelligent devices, there was no need to send paper through a large, intermediate location. Even the smallest agency could access The Travelers' host database directly. The presence of microcomputers in these offices meant that ratings applications and tables could be sent out on a floppy disk and accessed directly at the agent's office.

Microcomputers are making many of the traditional intermediary field-office functions obsolete. No longer does an insurance agent need to telephone a field office to obtain a life insurance quote from a mainframe computer; the calculation can be performed directly on a microcomputer by using software and rate schedules supplied by The Travelers. The processing can go to the data, and vice versa. No longer must a field office handle billing or claim inquiries. Agents can talk directly to the host to determine the status of accounts.

No longer does a provider (doctor, dentist, hospital) have to send The Travelers a claim on paper—only to be rekeyed. Money and time are saved by the company accepting the claims in "soft" form. Hospitals, many of the larger private practices, and service bureaus handling small practitioners send claims electronically via a number of media: tape, disk, emulation of 3270 binary synchronous communications (BSC), and asynchronous microcomputers.

If the parallel between delivering financial services and computing holds up, the next phase in technology might be termed "directed distribution," with standalone, dedicated microcomputers supported by large machines through intelligent and intermittent contact. The SNA emulator developed by The Travelers is a perfect example of directed distribution.

Network setting

The Travelers' SNA network integrates 11,000 minicomputers, microcomputers, and traditional terminals and printers of various types. This distributed hardware is linked to applications running on 17 IBM 308X-class mainframes at data centers in Hartford and in Atlanta, Ga. (Fig. 1). IBM front-ends (3705 and 3725) at the centers serve local boundary circuits and traffic concentrated from the rest of the country.

Each remote access point contains two front-ends linking the data centers with local boundary circuits. SNA's Multisystem Networking Facility (MSNF) is used to route interactive and batch traffic between the domains of the multiple hosts and the front-ends. The backbone network connecting the 31 front-ends consists of 50 intermachine trunks with 56-kbit/s capacity carrying MSNF links. A high-speed T1 circuit links Hartford and Atlanta. The resulting ring structures provide redundant paths for any failed link between a remote access point and a data center.

Boundary circuits between front-end processors and cluster controllers serve over 300 locations around the country. The network contains the equivalent of 612 boundary circuits with 9.6-kbit/s capacity each, including multiplexed links on higher-speed lines.

Nearly two-and-a-half million interactive transactions pass through the network during a typical workday. This traffic includes data related to claims, marketing quotes, electronic mail, management reports, and software development. At night, business data collected throughout the day is up-line loaded from the regional minicomputers to the data center. In the early morning, the network is used to transmit updates to files on the minicomputers. Much of the morning's traffic consists of print data sent to disks at the field offices.

In late 1983, The Travelers began considering ways to approach the growing population of microcomputers

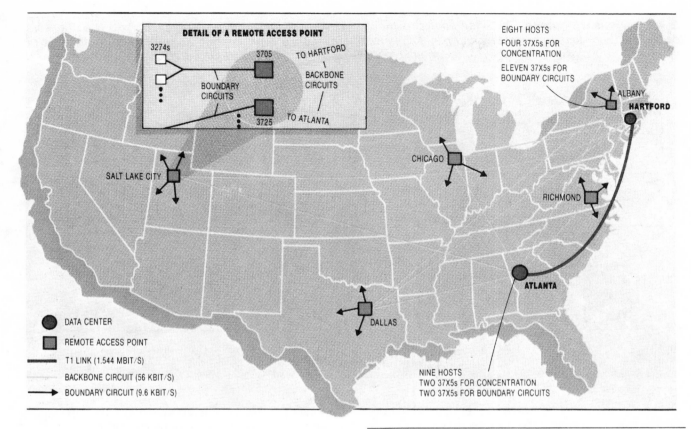

DETAIL OF A REMOTE ACCESS POINT

3274s

3705

TO HARTFORD

BACKBONE CIRCUITS

BOUNDARY CIRCUITS

3725

TO ATLANTA

EIGHT HOSTS
FOUR 37X5s FOR CONCENTRATION
ELEVEN 37X5s FOR BOUNDARY CIRCUITS

ALBANY
HARTFORD

CHICAGO

RICHMOND

SALT LAKE CITY

ATLANTA

DALLAS

NINE HOSTS
TWO 37X5s FOR CONCENTRATION
TWO 37X5s FOR BOUNDARY CIRCUITS

● DATA CENTER

■ REMOTE ACCESS POINT

▬▬ T1 LINK (1.544 MBIT/S)

── BACKBONE CIRCUIT (56 KBIT/S)

→ BOUNDARY CIRCUIT (9.6 KBIT/S)

1. Travelers around the country. The financial services company's large leased-line SNA network links 17 mainframe computers with 31 front-end processors. It strains SNA addressing limitations and is rapidly being supplemented (if not yet supplanted) by the dynamic duo, microcomputers and public data networks.

in agents' offices. Using public packet networks, which offer asynchronous dial access in hundreds of cities, appeared to be the best method of joining the geographically dispersed microcomputers and The Travelers' hosts. To verify this, The Travelers based an economic model on two assumptions:

■ Half of the total 2,000 users would have one 10-minute session with a host on each of 20 working days per month. The other half would be connected for 45 minutes a day.

■ Of the above users, 1,500 (75 percent) could access the public packet network with a local telephone call. The other 500 (25 percent) would use an 800 number directly to The Travelers, which would be less expensive than a long-distance call added to the packet-network charges.

Hourly rates for an 800 number were much higher than those of any of three packet-network vendors examined in early 1984 (Fig. 2). With discounts, the 800-number hourly rate of $19.33 averaged out to $16.10 an hour. In the model, the 2,000 users collectively spent 18,333 hours a month connected to the home office, for a total cost of approximately $295,000 using the 800 service.

Alternatively, three-quarters of the participating agents could be converted to public packet networks. The average situation was assumed to be a user in a medium-density city connecting to Tymnet. Discounts brought the average hourly charge from $6.25 to $5.09. The cost of sessions over the packet network, for 13,750 hours a month, was about $70,000. The remaining 4,583 hours a month using an 800 service would cost The Travelers $74,000. Thus, the total

would be $144,000, a monthly savings of $151,000 compared with 800 service. It was estimated that the public networks would save The Travelers 40 to 60 percent — over $1.5 million a year by the end of 1985.

General requirements

A means to take advantage of the economies of public data networks would have to offer certain features:

■ *End-to-end reliability.* Because financial data, such as policy information, claim statistics, and actual dollar figures, would be transferred across the network, end-to-end error detection and retransmission capabilities were needed. Simple parity checking or even a longitudinal redundancy check would not suffice. This sensitivity called for a cyclical redundancy check (CRC) akin to those used in synchronous and high-level data link controls (SDLC and HDLC). The complete path, including the local loop, required protection.

■ *3270 SNA access.* The Travelers had a large investment in business programs based on SNA's logical unit (LU) 2, which uses a 3270 data stream. These applications included claim and billing inquiries, policy rating and issuing, and electronic mail. An enormous amount of software would be immediately and economically usable by agents throughout the country if their microcomputers could appear to the hosts as LU 2 devices

2. An obvious difference. *This chart shows an hourly savings of $5 to $15, to be had by dodging 800 service in favor of public packet networks. An economic model based on these figures projected that The Travelers could save over a million dollars a year by the end of 1985 on dial-up 3270 SNA traffic.*

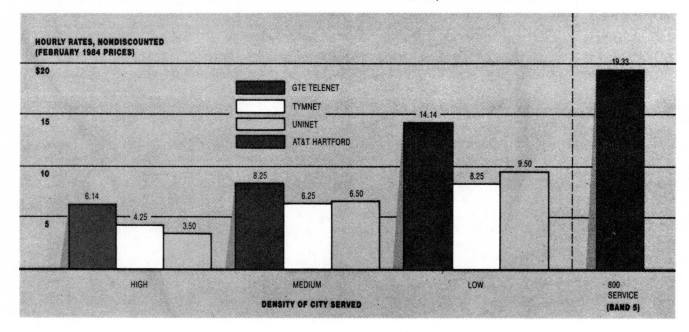

HOURLY RATES, NONDISCOUNTED
(FEBRUARY 1984 PRICES)

- GTE TELENET
- TYMNET
- UNINET
- AT&T HARTFORD

DENSITY OF CITY SERVED

while communicating through a packet network. Applications would not have to be rewritten to include asynchronous interfaces, access could include agents with microcomputers, and transmission costs could be cut significantly.

■ *File transfer capabilities.* The Travelers had been communicating for years with those agencies large enough to warrant a minicomputer. Before any interactive traffic, batch data was exchanged with the minicomputers using 3780 BSC.

Mapping logical record support into the microcomputer was an obvious need. The advantages of file transfer capability and the means for accomplishing it were well understood by The Travelers. For applications using data that does not have real-time immediacy, unattended overnight communications at reduced nonprime rates was the most economical solution. Such delivery can be timer-driven, that is, automatically sent to the host from the agent's office at roughly 8 P.M. and received from the host at 5 A.M.

■ *Program-to-program communications.* Perhaps the most interesting requirement came to light when The Travelers identified certain business transactions that called for host access under microcomputer control. These transactions could be processed, for the most part, by local microcomputer operators but could only be completed with a real-time connection to the host. To save on communications cost, it is necessary to minimize connect time.

It was determined that data communications controlled by a microcomputer program was the most economical method of handling these transactions. The communications savings would offset any software development costs. Also, productivity gains could be realized, since data collection can take up to six

seconds per screen if entered from a remote terminal but less than a second on a dedicated machine.

As an example of program-controlled communications, a user might do a dozen screens of data entry on a microcomputer, then edit and cross-validate the data locally. The microcomputer would dial the host automatically, transmit the screens, and then enter an interactive editing mode. With output data from the host captured on floppy disk, the program could disconnect from the host and allow the data to be displayed on screen, manipulated, or printed.

The host must complete those portions of an application that call for database access or raw computing power. The data entry part of existing host applications can be rewritten for microcomputers, with the back-end computation and database lookup remaining at the host. Emerging applications based on distributed data processing will make more creative use of the dual resources. Field-by-field editing, for instance, which would require too much data transfer to be done by the host, could easily be handled by a microcomputer.

Alternatives
Once The Travelers determined the economics for using public packet networks, the telecommunications group began searching for a way to meet the above requirements. Of the options it considered, The Travelers rejected those available off-the-shelf:

■ *3270 emulators.* Devices manufactured by third parties would have let microcomputer users access a host only through an 800 number, not through the more economical public data networks. The 3270 services offered by the network vendors themselves were little more than leased-line replacements between 3270 devices, requiring permanent, synchronous connections. Neither BSC nor SDLC was then supported in a dial-up mode by access ports on the public packet networks, and no such support was foreseen.

Even with dial-up 3270 available, problems in network management loomed. For example, on an initial dial-up SDLC connection, an identifying string of digits and letters is sent to the host. These exchanges of identification (XIDs) provide security against unauthorized log-ons and tell the host what kind of control unit is calling. The tables that deal with XIDs in IBM's Virtual Telecommunications Access Method (VTAM) must be as long as the number of dial-in devices. Managing such tables for thousands of microcomputers would have been a nightmare.

Another disadvantage of 3270 emulators is that they require a special circuit board and synchronous modem. These clearly would have been too expensive. Besides, users still might have needed an asynchronous modem to access other networks and data services, such as Dow Jones or Dun & Bradstreet.

■ *Host-end asynchronous protocol converters.* In late 1983, no appropriate protocol converters provided error detection and retransmission beyond mere parity schemes. Another problem was that such protocol converters emulate a 3270 screen on behalf of the terminal, requiring a microcomputer to "play dumb." Each time the terminal transmits a character, the protocol converter maps the character to the screen and echoes it back to the terminal. This echo function is an inherent part of all character-by-character protocol converters and cannot be disabled. Used with a packet network, such devices double character charges and yield unacceptable response times.

■ *Block-mode asynchronous protocol converters.* Although they were not available at the time, the current crop of products from companies like Simware Inc. and Renex Corp. could have done a portion of the job. However, they would not have met all of The Travelers' needs. Geared to supporting ASCII terminals, they cannot efficiently transfer binary data such as programs and spreadsheets. In addition, none provided program-to-program communications through an applications program interface (API).

■ *Starting from scratch.* Since nothing was then on the market to satisfy the company's requirements, The Travelers decided to write its own software. The home-grown code would have to use SNA's LU 2 for 3270 applications and permit asynchronous access over packet networks for dial-up microcomputers. SNA and X.25 would be joined in a "shot-gun marriage."

The task was to build a 3270 SNA emulator for the IBM Personal Computer that did not use SDLC (or any other synchronous protocol) for its data link control (DLC), but carried SNA data all the way to the microcomputer. As an intelligent device, the microcomputer could be programmed to make full use of this data.

A little-known DLC
Since SNA is a layered architecture, the DLC layer that transports the bit stream could be replaced by a protocol more suited to packet-switching networks. In this way, the lower layers of SNA could be replaced by

X.25 or even an asynchronous protocol. At both the host and the microcomputer, the higher SNA layers that interpret the bit-stream would remain the same.

SDLC is not the only data link control for SNA. Two years ago, IBM defined a Qualified Logical Link Control (QLLC) to let SNA data flow from one end of a synchronous X.25 network to the other. Replacing SDLC at both ends, QLLC preserves the higher-level SNA protocols. The link discipline is better known and may be more widespread in Europe, since IBM has emphasized SDLC in the United States.

QLLC allows an SNA PU 2 control unit (such as an IBM 3274) to use X.25. Packets flowing through the X.25 virtual call layer are used to carry SNA data and, when needed, SDLC commands. With QLLC software on each end of a virtual circuit, an IBM front-end processor and control unit can talk in X.25 protocol over a packet network. This little-known IBM link discipline allows SNA protocols to be transported to the control unit (and therefore to a microcomputer), letting the destination device emulate an SNA entity.

The Travelers' scheme was inspired by QLLC and by an IBM device that also uses raw SNA data, the 3270 Personal Computer. Ordinary 3274 control units perform screen-mapping and keyboard control for 3278 terminals using a coaxial-cable protocol known as Control Unit Terminal (CUT). SNA functionality, therefore, ends at the 3274. The 3270-PC, however, uses the Distributed Function Terminal (DFT) protocol to talk to the 3274. Under DFT, the 3274 is passive, relaying all SNA session data to the 3270-PC without modification. Thus, the SNA protocol is end-to-end.

The SNA emulator, instead of using the coaxial cable-oriented DFT protocol, formats data to leave via the asynchronous adapter in the microcomputer. From there the data passes to the asynchronous modem and then out into the network. The data stream ultimately presented to the host application is in LU 2.

The protocol defined
SNA emulation requires that the user's device receive actual SNA data. By developing true SNA emulation, The Travelers left the door open for future enhancements such as IBM's LU 6.2, a higher-level function that provides advanced program-to-program communications. With SNA layers present on both ends of a circuit, higher-level protocols can be changed as easily as the data link control. Such flexibility is not possible with simple protocol conversion, where data is transformed before it reaches the microcomputer.

To handle the multiple environments that data would be traveling through, The Travelers defined a block mode, full-duplex asynchronous protocol that uses a standard cyclical redundancy check (CRC) algorithm. This protocol is superimposed on, or embedded in, X.25 and SNA. Block mode is used for error detection. Each block presently transmits a frame 256 bytes long. (Preliminary tests with 512-byte blocks show acceptable error rates and low retransmission counts.)

For efficiency, the full-duplex protocol uses a sliding window, which permits multiple outstanding unacknowledged frames. The sliding window technique

3. Session establishment. *Elements in an SNA-emula-tion virtual circuit are activated in distinct phases: (1) emulation startup, (2) VTAM log-on, (3) host connec-* *tion, (4) user log-on, (5) CDINIT (initiation of a cross-domain session) and application* BIND, *(6) 3270 mode, and (7) relay program in passive mode.*

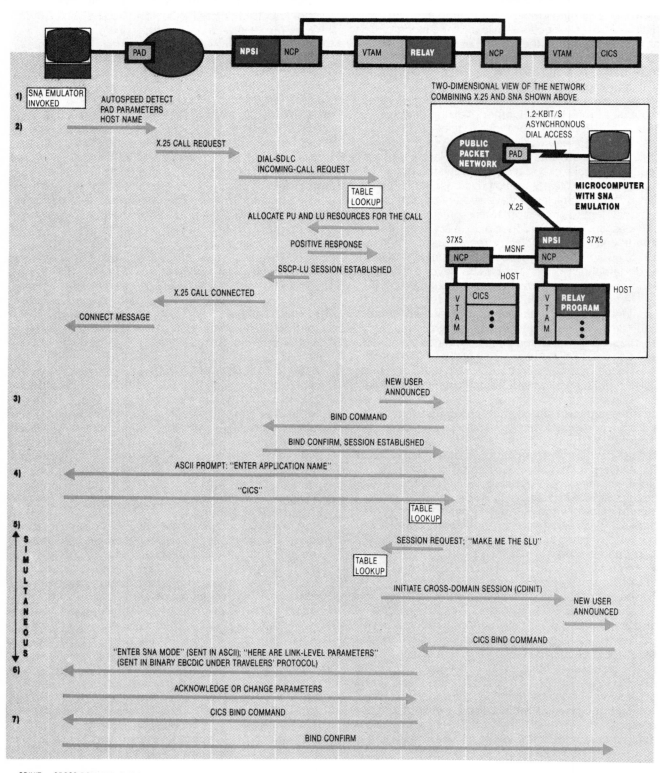

CDINIT = CROSS-DOMAIN INITIATION
CICS = CUSTOMER INFORMATION CONTROL SYSTEM
MSNF = MULTISYSTEM NETWORKING FACILITY
NCP = NETWORK CONTROL PROGRAM

NPSI = NCP PACKET-SWITCHING INTERFACE
PAD = PACKET ASSEMBLER/DISASSEMBLER
PU = PHYSICAL UNIT; LU = LOGICAL UNIT
SDLC = SYNCHRONOUS DATA LINK CONTROL

SLU = SECONDARY LOGICAL UNIT
SNA = SYSTEMS NETWORK ARCHITECTURE
SSCP = SYSTEM SERVICES CONTROL POINT
VTAM = VIRTUAL TELECOMMUNICATIONS ACCESS METHOD

boosts response time by negating the ill effects of propagation delay inherent in satellite or packet networks. End-to-end error control comes from a standard CRC algorithm of the International Telegraph and Telephone Consultative Committee (CCITT).

The Travelers' protocol is asynchronous between the microcomputer and the network but becomes embedded in X.25 packets between the network and the front-end and then becomes pure SNA on its way to the host application. The Microcom Networking Protocol (MNP) might have been used to safeguard the local loop, but it does not enjoy broad support. There are as yet few MNP access locations in the United States.

It takes four to Tango

The Travelers wrote two software packages to implement its protocol, an SNA emulator for the IBM PC and an "intelligent relay" that runs as a host VTAM application. With the addition of two standard offerings, namely a public packet network and IBM's Network Control Program (NCP) Packet Switching Interface (NPSI) in the 37X5, micro-to-mainframe SNA was off and running. An overview of the four components and how they relate is shown in the insert of Figure 3.

The SNA-emulation microcomputer software satisfies a number of needs. It provides standard microcomputer emulation of 3270, a file-transfer mechanism for upline and downline loading, an interface for PC-based application programs, and automatic log-on files for simplified startup. The host-based relay program runs as a nonprivileged VTAM application, one that contains no special hooks into either VTAM or the host's Multiple Virtual Storage (MVS) operating system.

The relay program handles microcomputer log-ons to host applications, local-loop error detection and retransmission, data compression, accounting, and security. It interfaces to NPSI and looks like a 3270 LU 2 terminal to the host application. With its host application interface, the relay program can talk to such IBM environments as the Information Management System (IMS), the Time Sharing Option (TSO), and the Customer Information Control System (CICS).

NPSI is an IBM program product for the 37X5 that coexists with NCP. The SNA-emulation technique uses the simplest standard form of NPSI support, with no special VTAM code. NPSI acts as a gateway for interfacing an X.25 network with SNA and provides integrated PAD support. That is, both the host-side X.29 and the terminal-side X.28 PAD functions are handled directly by NPSI.

Setting up a call

To support SNA emulation, NPSI must function transparently, without translating the eight-bit data passing through it from EBCDIC to ASCII or vice versa. An LU 1 interface is presented by NPSI to the relay program. Devices logically connected to NPSI virtual circuits therefore look to the host like a screenless keyboard/printer combination.

The role played by each of the components in SNA emulation can be illustrated by a typical call-establishment sequence (Fig. 3):

1. The microcomputer user invokes the SNA emulator and specifies an autolog-on command file. When the SNA emulator is initially invoked, it emulates a teletypewriter (TTY) to access the packet network over an asynchronous connection.
2. The SNA emulator reads commands from the autolog-on command file and interprets them. Typically, these commands would cause the microcomputer modem to dial, send the network an autospeed detect sequence, set the appropriate terminal-interface PAD parameters, and then specify the destination host name. NPSI translates the log-on request into SDLC and passes it to VTAM, which establishes a session with the microcomputer.
3. When connection to The Travelers' host occurs, VTAM tells the relay program that a new user wants to connect to it and creates a single NPSI session.
4. The relay program sends a prompt to the microcomputer, requesting that the user log on. The log-on information is sent out from the microcomputer (perhaps from the autolog-on command file).
5. Based on the log-on information, the relay program determines the LU 2 name and the destination host application. It sends a request to VTAM telling it to create a session with the destination program. This program can be anywhere in the MSNF network. If the application approves the user log-on, it sends a BIND command to the relay program.
6. While the relay program is setting up a session with the application, it sends a command to the microcomputer telling it to enter 3270 emulation mode.
7. When the application's BIND command is received by the relay program, it is forwarded to the microcomputer for verification and acknowledgment or negotiation. For the remainder of the session, the relay program functions as a passive passthrough for SNA information flows, acting only on the link-level protocol.

Terminating a session follows this procedure in reverse. When an UNBIND command is received by the relay program, it is forwarded to the microcomputer. When the microcomputer acknowledges the UNBIND, the acknowledgment is sent to the host application and the session is broken. Then the relay program can send a command to the microcomputer telling it to return to TTY emulation and display a prompt.

Microcomputer-based software

The two software components written by The Travelers bear closer examination. On the microcomputer, the SNA emulator is used to establish a single session with the host. The session, defined by LU 2, carries a 3270 data stream. Logically, multiple simultaneous sessions could have been provided using windows, but single-session emulation was satisfactory for The Travelers' bread-and-butter applications. The emulator provides:

■ *3270 functionality.* The microcomputer emulates a standard 3278-2 keyboard and screen with a 24- by 80-character display. There is also four-color 3279 support for the IBM PC color display.

■ *Reliability and speed.* The Travelers' protocol, upon which the relay program is based, implements end-to-end error detection and retransmission, allowing dial-up asynchronous communications with the same integrity as SDLC. It also uses a bit-compression algorithm that now achieves the equivalent of a 1.8-kbit/s throughput rate using 1.2-kbit/s modems at The Travelers.

These figures should not be misinterpreted. The hardware runs at 1.2 kbit/s, but characters are represented by a variable number of bits using a Huffman-coding algorithm and static tables. This algorithm increases the effective channel capacity in terms of characters per second, using standard hardware. Dynamic tables would have increased throughput, as well as complexity and processing overhead. The Travelers plans a more sophisticated Huffman scheme to further boost throughput.

■ *File transfer.* To fulfill this major requirement of The Travelers, the SNA emulator builds on a technique previously developed by IBM. It uses the same LU 2 structured field protocols that IBM implemented on its 3270-PC. IBM introduced structured fields for graphics support as a way to allow LU 2 sessions to carry data not intended for display. Because The Travelers used an existing IBM format, the same file transfer programs for IBM hosts that interface with the 3270-PC are also compatible with the SNA emulator.

Unlike most asynchronous protocol converters, the SNA emulator lets binary files traverse a packet network at the full transmission speed of the modem. Many other schemes implement binary file transfer by sending seven-bit ASCII characters with even parity to the IBM host. Each binary byte is represented as two ASCII characters for transmission, which means that the transfer effectively runs at half the modem speed. Since it uses IBM's structured fields, the SNA emulator can tell the packet network to transmit eight-bit binary data with no parity.

The IBM PC is ASCII-based. All 3270 functions are therefore done in ASCII and converted to binary EBCDIC to be transmitted. The public network, in binary transport mode, simply passes the data along. The network will thus refrain from interpreting the data. With pure binary file transfer, bit combinations that would otherwise mean STX, ETX, ETB, X-on/X-off and so forth to the packet network do not affect the network's virtual circuit.

■ *Application program interface.* The SNA emulator's API lets an application program running on the microcomputer communicate directly with a host application (Fig. 4). Through the API, the microcomputer program can pretend to be a terminal. Ordinarily, keystrokes from a 3270 terminal keyboard go into a logical screen buffer, a 24- by 80-character chunk of memory. (The logical screen buffer is at one end of an LU 2 session "pipe," with the host application at the other end.) Data generated by the microcomputer program goes through the API into the microcomputer's screen buffer. Besides writing data, the program can examine the contents of the buffer.

When the SNA emulator is inactive, so is the API, and the microcomputer keyboard and display are under the control of the local application program (Fig. 4a). During session establishment, the terminal gets asyn-

chronous TTY (teletypewriter-format) messages directly through pseudo link-level code (Fig. 4c). At other times, the host program has control of the keyboard and screen via the SNA emulation software (Fig. 4b). But when the API is active, a microcomputer application program can issue commands with parameters, known as function calls, to the SNA emulation code through the API (Fig. 4d). In this way, the program can read or modify the logical screen buffer in order to interact with the host, while controlling the screen and keyboard through the local operating system.

Structured fields are also supported via the API, so microcomputer applications can use the API for file transfer. The API can only simulate peer-to-peer communications, since it must rely on the LU 2 screen buffer. In the future, when IBM provides general host LU 6.2 support, the SNA emulator will no longer need to simulate keystrokes but will be able to pass parameters directly between programs using LU 6.2 commands called verbs. And because full SNA data travels to the emulator without first being interpreted, compatibility with LU 6.2 is not precluded. In fact, the API will probably be simpler when it incorporates LU 6.2, since it will not have to pretend to be a terminal.

■ *Secure printing.* The Travelers also uses the structured-field file transfer protocol, which is just an LU 2 extension, for printer output from IMS. Combining interactive terminal traffic and batch printer output onto a single session was an elegant way to get around

---

4. Emulation software. *Control of the user interface comes from within (A) or from the host via SNA (B) or async (C). An API gives an application the helm (D).*

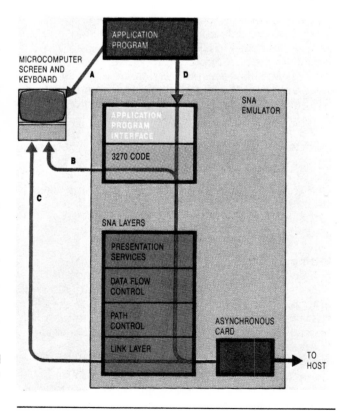

several tricky problems in security and implementation.

Since IMS is a queued operating environment, it is ill-suited for dial access. Dialing into IMS gives rise to two security problems. First, a user can get in under a prior user's ID if that user disconnected abnormally. Second, a user can receive an output queue's worth of leftover data that a previous user had sent to a printer.

To prevent occurrences of these problems, special security hooks were designed into the relay program in the host. When a new call comes in, the relay software notifies IMS of the new user and lets IMS clear an output queue. The software also tells the application program to prepare for a new session.

Normal SNA uses separate sessions for each user ID. Printers and terminals have separate IDs and thus run under separate sessions. While satisfactory with leased lines, where there is no danger of "crossed wires," this approach would be unacceptable for The Travelers' dial access to sensitive financial information. Besides, if the emulator were to handle printers and terminals separately, the security hooks needed by The Travelers would have to be much more complex, since clean-up messages would have to be sent for both sessions.

For these reasons, the developers of the SNA emulator wanted to find a way to use one session for both purposes. Luckily, IBM's structured field protocol, already part of the emulator, could transfer files consisting of nonscreen data directly to the printer in the same session as terminal traffic. The developers wrote an IMS program to intercept data that is meant to be printed from a user application and then to send it to the microcomputer in the structured field protocol.

The emulator "manages" two devices in a single session by transferring data to the disk and then printing it. At any given time, the SNA emulator is either in keyboard or file transfer mode. While data is down-line loaded to the disk, the keyboard is locked. Once the data is on disk, however, it can be printed without interrupting the user's session.

Host-based software

The relay program can play the role of one of three entities. Emulating VTAM, it creates log-ons for sessions with host applications; acting like the NCP, it handles error detection; and in its 3274 controller-mode, the program processes terminal communications. The tasks of the relay program are as follows:

■ *Log-ons.* Users gain access to IMS, CICS, TSO, and NCCF (Network Communications Control Facility) through the relay program. Just as VTAM creates connections between LU 2 terminals and host applications, the relay program logs onto applications on behalf of the virtual circuits coming to it through NPSI.

For each virtual circuit, the relay program appears as an individual LU 2 session to the host application. Certain applications, such as IMS and CICS, keep track of authorized users in "terminal" tables. With these applications, multiple LUs with dummy names must be generated, one for each potentially simultaneous session. It makes sense to define surplus table entries to prevent the relay program from refusing log-ons.

■ *Error detection.* The relay program supports the other

end of the microcomputer's error detecting and re-transmitting protocol. It does this by adding check sequences to SNA data units. For each virtual circuit carrying a user session, the program establishes one LU 1 session with NPSI and uses it strictly to send bytes to or receive bytes from the microcomputer.

When the relay program is in its NCP-like mode, it accepts function-management data in the form of request/response units (RUs) with their headers (RHs) from the host application via VTAM, adds a Travelers-defined transmission header (TH), divides the assembled unit into data link frames with a CRC field, and then sends the frames to the microcomputer. For data flowing from the microcomputer, the program accepts frames, checks the CRC, and, if acceptable, passes an assembled RU to VTAM for transmission to the host application.

■ *Optimization.* The relay program does two forms of optimization. It scans outbound RUs received from the host application and passes them through a 3270 RPA (repeat-to-address) optimizer. The RPA optimizer looks for character strings that repeat, such as blanks, dashes, or asterisks. It compresses the string to a four-byte transmission sequence consisting of the RPA command code, a two-byte ending address, and the character to be repeated.

Then the Huffman-coded bit-compression algorithm mentioned earlier is invoked as part of the data link protocol. The intent of this optimization is to keep the display time for typical screens in the 6-to-10-second range even when using 1.2-kbit/s modems. Without optimization, an average display might take 12 seconds or more to paint the screen. In addition to increasing productivity, compression lowers communications costs by reducing the number of packets traveling through the packet network.

■ *Security and accounting.* Several user-codable subroutine calls, known as installation exits, can be incorporated into the relay program for security and accounting. Installation exits allow tailoring of the application at well-defined points. The Travelers is currently using these exits to select specific LU names for IMS access. This allows an IMS application to associate the sessions with user IDs.

Use of mainframe hardware and software can be tracked by IBM's Systems Management Facility (SMF), a centralized MVS log. With the help of installation exits, the relay program in The Travelers' host sends accounting and performance information to SMF. In the future, these exits could check user IDs or passwords via the Resource Access Control Facility (RACF), an IBM-provided security package.

Triple-nested framing

The protocol's frame structure (Fig. 5) includes sequencing for a sliding window and two CRCs: one for the protocol header and one for the data. This structure is reportedly similar to framing in Tymnet's X.PC protocol. The Travelers' protocol functions end-to-end, above level 3 of X.25, the network layer. It also passes over SNA.

To let microcomputers talk to host applications at a

5. Framing. How can 3270 SNA, X.25, asynchronous, and binary data coexist? By enveloping the common frame "T" of The Travelers' protocol. T is constructed at the host by relay software and passed to the front-end processor in SNA format, where it is converted for transmission through a packet-switching network.

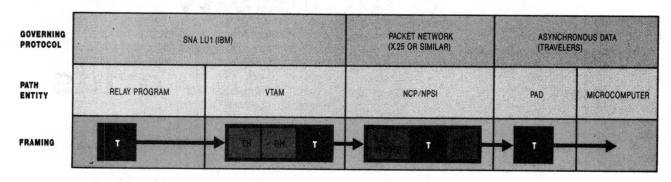

GOVERNING PROTOCOL	SNA LU1 (IBM)		PACKET NETWORK (X.25 OR SIMILAR)	ASYNCHRONOUS DATA (TRAVELERS)	
PATH ENTITY	RELAY PROGRAM	VTAM	NCP/NPSI	PAD	MICROCOMPUTER
FRAMING	T	TH RH T	T	T	

BYTES   **TRAVELERS' FRAME FORMAT**

Bytes	Field	Description	
1	STX	START OF TEXT FOR THE FRAME	
2	LENGTH	OF THE DATA PORTION (VARIABLE; COULD BE 0)	
2	SEQ	FRAME SEQUENCE NUMBER	
1	CMD	SIMILAR TO COMMAND FIELD IN SDLC OR HDLC	
1	•	RESERVED	
2	CRC1	TO VERIFY LENGTH OF DATA FIELD AND FIND CRC2	FRAME HEADER PORTION

			DATA PORTION (OPTIONAL)
2	MSGL	LENGTH OF SNA DATA	
1	OAF	ORIGINATING ADDRESS	
1	DAF	DESTINATION ADDRESS	
2	SEQ	SNA SEQUENCE NUMBER	
3	RH	SNA REQUEST/RESPONSE HEADER	
DATA	FMD	SNA/3270 USER DATA (VARIABLE LENGTH)	
2	CRC2	ERROR CHECK FOR ENTIRE FRAME	

MESSAGE HEADER

CRC = CYCLIC REDUNDANCY CHECK

FMD = FUNCTION-MANAGEMENT DATA

HDLC = HIGH-LEVEL DATA LINK CONTROL

NCP = NETWORK CONTROL PROGRAM

NPSI = NCP PACKET-SWITCHING INTERFACE

PAD = PACKET ASSEMBLER/DISASSEMBLER

RH = REQUEST/RESPONSE HEADER

SDLC = SYNCHRONOUS DATA LINK CONTROL

SNA = SYSTEMS NETWORK ARCHITECTURE

T = TRAVELERS' PROTOCOL FRAME

TH = TRANSMISSION HEADER

VTAM = VIRTUAL TELECOMMUNICATIONS ACCESS METHOD

level above SNA and X.25, the protocol embeds its frames within the frames or packets of the other two protocols. A frame "T" constructed according to The Travelers protocol can be carried along as SNA or X.25 data. There is actually a third level of protocol nesting: The data within T conforms to the LU 2 frame format.

This arrangement has several advantages. For example, LU 2 can be replaced by other formats, such as LU 6.2, without changing the network structure or user procedures. MNP could replace The Travelers' protocol at the link level. With MNP, error detection and correction over the local loop would no longer have to be performed by the host-based relay program. ∎

"Talking true SNA over async links" is based on an abstract by Mark A. Orenstein, who assisted in preparing the article. Orenstein, a director in the telecommunications area of The Travelers' data processing department, has been with the company since 1972. He has been involved with databases and data communications since 1974 and with the implementation of SNA since its inception. Orenstein conceived of and developed the SNA-emulation approach described above and directed the implementation of public packet networks at The Travelers. He holds an M. S. E. E. from MIT and a B. S. E. E. from Tufts.

Kelly McDonald, Brigham Young University, Provo, Utah

A university learns to link computing worlds the hard way

Academics with microcomputers and ASCII terminals have moved into the administration's former preserve, the IBM mainframe.

Necessity also being the mother of adaptation, Brigham Young University (BYU) has found increasingly sophisticated ways to give users of remote ASCII-based terminals and microcomputers access to the school's IBM mainframes. Beginning with a single request made six years ago, BYU can now accommodate nearly a hundred such devices, and is considering the purchase of an ASCII-only IBM machine. This growth has not come effortlessly.

Today, a network of computing centers throughout the university allows academic users to work with their traditional mainstay—the research-oriented machines of Digital Equipment Corp. (DEC)—while taking advantage of the unique strengths of IBM mainframes. Scholars in Provo and at remote sites can use the terminals or microcomputers now on their desks to access, through a network of data switches, the various computing resources on campus.

Dual origins
A large IBM 4341 mainframe, traditionally at the core of BYU's administrative data processing, has supported most of the school's financial requirements and has kept records of the campus's 26,000 students. Since direct access was the only available option when the administration's terminal network was developed, approximately 200 IBM 3270-type terminals connected to cluster controllers were linked to the mainframe.

Likewise, the academic community has, until recently, been accustomed to direct terminal attachment. Research, computation, and other scientific work at BYU has depended upon DEC computers ranging from small PDP-8 minicomputers to a large DEC System 10. Access to these machines was mainly through ASCII terminals such as DEC's VT52 and VT100.

Interconnection between these environments began

in 1979. BYU's support group, Computer Services, received a request for a terminal attachment to the IBM mainframe that could not be satisfied within the existing terminal network. This request came from a remote campus in Salt Lake City, 40 miles from the Provo, Utah, computer center. All previous terminals had been installed in locations that could be reached with a local coaxial cable connection. The computer center had no provisions, such as a communications controller, for supporting terminals at a greater distance. Therefore a search was begun for a solution that would be acceptable, yet reasonable in cost.

The desired solution to the problem would have utilized low-cost ASCII terminals with inexpensive telephone modems. Such a solution represented the lowest possible communications and terminal cost. When the request was made, IBM's 3705 communications controller did not offer 3270 terminal emulation, so ASCII devices connected to it operated in a character-by-character teletype mode. Microprocessor-based protocol converters that emulate 3270 cluster controllers were not generally available.

The first remote port
At that time, the only solution that could be found (besides using IBM remote 3270 terminals) was some type of communications processor located between the terminal and the host that would emulate the 3270 environment. In 1980, BYU chose a Data General Eclipse S-140 minicomputer to serve as a customized access controller to the IBM mainframe, which resided near it at the Provo site.

The decision to use the Eclipse was not made solely because it cost less than an IBM 3705. With some custom emulation software from Gamma Technology of Escondido, Calif., the Eclipse functioned like an IBM

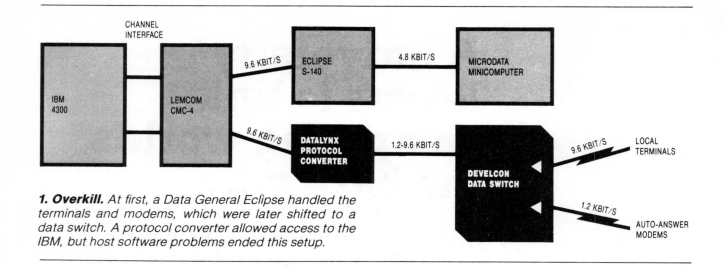

1. Overkill. At first, a Data General Eclipse handled the terminals and modems, which were later shifted to a data switch. A protocol converter allowed access to the IBM, but host software problems ended this setup.

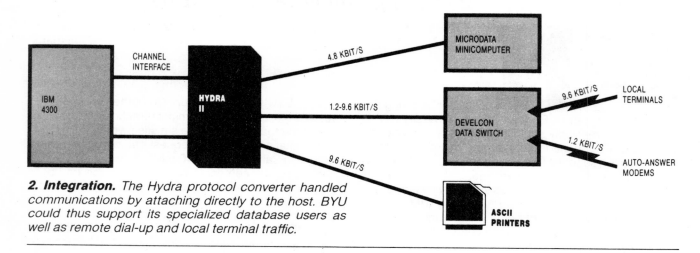

2. Integration. The Hydra protocol converter handled communications by attaching directly to the host. BYU could thus support its specialized database users as well as remote dial-up and local terminal traffic.

3271 cluster controller. ASCII terminals attached to the Eclipse could use this emulation software's translation and protocol conversion to reproduce the screen format of an IBM 3277 terminal. (The software searched the 3270 stream from the host for screen-addressing sequences, which it translated into equivalent ASCII cursor-controlling escape sequences for the particular terminal used.)

With this type of environment, the desired solution seemed to be reached. The remote campus could now call a modem on the Eclipse and have use of the emulation software through the same ASCII terminals that were dialing other non-IBM computers.

Expensive promise

The Eclipse still required a synchronous communications attachment to the mainframe in order to support its 3270 binary synchronous communications (BSC) protocol. Since only one BSC line was to be used, a powerful 3705 was not needed for the IBM attachment. The computer center leased a small, four-port communications controller from Lemcom Systems. The Lemcom CMC-4 allowed the Eclipse to be attached to the mainframe as an IBM 3271, but was not the overkill

in communications capability that a 3705 would have been.

If 3271 emulation was all that was planned, the Eclipse would have been too powerful a processor. It was envisioned that the Eclipse would eventually evolve into much more than just a terminal controller. There were hopes of developing other types of custom interfaces to the host through the Eclipse, including X.25.

As a first step, a custom interface was created for the Microdata computer. Various campus departments had been acquiring Microdatas to be used in specialized applications for several years. One such department, the financial aid office, still required some access to the student database on the IBM mainframe. Its Microdata was attached to the Eclipse, which contained special software for accessing the database. Local terminals were also linked to the Eclipse as were auto-answer modems for the remote terminals.

The other custom interfaces that were planned did not materialize. In fact, no other types of custom interfaces were even attempted. Programming the Eclipse to accept the Microdata was a complex task, yet it was far simpler than an X.25 interface would have been.

It soon became clear that the cost of the Eclipse and the communications controller did not justify the benefits of the terminals they supported. After an initial investment of $50,000 for the Eclipse and $4,000 for the emulation software, BYU was faced with recurring expenses totaling $1,100 per month for maintenance of the Eclipse and for leasing the Lemcom CMC-4. Due to the high ongoing charges, it seemed expedient to continue looking for a more cost-effective solution.

Early in 1982, an investigation was begun about the new protocol converters that were starting to appear on the market. These devices converted the IBM BSC data stream to asynchronous ASCII. Most of them emulated a 3271 cluster controller to the host in a manner similar to the Eclipse. Some early vendors, such as Datastream and PCI, offered units which supported eight asynchronous devices for $10,000 to $12,000. This obviously represented an attractive alternative to the Eclipse system which had been utilized on campus.

Unfortunate synergy

At about the same time that Brigham Young University was grappling with these remote terminal questions, a network was developing on campus (see "A campus of networks") which, together with IBM access, would bring security headaches. Faculty and administrators wanted access to campus computers besides the machines they were currently using. Still other users were interested in replacing their ASCII terminals or IBM 3270 terminals with personal computers. To satisfy some of these demands, a Develcon data switch was installed. The local terminals and auto-answer modems were moved from the Eclipse to the data switch (Fig. 1). For the first time, faculty, staff, and students could select applications on a variety of hosts.

Some of the users who were logging on to ASCII-based hosts through the data switch wanted access to the IBM mainframes, and with legitimate reason. The university therefore decided to purchase a protocol converter to put between the data switch and the IBM machine. But because of the confidential nature of the processing that is done on the administrative mainframe, it was important to restrict access to authorized users. A serious problem arose when various protocol converters were tested.

Tangled sessions

In many DEC machines, the operating system is intended to accept modems. Each port can handle a sequence of different user sessions. When a terminal user disconnects abruptly, the computer takes recovery steps to properly terminate the session. As a result, a number of the academic users had formed the habit of hanging up without signing off. In the IBM 3270 environment, however, each terminal is connected to a unique port on the controller by a coaxial cable. There is no provision for a controller port to be shared among multiple terminals.

The data switch appears to be a modem to the host by providing the interface control signals that the host would normally expect to receive from a modem.

Therefore, when an ASCII terminal disconnected from a protocol converter by breaking their connection through the data switch, there was no well-defined way for the protocol converter to notify the host of the disconnection.

Early versions of the protocol converter from Datastream and others simply did not provide the correct message or signal when a modem (or a data switch) disconnected from one of its asynchronous ports. The user had to completely log off from the host session before disconnecting. Otherwise, another user entering the same port could conceivably connect to an active session on the previous user's account.

Careful analysis of the 3270 terminal specifications finally revealed a method with which to notify the host that a disconnection had occurred at the protocol converter. In the 3270 protocol there is a status code known as "unsolicited device-end." This code is normally used to tell the host software that a 3270 terminal has just been powered on. This 3270 condition was originally intended to allow the software to display an initial screen to the user after the terminal is turned on. "Unsolicited device-end" was the closest signal that could be identified as an initialization sequence.

Fortunately, the IBM mainframe's Virtual Machine (VM) operating system was able to recognize this signal and log off any previous session at the terminal. The decision was immediately made to use this signaling method as a primary requirement for the selection of a protocol converter.

Short-lived solution

The evaluation process was by no means exhaustive. BYU examined units offered by Datastream, Atlanthus, Renex, Icot, and Local Data. At that time only two of the protocol converters, the C-80 from Atlanthus and the Datalynx-3270 from Local Data, offered the needed host signaling feature. The drop of data set ready (DSR) from the modem was the signal that triggered the protocol converter to send the "unsolicited device-end" signal to the host. Since C-80 terminal emulation did not work quite right with the particular terminal being used, the selection finally settled on Local Data's Datalynx. A two-port unit was comparatively inexpensive at $1,995.

The Datalynx emulated an IBM 3271 cluster controller as the Eclipse had done, and so it still required the Lemcom communications controller for the host connection. Figure 1 shows that the protocol converter could be attached to the IBM host as another 3270 controller. It did operate quite reliably, and the few remote and local campus users were generally satisfied with it.

In late 1982, Local Data announced a Datalynx-3274 which offered some enhanced capabilities. Local Data offered an attractive trade-in on the Datalynx-3270, and so the protocol converter was upgraded. As with any new device, there were a few early operational problems, but they were quickly resolved by the vendor. The biggest concern with the operation of the device eventually came with the support of the communications software in the IBM host.

A campus of networks

It would have been impossible to foresee that a request for remote access in 1979 was only the first step in a torrent of interconnection. Today, several types of data switches serve a campus population of over 1,000 terminals and microcomputers, which share approximately 300 host ports. The data-switch network provides interactive real-time access to host computers for terminal users. Another set of links provides background file transfer operations. And local networks are already in place, with more under consideration.

Two Gandalf PACX III switches have been installed in the science and computer buildings. They are primarily used by students in both departments to work on specialized machines. Other students access these switches from terminal rooms around the campus. The general faculty and administrative staff are served with three switches from Develcon Electronics, linked by T1 circuits. The operating software in the three Develcon switches permits them to interact with each other in such a way that they appear to the terminal user as one logical switching mechanism.

Any host computer that is attached to any of the Develcon switches can be made accessible to a terminal user on another one. There is no difference in the way the terminal user accesses hosts on remote switches from hosts on his local switch. For interaction between terminal users on the Gandalf switches and hosts on the Develcon switches, 9.6-kbit/s trunk lines have been established between the Gandalf and Develcon switches. Since these switches are of different manufacture, the link between them is not as completely transparent as the link between the Develcon switches. A Gandalf terminal user wishing access to a host on a Develcon switch must first request a conversation with the Develcon switch. The same holds true for Develcon terminal users who want to use Gandalf hosts.

CPU-to-CPU

Another important networking facility on campus consists of point-to-point BSC lines between various hosts on campus. This network, used to transfer various types of files between machines, is based on the remote spooling communications subsystem (RSCS) of IBM's Virtual Memory operating system. Where IBM hosts connect to other IBM hosts, the software interaction is straightforward. One RSCS system talks to another. When IBM hosts connect to DEC VAX computers, however, special software is necessary in the VAX. A software package from Argonne National Laboratories allows the VAX to participate in the RSCS network.

This network now provides file transfer for such applications as electronic mail, remote-job submission, and access to laser printing. For example, users of the VAX computers can submit job streams to the IBM mainframes or send files for printing on the laser printer at the administrative IBM 4381.

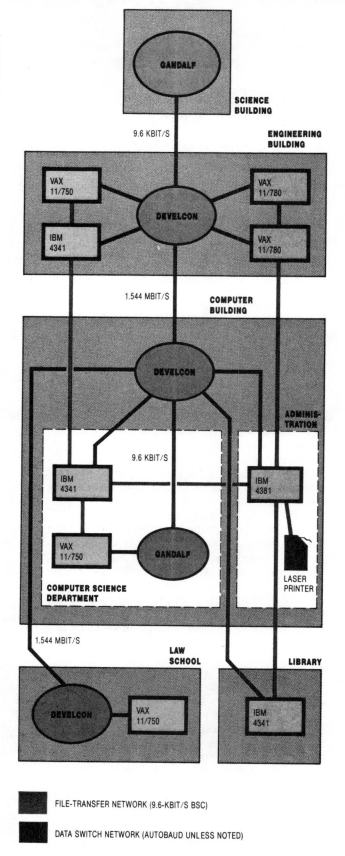

FILE-TRANSFER NETWORK (9.6-KBIT/S BSC)

DATA SWITCH NETWORK (AUTOBAUD UNLESS NOTED)

Apart from its file transfer network, the university has mainly been involved in IBM access from ASCII devices which consists of terminal-to-host communications. With the advent of microcomputers, however, this environment is rapidly changing. There is great interest in the development of local networks within campus departments. Several of these networks already tie microcomputers together in order for them to share data and printers. Most have been built using high-speed network hardware such as G-NET from Gateway Communications or S-NET from Novell Data Systems.

BYU's look ahead
These networks are not directly compatible with the existing data-switch network on campus. Yet many microcomputer users still require access to mainframe applications. At present, a microcomputer must have two network connections, one to its local network and another to the data switches. Because of the dual network connection requirement, the value of the local networks to the university has been diminished. When two different network connections (the local network and the data-switch interfaces) are required, the user must learn two different methods of interaction with network resources. This makes for a more difficult environment at microcomputer workstations and greater frustration for novice users. Some of the local network software, such as electronic mail, is not being used on campus because it cannot be delivered beyond the boundaries of the local network. Therefore, investigations are underway into means of linking the local networks directly to the rest of the campus machines.

Some manufacturers of local network hardware are developing gateways into established networks based on traditional IBM protocols such as binary synchronous communications or SNA (Systems Network Architecture). Another possible interface to the campus mainframes would be the development of a private X.25 packet network. Since the local networks are based on data packets, they could be adapted to the X.25 packet equipment that is available. At least this merits some investigation that has not yet been pursued by the campus.

The university is also considering a network connection to other universities. This would allow faculty and research personnel to communicate via electronic mail to their colleagues at other institutions. Several academic networks allow this type of capability of which Bitnet, a network of over 100 institutions, appears to be the most promising. Such a network connection would interface very well with the existing campus electronic-mail network. It would allow a faculty member to address messages to a colleague across the country as easily as is now done between buildings. From this new network connection should come an enhanced research environment for the university community.

IBM's VM operating system can accommodate remote 3270 terminals attached to 3271 controllers, but the reliability and support is less than ideal. Even with the Eclipse, the operations staff continually found that certain conditions occurred that would cause VM to disable the communications line. The situation was no better with the protocol converter. VM seems to provide little error recovery for exceptional conditions on the communications line. It simply stops polling the line and ignores the remote device. Operator intervention is then required to re-enable the communications line to the protocol converter.

Unaware
The computer operator was not always aware of this occurrence. As the number of users increased, the protocol converter was soon perceived by the users as an unreliable device even though most of the problem was in the host support software. It seemed incredible to BYU Computer Services that there should be so much difficulty with communications when the device was less than ten feet from the CPU.

There were other alternatives to these protocol converters that did not use remote communications software or expensive communications controllers. IBM offered a Series/1 minicomputer that attached directly to the mainframe channel. It emulated a 3272 local terminal controller. The Series/1 interacted with the host and then converted the 3270 terminal format into an ASCII data stream. The advantage to the direct channel attachment was speed and the freedom from the unreliable communications software. The Series/1 in every way acted like the 3272 channel attached controller it was designed to replace.

Success. . .for now
BYU rejected the Series/1 alternative because it seemed like a repeat of the Eclipse front-end that had begun its data communications shopping spree. A properly configured Series/1 for supporting 32 terminals cost in excess of $60,000.

In mid-1983, another protocol converter was introduced on the market, the Hydra II, manufactured by JDS Microprocessing. This device had one difference from the others in that it attached directly to the byte multiplexer channel rather than to a communications controller. It emulated an IBM 3272 control unit, as did the IBM Series/1. By that time, computer center management had a much better understanding of protocol converters and of how the devices supported ASCII terminals.

In the devices that had been evaluated, there were many different ways of supporting 3270 functions on ASCII terminals. During the evaluation of the Hydra, the ability to define and modify terminal definitions was deemed to be very useful. This was a feature that the Datalynx did not have. The most important reason for the decision to purchase a Hydra was the speed that the direct channel attachment provided. Earlier devices that had been evaluated had operated at speeds up to 9.6 kbit/s for data transfer with the host. If there were many ASCII terminals attached to the protocol converter, the host communications line became a bottleneck for data transfer. The Hydra II, attached to the byte multiplexer channel, could operate at 20,000 to 30,000 byte/s. This gave exceptionally good throughput when terminal activity on the device was high. A 16-port Hydra cost approximately $9,900.

The Hydra II offered three types of support for attached ASCII devices (Fig. 2). Like the other protocol converters, it allowed ASCII terminals to emulate IBM 3277s. It supported printers with IBM 1403 or 3211 line printer emulation. Finally, it offered a general I/O interface which provided unformatted read/write capabilities between host application programs and ASCII devices. This interface obviates the need to mimic a specific device which conforms to one of IBM's protocols. This interface was used to connect the Microdata minicomputer to the IBM mainframe.

The giant stirs

Due to the increased demands of ASCII terminal access to the IBM mainframes, the number of ASCII ports now available on the various IBM mainframes is approaching 100. A new IBM machine that is being installed in the university library will have only ASCII ports available to its users. No IBM 3270 terminals will be installed. This is due to the fact that most access to this machine will be from academic community members who have ASCII terminals and microcomputers.

IBM has now come full circle in providing ASCII terminal support. The company has most recently announced a model 7171 device controller that offers ASCII terminal attachment to the block multiplexer channel. Each controller can be expanded to support up to 64 ASCII devices at a very competitive price. Although this device has been slow to come to market, it should provide an attractive alternative to the earlier offerings from IBM.

The 7171 appears to be a low-cost implementation of the Series/1 that IBM has offered for some time. The IBM people have seen the popularity of this type of interface to their mainframes and are now providing the access that BYU originally sought some five years ago. If the 7171 proves to be a reliable device, it will surely open up the IBM world to the masses of ASCII terminals and microcomputers in the computing world. When that happens, more users will reap the benefits of interconnection that BYU has enjoyed, but hopefully without having to tackle the same problems. ∎

Kelly McDonald, manager of technical support and Planning for information systems services of Brigham Young University, graduated from that institution with a degree in Electronics Technology. He is currently doing graduate work in Computer Science.

Section 4
Management

Duncan Phillips, Perle Systems Ltd., Scarborough, Ont.

Picking the right strategy for protocol conversion

Confusion does not have to reign in the face of increasing hardware and software choices offered to data communications managers.

From hesitant beginnings in the mid-1970s, the protocol conversion industry has produced a multitude of companies competing for shares of what has become a very lucrative market.

As in most branches of the data communications industry, various degrees of success have been achieved by the developers and marketers of the wide variety of products in this sector of the market. While much attention has been paid to the basic reasons for using protocol conversion, too little focus has centered on some of the critical areas of various approaches. Such a focus may provide users with some of the questions to ask when making a buying decision on protocol conversion products.

For clarity, the discussion here revolves around the most common application of protocol conversion technology—the IBM 3270 world. Still, other communications protocols are becoming targets for the protocol converter vendors, and a few examples are discussed below.

Assuming that a decision has been made to examine protocol conversion as an option in expanding or replacing a communications network, the user should be familiar with the advantages that the products under consideration can offer: cost savings through the use of inexpensive or existing asynchronous terminals in a synchronous network; access to dial-up services; access to mainframes reachable through data switches or voice-data PBXs. However, in performing the conversion, or offering the additional functions, compromises have to be made. These areas must be considered carefully when selecting a protocol converter product.

In examining the effectiveness of the conversion product, it is necessary to have an appreciation of how and, probably more importantly, where in the terminal-to-host link the conversion process takes place. There are four classes of approach to protocol conversion, or four points within the network at which conversion occurs:

1. Host-resident software, which allows the host to communicate with devices that are not usually supported.
2. Controller replacement, where a hardware product replaces the cluster controller and attaches to the appropriate asynchronous terminals.
3. In-line conversion, which is a hardware product that attaches to the synchronous controller and usually connects to only one asynchronous device.
4. Terminal resident, where normally a combination of hardware and software is physically integrated into the asynchronous device (Fig. 1).

Host-resident software is fairly self-explanatory. This is a software package added to the host that supports asynchronous devices. It can be argued that this is not strictly protocol conversion, as no communications ever takes place using the original synchronous protocol. However, code conversion and terminal emulation still take place. This approach could offer greater cost savings than other solutions because no additional hardware is required.

Against this must be balanced the cost of multiple asynchronous ports on the host and the possible addition of processing overhead to the front-end processor as well as the potential increase in host memory requirements. Also, the newly acquired host software must be able to connect with the application and operating systems currently in use and those that may be released in the future.

Controller replacement is the most common type of protocol conversion product. As this is the solution most frequently proposed, we should examine the methodology and architectures a little more closely.

206

Many of the comments applicable here also apply to the in-line and terminal-resident protocol converters that will be considered later.

The replacement controller's function can be divided into two parts. First, it must connect to the host and appear as a normally supported IBM cluster controller. Typically, a protocol converter will emulate a 3274 or 3276 (or, in some cases, the 3271 or 3275).

The controller emulation function of the protocol converter responds to polls from the host, collects the received blocks until a full 3270 screen is in its buffer, then performs code conversion and passes data to the terminal handler part of the converter (and vice versa for data received from the terminal). An important consideration here is whether the converter can start transmitting to the terminal as soon as data for that terminal starts to be received from the host or whether the converter waits until all data for that terminal is received before transmitting to the terminal. Under the first scenario, there can be extended response times if the transmission speed to the terminal is low (2.4 kbit/s or lower). This may occur because the screen presentation has not been optimized (the protocol converter optimizes the transmission by examining the complete screen buffer and transmitting the data to the terminal with as few characters as possible); under certain circumstances the host can take up to 4 kbytes to write a 2-kbyte screen. Under the second scenario, problems can arise if the host link is low speed, such as 1.2 kbit/s or 2.4 kbit/s, as this can mean a long wait while the controller collects its data.

The second function of the controller is to emulate the IBM terminal. To do this, the controller first paints

the screen on the terminal and then accepts keystrokes from the terminal keyboard, interpreting the characters according to the data editing rules of the 3278. This is where the concept of keyboard mapping comes in. Keys that exist on the 3278 but not on the asynchronous terminal have to be emulated by escape sequences or control codes. Therefore, the converter must constantly monitor the incoming data checking for these sequences. The terminal handler now updates the screen presentation and, at the appropriate time, passes control to the emulator function of the converter, which forwards the data to the host. An important consideration here is the actual hardware architecture adopted by the converter manufacturer. There are generally two groups—the single processor architecture and the multiprocessor.

The single processor approach tends to result in a low-cost product. With the requirement for the one processor to handle all the converter's functions, however, this usually means a limit to the number of asynchronous ports, delayed response times, or throughput limitations. For the low-volume user with dial-up terminals, or perhaps two or three local terminals, this can still be a cost-efficient approach. With the increasing use by converter vendors of more powerful 16- or 32-bit processors, the limitation inherent in the single processor architecture is diminishing.

The multiprocessor approach typically uses multiple 8-bit processors, in most cases the Z80 or Z80A with one processor devoted to the host communications and one processor handling each asynchronous terminal or group of terminals. This architecture normally means a higher-cost product. But by remaining with

---

1. Different locations. A) An asynchronous software driver can reside in a host or front-end processor. B) A protocol converter can take the place of an SNA/SDLC 3278 controller. C) Converter may connect to a single ASCII device. D) A combination of hardware and software can reside within a terminal.

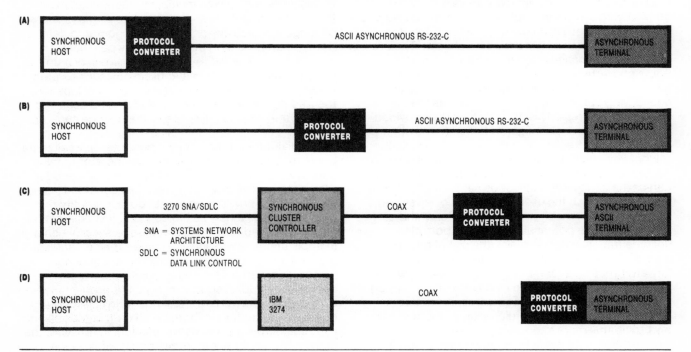

well-proven technology that offers economies of scale, such as the Z80, lower costs are being achieved by some of the multiprocessor converter vendors, with per-port costs approaching those of the single-processor offerings. The major advantages normally offered by the multiprocessor systems are higher numbers of terminal ports, faster response times, and greater overall throughput. The debate over response times and throughput versus cost does not normally apply to the third and fourth types of protocol converter — the in-line hardware and the terminal-resident solution.

The in-line protocol converter connects to the coaxial port on the IBM cluster controller and then to the asynchronous terminal or other device. In essence, its operation is similar to that of the controller replacement except that it takes data from a high-speed coaxial link instead of emulating a cluster controller. Applications exist where the network has cluster controllers already in the required locations and the number of asynchronous accesses needed in each location does not justify the addition of another controller.

Terminal-resident protocol conversion normally takes the form of additional hardware and software, which enable a terminal to communicate synchronously and to ape a 3270 terminal connected to the cluster controller or a cluster controller with one terminal attached. The most common manifestation of this approach occurs with microcomputers, where it is the addition of an expansion card, plus software, that makes possible the protocol conversion.

Problems and compromises
In examining the feasibility of the proposed network and products, it is necessary to be aware of potential problem areas — the reasons why some protocol converters work well in situations where others do not.

The first area in which compromises may be made is the configuration of the link between the protocol converter and the host. Typically, the communications port to be defined on the host has a large set of variables for which options must be chosen. The protocol converter configuration must be set to match. Some converter vendors take a simplistic approach to this problem by fixing the majority of characteristics and leaving options only on items such as line speed and polling address. This approach works, provided that the host can be configured to match the options.

Other vendors allow virtually any option within the link between host and converter. This is a much more flexible approach, but in order to make it work, each part of the configuration must be set correctly. This is the point at which the user normally involves systems programmers. What should be looked for at this stage to help eliminate potential problems is both clear documentation, which explains the use of and the effects of changing each parameter, and a straightforward procedure for making the necessary changes.

Typical restrictions on the host link include support for only one or two polling addresses, block size limitations, and lack of any diagnostics or error-recovery procedures.

Configuration restrictions on the terminal side are less common but still exist. Unless the user's current and future terminal population matches the restrictions imposed, it is advisable to look for a converter that can support a wide range of terminal types and any combination of communications features such as parity, line speed, and number of stop bits. Also, in the area of controller functions that are not supported, such restrictions as lack of extended-character attribute support are often significant because the eventual target terminal is not able to display attributes on a character-by-character basis. Be careful to look for such things as 3278 key functions that are not supported, absence of an NRZI (nonreturn to zero) option, or individual commands that are not recognized. This last deficiency usually manifests itself when the application and the converter appear to simply lock up. The host will have generated a command that the protocol converter does not recognize, the converter will not make the correct response and cause the host to resend the command, and the result is an indefinite loop that can be recovered only by restarting the converter.

Probably the most common complaint heard about protocol converters is the lack of performance — usually meaning delayed response times. This can be attributed to three factors. First, the speed of the synchronous link to the host may be the problem. For high throughput applications look for support for high speeds on this link. The next possible culprit is the speed of the link to the asynchronous terminal. Speeds up to 19.2 kbit/s are often supported for locally connected terminals, but if the user is dialing in at 300 bit/s or 1.2 kbit/s, then that is the speed for that facility. In this case, look for a converter that optimizes the screen presentation so as few data characters as possible are sent over the asynchronous link. The third troublemaker may be the converter itself. The processing overhead of handling the host protocol and simultaneously interacting with multiple terminals can mean that some converters, especially some single processor offerings, can achieve only very low aggregate data throughput. Less than 300 characters per second is not unknown. This is fine for the occasional dial-up user, but for higher volume applications such as gateways from a PBX or multiple local terminals, look for the total aggregate throughput that can be achieved, not just the maximum line speed that can be supported.

In a dial-up environment, it is possible for a call to be made to the protocol converter, the operator to have gone through the host's security procedures, and for the call to have accidentally been disconnected in mid-session. If the protocol converter does not notify the host and allows a new call to connect, it is possible for an unauthorized user to gain access to sensitive data. In applications where sensitive data is being handled, features such as auto-log-off are necessary on the protocol converter (it is possible for the protocol converter to add levels of security). For problem determination, the converters should perform self-tests on hardware and software, both on an on-going basis and by request from a supervisory function. In addition, the converter's ability to report diagnostic information (such as terminal and host status and whether the converter is being polled by the host) can provide useful information in an attempt to locate network problems that may be external to the protocol converter.

Another question to be addressed is whether the protocol converter can keep pace with any changes that may be made in the host architecture. Can new releases of software be installed easily by the user, by down-line loading from the manufacturer, or loading a new disk or tape, or is it necessary to return the unit for upgrade or fit new PROMS?

Traditionally, a protocol converter is placed between the asynchronous device or network and the synchronous host. As explained earlier, the converter itself provides the data editing capabilities of the emulated IBM terminal. The link between the converter and the asynchronous terminal is true full duplex. The converter, in fact, treats the terminal as two logically separate devices—the keyboard and the screen. Increasingly, data communications networks are using packet-switching technology, most noticeably in the use of public and private X.25 networks. To integrate a protocol converter into such a network can cause problems if hardware selection is made without an understanding of the protocol involved. Figure 2 shows two typical configurations.

Figure 2A shows the converter connected at the remote side of the X.25 network. The 3270 data stream from the host must be packetized by either a host-resident package such as NPSI (Network Packet Switch Interface) or DAS (Datapac Access Software) or by a suitable PAD (packet assembler/disassembler) either separated or integrated within the protocol converter. But there are potential problems:

■ The PAD may pass idle polls across the X.25 net-

work, resulting in diminished efficiency.
■ The converter-to-remote PAD may not be compatible with the host-resident software, as this software may handle part of the addressing of the X.25 network.
■ The hardware or software may limit X.25 options such as numbers of physical and virtual circuits, access to closed user groups, and so on.

Figure 2B shows the converter connected at the host side of the X.25 network. Here, the converter is communicating in full-duplex character mode over a half-duplex network. The result is a large number of single-character packets and thus high-packet charges and long response times. This problem can be resolved by using a converter which communicates with a suitable block mode terminal.

The future

The question has been raised about whether protocol conversion is still a valid approach given recent advances in data communications technology. But just as important are the price decreases of IBM's own terminal products and very aggressive marketing and pricing by some plug-compatible vendors. Along with this decrease in IBM pricing there exists a decrease in the price of the asynchronous terminal hardware, which means that the percentage hardware cost savings that a protocol converter can offer are being maintained, but the actual dollar savings are not as dramatic. It seems only recently that protocol converter vendors said that their product could allow a $1,200 terminal to replace a $3,000 IBM product. Now the claim is that the product will allow a $600 terminal to replace a $1,500 IBM product. IBM's own recent announcement of the 7171 protocol converter product, combined with these other factors, leads to the conclusion that a third-party protocol conversion proposal must contain sav-

---

2. Hardware placement. *A protocol mediating between a synchronous host and asynchronous terminals may be placed either (A) remote from the host or (B)* *remote from the asynchronous terminals; in this case, the PAD and protocol converter may be integrated into one unit.*

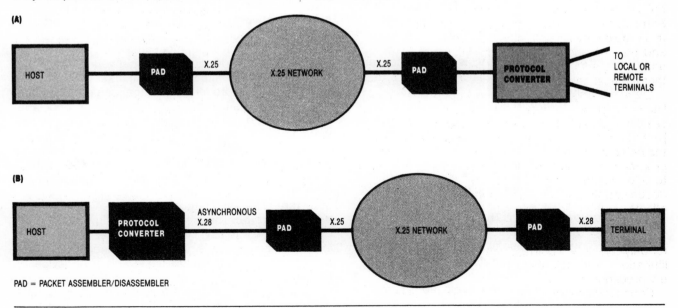

PAD = PACKET ASSEMBLER/DISASSEMBLER

ings and additional functions beyond the protocol converter's basic reason for being, the ability to use asynchronous communications.

There is an impressive list of added functions and extra benefits:

■ *Device independence.* A good example of this is IBM System/36 or System/38 users who are contemplating the expansion of their terminal networks but do not want to commit expenditure on hardware that may not be usable in the medium term because they are planning to migrate to a 4300 series mainframe. Several protocol converter vendors now offer both 5250 and 3270 terminal emulation using the same hardware, so that if the migration does take place, a simple upgrade of the converter hardware, or even just a software change, can convert all the terminals to 3270s.

■ *Multiple protocols and hosts.* Converters are available that give one terminal access to several different hosts or protocols, often simultaneously. Examples include setups that offer simultaneous 3270 and 3770 access for microcomputers to act as 3278s for enquiry and data entry and as RJE stations for data transfer; and also equipment that allows terminals to switch from one host to another with each host using a different protocol. Here the converter acts as a simple data switch in addition to performing its conversion functions.

■ *Additional security.* By the converter requiring a password procedure to be followed before allowing access to the host, it can add an additional layer of security.

Inactivity timeouts allow the protocol converter to disconnect a call that has no activity for a preset period of time—again, discouraging unauthorized use and saving idle connect time—freeing up the port for another user and saving dial-up telephone costs. A few converters also offer the U. S. National Bureau of Standards' Data Encryption Standard algorithm on the host link as an additional security feature.

■ *Programmable terminal support.* Allows the user to define custom keyboard layouts or redefine the screen presentation without changing the host software.

■ *Modifiable character sets.* Allow protocol converters at the hub of an international network deal with foreign languages.

■ *Printer passthrough.* This is a common buzzword in the protocol converter industry. It allows an asynchronous terminal with an auxiliary printer port to connect itself and a printer over one asynchronous line so that the host can address the two devices separately.

■ *Floating printer support.* Allows one printer defined to the host to be selected as required by any one of a number of remote users.

■ *Microcomputer support.* The micro-to-mainframe link is an application area which has spawned a large number of products, both software only and combined hardware and software. The protocol converter itself can provide the hardware connection without requiring the addition of synchronous communications hardware to the microcomputer. Products range from terminal

emulation to 3278 inquiry with data, file, and program transfer capability.

One final feature that can make a protocol conversion solution more acceptable (this has come mainly from terminal manufacturers rather than protocol converter vendors) is the advent of the low-cost asynchronous terminal with the 3270-look-alike keyboard.

Protocol conversion is a technology with a firm future. Admittedly, the increasing price competition is causing some vendors to review their offerings and marketing strategies. The results of this review are manifesting themselves in various ways, including the need to offer more and better features and functions in order to cost justify the product. In addition, with IBM legitimizing the protocol conversion product with the 7171 announcement, users are likely to see even fiercer competition between the major players in the industry. Sufficient hardware and software protocol conversion products have been delivered over recent years to ensure that the skills and technologies have been refined to the level where a buyer can have confidence in a product's ability to perform some of the more esoteric functions that are being promoted.

One word of warning, however. It is very easy to be led to the conclusion that a protocol converter must be fully loaded with every available feature in order to be a justifiable purchase. This is not true. For example, some of the lowest-cost protocol converters work extremely well in applications that require little in the way of throughput power or security, such as low-speed dial-up to public databases. A different kind of mistake can be made when a protocol converter is chosen that can act as a simple data switch. In this case, the real requirements of the network might be better satisfied by a high-throughput protocol converter used as an IBM gateway from a powerful data switch handling all asynchronous communications.

Wish list
This list covers some of the areas that the potential protocol converter user should be watching for:

■ *Local networking.* One or two protocol converter manufacturers offer some simple local processing for connected terminals, but most are waiting for some degree of standardization in local networks. Two notable exceptions are already on the market—one a multiport, multiprotocol product that can be interconnected through a token-passing network protocol, and the second a distributed network that uses a central unit communicating with small remote units by a private protocol. Each remote unit connects to a terminal, microcomputer or other device, and the central unit provides asynchronous and synchronous gateways to other networks, as well as handling local processing and storage for each remote device.

■ *Deconversion.* This is the ability to allow a real 3270 user to connect to asynchronous services or devices. Two approaches to this have recently been announced by vendors. The first is a low-cost single-user device that connects in the coax line between the 3270 terminal and its cluster controller, and provides a single asynchronous connnection. The second is a device that is situated in the communications line between the 3274 cluster controller and host front-end processor, and provides multiple selectable asynchronous connections sufficient for each terminal in the cluster.

■ **Combined coax and asynchronous.** Terminals on one controller. One such product is currently on the market, but the coax connection is not class A. It cannot yet mix 3270s and asynchronous terminals on the same controller.

■ **More sophisticated X.25 support.** Several vendors have already announced families of products that provide connection of 3270 clusters and asynchronous terminals over X.25 networks. More announcements in this area are certain to be made in the near future.

■ **Integrated security.** Such as proprietary error-detection and recovery protocols on the asynchronous side, integrated secure dial-back hardware, and built-in Data Encryption Standard.

■ **Office automation.** Packages such as DISOSS (IBM's document exchange program for data processing to office automation products) and architectures such as APPC (advanced program to program communication) will allow protocol converters to support various manufacturers' word processing and office automation packages.

■ **Other protocols.** Many of the current protocol converter vendors already offer products in areas other than the IBM 3270 world. The small protocol converter manufacturer is typically selling into a niche in the market, providing a solution to a data communications incompatibility problem that may be too small a market to warrant the interest of the larger competitors. Many of the larger manufacturers started with just such a strategy and have expanded into the lucrative but highly competitive 3270 world. Protocol conversion products have for some time existed in a number of other areas, such as IBM batch protocols (2780, 3780, 3770, HASP, 2741), Sperry Uniscope, Honeywell V.I.P., IBM point-of-sale and financial protocols (3600), NCR and Burroughs poll/Select protocols, and IBM 5250 (for System/34/36/38).

The 5250 world deserves a special mention. This is the major protocol used for remote communications on the IBM System/34/36/38. In terms of numbers of installed processors, this market outnumbers the 3270 market by a factor of approximately 10 to 1. Obviously, the System 34/36/38 user has a smaller network requirement than the mainframe user, but the significance of this market is indicated by the increasingly large number of vendors offering ASCII asynchronous-to-5251 products.

Other protocols are beginning to interest some of the major players in this market. Areas for which general purpose products may be launched in the not-too-distant future could well handle asynchronous-to-Wang-VS and microcomputer-to-IBM-Financial-Loop conversion. ■

Duncan Phillips, a manager with Perle Systems Ltd., has worked in the data processing and communications field for the past 13 years.

Jeff Elkins, Amdahl Corp., Sunnyvale, Calif.

Status reports yield key data for network planning

Today's network managers need surefire ways to gather, analyze, and present performance statistics. Here's how.

oncise, timely status reports are the cornerstone upon which network management bases future planning decisions. This planning consists of pairing new technologies and communications services with existing and future needs, as well as assessing the impact of projected corporate and network growth. Specifically, there are four basic aspects of such decision making: design, implementation, control, and planning.

Network design involves selecting the network architecture, line protocols, network components, and possible communications services, based on geographical distribution of nodes, traffic volume, and types of applications (inquiry/response and batch, for example). Performance requirements, response time, and availability are also defined during this phase.

After management selects the appropriate vendors to support the design, network implementation begins. Ideally, at this point controls are installed to monitor key network performance parameters. Periodic network status reports based on these parameters are essential for day-to-day network control.

One of the primary purposes of network status reports is to identify usage trends, which indicate the approach of thresholds, such as response time, that will ultimately affect network performance. These reports should also address immediate problem areas that currently jeopardize the network's performance objectives. For example, exceptional conditions, such as excessive error counts on communications lines or terminal control-unit failures, should be automatically reported. Tuning issues, such as congestion or device contention, and resource underutilization are other key issues that demand management's attention.

The generalized reporting scheme described in this article can be used on any network. The model merely provides a framework—within a management context—for making planning decisions. Accordingly, a prescribed sequence of steps must be followed. This article focuses on response time, resource utilization, network availability, and throughput. An application and evaluation of the model, in terms of its ability to monitor and report performance data, is included.

Figure 1 shows a diagram of a decision model used in the capacity planning process. The model depicts the logical flow of information in the management reports and how this data can be used to arrive at prudent decisions about the network.

At the top of the model is the actual network configuration. This connotes the particular combination of hardware and software chosen to ensure acceptable performance levels from the perspective of both the user and the management and technical staff responsible for maintaining the network. The configuration approximates the performance or service levels defined in the network's design phase. However, as is the case in most situations, such performance standards are all too quickly compromised. Nevertheless, it is the task of management and network technicians to deliver the best possible service to the user within the constraints of existing technologies and corporate budgets.

In the decision model (Fig. 1), the process directly below "network configuration" is involved in the parameter values for performance and resource usage. Note that arrows go both ways between the network's configuration and the observed performance levels. This indicates an interdependent relationship. The specified activity at this level is to gather empirical data about performance and usage. Hardware or software monitors can be used to collect this information.

During the model's next logical process, data is analyzed to reveal trends in usage levels. Thus, by

1. Keeping track. *Hardware and software are chosen to ensure desired performance. The charts reflect gathering and analyzing data and generating reports.*

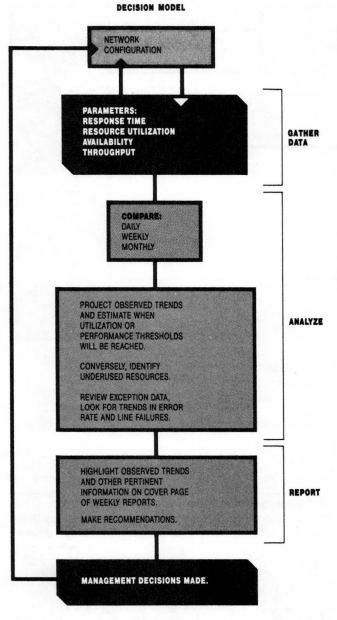

DECISION MODEL

NETWORK CONFIGURATION

PARAMETERS:
RESPONSE TIME
RESOURCE UTILIZATION
AVAILABILITY
THROUGHPUT

GATHER DATA

COMPARE:
DAILY
WEEKLY
MONTHLY

PROJECT OBSERVED TRENDS
AND ESTIMATE WHEN
UTILIZATION OR
PERFORMANCE THRESHOLDS
WILL BE REACHED.

CONVERSELY, IDENTIFY
UNDERUSED RESOURCES.

REVIEW EXCEPTION DATA,
LOOK FOR TRENDS IN ERROR
RATE AND LINE FAILURES.

ANALYZE

HIGHLIGHT OBSERVED TRENDS
AND OTHER PERTINENT
INFORMATION ON COVER PAGE
OF WEEKLY REPORTS.

MAKE RECOMMENDATIONS.

REPORT

MANAGEMENT DECISIONS MADE.

periodically comparing observed parameter values, network growth can be projected. As growth trends are uncovered, this information can be passed on to management as part of periodic status reports. Based on the reports, management then makes its decisions regarding the network configuration. For example, if the reports indicate that response time for a given line will reach unacceptable limits within three months, management should plan to provide greater throughput on the line by increasing the bandwidth, using a more efficient line protocol, or making some other configuration change in order to avert user dissatisfaction.

As an example, Amdahl, the Sunnyvale, Calif.-based computer manufacturer, is generating periodic status reports for its corporate network by employing an array of SNA (Systems Network Architecture) tools. These tools define collection points used in the data-gathering process. Collection points exist in the host, in the front-end communications processors, and in the terminal control units. The data is gathered and passed to host databases, where a combination of programs is used both to analyze, interpret, and correlate data and to produce reports. Figure 2 depicts this arrangement of collection points and host processing programs and indicates their interdependence.

Queuing theory has shown that a classic relationship exists between response time and the degree to which a line is being loaded (Fig. 3). The average delay increases dramatically after line utilization has reached 50 percent. If a network is slightly loaded, the average delay is simply the average response time. But, when utilization reaches 50 percent, average delay doubles because an average of one user or request for service is waiting in the queue at any given time.

NPM (Network Performance Monitor) is an IBM VTAM (Virtual Telecommunications Access Method) application that gathers usage and performance statistics for network resources. Information collected by NPM can be helpful in performance evaluation, capacity planning, and network tuning. The Network Performance Analyzer (NPA) is incorporated into the Network Control Program (NCP) to communicate with NPM for passing performance data to the host.

These NCP programs function as major nodes in an SNA network (Fig. 4) and are designated as SNA physical unit type 4. NPM runs in a single VTAM SSCP (System Services Control Point) in the host, yet it can communicate with all the NCPs simultaneously. Records collected by NPM are passed to SMF (System Management Facility) under the host operating system, MVS (Multiple Virtual Storage), and then to MICS (MVS Integrated Control System), a database management software product that uses SAS programming language. (MICS is marketed by Morino Associates Inc. in Vienna, Va.) MICS produces stock reports with SMF's NPM records and copies them into its own data sets.

By comparing utilization at fixed intervals, it is possible to project when unacceptable response time will be reached. And in some cases, underused lines are identified and eliminated from the network, thus realizing considerable savings.

The Response Time Monitor (RTM), a recent feature of IBM's 3274 terminal control unit, is also used in measuring response time. RTM operates in conjunction with another SNA network tool, NLDM (Network Logical Data Manager), which runs as a VTAM application and is invoked as a subsystem under NCCF (Network Communications Control Facility), a VTAM management application through which all SNA network tools can be controlled.

IBM 3274 control units with RTM can measure end-to-end response time (the elapsed time between a query from a network end point and receipt of a response) for individual terminals. The NLDM package sends requests for response-time statistics (in the form

2. Information drop-off. *Host processing programs and data collection points are used in the data-gathering process. Collection points exist in the host, in the front-end processors, and in the terminal control units. Data is gathered and passed to the host, where it is analyzed, interpreted, and correlated for reports.*

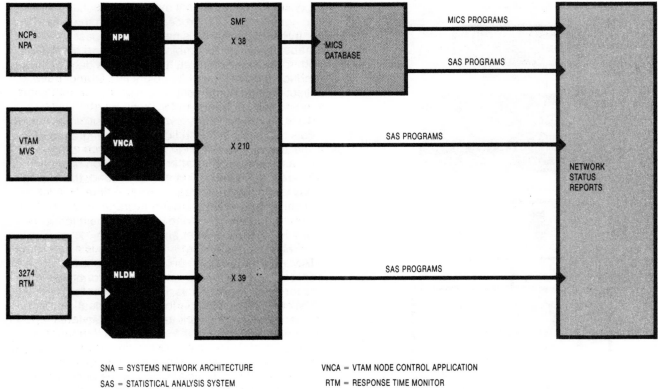

SNA = SYSTEMS NETWORK ARCHITECTURE
SAS = STATISTICAL ANALYSIS SYSTEM
NCP = NETWORK CONTROL PROGRAM
NPA = NETWORK PERFORMANCE ANALYZER
SMF = SYSTEM MANAGEMENT FACILITY
MVS = MULTIPLE VIRTUAL SYSTEMS
MICS = MVS INTEGRATED CONTROL SYSTEM

VNCA = VTAM NODE CONTROL APPLICATION
RTM = RESPONSE TIME MONITOR
NLDM = NETWORK LOGICAL DATA MANAGER

X 38
X 210 = RECORD TYPES (HEXADECIMAL)
X 39

of special packets called path information units, or PIUs). The controllers respond by returning the information in their own PIUs. RTM controllers are also capable of sending unsolicited messages about response time at the end of individual terminal sessions.

NPM is also capable of measuring and recording end-to-end response time for SNA sessions. This measurement can be broken down into two components: all delays to and from the host and host processing time itself. In fact, NPM's ability to segment response time allows the exact location of bottlenecks to be pinpointed. NLDM, on the other hand, gives a more precise figure for end-to-end response time but does not have the ability to segment it.

In addition to line utilization, NPM also measures and records statistics about front-end utilization. Both processing cycle and buffer utilization counts aid the capacity-planning function in projecting growth and planning for additional resources.

Availability, as perceived by the user, can be deduced from NPM line usage statistics. It is reasonable to infer that the line was down, for example, if usage for a given line is normally 40 percent each hour, and the

3. Queuing. *Existing models indicated a relationship between response time and the line loading. Average delay increases dramatically after usage exceeds 50 percent.*

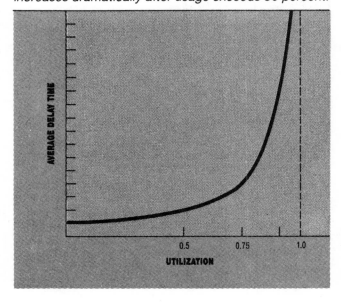

4. Major modes. *NCP software nodes function as major nodes in the SNA network architecture and are designated as physical unit type 4.*

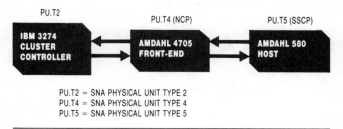

PU.T2

PU.T4 (NCP)

PU.T5 (SSCP)

| IBM 3274 CLUSTER CONTROLLER | AMDAHL 4705 FRONT-END | AMDAHL 580 HOST |

PU.T2 = SNA PHYSICAL UNIT TYPE 2
PU.T4 = SNA PHYSICAL UNIT TYPE 4
PU.T5 = SNA PHYSICAL UNIT TYPE 5

daily report shows that it dropped to 0 percent.

Another networking tool, VNCA (VTAM Node Control Application), holds the promise of yielding availability statistics. This tool's primary purpose is to automate NCCF operator functions and to offer dynamic, hierarchical status displays of individual resources within SNA domains. Since VNCA and NLDM are subsystems of NCCF, and NCCF is an extension of the network control function of VTAM, close attention must be paid to maintaining continuity between the various software release and maintenance levels of these software products to ensure VTAM's support of NCCF and NCCF's subsequent support of VNCA and NLDM.

As Figure 2 illustrates, VNCA does not maintain its own databases. Dynamic displays are created after VNCA has read certain control blocks within VTAM and MVS. It is possible, however, to turn on the SMF recording facility within VNCA. The SMF record type used is at the discretion of the user; it is not defined by the network architecture. Amdahl has elected to use record type 210 (hexadecimal), a record type specified by SNA, for VNCA records. MICS does not read and process VNCA SMF records, so Amdahl has written its own SAS programs to access this data.

There are some serious doubts about the viability of relying on VNCA for availability figures. VNCA is in-

voked by network operators under NCCF. For instance, if VTAM resources, such as communications lines, are activated or deactivated from a console other than the NCCF/VNCA console, VNCA will have no knowledge of the change in the status of the resources.

More misgivings
A second area of doubt concerns the reliability of the availability of the statistics themselves. VNCA samples VTAM and MVS control blocks based on timer parameters specified by the systems programmer. If the timer is set to one hour and a line is down for 45 minutes between sampling intervals, VNCA will show the line as being 100 percent available for that period. Setting timers for very short intervals gives a much more accurate picture of resource availability but greatly increases the number of central processing unit cycles required by the application to acquire the statistics.

Despite these problems, Amdahl is setting timers for fairly short intervals and producing rudimentary availability reports for its lines and other SNA nodes. These initial reports contain a calculated average of availability for lines and nodes within a 24-hour period.

The reliability or availability of a line has obvious performance implications. Some circuits are more reliable than others. International circuits, for example, tend to be the most unreliable. If periodic status reports that indicate the network's specified performance requirements for availability are consistently not met by a line, then the capacity planner and management should consider providing additional backup circuits from another common or international carrier.

Throughput refers to the amount of traffic per unit of time carried by a network. One objective of network control is to ensure that the network is passing as much traffic as possible. Transmission rate of information bits (TRIB), a network performance parameter, describes the effective rate of data transfer within a network. Many factors affect TRIB:
- Line speed and circuit bandwidth.
- Propagation delays.
- Modem delays.
- Whether terminals are multidropped or multiplexed.
- Serving speed or capacity of the front-end.
- Polling scheme.
- Error rates.

NPM collects byte counts for SDLC (Synchronous Data Link Control) and BSC (Binary Synchronous Communications) resources. Byte-count data for SDLC logical units includes not only user data but also SNA overhead, such as transmission header, request header, and a cyclical redundancy check. For SDLC physical units and links, byte count also includes overhead. BSC terminals, clusters, and line byte counts reflect overhead as well as user data. When using NPM statistics a certain percentage of the total must be subtracted in order to allow for overhead and get a more realistic idea of TRIB (see table). ■

Jeff Elkins received a B. A. from the University of California at Berkeley and an M. B. A. from Golden Gate University, San Francisco.

Software evaluation

CATEGORIES	NPM/NPA	NLDM	VNCA
A SUBSYSTEM OF NCCF	NO	YES	YES
CAN BE LOGGED ONTO FROM NCCF	YES	YES	YES
RESPONSE TIME END-TO-END, SEGMENTED	YES	NO	NO
RESPONSE TIME END-TO-END	YES	YES	YES
REQUIRES DEFINITE RESPONSE PROTOCOL	YES	NO	NO
RESOURCE UTILIZATION	YES	NO	NO
AVAILABILITY	YES*	NO	NO
THROUGHPUT	YES*	NO	NO

*USER CAN CALCULATE THESE STATISTICS WITH DATA COLLECTED BY THIS TOOL.

N. Dean Meyer, N. Dean Meyer and Associates Inc., Ridgefield, Conn.

How to design a nonrestrictive microcomputer policy

Telling users how to connect, not what to buy, can be politically and technically smart. Controls need not be coercive.

The proliferation of desktop computers in business and government is a mixed blessing for data communications and networking managers who get caught between the demands of users and upper management. Users want to buy and implement a variety of microcomputers. Being able to select their own machines often gives users greater job satisfaction and enhances their productivity. However, linking and supporting such diverse computers can be a real headache for management, which seeks integration. Managers want all computers in the organization to have the ability to exchange information and to appear to the user as a single, cohesive set of information tools.

Often, management will respond to the influx of small computers by issuing policy statements that limit the number of brands of hardware and software that the organization can use. This highly restrictive approach, however, usually draws a negative response from users. Considering that the technology can be purchased from a local retail store, such policy statements on company standards may have little impact. Strict controls make integration easier but often result in disgruntled, less-productive users. A policy that limits purchasing choices to the wares of only certain vendors seems to favor technology over business.

A more creative approach to microcomputer policy can guide users toward integrated computer networks without excessive restrictions. This philosophy can be summarized in the statement, "Tell people how to connect their computers to the network, not what computer to buy." In addition to minimizing the restrictions on users who wish to purchase microcomputers, the more liberal, business-oriented policy uses a carrot rather than a stick approach to gain user cooperation, and it leaves room for user innovation.

By drafting a microcomputer policy statement that is based on data communications, the information support staff can help strike a workable balance. Data communications managers, as part of that staff, can contribute the linchpin element of the policy: networking standards.

In addition to easing the integration of desktop computers into networks throughout the organization, a microcomputer policy can encourage the development of appropriate and high-payoff applications by users. Appropriate applications are those that meet the success criteria of the user's job and address issues relevant to corporate strategy. High-payoff uses of microcomputers lead to a significant impact on the bottom line, in terms of user and organization effectiveness. (They contrast with applications that only provide marginal productivity gains.)

Microcomputer policy statements can be used to advertise the services provided by the staff support group, to help users select applications appropriate for computing by individuals, and to clarify the office procedures that should be modified or defined to use microcomputers effectively. A comprehensive microcomputer policy statement addresses four topics (see table):
- Technological integration.
- Staff services.
- Appropriate applications.
- Office procedures.

The politics of policy
A microcomputer policy is more than a technical document; it reveals the attitude of the information support staff toward the users and describes the distribution of power between the two groups. The statement, therefore, often has political as well as

Elements of a successful policy

TECHNOLOGICAL INTEGRATION	STAFF SERVICES	OFFICE PROCEDURES	APPLICATIONS GUIDELINES
FILE TRANSPORT STANDARDS	**PEOPLE SERVICES**	HARDWARE AND DATA SECURITY	WHETHER TO PUT A RESOURCE ON A MICROCOMPUTER DETERMINED BY:
TERMINAL EMULATION	—DISCOUNTS, LICENSES	TREATMENT OF SOFTWARE LICENSES AND COPYRIGHTS	—TECHNICAL CONSTRAINTS, FOR EXAMPLE, MEMORY, SPEED
NETWORK PROTOCOL	—SOFTWARE NEWS, UPDATE	BACKUP PROCEDURES	—LEVEL OF OWNERSHIP OF DATA
—DATA TRANSPORT	—TRAINING, INFORMATION CENTER, HOT LINE	FILE-NAMING CONVENTIONS	—CENTRALITY, DEPENDENCE ON SUPPORT
—FILE INTERCHANGE	—APPLICATIONS DEVELOPMENT	PROBLEM DIAGNOSIS METHODS	
FILE CONTENT STANDARDS	—USER GROUPS	SOURCES OF PERIPHERALS, SOFTWARE, SUPPLIES	
SEQUENTIAL TEXT	—MAINTENANCE	ENVIRONMENTAL CONDITIONS: TEMPERATURE, HUMIDITY, POWER, INTERFERENCE	
FILE CONTENT STANDARDS	**NETWORK SERVICES**	ERGONOMIC WORK-SPACE AND FURNITURE DESIGN	
INTERFACE TO ARCHIVES	—ARCHIVAL, SHARED FILES	DOCUMENTATION OF USER-DEVELOPED OPERATING PROCEDURES	
SOFTWARE TRANSPORTABILITY	—PRINTERS, PLOTTERS, SLIDE MAKERS, SCANNERS	METHODS OF MOVING INFORMATION	
OPERATING SYSTEM STANDARD	—ACCESS TO MAINFRAME SOFTWARE AND DATA		
—HIGH-VOLUME SOFTWARE LICENSES	—ELECTRONIC MAIL		
—USER GROUPS	—GATEWAYS TO OUTSIDE DATABASE AND MESSAGE SERVICES		
CONSISTENT USER INTERFACE			
CONSISTENT HELP, COMMANDS, SCREEN INTERACTIONS			
FRONT-END INTERFACES			
—OPEN: WIDE COMPATIBILITY			
—CLOSED: CONSISTENT USE OF APPLICATIONS			
—USER INTERFACE STANDARD			
—PROTOCOLS FOR COMMUNICATIONS WITH BACK END			

technical impacts. Before considering any technical issues, policy setters must make a fundamental decision on the role of the information staff. The staff may be given a greater or lesser degree of control over microcomputer procurement and use. As Figure 1 suggests, each choice has its pros and cons.

On one end of the political spectrum, the information staff may attempt to gain strict control over microcomputer acquisition. This approach makes the staff's job much easier, since it is only necessary to support a few types of equipment and software, and integration capability can be mandated. Furthermore, in some organizations, central staff members are evaluated on their ability to control technology rather than to solve business problems. Thus, a restrictive microcomputer policy statement provides tangible evidence of their performance.

However, strict controls limit the freedom of users to tailor microcomputers to their unique business needs. Thus, high-payoff applications—which are always unique, because they pertain to a user's individual business mission—may be overlooked. Furthermore, when users are denied a larger role in the decision

process, their enthusiasm may be dampened and their willingness to cooperate destroyed. This severely inhibits innovative use of microcomputers within an organization and further limits business payoffs.

A 1983 study of 28 user organizations illustrates the danger of too much control over microcomputers. The study showed a negative correlation between the existence of microcomputer policy statements and the use of microcomputers. In the sample chosen, the median penetration of microcomputers was 1 percent of the white-collar workforce. Microcomputer penetration ranged as low as 0.2 percent and as high as 10 percent of that population. Those that had published microcomputer policy statements were twice as likely to be below median penetration as those that had not.

An overly restrictive microcomputer policy has other dangers as well. It often antagonizes users, particularly those with little experience in computing who do not recognize the business value of integrated computer networks. Information staff groups thus alienate the people they are supposed to support. Shaky relationships with users limit the ability of staff groups to deliver business-oriented applications for all types of computers, since the development of such applications requires a great deal of user involvement and local tailoring.

By jeopardizing their rapport with users, information staffs following a restrictive policy may be relinquishing long-term control over microcomputers. Desktop computers can be purchased from retail stores and funded by a manager's departmental budget. When users feel that microcomputer policies inhibit their ability to perform their jobs, they will naturally attempt an end-run strategy and bring nonstandard equipment into the organization without the approval of the information staff. Staff management cannot control such purchases without the willing cooperation of users.

The art's in being liberal . . .

On the other end of the political spectrum, users may be given complete reign over their choice of microcomputers. Such an approach usually results in a greater diversity of microcomputers. This "uncontrolled proliferation" greatly encourages user innovation, local tailoring, and applications that provide greater benefits to the user because they are custom made.

This route, however, makes the job of the central-information staff more difficult. The staff must be aware of a greater variety of equipment and software and must deliver local networks that support multiple telecommunications protocols. Thus, increasing the likelihood of high-payoff applications may incur greater costs by requiring more flexible networks. Greater user innovation demands more innovation from the central information staff.

While it may appear to give ground to users, the more liberal policy may actually lead to greater staff control. In addition to an official policy of "let them buy," management may provide a default standard. Users find this standard more attractive than being forced to accept decisions made by others. In this way, users turning to the staff for help in selecting a microcomputer may be steered to the brand favored by the company. But users are not told what to buy, and staff guidance is limited by the users' receptiveness.

By responding to business needs in a supportive manner and avoiding the stigma of being an obstacle to the procurement of microcomputers, staff groups can build a healthy working relationship with users. The credibility accumulated by serving people before worrying about technology can go a long way toward gaining user cooperation on standards. The goal of this less-restrictive approach is to have users follow staff guidance willingly, based on trust, rather than reluctantly, based on policy. Being liberal lubricates the social mechanism while laying a solid ground for collaboration between users and the information staff in integrating their machines into networks.

. . . but few know how

The more freedom, the more potential payoff. Unfortunately, though, the control-oriented approach is currently far more common. An exaggerated concern for control is the vestige of management styles that arose from data processing (DP) and management informa-

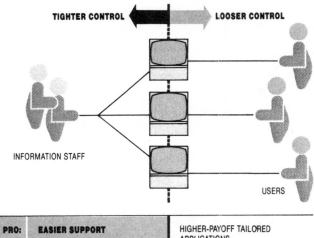

1. Staff vs. users. *Regardless of how the power is divided on microcomputer purchases, there are trade-offs. Letting users control their own destiny is better.*

TIGHTER CONTROL ◀━━━━ ▶ LOOSER CONTROL

INFORMATION STAFF

USERS

PRO:	EASIER SUPPORT	HIGHER-PAYOFF TAILORED APPLICATIONS
	EASIER INTEGRATION	MORE LONG-TERM CONTROL
	MORE SHORT-TERM CONTROL	BUILDS RELATIONSHIP WITH USERS
CON:	LOWER-PAYOFF GENERIC APPLICATIONS	NEED STAFF WITH MORE EXPERIENCE
	ANTAGONIZES USERS	NEED NETWORK PROTOCOL CONVERTERS

tion systems (MIS). Traditionally, these two environments engendered tight control and central direction. Heavy-handed management techniques were appropriate for highly structured and tightly integrated DP and MIS applications.

And yet desktop computers are decentralized. Integration in today's user-computing environment does not require that everyone have precisely the same hardware and software. The individual jobs of "knowledge workers" are different, lacking a common, uniform structure. Such workers can, therefore, use a variety of tools or techniques. Rather than hardware and software consistency, integration of user computing means tying microcomputers into networks that permit the exchange of messages and files.

Another key difference between traditional data processing and desktop computing is in the "ownership" of information. Microcomputers handle data at the personal, not the organizational, level. While the central information staff may control data stored on behalf of the entire organization, it cannot hold sway over information used by individuals and work groups. Furthermore, the applications are unique to the users' missions and jobs. The development of user applications requires a great deal of local tailoring. Thus, microcomputers warrant a management style that is different from the centrally directed approach required by large computers.

Most successful microcomputer policies fall somewhere between the free-for-all and stranglehold approaches. They balance restrictions with incentives for cooperation. In practice, the position of a microcomputer policy on this spectrum depends on the political strength of network managers and the information staff, the degree of centralization in the corporate culture, and the level of microcomputer awareness among users.

Analyze the organization, then set standards
To successfully bridge the gap between the desires of upper management and of users, the information staff must decide where the company is on the political spectrum. This means analyzing the corporation's present political climate and thinking about microcomputers in that context.

With an understanding of the political context, the staff can then begin writing its microcomputer policy. In practice, a policy consists of four parts: technologies, services, applications, and procedures. Technology is the area calling for the unique perspective and services of the data communications manager.

The setting of policy can influence both the selection and the integration of technologies. Selection policies are often the more controversial, since they dictate whether the staff members or the users have power over procurement. An approach to technological integration that is based on data communications offers the potential of a less-restrictive policy without sacrificing the compatibility of microcomputers with organizational networks. As suggested above, disputes over selection can be redirected by focusing attention on criteria for integration.

The levels of technological integration
Most larger organizations will have desktop computers, departmental minicomputers, and local networks, as well as organizational mainframes. These will eventually be tied together by telecommunications networks to deliver all of the many available information services through a single desktop workstation.

Users feel the effects of a lack of computer technology integration when they do not have easy access to data or to tools that reside on computers outside of their local areas (that is, outside of easy walking distance), or when they must learn an entirely different computer language to use these remote computer resources. The challenge in developing a microcomputer policy is to provide the greatest integration with the least restriction.

Limiting users' choices of vendors is an easy but undesirable way to ensure technological integration. Many staff groups attempt to limit their organizations to three vendors, generally some combination of equipment from IBM, Wang Laboratories Inc., Digital Equipment Corp. (DEC), Apple Computers Inc., and Hewlett-Packard Co. In its most restrictive form, the microcomputer policy limits the choice to a single vendor — in most cases, the one that supplied the organization's DP/MIS computer.

Greater freedom can be granted to users if the policymakers consider what kind of integration is desired and why. The information staff can then provide guidelines, such as data communications standards, for each level of integration, rather than simply naming an "acceptable" vendor and a list of approved prod-

ucts. There are four specific levels of compatibility: file transport, file content compatibility, software transportability, and a consistent user interface (Fig. 2).

■ **File transport.** A microcomputer should be able to exchange files with other computers in its network. Minimally, the machine must be able to emulate a terminal (either a standard asynchronous ACSII terminal or an IBM 3270 workstation) and to transfer files in both directions. File transfer through terminal emulation means that any character sent to the user's microcomputer can be simultaneously displayed on a screen and captured in a local file, and a file on the microcomputer can be transmitted to the mainframe as if it were being keyed in by the user.

Adopting such networking standards as Ethernet and others in the Institute of Electrical and Electronics Engineers (IEEE) 802 series facilitates the transfer of information between computers sharing a network. Standard networks are faster and easier to use than those that rely on terminal emulation.

Transferring a file on a standard network is simple compared with the elaborate procedure required if a desktop computer is simply emulating a terminal. With emulation, the user must do the following: leave the current application, enter terminal emulation mode, establish a connection and a job on the remote computer, open the file to be sent and another on the remote machine to receive, initiate the transfer, and monitor it until done. Standard networks permit remote file operations that resemble local ones, initiated with a single command.

As with microcomputers, the easiest means of controlling local networks would be to mandate a single vendor. However, no network handles all types of minicomputers, software, and peripherals. An application-level protocol standard such as X.400 could allow virtually any application package to work with any network. Until such standards are adopted by the hardware, software, and telecommunications industries, however, the choice of a local network must be based on the microcomputers and the applications software being used.

A common standard for a local network protocol is Ethernet (IEEE 802.2). IBM's token bus (IEEE 802.3) and token ring (IEEE 802.4) are alternative standards. An organization need not be limited to a single brand of network so long as all the local networks can be linked to the organization's backbone network. A mix of networks can be integrated through the use of "gateways" that convert between two or more network protocols.

Microcomputers may interact with mainframes either directly or through the use of network-based file servers. For their part, mainframe computers may use protocols such as IBM's Systems Network Architecture (SNA) or the CCITT standard X.25 for packet-switching networks.

In addition to the telecommunications linkage, integration requires that files be usable on various types of computers under a variety of operating systems. This presupposes a standard for file interchange. One such standard, offered by IBM, is called Document Interchange Architecture (DIA). Other network and computer vendors offer equivalent products. Currently, no industrywide standard is apparent.

Thus, at both the microcomputer and the local network levels, specification of communications protocols can substitute for restrictions to specific vendors. For example, a policy statement might require microcomputers to provide both terminal emulation with file transfer and compatibility with any local network that offers a gateway to the organization's network.

■ **File content compatibility.** The second level of integration addresses the content of files and the ability to move information between application software packages on various machines. Even when computers are physically attached to the same network, they may not be able to share information at all. And even if they do have the electronic ability to exchange files, they may not be able to interpret each others'. To do so requires that files used by various application packages have precisely the same format.

IBM offers one standard for the content of files: the Document Content Architecture (DCA). It specifies only the content of text files but is essential for communicating with IBM computers. In the world of mainframes, IBM's software product Distributed Office Support System (DISOSS) is emerging as the standard interface that enables users to exchange all types of documents with a central library or archive of computer files. Again, no industrywide standard exists.

In the microcomputer arena, trends in standard file formats are even less clear. Currently, the predominant standard is VisiCorp's Data Interchange Format (DIF). It is reasonable for the framers of a microcomputer policy to specify that application software be compatible with the DIF protocol. However, DIF is limited to structured data and does not standardize the exchange of spreadsheets or word processing documents. Of course, when the only requirement for integration is the ability to move information between machines on an occasional basis, standard sequential text files (unstructured ASCII or EBCDIC) or DIF files will often suffice.

■ **Software transportability.** A third level of integration addresses the transportability of software across computers. The purpose of this level of integration is not to carry a software product from one computer to another, as the sharing of software is generally prohibited by license agreements and copyright law. Its purpose is twofold: (1) to allow users familiar with software on one type of computer to use other computers without having to learn to use a new set of commands and (2) to simplify the movement of files among the various computers on the network.

In theory, if all computers in an organization are acquired from the same vendor, then software on any machine should run on any other machine. In reality, integration is never this easy. Few vendors provide a computer product line with complete software compatibility across all of their models. Therefore, this level of integration is not guaranteed by limiting the choice of vendors.

More user freedom can be granted by specifying microcomputer operating systems that are acceptable to upper management. For example, the British Civil Service supports the machines of 10 different microcomputer manufacturers, a large number for most information staffs, by allowing the purchase of any unit that can use Digital Research Inc.'s CP/M (control program for microcomputers) as its operating system. Currently, Microsoft's disk operating system, MS-DOS, is a de facto industry standard for 16-bit microcomputers.

While the degree of integration afforded by a single operating system is not required to establish an organizationwide network, standardizing microcomputer operating systems can allow users to take advantage of high-volume software licenses and discounts and can simplify the challenge of supporting users' common software needs. Operating system standards would also encourage users to share experiences through user groups and informal exchanges.

■ **Consistent user interface.** The fourth, most advanced level of integration addresses the commonality of the user interface across microcomputers and application software packages. Ideally, any workstation in the organization should allow the user to specify commands, point at items on the screen, and obtain help in consistent ways. Common user interfaces will facilitate learning as people are transferred between departments or explore new capabilities and applications. A consistent user interface may also allow the organization to benefit from common or generic training in the use of microcomputers.

Recently, a number of menu- or window-oriented user interface software products have been introduced. Because they stand between the user and the application software to provide consistent interactions, they are termed "front-end" interfaces.

Front-end interfaces, consisting of hardware, software, and protocols, can be either open or closed. "Open" means that the front-end is compatible with the variety of application programs currently on the market. A "closed" front-end is compatible only with application packages published by the front-end software's vendor or with those that meet the vendor's specifications.

Open front-end interfaces do little more than allow the user to portray multiple applications on the screen. Once the application is available in a window, the user interface unique to that application appears and performs just as the particular software author designed it. Hence, it is not consistent with software from other vendors. These windowing packages generally do not allow a user to run various applications simultaneously. They also provide only a very limited file integration, which allows the user to move text information from one window to another.

In closed front-ends, a consistent user interface can be enforced across application packages. Apple's announcement of the Macintosh microcomputer gives new hope to those interested in user interface integration. The Macintosh has a front-end architecture that, although "closed" in the sense of the above definition, is a published and supported interface that is open to

2. Levels of integration. *A microcomputer's ability to swap software or files, make sense of these files, or interact similarly with any users can all be standardized.* *By setting standards for whichever levels of integration are desired, greater freedom can be given to users over the acquisition of microcomputers.*

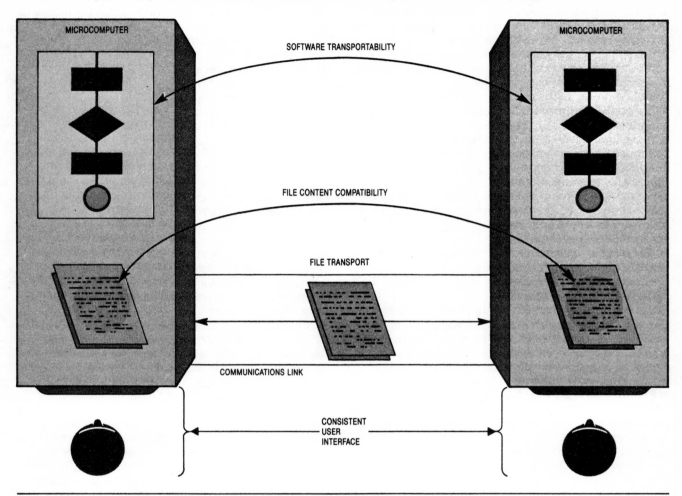

all software authors. As long as software authors use the front-end capabilities of the Macintosh, all of their software will interact with the user in consistent ways.

The Macintosh may provide the microcomputer industry with two types of standards: a generally accepted way to interact with users and a protocol for communications between the front-end user interface and application software. The Macintosh user interface is designed primarily for beginners rather than experts; however, the potential value of consistency from program to program and among users is at least as important as the interface's limitations. (The main limitation of this interface is speed, since the pull-down menus are slow and do not permit the bypassing of hierarchical menus through commands.)

Back-end functions, such as application programs, may share the user's workstation with the front-end, user interface software, although the trend may be to keep these functions on network resources, such as larger computers and file servers. The telecommunications protocol between the front-end software and the back-end networks is a critical requirement for integration, but one for which there are few standards. While

standards may exist within a single vendor's product line, such as the user interface to DEC's All-In-1 version 2 minicomputer-based office package, no industrywide protocol has yet been proposed. It is premature to propose a standard protocol between front- and back-end interfaces today, but this will be a key area to watch in the coming few years.

The rest of the policy

Technological integration allows for the support of nonstandard microcomputers and keeps their users from feeling "frozen out" of the corporate network. Still, the task of the support staff is eased if a majority of users choose the recommended, default machine. When they are otherwise free to choose their own machines, users can be enticed into using the de facto hardware and software. In parallel, members of the information staff can build their personal credibility with users in order to influence user-driven decisions. Data communications managers favoring the carrot over the stick approach will want to consider the inducements provided by the remaining three elements of a microcomputer policy.

First, the staff can provide human assistance (training, consulting, etc.) and services that are accessible over a network, such as electronic mail. Second, application guidelines help users (and staff) determine where in the network the application programs should reside (whether on the user's machine or on some larger, remote computer). Finally, users may want advice on how to handle the myriad office procedures being affected by computerization.

While researching and publicizing these areas requires an initial effort and expenditure, the long-term productivity, profitability, and even viability of an enterprise may hang in the balance. With the help of an adequate microcomputer policy, the information support staff can provide guidance and encouragement to all users.

The richest benefits from such a policy will accrue to users of computers that meet the company's integration standards. These benefits will thus provide a powerful reason to select accordingly. At the same time, the policy will also assist individuals for whom other machines are more appropriate.

Staff services

Without demanding adherence to standards, a microcomputer policy statement can advertise the services that make the compliance with such a standard attractive. Important services are those provided by information staff professionals and those on other computers accessible through the organization's network.

■ **People services.** The staff can do a number of things to encourage users to select company-standard machines. Discounts can be arranged on both hardware and software. The staff can disseminate software updates as new versions are released by the publishers. For software packages common to many users, the staff can develop and offer training courses and application ideas and procedures.

A hotline and information center can be set up to answer questions. The staff can facilitate the formation of user groups, which are useful as a means of disseminating information and encouraging user self-sufficiency. According to most organizations surveyed, user groups require very little time to manage. The staff can also arrange maintenance contracts and keep spare parts in-house for commonly used machines.

■ **Network services.** In addition to staff services, resources reachable through a network may provide added incentives for picking a machine that conforms to the policy's standards. Local networks may link users to mass storage devices for archival and for shared group files, with a decentralized but trained support staff available nearby to ensure proper information backup procedures. Networks may also provide print servers that give every user access to expensive, high-quality printers and graphical output devices.

Some organizations use local networks to distribute access to software that is licensed to run on a single computer. This is generally legal so long as the software processing is actually done on the computer for which it is licensed, and the remote workstations act only as terminals. These networks can also allow the use of software libraries that are licensed for downline loading. Some local computer networks also provide multimedia electronic mail among the attached microcomputers. These mail subnetworks may eventually be linked in a corporatewide electronic-mail network.

Services offered through the mainframes can also attract users. The most common example is host-based electronic mail, which requires only standard terminal emulation. When both network and file content protocols are implemented, the mainframe may enable the exchange of multimedia documents (for example, those combining text and graphics).

The user interface to electronic mail will be significantly improved by local message entry. Having the user interface run on a local machine means faster response time from the application than if transmission were involved, more screen control, and greater responsiveness on terminal input and output. The user will also benefit from the transparent, background transmission of messages through the network to the mainframe, sidestepping the complexities and delays associated with terminal emulation.

An area of particular interest to users is access to the organization's operating data on the central MIS computer. Executive users especially may wish to access selected data from the mainframe and download it onto a spreadsheet, on which they can juxtapose their plans with the actual results. Currently, this important capability is limited in ease-of-use. Generally, the file is transferred in terminal-emulation mode, and then the sequential file is transformed on the microcomputer into a spreadsheet format. This transformation process is awkward and may preclude direct use by executives.

In the past year, several vendors of mainframe database management packages announced microcomputer software to link to the mainframes. The linkage will allow the automatic retrieval and incorporation of mainframe data directly into microcomputer spreadsheets or databases, providing a powerful incentive to select standard microcomputers.

Network integration might also provide users with access to specialized input devices (such as optical character readers and video scanners) and expensive output devices (such as laser printers, slide makers, computer output to microfilm, and large plotters). Gateways to international hosts, Telex, and public packet networks can also be provided. The mainframe may also serve as an archive for microcomputer-generated files that can be converted into a standard format (such as DISOSS).

Of course, the information staff need not offer more services than it can effectively deliver. For example, it need not offer services on nonstandard machines with which it is unfamiliar. Support services can now be purchased from outside vendors as well as being provided in-house. If a user chooses a nonstandard machine and wishes to obtain support, the information staff should have the right to choose whether or not it wishes to bid on that support business. If the staff has the right to pass along to the user the cost of getting acquainted with a new type of equipment, the user can decide whether to purchase support from within the company or to go to a source outside the company.

Users frequently must decide whether to run a program on the mainframe or on the microcomputer. A microcomputer policy statement can provide guidance on the selection of appropriate applications for microcomputers

Applications guidelines

Running applications on the microcomputer whenever possible is generally the most cost-efficient approach. Computing cycles on the microcomputer are generally much cheaper than on the mainframe, since the microcomputer is a fixed-cost resource that will not become more expensive with use. Furthermore, a microcomputer gives the user a feeling of ownership and a maximum degree of control, while offloading the central staff and reducing the proverbial "DP backlog."

On the other hand, many applications should not run on microcomputers but rather reside on minicomputers or mainframes. The level of "ownership" of data is an important criterion for selecting the optimal location. Databases should be placed on minicomputers if they are shared by a work group or a department, or on mainframes if people throughout the organization must access them. Multi-user or shared microcomputers should be used only for personal or group data.

A second reason to place an application on minicomputers or mainframes is its dependence on support staff. Users are often too pressed for time to be concerned about proper backup procedures, and indeed they should not be burdened with these administrative tasks. Those applications that are critical to the operation of the business should be placed where the support staff can ensure proper maintenance and backup. Thus, even when a database is used primarily by one person, it should be placed on larger machines when it is critical to business operations and requires ongoing support.

Of course, technical issues have a bearing on where applications belong. Applications that require too much storage or memory for microcomputers must be placed on larger machines. The limited throughput of a microcomputer may also be of concern where complex calculations or extensive processing is required. Common examples of applications too large to fit on today's microcomputers include the statistical manipulation of large market research databases, sophisticated forecasting models, and the more powerful computer-aided design tools. The microcomputer policy may provide users with guidelines for how to calculate whether or not an application will fit on a microcomputer.

Office procedures

Finally, a microcomputer policy may provide guidelines on office procedures that surround the use of microcomputers. Workers will have to get used to different levels of security. Hardware protection calls for locking mechanisms and procedures for moving equipment into and out of buildings. Keeping data private may involve the use of hard-disk keys and handling procedures for disks with sensitive data, as well as file security. (Unfortunately, the lack of built-in operating system security on microcomputers precludes many of these measures.)

Guidelines should be established on the treatment of software licenses and copyrights. Users will want to know when it is and is not legal to make backup copies of software and documentation and to move software between machines. Backup procedures have to be set up to duplicate data files and to maintain transaction ledgers for an audit trail.

Helpful pointers can be offered in a policy statement about file-naming conventions; diagnosing, fixing, and reporting problems; where to obtain peripherals, software, and supplies; the regulation of environmental conditions (for the equipment); ergonomic workspace and furniture design; and how users should document the operating procedures they develop.

The use of data communications can be guided with procedures for moving data through networks. Gentle and supportive guidance for users can even include suggestions on when and how to physically ship disks.

A microcomputer policy might also suggest ways to identify new applications and measure their benefits. A particularly comprehensive microcomputer policy will also address the human resource implications of microcomputers, such as their impact on job definitions, grade levels, compensation, and promotability.

Conclusion

A microcomputer policy is far more than a technical guideline. It reveals a great deal about the attitude of the information staff toward users. A policy statement that does no more than limit the number of "acceptable" vendors of microcomputers shows a greater concern for technology than for business. In essence, it attempts to use power to ease the job of the central information staff, but it does so at the expense of user effectiveness.

On the other hand, a business-oriented microcomputer policy leaves as much room as possible for user innovation. It prescribes a minimum number of restrictions to ensure the integration of technologies. This approach shows a primary concern for business effectiveness and for a collaborative relationship between users and the central staff.

When policymakers understand the reasons for standards, policies can be made more liberal without threatening long-term network integrity. This involves specifying standards, in particular for data communications, where technological integration is desirable. A liberal microcomputer policy can do much to ensure good relations with users and a high payoff from microcomputers. ∎

N. Dean Meyer is a consultant in advanced office integration as well as managerial and professional networks and applications. He specializes in the management issues of program implementation, such as training, organizational planning, and managing change. From his "electronic cottage" in Ridgefield, Conn., Meyer hosts a management discussion group that meets via teleconferences.

A. L. Frank, California Software Inc., Santa Monica, Calif.

New tools address the problems of managing network facilities

Many networks are so vast that they cannot be properly monitored without special software tools. But how does a user choose one?

According to a recent market study, the vast majority of the large data communications centers in the United States cannot provide an accurate and up-to-date inventory of hardware and software by location. Managers at many of these data centers freely admit that they do not have answers when certain types of basic questions are asked: How long was a terminal down? What is the overall impact when a controller is down? What systems were affected? How long was IMS (Information Management System) available to a user over that last month?

In addition the market study indicated that computer/communications managers are no more informed about their networks' finances than they are about operations. For instance, while many do the best they can to verify invoices, they suspect that they sometimes overpay. Moreover, they admit to relying too heavily on the vendors to keep track of orders outstanding and to keep their networks running.

In recent years, however, a few vendors have released software packages that attempt to mitigate this crisis in the management of network facilities. Although the actual number of products is small, making choices is still difficult. Choosing between products requires an overall understanding of the many facets of facilities mangement as well as a thorough definition of a particular installation's management objectives.

In the past, properly managing network facilities could be accomplished without management tools or by using the schemes that came with the networks. Previously, a data network consisting of a few hundred terminals was considered large, but today the notion of large networks greatly exceeds that. As a result, the size and complexity of data communications neworks have simply outstripped management tools. Similarly, future networks may exceed the experts' current prediction.

Also contributing to the obsolescence of previous management tools is the fact that for many reasons—recent divestitures, new competitive ventures, and the merging of old and new technology—single-vendor networks are very rare. The typical problems associated with multiple vendors include incompatibility, coordination of new installations, and finger pointing when problems arise. Even more important, each vendor has at least one unique naming convention, billing methodology, maintenance process, and order-processing technique.

The communications environment is further complicated by a trend toward dispersed control. Today's technology supports local node control, and future methodologies will continue the transfer of control away from the central facility. For example, a user can replace an existing IBM 3178 with a microcomputer, and the change may not be apparent to the central facility. This trend toward decentralization presents both technical and administrative challenges.

The complexity of the recent spate of new products is a problem as well, and even industry specialists have difficulty tracking the gamut of available hardware and software methodologies. IBM alone offers hundreds (and perhaps thousands, depending on the product definition) of software products that affect the communications environment. A typical package for network control and management is likely to be responsible for more than a hundred types of software and hardware products and may be affected by hundreds of other resources.

The new products that attempt to address facilities management represent a variety of functionality, price, ease of use, and resource utilization. Before plunging

Categories. The 12 administrative functions of data center/communications network management cover four general management areas: inventory, problem, change, and finance. Although a number of software tools are available, the 12 functions are not necessarily met by each vendor's package.

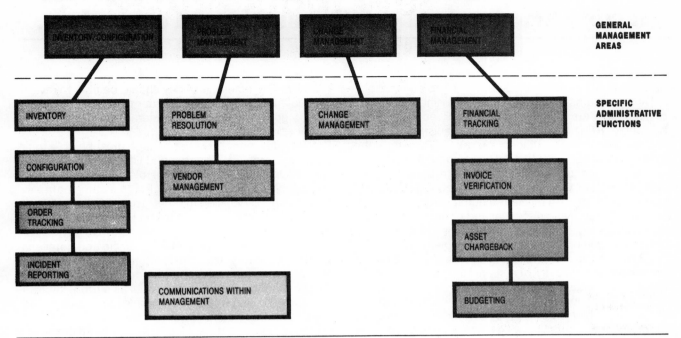

toward a decision about which management package should be installed (if any), a manager should analyze the various aspects of data center/communications network management. As the figure shows, there are four general management areas that a facilities management package should address; within these areas are 12 specific administrative functions that any particular installation may need.

Inventory/configuraton

Clearly, it is difficult to manage any set of resources without knowing where those resources are. So, the package should have a module that is devoted to capturing complete inventory information and the relationship of each element (hardware and software) within the network.

The inventory module should be able to function at more than one level. An initial implementation may provide for data capture at the level of the complete terminal. Future versions should be able to identify all features of the terminal including special keyboards, cables, and even screen sizes.

■ *Configuration.* The relationships or configuration of the hardware and software must be represented. This is important not only for the routine needs in configuration management and planning but also for effective problem and change management.

In installations without a sophisticated management tool, existing configuration data usually provides only a single network view. For example, a network control specialist may view the network from the port of a 3705 communications controller to the remote terminal control unit. By contrast, a CICS (customer information control systems) programmer may view the network

from the host to the logical terminal. Both of these views are valid, but neither alone provides for the total corporate needs. A central depository of configuration information is necessary.

The configuration tool should provide for a representation of all types of configurations, such as normal hierarchical networks, ring structures, and star networks. Additionally, this function should provide for order-related data so that the user can ascertain the company's position in a vendor's queue of back orders.

Batch reports are also important for providing hardcopy documents concerning configuration data, detailed inventory analysis, order analysis, and management summaries.

■ *Order tracking.* Hardware and software should be tracked from the time the order is placed. Ideally, on-order hardware and software should be directly entered into the inventory and configuration file with a special notation of its uninstalled status.

With this capability intact, an organization can provide vendors with a clear statement of its order and delivery expectations and require principal vendors to document any changes. This vastly improves the typical situation—most large users are totally dependent on their vendor account representatives to track order status.

Types of management

Most problem management methods provide a centralized facility (either manual or automated) for logging failure incidents in real time. Keeping good records is important so that a history of incidents and their patterns can be available. The last thing that busy

An analyst should be able to review existing historical problems across the network or in a specified facility before meeting with management or vendors.

network control center specialists want to do is stop solving problems in order to enter voluminous amounts of historical data. Thus, the method for recording must be simple. Additionally, very large organizations may require decentralized incident reporting. Therefore, the management tool should provide for input flexibility.

The historical data created by good reporting techniques is helpful when the network analyst is analyzing current incidents. An efficient mechanism for compiling and rapidly retrieving historical and configuration data is crucial to effectively solving problems. This will help network analysts determine, for example, whether a 3278 terminal is malfunctioning because it has failed or because it is a casualty of a separate (perhaps habitually) malfunctioning component.

An analyst should be able to review existing and historical problems across the network or in a specified facility prior to a meeting with management or vendors. The product ought to provide vendors with documented details of their own responsiveness so that problem control meetings can include quick reviews of problem status. Reports showing any level of detail for designated time periods and locations should be easily generated.

■ *Vendor management.* Keeping tabs on vendor-supplied maintenance is a whole management area in itself. How do you overcome a vendor's contention that the company was never notified of a problem, or that it has been responsive to a lingering problem? The only effective means for managing vendor relations is to detail the communications, contracts and actions associated with each problem and, when necessary, set up a mechanism for recording alarms and reports.

Almost every data center can recount a story of tracing a failure in the network to an undocumented software or hardware change. Change management software can project the impact of a change on the rest of the network as well as prepare a network for tracking the steps toward authorization and implementation of the proposed change.

Change authorization deals with questions about the approval cycle for changes. For example: Who must approve a change? What is the status of the approval? What is the justification for the change?

Change implementation concerns tracking the change itself, the elements involved, and their status. An important by-product is the ability to correlate changes to open problems and to the existing configuration. For example, a new problem with a CICS broadcast facility could, in theory, be the result of a recent change. An analyst should be able to review all of the the recent changes without difficulty. If CICS system programmers are about to go through a new

CICS system generation, they should be able to review scheduled future changes in order to alleviate multiple system generations. The management tool should document this entire process.

A facilities management package must be able to tie inventory, problem, change, and financial data together. One of the fundamental rules of operation for any decision support system is that the same data be available to all decision makers. Thus, the financial data should relate primarily to the fundamental inventory item.

Financial data can be ranked as basic and detailed for each inventory item. Basic information includes vendor name, contract (type, associated contracts, duration, costs), order data, as well as current information about depreciation, finance or lease accruals, and investment tax credits. Detailed information includes extensive contract data, historical cost notations and information required for budgeting, cost allocation, and cost analysis.

For each contract, the analyst must be able to determine some of the key terms and conditions. The package should also provide for warnings prior to contract expiration and checks for price protection. The financial analysts should be able to make a working copy of the inventory and financial data and prepare spreadsheets for up to a five-year period.

Costs should be allocatable to various groups or accounts within the organization. The financial analyst must be able not only to split the cost of a given item but also to provide for standard costs and any desired cost markups or markdowns.

Finally, it is essential that the analyst be able to verify invoices by using any procedure that produces an expected invoice. This requirement implies an ability for interactive analysis that goes beyond simply being able to review a hard copy of an expected invoice. Furthermore, it differs from an item-by-item search for each charge on the invoice in that it eliminates needless computer queries and reduces the time required to process invoices.

The batch reporting for the financial area must be extensive. It should include accrual, contract expiration, depreciation, investment tax credit, invoice (approved, pending, and not recieved), budget, and cost allocation data. This approach will greatly reduce the invoice verification time, virtually eliminate vendor overpayments, and provide for an enchanced ability for financial analysis.

A necessary but tedious and time-consuming task, inventory verification is an area that is quite vulnerable to fraud unless suitable control measures are implemented An ideal solution provides a detailed invoice-

Certain basic utilities should be built in: An audit trail, security maintenance, message broadcasts, and detailed help screens are invaluable.

processing scheme that ties the approval of invoices into the same inventory and financial information used elsewhere in the management tool. The cost justification of an invoice verification tool stems from its ability to substantially eliminate vendor overpayments.

Finance

■ *Cost allocation and asset chargeback.* The most effective way to maintain responsibility among data communications users seems to be to charge back the assets. The same financial information used for invoice verification can perform this function if a means for allocation to multiple cost centers, markups or markdowns, and/or standard costing are built in.

■ *Budgeting.* Too often budgets are planned in a static environment. A tool that brings budgeting alive is one that allows what-if scenarios to be planned against a copy of the live financial database. For example, suppose a manager wants to contemplate replacing all the 3278s with 3178s. A facilities management tool that can use a budget database should be able to cope with such a query.

■ *Communications within communications management.* It should go without saying that the group that is responsible for furnishing the technology that fosters the corporation's communications should have no problems with its own communications. The truth is that comprehensive, detailed information about data center and network performance is rarely available. Too often managers come to meetings with information drawn from numerous and often conflicting sources. Through reports generated from the information collected by the administrative tool, management can be working with a single body of reliable data.

Tool design

From this overview of necessary administrative areas, it is clear that a facilities administrative tool should operate from a single integrated database residing in the mainframe. If an incident is logged, it should be logged against a specific device that, in turn, is automatically identified according to its position within the configuration. Further, so much of the power of a management tool depends on integration across functions and multiple users for analysis, reliability, and reporting.

The tools should utilize existing mainframe security facilities, as well as provide for its own functional security. For example, the person who logs an incident against a 3178 should not be the same person who approves the rental invoice. More detailed field-level security should be available through user exits. Due to the need for such an implementation to coexist with

other major data processing software, it is necessary that the management tool utilize existing mainframe security packages.

The product should be table-driven. In order to maintain integrity, the product should make use of tables to define location codes, equipment identifiers, vendors, and so forth. The product should permit detailed and complete editing of data input to prevent incorrect entry. Furthermore, the tables must provide for truly integrated database integrity.

Beyond this, batch reporting should be controlled and provided from table-driven functions. These capabilities must permit efficient selection criteria as well as allow for concurrent report production while the interactive tool is active.

Certain basic utilities should be built in. An audit trail, security maintenance, message broadcasts, and detailed help screens are invaluable. Additional utilities are important, such as those providing for mass updates, prototype records, and database backup. If IBM announces a price decrease on normal 3178 maintenance, it is essential that a single entry be permitted to update the entire database. The product should also allow for documentation of all user procedures; the documentation should be easily accessible by all users associated with specified functions.

Of course, any implementation should be compatible with existing technology. In a normal IBM mainframe environment, the tool may best function if it is implemented in the primary IBM data access methodology, VSAM (Virtual Storage Access Method). In addition, sophisticated users should be given the means to customize screens and reports.

There is no single best solution for managing the communications environment. One solution that should probably be avoided is developing a tool in-house. It is unlikely that the cost of this development could be justified or that such a package will be as comprehensive as those on the market.

The best solution for one organization may include only some of the items discussed. Moreover, the organization's needs may change and expand. Thus, whatever tool is chosen should provide a base implementation scheme that readily provides for changes and growth. ■

A. L. Frank is the president and cofounder of California Software Inc. He had previously been director of corporate planning for Boole & Babbage. Frank received B. A. and M. A. degrees in operations research from Cornell University and a J. D. from Loyala University in Los Angeles. He is a member of the California Bar Association.

Carl N. Klahr, Fundamental Methods Associates Inc., Lawrence, N. Y.

An expert system can greatly reduce expenditures for telecommunications

Deregulation has made selecting long-distance circuits more confusing, but a microcomputer tool can foster smart choices.

Not surprisingly, the deregulated environment has created many new options for corporate communications managers. These emerging alternatives combine with improved multiplexing hardware to allow large cost savings in the operation of telecommunications circuits and network services.

Getting a handle on the new choices is particularly important for the thousands of corporations with annual telecommunications costs of $1 million or more for long-distance circuits and network services. Minimizing costs requires the proper selection, combination, and operation of circuits at the PBXs and the network switches of the corporate user. To help the manager make intelligent decisions in telecommunications alternatives, a number of software packages have recently emerged.

The choice of a telecommunications management tool is important. If the package employs proper economic optimization techniques, the user can reduce the cost of long-distance circuit facilities by as much as 20 percent. A management tool of this type should provide an interactive technical and mathematical consultant between the telecommunications analyst and the computer. Its knowledge base should include detailed technical expertise in economic optimization methods and in telecommunications. Of course, practical human judgment from the analyst is essential.

In such a package, data circuits and voice circuits should be selected together in a common optimization process. Although voice circuits on average comprise 85 percent of the total, the cost of the data circuits is significant. Even if the data circuits and voice circuits are not interchangeable, they should be planned together since they can be selected from a group of bulk channels (for example, multiplexed, or group discounted) whose cost per channel decreases with the number of channels in the group.

If voice and data channels can be substituted for each other, there is another reason for planning the voice and data circuits together. Principles of traffic engineering state that the number of circuits required to serve a given type of traffic is not a linear function of the amount of traffic. In other words, if a given amount of traffic requires a specific number of circuits, doubling the traffic will not require twice as many circuits. Because voice channels can provide backup facilities, substitutable voice and data channels can increase the reliability of data transmission, even if the data circuits do not transmit voice.

If the data circuits are switchable, they can be assigned from a common trunk group with voice circuits. Although the statistics of data circuits (for example, long occupancy time per message) will be different than those for voice, traffic engineering principles can include this when assigning circuits. There are also many situations in which the data can be multiplexed or packetized in order to mix voice and data on a single channel. In addition, continuing advances in channel compression and digital-voice transmission tend to enhance the economies of common optimization of voice and data transmission.

For several reasons, the economics of long-distance circuit optimization in a competitive multivendor environment are vastly different than those in the previous regulated environment. Many more vendors offer circuit alternatives, and they differ greatly in tariffs, geographic availability, and type of service (for instance, private-line, measured-use, and network service).

Advances in today's multiplexing equipment combine with the new multivendor environment to further reduce the cost of a single communications channel.

With this equipment, bulk groups of channels are extracted from a single wideband line and are operated together between two points. Such hardware is now available in proved and reliable equipment such as T1 links with advanced modulation, channel compressors, and statistical multiplexers.

Instead of setting up trunk groups with a single routing destination, network managers should set up trunk groups to exploit a variety of routing possibilities. Each trunk group can interface to other trunk groups for routing the calls to various traffic destinations, or to external network services that distribute the calls or data messages to their final destinations. In this way, the corporation can set up its own subnetworks. Because of the impact of bottlenecks, the allocation of traffic among various routes to the final destinations affects the maximum call-traffic volume. Consequently, capacity limitations on the various trunk groups affect the number of circuits that are needed, in accordance with the mathematical relations of traffic engineering.

The process of allocating traffic to trunk groups relies upon a discipline called mathematical programming — the minimization of a complex cost function that is subject to capacity constraints. This mathematical optimization process is well known in economic theory, but it must be modified when used for telecommunications facility management. Specifically, traffic engineering principles and the nonlinear nature of the line costs must be considered. Still, these complexities can be handled by a specialized package.

An expert system for choosing telecommunications options should give the communications manager the capability to:
■ Know and analyze call traffic.
■ Select the most effective circuit vendors.
■ Compute tariff costs automatically for individual and combinations of vendors.
■ Optimize the choice of circuits.
■ Automate calculations for traffic engineering and circuit economics.
■ Rate each PBX's long-distance circuit configurations.
■ Determine the most effective call-routing pattern.
■ Design the least-cost corporate network that meets user demands.

One approach to designing such an expert system is to base it around a series of spreadsheets, each performing a specific portion of analysis and design. The user should not have to concern himself with tariff data, traffic engineering, or logical layout of the analysis, all of which should be automated. Consequently, users could focus on the choices that they actually must make: vendors and services, customer calling patterns, least-cost routing possibilities, grade of service, and cost reductions.

Three strategies

To understand more fully how an expert system for telecommunications management might work, it is important to grasp the general principles of optimizing circuit costs. Overall, there are three basic strategies for reducing long-distance circuit costs in a multivendor environment.

First, the corporate telecommunications department should identify and install the most economical combination of circuits and network services at each PBX. The most cost-effective combination of circuits will depend on the unique call-traffic demand at the specific PBX. To choose the best combinations, the manager should be sure to:
■ Select low-cost vendors for the traffic demand.
■ Use bulk-priced channels.
■ Use recently developed multiplexed channels (T1 or statistically multiplexed, for example) derived from wideband circuits.
■ Identify the low-cost combinations of private-line vendors and/or network service vendors at appropriate gateways.

Second, these circuits and network services should be operated using the most efficient call-routing patterns at each PBX. The cost difference between an efficient and an inefficient routing plan is considerable. New routing methods should be used. (A derivation of efficient routing paths will be described below.)

Third, the designing of a least-cost configuration should be done with respect to the entire network of PBXs. In such a network, the internal and external call costs will be minimized.

Generating cost-effective circuit combinations requires a number of steps. The manager must tabulate all the traffic elements at each PBX. These traffic elements should be consolidated into a reasonable number of traffic groups — termed Traffic Destination Groups (TDGs) — each of which can be individually routed. Then the manager must examine the tariff alternatives for private-line groups. (Figure 1 shows the flow chart for selecting TDGs.)

Similarly, tariff alternatives for network services should be examined. These are matched at gateway locations and combined into user subnetworks called Circuit Facility Trunk Groups or CFTGs.

A number of factors must be considered in evaluating CFTGs. Specifically, the traffic offered by each TDG, the traffic offered each hour to the CFTG, and the routing tables specifying how data flows around the network all combine to produce overflow probabilities. The expert system must use all of this data as well as cost tables (both measured usage and fixed) to determine the monthly costs and grade of service of a PBX with a specified set of CFTGs (Fig. 2). In addition, the package must acknowledge the increased importance of user-defined subnetworks because of the increase in telecommunications options.

The package should also employ mathematical programming techniques to assist the user in routing optimization, which is also more important than in the deregulated environment. The optimal routing pattern can be obtained by a method called routing by allocation. This scheme entails allocating a certain fraction of the call traffic from each traffic destination group to each of the circuit facility trunk groups. An alternative to routing by allocation is routing by differential overflow. With this method, an attempt is made to place all of the call traffic on one trunk group, with the overflow going to another trunk group. That group's overflow would then go to another trunk group, and so on.

Completing the economic optimization procedure requires two types of cost tables. A measured-use cost table gives the cost for carrying each hour of traffic from each TDG on the measured-use network portion of each CFTG. A fixed-cost table contains the monthly fixed cost of the private-line portion of each CFTG. A telecommunications optimization tool must configure the circuits to minimize the total cost by trading off the fixed cost against the measured-use cost.

In addition to the cost tables, two types of traffic tables are used, one containing the offered traffic, one representing the carried traffic. The offered traffic—defined as the traffic offered to each PBX within a TDG—determines the activity of the PBX. The PBX then allocates this traffic to each of the CFTGs, in accordance with the routing pattern. The sizes of the circuit trunk group then determine the traffic carried by each CFTG, in accordance with the traffic engineering relations. It is the carried traffic that determines the grade of service. Thus, the offered traffic, the routing pattern, and the traffic engineering relations (all of which depend on the trunk group sizes) jointly determine the actual carried traffic. The purpose of mathematical programming is to minimize the total circuit cost by adjusting the trunk group sizes and selecting the optimal allocation of offered traffic through the routing pattern.

This procedure for optimizing the network circuits can be summarized in three basic steps: selection, evaluation, and optimization (Fig. 3). The circuit vendors, combinations of vendors, and user subnetworks must be selected, which involves choosing traffic destination groups and CFTGs. The cost and grade of service of the CFTGs at a PBX must be evaluated. Then, mathematical programming techniques modify the routing and adjust the trunk group sizes.

To insure that costs are minimized, this cycle can be iterated using different combinations of circuit vendors in the selection steps.

In addition to evaluating and optimizing each part of the network, the designer must also perform network

1. Paring down. *From the group of candidate Traffic Destination Groups (TGDs), the evaluation and screening procedure selects those most cost-effective.*

2. Thorough. *A proper analysis must include many different combinations of leased lines, network services, and multiplexed facilities.*

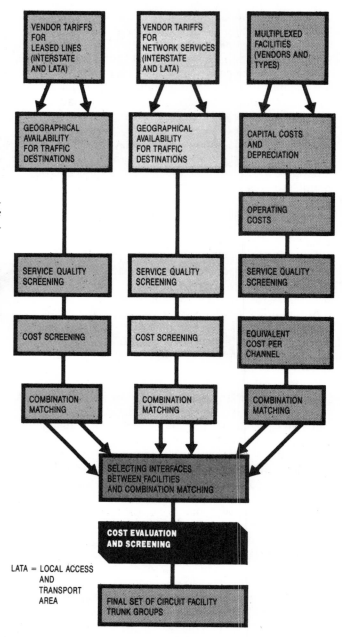

3. Never ending. *Network optimization is actually a cyclical process occurring in three distinct stages. After an initial selection of feasible alternatives, the designer's* *tool evaluates cost-effectiveness. If the tool includes network-optimization algorithms, it can usually cut costs even further.*

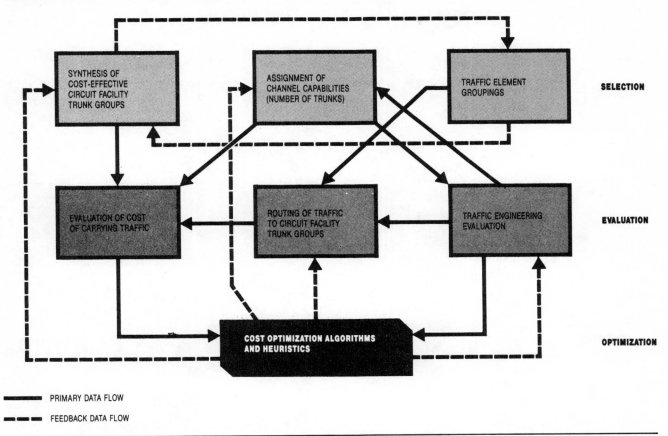

PRIMARY DATA FLOW

FEEDBACK DATA FLOW

optimization from the perspective of the entire network. (The network is defined to consist of a number of communications switches, each linked to its own set of node PBXs. The switches can communicate with a node that is not linked to it only by setting up a link through the switches that service those nodes.) The basic input data to this global optimization process is the node-to-node traffic matrix of the network. In the design of a minimum-cost network, the switch-to-switch traffic flows must be calculated in order to assess the cost of the circuit requirements. The primary requirement is to calculate the total circuit cost under many design variations, since the minimum cost under all design variations must be found. The variations to be considered include:
■ Vendor selection alternatives.
■ Number of switches.
■ Switch locations.
■ Switch-to-node associations.
■ Switch-to-switch link connections.
■ Trunk group size on each link.
   To allow the network manager to make the best network choice, an expert system should assist him or her in all phases of the design process. The manager will likely need to evaluate (and select) a specific circuit configuration, perform a differential evaluation in which differences between two circuit configurations or two

operating modes are sought, or optimize the configuration in an iterative process.
   An expert system for the reduction of telecommunications costs should have one module that evaluates a set of circuits (circuit configuration) assigned to a PBX. More specifically, such a module should calculate the call-overflow probability and the total cost for carrying the call traffic that the PBX users generate.

Several modules
Table 1 illustrates an input module for this type of calculation. In this particular example, the user specifies a calculation on the third hour of the day, using the second routing table (routing pattern B). Three types of data are needed for the calculation:
■ The traffic offered to the PBX by the users.
■ Tariffed costs (both measured use and fixed) for the circuit trunk groups that are being evaluated for the PBX.
■ Operating strategies selected for the PBX, such as the call-routing pattern for assigning calls to trunks, and the number of trunks of each circuit group.
   Each of these inputs could be available on a spreadsheet, having been prepared by other spreadsheets of the expert system. The user should be able to evaluate important statistics about a PBX (such as call-overflow probability or cost for each circuit group) for a variety

Table 1: Input to PBX circuit calculation

CONTROL PANEL

ITERATIONS	1	TRAFFIC HOURS	3
SCAN HOURS	2	ROUTING TABLE	2
INDEPENDENT HOURS	3	ACCUMULATED HOURS	1

TRUNKING FACILITIES

	NUMBER OF TRUNKS	DESTINATION	ROUTING PATTERN A	ROUTING PATTERN B
FACILITY 1	5	1	11796141	14680643
2	6	2	11718170	35621789
3	7	3	09252120	84259621
4	4	4	00309010	53689314
5	5	5	00663020	42671165
6	6	6	66264600	12399764
7	6	7	00214120	92837465
8	6	8	11416120	57382914

OFFERED TRAFFIC (ERLANGS)

	HOUR 1	HOUR 2	HOUR 3	HOUR 4	HOUR 5	HOUR 6	HOUR 7	HOUR 8
DESTINATION 1	4.76	5.71	8.09	7.14	6.19	8.09	7.14	0.47
2	5.71	6.85	4.85	8.57	7.42	9.71	8.57	0.57
3	6.19	7.42	5.26	4.64	8.04	10.52	9.28	0.61
4	8.57	10.28	7.28	6.42	5.57	7.28	6.42	0.85
5	4.76	5.71	4.04	7.14	6.19	4.04	7.14	0.47
6	5.71	6.85	4.85	4.28	7.42	4.85	8.57	0.57
7	6.19	7.42	5.26	4.64	8.04	5.26	4.64	0.61
8	5.71	6.85	4.85	4.28	7.42	9.71	8.57	0.57

COST PER TRAFFIC HOUR ($)

	FACILITY 1	FACILITY 2	FACILITY 3	FACILITY 4	FACILITY 5	FACILITY 6	FACILITY 7	FACILITY 8
DESTINATION 1	30.77	30.77	20.26	17.05	21.94	30.77	24.40	33.71
2	30.77	30.96	24.60	30.96	21.49	30.96	25.25	35.12
3	30.77	N/A	23.24	14.27	21.17	30.07	23.64	32.37
4	32.64	32.64	27.39	32.64	6.04	32.64	27.24	40.84
5	31.35	31.35	15.80	14.31	21.94	31.35	25.01	35.20
6	17.48	17.48	23.58	17.48	21.47	17.48	26.90	35.5
7	31.96	31.96	25.92	31.96	21.25	31.96	25.92	36.92
8	29.34	29.34	25.13	29.34	21.59	29.34	26.31	35.78
FIXED COST PER MONTH	6,854.2	5,483.6	2,078.04	272.52	24,799.5	1,472.6	0	0

N/A = NOT AVAILABLE BECAUSE THIS FACILITY CANNOT HANDLE THIS TYPE OF TRAFFIC.

of periods—a single hour, multiple hours, or a month. The user may want to vary the call-routing pattern, or the number of trunks per circuit group.

The offered traffic summarizes the users' call demands on the PBX and is presented in the form of a table that gives the total call traffic dispatched to each traffic destination for each hour of the day. The traffic volumes are given in ccs (hundred call seconds) or Erlangs. Computing these statistics requires data on the mean call length and total monthly traffic. Primary data of this type is available from SMDR (station message detail recording) summaries or from call-detail record summaries. This summary data is input into previous spreadsheets of the expert system that prepare the offered traffic table.

The tariffed costs for the circuit trunk groups also reside on the evaluation spreadsheet in the form of tables that are automatically copied from other spreadsheets of the system. The cost-per-traffic-hour table gives the variable costs on each circuit trunk group (the cost is proportional to the call traffic carried). The fixed-cost table gives the fixed costs

(monthly rentals) on the private lines of each circuit trunk group. The variable costs will depend on the traffic destinations since the tariffs are mileage dependent. They will, of course, partly depend on the locations of the PBX and the network gateway.

Table 2 shows the output of a calculation of the CFTG specified in Table 1. The summary section gives a variety of important statistics, including the overflow probability and the total communications cost for all of the facilities. The traffic engineering summary gives the traffic offered and overflow probability for each trunk. Also shown are the amount of traffic for each trunk carried for each destination, as well as summary statistics.

Several types of circuit trunk groups can be considered in today's competitive vendor environment. Point-to-point private lines, measured-use network services, and private lines interfaced to a measured-use network service at a gateway. A manager can consider many vendors, including Bell operating companies, for both the private line and the network services. The user can create his own subnetwork by interfacing one vendor's

Table 2: Output of PBX circuit calculation

CONTROL PANEL

ITERATIONS	1	TRAFFIC HOURS	3
SCAN HOURS	2	ROUTING TABLE	2
INDEPENDENT HOURS	3	ACCUMULATED HOURS	1

SUMMARY

31.73	=	LAST HOUR TRAFFIC CARRIED
0.28	=	LAST HOUR FACILITY OVERFLOW PROBABILITY
14,445.76	=	HOURLY MEASURED USAGE COST
14,445.76	=	CUMULATIVE HOUR MEASURED USAGE COST
55,406.22	=	TOTAL FACILITY MONTHLY COST FIXED + MEASURED, ALL TRUNKS
0.28	=	MAXIMUM HOURLY FACILITY
0.28	=	OVERFLOW PROBABILITY

FACILITY	NUMBER OF TRUNKS	ROUTING
1	5	14680643
2	6	35621789
3	7	84259621
4	4	53689314
5	5	42671165
6	6	12399764
7	6	92837465
8	6	57382914

TRAFFIC ENGINEERING SUMMARY (ERLANGS)

ORIGINATING TRAFFIC 44.52381

FACILITY NUMBER	1	2	3	4	5	6
TRAFFIC OFFERED	5.00	4.33	6.07	7.77	5.35	6.31
OVERFLOW PROBABILITY	0.28	0.14	0.19	0.56	0.31	0.28

CARRIED TRAFFIC

DESTINATION	1	2	3	4	5	6
1	0.18	0.86	1.22	0.88	0	1.08
2	0.25	0.50	0.57	0.10	0.08	0.59
3	0.81	0.48	0.23	0.31	0.88	0.60
4	0.66	0.48	0.90	0.65	1.15	0.40
5	0.36	0.21	0.61	0.38	0.08	0.09
6	0.08	0.20	0.28	0.46	0.73	0.59
7	0.76	0.20	0.77	0.15	0.57	0.34
8	0.44	0.74	0.30	0.43	0.17	0.80
TOTAL TRAFFIC CARRIED	3.57	3.71	4.92	3.38	3.68	4.51
MONTHLY COST/HOUR OF TRAFFIC ($)	2,324.58	2,037.28	2,383.39	1,582.63	1,281.05	2,744.31
TOTAL MONTHLY COST ($)	9,178.78	7,520.88	4,461.43	1,855.15	26,080.55	4,216.91

private lines to another vendor's measured-use network. The call cost will depend on the specific vendor tariff combinations, the mileage, mean call lengths, and monthly usage. These considerations must all be taken into account in calculating measured-use costs.

A telecommunications analysis tool greatly facilitates circuit evaluation if it automates the calculations of the tariff cost calculation and the offered traffic. The user can then focus on strategy selection and cost reduction.

As noted, a critical strategic variable in PBX cost reduction is the traffic routing pattern—that is, how the call traffic to each traffic destination group is routed to the various circuit trunk groups. To be maximally helpful, the evaluation spreadsheet must be designed to utilize many call-routing alternatives.

Two call-routing methods should be available, one based on the allocation of calls among the various

circuit trunk groups, the other based on overflow from one group to another. Furthermore, the package must be able to apply its various routing tables to different hours of the day or to different parts of the month. Significant cost reductions can often be achieved by varying the call-routing pattern.

In addition to guiding the user through the selection, evaluation, and optimization process for circuit configurations, the package should allow the evaluation of a multiswitched voice and data network in terms of both the monthly cost of operation and the grade of service. The user should be able to minimize the cost of a voice and/or data network within the constraint of various reliability criteria.

Table 3 shows some of the output of the cost-analysis module that performs this function. The network switch connections are shown, as are the links from switch to switch. An alternate network connection

Table 3: Network module

DIAGRAM NETWORK 1

SWITCHES

	SWITCH 1	SWITCH 2	SWITCH 3	SWITCH 4	SWITCH 5
LINKS 1 — 2	1 2				
2 — 3		2 3			
3 — 4			3 4		
4 — 5				4 5	
5 — 1	1				5

ALTERNATE NETWORK 2

	SWITCH 1	SWITCH 2	SWITCH 3	SWITCH 4	SWITCH 5
LINKS 1 — 2	1 2				
2 — 3		2 3			
3 — 5			3 5		
4 — 5				4 5	
5 — 2	2				5

CONFIGURATION OF NETWORK

NODES OF EACH SWITCH

SWITCH NUMBER	SWITCH NODE	NODE DESTINATION	NODE DESTINATION	NODE DESTINATION	NODE DESTINATION
1	1	1	2	3	4
2	5	5	6	7	8
3	9	9	10	11	12
4	13	13	14	15	16
5	17	17	18	19	20

INTERMACHINE TRUNKS

LINK SYSTEM COST ANALYSIS

	FROM SWITCH	TO SWITCH	LINK TRAFFIC BUSY HOUR	TRUNKS REQUIRED	AT&T 2000 LINK COST	MCI PRIVATE LINE LINK COST	AT&T 8000 LINK COST
LINKS 1 — 2	1	2	6.175	12	$1,646.79	$1,400.59	$12,695.52
2 — 3	2	3	14.525	22	3,089.72	2,626.16	12,741.88
3 — 4	3	4	18.39	27	13,301.94	10,839.98	13,985.50
4 — 5	4	5	13.92	21	6,593.82	5,437.37	16,676.50
5 — 1	5	1	3.36	8	2,992.32	2,454.57	11,909.59
TOTALS					27,624.61	22,758.79	68,009.02

MONTHLY TRAFFIC TOTALS (ERLANGS)

SWITCH-TO-SWITCH			TRAFFIC FLOW		
1 → 2	=	337	2 → 1	=	369
1 → 3	=	409	3 → 1	=	473
1 → 4	=	481	4 → 1	=	577
1 → 5	=	553	5 → 1	=	681
2 → 3	=	538.6	3 → 2	=	570.6
2 → 4	=	623.4	4 → 2	=	687.4
2 → 5	=	708.2	5 → 2	=	804.2
3 → 4	=	765.8	4 → 3	=	797.8
3 → 5	=	863.4	5 → 3	=	927.4
4 → 5	=	1,018.6	5 → 4	=	1,050.6

diagram is then given, and both schemes will be evaluated. The network configuration shows the association of nodes to switches, and the link trunkage design is evaluated for three vendors. The second vendor has the lowest cost. At the bottom are results for switch-to-switch traffic flows from which links and trunks can be designed for minimum cost.

If an expert system for telecommunications management has the facilities described, it can be used to directly analyze a number of recurring PBX and network problems, such as:

■ What are the effects on a PBX of changing the call-routing plans?
■ Can a new T1 link make significant cost reductions?
■ What is the trade-off between additional private lines' busy-hour overflow?

■ What are the effects of new traffic estimates on PBX and network circuit design? What are the effects of tariff changes?
■ Is it profitable to bring a new location into a corporate network?
■ What are the optimal network switch locations? The optimal network switch-to-switch links?
■ Should off-network connections completely bypass the network or should they leave it at the node closest to the destination? (These options are often referred to as head-end hop-off and tail-end hop-off.) ■

Carl Klahr was formerly the regional administrator for Telecommunications and Data Services for the U. S. General Services Administration.

Gabriel Kasperek, Kazcom Inc., Park Ridge, Ill.

Comparing various network management schemes

Some are hardware-based; some, software-based. Costs vary from hundreds to thousands of dollars. All minimize downtime.

No organization can afford downtime. This is why network control is a necessity. Networks and databases are regarded today as valuable corporate resources. In fact, a data communications network can be seen as an extension of business functions. If for some reason an organization cannot modify or access data, then it may not be possible to increase revenue or productivity. The user organization must attain maximum network availability (uptime) by pinpointing inefficiencies within the network.

The organization's communications staff, unlike networks, should not continue to grow in proportion to business. A larger staff does not always mean less downtime. Further, sheer numbers of personnel who can solve network problems are not easily found: The skill level needed and the skill level available are often far apart. In a decentralized computing environment, technically experienced people may be at each remote site to help resolve communications problems. This type of duplication must be avoided.

Ideally, an organization would like to take on personnel who are familiar with data communications concepts, place them in one centrally located network control, and have them be productive immediately in isolating and resolving problems. To gain this capability, the time and cost expended for training and retraining would not be considered significant.

Today, the training of one's own personnel is critical because there is no longer end-to-end service supplied by the telephone company. This alone is often reason enough for many organizations that want greater control to think of using network control techniques.

The network control center (NCC) as used in this article is defined as a centralized facility staffed with several persons equipped with specialized monitoring and diagnostic tools. The NCC's function is to manage all network problems and changes. This article discusses the techniques available to the NCC personnel to attain minimum downtime in data communications networks.

What it must do

In order to be effective, an NCC must provide these five basic functions:

- *Monitoring.* Give the manager or the operations staff an indication of a network-problem condition in real time. The operations staff must be able to monitor both the digital and the analog interfaces at all locations. This capability gets the staff out of the "react mode," typified by problem notification from a user calling into the center. By this time it is too late. With monitoring, problems can be acted on before they inconvenience the user.

For the staff to be productive, it cannot dedicate one or more members to this function. Instead, the monitoring function is automatic. The staff programs threshold levels for various parameters into the NCC equipment. If the levels are exceeded, an alarm informs the operations personnel.

- *Isolation.* With most communications problems, the greatest amount of corrective time is taken to find out where the problem is located. This process could involve several people. However, once a programmed threshold level is exceeded, problem isolation is almost automatic. Less time spent in isolating a problem translates to less downtime.

- *Restoration.* With the source of the problem identified, the staff reroutes circuits or substitutes hardware and/or software to restore the network to operation.

- *Performance measurement.* This is the information necessary to ensure the best possible network opera-

1. Dial backup. *A dedicated line may become inoperative either because it is causing too many transmission errors or because a discontinuity develops. Service may be restored by accessing another line on the switched network. This procedure can be supported by a modem or by external dial-backup units.*

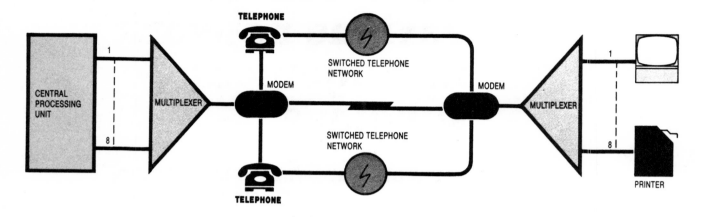

tion. This information tells whether there is under- or overutilization of resources. Certainly if resources such as leased lines are underutilized, the network's cost-effectiveness suffers. Or if resources such as multiplexers, front-end processors, and computers are overutilized, it may well affect user productivity. Performance measurement is a basic function that gives management personnel a tool to enable more effective use of its budget and processing resources. As with any monitoring function, it allows a marginally operating device to be pinpointed before it fails completely.

■ *Information management.* This is the ability to electronically store and retrieve all necessary network management data. To resolve problems, the operations staff must have ready access to information, such as the type of device, options used, serial number, and vendor. If the application of a communications link is in question, graphics displays on a CRT screen can be of great assistance. They would illustrate all network devices, with the destination terminations of each.

—continued—

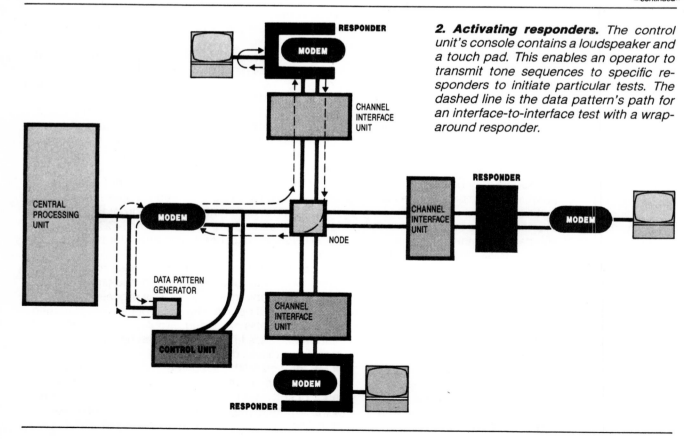

2. Activating responders. *The control unit's console contains a loudspeaker and a touch pad. This enables an operator to transmit tone sequences to specific responders to initiate particular tests. The dashed line is the data pattern's path for an interface-to-interface test with a wraparound responder.*

There is usually such a vast amount of information that maintaining such a database becomes a necessity.

To manage a network, the staff has various types of forms to complete. If these forms can be produced, changed, and stored electronically, network documentation may be readily updated, thus maintaining its accuracy.

Converting the paperwork

The information contained in these forms can be optimally manipulated by the database for hard-copy output. Manipulations on this stored data can show network trends, particularly what types of problems are occurring and how long they are taking to be isolated and solved. Certain vendors will be seen as having more frequent failures than others. Avoiding further integration of these vendors' products into the network will likely reduce future downtime.

All five basic functions should provide flexibility to accommodate changes and growth within the network. When a network grows, its management should be able to readily apply technologies to support these functions without having to redesign the network. And equipment in support of the functions must be more reliable than the equipment managed.

All five basic functions should be vendor independent. This, of course, is not always attainable. A vendor may not be able to support some of the functions. Also, it may be an organization's philosophy not to be locked into using just one vendor, even though that vendor supports all five basic functions.

The techniques

The control methods currently used in an NCC include dial backup, responders, patching, switching, intelligent modems, performance-monitoring, and host-based management. How dial backup supports the basic functions can be shown by assuming that a point-to-point multiplexer link exists with an aggregate dedicated link speed of 9.6 kbit/s. If this analog link were to open, it could take anywhere from one hour to a number of days to repair. In a business environment, even 15 minutes of downtime would probably be intolerable. One way to immediately bypass the failure is to access a line on the switched network. This can be accomplished by using dial-backup techniques. As illustrated in Figure 1, two telephone calls are initiated. The remote modem, sensing both ring signals on its analog interface, automatically goes into an auto-answer mode. A modem capable of functioning in both a dedicated and switched-network application is common to many vendors. Two telephone calls are necessary to establish a four-wire, full-duplex link. Two telephones may not be required: A dial-backup unit with one telephone can be used, reducing hardware. Further hardware reductions can be attained with one set of dial-backup hardware that can be patched into any dedicated failed link.

The advantages of this restoration method are the initial low cost in telephones and monthly access charges. This low cost may be countered by the possible high cost of toll charges. Even though these charges may accrue significantly, the application can be justified because service is restored.

A major disadvantage of dial backup is the lower transmission quality on the switched network at 9.6 kbit/s. Most likely, fallback to 7.2 or 4.8 kbit/s will have to be exercised—either automatically by the modems or manually by network personnel. Throughput may even be greater at the reduced data rates due to fewer retransmissions.

The dial-backup hardware is usually considered reliable. But an occasional test should be run to verify its operability and to keep operations personnel familiar with the procedures.

Reliability is one reason that organizations use leased DDS (Dataphone digital service) lines. If dial backup is desired here, the additional hardware required will be a modem at the local and remote sites and switching or patching to swap the RS-232-C interface connections.

For a look at an innovative dial-backup implementation on multidrop lines, see DATA COMMUNICATIONS, ''A novel approach to backing up a data network,'' December 1984, p. 183.

Responders

Illustrated in Figure 2 is a dedicated four-wire multidrop configuration. Via a control console, the responders allow an operator to perform specific tests of any remote drop. The selection process is accomplished by transmitting tones similar to those used on a push-button telephone: the DTMF (dual tone multi-frequency).

For example, the first sequence of tones selects a specific responder. The next tone initiates one of four tests by the responder: (1) Transmit a 1,004-Hz tone; (2) go into loopback; (3) ''quietly'' terminate (see discussion below); and (4) perform external digital loopback test (only on a wraparound responder).

Selecting test 1 allows an operator to determine if there is severe attenuation—typically greater than 16 dB in one direction—or a discontinuity on one side of a line pair at any remote drop.

Test 2 places a remote drop's modem into loopback by addressing its responder. Transmitting a 1,004-Hz tone from the console then determines if the line is continuous. This method is superior to that initiated by a channel interface unit (CIU). With the latter scheme, a transmitted 2,713-Hz tone triggers all remote CIUs into loopback. This could cause more confusion than control.

Isolating the source

Quiet termination (test 3) blocks the carrier signal from a streaming (uncontrolled carrier-signal) remote site, avoiding further interference to other users. It is accomplished by isolating the modem from the rest of the network and terminating the connection with its characteristic impedance of 600 ohms. But a problem similar to the one encountered earlier in transmitting the 2,713-Hz tone—which would put all remote modems in loopback and prevent a quiet termination of just one—can be avoided. By individually addressing and quietly terminating all responders but that of the problem modem, a remote analog loopback test may be performed on that modem.

Using a wraparound responder (test 4), an external digital loopback is performed. This test (Fig. 2) is equivalent to connecting pin 2 to pin 3 on a breakout box: a true interface-to-interface test. This technique enables an operator to isolate a defective remote terminal.

The main advantage to the user of responders is vendor independence. An organization can have any type of modem in an existing network and apply responders to quickly gain control. The test hardware costs about $500 to $800 (to do the tests described) and offers reliability higher than most other network control methods.

A disadvantage: All tests performed with responders interfere with normal transmission. Therefore, such tests would usually be performed during off-hours. Otherwise, normal traffic would have to be suspended. The console may provide the ability to exercise tests at a preprogrammed time.

A manual method
Patching enables restoration and reconfiguration without the inconvenience of making actual wiring changes. Patching is accomplished with patch cords plugging into jack pairs, making and breaking analog or digital connections. Typically there is a third jack for passive monitoring. Thus an operator can plug in digital or analog monitoring equipment on a noninterfering basis. Patching brings both analog and digital interfaces to one centralized location, enabling operators to work efficiently with both interfaces in proximity.

Another advantage of patching is that it readily accommodates network growth by the addition of patch modules. However, for every installation there is a practical limit to how much patching can be exercised. Once this limit is reached, another network control technique would have to be implemented.

Add-on patch panel modules must be of the same physical type as existing ones. Each vendor has its own type of plug, making it impossible to have different vendors' patching equipment coexist. Still, patching is vendor independent as far as the wiring interface to any data terminal equipment (DTE) or data circuit-terminating equipment (DCE) is concerned. Patching is the most common network-control technique because of its low cost ($70 to $80 per patch module), mechanical and electrical simplicity, ease of use, and ready applicability to various types of test equipment.

Dealing with more ports
Switching in an NCC exists on three levels: basic, intelligent (computerized), and matrix. Basic switching is much like patching in that its process restores a failed network. But when groups of 32 or more links need to be restored—as in the case of a multiplexer or front-end processor failure—basic switching is more efficient than patching. Activating one switch transfers an entire user group to another resource.

Common techniques in switching are A/B selection and sparing. A/B selection is straightforward: The operator selects either choice A or B, where either connection may be attached to a spare device or rerouted to another resource. The hardware typically is electromechanical, the connection held magnetically. This adds to the reliability: In case the power is lost to the switch rack, the connections will still be maintained. A/B selection can be combined with patching in one module to gain the capability of passively monitoring a transmission line.

Similar to patching, switching modules and panels may grow to an unmanageable extent. To forestall this situation, intelligence is added by placing a microcomputer card in the test chassis. An asynchronous terminal may be used to interface the switching array.

Working from afar
Unlike patching, remote switch arrays may be controlled by an operator terminal via a modem link, without human intervention at remote sites. To further enhance this operator interface, a microcomputer may be used. The commands will thus be more English-like, with the ability to store and retrieve information necessary to manage the network.

Sparing is a technique used in all three levels of switching to avoid one-for-one equipment duplication. Instead of a hot (activated) spare for every operating device, there is one spare for several devices. Figure 3 illustrates one-to-four modem sparing. A site may require no more than one spare for every 16 active devices, stretching the cost-effectiveness still further.

This sparing scheme, as it stands, has a disad-

---

3. One for all. *Sparing avoids equipment duplication, reducing costs. Illustrated is one-to-four modem sparing, without the capability of testing the spare.*

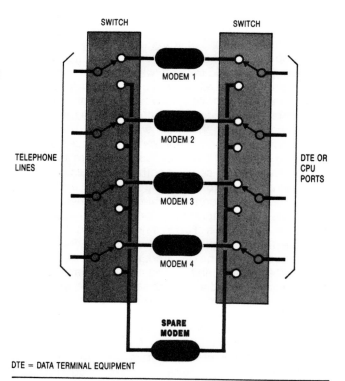

DTE = DATA TERMINAL EQUIPMENT

vantage: There is no convenient way one can test the spare modem's operability. What can be done, at a small additional cost (about $250 to $500), is to install a test bus that permits an operator to regularly test the spare to verify proper operation.

The extent of intelligent switching is restricted by associated hardware. Since most of this switching is of the A/B type, every port cannot be connected to every other port. If more flexibility is desired, matrix switching should be considered.

The more flexible way

Matrix switches can connect any port to any other port, or group of ports—activated by an operator using English-like commands at a terminal. The size of the matrix switch typically starts at 32 by 32, with 32-by-32 increments up to 512 by 512. If anything larger than this is required, a vendor can place switches in tandem. Some vendors are more flexible than others in matrix-switch size, also offering asymmetrical switches.

Figure 4 illustrates a matrix switch application. A large matrix switch at the central site can be linked to a smaller one at each remote site. The central switch— via a dedicated or dial-up link—accesses each remote switch, controlling all restoration and monitoring activity.

The matrix switch can provide the restoration of any DTE or DCE device, such as in modem and front-end processor sparing, either on an individual-port basis or for groups of 32 or more. If a matrix switch operates on digital ports, it can also monitor the RS-232-C leads between the DTE and DCE. When the DCD (data carrier detect) signal is not present for a programmed time (realistically, up to one minute), an alarm prompts an operator so that corrective action may be taken before receipt of a user's complaint call.

Figure 4 shows test equipment attached to the matrix switch. Thus, any user port may be connected as a test port. With this same connection at the remote matrix switch, a data pattern can be generated with a bit error rate tester (BERT) or data analyzer, while monitoring for possible errors. This application is a true interface-to-interface test, with all components at the remote digital interface accounted for.

Monitoring and restoration can also be accomplished at a modem's analog (line) interface. What is required is another type of interface card placed into the matrix switch. This adds about $300 to $500 to the switch's per-port cost, makes it more complex, and uses up more ports. Some vendors tackle analog restoration by placing equipment external to the matrix switch. (For more application information on matrix switching, see "Matrix switching: Quickest path to network restoral," DATA CCOMMUNICATIONS, May 1983, p. 137.)

Upgradability is a feature of a matrix switch. As a network grows, operators may not only need an easy-to-use tool to control the switch but also a database to store and manipulate information. Most matrix switch vendors can upgrade the network operator's workstation from an asynchronous terminal (for basic straight-forward switching needs) to a microcomputer and, if needed, to a minicomputer.

There is one potential problem. On one side of a matrix switch resides a user population; on the other, computing resources. What happens if the matrix switch fails? Vendors employ redundant power supplies, redundant logic, and equipment modularity to avoid catastrophic events. Even though these extras can be designed into a matrix switch, an organization may opt instead for a nonelectronic type of switch: an electromechanical matrix switch. In such a switch— unlike an electronic one—if power fails or a logic failure occurs, the switch maintains its connections. Thus, despite the inherent lower mean time between failures of any mechanical device, network-reliability requirements may mandate an electromechanical matrix switch.

Some disadvantages of an electromechanical matrix switch are related to its size. It would need to be about 40 percent larger than its electronic counterpart to be functionally equivalent. If its size were made competitive with that of the electronic matrix—by reducing the number of switching paths—the connections would be more likely to become overloaded (blocked) under maximum-traffic conditions.

The matrix switch provides many basic functions: monitoring, isolation, restoration, and information management. One of its most important characteristics is vendor independence.

The sidestream approach

Intelligent modems respond to an external processor's poll requests with status data. The modem informs the processor of any changes in its analog or digital interface. This is accomplished in one of two ways: in band or out of band. Out-of-band testing is accomplished by frequency-division multiplexing, allowing a separate portion of the bandwidth to be dedicated to diagnostics (DATA COMMUNICATIONS, "How network con-

---

4. Maximum control. *Here, one terminal controls connections to a local and a remote matrix switch. No personnel are needed to attach equipment to test ports.*

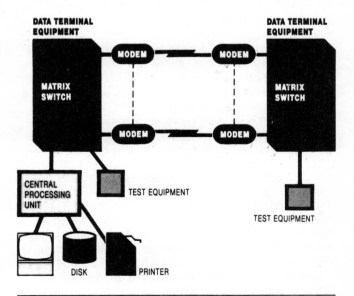

---

trol curbs downtime," July 1980, p. 52). In-band testing is seen in host-based network management.

The diagnostic approach that features a network of intelligent modems avoids the extensive use of external test equipment, thus simplifying the operator interface. The operator at one terminal can monitor both the analog and digital interfaces, set thresholds for alarm conditions, manipulate a database, and automatically run tests.

The tests can be interfering or noninterfering. The latter include monitoring the digital and analog interfaces for irregularities, displayed at the operator's terminal. Interfering tests, perhaps run during off hours, are all the varieties of loopback testing, with data patterns generated from the modems.

Almost all tester vendors provide a database that either exists at initial implementation or can be added when needed. As problems occur, the database produces forms on the CRT screen that the operator completes. With this information entered, plus the real-time diagnostic data transmitted by all intelligent modems, the database may be manipulated and displayed for trend-analysis purposes.

A vendor can either supply an intelligent modem or "wrap" intelligence around an already-installed nonintelligent one. The wraparound device is vendor independent. This method is an overlay process, useful—especially where an organization has multiple network vendors—for monitoring the analog and digital interfaces. All modems having internal intelligence must be from the same vendor, to minimize operations personnel's service-call efforts.

Just monitoring is not going to be sufficient with this technique. Operations can monitor and isolate the defective device, but then must restore the network. Therefore, many vendors usually combine some form of switching mechanism along with their intelligent-modem network.

Performance monitoring

A network must be designed for optimum performance at the least cost. As an organization's network evolves, management needs information-gathering tools to determine how the network is being utilized. For example, does remote location A need four more terminals and associated hardware and software? These and similar requests may have no quantified data for justification.

If management monitors the performance of remote site A, it may discover only 40 percent line utilization. Management would therefore deny the request for more terminals. By monitoring remote site B, management notices, say, at least double A's utilization. Remote site B therefore receives the needed resources—such as lines, terminals, multiplexers, and modems—to remain productive.

The organization's network traffic patterns change. Four months later, new observations note that site A has doubled its utilization. Also, there are plans for site A to work on a project that requires additional communications resources. Also, site B has decreased its utilization significantly—say, by half. Management takes underutilized lines and peripherals from site B

and transfers them to site A. What has been accomplished is a shifting of equipment, rather than having the budget eaten up unnecessarily by underutilized—or unneeded newly purchased—equipment and lines. In fact, an organization s data communications budget is not properly allocated unless quantified data is obtained by performance monitoring.

Other reasons to monitor performance:
- *Response times.* Does the user really undergo 25 seconds of response time? Performance monitoring will determine its validity and pinpoint any causes.
- *New hardware and software.* These may alter network performance.
- *Additional users.* These may degrade network performance.

Figure 5 illustrates an application of performance monitoring. Here, external equipment is placed near the front-end processor and local modems. Via a "Y" cable, the performance monitoring equipment taps in passively on pins 2 and 3, transmit and receive data, of the RS-232-C interface. The monitored data is then transmitted to a minicomputer that carries out all calculations and outputs the results to a printer or to disk storage.

This procedure can be applied to hundreds of lines. On the other hand, it may not be the most cost-effective, since it dedicates hardware and software for each line monitored. An alternative is to purchase a single portable unit and patch it into any line for which monitoring is desired. This is low-cost (typically $7,000) line monitoring for any size shop.

The mainstream approach

Some vendors provide software and load it into the user's mainframe for performance monitoring. Host-based network management must have hardware and software compatibility with all the network devices that it is intended to manage. For example, an operator might question if the DTR (data terminal ready) signal is active at a remote terminal's interface. Host-based network management has to communicate with the remote modem. This is accomplished with in-band diagnostics—which requires that user data be temporarily interrupted—that monitors the remote DTE interface and sends its status back to the host. This process is not vendor independent. All network devices en route must understand and route the diagnostic messages.

A major advantage of host-based management is its ability to achieve an end-to-end network perspective. Not only can operators discover hardware problems, they can also detect software problems in the network path to the remote terminal. But these benefits do not come free. Placing software packages on the mainframe uses CPU cycles that application programs may need. Mainframe performance will not be degraded as much—probably to an insignificant extent—if these packages are distributed onto several mainframes. (For greater detail on host-based network management, see "Net management choices: Sidestream or mainstream," DATA COMMUNICATIONS, August 1982, p. 91.)

Test instrumentation has taken on a new appearance. At one time an operator required many months

5. Composing the results. *A line monitoring unit captures two-way data at an RS-232-C interface. A minicomputer manipulates it into the desired format.*

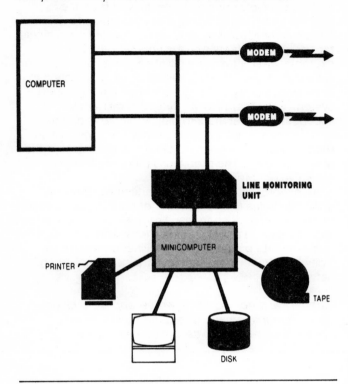

of training and expertise to use test equipment effectively. With the recently introduced test equipment, an operator can acquire the needed skills with little training—less than a day. Because the instruments are designed with the operator in mind, little retraining or reference to instruction manuals is needed. This is particularly important, because in a control center not all test equipment is used on a daily basis; diagnostic time being critical, the operator may not be afforded the luxury of referring to a manual when working with an infrequently used instrument .

Hand-held test equipment such as breakout boxes and some BERTs are comparatively easy to use to help isolate communications problems. Recent BERT developments have made the tester more intelligent by including, for example, buffers where data can be stored and manipulated. Network simulation and protocol decoding are achieved by placing ROM (read-only memory) into the BERT. This type of test equipment, along with simple tests provided by many modems, resolves most network problems. For greater capabilities, data analyzers are required. They include full network simulation and data recording, accomplished by the use of soft (programmable) keys. The only drawback with such test equipment is that it must be implemented manually.

Attempting to get greater control of the analog interface may require analog test equipment. After receiving ordered lines, an organization does not know for certain whether all of the lines are within specification. Exercising end-to-end tests verifies the current status of a line. This information is then stored, retrieved later when tests are exercised again, and compared to the new test's results to discover if the line's parameters have changed. The conclusions drawn from these comparison measurements better prepare the user to discuss problems with the telephone company. (For more detail about analog test equipment, data analyzers, and their application, see DATA COMMUNICATIONS, "What to look for in today's analog test equipment," November 1984, p. 219, and 'Data analyzers are sniffing out network snags," May 1984, p. 117.)

At one time an oscilloscope was standard test equipment. Today, because of the technical training required in its application, the oscilloscope is not always the best tool for isolating data network problems. However, it still has one big advantage: a visual indication. At an NCC, an oscilloscope can be placed in a rack along with analog switching or patching equipment. A modem's diagnostic-signal output (a separate output reserved specifically for oscilloscopes) can be patched or switched to an oscilloscope. Displayed on the oscilloscope is a representation of how the modem perceives the line. A trained operator views the display to determine if there is a problem with the transmission line. A major advantage of this technique is its visual approach and low cost (about $300).

Omens and futures
Certain trends in network management equipment are imminent or are already under way:
- An organization's network may be designed around large (with several hundred ports) statistical multiplexers that—besides their normal functions—also switch data to various resources. As this network grows, operations needs a tool to direct the statistics from all the multiplexers to one central location. Recently, a few multiplexer vendors released such an NCC tool. The supervisory ports on their multiplexers are terminated at an interface to a microcomputer. The micro's software manipulates the received data and displays it in various forms, including graphs. Other vendors will probably adopt this reporting technique.
- Intelligent-modem vendors and matrix-switch vendors will add performance-monitoring hardware and software to their existing products.
- The product line of network-control vendors is evolving and will include devices such as statistical multiplexers, T1 multiplexers supporting both voice and data, data switches, and local networks.
- If an organization integrates voice and data, management problems are cut significantly. One goal of voice/data integration is to avoid supporting two separate facilities. With one integrated facility, and with the problems being so similar, there is no longer the requirement for separate management tools.
- There will be many new vendors in test instrumentation providing innovations at lower cost. The microcomputer will increasingly become a test instrument. Perhaps with a touch-screen feature, an operator can readily select analog or digital test functions.
- Local network management tools will become avail-

able. Now that local networks have become more common, the operations staff needs tools to accomplish the five basic functions. The microcomputer has already been applied to local networks as an NCC tool. Data analyzers and similar devices will become available to pinpoint problems and to provide modeling techniques for network growth.

■ Many providers of database software for network management will appear. The software packages will be placed on microcomputers, minicomputers, and mainframes.

■ Carriers providing end-to-end services will continue to proliferate. If an organization goes with such a carrier, maintenance costs can be avoided. A carrier assures transmission and receipt of data for all users. This service includes managing the network that it leases.

■ Expert systems, a branch of artificial intelligence, can be applied with great advantage to an NCC. Expert systems already exist and are used with success in the medical and mining fields.

An expert system is a computer program that mimics a human expert. It uses methods and information acquired by that expert. The cost of an expert system—more than $50,000—can be justified in a typical data communications environment: With relatively few human experts available and an increasing demand for their expertise, the price of an expert's services is high.

(Whereas a salaried expert is paid $30,000 to $45,000 per year, a consultant is paid $500 to $1,200 per day.)

One type of expert system uses a knowledge base that consists of rules and facts derived from the existing knowledge and experience of experts. The rules are in the form of "IF A, THEN B," where A is a single fact or group of facts and B is another fact. For example, after a test on a point-to-point full-duplex link is executed, the following sequence of observations and conclusions can be incorporated into an expert system: DCD (data carrier detect) is missing for 10 seconds; the local modem passes self test; and the remote channel interface unit's loopback test is also passed. But there is no response to the self test of the remote modem. The problem is therefore identified as a defective remote modem.

An expert system can be enhanced by applying additional rules (those that do not conflict with present rules) if a network changes. Above all, this intelligence should reside in a sophisticated front-end processor—one with data processing capabilities—where it can "view" the main processor and the communications network. ■

Gabriel Kasperek consults, writes, and lectures on network management. One of his recent seminars covers hands-on troubleshooting techniques.

Jerrold F. Stach, Uninet, Lenexa, Kan.

Expert systems find a new place in data networks

Ever-growing networks pose unique problems to support personnel and to computer programs that mimic their knowledge. Such programs are now possible due to new hardware.

Originally a research area in the field of artificial intelligence, expert systems have become a controversial and vital part of computer science. Problem-solving programs have practical applications in medicine, geology, chemistry, and fault diagnosis. Research efforts are now under way to find new applications of expert systems for managing data communications networks.

Of these problem areas, only fault diagnosis seems to relate closely to computer networks. The use of expert systems in networks has previously been limited to diagnosis and maintenance, an area in which AT&T has produced a classic application. However, two other aspects of networking may be candidates for the use of expert systems: routing, now handled by heuristic algorithms, and supporting network operations.

Note that in computer science the area of expert systems is relatively new. Few good finished products exist, and a search of the literature indicates there is practically no precursor research for networking outside of diagnoses and maintenance. The advent of new computer hardware coupled with a class of intractable network problems would seem to offer the opportunity to employ expert systems in new ways. Applications research, but not development, is currently in progress.

An expert system (ES) is knowledge-based, resulting from an attempt to express human expertise in logical rules for decision making. It represents a peculiar human-to-machine relationship that makes the computer a close adjunct to the formal reasoning process. Emphasis in ES research has centered around the representation of knowledge as a practical matter; knowledge is scarce, and human experts are "expert" because they are knowledgeable. With the same knowledge as humans, say proponents of ES, the computer should be able to perform at the same level as humans, thereby extending their expertise.

ESs are distinct from artificial intelligence (AI), their progenitor. They attempt to solve difficult problems at an "expert" level of performance, doing the same job as the human expert, whereas AI is, in general, only an engineered facsimile of human behavior. ES designers must extract, articulate, and computerize the expert's knowledge prior to presenting a problem for solution. By contrast, robotics, which is one form of AI, is meant to approximate human performance.

In addition, an ES will often embody self-knowledge: the ability to recognize a previously encountered problem and to recall the prior solution. It can use this self-knowledge to reason about its own inferences and to provide the user with a justification for its conclusions.

The hardware opportunity

Several factors have led researchers to consider extending ESs to the data communications network. Topological design, routing, and network management in large networks have no tractable algorithmic solution for two reasons. First, very large networks are now being built with high degrees of interconnectivity and diverse transmission media, such as satellite, microwave, copper, and optical fiber. Each of these media has unique cost, performance, and reliability attributes. This variety complicates the design process.

The second reason is itself an impetus to employ an ES in the network: namely, technological opportunity. A variety of radically new architectures, such as parallel, fully or partially distributed (coupled or uncoupled), and those involved with bit-slice processors, are now available to designers of data switches. Earlier restrictions on memory and real time (which, to a software engineer, means the amount of time that can be allocated to a given process) may be overcome with these new architectures. The number of computing elements making network decisions can thus increase by an order of magnitude.

Scientists have always been plagued by results that were colored or constrained by their technological environment. Current monolithic architectures, such as those underlying traditional minicomputers, are limited in both memory and transaction processing rates. Advancements of these, such as the partially distributed, common-bus microcomputer architectures that constitute some fault-tolerant machines, can relax these bounds. Unfortunately, the performance of the single memory bank or central processing unit (CPU) in such designs tends to become sluggish, perhaps even before the bus or back-plane limit is reached.

Recently, however, more advanced hardware has started to become available. Both Bell Laboratories and Bolt Beranek and Newman announced new switch architectures. BB&N has developed a "butterfly" switch that uses a parallel matrix architecture. Bell Labs is developing a switch that handles both packetized voice and data. Uninet announced a network architecture built on a fully distributed/coupled machine from M/A-Com DCC.

Emerging computer architectures and new software disciplines such as ESs inspire researchers to apply technology to formerly intractable problems. The new parallel and distributed architectures offer to solve resource problems in large networks characterized by high event (interrupt or transaction) rates, increasing real-time requirements for network management and protocols, and memory requirements that grow with the network's size and software complexity.

Until now, these resource problems have dissuaded researchers from considering expert systems that reside in, and operate as part of, the network itself. Traditional ES applications run adjacent to the network, in standalone processors. Moving them into the network would only increase the network's computational overhead. Furthermore, it takes time for an ES to "reason out" a conclusion to a problem, implying still more overhead. Therefore, the new computing architectures that are available might enable network designers to consider expert systems.

Just as everything looks like a nail to the wielder of a hammer, there is a tendency to apply new technology to difficult problems simply because the technology exists. Why attack networking problems with expert systems and the newer hardware architectures? Because the increased size and versatility of contemporary wide-area networks require a processing power that is not met by currently available technology.

Three types of expert systems
The growth of networks obviously makes demands on the machines that comprise and manage them. Less frequently acknowledged is the increasing amount of work being asked of the people who design and operate these networks. As the data that they must process increases, their ability to handle it can also be enhanced by expert systems that can both present data more densely and offload numerous routine tasks

of synthesis and analysis. More sophisticated hardware makes it possible to implement an ES with advanced human/machine interfaces.

Different categories of ESs, namely diagnosis, control, and interpretation, can be applied to three different aspects of networking. Diagnostic ESs observe irregular behavior and try to infer the cause or causes of that behavior. Network impairments or outages might be examined by an "Expert Diagnostician," which would then coordinate work orders so that people could perform the actual repairs.

A control ES interprets the current state of its object and tries to predict its future state. Thus, an "Expert Router" could use its ability to monitor and predict a network's configuration to decide which path to use for each new call. Finally, an interpretation ES reviews observable facts and explains them by assigning them meaning. If an "Expert Operator" monitored and synthesized network events and statistics, it could augment human network-control personnel.

Expert systems are already being used in conjunction with such complex networks as AT&T's long-distance network. Diagnostic ESs are of particular interest to network architects because it is more difficult to diagnose impaired behavior than failure, since impaired performance is typically transient. Most established networks are plagued with at least one phantom problem that seems to abide for the life of the network. Repeated application of the ES to the impaired behavior using various hypotheses might well result in a reasoned conclusion regarding the cause.

An Expert Router would adaptively control the behavior of the network based on traffic, failure, and congestion, as does the conventional heuristic routing algorithm. However, a heuristic router can only optimize resource consumption locally. The goal of the Expert Router is to move toward global optimization.

Perhaps the most interesting potential application of an ES is the Expert Operator, which could process a greater number of events with reduced operator intervention. This application matches the ES interpretation category rather nicely, since a human expert could collaborate with a software engineer to codify and computerize knowledge about network operations. The Diagnostician's knowledge base is also human-based, unlike that of the Router; mathematical inference, not human knowledge, goes into routing decisions.

What's in an expert system
All expert systems are built from a common set of architectural components. Most implementations contain a subset of these components:
■ *Language Processor.* The human interface is provided by a Language Processor that allows problem-oriented communications between the user and the ES. The interface is generally implemented via a subset of English, although the context of networking provides an opportunity to supply it via graphics.
■ *Blackboard.* This component is a recording of intermediate conclusions and hypotheses that the ES manipulates in the course of solving the problem. Usually the steps taken to go from decision to decision

are also recorded here. When a human interrogator asks for justification of a conclusion, the ES works backward to show the logic behind its conclusion.

■ *Scheduler.* Since the Blackboard contains intermediate hypotheses and conclusions, there must be a component that schedules which rules to apply and in what order, because the problem changes as new facts become known to the ES.

■ *Interpreter.* This component is the key player determining how the ES actually does its job. It applies the rules that came from the human expert's knowledge to the problem in its current state.

■ *Justifier.* This final component brings the human being back into the loop by allowing the user to question the actions of the ES. In essence, the Justifier can trace backward through the Blackboard elements, one rule at a time, to explain why decisions were made.

Expert Diagnostician

Acting as a repair or work-order coordinator for the network, the Expert Diagnostician analyzes both failures and impairments, determines the probable cause, and specifies the repair or maintenance actions most likely to correct the problem. AT&T's arrangement is reported to be highly accurate, rarely misdiagnosing the problem. Expert Diagnosticians are failure-preemptive in the sense that they analyze impairments and attempt to preclude failure via preventive maintenance.

Underlying this type of ES is the premise that some unusual symptoms of network behavior must exist before a component fails. The ability to predict the cause of these symptoms is based on the integration of knowledge about symptoms, component mean-time-between-failure, and component historical behavior.

The goals of the automated diagnosis ES are:

■ To shorten the period of time required to detect the cause of unusual symptoms.

■ To assist the operator in taking appropriate action to deal with the imputed cause.

■ To identify distinct problems by effectively relating symptoms to causes.

This ES faces a time constraint, namely identifying and diagnosing a problem in a time period related to the problem's severity. That is, the computation needed to figure out severe problems cannot compromise their mean-time-to-repair. If it takes an ES longer to diagnose a problem than it takes a human being, the ES is counterproductive.

Figure 1 is a block diagram of the proposed Expert Diagnostician. Each network component is analyzed with respect to the performance of its peers. Contributing to the analysis are network measurements that reflect the current operating state of the various components. These measurements are not limited to operational status (up/down). They are intended to include indications of the load on the component. Despite the fact that components are predominantly solid state, the probability of component failure is still related to load (although correlation does not imply causality).

The ES analyzes these measurements in terms of a predictive failure database (a listing of how often, based on their specifications, the components are

1. What's down, Doc? In this diagnostic expert system, past, present, and future component behavior tell the interpreter what to tell the repair crew.

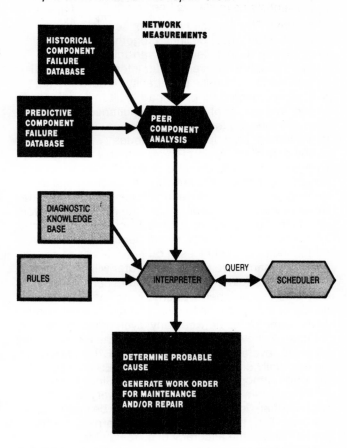

likely to fail) and a historical component-failure database of actual, logged performance. Even if no component has failed, the Interpreter may reason that the network reliability has dropped below some acceptable level and that a failure is imminent. Then the Scheduler determines which rule should be followed next and which action should be taken.

The final resolution is presented as a probable cause for the drop in reliability with a recommendation to schedule appropriate preventive maintenance. While repair would return the network to an acceptable reliability level, the preventive maintenance recommended by the ES is intended to pre-empt a potential future reduction in reliability.

The Expert Router

Part of the routing problem relates to the amount of information that arrives at the source of the routing decision. Networks of an earlier design only reported on the operational status of their components, but modern architectures are becoming instrumentation-rich, divulging information on CPU and buffer utilization, queue lengths, link occupancy, and so on. Since it is desirable to take more of the available information into account, traditional routing algorithms may become overwhelmed by the flood of factors.

An Expert Router might be used to approach global efficiency in network resource utilization. The premise underlying the Expert Router is that large networks contain significant amounts of extra capacity at any given time. This capacity exists for several reasons. Since all nodes must be linked together, more lines may have to be installed than warranted solely by traffic. Thus, the requirement for internodal connectivity can lead to a surplus of capacity. A network must also be engineered for peak load, built to handle the maximum number of expected simultaneous calls. Also, engineering for failure means redundant capacity in the form of backup lines and nodes.

The goal of the Expert Router is to use this capacity by increasing traffic over the existing network topology. A significant amount of network resources remains unused over time because the processes that allocate these resources are heuristic. As the number of factors on which route selection is based increases, the decisions made by a heuristic router become limited to a certain number of choices. If other routes exist between the same two points, the router will never pick them, since a rule-of-thumb algorithm can consider only a certain number of alternatives. That is, a heuristic router always tends to pick a relatively small number of the same paths between any given pair of nodes.

Figure 2 shows an overview of how the Expert Router employs several ES components. The Expert Router is conceptually different from traditional ESs because it operates without human intervention. Since it must make decisions approximately once every quarter-second, there is no time for humans to be involved. Yet, like other ESs, it uses a feedback or learning mechanism to adjust the accuracy of its reasoning.

The Expert Router capitalizes on the information that is discernible at call setup time. Particularly in X.25 networks, but also in networks like those running under IBM's Systems Network Architecture, a number of attributes of a future session are known at call-request time. The terminal and host pair are known, which means that the speeds of these devices are indicated. The other end's characteristics are discernible from the destination address of the call request.

By establishing a profile of the application and associating it with the speeds of the terminals, the Expert Router can quickly compute whether a call is delay-tolerant or not. For example, a point-of-sale terminal with a call duration of one transaction is not a candidate for the Expert Router because it needs the fastest and most direct route to its database. Also ruled out as a candidate is a computer that is accessing the network at 56 kbit/s and wants to transfer files to a machine running at the same speed because a call characterized by high-speed devices and a high bandwidth requirement is not delay-tolerant.

Conversely, many calls consist of low-speed terminals (300 bit/s) accessing relatively low-speed hosts (9.6 kbit/s). In this case, the time it takes to move information from the edge of the network to the host or terminal is relatively long compared with the time it takes to move the information from one side of the network to the other. Furthermore, the bandwidth

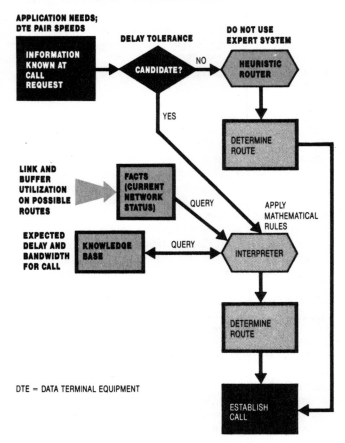

2. Where to go. *An Expert Router handles only those calls that can tolerate a certain delay. It picks a route mathematically by knowing the network's state.*

DTE = DATA TERMINAL EQUIPMENT

demand that the call can place on the network is naturally constrained by the bandwidth of the lines connecting the terminal and the host to the network. If the network gives its fastest route to a low-speed-in, low-speed-out call, it will only result in storing data at the destination edge of the network for the period of time it takes the host or terminal to retrieve the information from the network.

Such calls are candidates for the Expert Router, which attempts to predict the difference between how fast the network can move data from one side to the other and how fast the devices attached to the network can introduce or consume data. That is, it attempts to predict the maximum delay that the network can add to a call without compromising the performance of the devices involved in that call. Figure 2 shows that the information known at call-request time is sufficient for determining whether the call is a candidate for the Expert Router. If it is not, the resident heuristic router determines the best route for the call request to take.

Commensurate with the attributes of control ES applications, facts about the current state of the network are regularly presented to the Expert Router's Interpreter in the form of link and component status, link and buffer utilizations, and congestion information. The knowledge base contains profiles of calls according to the speed of the devices and the behavior of calls going to a given destination address. The Interpreter applies this data to determine the route.

In this case, route determination is not heuristic; it is, in fact, a bit peculiar. At any point in time, traffic patterns in wide-area networks are determined by the predominance of devices in geographic areas. The heuristic router can only generate a limited set of "good" routes between any two points in the network. The Expert Router looks at routes outside of this limited set. If any of these routes have delay and bandwidth attributes that match the performance requirements of the call requested, the Expert Router will assign the *poorest acceptable route* to that request.

This is a radical departure from the routing philosophy in use today, in which the path sought is the one with the least delay and the highest bandwidth. The Expert Router is an attempt to improve the probability that, if the next call request between the same two points requires high bandwidth and/or low delay, resources are available to the heuristic router. Otherwise, over time, the heuristic router might turn the best path into the worst one by directing all traffic over it. An Expert Router would thus protect a heuristic one from the consequences of its own decisions. In this way, users still receive acceptable service, while network resources are more efficiently allocated.

Research is under way to validate the concept of a "worst-path" router. A number of high risk areas, however, could invalidate this strategy. Clearly the Expert Router must operate in real time. It is unclear that this can be accomplished with current technology, since AI languages are not performance-oriented. Thus, it may not be possible to build expert systems that are fast enough. Furthermore, the rules used to compute the routes are not logical rules from human experts but mathematical ones yet to be developed.

In addition, there is some concern about the behavior of the Expert Router over time. Suppose that the majority of calls are determined to be candidates for expert routing. As the Expert Router continues to assign these calls over "longer" routes, it becomes more likely that links and nodes in those routes will be required by the heuristic router. Then the heuristic router may be blocked from using the routes in its repertoire, forcing it to refuse the call request.

Conflict between the expert and heuristic routers may perhaps be managed by using a learning mechanism. Figure 3 depicts such a mechanism for the Expert Router. Feedback comes in the form of network statistics on component utilization, numbers of calls on routes, link flows, congestion, and so on. From these a profile of global network utilization through time is created. This profile is evaluated against a set of success criteria provided by network engineers.

If the success criteria are met, the Expert Router is allowed to continue operating. If not, the network operator can turn off the Expert Router, and all routes will then be established by the heuristic router. The network-utilization profile, together with the actual call-behavior information (shown as "current facts" in Figure 3), is then submitted for engineering analysis.

3. How to learn. *The Expert Router learns from knowing the state of the network and what is expected. If not up to par, the Router is disengaged and studied.*

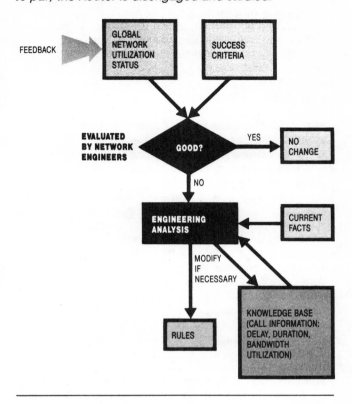

This analysis is likely to result in modification of the rules or the knowledge base, after which the Expert Router may be activated again.

Currently, human beings must view, interpret, and synthesize every network event and then take appropriate action. With increasing network size and complexity, a mental picture of the network can become frightfully unwieldy. ESs could presumably synthesize lower-level information and present intermediate conclusions. They could eventually present the network at a higher level of abstraction, allowing the operator to base decisions on less data.

An ES to assist the network operator

Running a large data network is a complex task, frequently requiring several operators at a time. In general, network components monitor some of the behavior of their own software and hardware and, to a lesser extent, the status and performance of their neighbors. Periodically, statistics are forwarded by network components to the operator. This information can also be delivered at the operator's request during network diagnosis. Events, such as changes in the state of the network's topology (component failure or recovery) or its performance (congestion), are forwarded to the operator as soon as they become known to a component. Over time, the operator generally sees a continuing series of messages.

At the first level of abstraction, the operator must interpret and analyze these messages in terms of each other and then apply the results of the analysis to a conceptual image of the previous state of the network. At the second level of abstraction, this application results in the determination of a course of action that the operator can take to correct the problem, such as further diagnosis or immediate intervention.

An ES may be applied to network operations at the first level of abstraction. At the second level, it may be possible to replace the Language Processor of the ES with a graphic interface.

Level one: The case for an expert system
Current operator support programs are not analytical; they simply present status messages. Despite the prioritization, coding, and display of events, it is the synthesis and interpretation of a group of messages, and not the messages themselves or their priority, that allow operators to react meaningfully to those events.

The goal of the ES is clearly not to replace the operator, even though developers may claim to have captured the human's expertise. Hopefully, by employing an ES as an extension of the human operator, it might be possible to reduce the number and types of operators required to run a large network, increase the accuracy of interventions, reduce the amount of information synthesis required for operator decisions, and reduce the time required to change the network.

One constraint is that operator capabilities must be enhanced, rather than left unaltered or actually impaired, by the ES. Some unforeseen fault in ES logic might send an operator off on the wrong track. The ES must work in concert with the operator, rather than be deceptive or misleading.

As with routing, an application of expert systems to operations presents a number of special problems that have not yet been solved. Those problems can best be understood after examining what happens at the operator station.

Successive, intelligent filtering
As the operator watches the console, a stream of messages—which include the originating component name, a message text, and a priority—is presented. This stream of discrete messages has three orders associated with it: 1) temporal priority, the order in which the message occurs in time relative to the other messages in the sequence; 2) explicit priority, an ordering of messages based on their severity codes in relation to those of other messages in the sequence; and 3) inferred priority, the message order the operator establishes during analysis of the message sequence. The messages may be presented to the operator in either temporal or prioritized fashion. However, the synthesis and interpretation of the messages allow operators to react meaningfully to network events.

To illustrate how these priorities are associated with message sequences, and to demonstrate the reasoning process desirable in an expert system, the information in Figure 4 was abstracted from the Uninet network control center message log.

The format of the messages used in the examples is as follows:

4. What went wrong. *In these sample log messages, the tip-off in case (a) was illegal frame addresses; in case (b), BCC errors mean line trouble.*

(A) NODE ISOLATION DUE TO NODE FAILURE

TEMPORAL ORDER				OBJECT NODE
ORDER	WEIGHT	SOURCE	MESSAGE	OR VALUE
1.	(8)	C1	PACKETS IN:	XXXX XXXX
2.	(8)	C1	CHARACTERS IN:	XXXX XXXX
3.	(7)	N1	ILLEGAL FRAME ADDRESS	(N2)
4.	(7)	N1	ILLEGAL FRAME ADDRESS	(N3)
5.	(3)	N2	LINK IS DOWN	(N1)
6.	(3)	N3	LINK IS DOWN	(N1)
7.	(1)	C1	NO RESPONSE TO NCC POLL	(N1)

EXPLICIT PRIORITY
REVERSE OF TEMPORAL ORDER

OPERATOR ANALYSIS
MESSAGES 1 AND 2 EXTRANEOUS
MESSAGES 3 AND 4 CRITICAL;
ILLEGAL FRAME ADDRESS ON BOTH LINKS CONNECTING
THE NODE TO THE NETWORK INDICATE PROBABLE NODAL
HARDWARE PROBLEM

INFERRED PRIORITY
MESSAGES (3, 4), (7)

(B) NODE ISOLATION DUE TO MULTIPLE TELEPHONE COMPANY FAILURES

TEMPORAL ORDER				OBJECT NODE
ORDER	WEIGHT	SOURCE	MESSAGE	OR VALUE
1.	(7)	N1	10 BCC ERRORS	(N2)
2.	(7)	N2	6 REJECTS RECEIVED	(N1)
3.	(7)	N2	4 REJECTS RECEIVED	(N1)
4.	(3)	N2	LINK IS DOWN	(N1)
5.	(7)	N1	5 BCC ERRORS	(N2)
6.	(3)	N3	LINK IS DOWN	(N1)
7.	(1)	C1	NO RESPONSE TO NCC POLL	(N1)

EXPLICIT PRIORITY
MESSAGES (7), (6, 4), (5, 3, 2, 1)

OPERATOR ANALYSIS
MESSAGES 2 AND 3 TOGETHER INDICATE A TELEPHONE COMPANY PROBLEM
MESSAGE 4 SUBSTANTIATES THIS JUDGMENT AS CORRECT
MESSAGE 5 IS PROBABLY A TELEPHONE COMPANY PROBLEM
MESSAGE 6 SUBSTANTIATES THIS JUDGMENT AS CORRECT
MESSAGE 7 HAS OCCURRED BECAUSE OF DISJOINT TELEPHONE COMPANY PROBLEMS

INFERRED PRIORITY
MESSAGES (1, 2, 3), (5), (4, 6)

BCC = BLOCK CHECK CHARACTER	N = NODE
C = CHANNEL	NCC = NETWORK CONTROL CENTER

(priority or weight) <message source>
<message text> <object node>
where the message source is the component issuing the event or statistic and the object node is the component on which the event is being observed.

The examples demonstrate the orders associated with a message sequence. In the first example (Fig. 4a), a node becomes isolated because of a hardware failure. Note that messages 3 and 4, indicating the receipt of illegal frame addresses, have a lower weight and explicit priority than messages 5 and 6 ("link is down") but more diagnostic value, representing a higher inferred priority in the operator's analysis.

Ideally, the ES should intercept and analyze the message stream. In the first example, it might report to the operator something to the effect of, "Node N1 isolated. Probable cause: communications processor failure. Both links show illegal frame address," and then inquire whether the operator would like to view a justification of the ES's reasoning.

In the second example (Fig. 4b), a node is isolated from the network due to multiple telephone company line failures. This example demonstrates the complexity of implementing an ES. As in the previous example, the same node N1 becomes isolated and fails to respond to the network control center poll. The ES would have to duplicate the human operator's ability to distinguish between these two outages.

The ES might analyze this message sequence and respond as follows: "Node N1 isolated. Restore link from N1 to N2 or N3. Apparent independent Telco failures on links to N2 and N3." As before, the operator would be offered a justification.

Special problems

In both examples, the temporal order of the messages figured predominantly in the operator's analysis. Time also relates to one of the unsolved problems in applying an ES to network operation. The message sequences used in the examples were carefully selected for their illustrative worth. However, in viewing the entire log as a single message stream, human engineers were able to determine the beginning and end of the message sequences that delineated a problem. The first obstacle in trying to build an ES for network operations is in establishing accurate rules for sampling the message stream arriving at the network control center. A way must be found to determine the beginning and end of an event set that can be presented to the ES as a unit to which to apply its rules.

A further problem lies beyond the sampling issue. Even a correctly delineated sample set may contain multiple distinct failures. If this is the case, presentation of the sample set to the ES might result in the recommendation of a single action to the operator that is totally inappropriate or that clears only one of the disjoint failures hidden in the events.

A third problem associated with the application of expert systems to network operations lies in their computational complexity. Complex problems require large knowledge bases, at least one of which must be the state of all components in the network. Therefore, search spaces for network problem solving tend to be large. The ES may thus require a fair amount of time to reason before reaching a conclusion and, thus, fail to reduce the time required for operator intervention.

In addition, the flow of events and statistics to the operator station is irregular. The interval between such reports depends largely on the number and types of problems that occur simultaneously in the network. In order to give the operator enough information to make valid decisions, designers tend to make networks instrumentation-rich. The ES cannot take one minute to reason a conclusion and to recommend action when policy calls for action within 30 seconds.

While there is a great desire to proceed with the prototyping of an ES, the scientists at Uninet have opted for the more prudent course of proving the premise and solving the special problems as a prerequisite for formulating an Expert Operator architecture. The application is ideal, since currently the operator is a human being with expertise that can be put into a formula. Problems unique to this applicaton include sampling, message arrival rate, and the time needed to search large knowledge bases, to reason, and to conclude. Also, it is necessary to find an adequate language with real-time performance capability before building a prototype.

Level two: The case for a graphic interface

The second level of abstraction requires the operator to analyze the message stream and to apply the results of the analysis to a conceptual image of the network. The operator must have a mental image of the network topology and apply to that picture updates garnered from messages. This method will not work forever because of the pace of network growth. Incorporating a graphic interface into the expert system permits designers to supplant the mental image with an up-to-date, three-dimensional network picture that the operator can rotate, turn, expand, and manipulate at will.

It should be noted that the examples presented show the ES assisting in the analysis of the network events and even recommending a remedial action. What remains fundamentally the same is the presentation of information to the operator. Use of the ES has reduced the amount of information required for the operator to prepare for intervention and, through application of the rule set, increase the accuracy of the intervention. Thus, the requirements stated for the first level of abstraction have been satisfied.

Notably, the thrust of the ES research in most of the literature does not adequately address the second level of abstraction. Surely it is important to provide the operator with a set of tools that make it easier to take the required action in a complex network. Current network management schemes require the operator to know the topology in a relational sense; that is, the operator must relate the symbolic name or address of a component to its location, connections to other components, and current status.

Diagnostic activity is still somewhat manual in that the operator must directly query the state of a component or execute a diagnostic program. Determining the state of a component is not a unary operation, since this state is based on a complex set of statistics. Aids must be provided to reinforce or even maintain the operator's conceptual image of the topology and its state as a single entity.

Current graphic techniques adequately support the presentation of three-dimensional objects. An immediate opportunity exists, therefore, to reinforce the operator's conceptual image of the network. Networks are intrinsically n-level hierarchies in three dimensions, exemplified by the hierarchical classes of trunks and central offices in the telephone network. Presenting the network to the operator in three dimensions can illumi-

5. What to do about it. *An Expert Operator isolates problems and informs the operator. It then offers an explanation of why the determination was reached.*

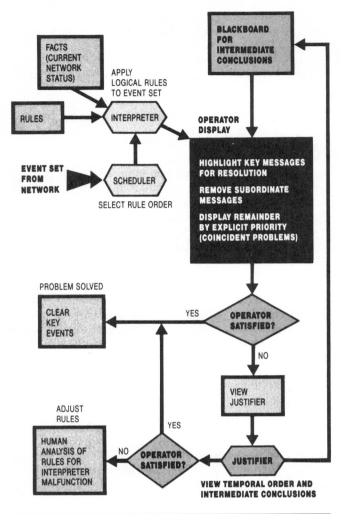

FACTS (CURRENT NETWORK STATUS)

APPLY LOGICAL RULES TO EVENT SET

RULES

INTERPRETER

BLACKBOARD FOR INTERMEDIATE CONCLUSIONS

OPERATOR DISPLAY

EVENT SET FROM NETWORK

SCHEDULER

SELECT RULE ORDER

HIGHLIGHT KEY MESSAGES FOR RESOLUTION

REMOVE SUBORDINATE MESSAGES

DISPLAY REMAINDER BY EXPLICIT PRIORITY (COINCIDENT PROBLEMS)

PROBLEM SOLVED

CLEAR KEY EVENTS

YES

OPERATOR SATISFIED?

NO

VIEW JUSTIFIER

ADJUST RULES

HUMAN ANALYSIS OF RULES FOR INTERPRETER MALFUNCTION

YES

NO

OPERATOR SATISFIED?

JUSTIFIER

VIEW TEMPORAL ORDER AND INTERMEDIATE CONCLUSIONS

nate relationships that might never be seen in two. Since this presentation does not free the operator from maintaining the conceptual relationship of component names or addresses to the represented topology, it is proposed that a pointer be provided that the operator could move freely along a three-dimensional network. It could also move under the direction of the ES. The pointer becomes a general-purpose tool for network operation when coupled with the ability to represent graphically the state of a component in the topology.

The command structure of the network management scheme can be freed from all but the simplest addressing considerations. In the examples, node N1 became isolated, once due to hardware failure and once because of transmission-line failure. In both examples, the three-dimensional representation of the topology would show the node isolated. The links connecting it to its neighbors would not be displayed. In the first example, the operator would move the pointer to the node and press a function key for nodal restart in order to restore the node. In the second example, the operator would

move the pointer to one of the faded links and execute a function key for link initialization. These cases, in which the operator's course of action is direct intervention, represent the simplest network use of a pointer.

The Expert Operator

For cases where the operator's course of action is to conduct further analysis, the pointer can be more closely coupled to the ES. As was done for the Router and Diagnostician, components of an ES can be mapped to the requirements of network operations. The object-oriented code corresponding to the pointer can be linked with a set of diagnostic programs. The principle behind this approach is to decouple the operator-initiated diagnostics from the human being so the operator can control the network in real time.

Figure 5 shows how the components in an ES architecture relate to the concept of successive, intelligent filtering and to the reasoning process of the network operator. The input to the Scheduler is the event set from the network, the same input as would ordinarily be presented to the human operator. Note that the Interpreter will interact with the operator whenever it realizes that a sampled set of events requires intervention. The intelligent pointer then acts on behalf of the operator by executing the diagnostics and presenting the results as an event set to the ES.

The operator might position the pointer to a place on the graph of the topology where diagnostics are to begin. The resulting sample sets are presented to the ES Scheduler. As they are processed, the pointer logically pauses at the component of the graph being analyzed. If the ES analysis finds that the sample is not

---

6. Why it said what it said. *The Expert Operator's explanation recaps its steps in reasoning, telling of its network explorations with an intelligent "pointer."*

LINK 3 (N1—N3) MARGINAL: DISPATCH TELEPHONE COMPANY TO LINK 3
POINTER DIAGNOSTIC COMPLETE

JUSTIFICATION?
  < OPERATOR INPUT: "YES" >

BLACKBOARD

OPERATOR DISPATCHES POINTER TO IMPAIRED NODE N1
POINTER TELLS EXPERT SYSTEM 97% POOL DEPLETION N1
POINTER TELLS EXPERT SYSTEM LINK 3 (N3) 88% OCCUPANCY
EXPERT SYSTEM DISPATCHES POINTER TO N3:
    POSSIBLE ROUTE CONGESTION

POINTER TELLS EXPERT SYSTEM 83% POOL DEPLETION N3
POINTER TELLS EXPERT SYSTEM LINK 3 (N1) 91% OCCUPANCY
POINTER TELLS EXPERT SYSTEM WINDOW RETRANSMISSION:
    27 LAST 100 ROTATIONS
EXPERT SYSTEM DISPATCHES POINTER TO N4:
    POSSIBLE ROUTE CONGESTION

POINTER TELLS EXPERT SYSTEM 48% POOL DEPLETION N4
POINTER TELLS EXPERT SYSTEM LINK 4 (N3) 52% OCCUPANCY
EXPERT SYSTEM CONSIDERS N4 WITHIN LIMITS
EXPERT SYSTEM REDISPATCHES POINTER TO N3

------------------------------CONCLUSION------------------------------

TELEPHONE COMPANY TRANSIENTS; PROBABLE CAUSE LINK 3 (N1—N3)

relevant to the problem, the pointer proceeds to the next sample point. When the sample is deemed to be significant, the pointer comes to rest at the position of significance and the ES presents the synthesis of the diagnostic samples to the operator, noting that they are tied to the diagnostic pointer.

Current schemes implement diagnostic programs by means of software commands, such as ROUTE, TRACE, or PROBE, which must be typed into the operator's console. Typically these programs return to the operator a set of statistics on a component-by-component basis. These may include data on link retransmissions, delay, buffer pool utilization, and so on. Coupling the pointer to the ES effectively decouples the operator from the diagnostic activity.

Figure 6 depicts how an operator might view intermediate results from the ES Blackboard. The ES displays, on request, its reasoning process and interaction with the pointer. The search starts at node N1, which the pointer finds overloaded. Under direction of the ES, the pointer proceeds to N3 and finds the situation to be critical. When the ES suspects the overload may be generalized, it tells the pointer to check another node, which turns out to be acceptable. The pointer ultimately returns to N3 for further diagnostics.

Conclusion
There is little doubt that the use of expert systems in network operations will soon be extended beyond those applications in the literature that relate to maintenance and diagnostics. As networks grow in size, not only by topology but also through the use of distributed computing architectures, a requirement to isolate the operator from the flow of events will become manifest. This is less likely when networks are built with monolithic computing architectures than when the network architecture distributes software functions over a large number of computing elements. In this case, for a given node or site, several computing elements, rather than merely one, will be reporting statistics and events.

Three-dimensional graphic representations of network topology are quite promising as a way to help the operator retain cognizance and control of the network, especially when supplemented with a window to view the internals of a given component. The pointer appears to be a useful mechanism for data manipulation. It is proposed that the graphic representation of the topology at the operator console be coupled with an expert system via the pointer, in support of the goals for an Expert Operator. ■

For further reading
Hayes-Roth, F. et al. *Building Expert Systems.* Addison-Wesley, 1983, pp. 16-18.
Wescott, J. et al. "Automated Network Management," *Proceedings of the IEEE Infocom '85,* March 1985, pp. 43-51.

Jerrold F. Stach is chief network scientist at Uninet, a US Telecom company. He is also an assistant professor of computer science, teaching at the University of Missouri-Kansas City.

Daniel Fidlow, Price Waterhouse, New York, N. Y.

A comprehensive approach to network security

This year's Karp Award winner for best Interface '85 conference paper outlines numerous network security techniques to help users design a security checklist.

The methods for protecting information passing the various points of a distributed processing network differ from those used to protect traditional batch transmission schemes, where nearby entry points are more easily secured. Exposures created by remote nodes, terminals, and circuits can be safeguarded with the proper techniques. The main security objectives of any computer service, distributed or batch, are the same:

1. Minimize the chance of intrusion at all via protective devices and procedures that would have to be overcome.

2. If intrusion does occur, ensure that it will be detected as soon as possible.

3. Be able to reconstruct the status, control information, and content of any transactions at the time of the intrusion, including all operator interventions that may have altered the network configuration. This reconstructive function will minimize damage and allow recovery.

What is the risk?

Wiretapping, or tampering with circuits and switching nodes, can be done by someone with modest technical training. Even in-house sites, which should be the easiest to secure, are often unprotected, with exposed telecommunications cable terminations. An intruder might connect a tap via a small isolation transformer out of sight, behind a termination panel. He or she might then connect the transformer to another line, at the end of which to operate in comfort perhaps dialing a connection to the tap from home.

Off-premises, a tap can be placed along any part of a terrestrial link, whether tower-to-tower microwave or land-line. If well hidden, it might not be discovered until the whole physical path of the link is traced. And even

then, discovery would only mean detachment of the device, not apprehension of the thief. Of special exposure to electronic interception are satellite down-links. Signal stealing would not require a physically attached device, but merely a receive-only earth station located anywhere within the footprint of the signal (thousands of square miles). Combined with a transmit device, information can be read, altered, and reentered without knowledge of the sender or receiver.

Of particular value to eavesdroppers is information that opens a range of new fraudulent opportunities, such as passwords and account numbers. The capture of confidential data by a competitor, such as customer lists or new product plans, can also be damaging.

Once a tap has been attached to a transmission line, the intruder would have the following options to introduce false data:

■ *Case 1.* There is no ongoing session between the host node and a valid terminal. Then the intruder, using authorization information obtained by eavesdropping, takes the identity of a valid terminal to establish a session.

■ *Case 2.* A session has been established by a valid terminal, but:

(a) The terminal is inactive, so the intruder can take these idle times for his or her own use.

(b) The terminal was active but has just sent a sign-off message to terminate the session. The intruder can intercept this "sign-off," continuing the session with unauthorized traffic.

(c) The terminal is active, sending and receiving live data. The intruder can transmit an error message to the terminal indicating that the host is down, and then continue the session in the terminal's name.

Exposures exist at the entry points of a network (terminals) analogous to those present along its con-

A summary of security measures

The table shown summarizes many of the precautions that can be taken to guard against potential threats with respect to the three major security objectives. In the interest of clarity, the table assumes that only one security measure is in place at a time. For example, if encryption is in place then there are no authentication or sequence numbers. The table also assumes that the intruder cannot bypass a security device by duplicating it (that is, if he changes text content, he cannot also manipulate the authentication word to mask the change). Justification for the entries is as follows:

■ *Encryption, entries 1, 3, and 5.* Since the data is encyphered, an intruder cannot read or modify it.

■ *Authentication, entries 10 and 11.* The data is in clear text, so an intruder can insert a false message or modify a real one on the circuit, but this will be detected at the receiving end. Authentication would be a box 8 entry for operations that calculate the testword before entering the message (assuming the intruder does not know the algorithm).

■ *Terminal sequence numbers (TSNs), entry 9.* These protect against duplication or loss of messages on the line as well as the insertion of a false message into a circuit by an intruder simulating the identity of a true terminal. TSNs are not in box 8 because they are usually calculated beyond the point of message entry. (Even if they are not, the interloper may know the proper TSN since it appears on a local printer, so TSNs offer little protection.)

■ *Acknowledgment of single messages or groups, entry 9.* This means that logical accept and reject responses are returned to the originator on a per-message basis, or that end-nodes periodically exchange message summary reports for comparison. As with TSNs, this control also protects against duplication or loss of messages on the line.

(Note that—although there is no separate row in the table for "stealing" a message, so that it never gets to the intended recipient in the first place and is thereby equivalent to being lost on the line—detection of this subversion is provided by terminal sequence numbers and logical acknowledgment of single messages or groups.)

■ *Passwords and log codes, entries 2 and 6.* An interloper cannot activate a terminal or initiate a session without the proper authorizations. Box 4 assumes that the session is already in progress, and thus not protected by passwords and log codes.

■ *Other terminal defensive measures, entry 6.* The measures include physical vs. logical terminal checks and, if "false" terminals are predefined in host tables, bypassing them in some other way.

■ *Operational safeguards, including entries 1 through 12.* The safeguards are physical security, awareness of network status, separation of functions, item-by-item and summary reconciliations, and privacy of information. For example, box 10 would be covered by attaching the source document to a copy of each delivered message and sending both to the originating department.

■ *Audit trails, entries 14 through 18.* Besides event records, exception logs, and journal tapes, these include system sequence-number assignment, computer console logs, and alarms-printer sheets.

Security measures vs. threats

THREAT	SECURITY OBJECTIVES		
	MINIMIZE THE CHANCE OF INTRUSION	QUICKLY DETECT INTRUSION	RECONSTRUCT STATUS AT TIME OF INTRUSION
READ MESSAGES ON A CIRCUIT	1 ENCRYPTION	7	13
INSERT FALSE MESSAGES AT A TERMINAL	2 PASSWORD AND LOG CODES	8 AUTHENTICATION	14 AUDIT TRAILS
INSERT FALSE MESSAGES INTO A CIRCUIT	3 ENCRYPTION	9 TERMINAL SEQUENCE NUMBERS ACKNOWLEDGMENT OF SINGLE MESSAGES OR GROUPS	15 AUDIT TRAILS
MODIFY REAL MESSAGES AT A TERMINAL	4	10 AUTHENTICATION ATTACH SOURCE DOCUMENT TO COPY OF DELIVERED MESSAGE	16 AUDIT TRAILS
MODIFY REAL MESSAGES ON A CIRCUIT	5 ENCRYPTION	11 AUTHENTICATION	17 AUDIT TRAILS
ATTACH A FALSE TERMINAL TO A NODE	6 PASSWORD AND LOG CODES OTHER TERMINAL DEFENSIVE MEASURES	12	18 AUDIT TRAILS

necting paths: input by an operator of false or changed messages. The table shown in "A summary of security measures" itemizes the risks: reading a message on a circuit, inserting a false message at a terminal or circuit (including attaching a false terminal at a node), and modifying fields in a real message at a terminal or circuit.

Eight general classes of security measures can be called upon to guard against these risks. The classes are encryption, key management, authentication, terminal (or message) sequence numbers, passwords and log codes (plus other terminal defensive measures), operational safeguards, and audit trails.

Encryption

If a line uses encryption devices, data passes along it in a scrambled form, rather than in clear text, so that it cannot be read by a line tapper. If a false message is inserted into the line in clear text, it would become scrambled at the receiving end. In 1977, the National Bureau of Standards adopted the Data Encryption Standard (DES), which defines a fixed transformation algorithm varied by a key. When DES is performed (in its simplest mode) by an encryption device, or "cryptor," each 64-bit block of clear text input is transformed by a secret, usually prestored key of 64 bits (56 for data plus 8 for parity), to produce the encrypted output.

Thus the same text encrypted with different keys will produce different data streams. To obtain the original text, the remote user passes the enciphered data through a cryptor, which contains the same prestored key. The sensitivity of DES is such that, even in this simplest mode, a single bit error in an encrypted block will cause the decrypted plain text block to have an average error rate of 50 percent (only that block is affected, since there is no error propagation between blocks).

Two other, more complex, versions of the DES are usually recommended. Both use the clear text and the key, plus a third simultaneous input to the cryptor — either the enciphered text block created by the prior round of inputs, or the prior bits of the enciphered text stream currently being created. Thus each encrypted block becomes a function of all the preceding blocks or bits of the message. For practical purposes, as long as the key is secure, DES can be regarded as unbreakable.

■ *Link vs. end-to-end encryption:* In a multinode network, in which a message traverses several nodes before reaching its end-point, the decision must be made whether to use link-oriented or end-to-end encryption. In the former, the message is independently encrypted/decrypted on each link; in the latter it passes entirely from source to destination node in encrypted form. Link-oriented encryption physically falls at layer 2 of the ISO reference model (Table 1), whereas end-to-end encryption logically falls at layer 6 (physically, it can be implemented anywhere from layers 4 through 7). Encryption between different layers is problematic because (without special engineering) the control portion of one layer will be encrypted by the

sender while expected in the clear by the receiver, or vice versa.

Several factors support link-oriented encryption. First, subversion of one link by knowing its key does not mean subversion of other links with different keys. Secondly, full text, including headers and routing information, can be encrypted on the links. With end-to-end encryption, these fields must be left in the clear, which implies dependence upon the software for encryption. The third factor is that link encryption is usually done by placing a cryptor box on the digital side of the modem at both ends of the line (Fig. 1), controlled by the same request-to-send/clear-to-send signals that control the modem. This frees the software from encryption tasks, so that ports on the data terminal equipment (DTE) would send and receive protocol characters in the clear. (For HDLC, this means that bit stuffing occurs before encryption at the source and removal occurs in clear text at the destination.) Lastly, for camouflage, a continuous stream of enciphered text can be placed on the links when they would otherwise be idle.

There are many arguments in favor of end-to-end encryption. Data remains encrypted within the nodes. (With link-oriented encryption, it is decrypted upon entering a node. Some or all of the intermediary links may be in the clear. Messages from the source node to a packet-switching network will also be in the clear on the access link, because the X.25 interface does not include an encryption function.) End-to-end encryption simplifies key distribution, in that only the end-nodes of each connection need be given keys. Also, in case of misrouting, the (incorrect) receiver gets encrypted data. Finally, cost can be directly apportioned to the end-nodes that use encryption, rather than having to be amortized across all users.

On balance, end-to-end encryption for multinode networks is quite attractive and does not preclude link-oriented procedures being superimposed upon it. Probably the strongest practical argument against it, however, is the built-in software dependence. It is easier to add encryption hardware than to modify software.

Key management

A complex security topic that has received surprisingly little popular attention is key management. The creation, assignment, distribution, and cancellation of keys is the most exposed part of the encryption process. Management can be either manual or automatic.

Manual key distribution is the usual method, and the cheapest. If a host communicates with 20 intelligent terminals on 20 point-to-point circuits, there could be up to 20 different keys to manage; i.e., a different bilateral arrangement for each user. The host site would generate the key and certify-mail or hand-deliver it by bonded courier to each user site with an effective key-change date (probably the next morning). The receiving site gets no notice when a new key will arrive. This unwieldy process could be simplified by using only four different keys, assigned to five different users each. But as the range of use of a single key increases, so does the amount of information exposed in case that key becomes compromised.

To implement a daily change, one can list a string of keys on a single sheet using sequential check-off as each one is consumed. Of course, this sheet should not be handled by anyone except the manager.

A very secure combination of manual and limited automatic key management is the independent generation, by different people, of two preliminary keys. They are then combined in a cryptor to become the final key. No one ever sees the key; it is stored only in the device and cannot be read out. The preliminary keys would also be separately delivered to the bilateral sites.

The main limitations of manual key management are the relative infrequency of key change, and the relatively small number of nodes that can be supported. Operations in which these limitations are unsatisfactory require automated key management, which means that the functions of generation and distribution are under control of the cryptors themselves, though initiated by a person. In the prior example of 20 point-to-point circuits, each with its own pair of cryptors, whenever a circuit is idle (as at system startup), an operator can set switches on the circuit's host-end cryptor, causing it to generate a new random key (which cannot be read out). The key, encoded under the prior key, is also sent to the remote cryptor. More secure, automated designs could replace the operator-initiated key change with downloaded instructions from the host. The key could then be changed on a per-connection basis.

Per-connection or per-session key change provides implicit validation that the intended end-nodes are communicating with each other (since an incorrect receiver would see encrypted data). It also removes the main reason for using different keys on different links of a link-oriented design, because key exposure on one link would no longer endanger all links. Thus the way is open to automate the whole key management scheme in a multinode network via a key distribution center (KDC). The KDC is a separate session management computer outside the network proper, in layer 5 of the ISO reference model. A source node tells the KDC the destination node with which it wants to establish a session. The KDC then assigns a key for that session and sends both nodes the same key, separately encrypted under the key used by each node's prior session. Alternately, the KDC could send two copies of the new key to the source node only, each enciphered according to the prior keys of each end-node, leaving it to the source node to forward the proper key to the destination node as part of session initiation procedures.

Authentication

Authentication is to a message what a parity bit is to a character or a block check character is to a data block. If the authentication field, calculated at the sending side and added to the message, cannot be recalculated on the receiving side to match, then the incoming message is not released or files updated until verification is correct. Typically, retransmission is requested or some other recovery procedure undertaken.

The authentication field—also called the testword or testkey—can be calculated by either a simple or complex algorithm. A trivial example, yet one still offering some protection for funds transfer messages, would be to add the number of thousands in the amount to the entry date. For example, if $1,234,567.89 is sent on September 18, the testkey is $1234 + 0918$, or 2152, verifying that these two fields, at least, were probably not changed. At the other end of complexity, all text can be passed through a DES operation, making each eight-character block of encrypted output a function of all preceding data input. Then the last block of output is fed back into the cryptor as further data and this final output taken as the authentication word. Of course, using DES, the same problem of key management arises as with regular encryption but, unlike encryption, here the total message passes the line in clear text; only the authentication field looks like gibberish.

Authentication is done earlier than encryption, and could be done as soon as the message is formatted from the original back office payment order. (This is the generic description we will use. As an example, it could be the corporate cash management department initiating a funds transfer from a lower- to a higher-interest bearing account.) But as a practical matter, it usually occurs as the message is entered into the sending terminal and protects from then on those fields that were used to create the authentication word. *continued*

Table 1: The structure of security

OSI REFERENCE MODEL LAYER	SECURITY FEATURE
7 **APPLICATION OR PROCESS CONTROL:** WHAT THE HOST DOES TO PROCESS THE DATA AT SYSTEM AND APPLICATION LEVELS	■ AUTHENTICATION ■ SYSTEM SEQUENCE NUMBERS ■ EVENT RECORDS
6 **PRESENTATION:** FORM IN WHICH THE DATA CHARACTERS ARE PRESENTED	■ END-TO-END ENCRYPTION (LOGICALLY AT LAYER 6; PHYSICALLY CAN BE IMPLEMENTED AT LAYERS 4 THROUGH 7)
5 **SESSION:** HOW A LOGICAL CONNECTION (SESSION) BETWEEN TWO END-NODES IS ESTABLISHED AND CONTROLLED FOR THE TRANSFER OF MESSAGES, INCLUDING RECOVERY	■ PER-CONNECTION AUTO-MATED KEY MANAGEMENT, ESPECIALLY VIA A KEY DISTRIBUTION CENTER ■ PHYSICAL VS. LOGICAL TERMINAL CHECK ■ PASSWORD AND LOG CODES ■ BATCH CONTROLS, SUCH AS END-NODES PERIODICALLY EXCHANGING SUMMARY REPORTS OF MESSAGE TYPES AND COUNTS FOR COMPARISON ■ CLOSE-THE-LOOP SESSION TERMINATION FUNCTIONS
4 **TRANSPORT, END-TO-END:** PER-MESSAGE CONTROL DURING THE SESSION	■ TERMINAL SEQUENCE NUMBERS ■ LOGICAL ACCEPT OR REJECT RESPONSES RETURNED TO THE MESSAGE ORIGINATOR
2 **DATA LINK CONTROL**	■ LINK-ORIENTED ENCRYPTION

The most direct way to detect loss, duplication, or fraudulent insertion of a message onto a line is by using message sequence numbers on a per-terminal basis. ("Terminal," of course, can mean anything from a teletypewriter through a computer.) Each message sent from the terminal to the host would carry its own monotonically increasing number in an input sequence number (ISN) field generated automatically by a one-up binary counter. Thus the first message of the day from a given terminal has ISN=1, the second has ISN=2, etc. The host checks this field for the expected ISN value; if correct, it accepts the message and, if incorrect, the host rejects it or takes some other exception action.

For example, if a message with ISN=2 gets lost on the line, the host will still be looking for it when the message with ISN=3 arrives. If the terminal sends a message with ISN=2 twice in a row, the host will be looking for ISN=3 when ISN=2 comes along again. Or if, after ISN=2 is sent, a fraudulent message with ISN=3 is inserted onto the line, a discrepancy will be detected when the terminal sends its next message, with ISN=3, while the host is expecting ISN=4.

In the host-to-terminal direction, each message carries an output sequence number (OSN) field, which is used in the same way. Thus each terminal has two sequence numbers associated with it: one for messages sent to the host—the ISN—and one for messages received from the host—the OSN. (Note that this orientation is reversed for the host: its OSN counter is for messages sent, its ISN for those received.) If the terminal end is concerned mainly with control rather than with security, the host can assign the terminal's ISN itself, which simplifies the input operation. This is common for nonintelligent stations, where the ISN has to be kept track of manually.

The terminal sequence number field is within the control portion of the message itself. That is, the ISN and OSN are implemented in layer 4 (or 5) of the ISO reference model. Terminal sequence numbers are not to be confused with the frame or flow control sequence numbers at lower layers. The ISN or OSN field should make each message unique to its associated terminal by line, and for some extended period such as one year. The 9-character format MMDDNNNNA will do this. MMDD defines month and day, NNNN—the terminal message sequence number proper—says that up to 9999 messages can be entered from (delivered to) the terminal that day. "A" is a logical identifier, different for each terminal on the line.

When doing an ISN/OSN implementation, a design question that must be resolved is, for what circumstances shall the numbers not be incremented? It is generally good practice to increment the ISN counter for both accepted and rejected inputs. An exception would be bad log codes and passwords where, for security, the ISN is not incremented. Conversely, it is good practice to increment the OSN counter only on successful deliveries; i.e., where redelivery will not have to take place. Otherwise, there might be gaps in the receiving terminal's OSN sequence (for example, if it never saw the start-of-message), or there might be

different OSNs for the same message (the first delivery was completed but, due to a final block check error, had to be resent). Redeliveries should be marked as possible duplicates regardless of the OSN.

At the end of the day, the host should generate and deliver to each terminal a traffic report containing three fields: the number of accepted messages received from the terminal that day (say 1,096), the number of rejected input attempts (say 24), and the final ISN (say 1,120). Note that, under the ISN incrementation rules described above, the last field would equal the sum of the first two. Also, according to the OSN incrementation rules, the OSN under which this report was delivered would equal the number of good deliveries to that terminal that day. Of course, there is no relation between the ISN and OSN fields of a given terminal.

Another design issue is the sort of resynchronization procedures to be used when a wrong sequence number is received. Good host practice when receiving an out-of-sequence ISN is to reject the input message and, if three bad numbers in a row occur, to lock out (logically disable) the sending terminal until manual procedures resolve the discrepancy. The terminal would also have to resolve a bad OSN before acting on a message. If the host failed, recovery procedures would send a message to each terminal giving the ISN and OSN counts that have been checkpointed (stored on disk) for it. The host then restarts from this point, which should be the latest, with correct numbers for each terminal.

Terminal sequence number use is limited to dedicated lines where each host port is associated with a predefined set of stations: from one (point-to-point circuit) to, say, 16 (multipoint circuit). But dial-in ports have no such predefined port-station assignment. Each dial-in connection should be given a port sequence number of the same format as above: MMDDNNNNA, where A is the port identifier and NNNN monotonically increases per connection. A separate sequence would be maintained for dial-out connections. The port sequence number may be sent to the dialing or dialed terminal as part of session setup interplay.

Passwords and log codes

Passwords are log codes for people, and log codes are passwords for terminals. In other words, the terminology is interchangeable but, for reference, we will call a "password" what a person uses to access the host, and a "log code" what a terminal uses. They are both prestored secret symbol sets that the host should check for legality, or match against, before further access is allowed. A password is often composed of several parts: the password proper, plus a user ID against which the password can be checked. The user ID is not appropriate for security purposes, because it is usually public information, such as an employee number, and cannot be changed easily, since much other information keys off it.

Implementation of passwords and log codes can range from single-level to pyramidal, where passing one level merely leads to the next. Passwords can be

1. Nesting. *Authentication is the security measure closest to the user or application. Link-oriented encryption, shown, follows the terminal sequence numbering (TSN).* *End-to-end encryption, implemented by software in the terminal or the host, would precede TSN assignment, making cryptor boxes unnecessary.*

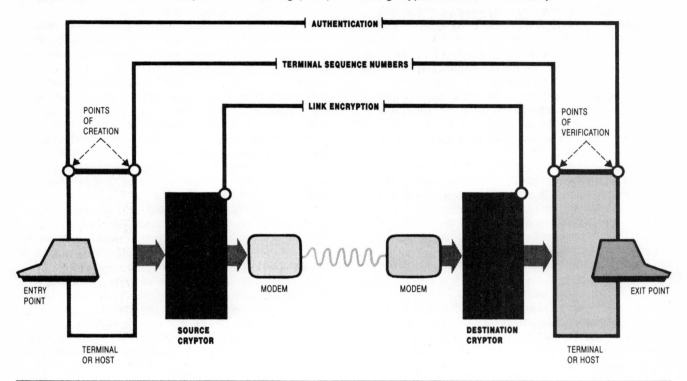

used to restrict access to various functions or transaction classes, so that only users owning those passwords can access the functions and classes. Each terminal may have a password/function table, used to determine which passwords will allow access to which functions. By generating similar password/function tables for every terminal, an overall security-access procedure would be defined. Given this capability, sensitive functions can be limited to designated terminals and persons. For example, a control terminal can be created to change the passwords and log codes of other terminals and be accessed by the department manager. Alternately, whole departments can have their workstations defined to access only processing functions particular to those departments.

When using passwords and log codes, it is advisable to follow certain operational guidelines. Log codes and passwords should not be trivial, such as might be guessed by an outsider. When typed in, they should not appear on the screen or printer. They should be changed at random, unannounced intervals, and again when an employee leaves. They should be available only to persons who use them and, if possible, not written down.

Who should know the passwords? In some applications, the user would not know his or her own—as with an invisible magnetic strip containing a personal identification number (PIN) on the back of a plastic card. In other applications, only the user knows the password, where a separate function is available allowing users to change their passwords upon request. Cash-dispensing

automatic teller machines (ATMs) combine both types: the customer must insert a PIN card, plus key in a secret code, before getting any money. Some computers in which the user assigns a code deactiviate it every 30 days, forcing the user to change it again.

To prevent unauthorized access, users should be encouraged to log out their terminals or deactivate their sessions when finished. The host should do this automatically when a terminal is left idle for, say, 20 minutes, and the user does not respond to prompts for reauthorization. Three successive bad attempts to log on to a terminal or validate a password should lock out or disconnect that terminal. More sophisticated security would lead the potential intruder into an interrogation entrapment routine. It might also be wise to cancel the valid password against which tries were made (if it can be determined from the user ID). Terminals should be logged out automatically by the host as part of recovery procedures following a failure.

■ *The hacker.* Random invasions by amateurs, with no special knowledge of the computer they are entering, should be little more than an annoyance. If properly implemented, passwords and log codes will screen out hackers. But, because of much recent publicity, hackers have diverted attention from the real threat: collusion by knowledgeable insiders. But at least the publicity has served to uncover how vulnerable distributed data networks can be.

Since the hacker's basic probe, after dialing in, is random-pattern password tries, the basic defense is automatic disconnection after three failed attempts.

What security must guard against above all else is a lucky hacker reading out the central password, log code, or file name directory. Therefore, these tables should not be maintained in a single central directory but, rather, stored in encrypted form in logically discrete areas. The encryption algorithm would be one-way: clear text to encryption, for password entry validation, but never reverse for recovering the encrypted passwords in clear form.

Even greater security is available if management feels the operational burden is justified. Automatic dial-back is the surest of these: upon receipt of a password, the host disconnects and dials back using a number prestored for that password. Unfortunately, overhead is incurred: the host picks up the cost of the call (unless a billing charge-back is used); overall time to connect is increased by a minute (if the host gets through on its initial dialing); and, of course, user terminals must have an acoustic coupler or auto-answer device.

Other terminal defensive measures
In addition to log codes, other terminal defensive measures include:

(a) Hardware protocol verification. This helps to ensure that the host is in contact with the right terminal (the one it thinks it is). The terminal ID can be made software invariant by storing it in a chip from where it is taken to answer a poll or select. The control unit / device address characters of the 3270 protocol can be protected in this way, as can the station address field of HDLC response frames. A programmer or terminal operator has no access to these characters, nor do they appear on the screen or printer. But they could be changed by swapping the address chip.

(b) Physical vs. logical check. The message format often contains symbolic fields indicating the source institution (company or department) and the inputting terminal. The host can validate these fields by checking the source institution symbolic field against the entering port, and by checking the terminal symbolic field against the hardware ID, discussed above.

(c) Format edit checks. The host should do other message checks such as on the transaction type, date, minimum or maximum limits on the values in fields where specific content is not defined, and so on. A tally field might be included where the sender gives the count of all data characters between start of header and end of text for the receiver to recalculate — a pseudo-authenticator. These edit checks would require an intruder to know the correct formats.

(d) Perform close-the-loop functions at the logical level, meaning that each action would have its acknowledgment. For example, each message sent could generate a short "accept" or "reject" data response at the receiving end. This is a logical response, not the protocol's positive and negative acknowledgments, ACK and NACK. Then a response received by a terminal when it sent nothing would alert it that a false message may have been entered elsewhere on the circuit under its identity. (But primarily logical responses are implemented for control, rather than security, and mean that the other end has now

taken responsibility for the message.)

Connections should terminate with some form of "Did you get it?" or "Are you still there?" In the telex world, this means tripping the receiver's answerback for verification before disconnecting. In the ISO reference model, layer 5 would perform this function depending on how session completion services are defined.

(e) What is to stop a person with proper password authorization from down-loading sensitive company information, such as a client list, to disk and passing it to a competitor? This is a particular risk associated with the increase in workstation-to-host interfaces. There really is no good answer beyond careful password management, but two other defenses are possible. Workstations could be built without disks. (But then, the printer might be used to steal information.)

Alternately, a company might keep sensitive files encrypted in the host and, upon receipt of the proper password, download them without decoding to reside encrypted on the workstation disk. The files would have to pass back and forth between the decode and encode functions in the workstation as entries are called to the screen, manipulated, and returned to disk. Obviously the overhead and operational inconvenience of this scheme may be very great.

(f) Are nonexistent terminals predefined in the host tables? This is a reasonable practice, done so that tables, or equivalent VTAM control blocks, need not be generated each time a terminal is installed. The potential risk is that, if entries in the table are made ahead of installation, an intruder terminal could be attached as one of the predefined identities. The best way to handle this is to ensure that these terminals are cut off in some other way, such as by password control (e.g., via LOGON EXIT facility in VTAM), or by being bypassed in the polling list.

Operational safeguards
Automated checks are no substitute for operational precautions and awareness. Telecommunications security grows from a careful mix of computerized and manual procedures. Among these procedures are:

(a) Physical security. To prevent unauthorized access, users should assign terminal areas their own dedicated, secure space, keep test keys and signature lists out of the way, and place the supervisor's office in view of the work area. Terminal locks should be considered, as well as magnetic card keys for operator identification.

On-premises transmission lines should be bundled away in conduits. Information flowing on them is particularly vulnerable because it may be low speed (unconcentrated) in the clear (unencrypted), and intact (not yet multiplexed). Cable closets should stay locked and unlabeled. Another idea is to make unscheduled visits along cable paths to see that they have not been tampered with (it should be known within the company that these spot checks are made).

The purpose of physical security is to prevent or minimize the opportunity for intrusion in the first place.

(b) Awareness of network status. The network, defined as circuits plus terminals, is always in flux: carrier failing/restoring, terminals not responding to polls and selects or being logical disabled, delivery queues building because an alternate route action was not completed properly, and so on. Greater risk accrues during abnormal operation, especially if the abnormalities go undetected. Therefore implementation, including software, should build in the functions to detect and "alarm" these network occurrences on a dedicated alarms printer, alerting users to especially sensitive conditions. Operators should initial the printout every 20 minutes or so to make sure it is being looked at and acted upon. This is part of the technical control function.

(c) Separation of functions. The priniciple here is that collusion is trivial by someone working alone, more difficult with a neighbor, and harder still when three people are involved. Therefore, where it is consistent with smooth workflow, different people should do different parts of the operation. For instance, separate groups should do key distribution, per-message testword calculation (if done manually), and message entry. In another case, message formatting should not be done by the same back office department that creates the payment order.

(d) Item-by-item reconciliation. The purpose of reconciliation is not prevention but detection of any lost or altered data as soon after the fact as possible. For example, operations should attach the source document to a copy of each delivered funds transfer message, and send both to the originating department for its own check-off procedures. No payment order should be accepted for transmission unless the originating department is specified in it. An auditor ought to be able to compare transactions against an edit list within 24 hours of posting.

In switching applications, the host should provide a report of individual transfers (one summary line per input or delivery) to senders and receivers for their own reconciliation. Such a transaction journal (which can be quite lengthy) could be delivered electronically at night, or printed locally and shipped to users the next morning. The batch analogy is the creation and mailing of customer advices.

(e) Crosscheck, or summaries, reconciliation. This precaution divides into operations and applications. For operations, communicating terminals could periodically exchange reports of message types and counts received for comparison. In the computer center, end-of-day totals for all traffic summed across terminals should equal the system message count maintained in a separate register.

In financial applications, the daily dollar total and number of messages accepted by the network can be struck to the dollar total and number of messages delivered plus those still in queue. With electronic shadow-posting, running debit and credit totals can be captured for use in before-and-after comparisons with the actual customer files to be created that night.

(f) Privacy of information. Knowledge of controls, tests for failures, and other privileged data should be limited to a minimum number of personnel. Sales reps need not have access to financial details, nor programmers to full technical specifications.

Audit trails

The purpose of audit trails is to allow the reconstruction, in sequence, of all actions and interventions that affected system components and states up to a given prior time. Audit trails are also used to trace the progress of any transaction throughout its lifetime in the network. Each node, port, and terminal that a message passed through should be identified and timestamped. Special delivery conditions and auxiliary messages generated should also be noted. Besides being good operational practice, the security reason for these trails is obvious. If tampering occurred, it is important to determine the state of the network at that time and the tracks that might have been left. Various audit trail tools should be built in as part of initial design:

(a) When any status or configuration is altered by operator command—computer or network equipment, circuits or terminals—this action plus the network's response and the time should be automatically printed on the computer console log or on the alarms printer sheets. The rolls should not be torn in order to preserve chronology; multipart paper can be used if sections have to be separated. Examples of operator commands to be noted are putting a circuit or concentrator on skip/hold, releasing skip/hold, entering or removing alternate-routing delivery, and so on. (Skip means to stop polling; hold, to stop selecting a device.) The principle is that nobody should be able to touch the network unrecorded, so that a whole day's interventions can be reconstructed.

A user terminal can be placed in the data center so that operations can see directly how customers are affected. (Sending the final broadcast or recovery message to this terminal will demonstrate how long everybody else took to get it.)

(b) The network should assign unique identification numbers to each transaction. For example, a system sequence number (SSN) of the form MMDDNNNNNN could be assigned to each message immediately upon input and remain associated throughout its life in the network. Originator and receiver would see this SSN in the message header or trailer. The NNNNNN begins at 1 at the start of the day, monotonically increasing for each accepted and rejected message. It is, of course, distinct from terminal sequence numbers (ISN and OSN).

The SSN is an explicit identifier and may not be needed for transactions whose internal data already makes them unique, such as a demand deposit account change (branch, account number, date, time, and transaction type).

(c) Besides the printout of alterations, another key audit and reconstructive tool is a set of magnetic tapes taken daily. This could be a single set of tapes, but logically we will describe it as three sets, each containing a subset of data taken from the preceding set. The three sets are the journal tape, the event record, and the exception log.

2. Applications. *Three bank-oriented scenarios—(a) electronic funds transfer, (b) data entry from a branch office like the one shown, and (c) dial-up microcomputers—differ widely in terms of their traffic and transaction value, so each presents a unique set of risks and security requirements for users.*

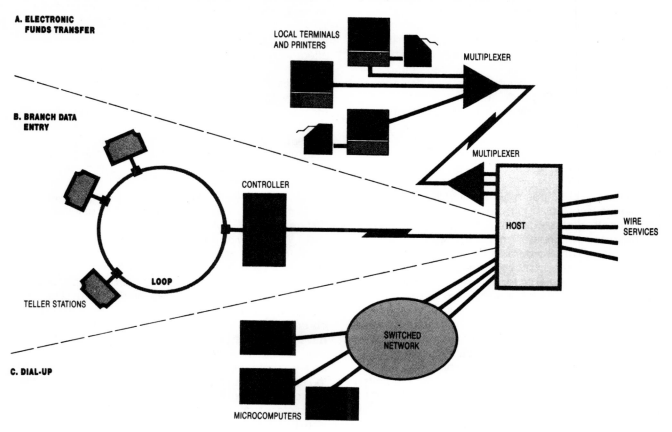

A. ELECTRONIC FUNDS TRANSFER

B. BRANCH DATA ENTRY

C. DIAL-UP

LOCAL TERMINALS AND PRINTERS

MULTIPLEXER

MULTIPLEXER

CONTROLLER

LOOP

TELLER STATIONS

HOST

WIRE SERVICES

SWITCHED NETWORK

MICROCOMPUTERS

The journal tape contains all message header, body, and trailer text. Volume-wise, it is by far the largest of the three sets. Its primary use is for retrievals.

The event record is the main set with which we are concerned. An "event" is defined as any inbound or outbound message. When an event occurs. a record is made of the occurrence. For example, suppose an entered transaction gets a positive logical response from the host, plus a final action, such as delivery of a requested report, or routing of the original message to another party.

In either case, three event records are created: one for the original report request or message entry, one for the host response, and one for the final action. If the final action is delayed, the network might send a notice to the user that it is still being worked on, or in queue. This notice would generate a fourth event record for the same transaction, and so on. These records are physically scattered over the event tapes but are logically tied together by the system sequence number. An off-line search program could verify that the event records are all there, answering the sender's question, "How do I know that my message was delivered?" (if the receiver lost the message). Besides an audit purpose, the event record tapes would be used to derive billing data and network utilization statistics.

The information "snapshot" in each event record

would typically include the transaction or message type, the date and time, the terminal sequence number (ISN or OSN) or port sequence number (if dialed), and the system sequence number. The originating or destination company or department would be recorded, as well as the terminal, if on a leased line. These are symbolic fields lifted from the message format or control block.

Also included in the event record are the user ID (but not password), usually entered by the operator; the message length (header + body + trailer character count); and special-condition delivery indicators, such as possible duplicate, alternate-routed, delayed, or multi-addressed.

Terminal state-change requests and notices, such as for log-on and log-off, are incoming and outgoing messages, so their events would be recorded. For example, the alarm generated by the automatic log-off of an idle terminal would be recorded.

The exception log contains all event records relating to anomalies such as unsuccessful password or log-on attempts, unauthorized transaction attempts, terminal lockouts, and test-word failures. Statistical summaries of these anomalies should be made for pattern investigation, in order to seek, for example, a correlation between them and operator actions.

Implementation of the event record and exception

log tapes involves reasonably small overhead. Typically, a 2,000-byte core buffer reserved to collect the events would be written to disk when full or on a time-driven basis. This would probably be a double buffered scheme, requiring 4,000 bytes. Implementing a separate exception log is for processing convenience; if use of the space is not justified, all of its information can be captured on the event record tapes.

(d) A remote auditor's terminal would allow monitoring of transactions, looking at queues on a last-in/first-out (LIFO) basis (most recent entries first), interrogating file status, flagging accounts for notice of special activity, and so on. Of course, the use of such a terminal must involve very special precautions.

Three examples

Figure 2 illustrates three typical bank applications involving money movement, and the following applications provide case studies covering telecommunications security features:

A. Funds transfer: From Back Office to Wire Service. In this application, payment orders are created by various back-office departments for delivery to a wire service. This traffic is two-way: funds transfer messages will be received as well as sent by the bank host via the wire services. It is characterized by a relatively low number of messages, each carrying relatively high dollar-value instructions.

A typical implementation might put several configurations of terminals and local printers in each back office department, and connect them through a multiplexer-pair to a wire-room host. Thus, effectively, each terminal is on a point-to-point circuit and the multiplexers are logically invisible. The host is responsible for all message editing and terminal control on the in-bank side. On the out-bank side, the host must meet the interface and security specifications of the funds transfer carriers—Fedwire, SWIFT, BankWire—and of telex. We are concerned here with security measures on the in-bank side.

B. Branch data entry: From Teller Stations to Host. In this application, each branch office teller and supervisor is equipped with an individual station. Terminals are used for the electronic entry of customer transactions (deposits, withdrawals, balance inquiry, transfer between accounts). Traffic is one way (teller-to-host for continuous update of the customer database and masterfile maintenance), and characterized by a high number of messages, each carrying relatively low dollar-value instructions.

Typically, each branch office has its own intelligent station controller connected, via a point-to-point link, to the host. The stations, on a loop with the controller, are logically invisible to the host; all its communication is with the controller only. The controller performs such functions as station management (password validation) and initial message format checks. Thus there are two sides to this configuration, from the stations to the controller and from the controller to the host, that must be secured.

The controller should have a capacity for limited off-line or standalone processing so that, in case of host failure, local customer transactions can continue. At restoral, the controller sends its accumulated messages to the host for master-file update. The station-to-controller side must also be flexible. The high-activity workflow of teller stations can be impeded by too much security; a balance must be maintained. For example, if a station breaks down, any other should be plug-to-plug replaceable, or the teller should be able to continue work at any other station. Therefore, cross-checks of teller ID with terminal ID would be inappropriate.

C. Dial-up microcomputers: This application is for home- or corporate-premises banking. It is one way, with the customer instructing the bank host to pay bills, move money between accounts, and so on. Transactions are characterized by relatively few messages in amounts ranging from low to high.

To offer this service, a bank creates appropriate software packages, putting them on copy-protected floppy disks for distribution to participants. The disks are differentiated only by secret exchange station identifier (XID) characters unique to each disk. To establish a connection, the disk is loaded and automatic dialing may occur. Interplay begins with an exchange of XID characters for host validation of a legal user. If good, other validation checks may follow. By their nature, dial-initiated transactions are much less secure than ones from dedicated lines because anybody, knowing the number and having a disk (perhaps stolen), can establish a session.

Table 2 juxtaposes eight security features against the three applications we have just described (A, B, and C). The features are rated as either recommended (1) or inappropriate (0), meaning not recommended, inapplicable, or unusual. "Recommended" does not mean that all of these safeguards have to be in place, but at least a selected subset should be.

Row 1 is encryption and its associated key management procedures. It applies to remote leased-line circuits (dedicated channels over distances) that may be part of A and B configurations. Thus, in A, if the host is located off-premises from the back-office departments, then that portion of the network should be encrypted; otherwise it need not be. In B, the controller-to-host link should be encrypted, though here the argument is less strong because of the nature of the traffic (a high volume of low dollar-value messages).

Another tradeoff for A and B is: does quasi-encryption already exist because of the nature of the transfer mechanism? That is, can the whole message be read off the link in consecutive characters, or is it already broken up? In packet switching, for example, different packets of the same message may take different physical paths. In multiplexing, the serial stream may be interlaced with characters from different transactions (for example, bits 16 slots apart in a time-division multiplexer). The weighting of these factors would be part of each encryption decision.

Row 2 is authentication or testword, strongly recommended for transfers of wire-service funds. The information needed for this end-to-end check could be inserted as early as the payment order is formatted.

Table 2: Security features for three applications

SECURITY MEASURE	APPLICATION			
	A. BANK SIDE OF FUNDS-TRANSFER WIRE SERVICES	B. BRANCH DATA ENTRY		C. DIAL-UP MICROCOMPUTERS
		STATION-TO-CONTROLLER LOOP	CONTROLLER-TO-HOST LINK	
1. ENCRYPTION	0, IF ON-PREMISE HOST 1, IF REMOTE HOST	0	1	0
2. AUTHENTICATION	1	0	0	0
3. TERMINAL SEQUENCE NUMBERS	0 (1 ON WIRE SERVICE SIDE)	0	1	0
4. PASSWORDS AND LOG CODES	1	1	OPTIONAL	1
5. PHYSICAL VS. LOGICAL TERMINAL CHECK	1	0	1	1
6. ACKNOWLEDGMENT OF SINGLE MESSAGES OR GROUPS	1	0	1	1
7. SYSTEM SEQUENCE NUMBERS	0 (1 ON WIRE SERVICE SIDE)	0	0	1
8. EVENT RECORD	1	0	1	1

1 = RECOMMENDED   0 = INAPPROPRIATE OR UNUSUAL

Authentication is particularly appropriate for the low volume of high dollar-value messages typical of wire-service traffic.

Row 3 is terminal sequence numbers. This form of protection and control is normal for the out-bank (wire service) side of A, but not for the in-bank side. It is recommended for B, controller-to-host, where "terminal" sequence number would mean "controller" sequence number. Loops from the teller station to the controller would not use it.

Row 4 is password and log code settings used to define terminal functions and/or their legal users. In B, besides teller stations, special function supervisory stations are needed. These are always "on-loop" to the controller but must be logically activated, per transaction, by the teller or supervisor inserting a plastic card. This implementation allows all stations to perform all functions (for flexibility), only restricted by the secret PIN-code password on each user's card. Whether or not the controller should have to log on for host access is optional to the implementation. This is really a computer-to-computer interface, so the controller might be regarded as always present.

In A, users would key in their passwords to log on for a session. In C, because of the exposed nature of dial-in connections from off-bank premises, several password layers might be required. For account inquiry, no password validation beyond the simple XID legality check that already took place would be requested. Corporate users making a mailbox pickup or retrieving prior messages would enter a single password that is validated against the XID. An account alteration would call for a second password to be validated against the XID. Account alteration is so sensitive that it might only be allowed via the host dialing back to the PC.

Row 5 is a physical vs. logical check for terminal validity. In C, the only crosscheck possible is XID vs. password, because dial-in connections are not associated with a preassigned port. From the controller to the host in B, validating the physical terminal ID embedded in the protocol is recommended, as well as crosschecking any symbolic abbreviations in the message header against their hardware counterparts. From the station to the controller, no such checks are appropriate. Application A calls for the same checks as in B, if they are available.

Row 6 is single or grouped message acknowledgements, end-to-end. In the former case, the example is logical accept or reject responses, mentioned earlier as close-the-loop functions. In the latter, the example is end-nodes periodically exchanging summary reports of message types and counts received for comparison (cross-check reconciliation). Some form of these logical acknowledgments is generally recommended.

Row 7 is system sequence numbers. In A, a quasi-SSN called the transaction reference number is often manually created by the originating department, put in the message field, and used for internal control. It is distinct from the true SSN that will be assigned on the wire service side. In B, the content of the message fields creates an implicit SSN so that another one is not required.

Row 8 is a taped event record of all incoming and outgoing transactions used for audit trails, billing, statistics, and off-line reconstruction of prior states. ■

Daniel Fidlow specializes in the Technology Management Services practice at Price Waterhouse. Formerly Fidlow was vice president of BankWire, the national funds transfer network. He has master's degrees in mathematics and management and is a lecturer at Pace University.

Section 5
Futures

Alan R. Severson, AT&T Information Systems, Lincroft, N.J.

AT&T's proposed PBX-to-computer interface standard

DMI provides T1 transmission between the two devices and supplies 23 user channels. Control is via ISDN common channel signaling.

Compatibility is one of the most important issues facing data communications companies. AT&T Information Systems has developed the Digital Multiplexed Interface (DMI) to establish an efficient interface between a computer and a PBX. DMI was developed in collaboration with Hewlett-Packard Co. and Wang Laboratories to help make a cost-effective link between workstations and hosts.

The interface, which is based on standard digital carrier schemes as transport mediums, uses standard channel and frame structures. In North America and Japan, the interface operates over 1.544-Mbit/s (T1) facilities to provide 23 data channels and one signaling channel, each comprised of 64 kbit/s. In Europe, the operation is over 2.048-Mbit/s facilities, which provide 30 data channels (in addition to one signaling and one framing channel) at the same 64-kbit/s rate. Within the data channels, DMI provides protocols to support data transport at all standard rates.

DMI's key benefits are that it:
■ allows 23 terminals in North America and Japan and 30 in Europe to simultaneously connect to a host computer over two twisted pairs of wires.
■ greatly reduces the cost, as in any multiplexer implementation, of interfacing a PBX to a host.
■ provides an interface between computers and PBXs that is consistent with the evolving architecture of the Integrated Services Digital Network (ISDN) interfaces being defined by the CCITT.
■ allows economical, high-speed (up to 64-kbit/s) access to hosts from terminals distributed over a digital PBX network.

DMI's elements that are key to tracking the evolving ISDN standards are common channel signaling and clear—that is, fully available to the user—64-kbit/s transmission. When the ISDN standards are estab-

lished, both PBXs and host computers can gracefully evolve to meet them. The DMI signaling channel will evolve to the ISDN "D" channel, which is specified as a message-oriented signaling channel that will enable access between hosts and PBXs.

DMI's most obvious application is to provide an efficient means of supporting switched access of EIA-interface-standard-equipped data terminals to a local host. However, because the interface is based on the use of standard digital carrier schemes for transport—such as T1 carrier—and the per-channel data formats support standard data transmission, several other configurations can be envisioned (Fig. 1).

As shown, terminal-to-host and host-to-host communications is supported. Terminals and host computers can be colocated or remote from each other. A user can establish communications with a host that is connected to the same PBX as his terminal or, through use of digital tie trunks between PBXs, with a host that terminates on another PBX.

The physical layer (in accord with the OSI model) for 1.544-Mbit/s facilities is based on the use of T1 carrier. The physical layer specifications conform to national and international standards for transmission facilities at the DS1 (the signal designation on T1 carrier) rate. The frame format consists of 24 eight-bit words (octets) and one frame bit, for a total of 193 bits per frame. Channels 1 through 23 carry data, and channel 24 provides signaling.

At 1.544-Mbit/s operation, DMI supports two uses of the framing bit: that used by existing carrier equipment, and the extended framing format proposed to the CCITT that is intended to replace the earlier channel-framing format in North America. In the extended framing format, the 8-kbit/s framing bit position is divided into three channels: 2 kbit/s for channel fram-

1. Supported applications. *With DMI applied between PBXs and computers, communications between hosts and between terminals and hosts is facilitated. Termi-* *nals and hosts may be either colocated or remote from each other. A user connected to one PBX may access a remote PBX's host via a digital tie trunk.*

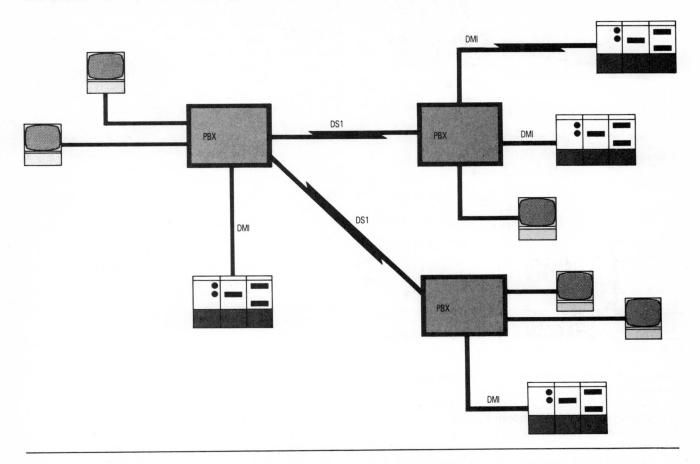

ing, 2 kbit/s for a cyclic-redundancy-check code (CRC-6), and 4 kbit/s for a data link. With this format, the CRC provides a means for performance monitoring of the facility and can ensure that synchronization is done on the valid framing pattern.

At 2.048 Mbit/s, DMI follows physical-layer international standards. The format consists of 32 octets for a total of 256 bits per frame. Channels 1 through 15 and 17 through 31 carry data. Channel 0 provides frame alignment, alarms, and network synchronization information. Channel 16 provides signaling.

Call control

DMI has a two-step approach to signaling. Step I, bit-oriented, is for initial implementation and is based on the widely used on-hook/off-hook tie-trunk signaling. Step II is a message-oriented scheme—a subset of the signaling procedures defined by CCITT Working Party XI/6 for ISDN. The two-step approach is necessary because of the time needed for the ISDN recommendations to become finalized.

DMI common channel signaling provides 23 or 30 channels free of traffic signaling bits, depending on trunk data rate. With 1.544 Mbit/s, conventional carrier telephony signaling—which was not designed for data transport—"robs" the least significant digit of

each channel in the sixth and twelfth frames. This scheme destroys any customer data contained in those bit positions within the applicable frames.

In Step I, DMI avoids this problem by using one of the 64-kbit/s channels to carry the signaling, clearing the entire 64-kbit/s bandwidth in the other 23 channels for customer data. This separate channel provides a multiplexing of the signaling bits that were formerly in each channel. In the 2.048-Mbit/s case, common channel signaling is already part of the standard. Step I for 2.048 Mbit/s uses standard European signaling.

For either interface case, standard on-hook/off-hook signaling sequences are used. The PBX and host recognize the off-hook signal as an incoming seizure signal. PBX-originated calls are placed by sending off-hook to the host for a particular channel. Host-originated calls use dial-repeating call setup, sending address digits to the PBX. Calls are answered with an off-hook signal and terminated with an on-hook signal.

Step II replaces Step I's analog-network-based signaling with a message-oriented procedure consistent with the ISDN recommendations for customer-access signaling. The signaling carries information concerning call setup, determination of call status, and invocation of special features such as address redirection (call forwarding) and calling-party identification. Step II pro-

2. A la mode. *DMI supplies three data formats, called modes. They provide for data transmission at a range of asynchronous and synchronous rates.*

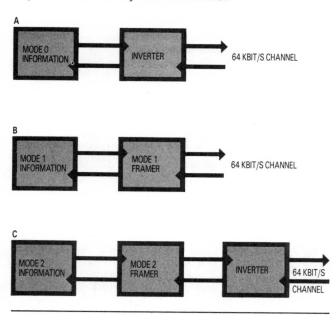

A

B

C

vides a communications link between the host and the PBX processors that is no longer limited to either an off-hook or on-hook indication. Now, the signaling link can supply additional information such as addressing, call waiting, and host status.

Synchronous and asynchronous

DMI provides three data formats—modes 0, 1, and 2—to convey user data. These formats provide for the transmission of synchronous data at rates of 300, 1.2K, 2.4K, 4.8K, 9.6K, 19.2K, 56K, and 64K bit/s; and of all asynchronous data at rates through 1.8 kbit/s, plus 2.4, 4.8, 9.6, and 19.2 kbit/s. The mode for each data channel is individually negotiated. Functional block

diagrams of the three modes are shown in Figure 2.

Mode 0 provides 64-kbit/s, full-duplex, synchronous transmission of user data. Mode 0's data is inverted (ones become zeros; zeros become ones) before transmission on the 64-kbit/s channel. This permits the use of an HDLC-based protocol to satisfy the ones-density requirements for operation on those 1.544-Mbit/s facilities that require sufficient pulses (ones) to maintain the transmission equipment's timing and synchronization. Because HDLC allows no more than six consecutive ones (flag definition), its inverse can then contain no more than six consecutive zeros.

Mode 1 (Fig. 3) provides 56-kbit/s, full-duplex, synchronous transmission of user data. Mode 1 is compatible with 56-kbit/s Dataphone Digital Service (DDS). Framing information from the 1.544- or 2.048-Mbit/s frame divides the data stream into individual octets for each of the 64-kbit/s channels. Within the Mode 1 data channels, each octet is subdivided into two fields. The first field consists of the first seven bits, which contain either customer data or a control-state code, depending on the contents of the second or status field. The latter consists of bit 8.

A "1" in the status field indicates data in the preceding seven bits (with bit 1 being the first received from the data source). A "0" in the status field indicates that the preceding seven bits contain a control-state code.

Mode 2 (Fig. 4) provides general data transmission at rates up to 19.2 kbit/s. It supports either asynchronous or synchronous data, full- or half-duplex operation, and existing data terminal interfaces. Mode 2 utilizes the same block delineation strategy as HDLC, allowing existing HDLC framing devices to be used in the hardware design. The same technique is used for both synchronous and asynchronous data.

In Mode 2, information from the 1.544- or 2.048-Mbit/s frame is not used to delimit user information. Instead, user information is divided into blocks of variable length that are delimited by a "flag" bit

3. Mode 1. *Framing information from the trunk frame divides the data stream into individual octets for each of the user's 64-kbit/s channels.*

4. Mode 2. *Here, the HDLC block delineation strategy is used. User information is divided into variable-length blocks delimited by flag patterns.*

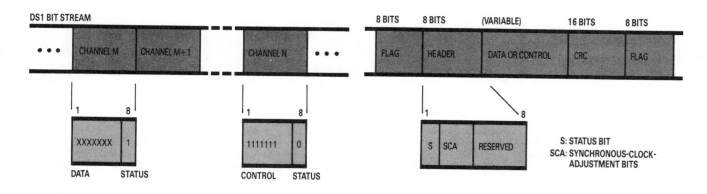

pattern: 01111110. A single flag may both terminate a block and begin the next block.

The ability to transmit information that has the same bit pattern as a flag (transparency) is preserved by "bit stuffing." The transmitter, as the last device in the sequence before the bit stream is supplied to the inverter, inserts a "0" bit following five consecutive "1" bits appearing anywhere between the opening and closing flags of a block. The receiver, after inverting the bit stream and searching for flag characters, removes any "0" bit that follows five consecutive "1" bits. In addition to block delineation, flags are used in a continuous stream during an active connection to fill the channel when there is no information to send.

Bit by bit

A header follows the opening flag of a block and contains information about the following data/control field. The header is one octet long. The first bit is a status bit that indicates whether the following data/control field contains data (status bit 1) or control information (status bit 0). The next four bits are used in a clock frequency adjustment technique that permits the transmission of synchronous data controlled by an external clock independent of the PBX clock. Bits 6 through 8 are reserved for future use.

The data/control field's length is variable and is implicitly determined by the block length. User data is packaged in the data/control field when the header status bit indicates data. For asynchronous data at any of the defined rates (300 to 19.2K bit/s), where character boundaries must be preserved, each octet in the block contains a single character.

Synchronous data is packed into the data/control field as it is received: Because of bit stuffing, each character may have more than eight bits. Of course, when the header status bit indicates control, control information appears in the data/control field.

There are two control messages in Mode 2 operation: handshake and update. Handshaking is the process of exchanging control messages between send-receive end-points to check compatibility and to initiate the process of entering the data-communicating modes. The handshake exchanges information such as working data rate, DCE or DTE end-point definition, synchronous or asynchronous operation, duplex or half-duplex operation, and the image of CCITT V.24/EIA RS-232-C interface control leads.

It is also necessary to send control messages during a Mode 2 data transmission to furnish information conveyed by the interface control leads and to signal a "break" condition (an interface signal consisting of at least 10 consecutive spacing intervals). This information is conveyed via the second control message type: update. Update messages are sent between send-receive end-points every two seconds and whenever a change of state is detected in an interface lead.

The next field, of 16 bits, contains a cyclic-redundancy-check (CRC), value calculated from the block's contents after the opening flag. This field is used for performance monitoring and to discard erroneous control information. The final field is another flag octet. ∎

Peter C. Janca, Digital Equipment Corp., Merrimack, N.H.

Comparing the two PBX-to-computer specifications

Although their means differ, CPI and DMI designers have the same end in mind: a standard for the interface to lessen costs now and in the future.

Last month Data Communications *published an article describing AT&T's Digital Multiplexed Interface (DMI) specification: "AT&T's proposed PBX-to-computer interface standard" (p. 157). There exists an earlier specification, the Computer-to-PBX, or CPI. Both specifications have been submitted to the Electronic Industries Association as the first step to obtaining a national—then an international—standard. One industry consultant says that computer makers would want a chip to meet both specifications, rather than have to design to either one or the other.*

In the wings is the CCITT's evolving ISDN controlling standard, which will probably be solidified by 1988. Some informed sources feel that the two specifications may well have merged by then, if not shortly thereafter. Whether or not they do merge, both DMI and CPI—or their merged version—will probably have to be redesigned to meet ISDN requirements, when they are finalized.

One prominent computer maker, Data General, has stated that it intends to support both specifications. Considering that this company was not involved in the design of either specification, its views are of considerable interest: "One's immediate reaction to predicting which interface will predominate is to blankly say that any standard backed by AT&T will eventually become the preferred one. This attitude is tempered when one is made aware of two situations.

■ *Products based on CPI are now in development by the major PBX and minicomputer vendors. This soon-to-be-installed base, coupled with the delayed availability of DMI-based products, makes CPI the only choice in the near future.*

■ *Because of its focus on the local Computer-to-PBX interconnection, CPI products can be developed more quickly as well as at a lower cost.*

"All this considered, CPI will see continued strong backing and heavy usage in the next one to five years. Eventually, when the ISDN becomes a reality, the independent PBX vendors will all be required to support DMI for connection to central offices. At that point, it seems likely that the PBX vendors' interest in perpetuating CPI as the exclusive computer-to-PBX standard will diminish.

"Eventually, DMI will be the obvious choice due to its compatibility with the future public communications networks [disputed herein], its flexibility for data and voice usage, and its compatibility with packet-switching techniques. It will, however, take a number of years before the networks for which DMI is tailored are in place.

"Meanwhile, it does not appear that support of CPI or DMI is a significant criterion for selecting office automation and communications gear. What is important is that whatever the user selects should offer the combination of connectivity, utility, and service at a price that makes sense."

The following article, by one of the designers of CPI, attempts to compare the two interface specifications as impartially as possible—considering the source. Some of the points may appear open to question, as, possibly, do some from the statements quoted above. If they do appear so to the reader, Data Communications *welcomes all substantive comments.* —RS

In July 1983, Digital Equipment Corp. (DEC) and Northern Telecom Inc. (NTI) announced the availability of the Computer-to-PBX Interface (CPI) specification: a technique to transport 24 simultaneous data channels over a four-wire T1-carrier link. Approximately eight months later, AT&T made known an alternative technique, called the Digital Multiplexed Interface, or DMI, to allow 23 channels over a T1 link.

This article describes the similarities and differences of the CPI and DMI approaches. Also included is the author's forecast of how and in what form these differences will be resolved.

The following is a list of the companies committed to building to each specification, as of this writing:

CPI	DMI
Digital Equipment	Data General
Data General	Honeywell
Prime Computer	Wang Laboratories
Wang Laboratories	Hewlett-Packard
Northern Telecom	AT&T
American Telecom	
InteCom	
Mitel	
Rolm	

Incidentally, the PBX manufacturers that have chosen CPI as their vehicle represent virtually all of the relevant (digital PBX) installed bases, and more than 90 percent of the current relevant PBX shipments.

CPI and DMI have similar objectives:
- Reduced cost
- Rapid availability
- Universal coverage and acceptability
- Reduced complexity

Their philosophical approaches, however, are somewhat different: DMI is described as moving to the Integrated Services Digital Network (ISDN) concept now, while CPI advocates stress the need for a solid working product at present and recommend use of ISDN in the next-generation product—when ISDN is more stable. These basic philosophical differences result in differing ways of addressing each objective.

Reduced cost

All digital PBXs today handle data as shown in Figure 1A. Voice and data are combined using a vendor-supplied data access module (or DAM—each manufacturer uses a different name for this device). The DAM may be a separate box or integrated within the maker's feature phone, but the function is the same for either case. The DAM conditions the data for the terminal (synchronous or asynchronous) to work over the synchronous link to the PBX.

These synchronous links are normally in multiples of 64 kbit/s because this rate is used to digitize voice and is typical for a PBX. (Some PBX manufacturers use different overall data rates to incorporate proprietary signaling.) The important point is that from the time the terminal connects to the DAM to the time data is available at the computer, on a circuit-by-circuit basis, the information is under the control of the PBX vendor's proprietary technique. If, for example, a user were to replace a PBX, proprietary DAMs would also have to be replaced.

As shown in Figure 1B, either specification moves the DAM function from a free-standing box to the commu-

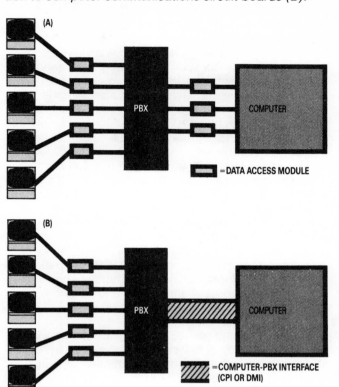

1. The old and the new. All digital PBXs today handle data as in A. Both CPI and DMI move their DAM function to computer communications circuit boards (B).

nications circuits of the computer. This allows use of standard T1 DS1 carrier techniques to multiplex up to 24 channels onto 4 wires. Both of these changes—moving the DAM functions, and T1-carrier multiplexing—can reduce costs, provided all PBX companies change their proprietary data techniques at the interface to a common standard. (If each computer maker must develop a separate interface for each PBX, most of the attractiveness disappears, due to higher overall development and support costs, and lower volumes per product.) CPI provides 24 channels, while DMI provides 23—both over the 1.544-Mbit/s T1-carrier link. Both specifications also are defined for CCITT standards, which yield 30 data channels over a 2.048-Mbit/s link.

The interfaces work only if both computer and PBX support the same standard. Each manufacturer builds and supplies the interface for its product. For example, the CPI link shown at Interface '84 required that NTI provide a circuit board that connected the PBX bus to the T1-carrier. The circuit board also had to make any conversions needed to change from NTI's data protocol to the CPI standard protocol. DEC provided a communications option that operated at T1 rates, decoded the data from the CPI protocol, and connected to the computer's bus. NTI and DEC have forecast that a complete CPI link (both PBX and computer sides) will be priced at less than half the current price of the same function using individual DAM equipment for the computer links.

Note that both CPI and DMI eliminate the separate and proprietary DAMs between computer and PBX. Neither addresses the problem of proprietary links and DAMs between a PBX and its connecting terminals.

Rapid availability

Market studies in 1981 concluded that a high-speed multiplexed interface, such as CPI, would be recognized by the market by 1983, and demanded by 1984. The high level of enthusiasm at Interface '84 and the emergence of DMI seem to confirm this forecast.

One step taken by both CPI and DMI developers has been to make the specifications open—nonproprietary and easily available—for manufacturers (CPI in July 1983; DMI in March 1984), although only CPI has announced a licensing process so far. With CPI available from either NTI or DEC, this process calls for a one-time $500 fee to NTI, with DEC not requiring any fee. Neither company charges royalties. There are currently about 65 CPI licensees.

Both specifications are based on T1, an existing, well-defined technique. Since CPI uses the current standard 24-channel T1 carrier (in-channel signaling), it can be switched on a channel basis and can work based on existing PBX makers' T1 hardware.

DMI can go over existing 24-channel T1 facilities but cannot be switched (the 23 + 1 CCITT technique will begin to be deployed in 2 years—at the earliest). It also requires new hardware by PBX makers. A critical factor in DMI's use is the PBX maker's willingness to begin development on the proposed 23 + 1 version of T-carrier.

Another required element is the ready availability of parts: DMI carries much of the complexity associated with ISDN, and several informed industry sources have stated that custom chips would be required to make DMI development feasible. Rockwell has announced that it will begin work on such chips. CPIs, on the other hand, are being developed today using currently available chips.

Universal coverage

Both CPI and DMI are designed to work throughout the world. Unfortunately, this is complicated by the fact that there are two standard techniques used in the world today:

■ In North America, Japan, and some other countries: T1, 24 channels, 1.544 Mbit/s.
■ In Europe and most of the rest of the world: CCITT, 32 channels, 2.048 Mbit/s

The North American standard places signaling and control for each channel within that channel, while the European standard moves this into two dedicated channels, leaving 30 channels available for data. Both T1 and CCITT standards transport voice in digital form, but neither is specified for data.

Both CPI and DMI have defined data protocols for both North American (T1) and European (CCITT) standards. DMI packages both sets of protocols within the same specification. The two CPI versions are in two documents. The European versions of both CPI and DMI are designed to work over 64 kbit/s clear (fully available to the user) channels and with common channel signaling. Both are also designed to work with ISDN as the evolving standard becomes a stable specification.

It appears that North American ISDN T-carrier will have 23 data and 1 common channel; the DMI specification is based on this assumption. However, the North American ISDN standard is still evolving, and the DMI specification will evolve with it.

There is a significant advantage to this approach. Assuming that ISDN-North America is stable, and assuming that facilities are commonly available to support it on market demand, DMI can be designed once and remain viable through the 1990s. This is especially attractive to designers and manufacturers.

CPI designers took a different approach for North America. Their conclusions are listed here.
■ ISDN is not yet stable enough to build to, even though its component parts are reasonably well understood. Any ISDN-based specification would require the designers to use parts that are not final, thus being subject to change; to invent new parts for areas not yet covered by ISDN discussions and work to convince ISDN standards bodies to adopt the chosen technique; and to differ from a proposed ISDN approach in places where it seems inappropriate for the task at hand—and then try to get ISDN changed. (In its presentation to the Electronic Industries Assn., AT&T stated that the DMI specification includes all of these required characteristics.)
■ A 64-kbit/s clear channel with common signaling is more attractive from a data transmission viewpoint, but there are no facilities and no PBX makers that handle it. None are expected prior to the late 1980s.
■ The critical measure of success would be in getting PBX and computer makers to accept the technique. This would happen only if it were based on something the majority already had, or were doing (such as 24-channel T1-carrier).
■ Market analysis showed customer demand would become heavy by 1984, and technical surveys revealed that each PBX maker was beginning to develop its own proprietary technique to handle data. It was determined that the market wanted a common technique to allow flexibility and freedom of choice that does not include proprietary techniques.

CPI designers decided that the most appropriate technique is one that is stable and buildable today. They recognized that ISDN is important, but felt that the five-to-seven-year lag before ISDN's availability in North America would leave too large a gap for buyers who want something now. They knew that almost any technique could be used, but decided to base the specification on something in place in a network today, and available from PBX makers. This resulted in a less "elegant" technical approach than with 64- kbit/s clear channel, but the end result is a straightforward specification that has already received acceptance by 90 percent of the relevant PBX market.

Although it is clear that manufacturers need to

decide which specification to use for their designs, it is not clear if the buyer cares whether one specification is "better" than the other. The appropriate ways for the buyer to compare appear to be price, availability, and universality. The first two are self-evident, but universality needs some discussion. Market research has shown very strong buyer preference for freedom of choice, rather than being locked into any one manufacturer's PBX-plus-DP package. The buyer wants to select what is best for him from a number of PBXs and from a number of computers; he then wants to readily interconnect the choices. The buyer also wants a standard used for his interconnection so that he is free to expand or change his PBX or computer installation in the future—with no drastic interface-concept changes.

The PBX problem
Both CPI and DMI have received public support from several computer vendors, so CPU buyers should have the required freedom of choice with either specification. However, CPI more readily passes the freedom-of-choice test on the PBX side: Several leading PBX vendors support it, but only AT&T supports DMI. CPI links between PBX and computer have already been developed and publicly demonstrated, so it will probably be the winner in time-to-market as well.

Both DMI and CPI follow the same reasoning. The use of an individual, external data access module for each channel, plus RS-232-C cables, plus line cards and computer multiplexing channels, becomes a mess to install, administer, and maintain. Figure 2 illustrates a current installation with only about 15 DAMs. Imagine 24, or 48, or more. Then imagine 24 such connections with a simple two-twisted-pair cable. This is the promise that both DMI and CPI offer.

Assuming anyone developing DMI chooses the same approach that is being followed in developing CPI products, the users of the PBXs and the computers will see no additional demands made on their machines. This is because the manufacturers will package the required CPI or DMI logic, firmware, and software within the new circuit cards themselves.

A less satisfactory alternative is to force the host to do some of the additional work needed to support the specification. For example, some CPI circuit boards require several "on-board" microprocessors to convert from T-carrier to CPU bus operation. The designers successfully resisted a temptation to pass some of this work along to the host. DMI appears considerably more complicated than CPI, so the temptation to burden the host will be even tougher to resist.

Relevant comparison
The table is based on the CPI and DMI specifications as submitted to the EIA, and on information conveyed during the respective presentations made on March 13, 1984. Other relevant information from public sources is shown in parentheses. The major elements are compared. Readers wishing a more detailed view are encouraged to obtain copies of both specifications (see below for details).

Both specifications address the issues of lower cost and reduced connection complexity. Both offer the attractive potential of open interconnect capability between computers and PBXs. It would appear that computer and PBX makers would have preferred that there be only one commonly used interface technique. However, it is a fact of life that there are two alternatives available today. The author believes that manufacturers would prefer to implement only one of the two, and that the majority of implementations will be CPI. Here's why:

■ PBX makers live in a world of cutthroat price competition and are looking for the maximum return on their investments. They tend to invest in the more stable and proven choices. Because CPI can take advantage of their existing T-carrier hardware, and is considered simpler and more stable, customers are already asking for CPI. The author predicts that PBX makers will continue with their existing CPI efforts.

■ All computer makers must develop new hardware, and are choosing to develop either CPI or DMI, or both. Since CPI requires no custom chips, CPI-based products will be brought to market much faster than DMI

2. The DAM picture. This is an installation with about 15 DAMs between the PBX and the computer. Cabling complexity multiplies as the number of DAMs increases to the often-encountered 24 or 48—sometimes even more. With CPI or DMI, all that is seen is a two-twisted-pair cable for each group of 24 connections.

Comparing interface factors

FACTOR	CPI	DMI
1. TRANSPORT MEDIA FORMAT	CURRENT 24-CHANNEL DS1/D3 (EUROPEAN VERSION USES CCITT 32-CHANNEL)	CURRENT DS1/D3, OR T1-EXTENDED FRAME FORMAT[1], OR CCITT 32-CHANNEL
2. NUMBER OF DATA CHANNELS	24, UNITED STATES 30, EUROPE	23, UNITED STATES[1] 30, EUROPE
3. FACILITY	EXISTING T1 OR PRIVATE	T1 OR PRIVATE[2]
4. MAXIMUM DATA RATES	19.2 KBIT/S ASYNC 56 KBIT/S SYNC (64 KBIT/S VOICE IN NORTH AMERICA AND EUROPE; 64 KBIT/S DATA IN EUROPE)	19.2 KBIT/S ASYNC 64 KBIT/S SYNC[2]
5. NUMBER OF DATA MODES	1 (STANDARD DS1/D3)	3 (MODE 0=64 KBIT/S, REQUIRES CLEAR CHANNEL. MODE 1=56 KBIT/S. MODE 2=UP TO 19.2 KBIT/S[3] USING HDLC)
6. DATA RATE ADAPTION TECHNIQUE	8-BIT DATA BYTES ARE STUFFED INTO T1 DATA CHANNEL[4]	UP TO 1.8 KBIT/S USES "BLIND SAMPLING." OVER 1.8 KBIT/S USES BIT STUFFING.[5]
7. SIGNALING	EXISTING STANDARD (A&B WITHIN EACH CHANNEL). SAME FOR ALL DATA MODES.	NEW: A BIT/S BUNDLED IN A 64-KBIT/S CHANNEL FOR THE INITIAL IMPLEMENTATION.
8. CAN T1 RULES BE MAINTAINED WITHOUT INDUCING DATA ERRORS?	YES	NO (AT 64 KBIT/S IN MODE 0 OVER CURRENT T1, DMI WILL INDUCE DATA ERRORS IF NEEDED TO MEET THE ONES-DENSITY RULE. AT&T RECOMMENDS THAT USERS SUPPLY A HIGHER-LEVEL PROTOCOL TO RECOVER FROM OR PREVENT THESE ERRORS.)
9. ERROR HANDLING	FORWARD ERROR CORRECTION THROUGH 9.6 KBIT/S.	ERROR DETECTION ONLY, THROUGH 19.2 KBIT/S.
10. MAINTENANCE	STANDARD T1 CONVENTION: INTERNAL LOOPBACK. IMPLEMENTATION GENERATES SAME SIGNAL AS DMI'S "BLUE."	REMOTE ALARMING; INTERNAL LOOPBACK DEFINED (BLUE SIGNAL)
11. CHANNEL FORMAT	CHARACTER-ORIENTED	PACKET-ORIENTED (HDLC)
12. EIA CONTROL SIGNALS	YES	YES (BUT NO EIA SECONDARY CHANNEL SIGNALING)
13. DATA INVERSION REQUIRED	NO	YES (ON CHANNEL-BY-CHANNEL BASIS IN MODES 0 AND 2)
14. NEW HARDWARE REQUIRED BY PBX MAKERS	NO	YES
15. NEW HARDWARE REQUIRED BY DP MAKERS	YES	YES
16. DEFINED FOR: —PBX TO HOST —HOST TO PBX —HOST TO HOST —PBX TO PBX	 YES YES YES YES	 YES YES YES, WITH PBX IN BETWEEN NO
17. SPECIFICATION STATUS	COMPLETE—CPI PRODUCTS HAVE ALREADY BEEN SHOWN.	DESCRIBED AS EVOLVABLE—COMPONENTS WILL BE DEFINED AS ISDN IS FURTHER DEFINED.

[1] REQUIRES FACILITY AND/OR HARDWARE NOT CURRENTLY DEPLOYED BY PBX MAKERS AND/OR NETWORK.

[2] DMI PROTOCOL INDUCES DATA RATE ERRORS IN SOME CASES. SEE FACTOR 8. FOR 64 KBIT/S, REQUIRES NONDEPLOYED HARDWARE.

[3] MODE 2 IS USED IN BOTH MODES 0 AND 1 AS A "HANDSHAKE" PROTOCOL.

[4] ALL 8 DATA BITS ARE PRESERVED AT ALL RATES.

[5] REQUIRES DATA-BYTE BUFFERING FOR SYNC AND ASYNC 19.2 KBIT/S AND LOWER RATES. FOR SYNCHRONIZATION, REQUIRES TRANSMISSION OF PHASE-CORRECTION INFORMATION.

products. The author believes that market acceptance of CPI products, coupled with its simpler development, will cause computer companies developing both specifications to gravitate to CPI, and those companies that have announced DMI developments will gradually swing over to CPI as well. Another factor to consider is that the manufacturers of an installed base of over 20,000 PBXs have committed to support CPI, while the installed PBX base that will support DMI numbers in the hundreds.

■ Basing the DMI specification on ISDN is admirable, but this will delay DMI's practical development. DMI developers must either wait until ISDN is firm in the aspects required for Computer-to-PBX interface (several years at best), or build a compromise now that is different in several areas from current ISDN recommendations. The former choice means that they will lose out in time-to-market, while the latter means they must probably change when ISDN becomes firm. Neither DMI nor CPI is in full accord with ISDN. Implementers of both DMI and CPI will have to change hardware and software to match the final ISDN specification. The magnitude of this task is expected to be comparable for both groups.

■ Both CPI and DMI have been submitted to the EIA. Although CPI is firm, and could be approved as early as mid-1984, the author forecasts that the EIA Committee (TR41.1) will first wish to study both specifications. Then it will probably wish to look at ISDN and how ISDN proposals could or should affect the interfaces under discussion. Drawing from experience gained in IEEE 802, the EIA will probably work toward having a next-generation specification to be available by around 1988. This specification will be able to draw on a far more firm ISDN specification (after the next CCITT plenary meeting in 1988), and will be able to incorporate experience gained from CPI (and possibly DMI) installations. This may seem like a long time, but it is consistent with the normal standards-body process. DMI may evolve more readily to the final ISDN standard, depending on how close its designers' guesses prove justified. There are mixed views on exactly how good their guesses are.

■ Market demand is strong today and will favor companies with products available immediately.

Readers who wish more information about the CPI and DMI specifications may obtain it from the following:

For CPI:
Peter C. Janca
Manager - PBX Program
Digital Equipment Corp.
Continental Blvd. - (MK02-1/C11)
Merrimack, N.H. 03054

For DMI:
Product Manager - DMI
AT&T Information Systems
Room 1F301
307 Middletown-Lincroft Rd.
Lincroft, N.J. 07738 ■

Marc H. Rudov, Telematics Resource Group, Wellesley, Mass.

Wanted: Concerned users to join ISDN (r)evolution

It's possible for users to determine the success of the integrated services digital network in the United States.

Information network users can influence ISDN regulatory and standards processes in the United States to the degree that they directly participate in these processes. Traditionally, users have played a small role in shaping communications policy in the United States, yielding this task to vendors of the equipment and services they purchase.

The ISDN evolution, and the user community's role in guiding it in the United States, demands a strategy for evaluating the standards and regulatory issues at stake.

For the majority of its evolution, the telephone network was modified and embellished at the common carrier's convenience and discretion. Furthermore, these exchanges were made, by and large, unbeknownst to the network's users. At this juncture, all major telephone companies have ISDN-deployment strategies, but find that without enthusiastic user demand, these strategies have limited value.

In the era of deregulation and competition, it is difficult for vendors to market new products and services without first understanding users' requirements and desires. Likewise, in some instances competition introduces so many choices to the user that he wishes there were, once again, a monolithic industry structure.

In today's telecommunications and data communications environment, users have two avenues for ensuring that their myriad choices for products and services are on common ground: standards and regulations.

ISDN is a digital communications medium evolving from the public switched telephone network. It will offer standard end-to-end connections and simultaneous support of voice and nonvoice services—all this through a single access. ISDN will benefit users and carriers alike because of the economies possible from using digital technology. It will also benefit users and carriers because it integrates voice, data, and video transmission in a single transport.

The fundamental building block of the ISDN is a 64-kbit/s pulse code modulation channel. Known as the B channel, or basic-access channel, it is designed to carry circuit-switched voice and circuit- or packet-switched data at 64 kbit/s or less.

The D channel is provided for out-of-band signaling of the B channel. It is a packet-switched channel that, typically, will operate at 16 kbit/s. The D channel, when not signaling for a B channel, may be used for low-speed data transmission, such as that employed in telemetry services.

The ISDN subscriber may obtain basic access (at 144 kbit/s, two B channels plus a D channel) or primary access (1.544 Mbit/s, or 23 B channels plus one D channel) to the network, on a switched, dynamic-allocation basis. Subscribers who desire a nonswitched circuit may access what is called the H0 channel, which operates at 384 kbit/s, or the H1 channel, which operates at 1.536 kbit/s. H0 and H1 channels may or may not include a D channel, depending upon the user's requirement for signaling.

Within the customer's premises, the CCITT recommendations require a balanced, metallic, four-wire transmission medium capable of transmitting bidirectionally at 192 kbit/s. This wiring is considered to be one continuous cable, with provisions for equipment and network terminations.

Most foreign countries, unlike the United States, which has the most deregulated telecommunications industry in the world, will design and deploy their own ISDNs through their respective government authorities—the Postal, Telegraph, and Telephone agencies, or PTTs. Some countries have established 25-year national plans and have created cabinet-level positions specifically for implementing their ISDNs.

In European countries, where analog technology lags considerably behind that of the United States and Canada, the ISDN evolution is seen as the vehicle for springing into the so-called information age of digital communications and attaining a level of service heretofore unknown there. The countries of the European Economic Community are embarking on a 10-year drive to improve Europe's antiquated telecommunications installations with a joint program called RACE (Research in Advanced Communications technologies for Europe).

By examining the deployment of ISDNs in other countries, users can better understand the benefits of ISDNs, the implications of government intervention in ISDN planning, and the value of their own involvement in the process of defining ISDNs in the United States.

The Canadian PTT, Telecom Canada, controls the communications industry in Canada and has chosen ISDN for the design concept of its telecommunications future. Its largest telephone company, Bell Canada, serves 60 percent of Canada's 16 million telephones in Quebec and Ontario provinces and in eastern sections of the Northwest Territories.

Bell Canada has been on the leading edge of digital communications technology for more than a decade. In 1972, Bell Canada offered the first digital leased-line network service in North America—Dataroute. In 1976, Bell Canada introduced Datapac, North America's first commercial public packet-switching network.

Telecom Canada now has the world's largest all-digital long-distance voice network and offers, through its telephone companies, services that eventually will be folded into an ISDN, such as electronic mail, voice mail, videotex, telemetry, and directory services. By 1990, Telecom Canada projects, 65 percent of local loops, 40 percent of local switches, and 85 percent of tandem switches will be digital.

In 1971, the French telephone network was considered hopelessly obsolete. Consequently, the French PTT declared that revamping and digitizing the network would become a national priority.

Currently, the French tout their telephone network as the most digitized and modern in the world. Sixty percent of France's short-distance transmission is digital, and more than 50 percent of tandem switches and approximately 45 percent of local exchanges will be digital by the end of 1985.

In its migration toward a national ISDN, the French PTT offers digital services such as Transfix, Transcom, and Transdyn. Transfix is a leased-line service that provides connection at data rates from 48 kbit/s to 2,048 Mbit/s. Transcom is a basic 64-kbit/s switched service, and Transdyn is a switched service with rates up to 1.92 Mbit/s.

The French PTT is introducing ISDN in rural Brittany, initially targeting small businesses and professional users. This approach is contrary to most other countries, which will seek large businesses in major cities to be the first users of ISDNs. The French project that 95 percent of the country will have ISDN connectivity by 1995.

Deutsche Bundespost (DBP), the West German PTT, plans to make West Germany an ISDN-using nation by 1990. Although West Germany is a latecomer to the digitization process—it did not begin digital transmission until 1970—it currently is instituting ISDN field trials to hasten the evolutionary process and expects to have 6 million ISDN subscribers by the year 2000.

The DBP recently established two field-trial centers—one in Mannheim and another in Stuttgart. Each pilot will include at least 400 subscribers and be connected to West Germany's public network in 1988, when the demonstration phase is completed. Using existing two-wire local loops, each pilot subscriber will have a single access for voice, data, text, and image transmission.

The Italian PTT, through its major telephone company, SIP, began its first ISDN trial in 1984, in Venice, involving four large companies as initial subscribers. The participants have access to 80-kbit/s full-duplex channels via two-wire local loops. The services available in the trial are telephone, videotex, and Teletex.

Using an ISDN-standard telephone terminal, with alphanumeric keyboard and alphanumeric display, the subscribers can monitor many new telephone functions. For example, a user can observe the cost of the call-in-progress, with continuous updating. In addition, the subscriber can verify on the readout the caller's number before he answers the call.

SIP estimates that all of Italy will be interconnected by an ISDN in 1990, when 90 percent of local loops will be digital and wideband services will be widely available.

Through Nippon Telegraph and Telephone (NTT), its quasi-PTT, Japan is developing a nationwide ISDN, due for completion in the year 2000, at an overall cost of $125 billion.

Japan, like West Germany, was late in migrating from analog technology. It introduced digital transmission in 1975. By 1990, however, NTT expects that 100 percent of its long-haul intercity links will be digital, as well as 60 percent of its tandem switches and 30 percent of its local switches.

The Japanese ISDN, which began operation in 1984, is called the Information Network System, or INS, and will be based on lightwave and satellite technologies. The INS, at present, accommodates 9,000 existing telephones, 400 digital telephones, and 1,100 data and facsimile terminals. Sevices offered by INS include telephone, Teletex, videotex, slow-scan video, data, telemetry, and facsimile.

Six thousand subscribers have been chosen by NTT to use and monitor INS services for six years. Residential subscribers constitute 64 percent of the group; business offices 29 percent; and retail establishments 7 percent.

British Telecom, the United Kingdom's PTT, now half-owned by the public, established a lead on the rest of the world in 1983 by actually marketing its ISDN concept as Integrated Digital Access (IDA). IDA will be marketed to large users, as British Telecom does not believe there is much benefit from ISDN usage, at this time, to the small user.

Table 1: Evolution of CCITT study groups

GROUP	1981-1984	1985-1988
I	DEFINITION AND OPERATIONAL ASPECTS OF TELEGRAPH AND TELEMATIC SERVICES	DEFINITION, OPERATION, AND QUALITY OF SERVICE ASPECTS OF TELEGRAPH, DATA TRANSMISSION, AND TELEMATIC SERVICES
II	TELEPHONE OPERATION AND QUALITY OF SERVICE	OPERATION OF TELEPHONE NETWORK AND ISDN
III	GENERAL TARIFF PRINCIPLES	GENERAL TARIFF PRINCIPLES, INCLUDING ACCOUNTING
IV	TRANSMISSION MAINTENANCE OF INTERNATIONAL LINES AND NETWORKS	TRANSMISSION MAINTENANCE OF INTERNATIONAL LINES, CIRCUITS, AND CHAINS OF CIRCUITS; MAINTENANCE OF AUTOMATIC AND SEMI-AUTOMATIC NETWORKS
V	PROTECTION AGAINST DANGERS AND DISTURBANCES OF ELECTROMAGNETIC ORIGIN	PROTECTION AGAINST DANGERS AND DISTURBANCES OF ELECTROMAGNETIC ORIGIN
VI	PROTECTION AND SPECIFICATIONS OF CABLE SHEATHS AND POLES	OUTSIDE PLANT
VII	NEW DATA COMMUNICATIONS NETWORKS	DATA COMMUNICATIONS NETWORKS
VIII	TERMINAL EQUIPMENT FOR TELEMATIC SERVICES	TERMINAL EQUIPMENT FOR TELEMATIC SERVICES
IX	TELEGRAPH NETWORKS AND TERMINAL EQUIPMENT	TELEGRAPH NETWORKS AND TERMINAL EQUIPMENT
X	(NONE)	LANGUAGES AND METHODS FOR TELECOMMUNICATIONS APPLICATIONS
XI	TELEPHONE SWITCHING AND SIGNALING	ISDN AND TELEPHONE NETWORK SWITCHING AND SIGNALING
XII	TELEPHONE TRANSMISSION PERFORMANCE AND LOCAL TELEPHONE NETWORKS	TRANSMISSION PERFORMANCE OF TELEPHONE NETWORKS AND TERMINALS
XIII	(NONE)	(NONE)
XIV	(NONE)	(NONE)
XV	TRANSMISSION SYSTEMS	TRANSMISSION SYSTEMS
XVI	TELEPHONE CIRCUITS	(NONE)
XVII	DATA COMMUNICATIONS OVER THE TELEPHONE NETWORK	DATA TRANSMISSION OVER THE TELEPHONE NETWORK
XVIII	DIGITAL NETWORKS	DIGITAL NETWORKS, INCLUDING ISDN

▨ INDICATES CHANGE IN TITLE

CCITT = INTERNATIONAL TELEGRAPH AND TELEPHONE CONSULTATIVE COMMITTEE

IDA will evolve from British Telecom's System X family of digital services, which range from packet-switching network access and digital leased circuits to satellite links. British Telecom expects the United Kingdom to have nationwide coverage of a digital network by 1988, when there will be 1,000 IDA access locations.

Subscribers in London will be the first to use IDA, with expansion planned to Birmingham and Manchester near the end of 1985, when service will be available from 60 access locations. Initial tariffs prescribe a $195 connect charge for single-line IDA and an annual $224 rental charge.

IDA will offer telephone; circuit-switched, packet-switched, and private-line data; Telex; Teletex; facsimile; slow-scan video; and videotex. In addition, British Telecom will market a variety of electronic mail and voice services through IDA.

The standards process

The primary group responsible for generating international ISDN standards is the CCITT (International Telegraph and Telephone Consultative Committee), one of seven ITU (International Telecommunications Union) organizations, headquartered in Geneva, Switzerland. The ITU, an international treaty organization, has been a specialized agency of the United Nations since 1948.

The objective of the CCITT is to establish recommendations, or standards, for end-to-end performance, interconnection, and maintenance of the world's networks for telephone, telegraph, and data communications. These recommendations are based on consensus, are not enforceable, and are ratified every four years at the plenary assembly. At the Eighth Plenary Assembly, held in October 1984 in Torremolinos, Spain, the I-Series recommendations (the "I" standing for ISDN), among others, were accepted unanimously by CCITT members.

Membership in the CCITT consists of four classes:
■ Government Administrations.
■ Recognized Private Operating Agencies (RPOAs).
■ Scientific or Industrial Organizations (SIOs).
■ International Organizations.

Voting in standards issues is a privilege reserved for the government of each member country, and each country is entitled to one vote. RPOAs, or common carriers, and SIOs—manufacturers and R&D firms—often represent their governments as technical contributors to the CCITT's standards process, even though they do not vote.

International organizations consist of standards groups, such as the ISO (International Organization for Standardization), and user groups, such as the International Air Transport Association (IATA) and the International Telecommunications Users' Group (INTUG). These organizations play a somewhat subordinated role to RPOAs and SIOs, and typically attend plenary assemblies out of general interest.

The ISDN subject has stimulated a new focus for the CCITT, and at the Eighth Plenary Assembly the titles of several CCITT study groups were modified to incorporate ISDN or acknowledge its effect on the overall

1. U. S. role in CCITT. *The United States' membership in the CCITT is held through the State Department's Bureau of Economic Affairs, Office of International Com-* *munications Policy, and is composed of one committee and five study groups. Study group membership is extended to all interested in telecommunications.*

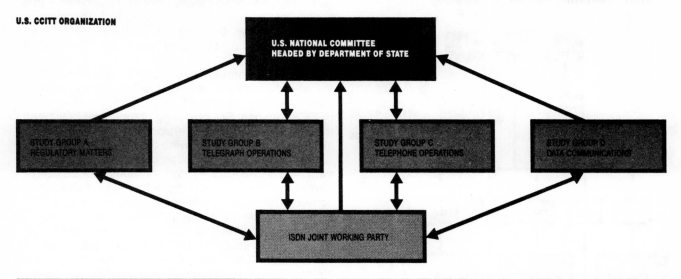

standards process. Table 1 lists the titles of the CCITT study groups for the 1981-1984 and 1985-1988 study periods, respectively, confirming this new focus.

Additionally, a new study group, "S," was created to examine the entire study group structure for possible revision at the Ninth Plenary Assembly. A key reason for this study is that ISDN developments are narrowing the distinction between voice and nonvoice services, thereby eliminating the need for separate efforts in these areas.

U. S. participation
Official membership of the United States in the CCITT is through the Department of State, Bureau of Economic Affairs, Office of International Communications Policy. The U. S. CCITT is composed of a national committee and five study groups: Regulatory Matters, Telegraph Operations, Telephone Operations, Data Communications, and the ISDN joint working group, as shown in Figure 1.

Membership in the U. S. CCITT study groups is extended to all parties interested in telecommunications, including users, carriers, manufacturers, national standards organizations, and government agencies. There are no dues, and membership is obtained through the chairman of the desired study group, not through the State Department.

The T1 Committee
An important source of U. S. ISDN standards-making is the T1 Committee, whose structure is shown in Figure 2. T1 is an independent organization, approved by the American National Standards Institute (ANSI), that develops interconnection standards for the U. S. telecommunications network. The T1 designation represents the ANSI nomenclature for committees—"T" for telecommunications, "1" for first T committee—and is not related to the 1.544-Mbit/s T1 specification.

Membership in the T1 Committee is open to all interested parties and currently comprises exchange carriers, interexchange carriers, resellers, manufacturers, vendors, government agencies, user groups, consultants, and liaisons. The T1 Committee employs the Exchange Carriers Standards Association, or ECSA, a trade association of wire-line exchange carriers, as its secretariat and administrative body.

Within the T1 Committee are six subcommittees, one of which is the T1D1 Subcommittee, devoted to ISDN standards work. T1D1 prepares ISDN-related positions and standards for submission to the U. S. CCITT. T1D1 further consists of three working groups:
- ISDN Architecture and Services (T1D1.1).
- Switching and Signaling Protocols (T1D1.2).
- Physical Layer (T1D1.3).

The X3 Committee
Since ISDNs incorporate data communications and other computer-related elements, such as the Open Systems Interconnection (OSI) reference model, the ANSI-approved X3 Committee also is involved in ISDN-standards contribution in the United States, along with the T1 Committee.

The X3 (Information Processing Systems) Committee creates standards in computers, information processing, peripheral equipment, and magnetic media. Its secretariat is the Computer and Business Equipment Manufacturers Association (CBEMA). A formal liaison exists between the T1 and X3 committees for creating ISDN standards.

Basic and enhanced services
One of the issues users must confront in subscribing to ISDNs is deciding where they would prefer that the bulk of ISDN-connection intelligence reside. From a regulatory perspective, this is exclusively the domain of the Federal Communications Commission, which, through

*2. **Important source.*** *The T1 Committee (unrelated to the 1.544-Mbit/s specification) is a key source of U. S. telecommunications interconnection standards.*

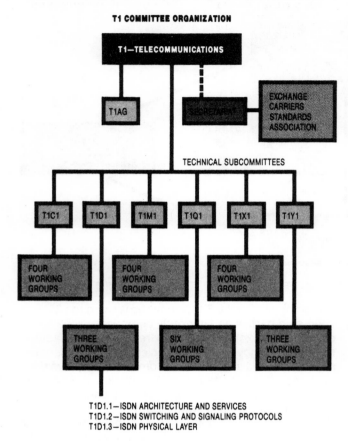

T1 COMMITTEE ORGANIZATION

T1—TELECOMMUNICATIONS

T1AG

SECRETARY

EXCHANGE CARRIERS STANDARDS ASSOCIATION

TECHNICAL SUBCOMMITTEES

T1C1 · T1D1 · T1M1 · T1Q1 · T1X1 · T1Y1

FOUR WORKING GROUPS

FOUR WORKING GROUPS

FOUR WORKING GROUPS

THREE WORKING GROUPS

SIX WORKING GROUPS

THREE WORKING GROUPS

T1D1.1—ISDN ARCHITECTURE AND SERVICES
T1D1.2—ISDN SWITCHING AND SIGNALING PROTOCOLS
T1D1.3—ISDN PHYSICAL LAYER

Computer Inquiry II, has established an ever-moving demarcation between basic and enhanced telecommunications services.

This demarcation, based largely on the 1980-vintage ability to distinguish between data-only and voice-only equipment, dictates the allowable sophistication of a network service and, consequently, the intelligence necessary in customer premises equipment (CPE) to interface with that network service.

According to Computer Inquiry II, basic services are those that provide transmission capacity for the transport of information and typically are offered by common carriers. An example of a basic service is POTS (plain old telephone service). Enhanced services are those offered juxtaposed with basic services. They necessarily alter the format, content, code, or protocol of a subscriber's transmitted information. An enhanced service requires computer processing to warrant its distinction—as in, say, voice mail and videotex.

Essentially, Computer Inquiry II was created to prevent large common carriers from using their monopolistic advantages to enter and, subsequently, dominate the information processing business. The original ruling dictated that common carriers be permitted only to route and switch the information they transport, and that enhanced services be offered by independent

providers or separate, unregulated subsidiaries of common carriers.

However, the basic premise of ISDN is to have both basic and enhanced services inextricably joined—true service integration—in a single transport. Therefore, the United States, because of regulatory impositions, appears unique in its contributions to the CCITT's ISDN standards.

Because the process of establishing separate subsidiaries by common carriers is redundant and expensive, as well as confusing to customers, the seven RBOCs (regional Bell operating companies) petitioned the FCC for protocol-conversion waivers, which would allow these carriers to provide their customers both X.25-to-X.75 (interconnection of separate packet-switching networks) and asynchronous-to-X.25 (CRT-terminal-to-packet-switching-network) protocol conversion. These are considered enhanced services.

Consistent with the Reagan Administration's emphasis on a free market, the FCC recently exhibited a willingness to reexamine past FCC decisions, especially Computer II, to determine whether outdated regulations are appropriate for current market conditions.

In December 1984 and March 1985, respectively, the FCC ruled in favor of the RBOCs' requests to perform both X.25-to-X.75 and asynchronous-to-X.25 conversions, dropping the separate-subsidiary requirement. These major decisions were a result of significant user demand for protocol-conversion services, which consequently obviate the intelligence required in the CPE to perform the same function.

Network-channel terminating equipment
Another stipulation of Computer Inquiry II is that common carriers may not sell CPE and basic services as a package. CPE, like enhanced services, must be sold by a separate subsidiary of the carrier.

Network-channel terminating equipment (NCTE) terminates a carrier's digital service on the customer's premises, providing electrical and mechanical maintenance (remote testing), and channel-provisioning functions for both the carrier and the user. The FCC ruled, due largely to protests from the Independent Data Communications Manufacturers Association (IDCMA), that NCTE shall be customer premises equipment and subject to competition on the open market. IDCMA's argument was that carriers had no inherent right to control a potentially lucrative equipment market such as NCTE.

Traditionally, NCTE was designed, built, installed, and tariffed by the common carrier, primarily AT&T. However, the FCC's ruling stated that there was no proof, as AT&T alleged, that independently manufactured and installed NCTE would harm the carrier's network. This ruling is contrary to the original CCITT ISDN concept of carrier-owned termination, which was modified to accommodate the United States.

Consequently, the T1 Committee is designing a new interface—to be positioned between the customer-owned NCTE and the end of the carrier's loop—that will affect only the United States' deployment of ISDNs.

While the concerns of carriers and manufacturers in

the NCTE issue are quite clear, those of the user community are not. After all, users ultimately bear the consequences of major decisions like this one. Perhaps users' input would have resulted in a different outcome.

Compatibility is key

Private networks are fashioned by communications users to fill a need not available from public networks, because of either technological or regulatory reasons, or both. Private networks consist of privately owned facilities or dedicated leased facilities and are used for local as well as long-haul voice and data traffic.

Because the majority of large users are public corporations, they are beholden to their stockholders. Stockholders are a very short-term-oriented group who care more about an investee's bottom line than about how the bottom line is derived.

An increasingly significant contributor to the bottom line is a company's communications network—from both cost and revenue perspectives. Therefore, these large users are motivated constantly to construct private networks that solve today's or yesterday's problems.

Faced with rapidly changing technology and the vicissitudes of regulatory fervor associated with changing administrations in Washington, the corporate communications manager is pressured to make difficult decisions about expanding his network that may prove, in the long run, to be fatal.

An ISDN standardization strategy is a logical and safe alternative to piecemeal insertion of network links—based on differing, proprietary solutions from every vendor. This will ensure that a user's private networks evolve with the technology and regulations of the time.

The FCC, for example, currently regards as questionable the future of private-line use. Because many private lines are being used to bypass the local exchange, the FCC believes MTS/WATS rates are priced uneconomically and should be reduced. The commission, furthermore, has established a $25 surcharge on private lines to compensate carriers for this unmeasurable traffic. Once the cost of MTS/WATS and private lines converge, the fate of uneconomic private-line usage, at least, will become dim.

Another consideration is that common carriers, both exchange and interexchange, are becoming more sophisticated with their private-line alternatives, especially those that resemble ISDN services. Illinois Bell, for example, is now offering legitimate ISDN services to large businesses that want to experiment with them. AT&T is marketing its new network service that will enable a customer to use the public switched telephone network as a quasiprivate network, by having statistically higher access to it than other users. These services give the users alternatives previously unavailable and are endorsed favorably by the FCC, too.

Since users will always have requirements for some form of private networks, they should give considerable thought to making these networks conform to ISDN standards. By striving for ISDN compatibility, users can reduce the risks related to network obsolescence and

Table 2: Key contacts

U.S. CCITT NATIONAL COMMITTEE
EARL S. BARBELY, DIRECTOR
OFFICE OF INTERNATIONAL COMMUNICATIONS POLICY
BUREAU OF ECONOMIC AND BUSINESS AFFAIRS
U. S. DEPARTMENT OF STATE
2201 C ST., N.W.
ROOM 5824
WASHINGTON, D. C. 20520
202-632-3405

ISDN JOINT WORKING PARTY
THIJS (TED) DEHAAS
SYSTEM PERFORMANCE STANDARDS AND DEFINITION
INSTITUTE FOR TELECOMMUNICATIONS SCIENCES
DEPARTMENT OF COMMERCE/NTIA
325 BROADWAY
BOULDER, COLO. 80303
303-497-3728

CHAIR, T1D1 SUBCOMMITTEE
WILLIAM F. UTLAUT, DIRECTOR
INSTITUTE FOR TELECOMMUNICATIONS SCIENCES
DEPARTMENT OF COMMERCE/NTIA
325 BROADWAY
BOULDER, COLO. 80303
303-497-3500

CHAIR, X3S3 SUBCOMMITTEE
BUD EMMONS
IBM CORP.
SYSTEMS COMMUNICATIONS DIVISION
P.O. BOX 12195 C71/651
RESEARCH TRIANGLE PARK, N. C. 27709
919-543-0062

NTIA CONTACT
DAVID J. MARKEY
ASSISTANT SECRETARY FOR COMMUNICATIONS
AND INFORMATION ADMINISTRATOR OF NTIA
DEPARTMENT OF COMMERCE
14TH ST. AND CONSTITUTION AVE., N.W.
WASHINGTON, D. C. 20230
202-377-1840

FCC CONTACT
WENDELL R. HARRIS
FCC/COMMON CARRIER BUREAU
INTERNATIONAL BUSINESS
1919 M ST., N.W., ROOM 534
WASHINGTON, D. C. 20554
202-632-3214

can better plan for future expansion.

The only way users will witness an ISDN evolution in the United States that matches both their technical and fiscal needs is by becoming active in creating standards and interacting with the three federal government bodies responsible for overseeing the U. S. ISDN evolution: the FCC, the Department of Commerce's NTIA (National Telecommunications and Information Administration), and the Department of State's U. S. CCITT National Committee (Table 2).

By helping create sensible alternatives for themselves, users lessen the burdens of excessive competition and regulation. Active user participation, along with manufacturers and carriers, will be the key to a successful ISDN evolution in the United States. ∎

Marc Rudov is the president of Telematics Resource Group, a Wellesley, Mass., firm that provides marketing consulting services to vendors in the communications industry. Rudov holds a B. S. E. E. from the University of Pittsburgh and an M. B. A. from Boston University.

Jerrold S. Foley, Burroughs Corp., Detroit, Mich.

The status and direction of open systems interconnection

The reference model still has seven layers, but its upper layers have acquired considerable detail. And there's more to come.

pen systems interconnection, better known as OSI, is solidly in place as a major business factor in interconnecting computers. The demand shown by major data processing users for implementation in banking, office automation, and manufacturing-process networking is a major factor in accelerating OSI into practical use. With increasing frequency, OSI is appearing in the plans of influential government and user organizations worldwide.

In the United States, the National Bureau of Standards (NBS) has defined a series of Federal Information Processing Standards, essentially identical to OSI, to be promulgated by the U. S. Department of Commerce and to be mandatory for the more than 30 federal agencies implementing DP (data processing) installations. General Motors has named OSI as a key factor of MAP (manufacturing automation protocol), its manufacturing DP structure.

General Motors also cosponsored with NBS an OSI network of various gear from different manufacturers at the NCC '84 show. A total of seven different manufacturers shared a common GM local network based on an IEEE 802 token-passing standard. OSI transport and file transfer protocols were demonstrated. A simultaneous, similar demonstration using an IEEE 802 CSMA/CD (carrier-sense multiple access with collision detection) local network involved seven additional manufacturers. These public demonstrations clearly show that OSI is more than blue-sky thinking; it is a down-to-earth answer to networking computers and terminals of all types and manufacture.

Statements from the Canadian Department of Communications show emphatic support for OSI, as do both France and the United Kingdom. In some instances, the U. K. is funding OSI implementation.

The U. K. government, in the interest of speeding the implementation of OSI by U. K. users and suppliers, has adopted its intercept strategy for guidance while higher OSI-layer protocols are under development. This provides interim solutions and assures a ready transition to the final OSI standard.

The U. S. Department of Defense (DOD) has been reviewing OSI protocols for suitability to its requirements. Since both the DOD TCP (transport control protocol) and the OSI transport protocol have strong ties to the Defense Advanced Research Project Agency, the prospect of interoperability or replacement of TCP is good. The North Atlantic Treaty Organization has indicated that OSI is central to its data communications planning. These market forces are propelling OSI out of the standards development phase and into accelerated implementation.

OSI is here to help

Applications in a production environment represent a substantial investment on the part of DP users. Assimilation of OSI into DP need not impact these existing applications at all. The visible effect of OSI will be primarily to make building new networks and expanding existing networks easier and less expensive in multivendor and multinational environments.

This application independence is due to the established OSI hierarchy of abstract definitions. The hierarchy chain consists of the reference model, the service description, and the protocol specification. This chain does not constrain implementations and, in turn, is transparent to implementation specifics. Only the user's OSI protocol implementations are concrete; conventionally, they will be handled by the operating system or executive program of the controlling computer or terminal. The applications that communicate should never be "aware" of whether the cooperating application is attached to its local processor or to a remote processor. The OSI developers' unwavering insistence on the fundamental implementation independence of OSI standards will perpetuate the independence of applications.

OSI developers are members of Subcommittee 16 (SC16) of Technical Committee 97 (TC97) — concerned with computers and information processing — of the International Organization for Standardization (ISO). This is a worldwide organization of national standards bodies. SC16 has organized itself into working groups (WGs), which are now:

- WG1 - The OSI reference model and general topics.
- WG4 - OSI management.
- WG5 - Presentation and application layers.
- WG6 - Session and transport layers.

There are 20 nations holding voting membership in SC16. The work on the physical, link, and network layers was assigned to SC6.

The CCITT is an international advisory body made up of the telecommunications authorities of national governments. As the CCITT was established by treaty, and as the need for governments' interoperation of data communications has been strongly felt, the CCITT has required unanimous consent to establish its recommendations (standards).

Both organizations have expanded their scopes — for OSI development, they fully overlapped. The need for close harmony was essential and has been met.

The financial investment in OSI by U. S. industry and government alone is estimated at upwards of $200,000 for just the June 1984 CCITT and ISO meetings. The same substantial measure of interest in OSI is met or exceeded by the U. K., France, and other countries. This should be taken seriously by any strategic planner in the data communications field.

Updating the architecture

SC16 has solved the problem of how to keep the stable OSI reference model abreast of technological advances. In setting up a formal list of registered questions for clarifying and interpreting the model, it became apparent that the same questions could be used for enhancements to the model. These enhancements are developed within the OSI architecture group and are acknowledged to be in accord with the existing model structure. They are certainly not disruptive to the development of protocols referenced to the model.

Final approval of the formal answers to the questions is reserved to the member nations, thus further assuring continuous stability of the model. Forty questions have been registered, with 15 receiving attention at the June 1984 OSI meetings. Other questions have been answered or rendered moot by recent enhancements.

Questions may originate within or outside SC16, such as from other standards organizations using OSI. The answers are made available for use along with the OSI reference model.

Substantial work on OSI addressing has taken place in support of an addendum to the reference model: A 50-page document was delivered at the June 1984 meetings. The addendum will be condensed, in har-

---

What the names mean

As ISO standards are developed, they receive different document names to indicate the phase they are in. Although these are not formal definitions, they should aid in understanding the process:

Working draft. The first stable document that contains all the technical features the developers affirmed as necessary. It may be a rough, unedited document, circulated principally within the working group that developed it.

Draft proposal. This is the result of technical correction and editorial refinement of the working draft. At this stage, and henceforth, the draft is registered with the ISO Central Secretariat and is circulated to all participating nations for ballot. Major technical comments may cause a second draft proposal stage. Some manufacturers begin implementing products at this stage.

Draft international standard. The comments of the member bodies on the draft proposal have been incorporated and further refinements are made. The document is circulated for member-body ballot. Only minor errors should remain to be corrected.

International standard. The document is now technically and editorially correct and corresponds to the ISO style. The standard is available in English, French, and Russian.

---

mony with the reference model, and specialists will define the addressing scheme for their layer.

The security addendum to the reference model emerged from the June meetings, with expectations of reaching draft proposal status in May 1985 (see "What the names mean"). New issues were brought in for study. They included access control, management functions, and a concern for the possibility of covert channels being used to bypass security provisions.

The OSI's Service Conventions, draft proposal 8509, was conceived as a guideline to development of future OSI service-description standards. It got a mixed reception because of the view that a formal definition technique would replace it. Further, the recent advances in the architecture and an error with respect to session services combined to send the standard back for a second pass through the draft proposal cycle.

Now that the initial concepts of OSI are in place, attention must be turned to conformance testing, to ensure the compatibility and interoperability of protocol implementations. This requires standardizing tests that can be used by worldwide organizations to ensure any given open system (operating methodology) will operate with other open systems. These tests may be used by many different groups: by vendors for verification of their products; by customers for assurance that products they buy will operate correctly with other OSI-conforming products; and by organizations offering third-party verification services.

The ISO's experts are optimally positioned to develop and standardize the OSI conformance tests. The active liaison between CCITT and ISO will substantially aid in producing mutually agreeable conformance test standards. ISO has already produced a checklist to guide protocol designers in this effort.

The protocol testing process checks the correctness of protocol data units (PDUs) and sequences of PDUs with respect to test scenarios. These scenarios are expressed as abstract service primitives: a set of functions that connects two adjacent layers, enabling each layer to provide service to the one above. This includes the ability of an implementation under test to correctly handle erroneous PDUs.

The protocol implementation being tested is treated as a finite-state machine. (A finite-state machine is a modeling technique for analytically defining the protocol entity so that it can be implemented in, for example, a chip. The "machine" is a basis for obtaining a formal protocol definition.) The finite-state machine must respond correctly to both the finite set of legal inputs and the infinite set of illegal inputs. While definitive and exhaustive, testing on this scale is clearly impossible. (How does one test for an infinite set of inputs?)

Practical conformance testing limits the inputs to a reasonable quantity—hundreds. It ensures that the inputs selected are somehow representative of the types in actual operation with which the protocol machine has to deal. (The protocol machine is a layer entity in the OSI model and is modeled as a finite-state machine.) The inputs to the protocol messages form a test driver. The responding protocol machine outputs are checked for correctness.

The protocol verification process has three essential parts: precise protocol specifications, validation of these specifications, and testing implementations. Concern here is for aspects of this process that are generally applicable and fundamental to procedural approaches to conformance testing.

To facilitate development of a satisfactory verification process for the emerging OSI protocols, the following steps are taking place:
■ The prose versions of OSI protocols are being rewritten using a formal description technique. This technique provides a precise and unambiguous protocol specification to define tests and to be used by a vendor in the implementation process.
■ The formal version of the protocol will be reviewed by the protocol originators to ensure the proper interpretations were made in going to the formal specification.
■ The formal version will eventually become the official protocol standard; the prose version will be retained as a tutorial supplement, possibly in an appendix.
■ Comprehensive test criteria, methodology, scenarios, and environments will be compiled and standardized by the test-process working group.
■ The completed test documentation will be reviewed by the responsible protocol working group.

It is essential that OSI protocol testing criteria be adopted internationally. Test procedures and parameters must be identical for each protocol implementation tested, regardless of where or by whom the testing is done. Users can more realistically expect interoperable communications products, and vendors will have a single, well-defined set of tests to verify their products for sale in all countries.

Formal description techniques make standards easier to implement and more convincingly interoperable. (These techniques are being standardized in ISO and CCITT.) The standards' original forms are in so-called natural language specifications. That is, they are expressed in a mixture of English, tables, and diagrams. This mode has not proven satisfactory: The ambiguous nature of natural language has often caused the interoperability of a heterogeneous network of implementations to be dependent on unique networkwide agreements. Retuning of implementations has been necessary to meet these agreements.

One formal technique, an extended finite-state-machine approach, is being used by a group of experts from the ISO and CCITT transport-level committees to formally define the transport protocol. This technique is based on the Pascal language with certain extensions, resulting in unambiguous and concise standards.

Meeting OSI requirements

A formal technique is also used to analyze the completeness, correctness, and efficiency of a specification in its standardization phase. In this phase, the technique is also useful to help determine that a specification meets the requirements of OSI and that it is consistent with other OSI specifications.

In the implementation phase, the formal version is useful to specify a product. In subsequent conformance testing, the formal version is also useful. In the testing activity that parallels the standardization and implementation phases, the formal protocol specification is essential to defining the test requirements, environment, procedures, and criteria.

Advances in the development of the OSI reference model are made following the fundamental rule that changes may not affect the standards based on the model or disrupt current work on OSI standards. Valuable improvements were made to the model and ratified by the end of 1983. The experts documented a clearer understanding of the concept of types, instances of application processes, and grouping of functions in the application layer (Fig. 1).

The three function groupings are the user element, the specific application service element, and the common application service element. The detailed structure of the network layer is also shown. Note the distinctions between an end system (the seven-layer configuration) and an intermediate one (the relay open system). These developments are discussed later.

Paralleling humanity

OSI management means getting and releasing OSI resources (such as connections, addresses, and files), intervening in the case of resource failure (including protocol state machine failure), account auditing, and access control. The parallel to human organization management is quite close. OSI management is subdivided into the concepts of application management, system management, and layer management. The definition of each and its current status is as follows:

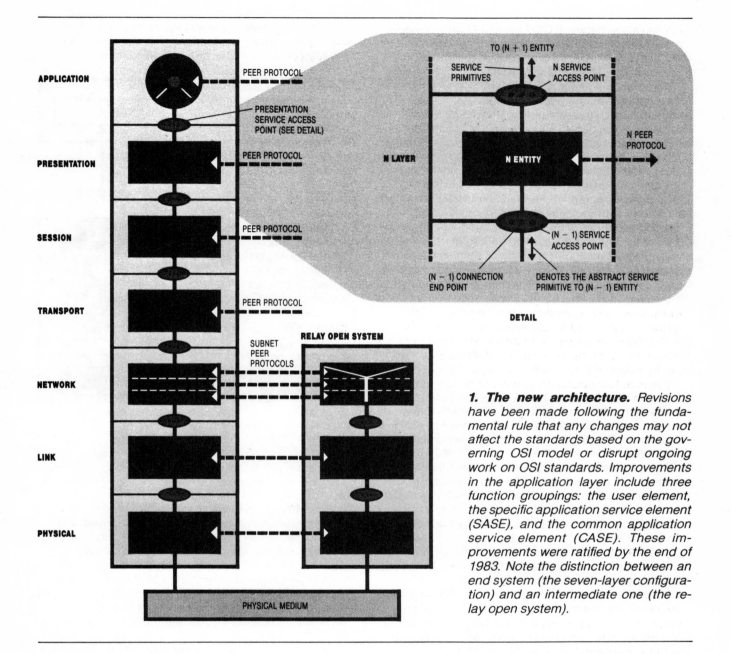

APPLICATION

PRESENTATION

SESSION

TRANSPORT

NETWORK

LINK

PHYSICAL

PEER PROTOCOL

PRESENTATION
SERVICE ACCESS
POINT (SEE DETAIL)

PEER PROTOCOL

PEER PROTOCOL

PEER PROTOCOL

SUBNET
PEER
PROTOCOLS

RELAY OPEN SYSTEM

PHYSICAL MEDIUM

TO (N + 1) ENTITY

SERVICE
PRIMITIVES

N SERVICE
ACCESS POINT

N LAYER

N ENTITY

N PEER
PROTOCOL

(N − 1) SERVICE
ACCESS POINT

(N − 1) CONNECTION
END POINT

DENOTES THE ABSTRACT SERVICE
PRIMITIVE TO (N − 1) ENTITY

DETAIL

1. The new architecture. *Revisions have been made following the fundamental rule that any changes may not affect the standards based on the governing OSI model or disrupt ongoing work on OSI standards. Improvements in the application layer include three function groupings: the user element, the specific application service element (SASE), and the common application service element (CASE). These improvements were ratified by the end of 1983. Note the distinction between an end system (the seven-layer configuration) and an intermediate one (the relay open system).*

Application management is concerned with those aspects of an application process represented in the user element (discussed later) and relevant to the communications and cooperation between applications. It is not related to the basic purposes of the cooperating applications. Application-management functions are located in the application layer.

System management is made up of functions—such as management of access rights, audit, and recovery—located in the application layer and is related to management of the OSI resources in all the layers.

Layer-management functions are related to the resources of their respective layers.

The current innovation in management-information exchange is to provide peer-to-peer layer-manager exchanges as well as exchanges between the management entities in the application layer. A three-layer relay or intermediate open system is explicitly part of the reference model. In such a scheme, exchange of layer-management information cannot possibly take place through an application layer—an application layer does not exist in an intermediate open system. In a seven-layer open system, if any layer were to stop functioning, then all layer managers in that OSI scheme would be unable to communicate.

This innovation has been accepted in principle by the OSI-management experts as answering many concerns, including those voiced by the IEEE 802 local-network committee members.

Comments from prospective OSI users are frequently concerned with OSI seeming to be oriented only to applications such as file transfer or sustained dialogs and neglecting brief transactions of a few hundred bytes or less. While the former require reliable connections of long duration, the transactional requirements can be efficiently satisfied using a single, brief, datagramlike transmission — dispensing with the reliability and accountability of connection-mode OSI.

To support the development of the new connectionless-mode OSI protocols, an addendum to the reference model has been developed that defines the relations between the layers and the layer features to be provided.

To elaborate, connectionless data transmission refers to isolated messages or data transfers that are independent of those transfers occurring before or after. (Actually some transfer association is often made by the application user.) This definition indicates that there is no retained state information, no acknowledgments, and no flow control. The requirements for this concept are quite similar to those of the datagram.

If the user finds this satisfactory for his application needs, connectionless transmission can prove more efficient than other transfer modes. Some current examples of uses for connectionless transmission are administrative messages, time and date announcements, real-time temperature, and stock price observations. A credit sale inquiry-update transaction would use two such transmissions.

Adding efficiency
Another basis for connectionless data transmission is in network-level operations. Many networks operate more efficiently and reliably if all the necessary control information accompanies a data unit rather than being held in every network node. When tandem networks from different carriers or of different types are involved, the effect of connectionless transmission on operating efficiency becomes more pronounced.

The connectionless program presently consists of projects to develop a network-level protocol and addendums to the OSI reference model, to the session protocol, and to the transport protocol. The link-level protocols have some potential to provide the connectionless mode service and may only require some partitioning into subsets.

Important architectural advances in the application layer have unified the ongoing application protocol work. These advances show the need for new projects on common application service elements, such as file transfer and management, and job transfer and manipulation. Service element groupings and protocol standards are now being developed as a result.

The application layer provides the sole means for application processes to access the resources of the OSI environment (Fig. 2): the collection of cooperating end systems for the defined period of cooperation.

The application layer is made up of the application entities that are used by one application process to transfer information between it and other application processes. The application entity obtains the remainder of the OSI services, in addition to those provided below the application layer, through the presentation services' access point.

The application process refers to the processing element for an application. The portion of this process

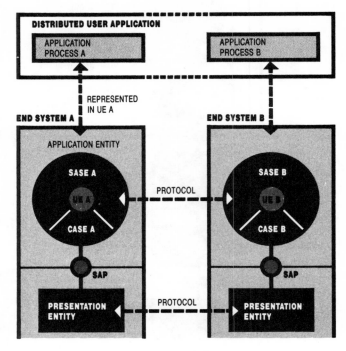

2. OSI environment. One application process transfers information to another via application entities, which obtain other services through their access point.

SASE = SPECIFIC APPLICATION SERVICE ELEMENTS
UE = USER ELEMENT
CASE = COMMON APPLICATION SERVICE ELEMENTS
SAP = SERVICE ACCESS POINT

that uses the application service elements is represented by the user element (Fig. 2). The shapes and relative positions of the application entity's subdivisions have no particular significance. The exact nature of how the user element represents the relevant portion of the application process is defined by the implementer. This determination has settled a long-standing issue of how the OSI user accesses the services of OSI.

The application needs determine which elements will be required from the service elements available in the application entity. This selected subset can vary according to the application being served by OSI.

The collection of application service elements to be used when associating one application with another is specified by the application context. The application context may be drawn from specific application service elements and common application service elements but must follow the rules for use of specific elements. The user element communicates with both specific and common application service elements.

Where messaging belongs
Designers have appropriately located protocols to use OSI services in the application layer. Notable among these protocols are the American National Standards Institute text preparation messages; interchange protocols of ISO Technical Committee 97, Subcommittee 18 (ISO/TC97/SC18); the European Computer Manufac-

turers Association message protocol family: message interchange distributed application, which is commonly known as MIDA; the CCITT X.400 series; and the NBS Federal Information Processing Series. Each of these development groups has devised its own architecture internal to the application layer.

The SC16 experts on OSI upper-layer architecture and the messaging experts have not performed a formal amalgamation of the general architecture of the OSI model and the various messaging architectures; it is not essential. The essential considerations are that the messaging protocols find the necessary services from the common application service elements and from those provided by or passed through the presentation layer, as appropriate. A further consideration is the suitability of the user element concept to the messaging protocols.

The presentation-layer standards have advanced to stable documents aided by the clarification of the upper layers' architecture, which has simplified the presentation layer. Where before many applications required their own presentation protocol, the revised upper-layer architecture permits use of a common presentation protocol. This reduces the potentially very large number—one for each application—of standard presentation protocols to one.

The capabilities of the presentation protocol are subdivided into named facilities. These are the connection, context, information-transfer, and terminal facilities. The presentation layer also provides transparent pass-through of session dialog management and synchronization to the application entity.

The context facility is particular to the presentation layer. Nothing similar to it exists in any other layers. In this facility, a base context is always active and never changing. It defines the presentation-control syntax and semantics and passes application-layer data transparently.

Above this default level of operation, a particular context related to the cooperating applications may be negotiated. This may consist of naming a common syntax to be used, naming a particular registered syntax, or describing a syntax that is neither. There are three syntaxes always to be considered in each context: the syntax for each end system and the transfer syntax between end systems. During the lifetime of a connection, context switching is supported by the presentation protocol if the cooperating application processes require the flexibility.

The information transfer facility also provides expedited data transfer, which is necessary for certain protocol control and management uses.

The session-layer services and protocol standards are stable documents with only the administrative phases remaining to make them international standards in ISO. The session-layer standards in ISO and CCITT are technically identical. Thus, the question of whether the standard is ISO or CCITT (an ISO standard is equivalent to a CCITT recommendation) has no bearing on interoperability.

The session layer is the lowest layer that has any direct interaction with the cooperating application entities. The session layer manages orderly data exchange, organizing and synchronizing the exchange essentially for the purpose of supporting associated cooperating applications. Session services depend on the provision of an essentially transparent data flow between end systems to be provided by the transport service. Strictly speaking, the session layer provides services to the presentation layer according to the hierarchical ordering of OSI; the presentation layer passes some session services transparently to the application layer and enhances others. The presentation layer itself uses the session layer to perform the intrinsic services of presentation: defining and interrelating the context(s) of the shared application.

In serving the application entities, the session entity functions include: session-connection establishment, supervision, and release; addressing; normal data transfer with flow control; expedited data transfer; and exception reporting. The unique functions of the session entity are for dialog management: Data-stream marks are used to synchronize normal dialogs and to recover synchronization of dialogs that may be interrupted or suffer unrecoverable errors.

There are several session-layer standards now in progress. Symmetric synchronization is being registered as a draft proposal as a result of the July 1984 ISO working group progress. Symmetric synchronization is most applicable when one end system issues a stream of messages and, for the sake of efficiency, does not want to wait for a response or acknowledgment following each message sent. Fine granularity in the ability to resynchronize—that is, resynchronizing on smaller segments of data—is obtained by using symmetric synchronization. This eliminates the necessity for resorting to an alternative (such as having to resend more data between wider-spaced synchronization points) that reduces performance efficiency.

"You're the tops"

The transport layer is the highest one in the model with application independence. Transport was conceived to be under the user's control to deliver data reliably without requiring detailed instructions or perplexing the user with details of how the transfer is achieved.

The transport-layer protocol has end-to-end significance, where the transport ends are entities located in the end systems (the seven-layer configurations). Thus capability, responsibility, and accountability for data delivery are located with the users.

The transport-layer protocol is divided into five classes, with classes 0 and 1 identified with teletex. Class 1, the minimum functionality class, is fully compatible with the CCITT's teletex Recommendation S.70.

Class 0 functions include getting and releasing, accepting or refusing transport connections; transferring data; and handling protocol errors. Class 1 adds the ability to handle multiple data units in one data unit and has an enhanced error recovery capability. Classes 2, 3, and 4 form a graded series with increasing capabilities; these classes may be multiplexed over a single network connection.

A class 2 transport entity may, in connecting with a

class 3 or 4, negotiate the higher-class entity down to the less-functional class 2. Similarly, six protocol options may be negotiated, including checksum (to confirm receipt of accurate data) and expedited data transfer. Given the protocol structure, the implementer can design the most flexible and efficient transport entity by comparing the quality of service required by the session layer to that provided by the network service. The implementer then selects the appropriate transport class and options to bridge the difference.

The implementer of an end system has the freedom, with the transport entity, to provide either a connection or connectionless service, handling either type of session mode. That is, mode crossover is supported in the transport architecture.

Class 4 of the transport-layer protocol is widely applied for a number of applications, experiments, and demonstrations. Its capabilities include the lower-class functions, plus detecting and recovering lost, duplicated, or out-of-sequence transport data units. The transport standards are stable and are undergoing completion of their administrative phases.

Making them uniform

The network layer is tasked with building on a wide variety of private and public network services, including X.25, X.21, local networks, domestic and international circuits, the public-switched telephone network, and leased lines. The network layer must take whatever network services are available and transform them into a uniform OSI network service, providing the specified network service primitives (functions that connect adjacent layers). In addition, the network layer must provide the global routing and relaying (switching) functions, including where several networks such as X.25 and local networks are connected in tandem.

Figure 3 illustrates one very real, relatively simple, but technically challenging, example of the network layer's function: End system A is on a local network with a gateway to an X.25 network to which cooperating end system B is attached. The transport entities must move data unaltered across the network service as though it were transparent.

Network addresses, and control functions and codes, must be translated (equalized) from local network expressions to X.25 equivalents to move the user data unaltered; the network-layer users are the transport entities. Service enhancements must be available to meet the user requirements and to equalize the services at both ends of the network connection.

The following services—or service elements—are provided by the network layer: network addresses, connections, connection-endpoint identifiers, and service-data-unit transfer (including expedited); quality-of-service parameters; error notification; sequencing; flow control; reset (optional); release of the connection; and receipt confirmation (optional and only to support existing features of X.25).

With the optional services, the intent of the designers is to have the user request the service. The network-service provider may honor the request or indicate that the service is not available at that time.

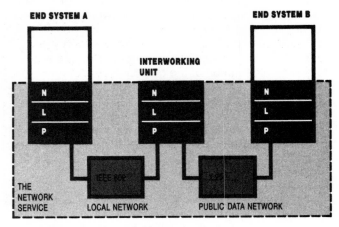

3. Network layer function. End system A is on a local network with a gateway to an X.25 network, to which end system B is attached.

N = NETWORK LAYER   P = PHYSICAL LAYER
L = LINK LAYER

More difficulties were encountered because considerations of gateways, PBXs, and ISDN (integrated services digital network) were injected. And, as in all of OSI, the reference model guidance and constraints had to be satisfied. Nevertheless, there has emerged a network-layer standard, ISO Draft Proposal 8648, which has accomplished its objectives.

Figure 4 shows the basic concepts of the network layer's internal structure. The developers have made it very clear that this structure does not depict sublayering, thus bypassing a great deal of development work that has defied agreement to date.

Conveying the functions

Note the subnetwork access protocol at the bottom of the network layer in Figure 5. It conveys the network layer functions needed to meet the requirements of subnetworks such as X.25, X.21, or a local network. In many X.25 networks, this protocol would be solely the "X.25 protocol" for that tariffed offering.

The next higher functional group supports the convergence functions using the subnetwork dependent convergence protocol (Fig. 5). This group adjusts upward or downward the services provided by the subnetwork access protocol, such as X.25.

The third group uses the subnetwork independent convergence protocol (Fig. 5) to accomplish the routing functions and finally constitute an internetwork protocol. The nesting of protocol data units follows the OSI practice: the subnetwork dependent convergence protocol's data unit nests inside the access protocol's data unit, and the independent convergence protocol's data unit nests inside the dependent convergence protocol's data unit. The internetwork routing via the independent convergence protocol is independent of the routing of an X.25 or circuit-switching subnetwork access protocol—in fact, none of the internetwork functions is visible to this protocol.

The capability for N-way (multiple-destination) con-

4. Inside the network layer. *The internal structure is divided as shown. Much contentious development work was bypassed by not depicting sublayering.*

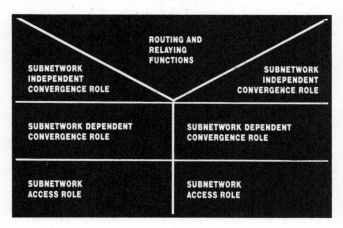

nections in OSI has become an active issue. One related concept under study is multi-endpoint connectionless-mode data transmission service in the network layer. Here, an independent network service data unit (self-contained) is transmitted to one or more network-service-access-point addresses or group ad-

dresses. The proposed service does not include flow control or confirmed (acknowledged) delivery. This is quite consistent with other connectionless services and is suitable where the network service has a quality level appropriate to the user needs.

A comprehensive set of protocols in the link and physical layers predated OSI. In fact, OSI was structured to be compatible with the established international link and physical standards.

The link-layer development primarily in support of OSI is the service description. This is expected to become an ISO standard and will be handled in ISO/TC97/SC6. Queuing, a significant new OSI concept, is introduced in the link services queue model (Fig. 6). This provides detail related to the real-world experience of delays and congestion.

Also note that an OSI data-link protocol operates point-to-point over a physical connection that may have uncorrected errors caused by line noise, connection dropouts, and interruptions. The link protocol must perform error correction and recovery, establishing the logical integrity of link-layer service.

The link layer can use either character-mode or bit-oriented protocols. The character-mode family is headed by ISO 1745; the bit-oriented, by ISO 4335, known as high-level data link control (HDLC). The ISO 4335 related standards include LAP (link access pro-

5. Nesting protocols. *The subnetwork access protocol conveys the functions required by subnetworks such as X.25 and local networks. The next higher, or subnetwork dependent convergence protocol, supports convergence functions. The third or subnetwork independent convergence protocol does the routing functions.*

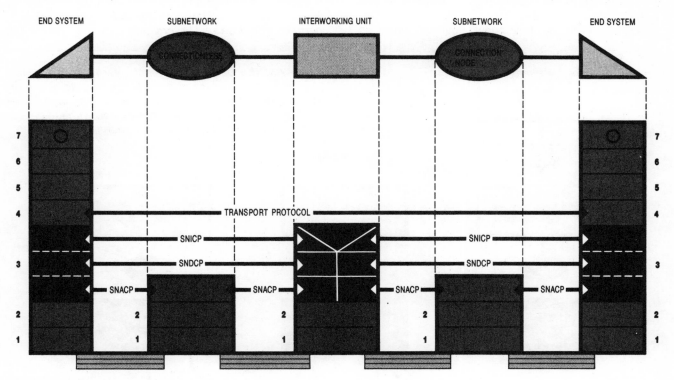

SNACP = SUBNETWORK ACCESS PROTOCOL
SNDCP = SUBNETWORK DEPENDENT CONVERGENCE PROTOCOL
SNICP = SUBNETWORK INDEPENDENT CONVERGENCE PROTOCOL

6. Link queue model. *The link protocol must perform error correction and recovery, and must generally establish the logical integrity of link-layer service.*

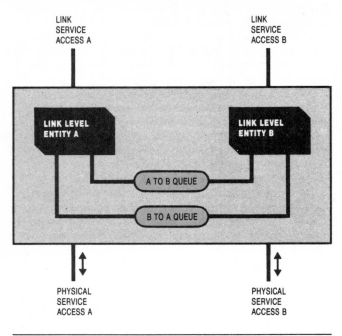

cedure) and LAPB of X.25 fame. Invariably, developments tend to be oriented to the HDLC group.

The physical layer encompasses established standards and concepts such as RS-232-C, RS-449, connectors such as ISO 2110 (for RS-232-C), and CCITT's V. and X. series. The layer's new section emphasizes that the physical layer is concerned with logical bits and does not cover analog conversions. The new architectural work on physical layer relaying (switching) and its control from the network layer is also more succinctly and understandably defined (Fig. 7) than in versions released earlier.

A physical layer service document, in keeping with OSI, is being prepared. This will fill the gap in the ranks of services documents and provide coordinating guidance in the rapid-paced developments in local networks, PBXs, and ISDN.

The reorganization of TC97 is well under way, reflecting the needs of changing technology in information sciences. The assignments of work to the subcommittees are established. The internal organization of SC21 (formerly SC16) will proceed carefully. The working groups have been brought into SC21 with their project assignments initially unchanged. The prime consideration is that the progress in standards development shall proceed unhindered.

The OSI management concepts and protocols require architectural work and protocol development. The simultaneous interworking of more than two open systems requires a great amount of work to be done; this is now in the early conceptual stages. Broadcast and N-way transmission have attained direction and are an indication of work to come. ■

Jerry Foley has been at Burroughs for eight years, where he is manager of communications networks, Systems Standards Engineering. He is also chairman of the U. S. Committee on OSI, and the founder of OSI work in the United States. He holds B. S. and M. S. degrees from Purdue University.

7. New at the bottom. *Physical layer relaying (switching) and its control from the network layer is now more succinctly and understandably defined. This layer's new section emphasizes that it is concerned with logical bits and does not cover analog conversions.*

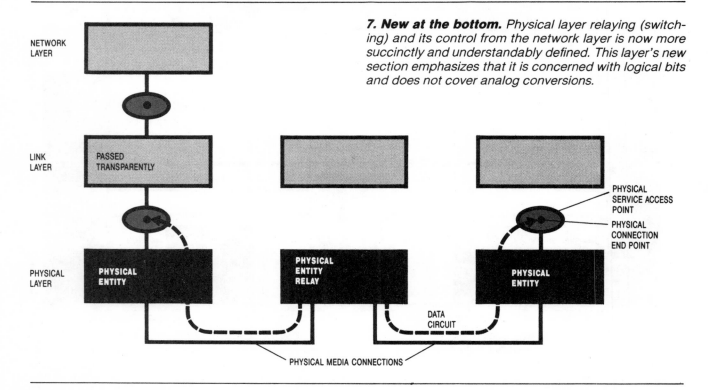

John M. McQuillan, McQuillan Consulting, and James G. Herman,
BBN Communications Corp., Cambridge, Mass.

Problems and opportunities in advanced data net architectures

What major design alternatives will be available to network architects for the next five years?

The changing data communications technology, regulations, pricing, and user requirements are the causes of both today's problems and opportunities in data network design. Some of the key developments of the last few years:

■ The AT&T divestiture has resulted in major disruptions in the planning and provisioning of telecommunications services—that is, both voice and data.

■ Lead times for getting service in the United States have grown, at times to as much as a year or more.

■ Local telephone company access charges have increased dramatically, as much as double or triple in some regions of the United States.

■ Long-distance and wideband services are becoming less expensive (by 10 to 20 percent per year), both for technical reasons and because of deregulation.

■ Large fiber optic networks are being installed in the United States and Europe, leading some observers to predict a glut of transmission capacity by the end of the decade.

■ Many carriers in the United States and Europe are shifting to measured service instead of dedicated lines or fixed-rate circuits.

With this background in mind, the authors recently investigated a number of different telecommunications technologies and services for a client. The findings can be summarized in two classes—those services that are especially attractive for the design of future private data networks, and those that offer little advantage.

Among the most attractive alternatives for the next five years is the development of software-controlled networks by AT&T and other carriers. An example of this is AT&T's Software Defined Network, which offers many of the advantages of a private network with additional customer control and flexibility—such as dynamically allocating bandwidth.

Another alternative uses V.32 modems capable of full-duplex transmission at 9.6 kbit/s over the public switched voice network. These devices, which debuted in 1985, offer service comparable to today's 300/1,200-bit/s modems at $2,000 to $3,000 and are available without ordering delays for any U. S. location.

A third alternative is access to private data networks obtained through national or regional packet networks. Such networks may have cost and performance advantages over the private lines in common use today.

Those not of the chosen

The authors have concluded that other technologies, services, and standards are less applicable:

■ High-speed digital services, at 1.544 Mbit/s in the United States or 2.048 Mbit/s in Europe, are not likely to be useful in most private data networks, since it is rare to find that much traffic flowing between two switching nodes. There do not appear to be any services planned in the "gap" between 64 kbit/s and 1.544 Mbit/s. Integrating voice and data thus appears to be the key to using the higher-speed, more cost-effective services.

■ Circuit-switched services at 56 kbit/s are attractive in theory but will not be widely available in the United States for several years. Small-scale experiments may be attractive here, but no major impact is foreseen.

■ Integrated Services Digital Network (ISDN) planning continues. Many ISDN advocates, especially in Europe, predict great things for the standard. However, the authors see major differences in the various national programs to build ISDN and many more years of development before the plans are fully realized. Most customers will not be greatly affected by ISDN until the late 1980s at the earliest.

■ Satellite services, once thought to be the wave of the

future offering limitless promise, are slowly being eclipsed by fiber optic technology. In the United States, several carriers are installing networks that are expected to consist of over 10,000 miles of fiber by 1986. The same kinds of projects are under way in many parts of Europe. Two transatlantic fiber cables are being installed. Satellite services now appear to be most useful for very long distances (1,000 miles or greater), broadcast communications, access to isolated locations, and providing diversity for increased reliability. Because fiber optic transmission has been slow to arrive in most parts of Europe, satellite services are especially useful there as an interim solution.

These observations about technology can be combined with the authors' conclusions on the prevailing thinking in telecommunications management: Most *Fortune* 500 customers are actively considering the integration of voice and data (see interview with OilCo below). The technology of T1 links and multiplexers makes this possible, while regulation and pricing trends make it a very desirable way to control costs. Also, bypass appears to be most useful when large amounts of traffic (indicated by the use of higher than 9.6 kbit/s or more than five voice lines) flow between hard-to-service or nearby locations (see BankCorp interview).

Another conclusion is that careful optimization of a large network (thousands of terminals) by a central staff may no longer be as effective as it was in the era of stable prices and predictable traffic (see interviews with OilCo and MidCo). AT&T points toward a new trend of "carrier management" rather than "network optimization"—the idea being that the carrier might be able to minimize costs in real time through a technique, such as a software-defined network (SDN), at least as well as the customer could by attempting optimal selection of individual lines. Ordering lines takes so long, traffic is so variable, and tariffs are so unpredictable that qualitative factors may dominate overall network planning. These factors include the ease of installation and the relationship of the user to the carrier.

Where go the smarts?

Furthermore, many organizations are reviewing the basic strategy of their networks: Should the intelligence (such as switching and control) be located on their premises or in the carrier's network? Some customers want to retain control (see OilCo interview), while others are best served by leaving the responsibility with the carrier (see BankCorp interview). This is equivalent to viewing AT&T as an intelligent network company on the one hand and a wire and cable company on the other.

Another key question for many organizations is the choice of public or private facilities for their telecommunications. Traditionally, many voice networks have relied on public switched services, while data networks have been built with dedicated private lines. Increasingly, customers are looking at private voice networks—with direct T1 interconnect among their digital PBXs—and public data networks. In the long run, the dominant trend seems to be toward hybrid

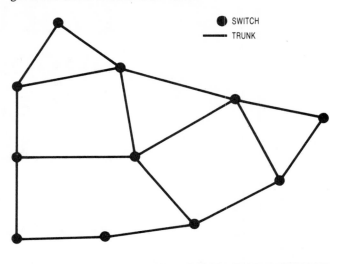

1. Reference network. *This is a simplified idealization of a current private network topology: a mesh of homogeneous trunk lines and switches.*

● SWITCH
— TRUNK

public/private networks (see MidCo interview). Remaining flexible, or "future-proof," is the byword for all the network planners interviewed.

One of the major U. S. petroleum companies, referred to anonymously here as OilCo, is recognized within its industry as applying many advanced-technology concepts through its innovative and insightful technical management. OilCo does not like the concept of a single large bill for telecommunications, such as might be provided with an SDN, because it is difficult both to unravel the cross-subsidization implicit in the bill and to charge back to the right users.

Overall, OilCo sees both significant benefits and disadvantages to SDN for various parts of the corporation. Therefore, it would be quite disruptive to introduce an SDN in its presently contemplated form. OilCo's current understanding is that the most limited version of SDN costs about the same as WATS does today, and that all the other intelligent services would cost more. Its present network costs 32 cents per minute, which is about 23 percent less than DDD (direct distance dialing).

This negative reaction to SDN does not mean that OilCo is not interested in some form of intelligent network with dynamic customer control. Its goals for such a network would include a constant economic charge and more readily understood billing and usage information for analysis and control. OilCo sees this happening sometime between 1988 and 1994. The key signposts for which they are watching include the behavior of the PUCs (public utility commissions) and the responses to AT&T filings on SDN.

One alternative to SDN pricing is the GTE advanced WATS service, which gives "banded" billing without volume bands per se. The GTE switch provides the ARS (automatic route select) function, which means that OilCo does not need to worry about pattern changes in its traffic (one of the selling points of SDN), just changes in overall volume. Thus, the GTE offering

2. Single heterogeneous. *The network could grow but remain as one, and it could evolve to include nodes and circuits of many different speeds and types.*

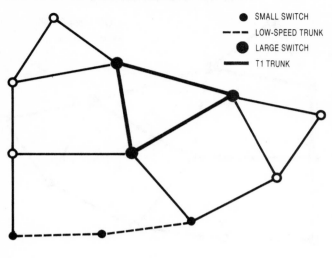

● SMALL SWITCH
- - - LOW-SPEED TRUNK
● LARGE SWITCH
—— T1 TRUNK

encapsulates much of the appeal of SDN for OilCo.

The company also expressed interest in intelligent networks offered by AT&T competitors, including that of Atlanta-based US Telecom. On the other hand, OilCo is not going to make changes in its network or vendors for just a 10 percent cost advantage.

Influenced by the public

Bypass is an issue that has received a great deal of attention within OilCo, but the conclusion is that bypass will probably not be an important alternative for the company. Consumer advocate groups are strong and well-organized locally, and they would make it very uncomfortable for OilCo if it engaged in much bypass. In fact, OilCo spoke of fears of "being crucified in the local newspapers." The reason for these fears and for the consumer interest is that bypass would reduce revenues of the local-exchange carrier, thereby causing an increase in local rates. For a prominent company such as OilCo, this public-relations disaster would offset any cash savings.

Bypass does not appear to be a practical alternative for OilCo except in rather limited and unusual circumstances. Specifically, it sees bypass (meaning its own installation, whether or not telephone company service is available) as helpful both for local interconnect and for access to wideband services. An example of the first type is a nine-mile T1 circuit OilCo installed because there was no local loop from downtown to its building. Similarly, at remote oil fields, it uses bypass because it has to. Basically, private networks are used for operational reasons, not to save money.

OilCo is a very large company (several billion dollars per year in revenues) but finds little incentive in the central sharing of telecommunications services. In fact, its managers have become firm believers in the virtues of decentralizing telecommunications responsibility. Again, they see that any resultant economies of scale and economies of sharing—for which they estimate

less than a 10 percent savings—are not worth the difficulty of building a highly coordinated centralized-management structure. In fact, OilCo feels that the 10 percent savings might well be outweighed by the expense of the additional central management. Further, the company feels it is nearly impossible to optimize today's networks to within 10 percent, for several reasons, including tariff and regulatory uncertainties and traffic unknowns.

OilCo's strategy is to:
■ Pick the technical architecture that best meets its anticipated future needs. This means integrated voice and data on high-speed digital trunks—T1 wherever cost-justified.
■ Leave till later the selection of vendors and products. Expect volatility, uncertainty, and political pressures. Be prepared to change the selection of vendors and products at any time. Stay short term in outlook.
■ Leave most decision making to local management. Optimization may be manageable at that level.
■ Go with public services wherever possible. Avoid squeezing the last 10 percent of cost by private optimization, since it is usually illusory or impossible.
■ Evolve toward a diverse network in 1990 with premises-based intelligence and dynamic control. Treat AT&T as a wire-and-cable company, rather than as an SDN supplier, and go with MCI and GTE wherever they are better. Avoid resellers who do not own their own transmission capacity. Use Intecom and other digital PBXs, but do not pick a single corporate standard.
■ Use bypass only where it is strongly indicated, such as in very local settings (under 20 miles) and in multiple-T1 traffic regions.

Keeping Telpak alive

The authors had a very helpful discussion with the telecommunications manager at a major regional bank (referred to anonymously as BankCorp). This bank enjoys a very favorable Telpak rate structure in its state and a set of bank requirements for voice and data that are well-matched to Telpak. (Telpak—a telephone company service not available in every state—offers discounts for multiple circuits between the same two points.) The BankCorp network appears to take advantage of these fortunate circumstances.

Furthermore, the telecommunications management has taken vigorous action to protect the Telpak offering in the face of repeated telephone company efforts to cancel it. Finally, management has adequate contingency plans in place to bypass telephone companies at various places in the network should that become necessary. Divestiture and technological advances have resulted in a difficult planning environment. BankCorp has done a fine job of planning, building, and operating a cost-effective telecommunications network.

The major finding is that BankCorp is a telecommunications customer of the Bell operating companies (BOCs) with characteristics well-matched to the BOCs' offerings—all of BankCorp's locations are population centers the BOC must serve, and traffic is roughly proportional to community populations. Even if tariffs rise considerably, BankCorp intends to plan the design of a BOC-based Electronic Tandem Network (ETN), a central-office switching configuration. (An ETN is a voice network based on customer PBXs.)

BankCorp does not appear to benefit as much as some organizations from such alternatives as bypass (no hard-to-service routes and not enough traffic concentration over short distances—less than 20 miles), premises-based ETNs (not enough purely local traffic), and AT&T's SDN (insufficient traffic fluctuations). Thus, BankCorp will attempt to work with the BOCs rather than against them. Of course, this has been the BankCorp strategy all along.

BankCorp is the second-largest telephone customer in its state, after the state government, spending over $10 million a year with various telephone companies. BankCorp is also a state banking leader. Thus, BankCorp is in an excellent position of strength when it comes to contractual discussions with telephone companies. Management has done an exemplary job of capitalizing on this strength to win concessions from the Public Service Commission and the telephone companies. The key accomplishment has been the defeat of all moves to drop the Telpak service. Management has used the leverage of BankCorp as a large and influential customer to keep the favorable rate structure in place.

A second important consideration in understanding the success of the BankCorp network is to recognize that its technical requirements for the network are quite uniform throughout the state. The main function of the network is to provide voice and data service to over 300 branches. Most branches look very much the same from a telecommunications standpoint. They require a few voice lines and a few data lines. All data service originates out of headquarters. The one major exception to this simple overview is that there are a small number of regional data centers for data capture and print. These can readily be handled by the same network. The major growth requirements for the network are the addition of new branches as the bank expands and the addition of new lines for new terminals as individual branches expand. The basic nature of the network need not change to accommodate this incremental growth.

Like a tree

BankCorp operates a single Telpak backbone network that reaches all its branches, and provides both voice and data services. The network is structured as a branching tree, with BankCorp headquarters at the root. Because of the nature of the bulk-discount Telpak tariff, most segments of the network have excess capacity. For example, if 100 circuits are required from A to B, the network would be configured with 120 (priced according to Telpak). What this means, in practice, is that much of the data traffic is carried at little or no incremental cost to BankCorp—the extra circuits would be paid for anyway.

The network has been designed with several important simplifications. Each of BankCorp's major data applications—teller, 3270, and ATM (automated teller

3. Two-level hierarchical. *The network could be comprised of a T1 backbone that is linked to many 56-kbit/s regional and metropolitan subnetworks.*

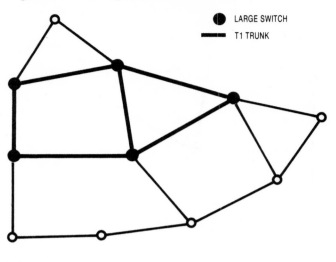

● LARGE SWITCH
▬ T1 TRUNK

machine)—is run on its own network, with its own circuits from headquarters to a branch. Most branches have one terminal on each network. The Telpak tariff provides economies of scale in pricing, so that the apparent inefficiency of running three separate lines all the way from headquarters to each branch is actually not inefficient.

There are none of the complications that might result from dual use of circuits in the daytime and at night for different functions. The multidrop lines usually run all the way to the local serving office before drops are made in a very small local area (a few miles radius), so there is no need for more advanced switching or multiplexing. In short, the network does not use very much in the way of advanced communications control hardware, and it does not need to do so.

It is interesting and important to note that while the "extra" Telpak circuits on the major traffic routes are being paid for anyway, they are not actually there until BankCorp orders them. Telpak is just a pricing policy and does not reflect the provisioning realities inside the telephone company. Thus, BankCorp is taking advantage of the economies of scale in the tariff itself.

Most conventional telecommunications planning centers around the search for economies of scale in the technology (such as the use of faster lines and bigger switches). BankCorp has chosen to seek economies of scale on the financial side, not the technical side. The principle is the same, with the financial side actually being easier for BankCorp, since the telephone company, rather than BankCorp, has the responsibility of managing the internals of the Telpak network.

The fact that BankCorp's network is actually three separate, rather simple networks is not to imply that its design and operation is an easy task. Rather, telecommunications management has wisely simplified the planning of this large and expensive communications entity. There are very few special cases, exceptions to the rules, or other labor-intensive projects. Management's attention has rightly been focused on operating the network to meet the bank's needs at a reasonable cost and with a small staff and streamlined operations, wherever possible.

Fill those requirements

BankCorp's strategy is based on meeting the two objectives of quality service and low cost. Management has met these objectives through concentration on a few key services. Recent user surveys confirm that the requirements of the regions are being met, and that local managements are satisfied with BankCorp's performance.

The second part of the strategy is to maintain BankCorp's strong bargaining position by conducting various experiments—primarily in local bypass—thereby sending a clear message to all parties that BankCorp is prepared to bypass the telephone companies if good service cannot be obtained from them at a reasonable price. It is essential that such experiments continue, and that BankCorp make good on one or two threats to bypass.

The authors were impressed by the quality of BankCorp's telecommunications planning. The network appears to be an excellent solution to the bank's requirements. It is based on strong bargaining for good financial terms and on operational simplifications, rather than technology-based economies and solutions. Many uncertainties remain for the telecommunications industry in the next five years; BankCorp is well-positioned to meet the challenges that lie ahead.

MidCo is the fictitious name of a prominent $6 billion-a-year conglomerate that participates in many different industries. MidCo can be considered to be a collection of about 100 diverse companies with very loose central management. The company focuses primarily on ser-

---

4. Multilevel hierarchical. *The network could consist of a two-level hierarchy plus LANs and 9.6-kbit/s (or lower) accesses to public data networks.*

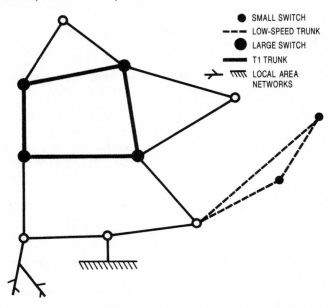

- ● SMALL SWITCH
- - - - LOW-SPEED TRUNK
- ⬤ LARGE SWITCH
- ▬▬ T1 TRUNK
- ⊼ ⊼⊼⊼⊼ LOCAL AREA NETWORKS

---

vices and activities relating to financial reporting and control.

MidCo has approached data communications on a decentralized basis. Each data center has installed its own network to meet its own specific requirements. There is very little information flowing between data centers, and little or no data communications coordination between them. One application dominates MidCo's present data communications approach: a large national query/response network for customers all over the United States. This network is much larger than any of MidCo's others.

Several MidCo affiliates have SNA (IBM's Systems Network Architecture) networks, but none of these is large (no more than three mainframes), and none is connected to any of the other MidCo networks. There is no common data network of any kind, but there is a common voice network. The corporate culture is such that the companies in the field suspect and resent any large build-up of staff or expenditure of funds in a central organization. They value their independence and would like to be left alone to run their own business and make money.

In 1983, the company established a task force to study its internal data communications. The task force developed a survey form to collect information on the applications supported by data communications, the hardware and software employed, current costs and problems, and future plans. The survey was mailed to over 100 MidCo people worldwide.

Current spending on data communications is not large for a company of MidCo's size and geographic distribution. (Typically, companies spend upwards of 0.5 percent of revenues on data communications.) The three most significant areas of spending analyzed by the task force were for leased lines supporting the query/response network ($120,000 per month), leased lines for 14 data centers' IBM networks ($70,000 per month), and total charges for the companywide electronic-mail network ($65,000 per month). (Note that the total cost of the terminals, computers, and associated communications equipment far exceeded—by about an order of magnitude—that of the communications lines. The study focused on line costs, because it was the one optimizable component of total costs.) When dial-up communications and purchased network services are added, the optimizable portion of MidCo's current costs reaches about $4 million annually.

Cannot improve

The task force concluded that there was very little opportunity to reduce cost or improve service if the management of data communications remained decentralized. Most of the discrete networks were well-optimized. Any gains were marginal and hardly worth the effort.

However, when the requirements of MidCo were viewed on a companywide basis, a different picture began to take shape. The requirements represented by the 14 discrete IBM networks were fed into an IBM modeling program that designed a companywide IBM network capable of interconnecting and supporting all 14 data centers in the domestic United States. This network would save leased-line costs, but the savings would be offset by newly incurred network-management costs.

When planned new requirements were added to the corporate network model, it became clear that MidCo had reached the data communications "critical mass" stage. By supporting the communications requirements for one new data center through the corporate network model—instead of installing another discrete network for the center—it was possible to save $450,000 a year. Four new leased lines planned by one division could be added to the network at a savings of $45,000 per year. Because of the geographic coverage provided by the network model, most new data communications requirements could be supported at significantly less cost if such a network were in place.

Much of the justification for changing the way MidCo manages data communications deals with future cost avoidance. By pooling requirements and sharing resources, MidCo as a whole can manage communications costs better than any single data center can on its own. One way is by sharing capacity and aggregating multiple low-speed circuits into more cost-effective high-speed circuits. By centralizing at least the planning and management aspects, MidCo can better position itself to deal with the post-divestiture world in which communications management has become significantly more complex.

Total information processing costs would be reduced if data centers would share applications. One division, through the network, could access an application that exists on another's machine, rather than purchase a second copy of software for itself.

Finally, there is a compelling argument for managing data communications on a companywide basis: The network model has shown that significant cost savings are possible by consolidating the 14 discrete IBM networks into one. One divison has an extensive query/response network in place today, with many hundreds of terminals throughout the country. The electronic-mail application is running on a third large network. The company is planning the best way to support IBM customers throughout the United States.

When this is all tallied, MidCo is looking at managing anywhere from four to 17 discrete data communications networks—all of which require and provide the same geographic coverage. If the planned new requirements are added to this picture, it is clear that MidCo should start managing data communications as a companywide resource.

While the cost benefits are not large today (less than a 10 percent savings), the task force felt that MidCo should begin to position itself to realize the cost savings that will be possible in the near future. Furthermore, the value of companywide networking extends to benefits that are difficult to quantify. Networking would enable such benefits as applications sharing, support of links between business operations in the field and staff-level management, and electronic-mail applications.

Networking could facilitate the development of indi-

5. Multihomogeneity. The configuration could be of several different, specialized networks. Simple, low-traffic gateways may connect them where needed.

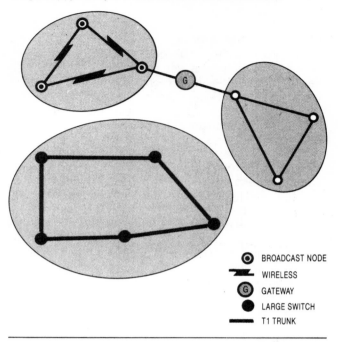

⊙ BROADCAST NODE
⟋ WIRELESS
Ⓖ GATEWAY
● LARGE SWITCH
▬ T1 TRUNK

vidual centers that could specialize with their own applications and avoid duplicate software purchases. Networking could also ease the data center disaster/recovery process and support the notion of regional data centers. Networking could be used to a competitive advantage if it provided fast and efficient links between MidCo's suppliers, distributors, and customers. Perhaps the benefit of managing data communications on a companywide basis that is most difficult to quantify is the strategic value of being able to move information quickly, accurately, and cost-effectively throughout the company.

Keep a lean staff
The task force made several recommendations on what MidCo should do over the next two years to improve its data communications position. These include building a small staff (no more than five people) at the company level to coordinate the planning, management, implementation, and operation of the company's data communications networks. This staff would have to draw heavily on support from the field for implementation and operations. (Because considerable resources would be required, a more realistic company-level staff of about 20 was not seen to be practical or acceptable to management at this time.)

Another recommendation was to develop long-range communications plans that would include the development of goals, organization, and roles and responsibilities. The plans would also include the design of an architecture and standards for MidCo's future communications networks.

A third recommendation was to temporarily adopt a two-network strategy:

6. Super gateways. *A configuration could evolve into networks connected by multifunction gateways and consolidated into a mesh "network of networks."*

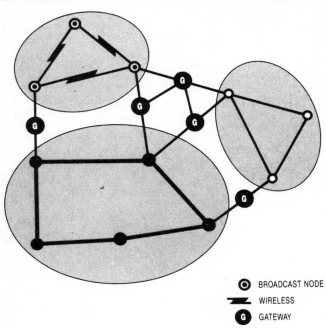

- ◎ BROADCAST NODE
- ⚡ WIRELESS
- Ⓖ GATEWAY

■ Implement a companywide IBM network interconnecting the major data centers in the domestic United States. This would be done with the planned new requirements in mind and in close cooperation with existing network designs to see if synergies exist.
■ Investigate the feasibility of extending the query/response network to support internal MidCo requirements, including the electronic-mail application.

In summary, there is considerable benefit to managing data communications on a companywide basis. In addition to future cost avoidance, efficient and cost-effective communications would improve revenues and provide a competitive advantage.

MidCo will continue to investigate the possibility of a corporate network combining voice and data, or a network combining the data traffic from several applications. The most attractive alternatives at this point include premises-based products similar to AT&T's Digital Access Cross-connect System (DACS) that combine the SNA traffic with other private lines.

There are certain basic issues that appear to be common in many network design decisions, including the three situations described above. These issues can be synthesized into a series of decisions about network architecture. The following six categories, each requiring several decisions, proceed from the most general topics—those with the broadest impact—to more specific issues:
1. Major policy questions.
2. Number of networks.
3. Structure of each network.
4. Network topology.
5. Switching technology.
6. Transmission technologies.

Decision: Network design charter—extended or not? Historically, the charter for telecommunications management in many organizations has included responsibility for long-distance services, but not for local communications, terminal equipment, or other customer-premises facilities. If this charter changes, it could have a major influence on network architecture.

Decision: Network architectural boundaries—where do they stop? The limits of network architecture must be clearly defined. For example, do they include host interfaces, host software, public services, or any local communications such as local area networks (LANs) and private branch exchanges (PBXs)?

Decision: Planning approach—active or reactive? Many networks are built around some original plan, often with detailed assumptions about the subscribers who would use the network. If these assumptions no longer correspond well with the realities, telecommunications management commonly chooses to react to users' requests. Developing a future architecture would be greatly facilitated if a definite target market of users were chosen initially, rather than the planners having to follow the market where it leads.

There is great value in responding to user needs. However, if the formal policy is actually to be one of maximum responsiveness, then the network architecture must be designed to accommodate unforeseen changes. Responsiveness is not inconsistent with good planning; therefore, planning efforts should evolve as users' needs develop.

Decision: One network or several networks? To date, most corporate data networks have evolved as a collection of networks, with some linked by gateways. This can continue, or they could be designed as a single network. Alternatively, the strategy could be to develop a collection of many more networks than are presently installed. There are several ways to break one network into different networks:
■ By traffic type, especially voice versus data and interactive data versus batch.
■ By community of interest, such as engineering and customer service.
■ By transmission medium, such as satellite, terrestrial, or local microwave.
■ By security level, especially in the military.
■ By switching and routing technology, such as circuit switching, datagram packet switching, or virtual circuit packet switching.
■ By geographical region, such as the United States, Europe, or the Pacific.
■ By data processing applications.

Decision: Unconnected networks or interconnected networks? Some of the divisions suggested above would lead to relatively low traffic levels between networks. This raises the possibility of several unconnected networks. In practice, isolating all constituent networks seems impractical. Rather, certain networks could remain independent from all others.

Decision: Simple gateways or super gateways? A more highly interconnected network of gateways, with the gateways forming a kind of network of networks, is another prospect. In this type of architecture, the super gateways assume the functionality of today's packet switches, including routing and congestion control.

Decision: Hierarchical or single-level topology? In striving for an architecture that permits rapid and flexible growth, one solution is building a network with two or more hierarchical levels. A "highway" scheme could provide for general long-distance connectivity, while at the next level down, "roadways" would be installed where traffic needs dictated.

This network structure presents certain concerns: For reliability reasons, for example, it must be possible to bypass the highways if they are unavailable and to reach the destinations entirely by roadways. Also, when network size grows into the thousands of nodes, this arrangement provides a simpler design and implementation than a single-level scheme.

Decision: Hierarchical or single-size switches? The highway discussed above can be constructed of a hub network of T1 lines, interconnecting regional packet switches. Compatible nodes will be needed to fully exploit these fast circuits. However, the presence of two different kinds of packet switches in the network introduces further operational complexities and adds to development and maintenance costs.

Decision: A few (tens), many (hundreds), or very many (thousands) switches? For simplicity's sake, it is tempting to design a network with relatively few switches, perhaps 10 or less. In this scenario, site operations costs fall, labor requirements are minimized, and topological design is simplified. However, this structure requires many expensive access circuits. (Generally, the fewer the switches, the longer—and therefore, the more costly—the access circuits.) Most importantly, this kind of network architecture lacks sufficient reliability—one switch failure affects many more subscribers than if there were more switches for the same number of subscribers.

An important question remains: Is a network with 100 nodes preferable to one with 1,000 smaller ones? The point of diminishing returns must exist for reliabilty. Certain trade-offs must be made between reliability and economy of scale.

Decision: Uniform access at each site or separate access for each subscriber type? Aggregating traffic at a given site takes advantage of economies of scale inherent in access-circuit tariffs and represents the future direction of ISDN. This is particularly true for locations that might require T1 offerings. If, for other reasons, the plan is structured in the form of a number of separate networks segregated by community of interest, it may be necessary to offer separate access points at a site, each requiring its own circuit.

Decision: Dynamic or fixed topology? New technologies—such as packet-satellite schemes using shared transponder capacity or AT&T's SDN—provide a dynamically controlled network topology. This appears to be an ideal answer to the need for rapid deployment of interconnections. It also promises, throughout the network, transmission costs lower than those of fixed topologies designed far in advance.

To exploit these new services, the architecture would have to be expanded to include some form of semi-

7. Shared trunking. *The configuration could evolve as a number of networks, segregated by applications or some other factor, but sharing common trunking.*

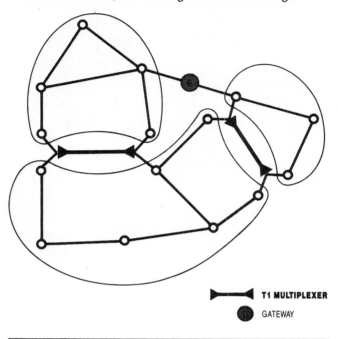

◄━━━► **T1 MULTIPLEXER**

● GATEWAY

automatic performance-monitoring and -modeling capability. This scheme would provide decision support for the manager invoking topological changes.

Decison: Vendor-supplied or internally provided dynamic topology? Some users are investigating establishing their own dynamically controllable circuit-switching capability. If technically feasible, this step could lessen dependence on AT&T while increasing network reliability.

Decision: Demand or dedicated services? In the past, most private data networks have been built exclusively with dedicated circuits. Demand services will include possibilities such as dial-up 56-kbit/s service. Although still new, these services appear very attractive. Even if switched 56-kbit/s service is not widely available for several years, there will soon be many vendors offering full-duplex 9.6-kbit/s modems for dial-up lines.

The decision to rely on demand services instead of dedicated lines for more than about 20 percent of the network would have major consequences for architecture. For example, a new real-time monitoring and control mechanism to manage such services would have to be designed and built. Necessarily, it would be computerized, since manual intervention would be too slow for the switching in each case.

This innovation could greatly affect the rest of the network technologies, including routing, congestion control, network monitoring and control, and security. There are also implications for network topological design. If demand services achieve their promise, then the topology could be altered in real time. New topological-design tools will be needed.

Decision: Integration at the switch or at the transmission level? There are two kinds of networks for integrated voice and data. The first performs integrated switching of traffic, bit by bit or packet by packet. The second is simpler: Separate switching is performed on two traffic types. Then, traffic is combined at the transmission level by some kind of multiplexing device.

Decision: Packet switching only or a hybrid of packet and circuit switching? Not all data traffic is suitable for packet switching. Furthermore, there are new traffic sources not previously considered in many data networks, such as facsimile and videoconferencing data. Such traffic poses an attractive addition to the network as a whole because, in principle, it can share the backbone with packet traffic.

At some point in the future most network designs should offer both packet and circuit switching. The real decisions are: *When* should both capabilities be present, and *how* should the transition to the new services be managed?

Decision: Broadcast or point-to-point services? Some transmission possibilities being considered permit broadcast communications in addition to point-to-point. This technique is attractive in certain circumstances. In a hierarchical network architecture, for example, a broadcast backbone creates flexibility in bandwidth allocation not present in a point-to-point network. It may offer a more cost-effective way of handling broadcast traffic, such as messages to large address lists. This usage requires new logic in the packet-switching subnetwork.

Such broadcast transmission may be somewhat less reliable than traditional approaches, because a single failure would eliminate many communications paths.

---

8. Dynamic control. *The network could be based on a scheme that provides dynamic reconfiguration in response to changes in traffic patterns and user needs.*

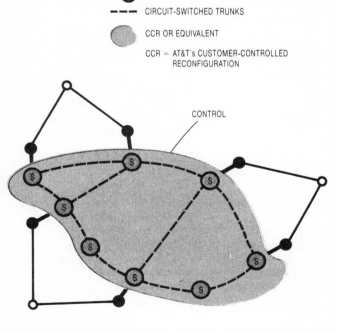

● SERVICE NODES OF CIRCUIT-SWITCHING NETWORK

--- CIRCUIT-SWITCHED TRUNKS

⬭ CCR OR EQUIVALENT

CCR = AT&T's CUSTOMER-CONTROLLED RECONFIGURATION

CONTROL

Satellite schemes seem especially vulnerable: They are subject to a single point of failure, the earth station or the satellite. However, a mix of broadcast and point-to-point offerings could be considered for most situations.

Decision: Use public data networks? If so, for access or as trunking? Public data networks (PDNs) could play an important role in many implementations. In the United States, public networks offer access to hundreds of locations on a cost-effective basis. Even if PDNs are not the primary means of subscriber access, they can provide rapid installation or expansion for users whose requirements are difficult to forecast. Now that the BOCs are able to offer packet networks and PADs (packet assemblers/disassemblers), the use of regional PDNs is likely to grow.

It is less likely that private data networks can use public X.25 facilities for interswitch trunking. Most private-network switches communicate over physical circuits, not virtual ones, so that the use of PDNs as trunks would necessitate some new development. Current interswitch protocols make no attempt to minimize circuit usage (because they were designed for dedicated circuits) and would be costly if operated over a public data network.

Nevertheless, most private networks will probably have numerous gateways to X.25 public networks so subscribers can access various public information services, databases, and document-distribution facilities.

Decision: Use T1 circuits? Clearly, both recent price reductions and wider installation of T1 circuits suggest increasing the use of these facilities. But some questions arise:
■ Should T1 circuits replace individual 56-kbit/s trunks on a case-by-case basis, or should a backbone network constructed entirely of T1 circuits be designed? In either case, improvements to routing and congestion control are needed.
■ Should T1 circuits be used as single channels or as a collection of multiple 56-kbit/s circuits?
■ Should bandwidth on T1 circuits be shared among several networks?

Decision: Dial-up access for terminals, for computers, or for neither? Many data communications networks today permit terminal users to dial in to network ports. Security and authentication needs must be met, often with passwords or dial-back schemes. With higher speeds available, either with 9.6- or 56-kbit/s switched digital service, it becomes practical to connect multi-user host computers by dial-up links. Several scenarios are possible, including partial-period use, dial backup for restoral, and parallel dial links for additional capacity. Each of these alternatives has implications for network architecture and protocols.

Decision: Use bypass or all-carrier services? Bypass of carrier facilities has become an important issue with the recent price increases for local service and the long installation lead times in some locations. Facilities bypass makes sense when the customer locations are hard to service by carrier offerings. It is also cost-effective for very short distances in some metropolitan areas (across a Manhattan street, for example). Bypass involves a trade-off between the problems of depending on the carrier and the headaches of managing facilities oneself.

The network architectures described and illustrated below indicate the range of choices for most designers at this time. The order of presentation proceeds from relatively simple architectures to more complex designs.

Architectural alternatives

To provide a frame of reference, Figure 1 provides an idealization of a present private data network topology: a mesh of homogeneous trunks and switches. Actually, this network diagram is simplified to omit the complexities of the several networks within most companies and government agencies and the associated access networks.

The network could grow simply by adding more of today's circuits and packet switches. The present topology would extend and enlarge without changing in its fundamental concept. T1 circuits, demand services, satellites, public data networks, and other new possibilities would not be included in this architecture.

The advantages of this conservative approach include: simplicity of planning and implementation; low implementation risk, although area routing and similar changes would be needed; new types of hardware and software not required, if expected traffic growth is modest (less than 25 percent per year); and a relatively reliable architecture.

The disadvantages include: placing definite limits on growth, although these limits are difficult to pinpoint in advance (problems are likely in routing, topological design, and network management); possible unsatisfactory performance of interactive traffic because of the large number of intermediate switches on the average path (this problem could be solved, but not without adding new circuits between the most distant pairs of switches—an expensive solution); possible unsatisfactory support of bulk traffic (the 56-kbit/s trunks must be shared by thousands of subscribers); and the many new services not exploited by this concept.

The present network could increase in scale by a factor of 10 to 20 simply either by installing much faster packet switches and circuits in place of today's equipment or by adding circuits and nodes in the same locations. The resulting network would support roughly the same number of nodes and lines as today, but it would have a greater traffic capacity. Terrestrial and satellite offerings in the T1 range would be used. PDNs probably would not be employed. Demand services might not be useful, except for AT&T's Accunet Reserved 1.5, a reservation offering for 30-minute usage blocks of T1 service.

The advantages of this network are as follows:
■ By maintaining network size, the many problems of larger network design, such as topological layout, routing, and network monitoring and control, are avoided.
■ This strategy would take advantage of significant economies of scale.

The disadvantages of this network are as follows:

■ It would not be cost-effective to increase the scale of all sites by the same factor, so some small switches and slow lines—especially overseas—would inevitably remain.
■ There are significant development costs and risks associated with the use of a new class of switches to build an entirely new network.
■ If the traffic is widely dispersed, this approach leads to increased costs for access circuits to the large switches.
■ Finally, this architecture threatens reliability for a network with, say, 10 times the present subscriber base. (Failure of one node or circuit would disrupt 10 times the previous number of subscribers.)

One heterogeneous network

The network could evolve into a single large network including nodes and circuits of many different speeds and types (Fig. 2). Many new services dicussed above would be utilized.

The advantages of this network are as follows:
■ In theory, such a network presents potentially the lowest cost and the best performance, since global optimization can be performed for the entire network.
■ Innovative services can be employed wherever they are appropriate.
■ Consolidating the total pool of communications resources in one network that is available to any subscriber enhances reliability.

The disadvantages of this network are as follows:
■ Such a network would not be simple to operate, monitor, and control.
■ Routing and congestion control might be difficult, since heterogeneity leads to greater possibilities for congestion wherever traffic flows encounter restrictive circuits or switches.
■ Implementation risk rises slightly when compared to the earlier alternatives. A gradual evolution from a network with all small components to one with mixed sizes minimizes this risk.

In a less ambitious step than the previous one, the network could be comprised of a T1 backbone linked to many 56-kbit/s regional and metropolitan-area subnetworks (Fig. 3). Some regions have high enough traffic volumes to justify T1 trunks locally. Demand services at both levels augment dedicated trunking. The scenario also includes satellites and two different sizes of packet switches, which are used in the backbone.

The advantages of this network are as follows:
■ Greater cost-effectiveness can be achieved with T1 service.
■ The simplicity of this structure makes planning, management, and control more straighforward.

The disadvantages of this network are as follows:
■ This structure may not function beyond the United States, where T1 circuits are not readily available.
■ A high-bandwidth backbone may not provide adequate reliability—one T1-circuit failure would disrupt service to 24 or more subchannels.

The multilevel hierarchical network could consist of a T1 backbone, many 56-kbit/s metropolitan and regional networks, plus LANs and low-speed (9.6 kbit/s or less) access to PDNs (Fig. 4). Each hierarchical level is clearly demarcated in topological planning. Several different-speed nodes, concentrators, bridges, and other switches are employed.

The advantages of this network are as follows:
■ The network's architectural boundaries extend into the local area.
■ At each level of the hierarchy, appropriate technology can be used without needing to support all of the network's different transmission technologies.
■ Cost-effective performance can be achieved by using megabit-per-second services.
■ A hierarchical network may be more easily managed by the traditional hierarchical approach to management present in many companies and agencies.

The disadvantages of this network are as follows:
■ This kind of approach may demand too much of a development effort, and, therefore, increase the risk of failure.
■ Reliability would require many links between components to bypass the simple hierarchical concept.
■ This structure may not function beyond the United States, since the required megabit-per-second circuits are not readily available.

Combining homogeneous nets
The network could be constructed of several specialized networks. If the traffic level between these networks is relatively low (using less than 9.6-kbit/s circuits), they can be connected by simple gateways. Individual network architectures would vary considerably, reflecting the geographical locations, traffic patterns, and performance requirements (Fig. 5). For instance, one might be highly centralized while another would be more distributed. Thus, each network would be homogeneous within its boundaries, but might radically differ from the other constituent networks in terms of the transmission media, speeds, or switching technology.

The advantages of this network are as follows:
■ Each network is kept to a manageable size and can be designed around present node and line technologies.
■ Implementation risk falls within each network.

The disadvantages of this network are as follows:
■ Overall implementation risk may increase because the integration of disparate networks into a functioning whole would represent a pioneering accomplishment.
■ Periodically, as individual networks grow, the overall network would need to be repartitioned — a difficult operation.
■ The individual networks do not enjoy the economy of scale inherent in a single network.

The network could become many networks, specialized as needed, interconnected by super (multifunction) gateways consolidated into a mesh "network of networks." The gateways perform many packet-switching functions — including routing and congestion control — treating the networks as virtual circuits between gateways (Fig. 6). As in the previous case, the networks might be quite disparate internally.

The advantages of this network are as follows:
■ The government protocol standard, TCP/IP (transmission control protocol/internet protocol), was specifically designed for this kind of internetwork application. The DARPA (Defense Advanced Research Project Agency) internetwork is based on this technology.
■ It might be possible to optimize architectures to particular purposes. For example, certain applications require quick response times — less than 0.25 second. A dedicated fast-response network could be provided for some subscribers, even though the expense would preclude it for the entire subscriber base.

The disadvantages of this network are as follows:
■ Such super gateways represent a relatively immature technology.
■ This architecture may not adapt well to commercially available protocols that were not designed with super gateways in mind.

Sharing trunks
The network could evolve as a number of separate networks, segregated by community of interest, technology, or other factors. All networks share common trunking facilities. These are typically built out of T1 circuits that can be allocated in 56-kbit/s channels to particular networks by using T1 multiplexers. Each network retains some number of dedicated lower-speed circuits for access to locations unique to its community (Fig. 7). Some networks are interconnected by gateways.

The advantages of this network are as follows:
■ Use of shared trunking and T1 facilities should result in significant cost savings.
■ Each network is kept to a manageable size and can be designed around present node and line technologies.
■ Implementation risk is reduced since the data switches are interconnected by 56-kbit/s subchannels, rather than by the T1 channels themselves.

The disadvantages of this network are as follows:
■ Segregating the user population may be impossible without generating excessive gateway traffic.
■ As individual networks grow, they may require repartitioning — a difficult operation.
■ Topological optimization becomes an even more complicated problem than it already is. (Circuit layout and optimization are more complex for networks with shared trunking than for individual networks.)
■ The sharing is fixed over time, so traffic on one network cannot "borrow" trunking from other networks in times of overload or network failure.

Demand services
The network could become a sparsely connected network of dedicated circuits, with a "minimum spanning tree" to connect major sites. Demand services could carry traffic efficiently, as needed. The dedicated backbone might be 56 kbit/s or T1. Demand services could serve all speed ranges. Public data networks could play a major role in this scenario.

The advantages of this network are as follows:
■ If practical, such a network might substantially lower

the costs, depending on the traffic volumes.
■ Rapid deployment would be achieved in response to changing user needs.
■ This network exploits the trends to measured service and to more intelligence in public services.

The disadvantages of this network are as follows:
■ The reliability of such an architecture is questionable, since it relies heavily on a small number of vendor services and on the continuing operation of a limited number of vendor control centers.
■ Contention for service may preclude access for priority traffic.
■ Demand services are not globally available, so this architecture would need to be combined with more conventional approaches overseas.

The network could be based on AT&T's Customer Controlled Reconfiguration (CCR) or some other third-party service equivalent to CCR. This would provide dynamic reconfiguration of the network in reponse to changing traffic patterns, user requirements, or network component availability. (AT&T's SDN and competitive services from other carriers also offer this capability. CCR is limited to direct customer commands entered at a keyboard; SDN has more capabilities, such as automatic procedures.) Megabit-per-second services could be employed, and CCR would control the use of the 24 subchannels on each T1 line (Fig. 8). Both satellite and terrestrial circuits could be employed, in addition to demand and X.25 services.

The advantages of this network are as follows:
■ This network promises lower costs by allowing purchased bandwidth to be directed at specific needs at specific times.
■ The network could be deployed with a high degree of flexibility.
■ With excess capacity, dynamic control can provide restoral after failures. Quality of service and reliability would improve over other schemes, as a result. High bandwidth could be allocated only as needed.
■ This approach could be used in conjunction with dynamic shared trunking for several networks.

The disadvantages of this network are as follows:
■ The implementation risk of this approach is difficult to analyze without more field experience with the CCR technology.
■ The CCR network control center is a single point of potential failure.
■ Topological optimization becomes more complicated.

A hybrid solution

The network could be designed with a high-speed (such as T1, where cost-justified) backbone using both packet and circuit switching. Dynamic trunking would be utilized with T1 channels wherever they are cost-effective. Individual 56-kbit/s subchannels would be dynamically assigned, either to packet switching or to circuit switching. A similar approach would apply to host-access circuits, which would support both types of data traffic simultaneously. Just as in the case of backbone trunking, CCR would be employed for T1 host-access lines (Fig. 9).

The advantages of this network are as follows:

9. Hybrid. A T1 backbone could use both packet and circuit switching, and individual 56-kbit/s subchannels would be dynamically assigned to either.

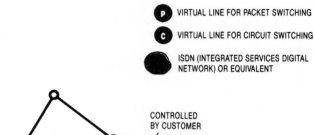

P — VIRTUAL LINE FOR PACKET SWITCHING

C — VIRTUAL LINE FOR CIRCUIT SWITCHING

● — ISDN (INTEGRATED SERVICES DIGITAL NETWORK) OR EQUIVALENT

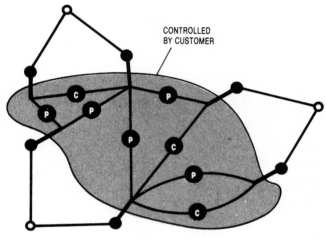

CONTROLLED BY CUSTOMER

■ This architecture neatly matches traffic characteristics with technical solutions.
■ It follows the PTT (Postal Telegraph and Telephone agency) trend to ISDN worldwide.
■ The network users would enjoy substantial economies of sharing.

The disadvantages of this network are as follows:
■ This new approach creates a sizable implementation risk. Several technical issues would need resolution, including the routing, topological design, and network management problems.
■ Integrated host access to the new services represents a new, unproven development.
■ The control of this network may also present a single point of potential failure, unless duplicate facilities are installed. ■

In a subsequent companion article, the authors will present a recommended architecture for one particular private network they recently helped to design. The proposed solution integrates three of the architectures described above.

Dr. John McQuillan, president of his own consulting firm, has authored over 100 papers, reports, and presentations on computer communications and office automation. He holds undergraduate and Ph.D. degrees in applied mathematics (computer science) from Harvard University. Jim Herman is director of the telecommunications consulting group at BBN Communications. He holds a B. A. in mathematics from Boston College.

Index

Index

Index

notes

notes

notes

notes

notes

notes